The *Gospel of Peter*

# Texts and Editions
# for
# New Testament Study

*Edited by*

Stanley E. Porter and Wendy J. Porter

VOLUME 4

# The *Gospel of Peter*

## Introduction, Critical Edition and Commentary

By

Paul Foster

BRILL

LEIDEN • BOSTON
2010

During the course of this project, the author received a period of research leave funded by the AHRC.

Arts & Humanities
Research Council

This book is printed on acid-free paper.

Library of Congress Cataloging-in-Publication Data

Foster, Paul, 1966–
 The gospel of Peter : introduction, critical edition, and commentary / by Paul Foster.
  p. cm. — (Texts and editions for New Testament study ; v. 4)
 Includes bibliographical references and index.
 ISBN 978-90-04-18094-9 (hardback : alk. paper) 1. Gospel of Peter—Criticism, interpretation, etc. 2. Gospel of Peter—Commentaries. I. Gospel of Peter. English & Greek. II. Title. III. Series.

 BS2860.P6F67 2010
 229'.806—dc22

                                                                    2010022100

ISSN  1574-7085
ISBN  978 90 04 18094 9

MIX
Paper from
responsible sources
FSC  FSC® C004472
www.fsc.org

PRINTED BY DRUKKERIJ WILCO B.V. - AMERSFOORT, THE NETHERLANDS

# CONTENTS

# PREFACE

During the course of writing a book such as this one many debts, both personal and academic, are accrued. Simple acknowledgement of names seems like poor recompense for the encouragement, the willingness to discuss ideas, and the interaction with my own published material that has fed into this volume. The sense of standing on the shoulders of previous luminaries has been keenly felt. Admiration for the work of Urbain Bouriant who, under what must have been difficult conditions, prepared the magnificent *editio princeps* of the *Gospel of Peter* has only increased as my own project progressed. The early scholars who published on the text did so with a rare combination of accuracy and alacrity which is a tribute to their industry, as well as being an aspiration to be followed. Figures such as Adolf von Harnack, Oscar von Gebhardt, Henry Barclay Swete, Armitage Robinson, and of a later generation Leon Vaganay have formed a cohort of able guides. Many of their original insights have an abiding validity. At points where I have disagreed with them, there has been a certain degree of trepidation and a desire to first ensure that their arguments are fully and fairly understood before putting forward rival proposals.

This study initially commenced as a post-doctoral project funded by the Arts and Humanities Research Board, and based in the University of Oxford. I would like to thank Prof. Christopher Tuckett for securing the funding for this project and for allowing me to continue with it when I was appointed to a full-time position at the School of Divinity in the University of Edinburgh. His support and intellectual stimulus during the initial phases of this book were invaluable. My fellow researcher and close friend on the project, Dr Andrew Gregory, has helped to focus the book in numerous areas. There is much I have learnt from his own scholarship, especially his work on *The Reception of Luke and Acts*, and his publications on Jewish-Christian gospels. My colleagues in the School of Divinity in Edinburgh deserve special mention. Prof. Larry Hurtado, Dr Helen Bond, Prof. Tim Lim, Prof. Hans Barstad and Dr David Reimer have probably endured more discussions and papers at research seminars on the *Gospel of Peter* than should befall any person in a lifetime, let alone over five years. I thank them for their patience and insights.

The *Gospel of Peter* has also helped me to develop many academic relationships. In particular I would like to express my thanks to Prof. Keith Elliott who has pressed me on various points, shown a strong interest in the project, and provided an outstanding model of scholarship. In particular, I would like to express my thanks for the confidence he put in me when he invited a then very junior scholar to present a paper at the textual criticism group of the annual SNTS meeting in Halle in 2005. That presentation addressed the recent identifications of certain manuscript fragments as witnesses to the *Gospel of Peter*. Two further friendships that have developed as a result of this research are those with Prof. Tobias Nicklas (Regensberg) and Dr Thomas Kraus. Their own scholarly publications on the *Gospel of Peter* are hugely important works, as are their other publications dealing with non-canonical texts and early manuscripts. They have provided me with many positive interactions regarding my work, and the collegial nature of their friendship has been of great encouragement. I would also like to acknowledge the support of Prof. Joseph Verheyden, formerly my co-chair of the Q Section of the SBL. He has taken an active interest in this project, contributed helpful suggestions, and has not reacted when I have smuggled in a reference to the *Gospel of Peter* during a paper ostensibly on Q! More recently, Prof. Francis Watson of Durham has commenced work on non-canonical gospels. He noted a number of typographical errors in various parts of this volume, and one important factual mistake. I wish him well with his own projects in this field, and thank him for his contribution to this book.

The publication of this volume in the prestigious TENTS series has been supported by the editor Prof. Stanley E. Porter (McMaster Divinity College). Like past luminaries, he dealt with the initial manuscript submission with great efficiency and accuracy. He has been unfailingly supportive throughout, and his suggestions to strengthen certain aspects of the volume have been most welcome. The editorial process at Brill was overseen by Ellen Girmscheid, who was extremely professional and supportive in all her work.

Finally, maybe not thanks, maybe not a traditional scholarly affirmation, but definitely acknowledgement and admiration for two unknown figures. The first is the author who, presumably in the second century, recast gospel traditions in a way that reflected his pastoral and pedagogical concerns for his contemporary believers. His work has left the legacy of a fascinating window into a world that would be wrongly labelled as either 'orthodox' or 'heretical', but more accurately reflects a form of belief that is both popular and pious. The second figure is an unnamed Egyptian Christian, maybe a monk from Akhmîm or maybe a lay believer, who died sometime between the sixth to ninth centuries. His love of a little codex meant it was interred with him, and consequently preserves a substantial fragment of the *Gospel of Peter*. Those who continue to cherish ancient texts and the study of manuscripts will have little difficulty in feeling an affinity with this unknown person. Though his name is long forgotten, his serendipitous preservation of this little codex has bequeathed an important treasure to modern scholars.

Paul Foster
29th June 2010
Feast Day of St Peter and St Paul

The following information was received from Prof. Dr. Johannes van Oort (Radboud Universiteit, Nijmegen & University of Pretoria) on 8 July 2010 relating to his trip to Egypt in 2010 where he attempted to locate the manuscript of the *Gospel of Peter* and the codex P.Cair. 10759.

"Between June 12–20 I did my utmost in Alexandria to see the *Gospel of Peter* manuscript, but without any real success. According to all my information, the manuscript is not in Cairo (neither in the Egyptian Museum, nor in the Coptic Museum, or in any of the other ones). Also, I have an explicit statement that it is not in the Graeco-Roman Museum in Alexandria. All my indications are that it should be in the Alexandria Library and during a week I visited this location every day. The people there looked in their treasures, but until now they could not find the manuscript."

# LIST OF ABBREVIATIONS

AB      Anchor Bible

*ABD*      David Noel Freedman (ed.), *The Anchor Bible Dictionary* (New York: Doubleday, 1992)

AnBib      Analecta biblica

AGJU      Arbeiten zur Geschichte des antiken Judentums und des Urchristentums

*ANRW*      Hildegard Temporini and Wolfgang Haase (eds.), *Aufstieg und Niedergang der römischen Welt: Geschichte und Kultur Roms im Spiegel der neueren Forschung* (Berlin: W. de Gruyter, 1972–)

ANTJ      Arbeiten zum Neuen Testament und Judentum

*Apoc*      *Apocrypha*

*APOT*      R.H. Charles (ed.), *Apocrypha and Pseudepigrapha of the Old Testament in English* (2 vols.; Oxford: Clarendon Press, 1913)

BDF      Friedrich Blass, A. Debrunner and Robert W. Funk, *A Greek Grammar of the New Testament and Other Early Christian Literature* (Cambridge: Cambridge University Press, 1961)

BET      Beiträge zur biblischen Exegese und Theologie

BETL      Bibliotheca ephemeridum theologicarum lovaniensium

*Bib*      *Biblica*

BICS.S      Bulletin of the Institute of Classical Studies Supplement

*BIFAO*      *Bulletin de l'Institut français d'archéologie orientale*

BINS      Biblical Interpretation Series

*BJRL*      *Bulletin of the John Rylands University Library of Manchester*

BNTC      Black's New Testament Commentaries

*BZNW*      *Beihefte zur Zeitschrift für die neutestamentliche Wissenachaft*

CAH      Cambridge Ancient History

*CBQ*      *Catholic Biblical Quarterly*

CBQMS      *Catholic Biblical Quarterly, Monograph Series*

*CBR*      *Currents in Biblical Research*

*CH*      *Church History*

ConBNT      Coniectanea biblica, New Testament

| | |
|---|---|
| DJD | Discoveries in the Judaean Desert |
| EHS | Europäische Hochschulschriften |
| *ETL* | *Ephemerides Theologicae Lovanienses* |
| *ExpTim* | *Expository Times* |
| FRLANT | Forschungen zur Religion und Literatur des Alten und Neuen Testaments |
| GCS | Die Griechischen Christlichen Schriftstellet der ersten Jahrhunderte |
| GCS.NF | Die Griechischen Christlichen Schriftstellet der ersten Jahrhunderte – Neue Folge |
| GKC | *Gesenius' Hebrew Grammar* (ed. E. Kautzsch, revised and trans. A.E. Cowley; Oxford: Clarendon Press, 1910) |
| *HeyJ* | *Heythrop Journal* |
| *HTR* | *Harvard Theological Review* |
| ICC | International Critical Commentary |
| *IEJ* | *Israel Exploration Journal* |
| IFAO | *Institut français d'archéologie orientale* |
| *JBL* | *Journal of Biblical Literature* |
| *JECA* | *Journal of Early Christian Studies* |
| *JEH* | *Journal of Ecclesiastical History* |
| *JRS* | *Journal of Roman Studies* |
| *JSHJ* | *Journal for the Study of the Historical Jesus* |
| *JSJ* | *Journal for Study of Judaism in the Persian, Hellenistic and the Roman Period* |
| *JSNT* | *Journal for the Study of the New Testament* |
| *JSOT* | *Journal for the Study of the Old Testament* |
| *JSP* | *Journal for the Study of the Pseudepigrapha* |
| JSPSup | *Journal for the Study of the Pseudepigrapha*, Supplement Series |
| JSNTSup | *Journal for the Study of the New Testament*, Supplement Series |
| *JTS* | *Journal of Theological Studies* |
| LCL | Loeb Classical Library |
| LDAB | Leuven Database of Ancient Books |
| LNTS | Library of New Testament Studies |
| LSJ | H.G. Liddell, Robert Scott and H. Stuart Jones, *Greek–English Lexicon* (Oxford: Clarendon Press, 9th edn, 1968) |
| MIFAO | Mémoires publiés par les membres de l'Institut français d'archéologie orientale |

| | |
|---|---|
| *MPER* | *Mitteilungen aus der Papyrussammlung der Österreichischen Nationalbiblothek* |
| NHC | Nag Hammadi Corpus |
| NICNT | New International Commentary on the New Testament |
| NIGTC | The New International Greek Testament Commentary |
| *NovT* | *Novum Testamentum* |
| NovTSup | *Novum Testamentum*, Supplements |
| NTL | New Testament Library |
| *NTS* | *New Testament Studies* |
| *NTTS* | *New Testament Tools and Studies* |
| OECCT | Oxford Early Christian Greek Texts |
| OTL | Old Testament Library |
| *OTP* | James Charlesworth (ed.), *Old Testament Pseudepigrapha* |
| *PG* | J.-P. Migne, (ed.), *Patrologia cursus completa Series graeca* (166 vols.; Paris: Petit-Montrouge, 1857–83) |
| *RB* | *Revue biblique* |
| SBLSP | Society of Biblical Literature Seminar Papers |
| SBLSS | Society of Biblical Literature Symposium Series |
| SC | Sources chrétiennes |
| *SecCent* | *Second Century* |
| SNTSMS | Society for New Testament Studies Monograph Series |
| Str–B | [Hermann L. Strack and] Paul Billerbeck, *Kommentar zum Neuen Testament aus Talmud und Midrasch* (7 vols.; Munich: Beck, 1922–61) |
| *TDNT* | Gerhard Kittel and Gerhard Friedrich (eds.), *Theological Dictionary of the New Testament* (trans. Geoffrey W. Bromiley; 10 vols.; Grand Rapids: Eerdmans, 1964–) |
| TENT | Text and Editions for New Testament Study |
| *TLZ* | *Theologische Literaturzeitung* |
| TSAJ | Texts and Studies in Ancient Judaism |
| TU | Texte und Untersuchungen zur Geschichte der altchristlichen Literatur |
| *VC* | *Vigiliae christianae* |
| WBC | Word Biblical Commentary |
| WUNT | Wissenschaftliche Untersuchungen zum Neuen Testament |
| ZAC/JAC | *Zeitschrift für antikes Christentum*/Journal of Ancient Christianity |

ZKT   *Zeitschrift für katholische Theologie*
ZNW  *Zeitschrift für die neutestamentliche Wissenschafte und die Kunde der älteren Kirche*
ZWT  *Zeitschrift für Wissenschaftliche Theologie*

# INTRODUCTION

## 1. The Text under Discussion

This book studies the text identified as the *Gospel of Peter*. A text bearing that name was known from the writings of various church fathers, but it was not until the discovery of a codex in 1886/87 that scholars identified an actual text which could plausibly be seen as a part of that gospel. The codex, although written on parchment, is classified by the papyrus reference P.Cair. 10759 and given the following inventory entry on the Leuven Database of Ancient Books:

> Alexandria, Bibliotheca Alexandrina (exhibited) [10759] = Cairo, Egyptian Museum CG 10759 (fol. 1–33).[1]

Unfortunately, contrary to this record, the codex is now missing. This has been confirmed in private correspondence with Tobias Nicklas and Thomas Kraus, as well as being the implication drawn from numerous unanswered e-mails and letters to the various institutions concerned. Notwithstanding this state of affairs, a set of excellent photographs of the text were taken by Adam Bülow-Jacobsen around 1981 and he has kindly given permission to reproduce these images in this book.[2] The detailed codicological discussions are based on those images.

Various fragments of text have also been identified as belonging to the *Gospel of Peter*. As will become apparent in the discussion in section six, it will be strongly disputed whether anything can be determined from such scanty fragments. The items that have been proposed as potentially having some possible relationship to the first text in P.Cair. 10759 discovered at Akhmîm are: P.Oxy. 2949 and P.Oxy.

---

[1] See http://ldab.arts.kuleuven.ac.be/ldab_text_detail.php?tm=59976&i=1 (1 September 2009). In more recent correspondence Thomas Kraus mentioned that Willy Clarysse of the LDAB once saw the codex on display in Alexandria, and that Clarysse has a contact person who has suggested that pages of P.Cair. 10759 are on display. However, Kraus states he received the following official response: 'In three emails the person responsible for the exhibitions and for the relevant collection of manuscripts claimed that the Alexandria library did not hold the Akhmîm codex.' (email correspondence of 20 April 2010).

[2] The photographs are also available electronically on the following website:http:// ipap.csad.ox.ac.uk/GP/GP.html (1 January 2010).

4009, both held in the papyrology collection in the Sackler Library
as part of the Oxford University Library Services holdings; P.Vindob.
G 2325, held in the Austrian National Library; P. Egerton 2 (+Papyrus
Köln 255), held in London at the British Library (and Universität zu
Köln);[3] and Ostracon (van Haelst 741), now missing. Of these textual
and artefactual remains only P.Oxy. 2949 shows any overlap with the
text discovered at Akhmîm, and here the overlap is only in the region
of two of the sixty verses contained in P.Cair. 10759. For this reason a
discussion of the text identified as the *Gospel of Peter* must focus upon
the nine pages of continuous text that occur as the first of the four
texts in the codex from Akhmîm.

The dating of P.Cair. 10759 has been debated. The four texts contained in the codex are not all written in the same hand, therefore
a range of different date must be assigned to each text, whereas the
dating of P.Cair. 10759 should only relate to its compilation and not
the composition of any of the individual texts it houses. Focusing on
the text of the *Gospel of Peter*, the most commonly proposed dating
of the text advanced by papyrologists since the discovery of the codex
has been sometime between the 7th to 9th centuries.[4] This both narrowed the range and moved it earlier than the 8th to 12th century
suggested in the *editio princeps*.[5] Even earlier datings have been suggested. Grenfell and Hunt proposed correcting the suggestion of Bouriant, advocating instead a dating of the 5th or 6th century.[6] This has
not been widely supported. Although not pushing back the boundaries
as radically, Cavallo and Maehler suggest a date 'near the end of the
VI century.'[7] Thus it appears that the consensus has settled on seeing

---

[3] For a discussion of P. Egerton 2 see T. Nicklas, 'Papyrus Egerton 2' in P. Foster
(ed.), *The Non-Canonical Gospels* (London: Continuum, 2008) 139–149; T. Nicklas,
'Papyrus Egerton 2', in T.J. Kraus, M. Kruger and T. Nicklas (eds.), *Gospel Fragments*
(OECGT; Oxford: OUP, 2008) 11–120; P. Foster, *The Apocryphal Gospels – A Very
Short Introduction* (Oxford: OUP, 2009) 105–111.

[4] See J. van Haelst's *Catalogue des papyrus littéraires juifs et chrétiens* (Paris: Publication de la Sorbonne, 1976), 597, no. 598.

[5] U. Bouriant, 'Fragments du texte grec du livre d'Énoch et de quelques écrits
attribués à saint Pierre', dans *Mémoires publiés par les membres de la Mission
archéologique française au Caire* (t. IX, fasc. 1; Paris: Ernest Leroux, 1892) 93.

[6] The proposals of B.P. Grenfell and A.S. Hunt are recorded in *Catalogue général
des antiquités égyptiennes du Musée du Caire No. 10001–10869*, 1903 (Nachdruck:
Osnabrück, 1972) 93.

[7] G. Cavallo and H. Maehler, *Greek Bookhands of the Early Byzantine Period AD
300–800*, BICS.S 47 (London: University of London, Institute of Classical Studies,
1987) 75.

the actual manuscript of the *Gospel of Peter* discovered at Akhmîm as being written at some point between the late 6th century and the beginning of the 9th century. The autograph of that text would come, of course, from an earlier period. Consequently, the evidence of church fathers in referring to a text bearing the name *Gospel of Peter* will be discussed in section eight as a means of fixing the date of composition for this text.

## 2. DISCOVERY OF THE TEXT

### 2.1. *Historical Context*

The discovery of the codex containing the text identified as a fragment of the *Gospel of Peter* needs to be seen as part of the larger archaeological endeavours of French scholars in Egypt.[8] It was towards the end of the period of French political favoured status in Egypt that the *Mission archéologique française au Caire* was established. This *Mission* was founded in 1881 by the French Government as a school of archaeology, but also for the purpose of research and publication of the findings from excavations.[9] Although the British occupation of Egypt limited the political relationship between Cairo and Paris, the French maintained a significance presence. The *Mission archéologique française au Caire* continued its scientific studies of the artefactual and literary remains of ancient Egyptian civilisations. The fruits of the *Mission's* findings were made accessible to the scholarly world through its own publication series known as *Mémoires publiés par les membres de la Mission archéologique française au Caire*. The first part of the first *tome*, which contained miscellaneous articles on Egyptian, Coptic and Arabic archaeology and antiquities, appeared under the direction Gaston Maspero in 1884, with the fourth and final part of the first *tome* being published in 1889.[10] This time lag illustrates the delay between

---

[8] P. Foster, 'The Discovery and Initial Reaction to the So-called Gospel of Peter', in T.J. Kraus and T. Nicklas, *Das Evangelium nach Petrus: Text, Kontexte, Intertexte* (Berlin: de Gruyter, 2007) 9–30.

[9] The *Mission archéologique française au Caire* 'was re-organized in 1901 on a lavish scale under the title *Institut français d'archéologie orientale du Caire*, and domiciled with printing-press and library in a fine building near the museum.' See: http://encyclopedia.jrank.org/AUD_BAI/AUTHORITILS.html (1 September 2009).

[10] G. Maspero (ed.), *Mémoires publiés par les membres de la Mission archéologique française au Caire*, tome 1, 4 vols. pp. 787 + plates (Paris: Ernest Leroux, 1884–1889).

discovery of various artefacts and texts and the time when details of these archaeological findings could be published.

## 2.2. *The Publication of the* Editio Princeps *of the* Gospel of Peter

It has often been suggested that the editor of the *editio princeps* of the *Gospel of Peter* failed to realise the significance of the first text contained in the codex discovered in a grave in Akhmîm. This conclusion is based upon the five to six year gap between discovery during the winter season dig of 1886–87 and the publication of a transcription of the codex in 1892. Rendel Harris is perhaps the most fulsome exponent of this point of view. He states,

> It is curious that the publication of this great discovery should have been so long delayed; the documents seem to have been found as far back as the winter of 1886–87, and there was certainly no need for five years' delay. But the reason of it is not far to seek. The French scholars, with some noble exceptions, are no longer interested in Biblical and Patristic criticism; and it is evident that they did not, at first, realise what they had found.[11]

Harris, however, was not alone in this view. Robinson, describing the discovery of the *Gospel of Peter* by the French Archaeological Mission at Cairo refers to 'its somewhat tardy publication.'[12] This perspective is best resisted for a number of reasons. First, this suggestion is made by those with an interest in the area of New Testament studies or Christian origins rather than recognizing that the interests of the members of the *Mission archéologique française* were broader, encompassing all aspects of the material and literary cultures of Ancient Egypt. Secondly, even among the four texts contained in the Akhmîm codex, Bouriant appears to have considered the fragments of *1 Enoch* to be the most significant find. In part this was due to the more extensive nature of the two fragments of *1 Enoch*, but this was not the only consideration. Rather Bouriant saw the fragments of *1 Enoch* as the more significant find since they provided the first extant evidence of the Greek text of

---

[11] J. Rendel Harris, *A Popular Account of the Newly Recovered Gospel of St Peter* (London: Hodder and Stoughton, 1893) 17–18.

[12] J.A. Robinson and M.R. James, *The Gospel according to Peter, and the Revelation of Peter: Two Lectures on the Newly Recovered Fragments together with the Greek Texts* (London: C.J. Clay and Sons, 1892) 15.

*1 Enoch.*[13] Thirdly, the wealth of material was itself a constraint to the speed at which individual items were published and this problem was not only experienced in relation to the codex discovered at Akhmîm.[14] Fourthly, in the *editio princeps* the first text is cautiously identified by Bouriant as possibly being the *Gospel of Peter*. Although one cannot be certain when during the period 1886–87 to 1892 this identification was made, or by whom, there is no reason to suspect that there was either delay or hesitation on the part of Bouriant in recognizing the text as potentially being an exemplar of the *Gospel of Peter*, which hitherto had only been known by title through references in various Patristic witnesses. Fifthly, Bouriant concludes his comments by supplying place and date details as being Cairo, November 1891.[15] This, perhaps, slightly reduces the perceived gap between discovery and preparation of the initial publication of the text. During this period Bouriant was involved with further winter season digs and publications.[16] Therefore, the gap between discovery and publication should not be taken as a failure on the part of the editors to perceive the potential significance of the text.

The circumstances surrounding the discovery of the codex are reported in extremely compressed form in the *editio princeps*. The winter season dig of 1886–87 was conducted under the leadership of Eugene Grébaut. This dig resulted in the finding of not one, but two

---

[13] He states, 'Les petits fragments que je viens de mentionner (Évangile et Apocalypse de Saint-Pierre, Évangile canonique) seront publiés en temps et lieu. L'importance de livre d'Énoch dont le texte grec n'est connu que par de courts passages rapportés dans Cédrénus et le Syncelle, est telle que je me suis décidé à commencer par lui la publication du manuscrit.' Bouriant, 'Fragments du texte grec du livre d'Énoch et de quelques écrits attribués à saint Pierre', 94.

[14] Publication under the series title *Mémoires publiés par les membres de la Mission archéologique française au Caire* continued until the appearance of tome 19 part 1 in 1894. After this the series and *Mission archéologique française au Caire* changed their names. The series became known as *Mémoires publiés par les membres de l'Institut français d'archéologie orientale du Caire*, and the next volume was published as number 52 in that series. This was to remove confusion between volume and part numbers. *L'Institut français d'archéologie orientale* continues to publish volumes in this series under the abbreviation *MIFAO*. According to their website the most recent volume in this series was published in 2002. See http://www.ifao.egnet.net/

[15] 'Le Caire, novembre 1891.' Bouriant, 'Fragments du texte grec du livre d'Énoch et de quelques écrits attribués à saint Pierre', 147.

[16] This is demonstrated by looking at his contributions to other volumes in the series *Mémoires publiés par les membres de la Mission archéologique française au Caire* especially for the period 1892–1894. During this period Bouriant contributed at least half a dozen articles to various volumes in this series.

ancient manuscripts. The other manuscript, published by Baillet in
the same volume of *Mémoires publiés par les membres de la Mission
archéologique française au Caire*, contained problems of an arithmeti-
cal and geometrical nature.[17] The remainder of the first part of tome
nine was devoted to the publication of what Bouriant describes as 'this
lastest manuscript', which occupied pages 93–147.[18] Thus, if the order
of presentation of texts within the volume is of significance, not only
did Bouriant consider the text of *1 Enoch* of greater significance than
those of the other three fragmentary texts,[19] but the placement of the
mathematical manuscript prior to the codex edited by Bouriant may
perhaps indicate that this was considered as being the more spectacular find.

Bouriant used two independent indicators to date the codex. The
first of these was based upon a palaeographical analysis of the four
texts contained in the codex. On this basis he concluded that the manuscript was not to be dated earlier than the eighth century and no
later than the twelfth century.[20] In conjunction with this date range,
Bouriant marshalled the location of discovery to corroborate this dating. He noted that the Christian cemetery at Akhmîm located upon
a hill serves as a datum for determining the period of interment of
the corpses. The graves range in date between the fifth and fifteenth
centuries with the earliest being found at the foot of the hill that at its
summit attains a height of 700 metres. The location of the grave containing the codex is described by Bouriant in the following manner:
'the tomb which contained the manuscript is found about 200 metres
up the hill in the north-east direction.'[21] While Bouriant acknowledges

---

[17] J. Baillet, 'Le papyrus mathématique d'Akhmîm', in *Mémoires publiés par les
membres de la Mission archéologique française au Caire* (t. IX, fasc. 1; Paris 1892)
1–90.

[18] Bouriant, 'Fragments du texte grec du livre d'Énoch et de quelques écrits attribués
à saint Pierre', 93.

[19] This may be further suggested by the observation that the heading Bouriant gives
to his publication on page 93 is 'Fragments du texte grec du livre d'Énoch' an abbreviated form of the description provided at the beginning of the volume. Moreover this
heading is used as a header on the odd numbered pages including those where the
other three documents are discussed.

[20] 'Seules, les particularités qu'on relève dans l'écriture ou dans la langue elle-même,
peuvent nous mettre sur la voie, et montrent que le manuscrit n'est pas antérieur au
VIIIᵉ siècle ni postérieur au XIIᵉ.' Bouriant, 'Fragments du texte grec du livre d'Énoch
et de quelques écrits attribués à saint Pierre', 93.

[21] 'le tombeau du propriétaire du manuscrit se trouve à environ 200 métres de la
colline dans la direction nord-est.' Bouriant, 'Fragments du texte grec du livre d'Énoch
et de quelques écrits attribués à saint Pierre', 93.

that this method cannot give an exact dating, nonetheless, he sees this as aligning with the dating suggested by palaeographical analysis.

Bouriant's introductory comments to both the *Gospel* and *Apocalypse of Peter* are far briefer than those given for the fragments of *1 Enoch*. He draws a comparison between the *Gospel of Peter* and *1 Enoch* noting that the former has a more cursive style of handwriting, and also preserves the more correct orthography.[22] He makes two further observations in his description. First he notes that the first text presents an account of the Passion of Christ which, 'as can be determined from the final phrase, formed a detached episode from the apocryphal gospel of St Peter.' Secondly, he comments that previous to this discovery no actual manuscript fragments of this text have been known.[23] Thus, the initial publication of this text contemplated no other possibility than identifying the first fragment as being a detached episode from the previously non-extant apocryphal *Gospel of Peter*. This point of view, introduced by Bouriant, has continued virtually unquestioned in subsequent scholarship.

## 3. History of Scholarship

### 3.1. *The Reception of the* Gospel of Peter *in England*

Knowledge of the text of the *Gospel of Peter* can first be referenced in England on the 17th of November 1892. Robinson and James give the following account in the preface to their volume. 'The Lecture on the "Gospel according to Peter" was given in the Hall of Christ's College on the 20th of November, three days after the text was first seen in Cambridge, in response to a general desire for information as to the new discovery.'[24] Although not with the same degree of specificity, this is corroborated by the opening comment in Swete's text: 'At the end of November, 1892, shortly after the appearance of M. Bouriant's *editio princeps*...'[25] Thus in England, Cambridge was the centre

---

[22] Bouriant, 'Fragments du texte grec du livre d'Énoch et de quelques écrits attribués à saint Pierre', 137.

[23] Bouriant, 'Fragments du texte grec du livre d'Énoch et de quelques écrits attribués à saint Pierre', 137.

[24] Robinson and James, *The Gospel according to Peter, and the Revelation of Peter*, 7.

[25] H.B. Swete, *The Akhmîm Fragment of the Apocryphal Gospel of St Peter* (London: Macmillan and Co., 1893) v.

of dissemination of the text known as the *Gospel of Peter*. Besides the works of Robinson and Swete, a third scholar from Cambridge was active in publishing a work treating the recent discovery of the text from Akhmîm. As its title suggests, Rendel Harris provided a popular account of the discovery and significance of the text with an accompanying English language translation, but no Greek text.[26]

### 3.1.1. *Henry Barclay Swete*

Swete was the most prolific among the Cambridge trio in his work upon this text. He produced three works dealing exclusively with the *Gospel of Peter*, each of which was an expansion on its predecessor. The first appeared towards the end of 1892 this was an edition of the Greek text 'published', apparently privately, for use by his students.[27] Copies of this initial work are not available in the Copyright Libraries of the United Kingdom, or in the collection of Swete's private papers maintained at Gonville and Caius where he was a Fellow.[28] This pamphlet was reprinted in early 1893, incorporating a number of corrections to the text. As Swete describes the pamphlet, 'This reprint was issued again in February, 1893, with some corrections obtained from the MS through the kindness of the late Professor Bensly, whose recent death has brought upon all studies of this kind a loss which is impossible to estimate.'[29] This pamphlet consists primarily of two parts: an introduction collecting Patristic references to a *Gospel of Peter*, and the Greek text of the first writing in the Akhmîm codex. It appeared under the title, *The Apocryphal Gospel of St. Peter, the Greek Text of the Newly Discovered Fragment*.[30]

The next contribution Swete made was to be his most enduring and comprehensive piece of scholarship on the Akhmîm fragment. His book length monograph, dated 'May 1893', consisted of thirty-eight pages of introductory material and thirty-four pages of textual

---

[26] J. Rendel Harris, *A Popular Account of the Newly Recovered Gospel of St Peter* (London: Hodder and Stoughton, 1893).

[27] In his preface to *The Akhmîm Fragment*, Swete makes mention of this work. 'At the end of November 1892 … I published for the use of students a tentatively corrected text of the newly discovered fragment of the Petrine Gospel' (v).

[28] Thanks are to be expressed to the librarians of Gonville and Caius for searching through the archive and verifying that a copy of this work is not held in their collection.

[29] Swete, *The Akhmîm Fragment*, v.

[30] H.B. Swete, *The Apocryphal Gospel of St. Peter, the Greek Text of the Newly Discovered Fragment* (London, Macmillan, 1893).

analysis. The first section covered twelve issues under the following titles: (i) Petrine writings; (ii) Relation of the fragment to the Canonical Gospels; (iii) Use of a harmony; (iv) Chronology of the Passion; (v) Allusions to the Old Testament; (vi) References to the fragment in Church-writers; (vii) Comparison with other *apocrypha*; (viii) Doctrinal tendencies of the fragment; (ix) Literary character; (x) Place of origin and approximate date; (xi) Description of the MS. and its probable age; (xii) Literature of the Petrine Gospel.[31] These introductory questions addressed by Swete became agenda setting for subsequent scholarship. Swete was in no doubt that the first text fragment discovered in the codex from Akhmîm was part of the text mentioned by the two Patristic authors he cites,[32] most notably by Eusebius[33] but also in a fleeting reference by Origen.[34] Swete asserted that '[t]here is no reason to doubt that the Akhmîm fragment was rightly assigned by M. Bouriant to the lost Gospel of Peter.'[35] Swete provided eight overlapping reasons for making such an identification, although not all can be said to be equally compelling. First, on internal evidence the text claims to be a personal account of Peter. Second, it appears to have been part of a complete gospel and not just a Passion account. Third, its tendency aligns with Serapion's account. Next Swete lists what he considers to be three docetic features: fourth, Jesus is addressed as ὁ κύριος or ὁ υἱὸς τοῦ θεοῦ; fifth, he is crucified without suffering pain; sixth, the resurrected body assumes supernatural proportions. Two further arguments are added. Seventh, the narrative is generally orthodox, which aligns with Serapion's initial assessment. Finally eighth, on internal evidence it should be dated to the second century.[36] Thus, although Swete acknowledges that Eusebius alone knows of six different texts that circulated in Peter's name,[37] this does not cause him to consider the possibility that more than one gospel-like text may have been associated with that apostolic figure. In part, this was due to the docetic features that Swete identified in the text. However, it might reasonably be asked whether these features would have been identified as particularly doectic if one were not already convinced of the

---

[31] Swete, *The Akhmîm Fragment*, see the table of contents, vii.
[32] See the discussion in Swete, *The Akhmîm Fragment*, ix–xii.
[33] Eusebius, *H.E.* 3.3.1–3 and 6.12.1–6.
[34] Origen, *Comm. on Matt.* x.17.
[35] Swete, *The Akhmîm Fragment*, xii.
[36] Swete, *The Akhmîm Fragment*, xii–xiii.
[37] Swete, *The Akhmîm Fragment*, ix.

identity of the text and thus sought to make it conform to Serapion's description?[38]

Swete's second section of his monograph consisted of three aspects: (i) an edition of the text with brief textual and exegetical notes under the passage to which they were referring;[39] (ii) an English translation of the text;[40] and (iii) two indices, referencing the Greek words in the fragment[41] and a subject index.[42] The brief notes often make highly significant and salient points. Thus, this compressed treatment, covering only twenty-four pages, still remains the nearest approximation to a commentary on the text in the English language.

The appearance of Swete's monograph did not entirely signal the end of his work on the *Gospel of Peter*. More than a decade after the publication of his landmark volume, he presented 'a lecture to the ladies assembled for Biblical study at Newnham College, Cambridge, on 5th August, 1907.'[43] The lecture was subsequently published under the title 'The Gospels in the Second Century', in *The Interpreter* later in the same year. Although this article tends not to be referenced in the literature on the *Gospel of Peter*, Swete makes numerous references to the Akhmîm text. While some of these comments reiterate thoughts in his earlier printed works, he also provides a number of new reflections on the text. He sees the first document in the Akhmîm codex as an example of a type of Gospel which 'was directly antagonistic to the Gospels of the Church, although largely based upon them. Such was the docetic *Gospel of Peter*.'[44] Furthermore, and in contradistinction from Harnack,[45] Swete argued that the Akhmîm text was not directly dependent on the works of Justin Martyr. His statements about the relationship between Justin and the *Gospel of Peter* were couched in far more tentative terms in his earlier work.[46] Thus, while Swete's major work on the Akhmîm fragment was completed in 1893, less than six months after the text first appeared in Cambridge, he continued to

[38] Swete, *The Akhmîm Fragment*, xxxvii–xliii.
[39] Swete, *The Akhmîm Fragment*, 1–24.
[40] Swete, *The Akhmîm Fragment*, 25–28.
[41] Swete, *The Akhmîm Fragment*, 29–32.
[42] Swete, *The Akhmîm Fragment*, 33–34.
[43] H.B. Swete, 'The Gospels in the Second Century', *The Interpreter* 4 (1907) 138–155.
[44] Swete, 'The Gospels in the Second Century', 139.
[45] Harnack, *Bruchstücke des Evangeliums und der Apokalypse des Petrus* (TU IX, 2, J.C. Leipzig Hinrichs, 1893).
[46] Swete, *The Akhmîm Fragment*, xxxiii–xxxv.

interact with the text and publish fresh ideas about its relationship to
the Canonical Gospels and the writings of Justin as late as 1907.

### 3.1.2. J. Armitage Robinson

Perhaps the first public lecture to be given to the topic of the *Gospel
of Peter* in England after the publication of Bouriant's *editio princeps*
must be attributed to Armitage Robinson. His alacrity in publishing
the text of this initial lecture is to be noted. The lecture given at Christ's
College on the 20th of November 1892, just three days after the text
was seen in Cambridge, was apparently followed only eleven days later
by the publication of a handsome hardback pocket-sized edition of
the lecture and the Greek text of the *Gospel of Peter*. The volume also
encompassed a similar treatment of the second text in the Akhmîm
codex, the Revelation of Peter. Robinson, in his preface dated the 1st
of December 1892, expresses his gratitude to the production team at
the University Press for their efficiency.

> For the rapidity with which this book has been published, without (we
> would fain believe) any consequent loss of accuracy in the printing, our
> thanks are due to the officers and workmen of the University Press.[47]

The preface also attests the death of F.J.A. Hort, the Lady Marga-
ret's Reader in Divinity at the University of Cambridge. Hort's death
occurred on the 30th of November 1892.[48] This chain of events estab-
lishes the speed at which the publication of the volume took place.
Less than two weeks after the appearance of Bouriant's *editio princeps*
Robinson and James had presented public lectures on the *Gospel* and
*Apocalypse of Peter* respectively, sent their manuscripts to the University Publishers, received and checked the proofs, appended a short
note in the preface referencing Hort's death, and had sent the proofs
back to the press for printing. As the book appears with a publication
date of 1892, it is to be assumed that the printing occurred equally
rapidly, being completed at most within a month of the writing of the
preface.

---

[47] Robinson and James, *The Gospel according to Peter, and the Revelation of
Peter*, 8.
[48] Robinson and James comment that 'This little book was finally corrected for the
press when we heard that he, whose latest message to us was permission to dedicate
it to him, had gone to his rest.' *The Gospel according to Peter, and the Revelation of
Peter*, 8.

This treatment of the *Gospel of Peter* falls into a number of sections. Although not divided under separate heads, Robinson initially discussed introductory issues such as Eusebius' record of Serapion's reaction to the *Gospel of Peter*, and the nature of Docetism.[49] The major component of the lecture consists of an English translation of the text, divided into fourteen chapters, with brief comments following each chapter of text.[50] Two observations need to be made. First, although the English text is divided into fourteen chapters the numbering goes astray at the end, with the final two chapters both being numbered as 'thirteen'.[51] However, if one looks at the numbering system with the Greek text presented at the rear of the volume, the fourteen chapters are correctly numbered.[52] Second, Robinson's 'comments' are perhaps best described as observation on the text, rather than presenting detailed commentary or philological notes of the type offered by Swete. These observations appear to have two central functions: to draw attention to any intertextual links with canonical gospels, apocryphal texts, or Patristic writings; and, to highlight perceived docetic features in the text. In respect to this last point, Robinson felt that this was exemplified at a number of points. These included the common arguments that the references to 'He held his peace as having no pain' (*Gos. Pet.* 4.10) and the cry of dereliction transformed into a description of power leaving the crucified Christ are obvious examples of docetic doctrine. In relation to this second example Robinson argues,

> 'The power' then, so often emphasised in S. Luke's Gospel in connection with the person of our Lord, is here, by a strange perversion of our Lord's quotation from Ps. xxii. I, described as forsaking Him: the Divine Christ is 'taken up,' the Human Christ remains upon the Cross. ...We are thus confirmed in the belief that this was the Gospel, as Serapion tells us, of the *Docetae*.[53]

To this Robinson added one further observation not widely taken up by subsequent commentators. He notes that the *Gospel of Peter* omits the words 'I thirst' from the crucifixion narrative. Robinson states, 'If

---

[49] Robinson and James, *The Gospel according to Peter, and the Revelation of Peter*, 13–16.

[50] This section of translation and commentary occupies pages 16–30.

[51] The two paragraphs numbered 'thirteen' are to be found on pages 28 and 29 respectively.

[52] The Greek text is presented on pages 83–88.

[53] Robinson and James, *The Gospel according to Peter, and the Revelation of Peter*, 21.

there is one word in the Canonical narratives of the Passion that is calculated to set our minds at rest on the question of whether our Blessed Lord truly felt the pain of Crucifixion, it is the word from the Cross, 'I thirst.'[54] Thus, this omitted detail is deemed highly significant in determining the docetic character of the text from Akhmîm, and this strengthens the equation that identifies this text with the *Gospel of Peter* depicted by Eusebius' narration of Serapion and his assessment of the Gospel in use at Rhossos. Obviously there is a certain circularity in this argument, and in many ways Robinson and his contemporaries found precisely that for which they were searching. This, however, is not to open the question of docetic tendencies in the Akhmîm text at this juncture, rather it illustrates that for Robinson the 'discovery' of such tendencies was a primary task in his comments on the text.

In the final part of this published lecture Robinson drew together a number of conclusions. First, that the discovery, like many contemporary discoveries, resulted in a text which was not unknown, rather it had previously been non-extant.[55] Secondly, the *Gospel of Peter* is an example of *Tendenz-schriften*, whereby the perspectives of the canonical gospels are 'wilfully perverted and displaced' to advance docetic doctrines.[56] By contrast, one is able 'to return to the Four Gospels with a sense of relief at his escape from a stifling prison of prejudice into the transparent and the bracing atmosphere of pure simplicity and undesigning candour.'[57] It is fully apparent that Bauer's critique of belief in a bedrock of orthodoxy which only subsequently was distorted by heresy needed yet to be heard.[58] Thirdly, Robinson tentatively suggested that the dating of the *Gospel of Peter* 'may be nearer to the beginning than to the middle of the second century.'[59] Fourthly, the author of the *Gospel of Peter* is acquainted with all four canonical

---

[54] Robinson and James, *The Gospel according to Peter, and the Revelation of Peter*, 20.

[55] Robinson and James, *The Gospel according to Peter, and the Revelation of Peter*, 30.

[56] Robinson and James, *The Gospel according to Peter, and the Revelation of Peter*, 31.

[57] Robinson and James, *The Gospel according to Peter, and the Revelation of Peter*, 32.

[58] W. Bauer, *Rechtgläubigkeit und Ketzerei im ältesten Christentum* (Tübingen: Mohr/Siebeck, 1934).

[59] Robinson and James, *The Gospel according to Peter, and the Revelation of Peter*, 32.

accounts, but 'uses and misuses each in turn.'[60] It is striking to note the
degree to which the rhetoric of these conclusions is shaped by a belief
in the pristine, tendency-free nature of the canonical gospels. At every
turn their superiority is asserted in comparison to their non-canonical
counterpart from Akhmîm. The final contribution made by Robinson
in this volume was an edition of the Greek text, with marginal references to parallels in the canonical gospels (and one reference to 1 Pet
3.19), along with a list of possible variant readings of the text at the
foot of the page. It appears that the list of variants was based on certain
perceived possible corrections to Bouriant's transcription, yet without
reference to any images of the manuscript since these were not available in late 1892.

### 3.1.3. J. Rendel Harris

Although the volume published by Harris is subtitled *A Popular
Account*[61] and contains no Greek text, it would be a mistake to under-
estimate his contribution to the early study of the text. Not only does
his book contain important insights in its own right, even more significantly his further textual work is referenced by other scholars. In his
preface Swete writes, 'To Mr J. Rendel Harris, Reader in Palaeography
at Cambridge, I owe not only many valuable suggestions during the
progress of my book, but much kind assistance in the final correction
of the proofs.'[62] In a similar vein, at one point, Robinson explicitly
acknowledges Harris' contribution in suggesting an emendation to the
text.[63] Subsequently the emendation could be seen to be correct when
images of the text became available. However, Harris is best known for
the volume that sought to make the contents of the first document in
the Akhmîm codex accessible to a wider audience.[64]

---

[60] Robinson and James, *The Gospel according to Peter, and the Revelation of Peter*,
33.

[61] The full title of the work is *A Popular Account of the Newly Recovered Gospel of
St Peter*.

[62] Swete, *The Akhmîm Fragment*, vi.

[63] Robinson and James, *The Gospel according to Peter, and the Revelation of Peter*,
17, fn. 1.

[64] Although the book has the appearance of being quite substantial, it should be
noted that the paper is thick and that even on its ninety-seven pages of description, the
margins are large and the space between lines is generous. In fact the contents could
have easily been contained in pamphlet instead of the impressive looking hardback
edition produced by the publishers.A quick count of a random selection of a number of pages indicates that full pages of typescript contain around 150 words. This

The book contains seven chapters of varying length and relevance
to the *Gospel of Peter*. The first chapter describes a number of then
recent manuscript discoveries as background to the find at Akhmîm.
The next chapter then outlines the discovery by the French Archaeological Mission, and includes Harris' exasperated question, 'Is there
any English Archaeological Mission in Egypt? and if not, why not?'[65] It
seems to be the case that he is only aware of three texts in the codex,
and has overlooked Bouriant's description of the 'actes de saint Julien'
which is written in majuscule script on the inside flyleaf pasted to the
rear board of the codex.[66] Next, an introductory outline to Docetism
is provided in chapter three, with alleged tendencies of this 'heresy' in
the Akhmîm text.[67] Then follows the English translation with marginal
references to canonical passages.[68] Chapters five and six investigate
respectively canonical,[69] and non-canonical sources behind the text.[70]
In relation to non-canonical texts, Harris discusses parallels between
the Akhmîm text and the *Diatessaron* as well as the writings of Justin
Martyr as a potential source. In relation to the *Diatessaron*, although
acknowledging that further research is necessary, Harris leans towards
the conclusion that Tatian's harmony is a source for the *Gospel of
Peter*. The similarity between the writings of Justin and the *Gospel of
Peter* is explained by Harris with greater certainty.

> I think the real explanation of these coincidences is that both Justin and
> Peter had a little text-book of fulfilled prophecies, to be used in dis-
> cussions with Jews. These Old Testament prophecies were taken from
> a Greek version, which was not the Septuagint, but was probably the
> version of Aquila the Jew, or some distinctly Jewish version.[71]

Although Harris did not follow up investigating these suggestions,
the theory is a further development in the discussion surrounding the
relationship between the writings of Justin and the first text in the
Akhmîm codex. In his brief conlusion, Harris alludes to traces not

---

is reduced for pages 43–56 where the translation of the text is presented with wider
margins to accommodate an occasional reference to the canonical gospels.

[65] Harris, *A Popular Account of the Newly Recovered Gospel of St Peter*, 15.

[66] Bouriant, 'Fragments du texte grec du livre d'Énoch et de quelques écrits attribués
à saint Pierre', 146.

[67] Harris, *A Popular Account of the Newly Recovered Gospel of St Peter*, 25–37.

[68] Harris, *A Popular Account of the Newly Recovered Gospel of St Peter*, 41–56.

[69] Harris, *A Popular Account of the Newly Recovered Gospel of St Peter*, 59–72.

[70] Harris, *A Popular Account of the Newly Recovered Gospel of St Peter*, 75–89.

[71] Harris, *A Popular Account of the Newly Recovered Gospel of St Peter*, 86.

only of Docetism in the *Gospel of Peter*, but also of Gnosticism and Marcionite teaching. Thus, according to Harris, the 'newly recovered Gospel of Peter' is tainted with heresy throughout its narrative, and reassuringly the four canonical gospels remain in the state of pristine purity first affirmed by Irenaeus.[72]

### 3.2. *French Scholarship after the* Editio Princeps

Early French scholarship on the *Gospel of Peter* was not as prolific as that in England or Germany, but nonetheless it proved to be highly significant. Following the publication of the transcription of the text in the first part of the ninth volume of *Mémoires publiés par les membres de la Mission archéologique française au Caire*, the same body took the opportunity to publish a fresh transcription of the first two texts, the *Gospel of Peter* and the *Apocalypse of Peter*, along with heliographic images of these first two texts. Corrections were also listed for the text of the fragments of *1 Enoch*.

### 3.2.1. *Adolph Lods*
The work of re-transcribing the first text in the Akhmîm codex was undertaken by Lods, another member of the *Mission archéologique française au Caire*. He stated clearly in his introduction that this was in no way to be seen as a criticism of the work undertaken by Bouriant. In fact Lods goes out of his way to laud the quality of work produced by his colleague. Not only does the tone appear fully sincere, but moreover, Lods describes the difficulties that faced Bouriant in his work. First, contrary to the suggestions levelled by both Robinson[73] and Harris,[74] Lods refutes any tardiness on the part of Bouriant. In fact he affirms the speed with which the task was brought to completion. He states that 'Bouriant received the manuscript some time after its discovery, that he immediately recognized its importance, he transcribed it quickly, then he translated it.'[75] Furthermore, Lods describes the lack

---

[72] Harris, *A Popular Account of the Newly Recovered Gospel of St Peter*, 95, 97.
[73] Robinson and James, *The Gospel according to Peter, and the Revelation of Peter*, 15.
[74] Harris, *A Popular Account of the Newly Recovered Gospel of St Peter*, 17–18.
[75] A. Lods, 'L'Évangile et l'Apocalypse de Pierre avec le texte grec du livre d'Hénoch. Text *publiés* en fac-similé, par l'héliogravure d'après les photographies du manuscrit de Gizéh' dans *Mémoires publiéss par les membres de la Mission archéologique française au Caire* (t. IX, fasc. 3; Paris: Ernest Leroux 1893) 217–231, 322–335. The page numbers are often cited as 217–235. This is fully understandable because page 322

of opportunity that was afforded to Bouriant to compare his initial transcription with the manuscript, and later when the manuscript was available it appears that his own transcript was not. Bouriant's decision was to publish these texts rapidly rather than slow the process with time consuming proof-reading.[76] Such facts perhaps give a partial insight into the difficulties encountered by the *Mission archéologique française au Caire* as they attempted to prepare proofs of archaeological reports for printing in Paris. The problem was exacerbated by the large amount of artefactual and textual material that was being processed, along with the delays encountered in sending their reports to Paris for publication.

Despite these factors, there is little doubt that the transcription prepared by Lods was a significant improvement in comparison to that which appeared in the *editio princeps*. The transcription confirmed a number of emendations that had been proposed by both English and German scholars. What, however, aroused the attention of the scholarly world was not the improved transcription, but the appearance of images of the first two texts in the Akhmîm codex. The plates that appear at the rear of Lods' work are heliographic images and not photographs in the modern sense. The term heliograph was originally given to the process invented by Niépce de St. Victor in 1826.[77] The process involves the formation of an engraving obtained by a process in which a specially prepared plate is acted on chemically by exposure to light. Although the process is not described in detail by Lods it was particularly suited to the imaging of static objects in an environment where the sunlight is brilliant and uninterrupted. Thus, taking the image of a manuscript in Egyptian sunlight was a particularly apt application of

---

follows page 231 without any intervening or lost material. The change to numbers in the three-hundred range is presumably due to an error in typesetting.

[76] '[I]l ne le revit plus et, quand il se décida à le publier, n'eut devant lui que sa première copie faite à la hâte. Quand, plus tard, le manuscrit redevint accessible, il ne put qu'y vérifier quelques passages; il aurait dû sans doute différer encore la publication, mais il lui sembla que les retards avaient trop duré et il se décida d'autant plus aisément à donner sa copie qu'il espérait y joindre à bref délai les fac-simile du manuscrit. Ici encore les délais ont été plus longs qu'il ne s'y attendait, pour des motifs sur lesquels il n'y a plus lieu de revenir.' Lods, 'L'Évangile et l'Apocalypse de Pierre avec le texte grec du livre d'Hénoch', 217.

[77] The Columbia Electronic Encyclopedia contains the following description of Niépce and his invention. 'Niepce, Joseph Nicéphore, 1765–1833, French chemist who originated a process of photography. In 1826 he produced the first known photograph, which he called a heliograph, using bitumen of Judea (a form of asphalt) on a pewter plate.'

this technique. The process required perhaps some 8 hours of bright sunlight to affix the image. These images circulated widely in other volumes besides that of Lods. Swete reproduced the *recto* and *verso* of leaf four, numbered as pages seven and eight respectively.[78] These served as frontispieces in Swete's volume. He acknowledges the generosity of the French publisher in allowing him to reproduce the two plate. 'Through the courtesy of M. Leroux I am able to enrich my book with a specimen of this facsimile.'[79] While Gebhardt knew of Lods' heliographic images, he had his own set of photographs (*Lichtdrucktafeln*).[80]

### 3.2.2. *Other French Contributions*

Perhaps the work that was most comparable to that of Harris in attempting to make the text of the *Gospel of Peter* accessible to a wider audience in the French speaking world was that of Meunier.[81] It comprised of a French translation with accompanying notes. In a similar vein, Sabatier discussed the relationship between the Akhmîm text and the canonical gospels.[82] Along with these volumes, French scholars produced a number of articles and notes of varying value. Most noteworthy were those of Lejay,[83] which appeared with a sample of the heliographic images, and the article by Semeria in *Revue Biblique*.[84]

### 3.3. *German Scholarship on the so-called* Gospel of Peter

Early German scholarship was intense, varied and highly stimulating. A variety of questions were addressed and a number of figures helped to shape the debate within the German context in much the same fashion as was done by Swete in England. Issues surrounding the sources employed by the first text in the Akhmîm codex were paramount, as was the exploration of potential docetic features. However, following

---

[78] Swete, *The Akhmîm Fragment*, see the two plates on unnumbered pages near the beginning of the volume.

[79] Swete, *The Akhmîm Fragment*, v.

[80] O. von Gebhardt, *Das Evangelium und die Apokalypse des Petrus. Die neuentdeckten Bruchstücke nach einer Photographie der Handschrift zu Gizéh in Lichtdruck herausgegeben* (Leipzig: J.C. Hinrichs, 1893).

[81] C. Meunier, *L'Évangile selon saint Pierre, traduction française avec notes* (Boulogne: Sociéte Typographique & lithographique, 1893).

[82] A. Sabatier, *L'Évangile de Pierre et les évangiles canoniques* (Paris: Imprimerie Nationale, 1893).

[83] P. Lejay, 'L'Évangile de Pierre', dans *Revue des études grecques* (1893) 59–84, 267–270.

[84] J.B. Semeria, 'L'Évangile de Pierre', *Revue Biblique* (1894) 522–560.

the publication of the heliographic images in Lods' volume, greater attention was paid to analysing the physical features of the manuscript. The debates surrounding the texts were made accessible to a wider audience through a number of scholarly discussions that were published within the pages of *Theologische Literaturzeitung*.[85] In part, it is no surprise that this development was covered so thoroughly by *Theologische Literaturzeitung* since one of its editors, Harnack, published the first German work on the *Gospel* and *Apocalypse of Peter*,[86] and his fellow editor wrote the review notices for volumes covering the topic including the book written by Harnack.[87]

### 3.3.1. *Adolf von Harnack*

Building upon, and expanding his earlier articles in *Sitzungsberichte der königl. Preussischen Akademie der Wissenschaften* entitled 'Bruchstücke des Evangeliums und der Apokalypse des Petrus',[88] Harnack published a short monograph, of the same title as the articles, describing both the *Apocalypse* and *Gospel of Peter*.[89] Although the volume has a publication year of 1893, the preface is dated by Harnack as 'Berlin, den 15. Dec. 1892.'[90] This volume was the first German book to be published on the subject. In it Harnack developed the convention of dividing the text into sixty verses.[91] Although apart from Bouriant's *editio princeps* the only work cited by Harnack was the Robinson and James volume, he had nevertheless consulted numerous scholars concerning his own work. He explicitly thanks the Bishop of Durham, Deissmann, Nestle, and Wellhausen.[92] Thus apart from fellow German scholars, it appears that by mid-December 1892, Harnack had managed to consult with Brooke Foss Westcott, the then Bishop of Durham concerning the new textual discoveries.

---

[85] A. Harnack and E. Schürer (eds.), *TLZ* 17 (1892) 609–614; (1893) 33–37.

[86] A. Harnack, 'Bruchstücke des Evangeliums und der Apokalypse des Petrus' *Sitzungsberichte der königl. Preussischen Akademie der Wissenschaften* (Berlin 1892) 895–903, 949–965.

[87] E. Schürer, *Theologische Literaturzeitung* (1892) 612–614.

[88] The two articles in *Sitzungsberichte der königl. Preussischen Akademie der Wissenschaften* appeared on the 3rd and 10th of November 1892.

[89] A. Harnack, *Bruchstücke des Evangeliums und der Apokalypse des Petrus* (TU IX, 2, J.C. Hinrichs: Leipzig 1893).

[90] Harnack, *Bruchstücke des Evangeliums und der Apokalypse des Petrus*, ii.

[91] This can be seen in the Greek text presented on pages 8–12 and is also followed in the German translation on pages 12–16.

[92] Harnack, *Bruchstücke des Evangeliums und der Apokalypse des Petrus*, ii.

In his introduction Harnack drew attention to a number of unique features contained in the first text of the Akhmîm codex. Whereas Bouriant had drawn attention to the first person narrative in v. 60,[93] Harnack observed that Peter also spoke in the first person in v. 26,[94] and saw this as further reason to identify the text as the *Gospel of Peter*. After presentation of the Greek text and the accompanying German translation, Harnack devoted his attention to exploring intertextual links. Having listed possible parallels he concludes, 'I have noted above, our evangelist appears to draw upon the canonical gospel and thus to be more recent than them.'[95] Thus, Harnack not only suggested that there is a literary relationship between the canonical gospels and the Akhmîm text, but at this stage of his thinking he saw the *Gospel of Peter* as being later than, and dependent upon the canonical accounts. However, his opinion on the relationship between the canonical gospels and the *Gospel of Peter* oscillated. At different stages of his academic career he believed either the canonical gospels or the *Gospel of Peter* to have the better claim to literary priority.[96] Apart from the canonical gospels, Harnack explored the parallels with the writing of Justin,[97] and the *Didascalia Apostolorum*. In relation to the latter, he argued that there is a clear case of literary dependency, but suggested that here the *Gospel of Peter* is acting as the source.[98] In addition to these texts Harnack also surveyed possible links between *Gos. Pet.* 36–40 and the form of Mark 16.4 preserved in codex Bobiensis;[99] the writings of Tatian;[100] and a number of weaker parallels.[101] Harnack's analysis is characterized by encyclopædic knowledge and close attention to detail. Thus, from the outset German scholarship approached the study of the

---

[93] Bouriant states, 'Le premier d'entre eux nous présente un récit de la Passion du Christ qui, comme nous l'apprend la dernière phrase, forme un épisode détaché de l'évangile apocryphe de saint Pierre.' Bouriant, 'Fragments du texte grec du livre d'Énoch et de quelques écrits attribués à saint Pierre', 137.

[94] Harnack, *Bruchstücke des Evangeliums und der Apokalypse des Petrus*, 2.

[95] 'Ich habe oben bemerkt, unser Evangelium scheine auf den kanonischen Evangelien zu fassen und also jünger wie diese zu sein.' Harnack, *Bruchstücke des Evangeliums und der Apokalypse des Petrus*, 32.

[96] For a description of this change of viewpoint see Semeria, 'L'Évangile de Pierre', 541–542 and section 7.1, *The So-called Gospel of Peter and the Canonical Gospels*, here.

[97] Harnack, *Bruchstücke des Evangeliums und der Apokalypse des Petrus*, 37–40.

[98] See the extended discussion on pages 40–45.

[99] Harnack, *Bruchstücke des Evangeliums und der Apokalypse des Petrus*, 46.

[100] Harnack, *Bruchstücke des Evangeliums und der Apokalypse des Petrus*, 45–46.

[101] Harnack, *Bruchstücke des Evangeliums und der Apokalypse des Petrus*, 46–47.

*Gospel of Peter* with methodological sophistication and a clear focus on detailed analysis of source critical issues.

### 3.3.2. *Oscar von Gebhardt*

Gebhardt's work was no less scholarly or meticulous than that of Harnack, but his emphasis was significantly different. With a preface dated 'Leipzig den 13. Mai 1893',[102] the volume represented a detailed palaeographical and codicological study. His work was based on an analysis of a set of photographic images the provenance of which is not fully explained,[103] but which differed from the heliographs in Lods' volume.[104] After the introductory discussion, Gebhardt gave a detailed description of the physical features of the codex and the use of *nomina sacra* as they occurred in the first text in the Akhmîm codex.[105] This was followed by a palaeographical analysis, which described the formation of the Greek letters in the text. Gebhardt drew attention both to consistent features as well as carefully describing aberrant forms. As is fully apparent from the photographs published in the volume by Kraus and Nicklas, the scribe of the text did not possess particularly consistent or even legible handwriting.[106] Based on his palaeographical analysis Gebhardt dated the first text in the Akhmîm codex to the ninth century. This dating aligned with the date proposed by Bouriant;[107] however, Gebhardt established a more secure basis for such a dating.

Following this close analysis of the physical features of the text, Gebhardt discussed a number of possible variant readings at points where the text is uncertain.[108] Often this was due to the poor formation of

---

[102] Gebhardt, *Das Evangelium und die Apokalypse des Petrus*, preface.

[103] Lods, 'L'Évangile et l'Apocalypse de Pierre avec le texte grec du livre d'Hénoch', plates.

[104] As he states, 'Einmal, meine ich, wird es vielen, welchen die kostspieligen Mémoires des französischen archäologischen Mission in Cairo nicht zugänglich sind, willkommen sein, die Petrusfragmente allein in einem Facsimile zu besitzen, und sodann kann ich nicht umhin, meine Lichtdrucktafeln für werthvoller zu halten, als die in den Mémoires enthaltenen Heliogravüren.' Gebhardt, *Das Evangelium und die Apokalypse des Petrus*, plates I–XX, 1.

[105] Gebhardt, *Das Evangelium und die Apokalypse des Petrus*, 7–10.

[106] See Thomas J. Kraus and Tobias Nicklas, *Das Petrusevangelium und die Petrusapokalypse: Die Griechischen Fragmente mit deutscher und englischer Übersetzung* (Berlin: Walter de Gruyter, 2004) plates.

[107] Bouriant proposed a wider range of dates, eighth to twelfth century. See Bouriant, 'Fragments du texte grec du livre d'Énoch et de quelques écrits attribués à saint Pierre', 93.

[108] Gebhardt, *Das Evangelium und die Apokalypse des Petrus*, 15–29.

letters by the scribe, although at some places the papyrus had become darkened, or there exists a hole in the page. Gebhardt's work concluded with a presentation of the text, a bibliographical list of works published to that point, and the reproduction of photographic images.[109] The strength of this volume lies in its unique study of the palaeographical and codicological aspects of the text. Such an analysis has not been undertaken again by later scholars to the same meticulous degree that Gebhardt focused on the physical features of the manuscript. While proposals have been made for an earlier dating of the text,[110] they fail to offer the same detailed study of palaeography. Consequently, the results often seem to be based on less scientific grounds than the conclusions presented by Gebhardt. It is for this reason that his contribution remains highly valuable, if unfortunately all too often neglected.

### 3.3.3. A. Hilgenfeld

Another significant and early contribution to the discussion in Germany was undertaken by Hilgenfeld in two articles and a short note, all of which appeared in *Zeitschrift für Wissenschaftliche Theologie*, although subsequent works have frequently failed to reference the short note.[111] In the first of these three articles Hilgenfeld presented the passage from Eusebius *H.E.* 6.12.3–5 (in Greek) outlining Serapion's reaction to the *Gospel of Peter* which was being used in Rhossos. Next he reproduced the Greek text of the first document contained in the Akhmîm codex. This was accompanied with a critical apparatus collating variants from four sources which are listed in the following form; 'B = Bouriant, C = Codex, D = Diels, H = Harnack.'[112] This list raises a number of questions. First it is not entirely clear what is meant by 'codex' since it is apparent in his final article that Lods' heliographs have only just become available to Hilgenfeld. Moreover, it appears that the emendations suggested by Diels had been gleaned from

---

[109] See Gebhardt, *Das Evangelium und die Apokalypse des Petrus*, 30–41 and plates I–XX.

[110] For a listing of various proposed dates see van Haelst's *Catalogue des papyrus littéraires juifs et chrétiens*, 597, no. 598.

[111] The three pieces are: A. Hilgenfeld, 'Das Petrus-Evangelium uber Leiden und Auferstehung Jesu', *ZWT* 36 (1893) part I, 439–454; 'Zu dem Petrus-Evangelium', *ZWT* 36 (1893) part II, 160; and, 'Das Petrus-Evangelium', *ZWT* 36 (1893) part II, 220–267.

[112] Hilgenfeld, 'Das Petrus-Evangelium über Leiden und Auferstehung Jesu', 440.

Harnack's work,[113] since Diels did not publish these independently.[114] Hilgenfeld's edition of the text with critical apparatus is then followed by brief observations and comments on the text.[115] These notes are primarily concerned with identifying parallels between the first document in the Akhmîm codex and the canonical gospels, although he does identify one extra-canonical parallel between *Gos. Pet.* 3.7 and Justin's *First Apology* (1.35).[116] The concluding paragraph re-asserts the case for seeing the document as originating in a second century context.[117]

The next contribution made by Hilgenfeld to the study of the Akhmîm text was a brief note in *ZWT*.[118] This note, however, further illustrates those works available to Hilgenfeld at the time of writing, for his ongoing textual work. Essentially the notice introduces a correction to the text of *Gos. Pet.* 2.5. Hilgenfeld's initial presentation of the text replicated an omission of the words καὶ παρέδωκεν αὐτὸν τῷ λαῷ πρὸ μιᾶς τῶν ἀζύμων τῆς ἑορτῆς αὐτῶν, initially omitted by Bouriant[119] and subsequently followed by Harnack.[120] As the note states, this correction had not been made by direct examination of the text, but through Robert Bensly's examination of the codex.[121] The same correction is made by Swete in his edition of the Akhmîm codex.[122] In his preface Swete also attributes this reading, and others, to the textual work of Bensly, 'This reprint was issued again in February 1893, with some corrections obtained from the MS. through the kindness of the late Professor Bensly, whose recent death has brought upon all studies

---

[113] Harnack, *Bruchstücke des Evangeliums und der Apokalypse des Petrus*, i.

[114] As Hilgenfeld stated, 'Den Abdruck des Herrn U. Bouriant (Mem. Publ. par les membres de la Mission archéol Française, T. IX, fasc. 1, 1892) hat A. Harnack (Sitzungsberichte der Kön. Preuss. Akademie der Wiss. zu Berlin vom 3 Nov. 1892), unterstützt von H. Diels, mehrfach verandert und, wie nicht anders zu erwarten war, auch berichtigen.' Hilgenfeld, 'Das Petrus-Evangelium über Leiden und Auferstehung Jesu', 440.

[115] Hilgenfeld, 'Das Petrus-Evangelium über Leiden und Auferstehung Jesu', 444–452.

[116] Hilgenfeld, 'Das Petrus-Evangelium über Leiden und Auferstehung Jesu', 447.

[117] Hilgenfeld, 'Das Petrus-Evangelium über Leiden und Auferstehung Jesu', 452–454.

[118] Hilgenfeld, 'Zu dem Petrus-Evangelium', 160.

[119] Bouriant, 'Fragments du texte grec du livre d'Énoch et de quelques écrits attribués à saint Pierre', 137.

[120] Harnack, *Bruchstücke des Evangeliums und der Apokalypse des Petrus*, 9.

[121] Hilgenfeld, 'Zu dem Petrus-Evangelium', 160.

[122] Swete, *The Akhmîm Fragment*, 3.

of this kind a loss which it is impossible to estimate.'[123] Bensly's death meant that he published no work on the Petrine gospel, but some of his textual observations have been preserved by others. Apart from this substantive correction, Hilgenfeld's note also records a smaller correction in v. 41.[124]

The third and final article that Hilgenfeld published on the Akhmîm text in *ZWT* reproduced and expanded upon his earlier work, as well as introducing a number of new features. The introduction acknowledged again Bensly's textual work undertaken while he was in Egypt, as well as mentioning the appearance of Lods' edition of the text with heliographic images.[125] The appearance of these heliographic images enabled further corrections to the text, which were presented in this third article. However, prior to giving the text, Hilgenfeld discussed a far greater range of Patristic evidence to link the text with a second century dating.[126] Next the text is presented with a more extensive set of readings assembled from the works of various German and French editions of the text, with Harris being the only representative of English scholarship. The sources for the apparatus as listed are, 'B = Bouriant, Bl. = Blass, D = Diels, Gbh. = v. Gebhardt, Hn. = Harnack, Hr. = Harris, Hg. = Hilgenfeld (in dieser Zeitschrift XXXVI, 4), L = Lods, Z = Zahn.'[127] Although Hilgenfeld did not list 'C = Codex' in this list as he had done in his original list, the symbol still persists in his apparatus with no clarification of its meaning. The remaining two sections in the article explored in detail the connections between the Akhmîm text and the canonical gospels, as well as looking at other textual traditions that may have been known to the author of the *Gospel of Peter*.[128]

### 3.3.4. *Other Early German Contributions*
While Harnack, Gebhardt and Hilgenfeld each made early, diverse and significant contributions to the study of the text that was identified as the *Gospel of Peter*, these three scholars are only representative of the vibrant and voluminous work that was undertaken in the German context. Appearing slightly after the books of Harnack, Gebhardt and the first two of Hilgenfeld's articles, the work of Zahn also presented an

---

[123] Swete, *The Akhmîm Fragment*, v.
[124] Hilgenfeld, 'Zu dem Petrus-Evangelium', 160.
[125] Hilgenfeld, 'Das Petrus-Evangelium', 220.
[126] Hilgenfeld, 'Das Petrus-Evangelium', 221–233.
[127] Hilgenfeld, 'Das Petrus-Evangelium', 233.
[128] Hilgenfeld, 'Das Petrus-Evangelium', 239–267.

edition of the Greek text with accompanying notes.[129] Another analysis of the relationship between the Akhmîm text and possible source material was provided by Hans von Schubert initially in German,[130] but also appearing later the same year in an English translation.[131] Also in 1893 Schubert published a fuller treatment of the text with translation and comments.[132] Alongside these works, a number of smaller articles appeared, usually without an edition of the Greek text. What is fully apparent from even a brief survey of German scholarship at this stage is that it was characterized by great energy and diversity.

### 3.4. *The Second Phase of Research*

The voluminous early interest in the text identified as the *Gospel of Peter* surprisingly dissipated at a rate almost equivalent to its appearance. A trickle of articles continued to appear between 1894–1897,[133] but thereafter there was almost a total loss of interest in the text for approximately thirty years. In the interim period the text was referenced primarily in collections of apocryphal texts, but not on its own.[134]

### 3.4.1. *V.H. Stanton (1900) and C.H. Turner (1913)*

Perhaps the major exceptions to this subsequent neglect were two articles that both appeared in the *Journal of Theological Studies* some thirteen years apart. The first of these by V.H. Stanton appeared in 1900 and explored the significance of the *Gospel of Peter* for discussing the emergence and recognition of the fourfold gospel canon.[135] In fact

---

[129] T. Zahn, *Das Evangelium des Petrus Das kürzlich gefundene Fragment seines Textes* (Erlangen-Leipzig: Deichert, 1893).

[130] H. von Schubert, *Das Petrusevangelium, synoptische Tabelle nebst übersetzung und kritischem Apparat* (Berlin, 1893).

[131] H. von Schubert, *The Gospel of St. Peter: synoptical tables, with translations and critical apparatus*, English trans. Rev. John Macpherson (Edinburgh: T&T Clark, 1893).

[132] H. von Schubert, *Die Composition des pseudopetrinischen Evangelium-Fragments* (Berlin: Reuther & Reichard, 1893).

[133] J.B. Semeria, 'L'Évangile de Pierre', *Revue biblique* (1894) 522–560; A.C. McGifferd, 'The Gospel of Peter', *Papers of the American Society of Church History* (1894) 99–130; C. Bruston, 'De quelques texts difficiles de l'Evangile de Pierre', *Revues des etudes grecques* (1897) 58–65.

[134] E. Klostermann, *Apocrypha I* (Bonn: J.C.B. Mohr, 1921); M.R. James, *The Apocryphal New Testament* (Oxford: OUP, 1924) 13ff; 90ff.

[135] V.H. Stanton, 'The Gospel of Peter, its early history and character considered in relation to the history of the recognition in the Church of the canonical gospels', *JTS* 2 (1900) 1–25.

Stanton prefaces his own investigation with an interesting note that attests the cessation of interest in this text.

> The publication by M. Bouriant in the autumn of 1892 of the fragment at Akhmim of the lost *Gospel of Peter* was followed, in our own country and others, by a shower of articles, lectures, editions, treatises, dealing with it, which, beginning in the last months of that year, continued throughout 1893, and gradually diminished in intensity and ceased in 1894.[136]

In apologetical tones, Stanton begs the indulgence of his readership for re-opening a subject 'which has lost all its freshness.' The main purpose of the article is to demonstrate that the *Gospel of Peter* is of a different 'class' from the canonical gospels.[137] Support for this conclusion is dependent upon four subsidiary arguments developed in the article. First, Stanton rejects both previous arguments that suggest that the *Gospel of Peter* was known and used by Justin Martyr, and also that Justin placed the *Gospel of Peter* on an equal footing with the gospels that he termed as 'apostolic memoirs.'[138] This is essentially the same conclusion as is reached in the discussion in this volume in regard to the suggested relationship between Justin and the *Gospel of Peter*, (although the possibility that the phrase phrase ἀπομνημονεύμασιν αὐτοῦ refers to the memoirs of Jesus is seen as being more plausible than Stanton allows).[139] Secondly, it is observed that the work does not have a decidedly docetic nature.[140] Thirdly, the dependence of the *Gospel of Peter* on all four canonical gospels is strongly advocated.[141] Fourthly, the *Gospel of Peter* can be related to the trajectory of Apocryphal Gospels which evidence creative retellings of familiar canonical stories. From this set of observations, it is suggested that while the *Gospel of Peter* is derivative upon the four canonical gospels, the character of the work is inferior to that of its predecessors.[142] Obviously there is a distinctively theological (or perhaps ecclesial) orientation in the arguments advanced in this article. Yet, nothwithstanding this, the criticism raised against some of the suggestions promoted in

---

[136] Stanton, 'The Gospel of Peter', 1.
[137] Stanton, 'The Gospel of Peter', 24–25.
[138] Stanton, 'The Gospel of Peter', 2–18.
[139] See section 8.1 below.
[140] Stanton, 'The Gospel of Peter', 20–21.
[141] Stanton, 'The Gospel of Peter', 21–23.
[142] Stanton, 'The Gospel of Peter', 23–24.

the first wave of publications on the *Gospel of Peter* makes for sober reflection.

The second major article to appear during this period of virtual neglect was C.H. Turner's investigation into the question '[i]s the Gospel of Peter an independent witness to the tradition of the Resurrection?'[143] After an extended discussion of potential parallels, he comes to the conclusion that it is 'infinitely more probable than not that he was acquainted with, and in his own Gospel made use of, all four Gospels of the Church.'[144] Moreover, Turner rejects the suggestion that the *Gospel of Peter* might be acquainted with a no-longer extant lost ending of Mark, since he argues that John's Gospel is the source used to round off the *Gospel of Peter*. In effect, Turner's conclusion echoes that of Stanton, namely that the *Gospel of Peter* is not a competitor to the priority of the four canonical accounts. While there may again be a theological motivation behind advancing this conclusion, this does not negate the cogency of the analysis undertaken by either Stanton or Turner, and their generally identical conclusions appears to stand irrespective of the motivation behind their investigations.

### 3.4.2. *P. Gardner-Smith (1926)*

After this period of at best sporadic interest in the text, during the mid to late 1920's two scholars, to a limited extent, re-opened interest in the *Gospel of Peter*. In his two part article of 1926, also published in the *Journal of Theological Studies*, Gardner-Smith questioned the dependence of the *Gospel of Peter* upon the canonical gospel accounts and sought to provide a basis for an early date for the text.[145] Although, surprisingly, not making any reference to Stanton's article and only one fleeting reference to Turner's detailed study,[146] Gardner-Smith argued precisely the opposite point of view to what was suggested in those two articles. His main point was that too much emphasis had been placed upon points of agreement rather than upon the independent features of the *Gospel of Peter*. This is a helpful place to observe that different scholars seem to understand 'literary dependence' in divergent

---

[143] C.H. Turner, 'The Gospel of Peter' *JTS* 14 (1913) 161–195.
[144] Turner, 'The Gospel of Peter', 187.
[145] P. Gardner-Smith, 'The Gospel of Peter', *JTS* 27 (1926) 255–271 and 'The Date of the Gospel of Peter', *JTS* 27 (1926) 401–407.
[146] Gardner-Smith, 'The Gospel of Peter', 264.

ways. For Stanton and Turner literary dependence does not require
showing that the *Gospel of Peter* is drawing on pre-existent written
tradition from the four canonical accounts at every point. Rather, they
only wish to demonstrate that at some places the *Gospel of Peter* drew
upon such material. This, they argued, suggests knowledge of those
accounts, but it does not disallow creativity on the part of the author
of the non-canonical text. However, for Gardner-Smith, it is the very
quantity of the divergences from the accounts of the fourfold corpus
of gospels that make it no longer tenable to maintain belief in literary dependence. He states, '[t]he many divergences of 'Peter' from the
canonical gospels are best explained, not by supposing that the author
had an inexplicable passion for tampering with his sources, but by
supposing that he did not know the work of Matthew, Mark, Luke
and John.'[147]

Having rejected the view that the *Gospel of Peter* was dependent
upon the canonical accounts in favour of the position that it independently drew upon the traditions behind the four gospels of the New
Testament, Gardner-Smith, in the second part of the article, turned
his attention to discussing the dating of this 'Petrine' text. He takes the
identity of the *Gospel of Peter* (mentioned in Eusebius' description of
Serapion) with the Akhmîm text as a given. Thus, he states, 'the last
decade of the second century' is taken as the upper limit for date of
composition.[148] According to Gardner-Smith's judgment '[t]he probability is very small that in 190 a church would read a book twenty
years old as one of the canonical gospels, and the Gospel of Peter must
have had a much longer history to explain the respect in which it was
held.'[149] The next important moment in tracing back the history of
the text is seen as being the writings of Justin Martyr. Without any
reference to the counterarguments raised by Stanton, Gardner-Smith
simply replicates the observations of Harnack and others concerning
potential parallels between Justin's writings and the *Gospel of Peter*. No
argument is presented for establishing the direction of dependence. It
is felt that the parallels show that the two writers are literarily related
and that it is self-evident that the *Gospel of Peter* is the predecessor.
For a second time in his article Gardner-Smith uses the spurious argu-

---

[147] Gardner-Smith, 'The Gospel of Peter', 270.
[148] Gardner-Smith, 'The Gospel of Peter', 401.
[149] Gardner-Smith, 'The Gospel of Peter', 401.

ment that a document must have been in circulation for at least twenty years before an author such as Justin would be able to make reference to it as an authoritative source. Without justification he again states, 'it is difficult to believe that Justin would use as the work of Peter a pseudonymous document that was less than twenty years old.'[150] Thus it is suggested in regard to the dating of the *Gospel of Peter* that 'the latest possible date for its composition is about AD 130.'[151] Yet this does not conclude the attempt to push the dating of the text earlier. Next Gardner-Smith marshals the hypothesis from the first part of the article, that the *Gospel of Peter* is independent of the canonical accounts. Sketching the tradition-history of some stories common to both the *Gospel of Peter* and the canonical gospels it is argued that the Petrine account could only have been written at a time before some of the elaborations and modifications contained in the four canonical accounts had become dominant. From such observations the following conclusion is advanced.

> A rough guess would suggest AD 90 as the date of the gospel, perhaps ten years earlier, possibly twenty years later, but the later date does not accord well either with the internal evidence, or with the respect which, if Justin knew it, the gospel enjoyed in the first half of the second century. The evidence fixed as a whole seems to fix the year 100 as the *terminus ad quem*.[152]

It is amazing to compare the conclusions of Stanton and Turner with those of Gardner-Smith. Although he does not interact explicitly with the work of his predecessors, his findings almost appear to be consciously designed to diametrically oppose their arguments. Turner's opening question was whether the *Gospel of Peter* was an independent witness to the resurrection,[153] and his conclusion was in the negative. Gardner-Smith states in his final paragraph 'that "Peter" is a very important witness to the traditions of the resurrection.'[154] Stanton devoted a considerable section of his article to arguing that there was not a demonstrable literary relationship between the writings of Justin Martyr and the *Gospel of Peter*.[155] By contrast, using the same

---

[150] Gardner-Smith, 'The Gospel of Peter', 403.
[151] Gardner-Smith, 'The Gospel of Peter', 404.
[152] Gardner-Smith, 'The Gospel of Peter', 407.
[153] Turner, 'The Gospel of Peter', 161.
[154] Gardner-Smith, 'The Gospel of Peter', 407.
[155] Stanton, 'The Gospel of Peter', 2–18.

set of potential parallels, Gardner-Smith has no hesitation in categorically affirming the existence of such a literary relationship.[156] What is
interesting is that Gardner-Smith finds slight points of contact (sometimes only a single shared word) to be compelling evidence for Justin's
dependence on the *Gospel of Peter*, but where there are more extensive
verbal parallels between the *Gospel of Peter* and the four canonical
accounts this is deemed not to constitute evidence of a literary parallel.
The methodological justification for such divergent approaches is not
altogether clear, and consequently this substantially weakens the case
being advocated by Gardner-Smith.

Another interesting feature of the positions articulated by Stanton,
Turner and Gardner-Smith is that in part they represent the current
divide in modern opinions concerning the *Gospel of Peter*. However,
at that stage there had been no attempt to formulate any theory that
equated to the 'Cross-Gospel' hypothesis. Crossan's suggestion that
the *Gospel of Peter* contains, embedded in it, an earlier source (regardless of what one considers to be the plausibility of this suggestion) is
without doubt the major difference between the way the debate was
conducted at the beginning of the twentieth century in comparison
to the terms in which it is currently being discussed. Nonetheless, the
fundamental divide remains between those who view the text as early
and independent of the canonical accounts, and those who advocate
its literary dependence upon the four canonical accounts and consequently usually support a later date at some point in the second
century.

### 3.4.3. *Léon Vaganay (1929)*

Léon Vaganay published his magisterial commentary on the *Gospel of
Peter* in 1929, with the second edition (which is usually cited in the
literature) appearing the following year in 1930.[157] Despite the breadth
of critical scholarship exhibited in this volume and the range of theological issues surrounding the text that are also discussed, it is the case
that too often this study is neglected in anglophone scholarship – often
to the detriment of the subsequent work. Notwithstanding the plau-
dits that Vaganay's work rightly deserves, in the eight decades since

---

[156] Gardner-Smith, 'The Gospel of Peter', 401–403.
[157] L. Vaganay, *L'Évangile de Pierre*, Études Biblique (Paris: Gabalda, 1st ed. 1929/2nd ed. 1930).

he wrote his commentary there have been significant advances not only in discussions surrounding the *Gospel of Peter*, but perhaps more importantly in the methodological approaches to the study of ancient Christian texts. Yet, surprisingly, the immense scholarship contained in Vaganay's work did not act as a catalyst for further research focused on the *Gospel of Peter*, instead it marked the end of any major work on the text for approximately forty years. Whether Vaganay's volume was the causal factor in this decline in interest, or whether it is coincidental may be debated, but a survey of bibliographies will show that apart from the *Gospel of Peter* being discussed in anthologies of apocryphal texts, it virtually disappeared from the scholarly horizon for more than four decades.[158] Vaganay's commentary will be used as one of the major dialogue partners in this commentary. For this reason a detailed discussion of its perspectives will take place at the appropriate points in the commentary contained in this volume.

### 3.5. *The Intervening Period – Relative Neglect (1930–1973)*

As mentioned above, during the period from the publication of the second edition of Vaganay's commentary until the appearance in 1973 of the only other commentary on the text, also in French but admittedly much briefer, there is somewhat of a void in scholarship on the *Gospel of Peter*. The lack of research during this forty years period commencing in 1930 is evidenced by the bibliography in Maria Mara's *Sources Chrétiennes* commentary.[159] She divides the literature into various periods. For the period after 1930 until the publication of her own volume in 1973 she lists only eight items under the heading *Études récentes*. If, however, compendia of apocryphal texts are set aside, then only three short articles have the *Gospel of Peter* as part

---

[158] Some of the more important collections of apocryphal texts containing the *Gospel of Peter* that were published between 1930 and 1970 include E. Klostermann, *Apocrypha I: 'Reste des Petrusevangeliums, der Petrusapokalypse und des Kerygma Petri* (KIT 3; Berlin 1933) although this was basically a re-issuing of an edition of the Greek texts of these three documents that originally appeared in print in 1903; A. de Santos Otero, *Los Evangelios Apocrifos. Colleccion de texyos griegos y latinos, version critica, estudios introductorios y commentaries* (Madrid: La Editorial Catolica, 1956); E. Hennecke und W. Schneemelcher (eds.), *Neutestamentliche Apokryphen in deutscher*, Band 1: Evangelien. Band 2: Apostolisches, (3rd ed., Tübingen: Mohr Siebeck, 1959).

[159] M.G. Mara, *Évangile de Pierre: Introduction, Texte Critique, Traduction, Commentaire et Index* (Sources Chrétiennes 201; Paris: Les Éditions du Cerf, 1973).

of their principal focus.[160] Yet it must be noted that even these three articles treat the *Gospel of Peter* in an extremely brief manner as a means to address other textual questions or to re-open the question of textual relationships.

However, in this intervening period one longer study was written, which is missing from many bibliographies due to the fact that it is an unpublished doctoral thesis. Submitted in June 1965 to the Harvard Divinity School, B.A. Johnson's dissertation was a study of 'The Empty Tomb Tradition in the Gospel of Peter.'[161] Its central thesis is that the 'women at the tomb' narrative is based upon a version of that story prior to its incorporation into Mark and that the 'guard at the tomb' story also 'existed prior to Mt and that it was actually an epiphany story which described the resurrection.'[162] In relation to the 'women at the tomb' account, Johnson contends that the *Gospel of Peter* does not show a knowledge of the developed form of the tradition with the twin apologetic concerns of the additional reference to the disciples (Mk 16.7) and the report of an appearance of the risen Lord. It is in relation to this last point that Johnson's thesis is weakest, for there is no appearance of the risen Lord in the final chapter of Mark unless one notes that, '[t]he longer ending of Mk (Mk 16.9) does provide an appearance of Jesus to Mary Magdalene on the morning of the resurrection.'[163] Johnson also draws attention to the fact that the *Gospel of Peter* in its version of the story of the women at the tomb contains many novelistic details. Taking these observations together, he concludes that this tradition was still 'alive and developing' and that the *Gospel of Peter* develops 'a form of the story that is older than any of the accounts in the canonical gospels.'[164] In reality, this conclusion is based solely on the lack of any parallel in the *Gospel of Peter* to the reference to the disciples in Mk 16.7. Johnson should, however, be acknowledged as generating much of the ensuing interested in the proposal that a unified pre-existing guard at the tomb story might

---

[160] G. Quispel and R. Grant, 'Note on the Petrine Apocrypha', *VC* 6 (1952) 31; A.F.J. Klijn, 'Het evangile von Petrus en de Westerse Text', *Nederlands Theologisch Tijdschrift* 16 (1961) 264–270; O. Perler, 'L'Évangile de Pierre et Méliton de Sardes' *RB* 71 (1964) 584–590.

[161] B.A. Johnson, 'The Empty Tomb Tradition in the Gospel of Peter', (Harvard: unpub. Th.D. thesis, 1965).

[162] Johnson, 'The Empty Tomb Tradition in the Gospel of Peter', 8.

[163] Johnson, 'The Empty Tomb Tradition in the Gospel of Peter', 22, n.15.

[164] Johnson, 'The Empty Tomb Tradition in the Gospel of Peter', 36.

account for the form of the story (again with novelistic expansions) contained in the *Gospel of Peter*.

### 3.6. *The Current Phase of Research*

Deciding where to cut the continuous fabric of history is always a subjective decision, but in many ways this is more obvious with the rebirth of interest in the *Gospel of Peter* evidenced by various scholarly treatments, initially starting slowly from the 1970s onwards. This rejuvenation of interest shows no sign of abating.

### 3.6.1. *Maria Mara (1973)*
Commencing slowly with mainly French and German scholarship, the 1970s saw the re-emergence of interest in non-canonical texts, with the *Gospel of Peter* being among the corpus of writings surveyed afresh. Mara's own commentary represented the first book length treatment of the text since Vaganay's magisterial work. In line with the general aims of the *Sources Chrétiennes* series the treatment she offers makes the text readily available in the original language with facing French translation, accompanied by relatively detailed notes and commentary (although nowhere near as detailed as Vaganay's treatment). One key issue for Mara, addressed in her introduction was the question of the identity of the Akhmîm text with the *Gospel of Peter* as known by Origen and Eusebius.[165] She sees it as being likely that the untitled Akhmîm fragment is to be identified with the text known to these two early Christian writers. With the caveat that the text may have undergone some changes in the transmission process, this appear to be the most probable conclusion from the available evidence.

However, it should be noted that Mara's handy-pocket edition is largely derivative upon the research and commentary of Vaganay and consequently does not represent a significant advance in the study of the text. Nonetheless, in many ways Mara's volume marks the opening of the current phase of research into the *Gospel of Peter* despite the fact that her commentary largely represents an epitome of early works on the text.

---

[165] Mara, *Évangile de Pierre*, 19, 35.

### 3.6.2. Jürgen Denker (1975) and Albert Fuchs (1978)

Following soon after the publication of Mara's commentary, two German volumes offered different treatments of the text. Denker ana-
lyzed the theological outlook of the text assessing theological issues
surrounding the text such as Christology.[166] By contrast, Fuchs' work
was primarily a lexical and grammatical tool for the study of the text.[167]
After the brief introduction, he provides a concordance to the *Gospel
of Peter* followed by three indices. The first lists all uses of χαί since
this word, along with the article, is not included in the concordance.
The second is an alphabetic listing of terms, and the third lists words
in order of frequency. There is a comprehensive bibliography of works
on the subject. Next follow two sections by Weissengruber on the date
of the *Gospel of Peter* based upon the use of the optative, the reappearance of which it is argued is not attested before the second century; the
text is consequently seen as being written during the second century
as suggested by Mara and Vaganay. The grammatical analysis suggests
the text is representative of typical Koine Greek, and hence a Syrian
provenance, as suggested by Vaganay, is deemed to be unlikely. In
many ways the usefulness of this volume has been surpassed by the
more recent work of Kraus and Nicklas which is a more up-to-date
reference tool.[168]

### 3.6.3. J.D. Crossan (1985, 1988)

The mid-1980s saw a full-scale revival of interest in the first text contained in the Akhmîm codex. In many ways this was sparked by J.D.
Crossan, primarily in his book *The Cross that Spoke*,[169] although he had
previously discussed the theory that the *Gospel of Peter* reflected earlier
stages of the Passion and resurrection tradition than that constained
in the canonical gospels in his earlier book, *Four Other Gospels*.[170] His
thesis was that the *Gospel of Peter* enshrined an earlier narrative, which

---

[166] Jürgen Denker, *Die theologiegeschichtliche Stellung des Petrusevangeliums. Ein
Beitrag zur Frühgeschichte des Doketismus*, EHS 23/36 (Lang, Frankfurt a.M., 1975).

[167] Albert Fuchs, *Die griechischen Apokryphen zum Neuen Testament. Bd. 1: Das
Petrusevangelium*, Studien zum Neuen Testament und seiner Umwelt B/2 (Freistadt:
Linz, 1978).

[168] Thomas J. Kraus and Tobias Nicklas, *Das Petrusevangelium und die Petrusapokalypse: Die Griechischen Fragmente mit deutscher und englischer Übersetzung*
(Berlin: Walter de Gruyter, 2004).

[169] J.D. Crossan, *The Cross that Spoke: The Origins of the Passion Narrative* (San
Francisco: Harper & Row, 1988).

[170] J.D. Crossan, *Four Other Gospels* (Minneapolis: Winston, 1985).

he labelled *The Cross Gospel*, and that this source pre-dates the canonical Passion accounts. This theory captured the interest of certain sectors of the New Testament fraternity. Thus, Crossan's work proved to be a harbinger of ideas that are still being pursued by certain scholars in relation to the *Gospel of Peter*.[171] The creative impetus of Crossan's work should not be under-emphasized, even for those who disagree with his major theses. Current work on the *Gospel of Peter* is still shaped in a large way in response to Crossan's theories.

### 3.6.4. *The Post-Crossan Period*

From this point onwards, discussion has continued at a steady rate with Crossan's own work defining much of the subsequent debate concerning the relationship of this non-canonical text to the canonical gospels. One of the earliest responses was made by Raymond Brown.[172] He rejects Crossan's supposition that the canonical gospels depend literarily on the *Gospel of Peter*.[173] His own thesis, however, is not simply the reverse of that position. First, Brown noted that there are only a few instances where there are sufficiently extended and close parallels which allow for the conclusion of literary dependence. Here Brown implicitly raised the important question of what precisely constitutes a case of literary dependence. It needs to be observed that this question remains unresolved in biblical scholarship, and this in part results in conflicting assessments of evidence. Brown appears to require a high level of correspondence between two texts before entertaining the possibility of dependence. This is potentially helpful since it excludes too high a degree of speculation and seeks to find demonstrable cases to borrowings. After documenting some striking divergences between the *Gospel of Peter* and the canonical accounts, Brown proposes that 'oral dependence of *GP* on some or all of the canonical Gospels'[174] best

---

[171] Paul Mirecki is a notable example of a scholar who has not only followed Crossan's hypothesis, but indeed has expanded its claims. He sees the first text contained in the Akhmîm codex, the Gospel of Peter, as itself pre-dating the synoptic gospels, rather than containing a source that antedates them. He states, 'The *Gospel of Peter* was a narrative gospel of the synoptic type which circulated in the mid-1st century under the authority of the name Peter.' (278). See P.A. Mirecki, 'Peter, Gospel of', in D.N. Freedman (ed.) *The Anchor Bible Dictionary*, volume 5, (New York: Doubleday, 1992) 278–281.

[172] R.E. Brown, 'The *Gospel of Peter* and Canonical Gospel Priority', *NTS* 33 (1987) 321–343.

[173] Brown, 'The *Gospel of Peter* and Canonical Gospel Priority', 333.

[174] Brown, 'The *Gospel of Peter* and Canonical Gospel Priority', 335.

accounts for the data. Brown is careful how he defines such orality. This is not the dependence upon some pre-Gospel traditions, but is described as a second type or orality which developed in the second century when Christians only heard the gospel accounts read aloud and consequently confused the details of the accounts. It is unclear how one would distinguish between this phenomenon and the case where a scribe may have read a gospel account firsthand and then subsequently drawn upon this from memory to write a text such as the *Gospel of Peter*. Again lack of knowledge about the mechanics of composition affects the categories that can be used to describe the formation of documents utilising source material.[175]

In relation to the story of the guard at the tomb contained in both the Matthean account and the *Gospel of Peter* Brown sees the continuous account in the latter text as not solely dependent on Matthew. Instead he argues that for '[t]his story GP may have drawn not only from oral memories of Matt but also from other ongoing oral traditions similar to that received in Matt at an earlier stage.'[176] It is, however, difficult to understand how Brown can so easily differentiate between these possibilities of oral and written tradition. Moreover, he seems to have ruled out the possibility that the author of the *Gospel of Peter* could actually have joined together the three separate scenes in Matthew.[177] This possibility will be discussed in the relevant sections of the commentary.

Brown's hypothesis concerning secondary orality, although not widely adopted in published discussion, has been supported in two subsequent studies. The first was in 1991 by Susan Schaeffer, Brown's doctoral student. In her unpublished thesis she built upon Brown's notion of a second type of orality whereby an author has knowledge of written gospels but composes his own later work without ready access to those texts. Schaeffer goes further than Brown in discussing the possibility that the author of the *Gospel of Peter* had previously seen written copies of the canonical gospels, but did not have access to these documents when composing his own account. Thus, during the

---

[175] For a discussion of orality in the formation and transmission of the synoptic tradition with specific reference to double tradition passages see, T. Mournet, *Oral Tradition and Literary Dependency: Variability and Stability in the Synoptic Tradition and Q.* (WUNT 2.195; Tübingen: Mohr Siebeck, 2005).

[176] Brown, 'The *Gospel of Peter* and Canonical Gospel Priority', 337.

[177] Brown, *The Death of the Messiah*, vol. 2, esp. 1317–1349.

composition phas, the author had to rely on memory and traditions derived from an oral culture.[178] Again, it is uncertain whether this constitutes a meaning distinction between oral and literary dependence. It appears that for Schaeffer, like Brown, literary dependence only takes place if a scribe is composing his text with an unrolled scroll or open codex containing the source material in front of the copyist. This definition is perhaps too restrictive.

The type of position advocated by Brown and Schaeffer has also been followed by Martha Stillman. In some ways Stillman's proposal is even more radical since she seeks to establish 'oral-only' dependence on the canonical accounts. Her study proposes establishing oral-only dependence be showing that 'GP uses words which are synonymous in meaning and sound almost identical to words found in parallel canonical verses, yet are different because they derive from different Greek roots.'[179] One thing that is lacking in her argument is a comparison of the way the synoptic gospels vary in their use of homophones with similar meanings, or changing compound to simplex verbal forms. It is suggested that the very features that Stillman finds conclusive for establishing 'oral-only' dependence are to be found in the synoptic accounts where literary dependence is widely recognized.[180]

There has also been support for the theories which investigates the relationship between the *Gospel of Peter* and the canonical accounts. Perhaps the three most prominent examples of following (or even extending) the proposals of Crossan are found in the scholarly discussions of Helmut Koester, Paul Mirecki and Arthur Dewey.[181] It should be stated, however, while perhaps not appearing in print as frequently as the theories of Crossan, Koester, Mirecki and Dewey, the dominant position held by scholars does nonetheless appear to be that of seeing the *Gospel of Peter* as dependent on one or more of

---

[178] S. Schaeffer, 'The Gospel of Peter, the Canonical Gospels, and the Oral Tradition', unpublished PhD dissertation (New York: Union Theological Seminary, 1991).

[179] M.K. Stillman, 'The Gospel of Peter: A Case for Oral-Only Dependency?', *ETL* 73 (1997) 114–120.

[180] Although for an attempt to problematise this assumption see Mournet, *Oral Tradition and Literary Dependency*.

[181] H. Koester, *Ancient Christian Gospels: Their History and Development* (Philadelphia/London: TPI/SCM, 1990) 216–231; P. Mirecki, 'Peter, Gospel of', in D.N. Freedman (ed.) *The Anchor Bible Dictionary*, volume 5, 278–281; Dewey has published a whole series of articles on this topic with the initial treatment being, A.J. Dewey, 'And an Answer Was Heard from the Cross', *Foundations and Facets Forum* 5.3 (1989) 103–111.

the canonical accounts. This latter position has been defended by Joel Green.[182] While not totally dismissing the possibility that the author of the *Gospel of Peter* had access to non-canonical gospel material, Green argues that 'we have found ample support for the conclusion that the canonical Gospels have been employed as sources in the writing of the Gospel of Peter.'[183] This conclusion appears to represent the majority position among scholars. Although this is not always reflected through the appearance of published opinion, personal discussions and public seminars at conferences provide at least anecdotal evidence that the dependence of the *Gospel of Peter* on canonical accounts is the more widely held position.

Another area of discussion in contemporary scholarship has been analysis of the Christology of the text. Following on from the work of Denker (see above), it has become increasingly recognized that the description of the extant text as being docetic is based more upon the comments of Serapion as reported by Eusebius (*H.E.* 6.12.2–6) than on the actual contents of this portion of text.[184] This debate was re-opened by Jerry McCant who concluded that the 'portion of GP which was discovered by Bouriant in 1886, taken as a whole, does not conceive of the death of the Lord docetically.'[185] Although discussing the question of docetism, Head effectively advances the debate beyond such narrow confines by noting how the popularizing Christology of the *Gospel of Peter* is combined with apocalyptic tendencies which most likely find their origins in Jewish mysticism.[186] This broadening of the categories being used to probe the Christology of the *Gospel of Peter* has also been a feature of recent study that looked at polymorphism as means of analysing the Christology of various early Christian texts.[187]

Therefore, although much recent discussion has continued to focus on two of the central questions of previous scholarship – the relationship to the canonical gospels, and the nature of the Christology

---

[182] J.B. Green, 'The Gospel of Peter: Source for a Pre-canonical Passion Narrative?', *ZNW* 78 (1987) 293–301. Obviously impressionistic measures are not as reliable as quantifiable data, but such impressions suggest most scholars see Green's arguments as more convincing than those of Crossan.

[183] Green, 'The Gospel of Peter: Source for a Pre-canonical Passion Narrative?', 301.

[184] For a full discussion of christological issues see section eight of this introduction.

[185] J.W. McCant, 'The Gospel of Peter: Docetism Reconsidered', *NTS* 30 (1984) 269.

[186] P.M. Head, 'On the Christology of the Gospel of Peter', *VC* 46 (1992) 209–224.

[187] P. Foster, 'Polymorphic Christology: its Origins and Development in Early Christianity' *JTS* 58 (2007) 66–99.

exemplified in the text – these questions have been broadened and answered in new ways. Other issues, such as the religio-cultural matrix in which the *Gospel of Peter* emerged, have also occupied the academic debate, though to a lesser extent. However, this range of issues and the fresh ways in which traditional questions are being addressed demonstrates renewed interest in the text and yields important new insights. One of the most significant recent publications *Das Evangelium nach Petrus* demonstrates this breadth of interest by addressing a number of new issues in relation to the text as well as seeking fresh responses to old questions.[188] Newer topic that are addressed in this volume include discourse analysis of the text, codicological analysis, the type of Greek used by the author, the interplay between tradition and memory, the place of the text in relation to other early Christian literature, reflections on the purpose of the text, and a study of the characterisation of Pilate. It is yet to be seen whether this volume of studies will re-shape the scholarly agenda in relation to the *Gospel of Peter*.

## 4. Numbering System

The Akhmîm fragment has been divided into smaller sections by several modern scholars using various systems of numbers. Unfortunately at least three numbering systems exist, which are not mutually exclusive, since they represent either larger divisions, i.e. 'chapters', or shorter units, i.e. 'verses'. Prior to the use of 'chapter' and 'verse' divisions, Bouriant simply used page and line numbers to refer to portions of the text. Thus, for the actual written text of the *Gospel of Peter* the numbers two to ten were used by Bouriant to denote the page numbers of the codex.[189] While there are no page numbers in the original text these can be designated by allocating the number one to the *recto* of the initial page (decorated with Coptic crosses and other ornamentation) and counting sequentially through the leaves until the final page, which is enumerated as page sixty-six. Also the inside back cover contains part of the text known as the *Martyrdom of St Julian*

---

[188] T.J. Kraus and T. Nicklas, *Das Evangelium nach Petrus: Text, Kontexte, Intertexte* (Berlin: Walter de Gruyter, 2007).

[189] The numbers are presented as Arabic numerals, indented and commencing the first line of each page of text, although they are printed continuously and not on separate pages in Bouriant's edition. See Bouriant, *Fragments*, 137–142.

(*of Anazarbus*), although this page is not usually numbered (in this case as sixty-seven) it is rather just referred to as the inside back cover. While such page numbering is a fairly straightforward process for the *Gospel of Peter*, the numbering of the second text causes difficulties. Since the text of the *Apocalypse of Peter* has been sewn into the codex upside down and back to front, the ending is to be found on page thirteen after the two blank pages that occupy pages eleven and twelve, whereas the text actually starts on page nineteen. Hence this explains Bouriant's system for the *Apocalypse of Peter* starting with the Arabic numeral nineteen and progressing in descending order until thirteen. Matters become more straightforward again after this. Page twenty is blank, twenty-one to sixty-six contain the two fragments of *1 Enoch*, and finally the inside back cover (or page sixty-seven) contains an account of the *Martyrdom of St Julian*.

An alternative system divides the text into small sense units. This system of versification was devised by Harnack, who explicitly claims credit for devising this system, stating that the versification stems from his own work.[190] This results in the text being split into sixty verses. Harnack also indented the text at nine places. These do not correspond to the nine pages of text that the *Gospel of Peter* occupies in the codex.[191] None of these indentations is numbered, nor is a description given of their purpose. It does, however, appear by observation that these are the points where Harnack saw major sense divisions or, in other words, the natural paragraph breaks in the text.

The final system in common usage breaks the text into fourteen larger sense divisions, which may for convenience be called 'chapters' (which distinguishes them from Harnack's nine paragraphs). The precise origin of this system is difficult to trace. It was in existence as early as the end of 1892, being used for the presentation of the Greek text in the volume by Robinson and James, and in all likelihood was the innovation of the editors.[192] They do not, however, explicitly claim to have devised this system, unlike Harnack who makes a statement concerning his introduction of the verse divisions into the text. While most of

---

[190] Harnack, *Bruchstücke des Evangeliums und der Apokalypse des Petrus*, 8.

[191] These indentations occur at the beginning of the following verses: 1, 6, 10, 15, 20, 26, 28, 35 and 50. See Harnack, *Bruchstücke des Evangeliums und der Apokalypse des Petrus*, 8–12.

[192] J.A. Robinson and M.R. James, *The Gospel according to Peter, and the Revelation of Peter: Two Lectures on the Newly Recovered Fragments together with the Greek Texts*, see pages 83–88.

Harnack's sense divisions correspond to chapter divisions (although the system of fourteen chapters breaks some of Harnack's larger units into smaller blocks of text), the correspondence is not perfect. For example Harnack's fourth paragraph ends at verse nineteen, with the form of the cry of dereliction that is unique to the Akhmim codex. It then commences its fifth paragraph, narrating post-death events, with the notice of the veil of the Temple being torn in two. In comparison Robinson's fourteen chapter system sees a closer link between the death and the tearing of the veil. Consequently its fifth chapter ends with the rending of the curtain, and the post-death narrative commences in chapter six with the Jews pulling the nails out from the hands of the corpse, at which instance an earthquake occurs. Further differences concerning where to break the text, can be detected at the beginning of paragraph six (verse 26) and chapter seven (verse 25), and the beginning of paragraph eight (verse 35) and chapter nine (verse 34). Also Harnack's final long paragraph (verses 50–60) is divided by Robinson into three shorter units: chapter 12, verses 50–54; chapter 13, verses 55–57; and, chapter 14, verses 58–60.

A numbering system that has not persisted in the secondary literature is the division of the text into twelve chapters, devised by Swete.[193] This is not greatly different from Robinson's chapter division. The points of difference are: (i) Verse five is split across chapters two and three; (ii) Swete's chapter eight runs from vv. 28–34, whereas Robinson places v. 34 in chapter nine; (iii) Swete's chapter nine is basically an amalgamation of Robinson's chapters nine and ten (although Swete includes v. 34 in the previous chapter); (iv) Swete's chapter ten corresponds to Robinson's chapter eleven; and (v) Swete's chapter eleven is a combination of Robinson's chapters twelve and thirteen. In effect, a couple of verses are placed in different sections and Swete on two occasions preferred to have two lengthier blocks (his chapters nine and eleven) which Robinson had presented as two shorter chapters. It is no longer possible to tell whether these differences were made independently, or as a conscious revision of Robinson's schema.

---

[193] This is represented in the presentation of the Greek text on pages 1–24, but is perhaps more readily observed in the English translation on pages 25–28. See Swete, *The Akhmîm Fragment*.

For ease of comparison much of this information can be tabulated, showing which of Harnack's sixty verses occur on each page and in each paragraph or chapter division.

Two points need to be made. First, the division of the verses into 'a' and 'b' sections that correspond to page numbers does not necessarily indicate a complete clause, or that the verse breaks approximately half way, only that a page ends somewhere within the body of the verse, and not where it ends. Second, Harnack indicates the page divisions using the terminology fol. 1$^v$, fol. 2$^r$, fol. 2$^v$, fol. 3$^r$,... fol. 5$^v$.[194] The superscripted 'v' and 'r' refers to the *verso* and *recto* of the pages of the codex.

More recently a further referencing system has been suggested by Dewey.[195] In effect he recognizes that a system of chapter and verse numbers is redundant since the verse numbering does not

Table 1. The different numbering systems referenced against Harnack's versification

| Page | Matching verses | Harnack's paragraphs | Matching verses | Robinson's chapters | Matching verses | Swete's chapters | Matching verses |
|---|---|---|---|---|---|---|---|
| 2 | 1–8 | 1 | 1–5 | 1 | 1–2 | 1 | 1–2 |
| 3 | 9–16a | 2 | 6–9 | 2 | 3–5 | 2 | 3–5a |
| 4 | 16b–25a | 3 | 10–14 | 3 | 6–9 | 3 | 5b–9 |
| 5 | 25b–30a | 4 | 15–19 | 4 | 10–14 | 4 | 10–14 |
| 6 | 30b–36a | 5 | 20–25 | 5 | 15–20 | 5 | 15–20 |
| 7 | 36b–43a | 6 | 26–27 | 6 | 21–24 | 6 | 21–24 |
| 8 | 43b–50a | 7 | 28–34 | 7 | 25–27 | 7 | 25–27 |
| 9 | 50b–55a | 8 | 35–49 | 8 | 28–33 | 8 | 28–34 |
| 10 | 55b–60 | 9 | 50–60 | 9 | 34–37 | 9 | 35–42 |
| | | | | 10 | 38–42 | 10 | 43–49 |
| | | | | 11 | 43–49 | 11 | 50–57 |
| | | | | 12 | 50–54 | 12 | 58–60 |
| | | | | 13 | 55–57 | | |
| | | | | 14 | 58–60 | | |

---

[194] See Harnack, *Bruchstücke des Evangeliums und der Apokalypse des Petrus*, 8–12.

[195] In his initial articles Dewey followed the traditional numbering system. The changed system occurs only in two later articles: A.J. Dewey, 'Resurrection Texts and the *Gospel of Peter' Foundations and Facets Forum* 10.3–4 (1994) 177–196; 'The Passion Narrative of the Gospel of Peter', *Forum* New Series 1.1 (1998) 53–69.

recommence at the start of each chapter. Thus in the existing system of quoting Robinson's chapter numbers and Harnack's verse numbers, the former is actually of no additional benefit, since each verse number uniquely and unambiguously denotes a separate section of text. Hence in Dewey's system the verse numbers recommence at the start of each new chapter. Therefore, *Gos. Pet.* 6.21, the opening verse in chapter six, would be referenced as *Gos. Pet.* 6.1 in Dewey's revised system.[196] While this brings the numbering system into line with the more familiar referencing system used for the biblical texts, and furthermore makes chapter and verse numbers vital in locating a portion of text, it is unlikely to be adopted. This is because the system dependent upon both Robinson's chapter and Harnack's verse numbers is entrenched in scholarship and also Dewey uses his new system without discussion or explanation.

## 5. Codicological and Papyrological Analysis

A study of the physical features of the codex in which the text known as the *Gospel of Peter* offers a number of important insights into the text and the social world in which it was written. First, it allows both the individual texts and the whole codex to be appreciated as an actual artefact belonging to at least one, if not more, specific historical contexts. Within these contexts such textual artefacts may provide insights into the way texts functioned and were transmitted.[197] Secondly, such a study assists in placing this specific volume of writings within the wider context of book production in the late antique period. Such appreciation of the technologies employed in book production may function as a clue to dating and location of production. Thirdly, it is important to appreciate the unique or individualistic traits of this specific codex. This enables the highlighting of some of the more uncommon features that mark out this collection of texts from other codices and writings known from the period following the emergence of the codex.[198]

---

[196] In particular see Dewey, 'Resurrection Texts and the *Gospel of Peter*' 178–180.

[197] See L.W. Hurtado, *The Earliest Christian Artifacts: Manuscripts and Christian Origins* (Grand Rapids: Eerdmans, 2006).

[198] The date of the emergence of the codex as a new technology is still disputed. There are examples of predecessors to the codex in the form of small wax covered wooden tablets held together by a cord passing through holes in the tablets to form a portable notebook. Moreover discoveries at Vindolanda show the existence of very

## 5.1. *Codicological Analysis*

The small codex which contains the *Gospel of Peter* is usually dated to around the seventh to nineth centuries on the basis of palaeographical analysis (hand-writing style), with some scholars suggesting a six or even fifth century dating.[199] It needs to be noted that this is a composite text codex which brings together texts written in various contexts and at different dates, rather than being a multiple text codex, that is a single codex prepared for the specific purpose of containing a determined collection of texts. This has ramifications for the whole notion of dating. The dating of the codex therefore is later than the three texts it brings together, but presumably earlier than, or co-terminous with the writing of the text of the *Martyrdom of St Julian*, which from the descriptions of the codex appears to have been written on the inside back cover after the formation of the codex (although it is possible that this was a previously written leaf stuck into the codex at a later date). Furthermore, study of the codex is of vital importance since it is the only certain context from which an actual fragment of the text which is likely to be the *Gospel of Peter* is known. Although the codex was discovered in a grave in a Christian cementry, the specific grave is no longer identifiable. Attempts to identify other fragments from Oxyrhynchus and elsewhere as part of the *Gospel of Peter* remain uncertain. Earlier patristic references to a gospel circulating under the name of Peter may offer some clues, but fail to describe the shape or contents of the text to which they refer. For these reasons the only solid piece of evidence that allows access to the text and and also provides any definite evidence of an ancient context in which this text was read is that of the Akhmîm codex. This artefactual evidence provides insight both into the text and of the textual nature of traditions that circulated in early Christianity. Moreover, it attests the preference for the codex in

---

thin slivers of wood used as a medium to receive ink, tied together with a cord to form a multiple leaf codex. Quintillian, however, appears to offer the first certain reference to a parchment multiple leaf notebook (*Inst. Or.* 10.3.31–32). These examples all tend to date from the first century CE. The widespread use of codex technology does appear to be an innovation that originated in Christian circles perhaps as an attempt to find a convenient format in which to accommodate collections of Pauline epistle and the fourfold gospel corpus. See Harry Y. Gamble, *Books and Readers in the Early Church: A History of Early Christian Texts* (New Haven/London: Yale University Press, 1995) 49–81; G.N. Stanton, *Jesus and Gospel* (Cambridge: CUP, 2004) 165–191.

[199] See the next sub-section for a discussion of the palaeography of the text.

Table 2. The contents of the Akhmîm codex

| Page | Contents |
| --- | --- |
| Inside front cover | Blank |
| 1 | Decoration, religious in nature, including Coptic crosses |
| 2–10 | The *Gospel of Peter* |
| 11–12 | Blank |
| 13–19 | The *Apocalypse of Peter* |
| 20 (13) | Blank |
| 21–66 | Two fragments from *1 Enoch* |
| Inside back cover | *Martyrdom of St Julian* |

Christian circles that had developed from the second century onwards, and the way texts themselves could become objects of piety.[200]

The book contains thirty-three unnumbered parchment leaves along with parchment pages glued to inner sides of both the front and back covers. Providing page numbers for the unpaginated codex enables the follow table of contents to be formed (with the inside cover sheets unnumbered). The bracketed page number is given to indicate the page number that the opening blank page of the second text would have occupied if it had been sewn in to the codex with the correct orientation.

Both the quality of hand writing and the amateurish compilation of this codex, lead to the suspicion that the text was not produced in a professional scriptorium, but was rather the product of a relatively unskilled individual, perhaps even the same person in whose grave the book was interred. It may be reasonable to speculate that this codex was for the private and personal use of the individual in whose grave it was discovered, rather than having any communal or corporate function. The texts originate from different sources and most likely have a pre-history prior to their incorporation into this codex collection, although nothing can be said about the way the texts might have been used prior to incorporation into the codex.

The following features can be noted. The dimensions of the parchment pages are: height 15.5–16.5 cm and width 12–12.5 cm. Although there are some partially damaged leaves these dimensions remain

---

[200] L.W. Hurtado, *The Earliest Christian Artefacts* (Grand Rapids: Eerdmans, 2006) see especially 43–94.

reasonable consistent throughout the codex. Consulting Turner's classification of the sizes of parchment codices, this codex is fairly atypical. It could either be placed in category ten, i.e. '*X Breadth* 15–12 cm. "*Square*"' or in category twelve, i.e. '*XII Breadth* 13–10 cm. *Not Square.*'[201] Turner lists only ten examples in category twelve, and interestingly only one has a height of less than 17 cm. By contrast, in category ten, although there are twenty-three examples, only seven of these have a breadth of around 12 cm. Of these seven, none have a height in excess of 15 cm. Thus it appears that the Akhmîm codex is neither truly square, nor does it properly align with the other examples in the non-square category of codices with a breadth in the range of 13–10 cm. The book in question is aberrant in terms of Turner's system and defies easy classification against known examples of ancient codices.[202] The left and right hand margins usually leave in the range of 0.5–1.0 cm of white space. The upper margin is more generous leaving on average between 1.5–2 cm of white space. This is regardless of whether a Coptic cross is present for decoration and occupying the central region of this upper space. The bottom margin is consistently much smaller, occupying on average around 0.5 cm. For each of the nine pages of the text it is possible to tabulate the sizes of the four margins. Again these are average measurements because the scribe is not meticulous in preparing standardized lines.

It needs to be noted that the measurement of the bottom margin on page ten is effected by the presence of a decorative motif.

Because of the loss or misplacement of the original volume, a detailed firsthand analysis of the physical production of the codex is no longer

Table 3. Margin sizes for the *Gospel of Peter* text in the Akhmîm codex

| Page | 2 | 3 | 4 | 5 | 6 | 7 | 8 | 9 | 10 | Average |
|---|---|---|---|---|---|---|---|---|---|---|
| Upper margin (cm) | 1.1 | 1.8 | 1.8 | 1.3 | 1.3 | 1.8 | 1.8 | 2 | 1.8 | 1.63 |
| Bottom margin (cm) | 1 | 0.7 | 0.6 | 0.4 | 0.6 | 0.5 | 0.6 | 0.5 | 0.5* | 0.54 |
| Left margin (cm) | 1 | 0.6 | 1.2 | 0.5 | 1.2 | 0.4 | 1.2 | 0.3 | 1.1 | 0.83 |
| Right margin (cm) | 0.5 | 0.5 | 0.5 | 0.4 | 0.4 | 0.7 | 0.7 | 0.5 | 0.2 | 0.48 |

---

[201] E.G. Turner, *The Typology of the Early Codex* (Philadelphia: University of Pennsylvania Press, 1977) see 26–30, esp. 29.

[202] See further Turner, *The Typology of the Early Codex*, 13–34.

possible. Thus it is necessary to rely on photographic evidence and previous descriptions. Yet even here there are problems, both because descriptions of the codex are incomplete and also because the bifolia appear to have been split into separate leaves to facilitate photography. However, the fact that the second document in the codex, the *Apocalypse of Peter*, is recorded as having been sewn into the codex upside-down and back-to-front provides strong evidence that this text comprised a different quire of sheets from the foregoing *Gospel of Peter* fragment. Turner has noted that there are two basic forms of codices, either the single gathering or multiple gatherings of quires. He notes,

> In the former type there is only one 'gathering' in the whole book, and it has become common to call this type a 'single-quire' codex. In the latter type, each set of folded sheets is 'gathered' together and stitched, i.e., the sets form 'gatherings.' One set of threads holds each gathering together. If a book has a binding, a second set passes horizontally through the first set and unites the gatherings; it is taken then through them across the spine of the book and secured to the front and back binding covers.[203]

The codex under discussion falls into this latter category. The first document, the *Gospel of Peter*, comprises three sheets, six leaves and twelve pages. It is no longer possible to tell for certain how these three sheets were gathering. From the photographs it is apparent that pages 9–12 represent a single bifolium. What cannot be determined, since the photographs reveal that the bifolia that constitute pages 1–8 have been split, is whether pages 1–8 represent two singletons, pages 1–4 and pages 5–8, or if a more complex arrangement is used. Peter van Minnen suggests that '[t]he first manuscript containing a fragment of the *Gospel of Peter* consists of a binio of two bifolia or four leaves or eight pages to which a bifolium consisting of two leaves or four pages was added.'[204] Given that the second text appears almost certainly to have been a gathering of two sheets, it is perhaps more likely that the scribe was capable of gathering sheets together. Hence van Minnen's suggestion represents the most likely arrangement of the gathering of the three bifolia. The first page is decorated with Coptic crosses and the final two pages are blank, thus leaving nine pages of

---

[203] E.C. Turner, *The Typology of the Early Codex* (Pennsylvania: University of Pennsylvania Press, 1977) 55.

[204] Peter Van Minnen, 'The Akhmîm Gospel of Peter', in T.J. Kraus and T. Nicklas, *Das Evangelium nach Petrus: Text, Kontexte, Intertexte* (Berlin: Walter de Gruyter, 2007) 53–60.

written text. The next gathering consists of two sheets, four leaves and eight pages. Since this gathering is sewn in upside-down and back-to-front it finishes with a page containing no writing, nor any decoration. It is possible that page twenty, which is actually the initial page of the text had been left blank for decoration to be added at a later stage. For some unknown reason this never occurred. The text of the *Apocalypse of Peter* then starts on page nineteen and is read backwards to page thirteen, with page twenty blank.

The two fragments of *1 Enoch* pose greater problems for reconstructing the codicology of this volume. Photographs of these pages are available on-line.[205] The second fragment, written in a smaller majuscule script, is listed by van Haelst as occupying pages 51–66.[206] Yet the on-line images show only fourteen pages of the neater smaller majuscule script, rather than the sixteen implied by the listing of van Haelst. However, the on-line photographs show forty-four pages of text instead of the forty-six listed in the various publication reports. Hence it appears that two pages of images are missing. Whether these had gone missing between the discovery of the codex and the process of photographing it in the 1980's, or if for some technical reason the images were not made or not listed on the internet is not easy to determine.[207]

Nonetheless, if one is to trust the listing of van Haelst this would result in the two missing pages being part of the smaller neater majuscule writing of the second fragment. This then appears to have been a gathering of four bifolia, producing the required eight leaves and sixteen pages. The first fragment occupies thirty pages, which is somewhat problematic since this number when divided by four (the number of pages to a sheet) does not yield an integer as the result. Instead it appears to comprise seven and a half sheets of parchment. The use of split sheets, however, is not unevidenced, alternatively this could

---

[205] http://ipap.csad.ox.ac.uk/Apocrypha-Pseudepigrapha.html (1 January 2010).

[206] van Haelst, *Catalogue des Papyrus Littéraires Juifs und Chrétiens*, 575, page 202.

[207] According to Van Minnen the fragments of *1 Enoch* consist of three quires. These were all original quaternios (four bifolia, eight leaves, sixteen sheets). However, he proposes that the first of these quires of *1 Enoch* has shed its first leaf, prior to the manuscript being interred in the grave. The next quaternio quire is written in the same hand as the preceding quire. However, the final quire is written in a different hand. See Van Minnen, 'The Akhmîm Gospel of Peter', 56.

be due to the loss of a leaf.[208] It is perhaps most likely that these thirty pages were originally formed from two quaternios, each of sixteen pages with the first having shed a leaf which accounts for the loss of the original two pages of the first gathering.

However, the online photographs presented on the final page of images list two sets of pages as 'Pages 20–21 (duplicate copy of 19:3:3–21:7:2).' Precisely what the page numbers refer to is unclear. Since the text of *1 Enoch* commences on page twenty-one of the codex, it would initially appear that these are not pages of the entire codex, unless the page of decorations at the beginning of the codex have not been numbered (in which case this could be a single leaf at the beginning of the document *1 Enoch*. Alternatively, these could represent page numbers counted from the beginning of the pages of the first fragment of *1 Enoch*. In this case, this would represent a loose leaf inserted in the document, but one would require an even number of pages to precede this leaf, so it should be numbered initially with an odd number, not an even number such as twenty. Thus in the face of incomplete evidence and a missing codex caution is required. There is no way of determining the exact physical structure of the codex at the point it contains the text of *1 Enoch*, although the most likely suggestion is that it was composed of three quires each originally comprising of sixteen pages. However, what can be stated with confidence is that this volume was a multiple quire codex and hence exemplifies Turner's general statement that '[i]t is worth noting that no example of a single-quire codex of parchment has yet been identified.'[209]

Preparation of parchment was an involved process. After flaying the slaughtered animal, the skin was soaked in a lime solution. From the inner side the fleshy residue was removed, while a careful scraping of the epidermis from the hair side by close shaving prepared the outer side. This was then followed by washing and drying on a wooden frame. Further shaving could then be undertaken to reduce thickness and unevenness in the prepared pages. Gamble notes the difference in the two sides of the parchment sheet. Like papyrus, the two sides of a parchment sheet differed: the flesh side was lighter and smoother and thus the better side for writing (and so constitutes the *recto*) though

---

[208] See Van Minnen, 'The Akhmîm Gospel of Peter', 56.
[209] Turner, *The Typology of the Early Codex*, 58.

Table 4. Arrangement of rough and smooth surfaces of parchment sheets

| Page number | 1 | 2 | 3 | 4 | 5 | 6 | 7 | 8 | 9 | 10 | 11 | 12 |
|---|---|---|---|---|---|---|---|---|---|---|---|---|
| Parchment side | R | S | S | R | R | S | S | R | R | S | S | R |

the rougher, more absorbent hair side held the ink better.[210] When a sheet was folded, however, to form a codex the smooth side alternated between being either the *recto* or *verso*, so the distinction Gamble makes is not entirely correct. The photographs of the Akhmîm codex are not altogether helpful in determining the smooth flesh side (S) and the rougher hair side (R). The following table is an attempt to classify the sides based on the appearance given by the photographs for the first text.

It therefore appears that the person who prepared the sheets for the first gathering in the codex arranged the leaves so smooth sides faced smooth sides, and rough sides faced rough side.

A further feature which needs to be documented is the fact that all four texts contained in the document are written in single columns of text. This perhaps places this codex in a more unusual category of codices since Turner observed that 'the double column was a favoured format for a parchment codex.'[211] However, the existence of single-column parchment codices, although less common, is nevertheless not infrequent. By contrast, the occurrence of double-column (or multiple-column) papyrus codices is relatively infrequent. Thus the fact that the four texts contained in this volume are presented in single column format may reflect the exemplars that are being copied (perhaps written on papyrus). This is perhaps not that likely since there is little to suggest that scribes were in the business of reproducing facsimile-type copies of texts. More plausible is the suggestion that the single columns have been employed here since the page size of this codex, although not miniature, is still small.

As the first two texts may be from the same hand, it is worth comparing some of the features of these texts.[212] Prior to considering the shapes of letters which may show considerable variation in the same text even when written by the same hand, it is helpful to first consider

---

[210] Gamble, *Books and Readers in the Early Church*, 46.
[211] Turner, *The Typology of the Early Codex*, 35.
[212] See the two entries 575 and 598 in van Haelst, *Catalogue des Papyrus Littéraires Juifs und Chrétiens*, 201–202, 212.

Table 5. Lines of text per page for the *Gospel of Peter* and the *Apocalypse of Peter*

| Page number | Lines per page |
|---|---|
| 2 | 19 |
| 3 | 18 |
| 4 | 18 |
| 5 | 17 |
| 6 | 17 |
| 7 | 17 |
| 8 | 17 |
| 9 | 17 |
| 10 | 14 + final decoration |
| 11–12 | Blank |
| 19 | 19 |
| 18 | 19 |
| 17 | 20 |
| 16 | 19 |
| 15 | 18 |
| 14 | 18 |
| 13 | 16 |

some of the physical features of these two texts to see if any common patterns emerge. Therefore, first considering scribal habits one can count the number of lines per page:

Omitting pages nine and thirteen from the calculation, since they are the final pages of text in the *Gospel* and *Apocalypse of Peter* respectively and are not complete pages of text, overall the average number of lines per complete page of text is 18.07 (to 4 sig. figs) or 18 lines to the nearest whole number.[213] For the *Gospel of Peter* alone the average is 17.5 lines per page.[214] By comparision the average for the *Apocalypse of Peter* is slightly higher at 18.83 (to 4 sig.figs.).[215] This would suggest that the number of lines per page is close enough not to exclude the possibility that the same scribe was responsible for both texts.

The scribe's penmanship is highly variable. Apart from the changeable manner in which he forms the same letters, this is also exemplified by the difference both in the size of letters and the number of letters he

---

[213] Taking a simple arithmetic average 253/14 = 18.07 (to 4 sig. figs.).
[214] That is 140/8 = 14.5.
[215] That is 113/6 = 18.83 (to 4 sig. figs.).

fits on each line of the text of the *Gospel of Peter*. Representing such variation is not always totally straightforward since the text has the occasional lucuna, also there are supralinear letters are inserted at two points and this is coupled with some sections where it is difficult to read the actual writing that is present in the manuscript. This may lead to some dispute about counting the actual letters present on a given line. Fortunately such problems do not greatly beset the text, so that there are not huge problems in carrying out a letter count. Some places where there are problems will be noted, while with others the letters will be counted based on the most likely reconstruction without note. The number of letters per line is recorded for each page. It will be observed that these tabulated results clearly confirm the visual impression for detecting points in the text where the scribe chose to sharpen or trim his pen (marked with a double asterisk). This has resulted in much finer letter formation and consequently a greater number of letters per line of text.

From this table a number of significant features can be noted. First, although the average number of letters per line for individual pages varies between a maximum of 42.11 and a minimum of 35.88, the variation appears to be due to the sharpness of the point of the pen. The initial page of text (page two) appears to have commenced with a sharpened pen. For the first two pages (pages two and three) the average number of letters per line is above forty characters. On the third page there is a significant decrease due to the broader strokes of the blunter pen requiring more room for each letter. Thus, for pages four to seven the average number of letters falls in a relatively tight range of a maximum of 37.82 down to a minimum of 35.88. Before commencing page eight the scribe had obviously either sharpened his pen or replaced it with another newly sharpened writing implement. Here the average letters per line increases to above forty-one for two pages. Yet after these two pages there is a marked decrease yet again as the pen becomes blunt. The average on the final page falls to 37.79. A more professional scribe may have sharpened his instruments more frequently to maintain a higher level of consistency.[216]

Two places have been noted with an asterisk in the table, line one page three and line four page ten. These are both places where supra-

---

[216] There is little discussion in the secondary literature of scribal practices in relation to the preparation and maintaince of their writing tools.

Table 6. Letters per line for the *Gospel of Peter*

| Page | | | | | | | | | | Line number | | | | | | | | | | Average |
|------|---|---|---|---|---|---|---|---|---|----|----|----|----|----|----|----|----|----|----|---------|
| | 1 | 2 | 3 | 4 | 5 | 6 | 7 | 8 | 9 | 10 | 11 | 12 | 13 | 14 | 15 | 16 | 17 | 18 | 19 | |
| 2 | 39 | 43 | 42 | 41 | 43 | 42 | 45 | 43 | 40 | 42 | 43 | 41 | 38 | 41 | 45 | 47 | 48 | 42 | 35 | 42.1053 |
| 3 | *41 | 40 | 41 | 42 | 44 | 40 | 43 | 41 | 40 | 36 | 40 | 38 | 40 | 39 | 37 | 40 | 42 | 37 | | 40.0556 |
| 4 | 39 | 37 | 36 | 38 | 38 | 36 | 37 | 37 | 37 | 36 | 38 | 33 | 34 | 36 | 36 | 36 | 39 | 39 | | 36.7778 |
| 5 | 36 | 37 | 39 | 39 | 35 | 39 | 42 | 37 | 38 | 42 | 37 | 40 | 40 | 36 | 36 | 37 | 33 | | | 37.8235 |
| 6 | 37 | 34 | 36 | 36 | 34 | 37 | 38 | 37 | 38 | 34 | 34 | 38 | 36 | 35 | 36 | 35 | 35 | | | 35.8824 |
| 7 | 33 | 34 | 37 | 33 | 38 | 39 | 42 | 36 | 37 | 36 | 37 | 33 | 37 | 34 | 38 | 39 | 35 | | | 36.3529 |
| **8 | 42 | 41 | 39 | 45 | 41 | 41 | 44 | 44 | 45 | 46 | 41 | 39 | 40 | 39 | 44 | 40 | 40 | | | 41.8235 |
| 9 | 39 | 44 | 48 | 41 | 42 | 39 | 45 | 45 | 42 | 40 | 41 | 38 | 37 | 39 | 39 | 39 | 40 | | | 41.0588 |
| 10 | 37 | 36 | 37 | *41 | 35 | 41 | 37 | 40 | 37 | 42 | 40 | 34 | 33 | 39 | | | | | | 37.7857 |

linear letters have been inserted into the line of text. If these supralinear letters were omitted from the statistics then the respective averages would be 40.00 for line one of page three and 37.64 for line four of page ten. The decision to include or omit these letters makes relatively small variation to the averages.

The overall average of letters per line for the whole document is 38.91 (to 4 sig. figs.), calculated by dividing the total number of letters, 5992, by the total lines of text, 154. The fact that the greatest variation is above the mean shows that fewer lines have a greater number of letters than the number of lines with a lesser number of letters than the mean. In other words, once the pen has become blunt after writing the initial two pages with the freshly sharpened instrument, there then occurred a marked drop in the number of letters per line. The scribe appears to be happy to retain these broader writing strokes for a number of pages, since there is not as rapid a deterioration after the initial loss of the fine letter strokes.

The sizes of letter will be discussed more fully in the textual notes that accompany each section of commentary. The length of each line is approximately in the range 10.5 to 11.5 cm. Thus taking the central point 11 cm as the average length, and the calculated average of 38.91 letters per line, then on average each letter occupies 0.28 cm (to 2 sig. figs.). Obviously there is huge variation here from an iota that is less than 0.1 cm wide or an omicron that can be written as little more than a point, in comparison with some of the more expansive omegas or final form sigmas.

### 5.2. *Palaeographical Analysis*

A number of different scribal hands are present in the four texts that comprise the documents in this slim codex.[217] Commencing this discussion by considering the fourth text in the codex, it needs to be noted that there are no readily available photographs of the fragment of the *Martyrdom of Julian*. However, van Haelst gives the following description. 'Parchment. Leaf of a codex glued in the cover of the codex described at 575: about 15 × 12 cm; a full page; 22 lines on

---

[217] The four documents are listed by van Haelst with the following respective entry and page numbers. van Haelst, *Catalogue des Papyrus Littéraires Juifs und Chrétiens*, entry 575, 598, 617, 707, page 201–202, 212, 219, 257.

each side.'[218] It appears that the decription of this text as occupying '22 lines on each side' is incorrect. The original publication report stated that, 'Finally, on the interior cover of the binding of the manuscript, is found glued a leaf covered with a beautiful script in majuscule and which must have belonged to a book containing the Acts of Saint Julian.'[219] There then follows a transcription of the twenty-two short lines of text. The original publication report gives no indication that the leaf had been written on the reverse. Rather it simply describes a leaf written on one side containing twenty-two lines of text. This had been glued to the interior back cover of the codex, and the text is transcribed by Bouriant.[220]

The third document in the codex comprises of two fragments of *1 Enoch* written in different majuscule scripts. The significance of this text at the time of discovery was that it provided the first witness to the text of *1 Enoch* written in Greek. The contents and hands responsible for the two sections are described by van Haelst in the following manner. 'pages 21–50: *Enoch* 19, 3; 20, 2–21, 9 and 1, 1–16, 22 in a square majuscule, rather irregular; pages 51–66: *Enoch* 16, 22b–32, 6 in a smaller majuscule.'[221] It is fully apparent that the majuscule hands of the fragments of *1 Enoch* and the *Martyrdom of Julian* differ greatly from the cursive writing that is used for the first two texts in the codex. The hands in these two documents also deviate from each other. Thus the final two documents are the work of three different scribes.

The dating of the first text in the codex has also been debated. The most commonly advanced range of dates falls between the 7th and 9th centuries.[222] Grenfell and Hunt suggested dating the text to the

---

[218] B.P. Grenfell and A.S. Hunt are recorded in *Catalogue général des antiquités égyptiennes du Musée du Caire No. 10001–10869*, 1903 (Nachdruck: Osnabrück, 1972) 93.

[219] Bouriant, 'Fragments du texte grec du livre d'Énoch et de quelques écrits attribués à saint Pierre', 146.

[220] In his discussion Van Minnen provides the following assessment of the hand responsible for the *Martyrdom of Julian*. 'The handwriting is the most literary in the codex and can be securely dated to the first half of the seventh century, which would therefore be the *terminus post quem* for the composition of the codex, unless the last leaf was not original to the codex but was added at a later date to strengthen the back cover.' Van Minnen, 'The Akhmîm Gospel of Peter', 56.

[221] van Haelst, *Catalogue des Papyrus Littéraires Juifs und Chrétiens*, entry 575, page 202.

[222] This dating is suggested by Swete, Robinson, Lods, Omont, Vaganay, Mara, although it should be noted that this has both narrowed and lowered the initial suggestion of Bouriant that the handwriting dated to the 8th to the 12th centuries.

5th–6th century, whereas the Leuven database of ancient books, apparently drawing upon the analysis of Cavallo and Maehler,[223] places the range a century later, 6th–7th century.[224] While without the actual manuscript it is impossible to come to a firm conclusion, it does appear that a date of the late 6th to the early 9th century provides a highly probable period for the composition of the text. This takes into account both the archaeological evidence provided by the location of the grave, and the varying suggestions of palaeographers who have analysed the text.

The first two texts are both written in similar type scripts with a tendency towards cursive writting. Establishing the identity, or otherwise, of these hands is made more problematic by the deviations of letter forms that occur within each document. However, more features are shared which suggests that the same scribe is at work in both cases. First, on the opening page of text of both documents a similar form of the Coptic cross decoration is employed. Secondly, both documents exhibit a similar range of words that are written as *nomina sacra*: these are, κύριος, θεός, ἄνθρωπος, in both texts. Thirdly, both texts omit the final ν at line endings and indicate this with a horizontal supralinear stroke. Fourthly, and perhaps of greatest significance, letter shapes and unusual combinations of letters often occur with nearly identical graphic representations. A number of examples of this phenomenon could be listed. One of the most striking examples is the graphic form of the double lambda as it occurs in the same word πολλοί, in *Gospel of Peter* 14.58 and *Apocalypse of Peter* 1.1. There is little attention paid to producing a bilinear hand in either text.[225] Both texts are inconsistent in the use of ligatures, although common elements occur (although without uniformity) such as the use of the elongated central crossbar of the epsilon to function as a ligature. Thus, it may be concluded that the same scribe is responsible for both texts, and that his writing practices can be documented in both writings.

It is not possible to tell if the skeletal remains with which the text was interred belonged to the scribe responsible for any of these texts,

---

[223] Cavallo and Maehler, *Greek Bookhands of the Early Byzantine Period A.D. 300–800*, 75.

[224] http://ldab.arts.kuleuven.ac.be/ldab_text_detail.php?quick=LDAB%201088

[225] See the plate of the writing exercise with parallel lines that is presented in E.G. Turner, *Greek Manuscripts of the Ancient World*, second ed., revised and enlarged by P.J. Parsons (Bulletin Supplement 46; London: University of London, Institute of Classical Studies, 1987) example 4, 32.

or even if he was the person who bound them together. It is perhaps attractive to see this burial keepsake as having some close connection with the dead man, but sometimes attractive proposals are not necessarily correct answers.

## 6. Suggested Early Fragments of the 'Gospel of Peter'

Without doubt Dieter Lührmann has done more than any other scholar in attempting to establish a firmer textual base for tracing the origins of the first text in the Akhmîm codex back to the second century. A number of his articles advancing these claims have been published, and most recently these ideas have been collected and summarised in chapters of two separate volumes.[226] Recently, a debate has emerged concerning the identifications made by Lührmann, with Foster suggesting the fragments suggested as belonging to the Gospel of Peter cannot be thus identified with any level of confidence or objectivity.[227] Foster's attempt to question this hypothesis led to two printed replies by Lührmann in which, among other things, he states that Foster can never have seen the two Oxyrhynchus fragments that form part of the discussion.[228] In a brief reply, Foster stated that he had indeed worked directly with the Oxyrhynchus fragments and this could be confirmed by consulting the curators of the Oxyrhynchus fragments in Oxford. Despite Lührmann's two replies, the substantive question of whether there are early witnesses to the Gospel of Peter remains open. P.Oxy. 2949 is the most likely possibility of an extant manuscript fragment preserving some form of the Gospel of Peter prior to the date of the Akhmîm text. It is the substance of this important question that is considered in detail below.

---

[226] D. Lührmann, *Fragmente apokryph gewordener Evangelien in griechischer und lateinischer Sprache* (Marburg theologischer Studien 59; Marburg: Elwert, 2000) 72–95. D. Lührmann, *Die apokryph gewordenen Evangelien: Studien zu neuen Texten und zu neuen Fragen* (NovT Supp. 112; Leiden: Brill, 2004) 55–104.

[227] P. Foster, 'Are there any Early Fragments of the So-called *Gospel of Peter?*', *NTS* 52 (2006) 1–28.

[228] D. Lührmann, 'Kann es wirklich keine frühe Handschrift des Petrusevangeliums geben?: Corrigenda zu einem Aufsatz von Paul Foster', *NovT* 48 (2006) 379–383; and 'Die Überlieferung des Petrusevangeliums' in T.J. Kraus and T. Nicklas, *Das Evangelium nach Petrus: Text, Kontexte, Intertexte* (Berlin: Walter de Gruyter, 2007) 'Postscriptum', 48–51.

## 6.1.  *P.Oxy. 2949*

This text consists of two small fragments, the larger of which does have certain affinities with *Gos. Pet.* 2.3–5a. Although these fragments were discovered by Grenfell and Hunt at Oxyrhynchus during one of their winter digs between 1897 and 1906, the sheer amount of material excavated meant that publication did not take place until 1972.[229] Palaeographically, according to Coles the editor of these fragments for the Oxyrhynchus volume in which they appear, the handwriting should be assigned to the 'early third or possibly the late second century.'[230] Interestingly, most scholars who have made use of the assessment of dating provided by Coles, simply give the dating mentioned in the subheading 'late second or early third century.'[231] Consequently they miss the fact that Coles put the third century dating first in the body of his discussion, and only haltingly introduced the possibility of a late second century dating. Koester exemplifies this trend.

> No other manuscript or fragment was known until Dieter Lührmann discovered that two small papyrus fragments from Oxyrhynchus, written ca. 200 CE, which had been published in 1972, actually belonged to the Gospel of Peter. This confirms a *terminus ad quem* for the composition of the *Gospel of Peter* of 200 CE.[232]

From this summary statement it would appear that Koester has not read Coles' report on P.Oxy. 2949 closely. Apart from the fact that Koester turns the more flexible date of ca. 200 CE turns into an absolute *terminus ad quem*, more importantly, he also fails to acknowledge that Coles had in fact cautiously suggested affinities between the *Gospel of Peter* and P.Oxy. 2949. Thus, not only is Coles' sober note of caution lost when these papyrus fragments are mentioned subsequently by scholars, moreover, there is often a failure to acknowledge that Coles was the first to mention a possible connection between the two fragments he published and the Akhmîm text. He presented the tentative relationship in the following terms,

---

[229] R.A. Coles, '2949. Fragments of an Apocryphal Gospel(?)', in G.M. Browne (ed.), *The Oxyrhynchus Papyri*, vol. 41 (Cambridge: CUP, 1972) 15–16.

[230] Coles, '2949. Fragments of an Apocryphal Gospel(?), 15.

[231] Coles, '2949. Fragments of an Apocryphal Gospel(?), 15.

[232] H. Koester, *Ancient Christian Gospels: Their History and Development* (London/Philadelphia: SCM/TPI, 1990) 216–217.

The larger of these fragments relates the story of Joseph of Arimathaea's request to Pilate for the body of Jesus, in a version which is not that of the canonical Gospels. Among the Apocrypha its closest resemblances are to the Gospel of Peter, §2, although even from this it has considerable variations.[233]

By contrast, Lührmann makes much more positive claims about identifying P.Oxy. 2949 as an early fragment of the text discovered at Akhmîm. While he acknowledges divergences between P.Oxy. 2949 and P.Cair. 10759 (verses 3–5), it is argued that this freedom with the transmission of the text is due to the fact that it circulated before fixed notions of canonicity had been developed. Thus there were no external controls preserving the form of the text.[234] In order to assess the merits of the claim advanced by Lührmann it is necessary to look in detail at the proposed parallel between P.Oxy. 2949 and P.Cair. 10759 verses 3–5. It needs to be acknowledged that there are obviously points of contact between these passages, but it is suggested that these are not strong enough to allow the conclusion that the Akhmîm text necessarily represents the same text form as P.Oxy. 2949.

This parallel has been set out by numerous scholars, in some cases without the level of reconstruction being acknowledged, especially for the lacunae in P.Oxy. 2949. For this reason it is necessary to present both a transcription of the text as well as the photographs of the Oxyrhynchus fragments.[235] Although the discussion has correctly centred on the larger of the two fragments, it is helpful to first look at the reconstruction of the smaller fragment given by Coles and duplicated by Lührmann.[236]

---

[233] Coles, '2949. Fragments of an Apocryphal Gospel(?), 15.

[234] D. Lührmann, 'POx 2949: EvPt 3–5 in einer Handschrift des 2./3. Jahrhunderts', *ZNW* 72 (1981) 216–226, 225.

[235] The reconstructions that follow, for both P.Oxy. 2949 and 4009, are based upon direct analysis of the papyrus fragments held in the Oxyrhynchus Papyrology Collection of the Sackler Library in Oxford. Special thanks are due to Nikolaos Gonis who was both most obliging and generous with his time. The photographs of P.Oxy. 2949 and 4009 that are reproduced in this paper have been downloaded from the official website http://www.papyrology.ox.ac.uk/ (homepage), and are freely available for use in the public domain.

[236] Lührmann, 'POx 2949: EvPt 3–5 in einer Handschrift des 2./3. Jahrhunderts', 219.

Table 7. Coles' transcription of the smaller fragment of P.Oxy. 2949

| Line number | Coles' transcription |
|:-----------:|:--------------------:|
| 1. | .μου[ |
| 2. | πειλ[ |
| 3. | τισα[ |
| 4. | μεν̣[ |
| 5. | [ |

Here letters that are uncertain have been indicated by Coles using the standard convention of a dot under the uncertain letter. Yet even in this reconstruction, as comparison with the photograph shows there are other uncertain letters besides those indicated with the dots. On the first line only the omicron is certain. On the second line the final letter has only a partial upward stroke and hence is not necessarily the lambda (λ) which Lührmann uses to reconstructs a further reference to Πειλᾶτος. Similarly on the third line the alpha cannot be read with any degree of certainty. On the fourth line there is a hole in the text after the μ and the letters εν suggested by Coles are highly speculative. A more accurate portrayal of the visible text would be:

Table 8. Revised transcription of the smaller fragment of P.Oxy. 2949

| Line number | Transcription |
|:-----------:|:-------------:|
| 1. | .μου̣[ |
| 2. | πει.[ |
| 3. | τισ.[ |
| 4. | μ.[ |
| 5. | [ |

The accuracy of this transcription can be assessed by a comparison with the photograph of the fragments. The fragment has at most ten certain letters, and even two of these are somewhat problematic reconstructed letters on the first line. It is not being argued here that Coles' reconstructions are necessarily incorrect.[237] Rather, the aim is to draw attention to the hypothetical nature of these reconstructions, which form the basis for identifying P.Oxy. 2949 with the Akhmîm text.

---

[237] Coles, '2949. Fragments of an Apocryphal Gospel(?), 15–16.

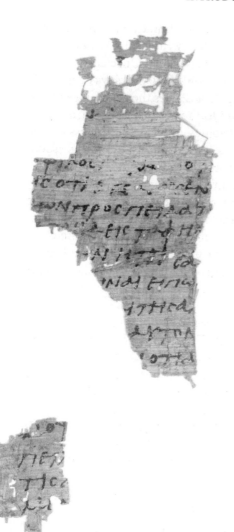

Although these two fragments are always treated together as part of the same text, there is little indication given in the literature concerning the basis on which this decision has been made. There are similarities in the shapes of letters in both fragments, especially in terms of the overlap between the tau and iota, where the horizontal cross bar of the tau intersects the vertical stroke of a following iota. Coles notes that the fibres do not allow an alignment of these two fragments.[238] There does not appear to be any record, either in print or in the Papyrology reading room of the Ashmolean, describing whether these fragments were discovered together *in situ* or if the connection was made by Grenfell and Hunt, or perhaps a later scholar, or even by Coles himself.

Figure 1. The two fragments of P.Oxy. 2949.

The positioning of this fragment is equally problematic. Crossan places the smaller fragment on the right-hand side of the final five lines of the larger fragment.[239] Here it is apparent that he has not consulted either the papyrus fragments or the photographs. The white space on

---

[238] Coles, '2949. Fragments of an Apocryphal Gospel(?), 15.
[239] Crossan, *The Cross that Spoke* (SanFrancisco: Harper & Row, 1988) 8.

the left-hand side of the smaller fragment shows that it is the commencement of new lines of a text which is written in *scripta continua* and not the continuation of existing lines of text. Once again, examination of the photographic evidence shows that Coles was correct in his judgement that 'The smaller fragment (2) has the beginnings of five lines, and probably should be placed to the lower left of (i) [*sic*[240]].'[241]

Thus the smaller fragment contributes little to the discussion for three reasons. First there is the issue of the uncertainty of its placement in relation to the larger fragment. Second, it contains at most ten undisputed letters. And third, the only complete word it may preserve, τις, is not of great enough significance to establish a link with the text of P.Cair. 10759. Therefore, the text of the larger fragment must be analysed to see if the parallels it has with the Akhmîm text are close enough to suggest that there are two witnesses of the same textual archetype. The reconstructions proposed by Crossan and Lührmann can be tabulated in the following form.

Table 9. Crossan's presentation of the parallel[242]

| P.Oxy. 2949 | | *Gospel of Peter* 2:3–5a |
|---|---|---|
| 1. ]τ̣[ | | |
| 2. abraded | | |
| 3. ]ν..[ | | |
| 4. abraded | | |
| 5. ]ὁ φίλος Π[ε]ιλά̣[τ]ου̣ [ | | ὁ φίλος Πειλάτου |
| 6. ] ι̣ς ὅτι ἐκέλευσεν [ | | εἰδὼς ὅτι στωυρίσκειν |
| 7. ελ]θὼν πρὸς Πειλᾶτο̣[ν | | ἦλθεν πρὸς Πειλάτον |
| 8. ]τ̣ὸ σῶμα εἰς ταφὴν [ | | τὸ σῶμα τοῦ κυρίου πρὸς ταφήν |
| 9. Ἡρῴδ]ην ἠτησα[το | 14. μου[ | πρὸς Ἡρῴδην ἤτησεν αὐτοῦ |
| 10. ] ηναι εἰπὼ[ν | 15. Πειλ[ατ | [ἔφη] ἀδελφε Πειλᾶτε |
| 11. ]αιτησα [ | 16. τις α[ὐτὸν | τις α[ὐτὸν ἠτήκει |
| 12. ]αὐτὸν [ | 17. με̣ν | αὐτὸν ἐθαπτομεν |
| 13. ] ὅτι α[ | 18 [. | ἐπεὶ |

---

[240] The confusion between numbering the larger fragment with a Roman numeral and the smaller fragment with an Arabic numeral is due to Coles.

[241] Coles, '2949. Fragments of an Apocryphal Gospel(?)', 15.

[242] Crossan, *The Cross that Spoke*, 8.

A number of points need to be made in relation to the way Crossan presents this data. First, he seems unconcerned that the required breaks in the *Gos. Pet.* produces widely divergent line lengths, with the shortest complete line having 14 letters whereas the longest line has 24 letters. Second the placement of the smaller fragment, on the right-hand side of the larger fragment seems arbitrary, and while the smaller fragment contains a few letters that align with the Akhmîm text, no explanation is given to explain how lines 10–13 of the larger text are to be accounted for against the Akhmîm wording.[243] Third, and most tellingly, when one examines the actual papyrus fragments that form P.Oxy. 2949 one is struck by the extent of reconstruction that has occurred to produce greater conformity between the Oxyrhynchus fragments and the Akhmîm text.[244]

Lührmann makes much of the correspondence of the phrase ὁ φίλος Πειλάτου. He states that this 'friend' is Joseph of Arimathea in both texts. While this is obviously the case in the Akhmîm text where he

Table 10. Lührmann's presentation of the parallel[245]

| P.Oxy. 2949 | | *Gospel of Peter* 2:3–5a |
|---|---|---|
| 5. ]ὁ φίλος Π[ε]ιλα̣[τ]ου [ | 3 | ὁ φίλος Πειλάτου καί |
| 6. ] ς ὅτι ἐκέλευσεν[ | | εἰδὼς ὅτι στωυρίσκειν |
| 7. ελ]θὼν πρὸς Πειλᾶτο[ν | | ἦλθεν πρὸς τὸν Πειλάτον |
| 8. ]τ̣ὸ σῶμα εἰς ταφήν[ | | τὸ σῶμα τοῦ κ(υρίο)υ πρὸς ταφήν |
| 9. Ἡρώδ]ην ἠτησα[το | 4 | πρὸς Ἡρώδην ἠτησεν |
| 10. ]ηναι εἰπώ[ν | 5 | ἔφη? |
| 11. ]ητησα [ | | ἠτήκει? |
| 12. ]αὐτὸν[ | | αὐτὸν ἠτήκει ? αὐτὸν ἐθάπτομεν? |
| 13. ] ὅτι α[ | | ἐπεί? γάρ? |

---

[243] Again compare the treatment of Kraus and Nicklas. While in general they accurately indicate the uncertain letters in P.Oxy. 2949 on occasions they fail to mark reconstructed letters. See in particular ἐκέλευσεν on line 6, where the middle letters of the word have been abraded. See Kraus and Nicklas, *Das Petrusevangelium and die Petrusapokalypse*, 55–58.

[244] In particular large amounts of the text of the P.Cair. 10759 are omitted, thus making the correspondences appear proportionally greater than the divergences.

[245] Lührmann, 'POx 2949: EvPt 3–5 in einer Handschrift des 2./3. Jahrhunderts', 218.

is explicitly named (but simply as 'Joseph', not 'of Arimathea'), this is only the case for P.Oxy. 2949 if one has already decided that the two manuscripts represent the same base text. Having made this decision Lührmann sees this as a strong basis for asserting the identity of P.Oxy. 2949 with the Akhmîm text. However, if the possibility is even entertained that these two manuscripts do not represent the same text, then there is no need to automatically conclude that the 'friend of Pilate' mentioned in P.Oxy. 2949 is necessarily Joseph of Arimathea.

In many ways both the parallels of Crossan and Lührmann are misleading for two reasons. First, they include reconstructed letters that cannot be identified with certainty from the manuscript, and second they omit portions of the Akhmîm text, thereby making the correspondence appear far greater than is actually the case. A comparison is presented below that rectifies both of these problems. It contains only the certain letters in the larger fragment [P.Oxy. 2949 (i)] and parallels this to the complete text of verses 3–5a of P.Cair. 10759.

The true extent of the parallel is now apparent and most importantly it is possible to see the variation as well as the agreement. Lines 9–13 offer very little evidence for concluding that the two manuscripts represent the same base text, and even if it were felt that these texts exhibited literary dependence it would have to be admitted that large scale alterations had occurred in the transmission process.

The most important change is the absence of the name Pilate from line 5, although given its occurrence in line 7 it is not unreasonable to assume from the partial remains of other pen strokes that it may have been present here also. While there may be traces of a lambda, the rest of the letters are totally abraded, although the vestiges of a Π may

Table 11. Revised transcription of the larger fragment compare to *Gos. Pet.* 2:3–5a

| P.Oxy. 2949 | | *Gospel of Peter 2:3–5a* |
|---|---|---|
| 5. | φίλος       ο | ὁ φίλος Πειλάτου καὶ του κ(υρίο)υ |
| 6. | ς ὅτι ἐκ    σεν | καὶ εἰδὼς ὅτι στωυρίσκειν αὐτὸν μέλλουσιν |
| 7. | ων πρὸς Πειλᾶτ | ἦλθεν πρὸς τὸν Πειλᾶτος καί ᾔτησε |
| 8. | μα εἰς ταφὴν | τὸ σῶμα τοῦ κ(υρίο)υ πρὸς ταφήν καὶ ὁ Πειλᾶτος |
| 9. | ν ᾔτησα | πέμπας πρὸς Ἡρώδην ᾔτησεν αὐτοῦ τὸ σῶμα |
| 10. | ηναι εἰπὼ | καὶ ὁ Ἡρώδης ἔφη ἀδελφε Πειλᾶτε εἰ καὶ μή |
| 11. | ιτησα | τις αὐτὸν ᾐτήκει |
| 12. | αὐτὸν | αὐτὸν ἐθαπτομεν |
| 13. | ὅτι α | ἐπεὶ καὶ σάββατον ἐπιφώσκει |

perhaps be made out. The name Πειλᾶτος does occur partially in line 7, and one may confidently conclude that this text does mention Pilate, a tomb (line 8) and a friend (line 5). It is not impossible that P.Oxy. 2949 is a reworking or summary of Luke 23.7–12 where Herod is described as forming a friendship with Pilate, and the tomb is also mentioned. This is not possible to confirm on the basis of the larger fragment, but if one wishes to identify the friend in line 5, Herod is at least an equally plausible candidate as Joseph of Arimathea.[246]

Also highly significant is the total lack of correspondence between the two texts in lines 10 to 13, apart from the shared αὐτόν in line 12. Here P.Oxy. 2949 and the Akhmîm codex completely diverge. This perhaps argues more powerfully against identifying the two textual witnesses as representing a common text, rather than the tendency to allow the fleeting similarities in lines 5 to 8 to suggest the opposite conclusion. It is not impossible that these similarities in lines 5 to 8 may be accounted for as being due to a short shared tradition, either oral or written. However, the correspondences may equally be due to a coincidental reworking of the synoptic tradition.

Alternatively, one may wish to maintain that the papyrus and the Akhmîm text represent different versions of the same text. This appears to be basically the position held by Treat when he states, 'The Akhmîm excerpt is not a simple witness to the state of the *Gospel of Peter* at the end of the second century. Rather, the *Gospel of Peter* appears to be an evolving literary tradition, of which we have traces at two points in its development.'[247] Obviously the array of similar or the same words is striking, especially in lines 5 to 9 of the larger fragment. Such similarity leads Kraus and Nicklas to observe that P.Oxy. 2949 is most likely a source or tradition from the second or third century that is utilized by the *Gospel of Peter*.[248] However, the fact that there are virtually no similarities in lines 10 to 13 strongly suggests that the tradition represented in lines 5 to 9 has been removed from its original context and

---

[246] Here Coles is over-confident in his assessment that 'The larger of these fragments relates the story of Joseph of Arimathea's request to Pilate for the body of Jesus, in a version which is not that of the canonical Gospels.' (Coles, '2949. Fragments of an Apocryphal Gospel(?)', 15). Coles is only correct if the P.Oxy. 2949 is the *Gos. Pet.* and hence the name of Joseph of Arimathea may be supplies. The circularity in such reason is fully apparent.

[247] J. Treat, 'The Two Manuscript Witnesses to the Gospel of Peter', *SBLSP* (1990) 391–399, 398.

[248] Kraus and Nicklas, *Das Petrusevangelium and die Petrusapokalypse*, 58.

placed in a new literary context, or has evolved significantly by the time of the Akhmîm form of the text. Hence, although the highly fragmentary nature of the text must be acknowledged, it is more probable that material in lines 5 to 9 of P.Oxy. 2949 represents shared tradition, rather than a different version of the *Gospel of Peter*.

If one were to accept what appears to be Treat's underlying assumption, namely that short snatches of shared text indicate literary identity, then presumably the much higher level of agreement between the Akhmîm text at 8.28–33 and Matt 27.62–66 (the request by Jewish authorities for a guard on the tomb) should be read as a third point of reference in the evolving literary tradition of the *Gospel of Peter*, or perhaps one should call P.Oxy. 2949 and P.Cair. 10759 'reworked Matthew' (or to go a stage early, 'rewritten Mark')! Obviously this is to be resisted since the Akhmîm text has not expanded Matthew in a facile manner.[249] Rather the author has both rewritten and rearranged Matthean material in such a manner that his own redactional imprint is left on the version of the Passion as he tells it. In terms of a relationship between P.Oxy. 2949 and P.Cair. 10759 the fragmentary nature of the Oxyrhynchus text makes it much more difficult to determine the nature of such a connection. What can be said is that the tradition in P.Oxy. 2949 has been substantially modified in the overlapping section in lines 5 to 9 and that the total divergence in lines 10 to 13 suggests this material has also been placed in a new context. Since this is akin to what the author has done with canonical gospel traditions, consistency demands that one refrains from the temptation to describe the papyrus and the Akhmîm text as different versions of the same

---

[249] No hard and fast rules can be drawn here. Rather a continuum of relationships needs to be established. At one extreme might be the type of relationship that exists between the scribe of P[75] and B, where there is an extremely high level of correspondence. Further along the spectrum may be placed the form of the text of Acts found in Bezae [see E.J. Epp, *The Theological Tendency of Codex Bezae Cantabrigiensis in Acts*, SNTSMS 3 (Cambridge: CUP, 1966)]. In both these examples one is speaking of different versions of the same base text. More problematic would be the relationship between the Greek fragments P.Oxy. 1, 654 and 655 and the Coptic form of Gospel of Thomas. Next one could consider the relationships between the synoptic gospels. Here the scholarly discourse would describe Matthew and Luke not as variant forms of Mark, but rather as new texts in their own right with different redactional concerns. The use of Mark by the later synoptic evangelists is seen as a source for a new entity and not as the base-form of an expanded text. It must be remembered that the Synoptic gospels, at times, show a far greater level of correspondence both in wording and sequence than can be determined for the short text of (larger) fragment of P.Oxy. 2949.

text. Instead it is better to understand that Akhmîm text has taken an existing tradition and reworked it into a composition that has its own redactional concerns.

Thus, in summary, Lührmann may initially appear to do better in his reconstruction than Crossan, since he avoids the fundamental blunder of placing the smaller fragment to the right of the larger, and instead suggests it represents the commencement of lines 11–14.[250] However, this runs into the problem of commencing line 11 with μου, which is unparalleled in P.Cair. 10759. Also the line lengths remain widely divergent in length. Finally, Lührmann reconstructs a text of P.Oxy. 2949 that has 238 letters, of which on his own estimate only 63 are shared.[251] It should be noted that 2 of these 63 letters are bracketed, indicating they are not readable on the papyrus. However, there are at least another 17 letters that highly uncertain. This leaves the identification based on 44 shared letters out of a text of 238 letters, or an 18.49% (to 4 sig. figs.) correspondence between the texts. Perhaps others would feel more caution should be exhibited, rather than concluding that P.Oxy. 2949 is a fragment of the same text discovered at Akhmîm.

Since the appearance of Foster's article which challenged the identification of various fragments and artefactual remains as either part of the *Gospel of Peter* or witnessing to the existence of the text at an earlier date,[252] there have been a number of articles that have interacted with aspects of this debate. Specifically in relation to Foster's discussion of P.Oxy. 2949, Thomas Wayment stated that, '[s]everal other readings are called into question in Foster's minimalistic reconstruction, as well as the text of the smaller fragment, which Coles originally placed to the bottom left of the original fragment.'[253] One of the particular instances that is identified by Wayment as a major part of his argument is that 'Foster subsequently removed the reference to Pilate in line 5 completely.'[254] Unfortunately, Wayment failed to copy

---

[250] See Lührmann, *Fragmente apokryph gewordener Evangelien in Griechischer und Lateinischer Spracher*, 85.

[251] See the note next to the reconstructed text. Lührmann, *Fragmente apokryph gewordener Evangelien*, 85.

[252] Foster, 'Are there any Early Fragments of the So-called *Gospel of Peter*?', 1–28.

[253] Thomas A. Wayment, 'A Reexamination of the Text of *P.Oxy.* 2949', *JBL* 128 (2009) 375–382, here 375.

[254] Wayment, 'A Reexamination of the Text of *P.Oxy.* 2949', 378.

Foster's reconstruction accurately. As stated in response to the mis-transcription:

> Unfortunately Wayment's conclusion is the result of a fundamental mistake. He has failed to reproduce my transcription accurately. He has omitted two letters and one of these is crucial, since it undermines his argument in its entirety. I do in fact transcribe the *omicron* on line 5 in the name which has probably been correctly reconstructed as Πειλάτου by both Coles and Wayment. Moreover, Wayment also fails to reproduce the *alpha* on line 13 of my transcription, although in this case he does not base any argument on that letter.[255]

While Wayment's application of multispectral imaging techniques to read more of the abraded writing on the papyrus fragment is welcomed, his mis-transcription invalidates the argument he advances. He suggests that P.Oxy. 2949 is potentially either a commentary on the *Gospel of Peter* or an oral report of the text. This allows him to account for the deviations from the Akhmîm text. However, the basis for making this suggestion must be questioned. Given that P.Oxy. 2949 preserves a shorter and at times significantly different form of the text, it appears more likely that the tradition preserved by the papyrus fragment is earlier and represents an alterative development of a narrative that originated ultimately with the canonical gospels. By contrast, Wayment's highly innovative suggestion that P.Oxy. 2949 is a commentary on the *Gospel of Peter* is of course not impossible. However, given the available evidence contained in the papyrus fragment, this suggestion does not seem to have a significant degree of probability. This is because the legible portion of P.Oxy. 2949 does not provide any support for reading this text as a commentary. Wayment's hypothesis appears to be introduced to explain away certain very noticeable deviations between P.Oxy. 2949 and P.Cair. 10759. Furthermore, it is based on the assumption that a text of the *Gospel of Peter* was already available to a putative commentator. In turn, this assumption is then used to argue that the *Gospel of Peter* was already in existence prior to P.Oxy. 2949. Such circularity is not compelling.

---

[255] P. Foster, 'P.Oxy. 2949 – Its Transcription and Significance: A Response to Thomas Wayment', *JBL* 129 (2010) 173–176.

## 6.2. *P.Oxy. 4009*

The evidence Lührmann adduces in support of the first text from the Akhmîm codex having manuscript support in the second century is even more speculative in the case of P.Oxy. 4009, than was the case for P.Oxy. 2949. Together with Parsons, Lührmann edited this fragment in the Oxyrhynchus series.[256] His argument for identifying this text with the *Gospel of Peter* can be summarised in the following manner.[257] P.Oxy. 4009 parallels a dialogue between Jesus and Peter which is recorded in 2 Clem 5.2–4. Yet, unlike the version contained in 2 Clem 5 where the dialogue is reported in the third person, in P.Oxy. 4009 Peter, according to Lührmann, speaks in the first person. This is similar to the two places in the Akhmîm text where Peter speaks in the first person. Hence, it can be concluded that P.Oxy. 4009 represents a no longer extant part of the exemplar for P.Cair. 10759, and consequently is a second century witness to the *Gospel of Peter*.[258] Yet this argument is far more convoluted than the preceding summary suggests.[259] In part this is due to two major factors. First the identification made between P.Oxy. 4009 and 2 Clem 5.2–4 is precarious because of the highly fragmentary nature of the papyrus manuscript. Second, there are other versions of the traditional saying about serpents and doves which occur in Matt 10.16b,[260] G.Thom. 39, and also in a highly fragmentary form in the Greek fragments of G.Thom. (P.Oxy. 655, col.

---

[256] D. Lührmann and P.J. Parsons, '4009. Gospel of Peter?' in *The Oxyrhynchus Papyri*, vol 60 (Cambridge: CUP, 1994) 1–5.

[257] For the argument supporting the identification of this fragment with the Gospel of Peter, see D. Lührmann, 'POx 4009: Ein neues Fragment des Petrusevangeliums', *NovT* 35 (1993) 390–410.

[258] To give his argument in full in order to clearly represent his views Lührmann states, 'POx 4009 ist ein kleines weiteres Fragment, das unsere insgesamt eher zufällige Kenntnis der frühen nicht kanonisch gewordenen Jesusüberlieferung bereichert. Es eröffnet überraschende neue Perspektiven, ohne die Rätsel auch nur des Petrusevangeliums zu lösen. Vergleichbar ist es einem (halben) Stück aus einem Puzzle, dem es zusammen mit anderen zwar zugehört, dessen meiste Teile und vor allem das Gesamtbild aber verlorengegangen sind.' Lührmann, 'POx 4009: Ein neues Fragment des Petrusevangeliums', 410.

[259] As Kraus and Nicklas note, 'Des Weiteren sind Herkunft und Werden des Apophthegma in II Clem 5,2–4 ebenso komplex, wie sie Ausgangspunkt unterschiedlicher Hypothesenbildungen sind.' (Kraus and Nicklas, *Das Petrusevangelium and die Petrusapokalypse*, 63).

[260] Although Matt 10.16a is paralleled by Luke 10.3, the serpents and doves saying is not present in the Lukan account.

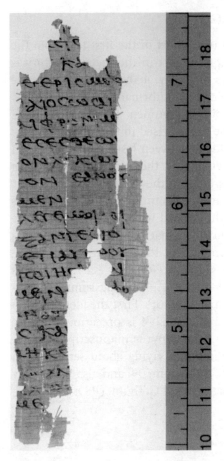

On the eleventh line are the key words for Lührmann's thesis λεγει μοι. Although this reading is reasonably secure, it is curious that the scribe has formed a smaller omicron in the word μοι than at many other points in the text. However, at the end of line sixteen there is an omicron of even smaller size.

Figure 2. The *Recto* of P.Oxy. 4009.

ii.11–23).[261] It is likely that the introductory warning that the disciples are being sent like sheep into the midst of wolves was part of the Q source.[262] To this saying, Matthew appears to have joined the free float-

---

[261] For a discussion of P.Oxy. 655 see B.P. Grenfell and A.S. Hunt, '655. Fragment of a Lost Gospel', in B.P. Grenfell and A.S. Hunt (eds.) *The Oxyrhynchus Papyri* IV (London: Egypt Exploration Society, 1904) 22–28 and Plate II at the rear of the volume.

[262] Kloppenborg et al. reconstruct the Q version in the following way, [ὑπάγετε] ἰδοὺ [()] ἀποστέλλω ὑμᾶς ὡς (πρόβατα) ἐν μέσῳ λύκων (). See J.M. Robinson, P. Hoffmann and J.S. Kloppenborg, *The Critical Edition of Q: Synopsis including the Gospels of Matthew and Luke, Mark and Thomas with English, German and French translations of Q and Thomas* (Minneapolis/Leuven: Fortress/Peeters, 2000) Q 10.3, 162.

ing piece of tradition about the serpents and doves. This conclusion is supported by the observation that in G.Thom. the serpents and doves saying occurs in a different context. Therefore it is not implausible to see the serpents and doves saying as an independent piece of oral tradition that was used independently by both Matthew and Thomas.

Now, after these preliminary remarks, it is necessary to look at the manuscript evidence provided by P.Oxy. 4009 in order to assess the merits of the thesis advocated by Lührmann. In particular, two claims Lührmann makes for P.Oxy. 4009 will be questioned. First, the claim that it represents the same dialogue as 2 Clem 5 will be analysed. Secondly, the basis of the conclusion drawn from this identification will be questioned, namely that P.Oxy. 4009 is a fragment of the *Gospel of Peter*.

A serious problem for Lührmann's thesis is the identification he makes between the text of P.Oxy. 4009 and 2 Clem 5.2–4. First it should be noted that while the *verso* (defined as the side where the writing is perpendicular to papyrus fibres) contains a *nomen sacrum* and hence, according to Lührmann, 'identifies this as a Christian text',[263] nonetheless in contrast to the *recto*, he concludes with Parsons in the *editio princeps* that '[w]e have not found any similar basis for reconstructing V[erso].'[264] What is amazing about this statement is that in his 1993 *Novum Testamentum* article, which is referenced in the *editio princeps*, Lührmann does in fact suggest partial reconstructions for the *verso* and hence suggests that it also represents part of the text of the *Gospel of Peter*. Nonetheless, while stating that a reconstruction of the text contained on the *verso* is impossible,[265] Lührmann reconstructs various synoptic type words and hence concludes that P.Oxy. 4009 (both *recto* and *verso*) is a new fragment of the *Gospel of Peter*.[266] The lack of any continuous text or rarely used words on the *verso* means that the conclusion articulated with Parsons remains in force, namely, no secure identification is possible.

The *recto* potentially offers more promising results since there are, according to Lührmann, both similar combinations of words used in

---

[263] Lührmann and Parsons, '4009. Gospel of Peter?' 1.

[264] Lührmann and Parsons, '4009. Gospel of Peter?' 1.

[265] 'Eine Rekonstruktion des Textes des Verso ist also ausgeschlossen', Lührmann, 'POx 4009: Ein neues Fragment des Petrusevangeliums', 403.

[266] 'daß POx 4009 (Recto und wohl auch Verso) ein neues Fragment des Petrusevangeliums ist.' Lührmann, 'POx 4009: Ein neues Fragment des Petrusevangeliums', 404.

the synoptic tradition and also, apparently, a first person narrative. Lines 5 and 6 are correctly transcribed by Lührmann as follows:

Line 5      ] . αιοσωσαι[
Line 6      ] αιφρονιμ.[

The reconstruction offered is made on the basis of parallels contained in Matt 10.16b, P.Oxy. 2.19–23 and G.Thom. 39.

Line 5      γείνου δὲ ἀνέ]ραιος ὡς αἰ [πε
Line 6      ριστεραί κ]αὶ φρονιμο[ς
Line 7      ὡς οἱ ὄφεις [

First, it should be noted that inexplicably a rho appears with the manuscript text at the beginning of line 5 and an omicron at the end of line 6. These letters are not uncertain, they are in fact non-existent as the photograph of the manuscript makes patently clear.[267] Second, if the reconstruction is correct, this differs in comparison to the unified testimony of Matt 10.16b, P.Oxy. 2.19–23 and G.Thom. 39, all of which refer to 'serpents' and then 'doves'. The reconstruction continues for the lines 7 and 8 in the following fashion:

Line 7                  ]ἔσεσθε ὡς[
Line 8      ἀρνία ἀνὰ μέ]σον λύκων[

This reconstructs a saying similar to Matt 10.16a, but places it after the saying that parallels Matt 10.16b. This is further complicated by the fact that while the combination of these two sayings may be explained by appeal to their conjunction in Matt 10.16, P.Oxy. 4009 does not use the Matthean term πρόβατα, but the Lukan term ἀρήν. Yet Luke does not have a parallel to Matt 10.16b. So it appears the author of P.Oxy. 4009 so far, if the reconstruction is correct, has presented a version of Matt 10.16b, but reversed the Matthean and Thomasine order of serpents followed by doves. Next he has appended the first of the sayings Matthew had redactionally joined, but in the opposite order. Moreover, he has chosen to adopt Lukan terminology ἀρήν in preference to Matthean term πρόβατα. The handiwork, however, is not yet completed. The wolf-lambs metaphor is employed in 2 Clem 5.2–4 in a dialogue between Peter and Jesus. Lührmann notes simi-

---

[267] At the beginning of line 5 there may be the curved stroke that are the partial remains of a rho, but this could also be an omicron.

larities between his reconstructed text and the passage in 2 Clem, but the points of contact with the actual text contained in P.Oxy. 4009 are minimal. The text in 2 Clem has no parallel to the serpents-doves logion, it does use the term ἀρνία, but it must be remembered that this is a reconstructed element in P.Oxy. 4009. In fact the only significant shared word is λύκων. In fact, one might as well suggest that the pastoral concerns that are present in 2 Clem are modelled on the Miletus speech in Acts, especially 20.29 with its reference to wolves, and that this is perhaps coupled with the charge to Peter in Jn 21.15 βόσκε τὰ ἀρνία μου.

Despite the improbability of this link with 2 Clem 5.2–4 Lührmann must insist upon this because 2 Clem 5.2–4 mentions Peter by name. This then enables him to interpret his own reconstruction of lines 11–14 of P.Oxy. 4009 as a reference to Peter, and consequently to identify the text as a hitherto non-extant fragment of the *Gospel of Peter*.[268] The proposed reconstruction is:

Line 11   ὁ δὲ ἀποκριθεὶς ]λέγει μοι οἱ
Line 12   λύκοι σπαρά]ξαντες τὸ
Line 13   ἀρνίον οὐ]κέτι αὐτῷ οὐ-
Line 14   δὲν δύνανται ]ποιῆσαι

To quote the more cautious form of the argument that Lührmann offers in conjunction with Parsons based on the identification of the referent of λέγει μοι being Peter:

> We have two clues to the precise provenance. (i) R[ecto] 11 suggests a first person narrative. (ii) R 9 ff., the *logion* of the wolves and the lambs, shows an extended text that recalls the version quoted (from an apocryphal gospel) in 2Clem. 5.2–4. There we have a third person narrative, which quotes a dialogue between Jesus and Peter. If it is again Peter who speaks in our text, but as narrator himself, we could assign 4009 to the *Gospel of Peter*; the Akhmim fragment, PCair 10759.[269]

There are a number of statements here which are either misleading or circular. First while the λέγει μοι reference does suggest some form of first person narrative this cannot be deemed to be an extended narrative. Only if the reconstruction is correct is this the case, but this is

---

[268] See in particular Lührmann, 'POx 4009: Ein neues Fragment des Petrusevangeliums', 394–396.

[269] Lührmann and Parsons, '4009. Gospel of Peter?' 1–2.

certainly not *a priori* the case. Second, the comment in brackets that 2 Clem is quoting an apocryphal gospel is highly dubious. The source of the narrative in 2 Clem is not stated and it is not possible to determine whether the author is reworking oral, non-canonical or canonical gospel traditions (or even a combination of these). Alternatively, there could be a large amount of redactional creativity occurring. Third, the shared vocabulary between P.Oxy. 4009 and 2 Clem is not significant. The most striking similarity is the term λύκων/λύκοι, but even here the forms differ. Lührmann's identification of P.Oxy. 4009 as an unparalleled fragment of the *Gospel of Peter* is based on a chain of highly speculative reconstructions, identifications and implausible textual relationships. In no way can P.Oxy. 4009 be viewed as giving firm support for the existence of an exemplar of the Akhmîm text in the second century. Concern over such an approach has been raised by Pheme Perkins. She states,

> Sometimes a scholar is so anxious to put the new fossil or text into a particular hole in the known data that differences between the reconstruction and what is really in the record are fudged. Such tendencies have been exhibited by scholars who rushed to claim that very small fragments of Gospel material are from missing parts of *Gos. Pet.*, for example. More cautious scholars insist that these fragments be referred to by their museum numbers until such time as more secure evidence for the alleged connection is discovered.[270]

Perkins cites Foster's previously published work questioning Lührmann's theories as an example of cautious scholarship.[271] The motivation for identifying P.Oxy. 4009 as a part of the *Gospel of Peter* appears to relate to the desire to claim this was a gospel that recounted both the ministry and passion of Jesus. For this reason one must remain sceptical about such exaggerated claims.

Subsequent to Lührmann's work, a detailed attempt to reconstruct the *verso* of P.Oxy. 4009 has been undertaken by Matti Myllykoski, with his argument set out in two articles.[272] The first of these articles is the more significant for the present discussion since it is there that the

---

[270] P. Perkins, *Introduction to the Synoptic Gospels* (Grand Rapids: Eerdmans, 2007) 288; and 266–267.

[271] Perkins, *Introduction to the Synoptic Gospels*, 288, n. 1.

[272] M. Myllykoski, 'The Sinful Woman in the *Gospel of Peter*: Reconstructing the Other Side of P.Oxy. 4009', *NTS* 55 (2009) 105–115; and M. Myllykoski, 'Tears of Repentance or Tears of Gratitude? P.Oxy. 4009, the Gospel of Peter and the Western Text of Luke 7.45–49', *NTS* 55 (2009) 380–389.

proposed reconstruction is initially presented with supporting arguments for identification of this text with the *Gospel of Peter*. First Myllykoski cites the opinions of Lührmann, 'a reconstruction of the verso is excluded', Foster, 'no secure identification is possible', and he notes that 'Kraus and Nicklas have given up all attempts to make sense of the other side.'[273] In opposition to this, Myllykoski constructs his argument in a number of stages. Initially he states that 'Lührmann has made a good case for P.Oxy. 4009 being a fragment of the *Gospel of Peter*.'[274] Then quite plausibly arguing that the two sides belong to the same continuous narrative, it is tentatively suggested that the *verso* is likewise a witness to the *Gospel of Peter*. Next Myllykoski transcribes and reconstructs the *verso* but notes that his 'transcription of the unknown side runs differently at some points from that of Lührmann and Kraus and Nicklas. He presents his transcription with bolded letters representing actual text and reconstructed letter in plain typeface in the following form, alongside the proposed parallel to Luke 7.45–50.

Myllykoski does admit that 'some *uncertainities* remain as regards the precise wording of the lost letters in each line.'[275] While it would be churlish to simply criticise a much needed attempt to reconstruct the *verso* of P.Oxy. 4009, it is only fair to Myllykoski to accurate quantify the degree of fit between the fragmentary text and the reconstruction. There may be a few points of disagreement concerning the actual transcription of the letters preserved in the manuscript. For example, the final two letters on line four are transcribed by Myllykoski as το. This is almost certainly incorrect. The first letter is probably γ, or less likely υ, and the second letter has so little of its shaped preserved that all that can be stated is that there is a slight curved stroke on the right-hand side.[276] Yet, while correct transcription is important in its own right, the major issue is that of the reconstruction.

Considering the significant feature of the reconstructed lines in sequence, the following set of observations can be made. In relation to the non-extant line 1, the highly significant term μύρῳ is introduced

---

[273] All citations taken from Myllykoski, 'The Sinful Woman in the *Gospel of Peter*', 108–109.

[274] Myllykoski, 'The Sinful Woman in the *Gospel of Peter*', 108.

[275] Myllykoski, 'The Sinful Woman in the *Gospel of Peter*', 115.

[276] For alternative transcriptions see Lührmann and Parsons, '4009. Gospel of Peter?' 2, and Kraus and Nicklas, *Das Petrusevangelium and die Petrusapokalypse*, 60.

Table 12. Myllykoski's reconstruction of the *Verso* of P.Oxy. 4009

| P.Oxy. 4009, unknown side | Luke 7.45–50 |
|---|---|
| μύρῳ ἤ-<br>λει]ψε[ν καὶ οὐ διέλ(ε)ιπεν<br>το]ὺς[ πόδας μου φιλοῦσα.<br>σὺ δὲ τὸ[ ἔλαιόν ἐμοὶ οὐ<br>5  παρέσχ[ες οὐδὲ εἰσελ-<br>θοντι μ[οι φίλημα ἐδώ-<br>κας. διὰ[ τοῦτο λέγω σοι<br>ὅτι ἀφέ(ι)ω[νται αὐτῇ πολ-<br>λαὶ ἁμα[ρτίαι<br><br>εἶπον δὲ<br>10  αὐτῷ ἐκ [τῶν συνανακεί-<br>μενων· [Διὰ τί ἐν τῷ ὀ-<br>νόματί [σου ἁμαρτίας<br>ἀφεῖς, κ(ύρι)ε; [<br>]ουθ[<br>15  ]αμαι[<br>]προ.[<br>].πn.[<br>] ν [<br>] αι[<br>20  ].......[ | (45) φίλημά μοι οὐκ ἔδωκας· αὕτη<br>δὲ ἀφ' ἧς εἰσῆλθον οὐ διέλιπεν<br>καταθιλοῦσά μου τοὺς πόδας.<br>(46) ἐλαιω τὴν κεφαλήν μου<br>οὐκ ἤλειψα· αὕτη δὲ μύρῳ<br>ἤλειψας τοὺς πόδας μου.<br>(47) οὗ χάριν, λέγω σοι,<br>ἀφέωνται αἱ ἁμαρτίαι<br>αὐτῆς αἱ πολλαί, ὅτι ἠγάπησεν πολύ·<br>ᾧ δὲ ὀλίγον ἀφίεται, ὀλίγον ἀγαπᾷ<br>(48) εἶπεν δὲ αὐτῇ, Ἀφέωνταί σου<br>αἱ ἁμαρτίαι. (49) καὶ ἤρξαντο<br>οἱ συνανακεί-<br>μενοι λέγειν ἐν ἑαυτοις, Τίς οὗτός<br>ἐστιν ὃς καὶ ἁμαρτίας<br>ἀφίησιν;<br><br><br><br><br>(50) εἶπεν δὲ πρὸς τήν γυναῖκα, Ἡ<br>πίστιςσου σέσωκεν σε· πορεύου εἰς<br>εἰρήνην |

which forms a parallel with the same term in Lk 7.46. There is no palaeographical basis on which to propose this reconstruction. In line 2, the two extant letters ψε are not paralleled in combination in the text of Lk 7.45–50, which Myllykoski sees as the basis of his reconstruction. However, he notes that a variant reading, preserved in the witnesses D W 079 sy, supports the reading αὕτη δὲ μύρῳ ἤλειψεν (Lk 7.46b).[277] This introduces the necessary letter combination, and this

---

[277] Myllykoski lablels this reading Western, however, the witnesses W and 079 are classified as category III by Aland and Aland, 'manuscripts of a distinctive character with an independent text' and not as category IV 'manuscripts of the D text' K. Aland and B. Aland, *The Text of the New Testament* (2nd ed.; Grand Rapids: Eerdmans, 1989) 106.

then becomes the basis for reconstructing the entire phrase. However, this phrase appears to occur somewhat earlier in the reconstructed narrative of P.Oxy. 4009, than it does in any textual form of the Lukan parallel. With line three, the letter combination υς is unremarkable even when used to reconstruct the accusative plural form of the article. The suggestion that line 3 produces a parallel with the form found in the Old Latin manuscript e is a flawed observation.[278] First the Latin of course has no parallel utilising the definite article, second this requires retroversion back into Greek, and thirdly Myllykoski cobbles together partial parallels from various witnesses without being able to demonstrate a continuous parallel to any known text form. Myllykoski treats lines 4–7 together. None of the surviving text in P.Oxy. 4009 parallels any element in the narrative from Lk 7.45–46, with the possible exception of the final μ on line 6 paralleling the initial letter of the word μου, although this is reconstructed as μοι rather than μου. This single corresponding letter may not be seen by many as constituting particularly strong evidence. Lines 11–13 provide what may be considered relatively as the strongest evidence. Although with a different case ending the -μενων may parallel the ending of συνανακείμενοι, although such passive or middle participal endings are very common. The ἀφεῖς may also be a reworked parallel of ἀφίησιν (Lk 7.49), although Myllykoski does not acknowledge that the letters in P.Oxy. 4009 are somewhat defective, the initial two letters αφ are not clearly visible.

In terms of complete words that are preserved on the *verso* of P.Oxy. 4009 (adopting here Myllykoski's transcription), the following nine words can be identified: σύ, δέ, τό, διά, ὅτι, αὐτῷ, ἐκ, ἀφεῖς, κ(ύρι) ε. In terms of exact correspondence two words match words found in Luke 7.45–50: δέ and ὅτι. In terms of partial correspondence but with altered case or verbal forms there are potentially four shared terms: σύ, τό, αὐτῷ, ἀφεῖς. With the second person pronoun σύ which occurs in nominative form on the *verso* of P.Oxy. 4009, there may be parallels with the gentive and dative forms found in Luke 7.45–50. Although the neuter article τό is not present, other forms of the definite articles are found – but this is obviously of little significance. The parallel between αὐτῷ and αὐτῇ, is not significant, and the change in gender undermines any potential link. Lastly, as has already been noted, the relationship between ἀφεῖς and ἀφίησιν is problematic because the

---

form in P.Oxy. 4009 is not fully preserved. The remaining two words, ἐκ and κ(ύρι)ε are not paralleled. The absence of the preposition ἐκ is inconclusive. However the absence of the term κ(ύρι)ε, written as a *nomen sacrum* in P.Oxy. 4009, tells against Myllykoski's proposal. This is because the most significant of the nine preserved words is absent from the proposed parallel with the Lukan pericope.

The second article published by Myllykoski advocates the theory that 'the *Gospel of Peter* used manuscripts that represent the Western text of the earlier Gospels.'[279] Obviously there are a number of highly contestable statements in this short citation concerning both the Western text and the *Gospel of Peter*. Without engaging in these important but somewhat tangential issues one can focus on the actual argument. Myllykoski continues by stating that the 'most notable Westen feature, the omission in P.Oxy. 4009 of Luke 7.47b–48, is no coincidence.'[280] However, detailed examination of the surviving text reveals that there is no correspondence of exact terms beyond the two words δέ and ὅτι. Thus the extant text not only omits Luke 7.47b–48, but appears to be devoid of any correspondence to any extant form of Lk 7.45–50. It is strange that Myllykoski has not set his reconstruction of the *verso* of P.Oxy. 4009 against the form of Lk 7.45–50 preserved in codex Bezae, instead utilising the text of NA[27]. The only parallels that exist between the *verso* of P.Oxy. 4009 and Lk 7.45–50 occur only at places where Myllykoski has reconstructed the non-extant portions of the text. By contrast, at every place where text survives on the *verso* of P.Oxy. 4009 Myllykoski is forced to explain why the extant material does not parallel Lk 7.45–50. Perhaps the most generous assessment that can be made is that his proposed reconstruction, his identification with Lk 7.45–50, his suggestion that this parallel reflects the Western text form of that pericope, and his theory that the tradition has been reworked and incorporated into the *Gospel of Peter*, are ultimately not persuasive due to the lack of evidence within the papyrus fragment to support such wide-reaching theories.

For the sake of completeness, the image of the *verso* of P.Oxy. 4009 is provided below. This is accompanied by a transcription of the text. This will allow comparison with transcriptions undertaken

---

[279] Myllykoski, 'Tears of Repentance or Tears of Gratitude?', 380.
[280] Myllykoski, 'Tears of Repentance or Tears of Gratitude?', 380.

The *Verso* of P.Oxy. 4009

Transcription of the *Verso* of P.Oxy. 4009

]ψε[

]υς[

συ δε γ [

5  παρεσχ[

θοντιμ[

καςδια[

οτι αφ°ια[

λαι αμα[

10  αυτω εκ[

μενων[

νοματ[

αφεις κ̄ε[

]ουθ[

15  ]α̣μαι[

]προ.[

].πη.[

] ιν [

] α̣ι[

20  ].......[

Figure 3. The *Verso* of P.Oxy. 4009.

by Lührmann and Parsons,[281] Kraus and Nicklas,[282] and Myllykoski.[283] Like the former two transcriptions, but unlike the later, uncertain or incomplete letters will be marked using the standard convention of a dot placed under the letter. This has been used with the earlier transcriptions in previous sections.

[281] Lührmann and Parsons, '4009. Gospel of Peter?' 2.

[282] Kraus and Nicklas, *Das Petrusevangelium and die Petrusapokalypse*, 60.

[283] Myllykoski, 'The Sinful Woman in the *Gospel of Peter*', 114–115; and Myllykoski, 'Tears of Repentance or Tears of Gratitude?', 380–381.

Among the canonical gospels this text mos closely parallels Mark 14.27–30 On line the name Peter occurs in abbreviated forn πετ written in red ink, with red dots writ ten above the π and the τ of the πετ.

Figure 4. P.Vindob. G 2325

## 6.3. *P.Vindob. G 2325*

The fragment of text designated P.Vindob. G 2325, also known as 'the so-called Fayyum Fragment' consists of seven lines of text, although the seventh line consists only of the tops of perhaps at most three letters.[284] The text was discovered in Vienna, by Bickell, in the papyrus collection of Archduke Rainer in 1885.[285] It was published later that same year, with a subsequent note appearing the following year.[286]

Although there are abrasions on the first line, and while line seven is virtually non-existent, the rest of the text is reasonably clear and contains an obvious parallel to the tradition contained in Mk 14:27–30, but in a shorter form. The text may be transcribed as follows:

| Line 1 | ] αγειν ως[   ]τι[ |
| Line 2 | ]τη νυκτι σκανδαλισ[ |
| Line 3 | ]το γραφεν παταξω τον[ |

[284] For a recent discussion of this text see, T.J. Kraus, 'P.Vindob. G. 2325: Das sogenatte Fayûm-Evangelium – Neuedition und kritische Rückschlüsse', *ZAC* 5 (2001) 197–212; S.E. Porter and W.J. Porter, *New Testament Greek Papyri and Parchments: New Editions: Texts*, 2 vols. Mitteilungen aus der Papyrussammlung der Österreichischen Nationalbibliothek (Papyrus Erzherzog Rainer) Neue Serie XXIX, XXX. Folge (MPER XXIX, XXX), (Berlin: De Gruyter, 2008) for P.Vindob. G 2325 see vol. 1, 291–294 and for the plate see vol. 2, plate 62, Tafel XLVII.

[285] G. Bickell, 'Ein Papyrusfragment eines nichtkanonischen Evangelium', *ZKT* 9 (1885) 498–504.

[286] G. Bickell, 'Ein Papyrusfragment eines nichtkanonischen Evangelium', *ZKT* 9 (1886) 208–209.

Line 4        ]ροβατα διασκορπισθης[
Line 5        ]υ πετ και ει παντες ο[
Line 6        ]. αλεκτρυων δις κυκ[
Line 7              ]πα ν[

Standard reconstructions of this text sensibly base the completions of the lines on the text preserved in Mark 14:27–30 since this offers the closest parallel, despite hypotheses to the contrary.[287] Therefore, P.Vindob. G 2325 is most plausibly seen as an abbreviation of the Markan account.[288] Lührmann's identification of this text as yet another previously non-extant fragment of the *Gospel of Peter* depends on his proposed reconstruction of the end of line 4 and the beginning of line 5. The majority of reconstructions of this portion of the text read as follows (with only minor deviations).[289]

Line 4        ] ροβατα διασκορπισθησ[εται εἰ
Line 5   πόντος το]ῦ Πέτ(ρου) καὶ εἰ πάντες ο[ὐκ ἐγὼ λέ

Thus the end of line 4 and the beginning of line 5 contain a typical genitive absolute clause 'When Peter said…' By contrast, Lührmann offers the following reconstruction which differs in one element, the proposed completion of the second word of line 5.

---

[287] See in particular the meticulous work of Thomas Kraus on this fragment. T.J. Kraus, 'P.Vindob.G 2325: Das sogenannte Fayûm Evangelium – Neuedition und kritische Ruchschlüsse', *JAC/ZAC* 5 (2001) 197–212; updated with *addenda*, 'P.Vindob.G 2325: The So-called Fayûm Gospel – Re-Edition and Some Critical Conclusions', in idem, Ad fontes: *Manuscripts and Their Significance for Studying Early Christianity* (TENT 3; Leiden: Brill, 2007) 69–94; 'P.Vindob.G 2325: Das so genannte Fayûm Evangelium', in T.J. Kraus und T. Nicklas (eds.), *Das Petrusevangelium und die Petrusapokalypse. Die griechischen Fragmente mit deutscher und englisher Übersetzung* (GCS.NF 11 = Neutestamentliche Apokryphen 1; Berlin: de Gruyter, 2004) 65–69; 'P.Vindob.G 2325: Einige Modifikationen von Transkription und Rekonstruktion', *JAC/ZAC* 10 (2007) 383–385. T.J. Kraus, 'P.Vindob. G 2325', in T.J. Kraus, M.J. Kruger, and T. Nicklas (eds.), *Gospel Fragments* (OECGT; Oxford: OUP, 2009) 219–227, see plate 9 after page 236; T.J. Kraus, 'The Fayum Gospel' in P. Foster (ed.), *The Non-Canonical Gospels* (London: T&T Clark, 2008) 150–156.

[288] This perspective is shared by Kraus and Nicklas. 'Einer Zuordnung von P.Vindob.G 2325 zum PE wird deshalb, und weil auch der erhaltene Text des Fragments nicht durch einen anderen, dann dem PE zugerechneten Textzeugen belegt ist, hier nicht zugestimmt.' (Kraus and Nicklas, *Das Petrusevangelium and die Petrusapokalypse*, 68). See also the comments of W. Schneemelcher, *Neutestamentliche Apokryphen in deutscher Übersetzung* (5. Auflage: Tübingen: J.C.B. Mohr [Paul Siebeck], 1987) 87.

[289] See for instance Kraus and Nicklas, *Das Petrusevangelium und die Petrusapokalypse*, 66.

Line 4       ] ροβατα διασκορπισθησ[εται εἰ

Line 5   πόντος ἐμο]ῦ Πέτ(ρου) καὶ εἰ πάντες ο[ὐκ ἐγὼ λέ

This genitive absolute clause (When I, Peter, said…) forces the narrative into a first person form with Peter as the subject.[290] Leaving aside the arbitrariness of this reconstruction, a fundamental point tells against Lührmann's argument. The Markan text clearly provides a model on which to base the line completions and strong reasons must be proposed to deviate from the forms it offers. Mark 14.29 is part of a third person narrative where the name Peter is used with the definite article, ὁ δὲ Πέτρος ἔφη αὐτῷ· εἰ καὶ πάντες σκανδαλισθήσονται, ἀλλ' οὐκ ἐγώ. Secondly, red ink is not unique to this papyrus fragment. P.Oxy. 840 contains a number of red ink marks. It uses red ink in four ways. Red circles are used to highlight punctuation marks; red outlines are placed over the black supralinear strokes in *nomina sacra* but the letters themselves are not written in red; enlarged black letters are re-inked in red; and, red outlines are given to accents and breathing marks.[291]

However, even if the letters πετ were taken to be some type of special abbreviation, this feature does not make the narrative more likely to have Peter speaking in the first person. In this case Lührmann's reconstruction stretches credulity and he appears to have failed to take heed of Schneemelcher's warning 'the brevity of the fragment forbids sure statements of any kind: the completions also remain questionable.'[292] There is, therefore, no firm basis for identifying P.Vindob. G 2325 as being a fragment of the *Gospel of Peter*.[293]

---

[290] Lührmann, *Fragmente apocryph gewordener Evangelien in Griechischer und Lateinischer Sprache*, 81. Also Lührmann suggests 'eine kleine Änderung daran jedoch macht Petrus zum ebenso möglichen Ich-Erzähler auch dieses Textes: εἰπόντος ἐμο]ῦ Πέτ(ρος) καὶ εἰ πάντες ο[ὐκ ἐγώ.' See *Die apokryph gewordenen Evangelien*, 89.

[291] For a fuller discussion see M.J. Kruger, *The Gospel of the Savior: An Analysis of P.Oxy. 840 and Its Place in the Gospel Traditions of Early Christianity* (Leiden: Brill, 2005) 48–49. Primarily colour seems to function as an aid to the reader to highlight text which would either need to be read differently to what was written, or to draw attention to a reading mark such as an accent, breathing or section break.

[292] W. Schneemelcher, *New Testament Apocrypha*, vol 1: Gospels and related writings, trans. R.McL. Wilson (Louisville: WJK Press, 1991) 102.

[293] As Kraus and Nicklas state, 'Übrig bleibt dann *P.Vindob.G* 2325 als Teil eines nicht näher bekannten Evangeliums aufzufassen, das auf mit den Synoptikern gemeinsamen Traditionen beruht, bzw. es als Harmonisierung, Paraphrase oder rein Exzerpt eines synoptischen Stoffes anzusehen.' (Kraus and Nicklas, *Das Petrusevangelium and die Petrusapokalypse*, 68).

## 6.4. *Ostracon (van Haelst Nr. 741)*

The original publication of this ostracon was undertaken by Jouguet and Lefebvre,[294] with an excellent recent discussion being undertaken by Kraus which dicusses the most pertinent issues in relation to the *Gospel of Peter*.[295] It was discovered at Thebes and was assigned a date of sixth to seventh century. This ostracon is described by van Haelst in the following manner.

> Ostracon presenting the form of a triangle: 8 × 9.5 × 14.5 cm; on the convex face, 6 lines of a liturgical text; on the concave face a portrait of St. Peter with the unexpected legend ὁ ἅγιος Πέτρος ὁ εὐαγγελ[ισ]τ[ής]. 6th–7th century. Thebes.[296]

For Lührmann the combination of the name Peter and the description 'the evangelist' provides corroboration that Peter was known as the author of a gospel.[297] Two points tell against too quickly concluding that this is a reference to Peter as the writer of a gospel that circulated in his name. As Lührmann acknowledges, the term εὐαγγελιστής, is used in the NT three times (Acts 21:8; Eph 4:11; 2 Tim 4:5) and in none of these cases is the term designating the author of a literary work of any kind. Rather, it denotes the role of those engaged in the proclamation of the Christian message; Philip in Acts 21:8, as well as a general description of the role in Eph 4:11 and 2 Tim 4:5. Lührmann, however, argues that this usage was not the primary meaning of the term from the second century onwards.[298] Consultation of Lampe's *A Patristic Greek Lexicon* demonstrates conclusively that this is not the case.[299] Although the term is often used to denote one of the Four Evangelists, there is a widespread, persistent, and, based on the evidence cited by Lampe one may perhaps say, predominating usage of

---

[294] P. Jouguet and G. Lefebvre, 'Deux ostraka de Thèbes', *Bulletin de Correspondance Hellénique* 28 (1904) 205–209.

[295] T.J. Kraus, 'Petrus und das Ostrakon *van Haelst 741*', *ZAC* 7 (2003) 203–211.

[296] J. van Haelst, *Catalogue des Papyrus Littéraires Juifs et Chrétiens*, 268, number 741.

[297] Lührmann states, 'Gemeint ist vielmehr, wie bereits die Herausgeber interpretiert haben Evangelist als Autor eines Evangeliums entsprechend dem in 2. Jh. sich ausbildenden Sprachgebrauch, also der Verfasser des εὐαγγέλιον κατὰ Πέτρον.' D. Lührmann, 'Petrus als Evangelist – ein bemerkenswertes Ostrakon', *NovT* 43 (2001) 348–367, 349–350.

[298] See also Lührmann, *Die apokryph gewordenen Evangelien*, 92.

[299] See the entry for εὐαγγελιστής in G.W.H. Lampe (ed.), *A Patristic Greek Lexicon* (Oxford: OUP, 1961) 559.

The concave side of the ostracon showing
the face of Peter with upraised hands.

Figure 5. Ostracon (van Haelst Nr. 741).

the term to refer to those who preach the gospel, cf. Chrys. *Hom. 1.1
in Rom.*; Eus. *H.E.* 5.10.2; Ath. *Dial. Trin.* 1.12.

The second point, which Lührmann does not consider, is the association of Peter as the source of information for Mark's gospel. As
Eusebius reports the tradition he transmits from Papias, Μάρκος μὲν
ἑρμηνευτὴς Πέτρου γενόμενος, ὅσα ἐμνημόνευσεν, ἀκριβῶς ἔγαψεν (*H.E.*
3.39.15). The tradition associating Peter with Mark is also known from
the anti-Marcionite prologue, Irenaeus (*Adv. Haer.* 3.1.1) and Clement
of Alexandria (*H.E.* 6.14.6–7).[300] Thus, if the description of Peter as ὁ
εὐαγγελιστής is, as Lührmann suggests, a reference to his role in the
composition of a gospel, there is greater weight of Patristic testimony
associating Peter with Mark's gospel, than with a gospel that circulated
in his own name.

Lührmann also reconstructs the liturgical text on the convex side
of the ostracon and from this he finds further support for his thesis
that Peter is being referred to as author of a gospel.[301] At a number

---

[300] For further discussion of traditions associating Peter with the writing of Mark's
Gospel see R.A. Guelich, *Mark 1–8:26*, WBC 34A (Dallas: Word, 1989) xxvi–xxix.
[301] Since the ostracon now appears to have gone missing, one must rely on the
transcription provided in the original publication.

of places the six lines of rough script are not easy to decipher. The following transcription and reconstruction was proposed by Jouguet and Lefebvre:[302]

Line 1 ..........
Line 2 προ]σκυνήσω
Line 3 προσκυνήσο]μεν αὐτὸν
Line 4 τὴν μη]τέρα Μ(αρία)ν
Line 5 κα]ταλαβοῦ[σα
Line 6 ]μεν

The major problem with this reconstruction is the reading of the ρ on line 4, where the letter is perhaps more likely to be υ. Also the *nomen sacrum* Μν is not one of the group of fifteen words usually abbreviated and it is lacking the supralinear bar. This form, however, is represented in later iconography, often in depictions of Madonna and Child. Hence, this *nomen sacrum* is not unattested, although it usually occurs with a supralinear stroke.

Because of these difficulties Lührmann has proposed an alternative reconstruction.[303]

Line 1 προ]-
Line 2 ]σκυνήσω-
Line 3 μεν αὐτὸν
Line 4 τ(ὸ) εὐ(αγγέλιον)[304] α(ὐτοῦ) μέ-
Line 5 ταλαβω-
Line 6 μεν.

This reconstruction seems to introduce more problems than it solves. First why has the scribe introduced three non-standard abbreviations on line four? It is uncertain that the meaning of such a text would be followed by ancient readers. At the end of line 5 the reported discernable letters ου are replaced by ω. This allows the introduction of a

---

[302] P. Jouguet and G. Lefebvre, 'Note sur un Ostrakon de Thèbes', *Bulletin de Correspondance Hellénique* 29 (1905) 104.

[303] Lührmann, 'Petrus als Evangelist – ein bemerkenswertes Ostrakon' 353.

[304] Lührmann's initial reconstruction duplicated the α on line 4, and thus appears to present two alphas as part of the text contained on the ostracon. See Lührmann, 'Petrus als Evangelist – ein bemerkenswertes Ostrakon' 353. However, in his summarised version of this article the first alpha is included in the brackets of εὐ(αγγέλιον). Lührmann, *Die apokryph gewordenen Evangelien*, 97.The corrected form of the reconstruction is presented here.

hortatory subjunctive form. Once again, Lührmann presents an implausible reconstruction of a fragmentary text and appears to force into that text a reference to Peter's gospel by arbitrarily taking individual letters and treating them as abbreviated forms. Therefore, the ostracon (van Haelst Nr. 741) does not provide a reference to the *Gospel of Peter*.

## 6.5. *P.Egerton 2*

Apart from Dieter Lührmann, one other scholar has advanced claims for an early papyrus fragment being part of the *Gospel of Peter*. In two articles published in the 1980's David Wright suggested that P.Egerton 2, the *Unknown Gospel*, is in fact a fragment of an otherwise no longer extant portion of the *Gospel of Peter*.[305] This thesis does not appear to have gained acceptance with other scholars, and even Lührmann, while speaking warmly about what Wright has attempted, states that without further textual evidence his thesis cannot be accepted.[306] It is interesting to note the implied weakness that Lührmann detects in Wright's thesis. Namely, the lack of clear parallels between P.Egerton 2 and the Akhmîm text, and basing the conclusion on similarities of style and vocabulary alone. Such criticisms could easily be levelled against Lührmann's own identifications of P.Oxy. 4009 and P.Vindob G 2325 as fragments of the *Gospel of Peter*! Nicklas is also unpersuaded by the suggestion that P.Egerton 2 is a fragment of the otherwise non-extant part of the *Gospel of Peter*.[307] Listing four texts, the *Gospel of the Egyptians*, the *Gospel of the Hebrews*, the *Gospel of Basilides* and the *Gospel of Peter*, he states, '[a]ll prior attempts to attribute the text to an otherwise known piece of apocryphal literature have failed.'[308]

---

[305] The two articles in question are, D.F. Wright, 'Apocryphal Gospels: "The Unknown Gospel" (Pap Egerton 2) and the Gospel of Peter', in D.W. Wenham (ed.), *Jesus Tradition Outside the Gospels* (Sheffield: JSOT Press, 1984) 207–232; and, 'Papyrus Egerton 2 (the *Unknown Gospel*) – Part of the Gospel of Peter?', *Second Century* 5 (1985–1986) 129–150.

[306] 'David F. Wright hat versucht, PEgerton 2 als Bestandteil des Petrusevangeliums zu bestimmen. Er argumentiert freilich sehr vorsichtig und will als Ergebnis lediglich festhalten, daß eine Zugehörigkeit nicht auszuschließen sei…weitere neue Textfunde können hier eigentlich nur neue Überraschungen bieten.' Lührmann, *Die apokryph gewordenen Evangelien*, 139.

[307] For a recent comprehensive treatment of P.Egerton 2 + P.Köln 255 see T. Nicklas, 'The "Unknown Gospel" on Papyrus Egerton 2', in T.J. Kraus, M.J. Kruger, and T. Nicklas (eds.), *Gospel Fragments* (OECGT; Oxford: OUP, 2009) 11–120.

[308] Nicklas, 'The "Unknown Gospel" on Papyrus Egerton 2', 101, n. 17.

Wright's argument is indeed stated in cautious terms, and unlike Lührmann he advances his claim only as a possibility. In his first article Wright alludes to the possibility that P.Egerton 2 and the Akhmîm text are both fragments of the *Gospel of Peter*. He notes,

> In working on these texts [i.e. P.Egerton 2 and the Akhmîm text] for this study, I reached the conclusion that the possibility of *UG*'s [Unknown Gospel = P.Egerton 2] being part of the lost pre-passion section of *EvP* has been too lightly dismissed. I hope to reopen this question elsewhere. The present study, however, treats them as unconnected texts, in accord with the unanimous consensus.[309]

In his second article Wright attempted to demonstrate the similarity between P.Egerton 2 and the Akhmîm text on two fronts. First, he considered general features, then secondly he analysed the vocabulary and style of the two documents. In terms of general features he noted that both documents: (i) are closely related to both Johannine and Synoptic gospel traditions;[310] (ii) display unfamiliarity with Palestine and Palestinian Judaism;[311] (iii) have an anti-Jewish apologetic tendency;[312] and (iv) have been presented as works of popular Christianity.[313] These general features alone are hardly conclusive since many of these features already occur in the canonical gospel texts, so it would be a simpler solution to propose that the two texts are independently drawing upon such canonical gospels.[314]

Potentially more significant are the observations offered in relation to shared vocabulary and style. Wright, however, offered a caveat at the outset of his analysis, which while eminently sane, seriously limits the likelihood of the identification he makes. He states,

> Unfortunately, a comparison of their [i.e. P.Egerton 2 and the Akhmîm text] language and style encounters major limitations. They contain

---

[309] Wright, 'Apocryphal Gospels: "The Unknown Gospel" (Pap Egerton 2) and the Gospel of Peter', 228, fn 4.

[310] Wright, 'Papyrus Egerton 2 (the *Unknown Gospel*) – Part of the Gospel of Peter?', 134–136.

[311] Wright, 'Papyrus Egerton 2 (the *Unknown Gospel*) – Part of the Gospel of Peter?', 136–137.

[312] Wright, 'Papyrus Egerton 2 (the *Unknown Gospel*) – Part of the Gospel of Peter?', 137–138.

[313] Wright, 'Papyrus Egerton 2 (the *Unknown Gospel*) – Part of the Gospel of Peter?', 139–141.

[314] On the nature of the dependence of the so-called Gospel of Peter on canonical gospel texts see M. K. Stillman, 'The Gospel of Peter: A Case for Oral-Only Dependency?', *Ephemerides Theologicae Lovanienses*, 73 no. 1 (1997) 114–120.

different kinds of material, so we should not be surprised to find differences of the same kind as obtain between the narratives of the passion and resurrection and the accounts of the teaching and work of Jesus in the canonical Gospels, or at least in the Synoptics. Furthermore *UG* is a small text, whose reconstruction is at points quite tentative... Finally, assessments of style cannot avoid some element of subjectivity.[315]

This sober reflection demonstrates the caution with which Wright approaches his task, but it also calls into question the very validity of the endeavour. For instance, the comments on the double vocative, δίδασκαλε Ἰησοῦ (P.Egerton 2.33; 45) while structurally an interesting parallel to ἀδελφέ Πειλᾶτε (*Gos. Pet.* 2.5), is not a feature, as Wright himself shows, that is unique to these documents.[316] Hence its value for arguing the two manuscripts are fragments of the same text is dubious. Similar conclusions could be drawn about the other stylistic features Wright advances in support of his arguments. The assessment of shared vocabulary may likewise show the two texts inhabit the same conceptual world, but it falls far short of proving the two manuscript fragments are part of the same continuous original text.

In fairness to Wright, as he acknowledges, he 'did not set out to prove the identity of *UG* and *EvP.*'[317] Rather he concludes that 'their distinctive vocabularies are not incompatible with the hypothesis of identity.'[318] One does, however, wonder if a fragmentary portion of, say, the Gospel of Matthew were compared with P.Egerton 2 or the *Gospel of Peter* whether one would be forced to conclude that those vocabularies would not be incompatible with the hypothesis of identity? It is for this reason that Wright's cautiously argued thesis remains unconvincing, and perhaps the most positive assessment is that the identity of P.Egerton 2 with the Akhmîm text has been shown not to be a total impossibility.

---

[315] Wright, 'Papyrus Egerton 2 (the *Unknown Gospel*) – Part of the Gospel of Peter?', 141.

[316] The reference to Τωβιτ ἀδελφέ (LXX Tobit 5.11) demonstrates the existence of double vocatives in other passages. Moreoever, Wright's argument about ἀδελφέ being 'weight bearing rather than merely conventional' appears to be somewhat forced. Wright, 'Papyrus Egerton 2 (the *Unknown Gospel*) – Part of the Gospel of Peter?', 142.

[317] Wright, 'Papyrus Egerton 2 (the *Unknown Gospel*) – Part of the Gospel of Peter?', 149.

[318] Wright, 'Papyrus Egerton 2 (the *Unknown Gospel*) – Part of the Gospel of Peter?', 149.

### 6.6. Conclusions

Five separate pieces of textual evidence have been identified by scholars as either fragments of the *Gospel of Peter*, or in the case of the ostracon a witness to Peter's role as a gospel writer. The most cautious approach is exhibited by Wright, who in relation to P.Egerton 2 adjudged that the verbal and stylistic similarities would not preclude identifying this fragment and the Akhmîm text as two parts of a no longer fully extant *Gospel of Peter*.[319] While concurring with Wright that his hypothesis is not a total impossibility, its degree of probability remains extremely low.

The most active proponent for identifying fragments and references to the *Gospel of Peter* is Dieter Lührmann. Of the four pieces of evidence he sees as being significant three have no overlap with the Akhmîm text. The ostracon has a description of Peter as 'the evangelist' on its concave face. As has been argued, the term does not necessarily denote the 'author' of a gospel even from the second century onwards, and, even if it did, it could quite plausibly refer to the widespread Patristic tradition describing Peter's role in the composition of Mark's gospel. The convex side contains six partial lines of a liturgical text. Here Lührmann's completion of the lines, especially taking letters as unusual abbreviations, is totally unconvincing. The text on the ostracon contains no reference to Peter's gospel. Equally spurious is his attempt to make P.Vindob. G 2325 read as a first person narrative. There is no good reason to reconstruct the text in such a manner, thereby deviating from the form preserved in Mark's Gospel. Similarly, the identification of P.Oxy. 4009 as an otherwise non-extant fragment of the *Gospel of Peter* is based on a series of convoluted and implausible arguments. Claims that P.Oxy. 4009 is a fragment of the *Gospel of Peter* appear to stem, at least in part, from a desire to show that non-canonical account to have been more extensive than a passion narrative. The one text that shows a partial overlap with part of the Akhmîm text is P.Oxy. 2949. Yet even here the divergences are far greater than the similarities. The lack of correspondence between lines 10 to 13 and the Akhmîm text suggests that the material in lines 5 to 9 has been placed in a different context than that in P.Oxy. 2949. Thus,

---

[319] See Wright, 'Papyrus Egerton 2 (the *Unknown Gospel*) – Part of the Gospel of Peter?', 129–150.

it is more plausible that lines 5 to 9 represent a shared tradition, rather being a different form of the same text.[320]

These negative results mean that it is no longer possible to assert that the first text discovered in the Akhmîm codex is definitely a witness to an archetype dating to the second century. Furthermore, the tendency to associate texts with the apostle Peter[321] means one should exercise caution before too quickly identifying the Akhmîm text with the *Gospel of Peter* that Serapion declared open to docetic interpretation. While this may remain the most likely hypothesis, the case is uncertain due to the lack of a title on the Akhmîm text, and the absence of any parallel text.

Kraus and Nicklas observe in their discussion of P.Oxy. 4009 that first person narratives with Peter being the subject are not unique to the Akhmîm codex.[322] One example is particularly instructive, since throughout its narrative the first person form is used by Peter. A striking parallel exists between the *Gospel of Peter* 14.60 ἐγὼ δὲ Σίμων Πέτρος and the statement in *NHC* VI.1 'And I, Peter,...'[323] Thus, while Peter speaking in the first person in the Akhmîm text on two occasions (7.27 and 14.60) is perhaps suggestive for those who wish to identify this text with the *Gospel of Peter* mentioned by Serapion, nonetheless this remains a supposition since a number of other extant texts employ first person narratives in relation to the character of Peter. Perhaps further textual discoveries might potentially assist in providing evidence to support this hypothesis. In the meantime greater caution is necessary. Perhaps all one can say with certainty is that the first text from the Akhmîm codex provides a sixth to ninth century manuscript which contains a passion and post-resurrection narrative with heightened miraculous element and sensational details. To make claims about the pre-history of this text in the second century (or even

---

[320] Stillman, 'The Gospel of Peter: A Case for Oral-Only Dependency?', 114–120.

[321] These include Mark's Gospel, 2 Peter, various Apocalypses and Acts.

[322] 'Zudem ist der Akhmîm-Codex nicht das einzige Zeugnis für einen Ich-Erzähler Petrus (z.B. I und II Petr; äthApkPetr 2; Akten des Petrus und der Zwölf 1,30–31 [*NHC* V[*sic.*],1]) und ist der Gebrauch der ersten Person als Erzählperspektive natürlich nicht exklusiv auf das PE beschränkt.' Kraus and Nicklas, *Das Petrusevangelium and die Petrusapokalypse*, 63.

[323] See the translation of D.M. Parrott and R.McL. Wilson 'The Acts of Peter and the Twelve Apostles (VI,*1*) in J.M. Robinson, *The Nag Hammadi Library in English* (4th rev. ed., Leiden: Brill, 1996) 287–294, 289.

earlier) is to go beyond the available evidence, and in fact may be ret-rojecting this text into a period when it did not exist.

## 7. The 'Gospel of Peter' and the Emerging Corpus of Petrine Writings

The *Gospel of Peter* shows no demonstrable awareness of the canonical Petrine epistles.[324] In this sense it may be fair to assert that the original author of the text reflects no knowledge of a growing corpus of Petrine literature, nor a desire to locate the gospel text in that stream. Rather, he presents his re-cast gospel as a free-standing authoritative text, legitimated by the status of Peter himself. As is argued elsewhere in the introduction, the *Gospel of Peter* does, however, draw directly on Mark's gospel. The testimony of Papias asserts a strong Petrine con-nection with the Markan text. However, the author does not exploit this connection in the surviving portion of text. Therefore, any attempt to link the *Gospel of Peter* with wider Petrine traditions via Papias' testimony concerning Mark does not appear secure.

### 7.1. *Petrine Apocalypses*

Notwithstanding this lack of explicit linkage between the *Gospel of Peter* and other Petrine texts, the gospel text does reflect the larger phenomenon of a growing interest in the early Christian movement of creating a body of literature around the figure of Peter. One of the most obvious examples occurs in the Akhmîm codex itself, where the gospel text is immediately followed by a text known (although not uniquely) as the *Apocalypse of Peter*. In this text Peter is not explicitly named, however, the text opens with a dialogue which is set within the context of the canonical transfiguration story. The dialogue is reported in the first-person, initially plural with the narrator reporting the expe-rience of himself and his fellow disciples, but soon breaks into a first-person singular dialogue and although the 'I' remains unidentified it

---

[324] In his edition of the Greek text, Robinson did note a parallel between 1 Pet 3.19 and *Gos. Pet.* 10.41. Here there is obviously some related shared tradition of Christ preaching to the beings in the underworld in the period between his death and resur-rection. However, there is only one shared term in common, ἐκήρυξεν/ἐκήρυξας. For a further discussion of the relationship see the comments on 10.41b.

is perhaps most plausible to identify the speaker as Peter.[325] The text reports a firsthand vision initially of heaven and then the torments of what is labelled the place of chastisement (*Apoc. Pet.* 6). The description of the second location is reported in far greater detail, with the author giving vivid and gruesome portrayals of the various tortures that await those who find themselves in such a place.[326] Given the proximity of this fragmentary text to that of the *Gospel of Peter* in the Akhmîm codex, the similarity in the use of first person narrative, the fact that the vision of hell is reported within a scene from the synoptic gospel tradition, it perhaps somewhat surprising that it has not been more widely suggested that these two fragments may be part of the same text.[327] Presumably this is because ancient authors speak of separate texts known as the *Gospel* and *Apocalypse of Peter* and given the generic differences between the texts connection of these two fragments may seem problematic.

The interest in this apocalypse is widespread. The more expansive Ethiopic version of the *Apocalypse of Peter* contains a section paralleling the Akhmîm fragment. It is not certain whether the Akhmîm fragment has been excerpted from a longer Greek text of the *Apocalypse of Peter* or whether this shorter form has undergone expansion.[328] Either way the text demonstrates the interest in the figure of Peter and the tendency to present revelatory perspectives as having been mediated through the most prominent of the Apostles. In fact this Ethiopic version of the textual tradition explicitly names Peter, and the narrator

---

[325] In the first four verses, the entire speech may be attributed to Jesus. This is obviously the case in verse 4, where the narrator opens with the description, 'and the Lord continued and said'. The note of continuance probably implies the preceding material was also spoken by 'the Lord'. However from verse 5 onwards an unidentified character reports the collective response of the twelve disciples, and then uses the first person pronoun as a self-reference at various points throughout the text (i.e., verses 9, 12, 14, 15, 21, 25, 26).

[326] James, *The Gospel According to Peter and the Revelation of Peter*, 68–69.

[327] Those who have entertained the possibility include T. Zahn, 'Kanon des Neuen Testaments', *Realencyclopädie für protestantische Theologie und Kirche* 9 (1901) 779 (in passing); M.R. James, 'A New Text of the Apocalypse of Peter' *JTS* 12 (1911), 573–583; A. Dieterich, *Beiträge zur Erklärung des neuentdeckten Petrusapokalypse* (2nd ed.; Leipzig: 1913 [first ed. 1893]) 10–18. This option has also been discussed by R. Bauckham. 'The Apocalypse of Peter: An Account of Research', *ANRW* II.25.6 (1988) 4712–4750; and most recently T. Nicklas, 'Zwei Petrinische Apokryphen im Akhmîm-codex oder Eines? Kritische Anmerkungen und Gedanken', *Apocrypha* 16 (2005) 75–96.

[328] The first alternative is favoured by James. M.R. James, *The Apocryphal New Testament* (Oxford: Clarendon Press, 1924).

self-identifies himself as 'I, Peter' on a number of occasions throughout the text.

Apart from this strand of the apocalyptic Petrine tradition, there
also exists among the codices discovered at Nag Hammadi another
text that has been named the *Apocalypse of Peter*.[329] As the editors
describe this text, it is 'a pseudonymous Christian Gnostic writing that
contains an account of a revelation seen by the apostle Peter and interpreted by Jesus the Saviour. The persecution of Jesus is used as a model
for understanding early Christian history in which a faithful gnostic
remnant is oppressed by those "who name themselves bishops and
also deacons."'[330] This writing bears no relationship to the text represented by the Akhmîm fragment and the larger Ethiopic version. Nor
is it related to the other writing of the same name that is extant only
in Arabic.[331] The Nag Hammadi text preserves a dialogue between the
risen Christ and the first person narrator who is addressed as 'Peter'.
Its concerns are different to the other apocalypses of the same name.
Primarily it attempts to legitimate the christological perspective of
Jesus being a docetic redeemer. By the time of its writing there is a
clear demarcation between its outlook and that of its 'orthodox' opponents. Nonetheless, both parties are obviously engaged in a battle to
claim Peter as the originator of their competing traditions.

Even as late as the eighth century texts were being written that pur-
ported to preserve first peson speech of Peter. The Syriac *Gospel of the
Twelve Apostles* has a section containing a revelation of Simeon Kepha.
Having been 'moved by the Spirit' Peter undergoes bodily transformation in the form of enlargement. He then utters a revelation discourse
that is loaded with eschatological themes with certain sections poken
in the first person voice.

### 7.2. *The Preaching of Peter*

Moving away from apocalypse literature, other writings of various literary genres circulate under the name of Peter. The *Preaching of Peter*
(also known as *Kerygma Petrou*) survives only as a dispersed collection

---

[329] This is the third text in codex seven, i.e. Nag Hammadi VII,3. See J.M. Robinson
(ed.) *The Nag Hammadi Library in English* (Leiden: Brill, 1996) 372–378.

[330] J. Brashler, 'Apocalypse of Peter (VII,3)' in Robinson (ed.) *The Nag Hammadi
Library in English*, 372.

[331] F. Wisse, 'Peter, Apocalypse of (NHC VII,3)', in D.N. Freedman (ed.), *Anchor
Bible Dictionary*, vol. 5, (New York, Doubleday, 1992) 268–269.

of fragmentary citations in the writings of Clement of Alexandria primarily,[332] but also in some brief references made by Origen. The fragmentary nature of the surviving material means that little can be said about the contents, extent or structure of the work. It appears to have preserved a series of sermons purportedly preached by Peter. Clement considered the work genuine and may have seen it as providing exemplary sermons. Corley suggests that it 'may have included christological sections which utilized OT passages in its Christian interpretation of Jesus death and resurrection.'[333] While precise conclusions remain uncertain due to the partial remains of the text, it illustrates the way the supposed words of Peter functioned paradigmatically for early Christian preaching.

## 7.3. *Apocryphal Acts*

Most likely an imitation of the form of the canonical Acts of the Apostles, the Apocryphal Acts portray events, either noteworthy or miraculous, in the careers of various prominent apostles. Five early Apocryphal Acts survive, which are associated with the apostles, Andrew, John, Paul, Thomas and, of course, Peter. A complex relationship exists between the texts of a number of these Acts. These texts reflect varying theological perspectives that may be in some cases in competition with one another.[334] The *Acts of Peter* records a miracle contest that takes place in Rome between the arch-heretic Simon Magus and the chief apostle Peter. Probably composed during the second half of the second-century the *Acts of Peter* represents an early example of the tendency to produce texts that enhance the prestige of the apostle or exploit Peter's apostolic status to further the theological perspectives embodied in the text. This text also represents

> an important source for much of the later Petrine literature. The Pseudo-Clementine Romances show a general familiarity with the *Acts of Peter* and maybe designed to fit into the period between Peter's activity in Jerusalem and his journey to Rome. The *Acts of Peter* follows the Clem-

---

[332] See Clement, *Stromateis* 1.29.182; 2.15.68; 6.5.39–41; 6.5.43; 6.6.48; 6.7.58; 6.15.128; see also *ecl.* 58).

[333] K. Corley, 'Peter, Preaching of', in D.N. Freedman (ed.), *Anchor Bible Dictionary*, vol. 5, (New York, Doubleday, 1992) 282.

[334] See P. Foster, 'Polymorphic Christology: Its Origins and Development in Early Christianity', *JTS* 58 (2007) 90–93.

entine *Recognitions* in the Vercelli manuscript.... The *Acts of Peter* also
lies behind alternative accounts of Peter's death in Pseudo-Hegesippus
and in the Pseudo-Marcellus texts, the *Passion of Peter and Paul*, and the
*Acts of Peter and Paul*.[335]

Such a trajectory reveals a phenomenon that progressed rapidly from
the second-century onwards of creating texts that drew upon the
authority of Peter to enhance their circulation, reputation and authoritative standing.

As is noted above, the *Acts of Peter* led to the composition of a number of other Acts. Again, it is possible to see a highly creative strand
in Christian thinking and theology that centres on the figure of Peter.
Here one of the functions of the text is address certain contemporary
concerns such as 'the restoration and maintenance of faith in the face
of competition from other cults.'[336] This is achieved by retrojecting
those concerns into the context of Peter's life, especially in the form of
the narrated miracle contest between Peter and Simon Magus (characterized in much early Christian literature as the arch-heretic). Another
text in this genre, the *Act of Peter* (in the singular) recounts the story of
Peter's virgin daughter who is paralyzed in response to Peter's prayer
to preserve her virginity.[337] Here the story is narrated for the apparent
promotion of encratic ideology.[338] Similarly, with the growing interest
in Christian martyrology, the final chapters of the *Acts of Peter* circulated separately and no doubt furthered the development of a theology of martyrdom.[339] This text then took on a life of its own and was
expanded into the Latin elaboration known as the *Passion of Peter*.[340]
The hagiographical and martyrological traditions which developed in
a Roman context around claims of dual apostolic foundation are witnessed in the ongoing expansions of Acts and martyrdom texts. Both

---

[335] R.F. Stoops Jr., 'Peter, Acts of', in D.N. Freedman (ed.), *Anchor Bible Dictionary*,
vol. 5, (New York, Doubleday, 1992) 268.

[336] Stoops, 'Peter, Acts of', 267.

[337] The text is contained in P.Berol. 8502, preceded by three other tractates: *Gospel
of Mary*, *Apocryphon of John*, and *Sophia of Jesus Christ*.

[338] See M. Krause, 'Die Petrusakten in Codex VI von Nag Hammadi', in M. Krause
(ed.), *Essays on the Nag Hammadi Texts in Honour of Alexander Böhlig* (NHS 3;
Leiden: Brill, 1972) 36–58.

[339] For discussion of martyrdom traditions relating to Peter see O. Cullmann, *Peter:
Disciple, Apostle and Martyr: A Historical and Theological Study* (2nd ed.; London:
SCM, 1962).

[340] E. Amann, 'Les Actes de Pierre', *DBSup* 1 (1982) 496–501.

the shorter *Passion of Peter and Paul* and the longer *Acts of Peter and Paul*, both dating from around the sixth or seventh century, combine various earlier traditions in to a larger foundational narrative which seeks to legitimate claims of the apostolic primacy of the Roman see.[341]

## 7.4. *Epistolary Literature*

Apart from the two canonical epistles attributed to Peter, other letters circulated that were penned in the name of Peter. Apart from the *Epistula Petri* at the beginning of the Pseudo-Clementines, the *Letter of Peter to Philip* is another example of this genre of writing. Originally extant as part of the Nag Hammadi collection of codices (NHC VIII, 2) a second fragmentary copy has been recovered as the opening tractate in the Tcachos codex which also contains the *Gospel of Judas*.[342] Both texts are written in Sahidic Coptic, but the titular forms are slightly different. The Nag Hammadi version opens with a titular superscript that 'is more periphrastic and descriptive of the opening of the text…"The Letter of Peter which he sent to Philip" (132,10–11).'[343] By contrast the version in Codex Tchacos has a titular subscript 'Letter of Peter to Philip'. The epistle seeks to legitimate its 'gnostic' outlook by associating such views with the figure of Peter.

## 7.5. *Conclusions*

This brief survey is far from an exhaustive or complete catalogue of texts written in Peter's name, or of literature where Peter is a prominent figure. What it has sought to demonstrate is that the *Gospel of Peter* stands as part of a larger literary phenomenon where texts are generated around Peter as a central protagonist or the authority behind the text written often in his name. In many ways this is unsurprising, and reflects the phenomenon of pseudepigraphical literature which is

---

[341] For further discussion of links between the *Gospel of Peter* and the *Acts of Peter* see István Czachesz, 'The Gospel of Peter and the Apocryphal Acts of the Apostles: Using Cognitive Science to Reconstruct Gospel Traditions', in T.J. Kraus and T. Nicklas, *Das Evangelium nach Petrus: Text, Kontexte, Intertexte* (Berlin: de Gruyter, 2007) 245–261.

[342] Rodolphe Kasser and Gregor Wurst (eds.), *The Gospel of Judas together with the Letter of Peter to Philip, James, and a Book of Allogenes from Codex Tchacos – Critical Edition*: Introductions, Translations, and Notes by Rudolphe Kasser, Marvin Meyer, Gregor Wurst, and François Gaudard (Washington DC: National Geographic, 2007) esp. 79–109.

[343] Kasser and Wurst (eds.), *The Gospel of Judas – Critical Edition* 79.

widely attested in contemporary ancient literature and beyond. This overview of Petrine literature amply illustrates the ongoing production of texts either centred on Peter of written in his name. This growth is consonant with the increasing prestige that Peter enjoyed a primary source of authority and with his link with the Roman see.

## 8. POTENTIAL PATRISTIC REFERENCES TO A 'GOSPEL OF PETER'

Since the publication of the Akhmîm codex in 1892 with the suggested identification of the first text as the *Gospel of Peter*, scholars have collected potential references to this text from the Patristic sources. Initially this was primarily an exercise in finding explicit references to a gospel attributed to Peter, rather than looking for intertextual allusions shared by the first text in the Akhmîm codex and other early Christian texts. However, in the desire to find ever earlier references to this text, scholars focused more on the citation of passages from the *Gospel of Peter* in other Patristic texts, albeit with limited degrees of success. The detection of allusions is a slightly different task to that of finding direct references, so here the emphasis will fall on those cases where texts have been seen as explicitly referring to the *Gospel of Peter*. Yet even with the cases of alleged citations there are, nonetheless, marked differences between the various examples. Such differences will be highlighted in the discussion of the individual texts that follow. In this section of the introduction the concern is threefold: to catalogue such potential Patristic references to a *Gospel of Peter* that have been suggested by various scholars; to present the relevant portion of text both in its original language and in translation; and, to briefly comment on the relative merit of each suggested identification.

### 8.1. *Justin Martyr*

Some scholars have detected a direct reference to the *Gospel of Peter* in Justin's *Dialogue with Trypho* 106.3. This identification is contested, not only because a phrase such as 'the memoirs of Peter' could reflect the tradition that Mark's gospel was actually the transcription of Peter's recollection, but also because the actual phraseology used by Justin is highly ambiguous. Justin writes,

καὶ τὸ εἰπεῖν μετωνομακέναι αὐτὸν Πέτρον ἕνα τῶν ἀποστολῶν, καὶ γεγραφθαι ἐν τοῖς ἀπομνημονεύμασιν αὐτοῦ γεγενημένον καῖ τοῦτο, μετὰ τοῦ καὶ ἀλλους δύο ἀδελφούς, υἱοὺς Ζεβεδαίου ὄντας, ἐπωνομακέναι ὀνόματι τοῦ Βοανεργές, ὅ ἐστιν υἱοὶ Βροντῆς·...[344]

And when it is said that he changed the name of one of the apostles to Peter; and when it is written in the memoirs of him that this so happened, as well as that he changed the names of other two brothers, the sons of Zebedee, to Boanerges, which means sons of thunder;... (Justin, *Dial.* 106.3).

Debate has arisen concerning the referent of the third person singular genitive pronoun that follows the term ἀπομνημονεύμασιν.[345] It has been variously suggested that the phrase ἀπομνημονεύμασιν αὐτοῦ refers either to the memoirs of Jesus or of Peter. Traditionally the former option has been preferred, with the standard English language edition indicating this by capitalizing the pronoun, i.e. 'the memoirs of Him'.[346] In opposition to this interpretation, Pilhofer argues strongly for understanding the pronoun as referring to Peter.[347] Primarily Pilhofer bases his argument on the other uses of ἀπομνημονεύματα found in Justin's writings. The term occurs fifteen times in total,[348] and apart from this occurrence it usually occurs in close connection to a reference to the apostles in the plural (e.g. ἀπομνημονεύμασιν τῶν ἀποστολῶν *Dial.* 100) or in the absolute form τῶν ἀπομνημονευμάτων *Dial.* 105. As is apparent from the absolute form, this has become an abbreviation of the fuller title 'memoirs of the apostle', conveniently designated as 'the memoirs'. However, Pilhofer takes the replacement of a collective reference to the apostles in *Dial.* 106 by the singular pronoun αὐτοῦ

---

[344] For the Greek see M. Marcovich (ed.), *Iustini Martyris: Apologiae pro Christianis, Dialogus cum Tryphone* (combined edition; Berlin: de Gruyter, 2005) 252.

[345] W.R. Cassels argues extensively for the phrase ἀπομνημονεύμασιν αὐτοῦ being understood as a reference to the *Gospel of Peter*. See *The Gospel according to Peter: a study by the author of 'Supernatural Religion'* (London: Longmans, Green and Co., 1894) 20–25.

[346] Roberts & Donaldson (eds.), 'Dialogue with Trypho' in *Ante-Nicene Fathers*, vol. 1, P. Schaff (trans.) 'The Apostolic Fathers with Justin Martyr and Irenaeus' (Edinburgh: T&T Clark, 1893).

[347] Directly in relation to *Dial.* 106.3 Pilhofer argues that, Justin hier in der Tat vom Petrusevangelium spricht; denn zieht man die Zitierweise des Justin in Betracht, so wird man es wohl für möglich halten, daß er eine Geschichte aus dem Petrusevangelium mit einer anderen zusammenbringt, die möglicherweise nicht aus dem Petrusevangelium stammt, ohne dies näher zu kennzeichnen. P. Pilhofer, 'Justin und das Petrusevangelium', *ZNW* 81 (1990) 68.

[348] *1 Apol.* 66; 67; *Dial.* 100; 101; 102; 103 (2x); 104; 105 (3x); 106 (3x); 107.

as showing that one member of the group is being described, namely Peter who was mentioned in the previous clause.

Stanton, likewise, after a careful and qualified discussion, leans slightly in favour of taking the pronoun as referring to Peter. He, however, does not draw the conclusion advanced by Pilhofer that this constitutes a reference to the *Gospel of Peter*, instead he suggests that 'Justin is here referring to Peter's memoirs, i.e. Mark's Gospel.'[349] Thus, Stanton marries Justin's comment with the early tradition known through the writings of Papias and other Church Fathers, that Mark was the amanuensis of Peter. What Pilhofer does not entertain is the possibility that the genitive αὐτοῦ does not depict a possessive relationship, but is functioning as an objective genitive. In this sense Justin could be referring to 'the memoirs [of the apostles] about Jesus (or Peter)', where the bracketed reference to the apostles is implied, as is elsewhere the case with the shorter form that Justin only uses in *Dial.* 105–107. Furthermore, on grammatical grounds the pronoun αὐτοῦ is far more likely to refer to the same person who changes the names of the sons of Zebedee, since the infinitive ἐπωνομακέναι assumes Jesus as its subject without signalling any change from the previous subject designated by the pronoun αὐτοῦ. Thus, the case Pilhofer advances is not compelling since it depends upon a grammatically unlikely reading of the text, and also creates a reading that stands in tension with other uses of the phrase ἀπομνημονεύμασιν τῶν ἀποστολῶν/τῶν ἀπομνημονευμάτων as it occurs in Justin's writings.

### 8.2. *Melito of Sardis*

Melito was bishop of Sardis in the latter half of the second century and a prominent theological writer. He is remembered as a leading proponent of the Quartodeciman position regarding the dating of Easter. Eusebius preserves the names of many of his works (*H.E.* 4.26.2–4) the majority of which are no longer extant. Among the works thought to have perished was περὶ πάσχα, 'concerning Pascha'. Eusebius describes 'the two books On the Pascha', but Hall has argued that this designation refers not 'to separate works, but more naturally suggests a single work in two parts.'[350] Fragments of this hitherto non-extant text were

---

[349] G.N. Stanton, *Jesus and Gospel* (Cambridge: CUP, 2004) 101.
[350] S.G. Hall, *Melito of Sardis: On Pascha and Fragments* (Oxford: Claredon, 1979) xix.

discovered as early as 1936, but it was not until the publication of a Greek copy of the homily, lacking only the first page and preserved in the papyrus codex known as Bodmer XIII, that an accurate picture of its contents emerged. In essence what this text preserves is tractate or sermon for a Quartodeciman celebration of the Pascha (or Easter).

Soon after the appearance of this text it was suggested that parallels existed with the *Gospel of Peter* discovered at Akhmîm. In 1964 Othmar Perler published a short article noting perceived similarities between the two texts, and drawing the conclusion that Melito knew and drew upon the *Gospel of Peter* in his paschal discourse.[351] The first example of literary dependence presented by Perler involves the non-washing of hands by the Jews reported in the opening line of the Akhmîm text (*Gos. Pet.* 1.1). It is noted that in *Peri Pascha* 71 Pilate's act of handwashing is described, ἐφ᾽ ᾧ Πιλᾶτος ἐνίψατο τὰς χεῖρας. Obviously this detail by itself is insufficient to establish dependence. First the extant portion of the Akhmîm text does not report Pilate washing his hands (although admittedly this was almost certainly the incident that preceded the opening line of preserved text); and secondly, Pilate's handwashing is known from the canonical accounts (Matt 27.24) so dependence on the *Gospel of Peter* cannot be conclusively established. However, Perler states that elsewhere *Peri Pascha* depicts the refusal of the Jews to wash their hands. 'That the Jews (and Herod) refused to wash their hands is stated explicitly in section 77 of *Peri Pascha*, although using another term.'[352] The 'other term' that Perler refers to is the phrase οὐδὲ ἀφωσίωσαι τῷ δεσπότῃ, ('nor have you cleared yourself before the master'). Not in this phrase, nor in the wider context, is there any reference to hand-washing, water, Pilate or Herod, and although 'Israel' is designated, the term 'Jews' does not occur. Moreover, the scene depicted is the crucifixion, not the trial. That Perler can describe this as an 'explicit' reference to the *Gospel of Peter* 1.1 makes one wonder how slight the parallel would have to be before it was classed as being implicit!

A second example involves Herod's role in the trial scene, which is seen as a further point of contact between the two texts. In *Peri Pascha* there is a catalogue of pronouncements against the Jews with each

---

[351] O. Perler, 'L'Évangile de Pierre et Méliton de Sardes', *RB* 71 (1964) 584–590.

[352] 'Que le Juifs (et Hérode) aient refusé de se laver les mains, PP le dit explicitement au n° 77, bien qu'avec un autre terme.' Perler, 'L'Évangile de Pierre et Méliton de Sardes', 585.

line of the stanza introduced by the term πικρός 'bitter'. The seventh repetition of the twelve listed aspects of bitterness states πικρός σοι Ἡρώδης ᾧ ἐξηκολούθησας, 'bitter for you Herod whom you followed' (*Peri Pascha* 93 line 686). Perler argues that 'This is in full conformity with EP. None of the canonical Gospels mentions this order of king Herod…EP and PP, on the other hand, allocate the entire blame only to the Jews and to Herod.'[353] Again there is no terminological parallel between these two portions of text apart from the occurrence of the name Herod.

What Perler has failed to take into account is the way in which increased wider anti-Jewish sentiment during the second century and beyond attribute increased blame and participation in the events of the Passion to the Jewish leaders, rather than to the Romans. Such heightened anti-Jewish polemic is not unique to *Peri Pascha* and the *Gospel of Peter* alone, and in the absence of clear terminological parallels it is over-confident to suggest literary dependence. Not many scholars have followed Perler's assessment that Melito shows demonstrable knowledge of the *Gospel of Peter*, although Hall in his edition of *Peri Pascha* multiplies the references to the *Gospel of Peter* in his lists of parallels virtually without comment.[354] Also, although being more circumspect in her assessment, Cohick entertains the possibility of literary dependence: 'Though not a quotation, there may be allusions to the Gospel of Peter 3.6 in *PP* 72, with its blame of Jesus' death laid at "Israel's" feet and to Gospel of Peter 6.21 in *PP* 79, referring to the sharp nails used in the crucifixion.'[355] What is particularly striking is that while Perler, Hall and to a lesser extent Cohick, all see literary dependence between *Peri Pascha* and the *Gospel of Peter* (a questionable conclusion in itself) it is simply taken for granted that the *Gospel of Peter* is the earlier work without any attempt to justify this conclusion. Thus Perler's attempt to find early Patristic citations of the *Gospel of Peter* in the writings of Melito remains far from being plausible, let alone being established.[356]

---

[353] 'C'est en pleine conformité avec EP. Aucun des évangiles canonique ne mentionne cet ordre du roi Hérode…EP et PP, par contre, attribuent toute la faute aux seuls Juifs et à Hérode.' Perler, 'L'Évangile de Pierre et Méliton de Sardes', 586.

[354] Hall, *Melito of Sardis: On Pascha and Fragments.*

[355] L.H. Cohick, *The* Peri Pascha *attributed to Melito of Sardis Setting, Purpose, and Sources* (Brown Judaic Studies 327; Providence: Brown University, 2000) 89, fn 1.

[356] The question of the putative relationship between the Gospel of Peter and Melito's *Peri Pascha* is discussed at length in Thomas R. Karmann, 'Die Paschahomilie des

## 8.3. *Origen*

Writing nearly a century later, Origen provides a much more secure reference to a text known as the *Gospel of Peter*. In his *Commentary on Matthew*, while discussing the reference to four named brothers and a group of unnamed and unnumbered sisters (Matt 13.55–56), Origen mentions the point of view that these siblings were half-brothers and sisters. That is the so-called Epiphanian explanation, which sought to remove this textual obstacle to the notion of the perpetual virginity of Mary.[357]

> Τοὺς δὲ ἀδελγοὺς Ἰησοῦ φασί τινες εἶναι, ἐκ παραδόσεως ὁρμώμενοι τοῦ ἐπιγεγραμμένου κατὰ Πέτρον εὐαγγελίου ἢ τῆς βίβλου Ἰακώβου, υἱοὺς Ἰωσὴφ ἐκ προτέρας γυναικὸς συνῳκηκυίας αὐτῷ/ πρὸ τῆς Μαρίας.[358]

> But some say the brothers of Jesus are, from a tradition based upon the Gospel according to Peter, as it is entitled, or the Book of James, sons of Joseph from a former wife, who was married to him before Mary. (Origen, *Comm. on Mt* x.17).

That the phrase κατὰ Πέτρον εὐαγγελίου is intended, as is clear from the use of the term ἐπιγεγραμμένου, to be read as the title of a literary document. This is also supported by the fact that it stands in parallel with another source which is designated as 'the Book of James'.[359] This is an even more explicit designation of a written text. This passing comment as it stands in Origen's exegetical treatment of the first gospel clearly shows that he claims to know a written text entitled the *Gospel of Peter*.[360]

---

Melito von Sardes und das Petrusevangelium', in T.J. Kraus and T. Nicklas, *Das Evangelium nach Petrus: Text, Kontexte, Intertexte* (Berlin: de Gruyter, 2007) 215–235.

[357] This is distinction to Jerome's contention that these 'brothers' and 'sisters' were in fact cousins, and not children of Joseph from a previous marriage. See Jerome, *The Perpetual Virginity of Blessed Mary: Against Helvidius*.

[358] For the Greek text see E. Klostermann and E. Benz (eds.), *Origenes Werke: Zehnter Band, Origenes Matthäuserklärung*, GCS 40 (Leipzig: J.C. Hinrichs, 1935) 252.

[359] This document is usually understood to be the text now known as the *Protevangelium of James*, which in its ninth chapter refers to Joseph's sons from a prior marriage. In conversation with the high priest named Zacharias to whom it has been revealed that the aged Joseph should take the young Mary as his ward, Joseph responds, 'I have sons and am old; she is but a girl' (*Prot. James* 9.2).

[360] For a discussion of Origen's knowledge of non-canonical texts see J. Rüwet, 'Apocryphes dans l'œuvre d'Origènes', *Biblica* 25 (1944) 143ff.

Furthermore, it can be seen that from Origen's perspective this text contained a tradition that explained the reference to siblings of Jesus in the canonical gospels as actually denoting step-brothers and sisters born to Joseph and a previous wife. Such a detail is not present in the extant portion of the first text discovered in the Akhmîm codex.[361] This is not necessarily problematic, since that manuscript only preserves the part of the text which relates to the passion. If the *Gospel of Peter* actually represented a full length gospel text paralleling the structure of the canonical accounts, then one might expect this detail to perhaps be recounted at a much earlier stage, as is the case with the location of the story under discussion from Matthew's gospel and paralleled in Mark. Furthermore, if Origen's description is deemed to be accurate, and the document he describes represents the same text as preserved in the initial place in the Akhmîm codex, then this might have important ramifications for decisions pertaining to the dating of the document. The necessity of finding an exegetical explanation in support of the notion of the perpetual virginity of Mary does not fit well with the first century, but does in fact reflect the debates of the late second century and third century onwards.

### 8.4. *Eusebius of Caesarea*

Without doubt the most important testimony to the existence of a text circulating under the title of the *Gospel according to Peter* is to be found in the *Historia Ecclesiastica* of Eusebius. It is possible only to suggest an approximately dating for this work for three reasons. First, the length of this text probably means that it was composed over an extended period; secondly, there is not enough known about Eusebius' life to accurately determine the chronology of his writings, and lastly, the *Historia Ecclesiastica* almost certainly went through a number of editions with earlier material revised in existing sections and books being added at the end of the work to bring it up-to-date with contemporary events.[362] Notwithstanding these limitations references to

---

[361] This point is noted by Girod, '*L'Évangile selon Pierre* ne nous est pas parvenu, sauf dans un court fragment racontant la Passion et la Résurrection de Jésus.' R. Girot, *Origène: Commentaire sur l'Évangile selon Matthieu*, SC 162 (Paris: Les Édition du Cerf, 1970) 216.

[362] For a discussion of the various recensions of Eusebius' *Historia ecclesiastica* see E. Schwartz & T. Mommsen, *Eusebius' Werke 2: Historia ecclesiastica* GCS (3 vols; Leipzig: J.C. Hinrichs 9.1, 1903; 9.2, 1908; 9.3, 1909) 9.1, lvi. A discussion of the theory

the *Gospel of Peter* in the *Historia Ecclesiastica* almost certainly appear to belong to the initial recension of this text. This edition is likely to have been completed around the time of the Edict of Tolerance in 311 CE. This helpfully provides the terminal date for the writing of these references, and it can thus perhaps be assumed that they were initially written as part of the first edition of this work at some stage during the first decade of the fourth century.

Eusebius make two references in the *Historia Ecclesiastica* to the *Gospel of Peter*. The first occurs in book three in a general discussion about the literary works that are attributed to the apostle Peter. Although Eusebius knows of both epistles now contained in the New Testament, as well as a range of other texts bearing Peter's name, he accepts only one, the so-called First Epistle, as 'covenantal' or canonical, ἐνδιάθηκον.

Πέτρου μὲν οὖν ἐπιστολὴ μία, ἡ λεγομένη αὐτοῦ προτέρα, ἀνωμολόγηται, ταύτῃ δὲ καὶ οἱ πάλαι πρεσβύτεροι ὡς ἀναμφιλέκτῳ ἐν τοῖς σφῶν αὐτῶν κατακέχρηνται συγγράμμασιν· τὴν δὲ φερομένην δευτέραν οὐκ ἐνδιάθηκον μὲν εἶναι παρειλήφαμεν, ὅμως δὲ πολλοῖς χρήσιμος φανεῖσα, μετὰ τῶν ἄλλων ἐσπουδάσθη γραφῶν. τό γε μὴν τῶν ἐπικεκλημένων αὐτοῦ Πράξεων καὶ τὸ κατ' αὐτὸν ὠνομασμένον εὐαγγέλιον τό τε λεγόμενον αὐτοῦ Κήρυγμα καὶ τὴν καλουμένην Ἀποκάλυψιν οὐδ' ὅλως ἐν καθολικοῖς ἴσμεν παραδεδομένα, ὅτι μήτε ἀρχαίων μήτε μὴν καθ' ἡμᾶς τις ἐκκλησιαστικὸς συγγραφεὺς ταῖς ἐξ αὐτῶν συνεχρήσατο μαρτυρίαις.[363]

Of Peter, one epistle, that which is called his first, is admitted, and the ancient presbyters used this in their own writings as unquestioned, but the so-called second Epistle we have not received as canonical, but nevertheless it has appeared useful to many, and has been studied with other Scriptures. On the other hand, of the Acts bearing his name, and the Gospel named according to him and Preaching called his and the so-called Revelation, we have no knowledge at all in catholic tradition, for no ecclesiastic writer of the ancient time or of our own has used their testimonies. (Eusebius, *H.E.* 3.3.1–2).

---

suggested by Schwartz can be found in K. Lake, *Eusebius Ecclesiastical History*, LCL 153 (Harvard: HUP, 1926) xix–xxvii.

[363] For the Greek text see Schwartz & Mommsen, *Eusebius' Werke 2: Historia ecclesiastica GCS* 9, 188–190.

Such a comment reveals a threefold classification of texts attributed to Peter: (i) the undisputed writings, here the only example is the First Epistle; (ii) disputed writings which although perhaps not receiving wide recognition as being canonical nevertheless can be viewed as helpful, here the Second Epistle; and (iii) the rejected writings at least from the perspective of the 'orthodoxy' represented by Eusebius, with the four texts listed in this category being the *Acts, Gospel, Preaching, and Revelation of Peter*. Thus, this passage attests the existence of a text know as the *Gospel of Peter*. Furthermore, it shows that this text was rejected by at least some strands of emergent orthodox Christianity, yet nothing of its contents is described here.

More fulsome is Eusebius' second and final reference to the *Gospel of Peter*. This occurs in the sixth book of his *Historia Ecclesiastica*, again apparently written as part of the first recension of this work and published initially around 311 CE. Describing the works of Serapion, Bishop of Antioch around the last decade of the second century and maybe into the opening decade of the third century, Eusebius lists a literary work described as a λόγος entitled, 'Concerning what is known as the *Gospel of Peter*'. Because this text is the most extensive surviving testimony concerning the *Gospel of Peter* and also as it will be referred to in the discussion at subsequent points its full text is provided here.

ἕτερός τε συντεταγμένος αὐτῷ λόγος Περὶ τοῦ λεγομένου κατὰ Πέτρον εὐαγγελίου, ὃν πεποίηται ἀπελέγχων τὰ ψευδῶς ἐν αὐτῷ εἰρημένα διά τινας ἐν τῇ κατὰ Ῥωσσὸν παροικίᾳ προφάσει τῆς εἰρημένης γραφῆς εἰς ἑτεροδόξους διδασκαλίας ἀποκείλαντας· ἀφ' οὗ εὔλογον βραχείας παραθέσθαι λέξεις, δι' ὧν ἣν εἶχεν περὶ τοῦ βιβλίου γνώμην προτίθησιν, οὕτω γράφων·

ἡμεῖς γάρ, ἀδελφοί, καὶ Πέτρον καὶ τοὺς ἄλλους ἀποστόλους ἀποδεχόμεθα ὡς Χριστόν, τὰ δὲ ὀνόματι αὐτῶν ψευδεπίγραφα ὡς ἔμπειροι παραιτούμεθα, γινώσκοντες ὅτι τὰ τοιαῦτα οὐ παρελάβομεν. ἐγὼ γὰρ γενόμενος παρ' ὑμῖν, ὑπενόουν τοὺς πάντας ὀρθῇ πίστει προσφέρεσθαι, καὶ μὴ διελθὼν τὸ ὑπ' αὐτῶν προφερόμενον ὀνόματι Πέτρου εὐαγγέλιον, εἶπον ὅτι εἰ τοῦτό ἐστιν μόνον τὸ δοκοῦν ὑμῖν παρέχειν μικροψυχίαν, ἀναγινωσκέσθω· νῦν δὲ μαθὼν ὅτι αἱρέσει τινὶ ὁ νοῦς αὐτῶν ἐφώλευεν, ἐκ τῶν λεχθέντων μοι, σπουδάσω πάλιν γενέσθαι πρὸς ὑμᾶς, ὥστε, ἀδελφοί, προσδοκᾶτέ με ἐν τάχει. ἡμεῖς δέ, ἀδελφοί, καταλαβόμενοι ὁποίας ἦν αἱρέσεως ὁ Μαρκιανός, <ὃς> ἑαυτῷ ἐναντιοῦτο, μὴ νοῶν ἃ ἐλάλει, ἃ μαθήσεσθε ἐξ ὧν ὑμῖν ἐγράφη, ἐδυνήθημεν [γὰρ] παρ' ἄλλων τῶν ἀσκησάντων αὐτὸ τοῦτο τὸ εὐαγγέλιον, τοῦτ' ἐστὶν παρὰ τῶν διαδόχων τῶν καταρξαμένων αὐτοῦ, οὓς Δοκητὰς καλοῦμεν (τὰ γὰρ πλείονα φρονήματα ἐκείνων ἐστὶ τῆς διδασκαλίας), χρησάμενοι παρ' αὐτῶν διελθεῖν καὶ εὑρεῖν τὰ μὲν πλείονα τοῦ ὀρθοῦ λόγου τοῦ σωτῆρος, τινὰ δὲ προσδιεσταλμένα, ἃ καὶ ὑπετάξαμεν ὑμῖν.

καὶ ταῦτα μὲν τὰ Σεραπίωνος.[364]

And another book has been composed by him: *Concerning the so-called Gospel of Peter*, which he has written refuting the false statements in it, because of certain in the community of Rhossus, who on the ground of the said writing turned aside into heterodox teachings. It will not be unreasonable to quote a short passage from this work, in which he puts forward the view he held about the book, writing as follows:

For our part, brothers, we receive both Peter and the other apostles as Christ, but the writings which falsely bear their names we reject, as men of experience, knowing that such were not handed down to us. For I myself, when I came among you, imagined that all of you clung to the true faith; and without going through the Gospel put forward by them in the name of Peter, I said, "If this is the only thing that seemingly causes captious feelings among you, let it be read." But since I have now learnt, from what has been told me, that their mind was lurking in some hole of heresy, I shall give diligence to come quickly to you; wherefore brothers expect me to come quickly. But we, brothers, gathering to what kind of heresy Marcianus belonged (who used to contradict himself, not knowing what he was saying, as you will learn from what has been written to you), were enabled by others who studied this very Gospel, that is, by the successors of those who began it, whom we call Docetae (for most of the ideas belong to their teaching) – using [the material supplied] by them, were enabled to go through it and discover that the most part indeed was in accordance with the true teaching of the Saviour, but that some things were added, which also we place below for your benefit.

Such are the writings of Serapion. (Eusebius, *H.E.* 6.12.2–6).

---

[364] Again, for the Greek text see Schwartz & Mommsen, *Eusebius' Werke* 2: *Historia ecclesiastica* GCS 9.

This extended statement concerning the *Gospel of Peter* is best ana-
lyzed in two parts. First, the comment made by Eusebius pertaining to
Serapion's writing against this gospel text, and secondly, the contents
of the actual citation allegedly drawn directly from the work penned
by the Bishop of Antioch. While the accuracy and reliability of Eusebius' citations is sometimes questioned, there is no obvious reason
to do so here. In fact, the differences between Eusebius' introductory
comments and the contents of the citation support the argument that
here the excerpt from Serapion's work has been accurately presented,
since Eusebius has not apparently reworked the text to conform to his
own interpretation of its meaning.[365]

Eusebius attributes a work entitled *Concerning the so-called Gospel of Peter* to Serapion. This writing is reported as being a refutation
of the ideas contained in the *Gospel of Peter*. The necessity for such
a text is said to have arisen from the spread of heterodox teachings
among the Christians at Rhossos which stem from the gospel written in Peter's name. Thus, root and branch, Eusebius attributes a perceived widespread deviation from orthodoxy at Rhossos to the ideas
contained in the *Gospel of Peter*.

By contrast the quotation given from Serapion illustrates more hesi-
tancy in identifying the text as heretical. It appears that the *Gospel of
Peter* is not itself the source of the perceived deviant teaching. Rather,
successors of those who introduced the text at Rhossos, labelled by
Serapion as Docetae, used this text albeit with their own additions to
promote teachings deemed to be heterodox. This is also the conclusion
Bardy draws after a close reading of the text.[366] Furthermore, a certain
Marcianus appears to have been the leader of this faction at Rhossos.
Although he is otherwise unknown, this in itself is not sufficient reason
to amend the name to that of famous heterodox figure Marcion.[367] In
fact Serapion, in opposition to his opening statement concerning the

---

[365] Swete provides a harmonising reading of Eusebius' comments and the citation
from Serapion's work, allowing one to fill the gaps of the other. Thus he concludes
concerning Serapion's treatise that 'It appears to have been a pastoral letter addressed
to the clergy or people of Rhosus, consisting of a general criticism of the Gospel followed by extracts from it. The passage preserved by Eusebius explains the circumstances under which the letter was written.'

[366] 'Les docètes donc parle Sérapion ne sont pas, semble-t-il, ceux qui ont introduit
l'Évangile de Pierre, mais leur successeurs.' G. Bardy, *Eusèbe de Césarée: Histoire
Ecclésiastique, Livre V–VII Texte Grec Traduction et Notes* SC 41 (Paris: Les Édition
du Cerf) 103, note 8.

[367] Bardy, *Eusèbe de Césarée*, 103, note 7.

rejection of writings that falsely bear the names of apostles, appears to support his initial assessment of the document made while in Rhossos. Namely that for the large part it accords 'with the true teaching of the saviour.' Thus Serapion's comments attest a two-stage textual history: (i) an original generally orthodox document which reflects the teachings of the saviour; (ii) a second edition expanded containing statements supportive of a docetic outlook was circulated subsequently after an unspecified period of time.

It may be the case that Serapion's more nuanced explanation enables a firmer identification to be made between the fragment of the first text discovered at Akhmîm and the document mentioned in the writings of Eusebius. If this is the case, then it is perhaps more plausible that the version of the text which is preserved in the codex is in fact a witness to the first edition of the *Gospel of Peter* since there are no blatantly docetic features, despite initial suggestions by some scholars to the contrary.[368] Moreover, the fact that Eusebius does not replicate the list of troublesome elements contained in the expanded form of the *Gospel of Peter* as listed by Serapion, means that the possibility remains that there were two somewhat divergent forms of this text.[369]

## 8.5. *Rufinus*

Usually omitted from such discussions, the testimony of Rufinus to the existence of the *Gospel of Peter* should not be neglected, since it is the earliest extant attestation of this text in the Western Church. Although born in northern Italy and initially schooled in Rome, Rufinus visited Egypt spending time in the monastic communities of Upper Egypt and 'also studied for several years in Alexandria under Didymus the Blind, and was deeply influenced by his Origenism.'[370] Despite being an original theological writer, his legacy stems from his work as a translator of Greek works into Latin. For the present discussion his translation of Eusebius' *Historia Ecclesiastica* is of significance.

---

[368] The case for detecting docetic elements in the Akhmîm codex was articulated by Swete, *The Akhmîm Fragment*, xxxviii. Such suggestions have been countered by J. McCant, 'The Gospel of Peter: Docetism Reconsidered', *NTS* 30 (1984) 258–273. See also the section on 'Docetic Christology and the Gospel of Peter' in this volume.

[369] As Kraus and Nicklas state, 'Zwar ist ein Bezug wahrscheinlich, trotzdem kann damit aber eine Datierung der Schrift Serapions *nicht* mit absoluter Sicherheit als *Terminus ante quem* für die Entstehung des durch Akhmîm-Text repräsentierten PE gesetzt worden.'Kraus und Nicklas, *Das Petrusevangelium und die Petrusapokalypse*, 16.

[370] 'Rufinus, Tyrannius or Turranius' in *ODCC*, 1433.

This is characterized by its free rendering of the base text along with
the addition of two further books that continue the narrative until
the death of Emperor Theodosius in 395. While an exact dating of the
work is not possible Rufinus' death in 411 provides an upper limit
for its composition, which must have been completed either in the
last decade of the fourth century or the first decade of the fifth century. To accommodate the additional material contained in his books
ten and eleven, Rufinus greatly abbreviates the material in Eusebius'
book ten, preferring to give his own account of the events of the Arian
controversy.[371] As the first account of church history written in Latin,
this work exerted great influence upon the subsequent scholarship of
the Western Church. The passages that refer to a gospel composed in
Peter's name do not deviate greatly from their Greek parallel. For this
reason only the Latin of the longer reference is provided here.

> sed et ille liber venit ad nos, quem scribit de euangelio Petri, ubi
> arguit quaedam falsa in eo conscripta, emendare cupiens fratres,
> qui erant apud Rossum, qui per occasionem scripturae ipsius in
> haeresim declinabant. dignum tamen mihi videtur pauca quae-
> dam de eius libello inserere, ex quibus innotescat, quae fuerit eius
> de ipsa scriptura sententia. scribit ergo in quodam loco ita:
>
> Nos enim, fratres, et Patrum et alios apostolos recipimus sic ut
> Christum. quae autem sub eorum nomine falso ab aliis conscripta
> sunt, velut gnari eorum sensus ac sententiae declinamus, scientes
> quod talia nobis non sunt tradita. ego enim cum essem apud
> vos, putabam omnes rectae fidei esse inter vos et non decurso
> libello, qui mihi offerebatur, in quo nomine Petri conscriptum
> euangelium ferebatur, dixi » si hoc est solum, quod inter vos
> simultatem videtur inferre, legatur codex. « nunc autem com-
> perto, quod hi, qui codicem illum legi debere adserunt, prospectu
> cuiusdam occultae haereseos hoc fieri poposcerunt, sicut mihi
> dictum est, festinabo iterum venire ad vos et expectate me cito.
> nos enim novimus, fratres, cuius haereseos fuerit Marcianus, qui
> etiam sibi ipsi contrarius extitit, non intellegens quae loqueretur,
> quae etiam vos discetis ex his, quae scripta sunt vobis, investigate
> per nos ab illis, qui hoc ipsum euangelium secundum illius tra-
> ditionem didicerant, et successores extiterunt scientiae eius, quos

---

[371] For further discussion on Rufinus' unique material in books ten and eleven see,
Philip R. Amidon, *The Church History of Rufinus of Aquileia* (Oxford: OUP, 1997).

nos δοκητὰς vocamus, quia in hac ipsa doctrina illorum sunt quam plurimi sensus et ab ipsis mutuati. nam certum est, quod plurima secundum recti rationem sentiunt de salvatore, alia vero aliter, quae et subiecimus.

Haec Serapion scribit. (Rufinus, 6.12.2–6)[372]

The text offers a close translation of the Greek written by Eusebius. Rather than offering any fresh information, the Latin edition ensures that knowledge of the existence of a *Gospel or Peter* would have become more widespread from this point onwards.

### 8.6. *Jerome*

Among Jerome's writings, in around 392–393 he composed a work under the title *de viris Illustribus* which provides short biographies of one-hundred and thirty five of the most prominent Christians from the post-Easter period down to Jerome's own day. Without concerns for modesty Jerome concludes this gazetteer with an autiobiographical portrait listing his place of birth and the various works he had composed up until that stage of his life (*de vir. Illustr.* 135). It is, however, the very first entry in the list dealing with Peter, which makes reference to an apocryphal gospel written in the apostle's name.

> Simon Petrus...scripsit duas epistolas quae catholicae nominata, quarum secunda a plerisque eius negatur propter stili cum priore dissonantiam. sed et Euangelium iuxta Marcum, qui auditor eius et interpres fuit, huius dicitur. libri autem e quibus unus Actorum eius inscribitur, alius Euangelii, tertius Praedicationis, quartus Ἀποκαλύψεως, quintus Iudicii, inter apocryphas scripturas repudiantur. (*de vir. Illustr.* 1)

> Simon Peter...He wrote two epistles which are called catholic, the second of which, on account of its difference from the first in style, is considered by many not to be by him. Then too the Gospel according to Mark, who was his disciple and interpreter, is ascribed to him. On the other hand, the books, of which one is entitled his Acts, another his Gospel, a third his Preaching, a fourth his Revelation, a fifth his Judgement are rejected as apocryphal.

---

[372] For the Latin text see Schwartz & Mommsen, *Eusebius' Werke 2: Historia ecclesiastica* GCS 9, 545 and 547.

In this section of the entry dealing with Peter, Jerome presents a catalogue of writings ascribed to him. He notes the difference of opinion surrounding the authenticity of 2 Peter, and basically divides a first group of writings from a second set, the latter being described as 'apocryphal' and hence rejected. Among this second group he mentions a 'gospel' that circulates in Peter's name which is clearly not the gospel of Mark. Nothing is stated concerning the contents of this work. This testimony is remarkably similar to the catalogue provided by Eusebius (*H.E.* 3.3.1–2), although Jerome's list of works in fuller. Thus Jerome discusses the Gospel of Mark as being ascribed to Peter, and in the apocryphal list he mentions a *Judgement* text which likewise is not present in the list of Eusebius.

## 8.7. *Didymus the Blind*

An often overlooked manuscript discovery is that of the cache of codices uncovered at Tura 10 miles from Cairo in 1941. As part of the preparatory work to excavate an ammunition dump in a series of disused tunnels the clearing process unearthed a collection of papyrus manuscripts in quarry 35. Although the discovery was subjected to apparently heavy pilfering, a number of important exegetical works attributed to Didymus of Alexandria were discovered that had previously not been known in extant form. The most important of these for the present discussion was his *Commentary on Ecclesiastes*, which in its condemnation of the reading of apocryphal gospels explicit names the *Gospel of Thomas* and also apparently the *Gospel of Peter*, although the manuscript is tantalizingly defective at the point were the name Peter occurs. As photographs of the text are unavailable it is not possible to assess the certainty of the restoration of the name as being that of Peter. If the reconstruction is valid, then this attests the ongoing circulation and use of the *Gospel of Peter* during the fourth century.

> καὶ τοῦτο δὲ πρὸς τοῖς εἰρημένοις ἔτι λεχθήτω, ἐπεὶ πολλάκις τινὲς
> ψευδογρα[φοῦσιν] βίβλια καὶ καταχρῶνται προσηγορίαις. ὁ Κλήμης
> γοῦν πολλὰ λέγει ερ[...] βιβλία ψευδεπίγραφα παρέστησεν διὰ
> π[ο]λλῶν· πολλὰ γὰρ καὶ ἀναγν[ο]ὺς καὶ μνημονεύων ὁ ἀνὴρ καὶ
> ἐπιστάμενος ἔδειξεν ὅτι προσέθηκαν βιβλίοις ἀλλ[οτ]ρ[ίοις τ]ι[ν]ὲς
> ἀλλόκτ{τ}ά τινα, ἔνιοι δὲ καὶ ὅλους λόγους συντάξαντες ἀνέγραψαν.
> διὰ τοῦτο γοῦν καὶ ἡμέτερος λόγος ἀπαγορεύει τὴν ἀνάγνωσιν τῶν
> ἀποκρύφων, ἐπεὶ πολλὰ ἐ[ψευ]δογραφήθη καὶ γράψας τις ἐπέγραψεν
> αὐτὸ εὐαγγέ[λι]ον εἰ τύχοι κατὰ Θυμᾶν ἢ κατὰ Πέ[τρον].

And let this also be spoken to the peaceful, since frequently certain people are falsely writing books and they make full use of assigned names. Clement at least says that many...pseudepigraphical books are affirmed by many. For this man also read and remembered many, having set about to show that they added to books some other things that belonged to certain others, but some also read other things which they have composed. Because of this he forbade us to read the apocrypha since many had been falsely written and signed a certain name to the title of the gospel, for example 'according to Thomas' or 'according to Peter'. (Didymus the Blind, *Comm. Eccl.* 1.1–8).

This text shows a comprehensive distrust both on the part of Didymus and Clement, who is cited as an authority, in relation to the reading of apocryphal texts. The *Gospel of Thomas* is cited as a text that falls into this class of falsely attributed texts with additional traditions. The implication is that these are traditions additional to those contained in the four canonical accounts. The title of the work that follows *Thomas* is lacunose, but according to the transcription the text does preserve the first two letters a name that could potentially be that of Peter, i.e. Πέ[τρον]. Nothing of the content of this work is described, only the general assessment that it is not trustworthy and should not be read.[373]

## 8.8. *Theodoret of Cyrus*

At the request of a high official named Sporacius, Theodoret compiled a *Compendium of Heretical Accounts* (*Haereticarum fabularum compendium*), including a heresiology (books i–iv) and a 'compendium of divine dogmas' (book v). This work appears to have been written shortly after the Council of Chalcedon in 451.[374]

Οἱ δὲ Ναζωραῖοι Ἰουδαῖοί εἰσι τὸν Χριστὸν τιμῶντες ὡς ἄνθρωπον δίκαιού καὶ τῷ καλουμένῳ κατὰ Πέτρον εὐαγγελίῳ κεχρημένοι.

---

[373] Kraus und Nicklas, *Das Petrusevangelium und die Petrusapokalypse*, 19.

[374] As Moreschini and Norelli observe, 'It is dedicated to Sporacius, a *comes*, at whose request it was written. Spracius, an imperial commissioner delegated to the Council of Chalcedon in 451, was consel in 452; since the latter office is not mentioned, the work must go back at least to 453; a *terminus post quem* of 451 is indicated by the reference in the introduction to the rooting out of the most recent heresy, that of Eutyches.' C. Moreschini and E. Norelli, *Early Christian Greek and Latin Literature: A Literary History*, vol. 2, From the Council of Nicea to the Beginnings of the Medieval Period (Peabody, Mass.: Hendrickson, 2005) 171.

> But the Nazoreans are Jews, who honour Christ as a righteous
> man, and they have made use of the so-called gospel according
> to Peter. (Theodoret, *haer.* 2.2)

As an aside to the description of the Nazoreans, whom Theodoret
describes as Jews, he mentions their penchant for reading a text he
describes as 'the so-called gospel according to Peter.' Nothing is stated
about the contents, nature or provenance of this text. Rather, it is
assumed that the title itself conveys a recognition that use of this text
is a deviant practice, at least from the perspective of the orthodoxy
of the fifth century. The first patristic references to the Nazoreans as
a distinct group occur in the fourth century. Epiphanius describes
the group as law observant (*Pan.* 29.5.4; 29.7.5; 29.8.1ff.) and also
notes there practice of reading the Gospel of Matthew in Hebrew
(*Pan.* 29.9.4).[375] Jerome, likewise, categorizes the group as law observant (*Comm. Isa.* 8.11–15; *Comm. Ezech.* 16.16). Moreover, he makes
repeated reference to a gospel used by this group. It is important to be
careful about the terminology Jerome employs. He describes a gospel
that the Nazoreans read rather than a *Gospel of the Nazoreans*, and
in fact Jerome suggests that some of the gospel fragments that have
been given separate titles in the modern period are in fact identical.[376]
Thus he states, 'in the gospel which the Nazoreans and the Ebionites
use, which we have recently translated out of Hebrew into Greek, and
which is called by most the authentic Gospel of Matthew...' (*Comm.
Matt.* 12.13).[377] Regardless of the answer to the intractable question
concerning the number of separate 'Jewish-Christian' gospels, apart
from the comments of Theodoret, there is no other testimony that
documents the use of the *Gospel of Peter* by the Nazoreans. In fact
given the anti-Jewish perspective of the *Gospel of Peter* its use by a
supposedly law-observant group may appear somewhat problematic.
However, what may appear a problem to modern scholars may not
have been seen as problematic by ancient readers.

---

[375] For a wider discussion of the Nazoreans and the gospel associated with that
group see Andrew Gregory, 'Hinderance or Help: Does the Modern Category of "Jewish-Christian Gospel" Distort our Understanding of the Texts to which it Refers?'
*JSNT* 28.4 (2006) 387–413, esp. 408–409.

[376] Gregory, 'Hinderance or Help?' 402–404.

[377] See Henneke and Schneemelcher (eds.), *New Testament Apocrypha*, vol. 1, 160.

## 8.9. Decretum Gelasianum

Although attributed to Gelasius I, bishop of Rome from 492 until his death on the 19th of November 496, the so-called *Decretum Gelasianum* is now recognized to be a pseudepigraphical compostion stemming from the sixth century.[378]

> Cetera quae ab hereticis sive scismaticis conscripta vel praedicata sunt, nullatenus recipit catholica et apostolica Romana ecclesia; e quibus pauca, quae ad memoriam venerunt et a catholicis vitanda sunt, credidimus esse subdenda:
> *Item notitia Librorum apocryphorum [qui non recipiuntur]*
> …Euangelium nomine Petri apostoli. (*Decret. Gelasian.* V, de libris recipiendis)[379]

> The remaining writings which have been compiled or been recognised by heretics or schismatics the Catholic and Apostolic Roman Church does not in any way receive; of these we have thought it right to cite below a few which have been handed down and which are to be avoided by catholics:
> Likewise apocryphal books which are not to be received
> …the gospel in the name of the apostle Peter.

This is excerpted from an extended list of proscribed writings. There is neither any indication of the contents of this work, nor any explicit statement concerning why it is to be rejected. While one may hope that such a rejection was based upon its undiscussed contents, other external factors may have been more significant. These include the fact that its alleged authorship had not gained wide acceptance along with the historical precedent set by previous ecclesial writers in rejecting this text. While the title is known, it is perhaps likely that the author of the *Decretum Gelasianum* did not have any firsthand knowledge of this text.

---

[378] H. Leclerq, Gelasien (Decret), article in F. Cabrol (ed.), Dictionnaire D'Archeologie Chretienne et De Liturgie, (Paris : Letouzey et Ané, 1907–1953, vol. 6 [G-Gotha], 1924) Vol 6 (G-GOTHA), 722–747. Puts the case for sixth century authorship and reviews the secondary literature on the topic.

[379] The text is taken from the critical edition of E. von Dobschütz, Das Decretum Gelasianum: De Libris Recipiendis et Non Recipiendis, TU XXXVIII (Leipzig: J.C. Hinrichs, 1912).

## 8.10.  *Conclusions*

To summarise the results of this discussion, it is the case that the degree of clarity and certainty of the suggested explicit witnesses to a text known as the *Gospel of Peter* varies greatly. Contrary to certain suggestions, there is nothing in the writings of Justin or Melito of Sardis that makes their knowledge of this text even probable. Later writers bear witness to a text circulating under the name *Gospel of Peter*. Such writers include Origen, Eusebius of Caesarea, Rufinus, Jerome, Didymus the Blind and Theodoret of Cyrus, Some of these writers give information about the contents or nature of the text. Thus Origen states that it referred to the siblings of Jesus as half-brothers and sisters from Joseph's previous marriage. Theodoret understands the theological outlook of the text to be acceptable to the Nazoreans, and Didymus, if he in fact mentions this text, declares it to be untrustworthy. The only slightly more detailed information is preserved in the writings of Eusebius, which in turn were translated and transmitted in Latin by Rufinus.

## 9.  Literary Relationships

Examples of literary dependence between the *Gospel of Peter* and texts such as the canonical gospels, the writings of Justin Martyr, Tatian's *Diatesseron* or some other gospel harmony, the *Epistle of Barnabas* or other writings from church fathers of the second century, have been variously asserted or denied by a range of scholars. What is needed, however, before making such claims is a methodology for establishing literary dependence between two texts, and a definition of what constitutes such a phenomenon. Perhaps the strongest form of literary dependence occurs when a writer is composing his work with a copy of another text open in front of him and excerpting passages for incorporation into the new writing. This can be done explicitly, such as in the case of Origen's refutation of Celsus,[380] Matthew's formula

---

[380] See F. Young, L. Ayres and A. Louth, *The Cambridge History of Early Christian Literature* (Cambridge: CUP, 2004) 127, which notes that *Contra Celsum* was written as a refutation of Celsus' tractate '*The True Doctrine* which attacked Christianity, and which had been written some time in the second century by an unknown Middle Platonic philosopher named Celsus. In the preface, Origen tells his audience that Ambrose requested this rebuttal be written (*Contra Cel.* pref. 1); that Celsus' work was entitled *The True Doctrine* (*Contra Cel.* pref. 1); then throughout the refutation he cites the arguments of Celsus with phrases such as 'Celsus' first main point…' (*Contra*

quotations,[381] or the preface to the Lukan gospel.[382] Alternatively, it may occur without disclosure of source material to readers, as with Matthew's reworking of Mark,[383] or the incorporation of the *Didache* into the *Apostolic Constitutions*.[384] Literary dependence can also encompass the case of a writing drawing upon a literary work from memory. This may well account for the relative freedom with which a number of the patristic writers cite scriptural texts in their own writings. In particular, this is almost certainly the case in the seven genuine epistles of Ignatius, where the author is likely to have been forced to draw on the repository of texts contained in his memory, since during his transportation to Rome he presumably did not have ready access to the various writings cited in the epistles.[385]

Demonstration of literary dependence between two texts would appear to require one of two factors to establish the case. First, there could be explicit acknowledgement of source material. This would show both dependence and direction of borrowing. In the absence of such direct evidence, the second possibility is to observe significant portions

---

*Cel.* 1.1); 'Next he says…' (*Contra Cel.* 2.1); 'After this he urges…' (*Contra Cel.* 9.1) and so on. Thus enabling the reconstruction of a large portion of the original work. Thus Chadwich can conclude, 'Origin's method of quoting his opponent sentence by sentence, paragraph by paragraph, has ensured that a substantial part of the work has been preserved in its original wording.' H. Chadwick, *Origen: Contra Celsum* (Cambridge: CUP, reprinted ed. 1965) xxii.

[381] G.M. Soares Prabhu, *The Formula Quotations in the Infancy Narrative of Matthew*, AnBib 63 (Rome: Pontifical Biblical Institute, 1976); G.N. Stanton, *A Gospel for a New People* (Edinburgh: T&T Clark, 1992) 353–363; W.D. Davies and D.C. Allison, *A Critical and Exegetical Commentary on the Gospel according to Saint Matthew*, vol. 1 chaps. *I–VII*, ICC (Edinburgh: T&T Clark, 1988) 190–195.

[382] Bovon recognizes that 'Luke is the only evangelist who sets forth in a prologue the motivation, purpose, and method of his work.' F. Bovon, *Luke 1: A commentary on the Gospel of Luke 1:1–9:50*, Hermeneia (Minneapolis: Fortress, 2002) 15.

[383] The central assumption of the two-source theory, the priority of Mark and subsequent use of that account by both Matthew and Luke, is assumed throughout this commentary. For an articulation and defence of this position see B.H. Streeter, *The Four Gospels* (London: Macmillan, 1924) esp. 151–198; J. Kloppenborg Verbin, *Excavating Q: The History and Setting of the Sayings Gospel* (Minneapolis/Edinburgh: Fortress/T&T Clark, 2000) 11–54.

[384] As Bradshaw et al. note, the *Apostolic Constitutions* 'reworks and weaves together several older sources, chief of which are the third-century church order known as the *Didascalia Apostolorum* (forming books 1–6 of the work), the *Didache* (in book 7), and the *Apostolic Tradition* (in book 8).' P.F. Bradshaw, M.E. Johnson and L.E. Phillips, *The Apostolic Tradition*, Hermeneia (Minneapolis: Fortress, 2002) 9.

[385] See P. Foster, 'The Epistles of Ignatius of Antioch and the Writings that later formed the New Testament', in A. Gregory and C.M. Tuckett (eds.), *The Reception of the New Testament in Apostolic Fathers* (Oxford: OUP, 2005) 185.

of shared text. In such cases, some form of dependence may be probable. However, a number of further steps are required before a firm case can be established. It is possible that rather than being directly dependent the similarity may be explained by some intermediate relationship, such as a shared oral tradition or common written source.[386] Another issue is the lack of agreement concerning what constitutes a 'significant portion of shared text.' This cannot be determined simply in terms of the length of a shared phrase. Two texts that might recount a mundane event in verbally identical or similar terms, such as 'I went to the market to buy fish today', may be totally unrelated in literary terms. By contrast, references to the baptism of Jesus that state that it occurred to 'fulfil all righteousness' have a marked probability of being dependent on the Matthean account of the baptism story.[387] So apart from the length of shared text, the rarity of common vocabulary, similarity of context, and factors that make it likely that the authors inhabit the same literary and linguistic community increase the probability of textual borrowings.

This still leaves the question of direction of dependence. If an author does not state his dependence on his source, or if the potentially related works are not unambiguously datable, then internal and external factors need to be considered. Internal factors may include the identification of the rewriting of confused or theologically problematic passages, embellishments to the tradition, or the introduction of anachronistic features. The problem with such judgments, as E.P. Sanders so clearly illustrated, is that often the tendencies of later works do not move uniformly in the same direction.[388] Thus, one may ask if a longer passage

---

[386] An example of the latter phenomenon is best attested by the Q hypothesis, where the similarity of wording in a number of double tradition passages shared by Matthew and Luke, cannot account for the alternating primitivity of the sayings between the versions of the parallel sayings in the first and third gospels, or for the the two evangelists placing double tradition material in different Markan context if one were to postulate direct dependence of either evangelist on the other. See further on this in C.M. Tuckett, *Q and the History of Early Christianity: Studies in Q* (Edinburgh: T&T Clark, 1996) 16–39; and P. Foster, 'In it Possible to Dispense with Q?' *NovT* XLV (2003) 313–337.

[387] This example is not chosen at random. It is cited in Ignatius, where in the context of discussing Jesus' baptism he states that it was done 'in order that all righteousness might be fulfilled by him' (Ignatius, *Smyrn.* 1.1). This citation of an element that is found only in Matthew's Gospel presents a strong case for direct literary dependence between these two texts.

[388] E.P. Sanders, *The Tendencies of the Synoptic Tradition*, SNTSMS 9 (Cambridge: CUP, 1969).

a sign of a later embellishment, or is the shorter version of the parallel text an illustration of removing problematic features. Such problems are often most difficult when texts are temporally proximate. With the passage of time, later authors often betray themselves by inserting anachronistic details.[389] External factors may include papyrological and codicological features of manuscript witnesses, a comparison of the outlook of the text with known theological discussions in different periods, and a sense of the wider context in which the respective texts may have been composed.

While there might be a certain degree of subjectivity in this process, nonetheless, if one develops a cumulative argument based on a range of factors then a stronger case can be mounted for establishing the more plausible direction of literary dependence. Since the *Gospel of Peter* text is both undated and does not acknowledge any literary debts in the extant portion of the narrative, it becomes necessary to build such a cumulative case for establishing both any putative dependences, as well as arguing for the direction in which such dependence may operate. The events contained in the narrative do themselves obviously assist in establishing at least the direction of dependence with one corpus of source texts. Since the passion of Jesus post-dates the OT, it is obviously the case that any parallel with OT texts is likely to show that the Akhmîm text is dependent on these writings and not *vice versa*. Yet even here there is a complication. At a number of points the text shows affinities with readings preserved from Symmachus' recension of the LXX Psalms.[390] Theoretically it could be possible that the Akhmîm tradition had influenced this author, rather than the reverse. This, however, appears improbable, since it is unlikely that the Jewish scholar Symmachus would be influenced directly by the *Gospel of Peter*, although there could be a shared tradition behind the text of the non-canonical gospel and the recension of LXX by Symmachus made around the beginning of the third century CE. This case aside, in looking at texts which like the Akhmîm text also post-date the passion, it becomes necessary first to establish a case for literary dependence on

---

[389] Famously in Judges the repeated statement 'and there was no king in Israel in those days' (Jdg 17.6; 18.1; 19.1; 21.25), betrays knowledge of a later period when the monarchy was the political form of governance over Israel.

[390] See the discussion in the commentary at the following places G.Pet. 10.39 (cf. LXX σ Ps 43(44).19); and G.Pet. 11.43 (cf. LXX σ Ps 2.2; 30.14).

the basis of shared vocabulary and other stylistic features, and then to
account for the direction of that dependence.

### 9.1. *The* Gospel of Peter *and the Canonical Gospels*

In discussions of literary dependency the greatest energy has been
expended in establishing claims either for or against a literary relationship with the gospels of Matthew, Mark, Luke and John. Even those
who accept such a relationship do not agree concerning the direction
of such a line of borrowing.

After the appearance of Bouriant's *editio princeps* a series of works
appeared that supported the idea that the author of the Akhmîm text
knew the canonical accounts. It was assumed that this author had
intentionally reworked the canonical traditions to create a fresh version of the events of the passion and resurrection (and perhaps also
the prior events in the gospels). Although acknowledging the apparently new elements in the narrative, Swete nevertheless concluded that
'there is nothing in this portion of the Petrine Gospel which compels
us to assume the use of historical sources other than the canonical
gospels.'[391] Robinson was even more direct in his assessment that the
author had used the canonical accounts as his source material:

> Lastly, the unmistakeable acquaintance of the author with our four evan-
> gelists deserves a special comment. He uses and misuses each in turn. To
> him they all stand on equal footing. He lends no support to the attempt
> which has been made to place a gulf of separation between the Fourth
> Gospel and the rest, as regards the period or area of their acceptance
> as Canonical. Nor again does he countenance the theory of the contin-
> ued circulation in the second century of an *Urevangelium*, or such as a
> prae-canonical Gospel we feel must lie behind the Synoptists. He uses
> our Greek Gospels; there is no proof (though the possibility of course is
> always open) that he knew of any Gospel record other than these.[392]

While one may feel that Robinson's defence of the canonical accounts
and the relative denigration of the Akhmîm text are motivated by his
theological outlook, as is his judgment that there was already a developed canonical status afforded to the fourfold collection, nonetheless

---

[391] Swete, *The Akhmîm Fragment*, xv.
[392] Robinson and James, *The Gospel according to Peter, and the Revelation of Peter*,
32–33.

it is impossible to doubt that he viewed the *Gospel of Peter* as literary dependent on all of the canonical accounts.

Such a point of view was not confined to English speaking scholarship on the text. Later, German scholars writing about the text immediately after its publication came to similar conclusions in relation to this issue. Zahn concludes that the narrative is dependent on the canonical gospels.[393] This conclusion was initially shared by Harnack who stated, 'I noted above, that our gospel seems to utilize the canonical gospels and consequently to be later than these.'[394] Later, he altered his thinking, noting the deviations contained in the text in comparison with the canonical accounts.[395] A further oscillation in thinking took Harnack back to his starting position.[396] Although documenting the diversity of opinion in regard to the relationship between the *Gospel of Peter* and the canonical tradition,[397] Semeria supported the view that the Akhmîm text was both posterior to, and drew upon the canonical accounts. Three conclusions led to this observation. First, there were features unique to each of the canonical accounts in the *Gospel of Peter*. Secondly, a theory of oral dependence did not provide a more plausible explanation of the textual similarities. Thirdly, alongside the resemblances he recognized both deviations and even contradictions in comparison to the canonical narratives.[398] Thus, with the exceptions of a few dissenting voices, such as Reinach,[399] there was general prevailing consensus that the Akhmîm text had utilised the canonical gospels in the composition of its account.

---

[393] See Zahn, *Das Evangelium des Petrus*, 20.

[394] 'Ich haben oben bemerkt, unser Evangelium scheine auf den kanonischen Evangelien zu fassen und also jünger wie diese zu sein.' Harnack, *Bruchstücke des Evangeliums und der Apokalypse des Petrus*, 32; cf. the article by Harnack in *Sitzungsberichte* (1892) 895.

[395] Harnack noticed the way the author's account creates distance between the manner in which the canonical authors present their account of the events. 'In der Erzählung steht unser Verfasser dem 4. Ev. äusserlich betrachtet am fernsten.' Harnack, *Bruchstücke des Evangeliums und der Apokalypse des Petrus*, 35.

[396] Harnack, *Theologische Literaturzeitung* (1894) col. a; and *Revue critique*, (12 mars 1894) 207.

[397] Semeria, 'L'Évangile de Pierre', 541–542.

[398] Thus Semeria stated that the most probable explanation was 'que le pseudo-Pierre a connu et même utilisé les évangiles canoniques', but he accompanied this with a note of caution, 'la certitude restant toujours un desideratum qu'il ne nous est pas donné de réaliser.' Semeria, 'L'Évangile de Pierre', 550.

[399] S. Reinach, 'L'Evangile de saint Pierre', *La République française* (5 janv. 1893).

Kirsopp Lake, writing in 1907 on the historical evidence for the resurrection, made the following statements concerning the interrelationships with the canonical gospels. Suggesting a date of composition between 100–130 CE. Lake stated,

> It seems certain that it [*Gospel of Peter*] made use of Mark, and according to most writers probably of Matthew, but that it shows knowledge of Luke and John is doubtful (to my own mind improbable), and various details of more or less legendary character have been added from other sources which cannot be identified. It is impossible to say exactly whether the sources which it used were textually identical with the canonical gospels or were recensions earlier than any now extant.[400]

However, Lake's primary point, based on the commonality of the name Levi the son of Alphaeus in Mark 2.14 and *Gos. Pet.* 14.60, was to argue that the non-canonical gospel made use of the lost ending of Mark's gospel. 'I am therefore inclined to accept the suggestion that "Peter" was acquainted with and used the lost conclusion of Mark.'[401] Notwithstanding the fact that many scholars now feel that the gospel ending at Mark 16.8 forms a satisfactory conclusion,[402] nevertheless Lake's argument is substantially weakened by the fact that the resurrection scene anticipated in *Gos. Pet.* 14.58–60 would appear to be most closely aligned to material in Jn 21, where Peter himself is a prominent character in the narrative.

Six years later, in January 1913, Lake's arguments were debated in print by C.H. Turner.[403] Again the key question in thar article was whether discovery of extra-canonical provided independent testimony to the resurrection. Thus Turner frames his question in the following manner. 'Is the Gospel of Peter an independent witness to the tradition of the Resurrection?'[404] Turner rejects claims that the text provided independent testimony. Instead he states,

> we have in this so-called Gospel of Peter a very early testimony to the combined use of all four Gospels of the Church. It would be an anachronism to speak of this common use as exactly a recognition of the canonical

---

[400] K. Lake, *The Historical Evidence for the Resurrection of Jesus Christ* (London: Williams & Norgate, 1907) 149.

[401] Lake, *The Historical Evidence for the Resurrection of Jesus Christ*, 162.

[402] See in particular J.L. Magness, *Sense and Absence: Structure and Suspension in the Ending of Mark's Gospel* (SBLSS; Atlanta: Scholars, 1986).

[403] C.H. Turner, 'The Gospel of Peter', *JTS* 14 (1913) 161–195.

[404] Turner, 'The Gospel of Peter', 161.

authority of the Gospels, if 'Peter' is correctly dated at about 125 AD, since at that date the idea of canonical authority of the New Testament books, even of the Gospels , was still only in the making.[405]

In his conclusion, declaring it 'infinitely more probable than not' that the *Gospel of Peter* was acquainted with the four canonical gospels, Turner rejects dependence on the lost ending of Mark, and instead sees the final sequence as related to the last chapter of John's Gospel. Thus scholarly opinion gravitated towards expressing the dependence of the Akhmîm text on some number of the canonical accounts.

This question was re-opened in 1926 by Gardner-Smith.[406] He wrote in response to the opinion expressed in James' compendium of apocryphal writings where it was stated, '[t]he Gospel of Peter uses all four canonical gospels.'[407] By contrast, taking suggested literary parallels from each of the four gospels in turn Gardner-Smith argued in every instance 'the similarities which exist between the canonical accounts and the apocryphal gospels can be explained on the hypothesis that all the evangelists, including 'Peter' collected the floating traditions with which they were familiar and made of them the best narrative they could.'[408] Leaving aside what appears to be the implied subtext of the argument that there is also no literary relationship between the canonical accounts, only a shared pool of oral traditions, it is helpful to look at a few examples where Gardner-Smith dismisses the case for literary relationship. Considering the story of the guard-at-the-tomb (Matt 27.62–66; 28.4, 11–15//*Gos. Pet.* 8.28–11.49) and in particular the shared phrase 'lest his disciples come and steal him', Gardner-Smith draws the following conclusion:

> That a common phrase should appear in different versions of a tradition is not at all surprising; the Jews must have given some reason for the request, and what other reason other reason could they have given than this? It is difficult for two people to tell the same story without using some common words and phrases, but if they differ in matters of fact the probability is that the one is not repeating the narrative of the other.[409]

---

[405] Turner, 'The Gospel of Peter', 173.

[406] P. Gardner-Smith, 'The Gospel of Peter', *JTS* 27 (1926) 255–271, and 'The Date of the Gospel of Peter' *JTS* 27 (1926) 401–407.

[407] M.R. James, *The Apocryphal New Testament* (Oxford: OUP, 1924) 90.

[408] Gardner-Smith, 'The Gospel of Peter', 270.

[409] Gardner-Smith, 'The Gospel of Peter', 261.

What Gardner-Smith has not considered as a control against which to test his claims was the case where ancient authors declared their dependence on a written source, but nonetheless show considerable reworking of the earlier material. Moreover, it appears that he required exact duplication of an extended literary parallel before he would consider admitting literary dependence as being likely. It is unsurprising with such unrealistic strictures that he decided against the literary dependence of the Akhmîm text on the canonical accounts, and apparently against literary dependence between the synoptic gospels. In perhaps what is the strongest example of literary relationship between the *Gospel of Peter* and the canonical accounts, that between the material in Mark 16.5–8//*Gos. Pet.* 13.55–57, Gardner-Smith rejects a direct connection between these sources. He states, 'Even in this passage in which the Petrine account corresponds most nearly to that of Mark his source was not our gospel, but an independent tradition in some respects inferior to Mark, but in other respects exhibiting traces of an earlier form of the narrative than that incorporated in the second gospel.'[410] Thus in a passage where he is forced to concede close correspondence, Gardner-Smith refuses to draw the most natural conclusion. Instead he argues for independent oral tradition as explaining the similarities, and exact parallels in language being produced by limited vocabulary options in recounting differing versions of the same event.

Next to consider in detail the question of the relationship between the canonical accounts and the *Gospel of Peter* was Vaganay in the introduction to his magisterial the *Gospel of Peter* commentary.[411] He investigated the relationship between multiply attested passages in the canonical gospel tradition alongside similar details from the Akhmîm text.[412] Following this analysis he turned his attention to details which are unique in each of the canonical accounts.[413] This introduced a heightened level of sophistication into the discussion, since it allowed unique redactional features of each evangelist to be compared with parallel passages in the *Gospel of Peter*. While this had not been absent in earlier treatments, Vaganay's system of classification assisted the process of coming to a decision on the issue of the use of a specific gospel. In effect he anticipated the criterion articulate by Köster for

---

[410] Gardner-Smith, 'The Gospel of Peter', 270.
[411] Vaganay, *L'Évangile de Pierre*, 43–75.
[412] Vaganay, *L'Évangile de Pierre*, 44–46.
[413] Vaganay, *L'Évangile de Pierre*, 46–65.

establishing literary dependence, namely the presence of a clearly unique redactional element in a later text. Discussing the method for the purpose of demonstrating the dependence, or otherwise, of the Apostolic Fathers on the canonical gospels Köster states, 'thus the question of dependence hinges upon whether one is able to find use of an evangelist's a redactional work.'[414] Without cataloguing each of Vaganay's conclusions for the individual gospels, his opinions on Mark and John are representative. In relation to Mark he states, 'All things considered, it appears certain that our author used the Gospel of Mark and there is some chance that he knew it in its current form.'[415] In regard to the fourth gospel, Vaganay is equally certain that the author of the *Gospel of Peter* had knowledge of this document, but it is a different type of dependence to that which exists with the synoptics. Rather than looking for too narrow a comparison of direct material dependence, Vaganay sees the imprint of the Johannine account embedded in the narrative at a deeper level.[416] The problem with this outlook is that in comparison with the analysis Vaganay utilizes for comparison with the synoptic gospels, this introduces a much less clearly defined criterion for establishing dependence. Rather he appears to base this claim on far less tangible textual similarities.

For over half a century little was added to this debate, with major handbooks dealing with apocryphal texts tending to favour the case for dependence.[417] In the 1980s Koester[418] and Crossan re-opened the question in various works. Partitioning the *Gospel of Peter*, Crossan separated three units which he argued were independent of the three canonical accounts, from three further units which were dependent

---

[414] As Köster states, 'so hängt die Frage der Benutzung davon ab, ob sich in den angeführten Stücken Redaktionsarbeit eines Evangelisten findet.' H. Köster, *Synoptische Überlieferung bei den Apostolischen Vatern*, TU 65 (Berlin: Akademie Verlag, 1957) 3.

[415] 'En somme, il paraît certain que notre auteur a utilisé l'évangile de Marc et il y a quelque chance pour qu'il l'ait connu dans sa forme actuelle.' Vaganay, *L'Évangile de Pierre*, 54.

[416] Vaganay concludes, 'On arrive à sa convaincre que notre faussaire dépend de Jean en quelque manière.' Vaganay, *L'Évangile de Pierre*, 65.

[417] See, C. Maurer, 'The Gospel of Peter' in Hennecke and Schneemelcher (eds.), *New Testament Apocrypha* (Eng. edition, vol. 1, 1963) 180.

[418] See H. Koester, 'Apocryphal and Canonical Gospels', *HTR* 73, 105–130.

Table 13. Crossan's redactional layers in the *Gospel of Peter*

| Independent tradition | Redactional preparation | Dependent tradition |
|---|---|---|
| GP 1 (1:1–6:22) | with 2:3–5a for | GP 2 (6:23–24) |
| GP 3 (7:25–9:34) | with 7:26–27 for | GP 6 (14:58–60) |
| GP 4 (9:35–11:49) | with 9:37 and 11:43–44 for | GP 5 (12:50–13.57) |

upon the canonical gospels. He represented these layers in the following tabulated form:[419]

Thus Crossan proposed that the document contains three layers of material. An early source he termed 'the Cross Gospel',[420] which pre-dated and was utilised by the canonical accounts in framing their narratives of the passion. Next, preparatory material presumably redactional in nature was added, apparently at the same time as the traditions that had been formed out of canonical materials. And lastly, the dependent traditions were woven into the more primitive narrative. The earliest layer still retained the bulk of the material contained in the Akhmîm manuscript, some forty-seven of the sixty verses. The three blocks of dependent tradition constitute material that is demonstrably literarily related to the canonical accounts. Crossan argues that the story preserved in the three blocks of independent tradition results in a 'careful narrative logic.'[421] It is questionable, however, whether one obtains a demonstrably improved coherence in the narrative through the removal of the blocks of 'dependent tradition'. Brown is sceptical of the criterion of 'better-flowing narrative' as a useful datum for establishing direction of literary dependence. He observes that '[w]hen there are diverse forms of a story, judgments about which form constitutes the better narrative tend to be subjective.'[422] He then asks a question that first appeared in relation to the claims of form criticism: namely whether the earlier form is better attested by a smooth and sequential account that attracts additional superfluous details, or by a

---

[419] This representation of his theory is draw from J.D. Crossan, *Four Other Gospels* (Minneapolis: Winston Press, 1985) 134.

[420] The term 'cross gospel' was not coined by Crossan in his earlier work *Four Other Gospels*, 124–181. The term is, however, fully in evidence by the time Crossan's more extensive treatment of the topic appeared, *The Cross That Spoke: The Origins of the Passion Narrative* (1988), see especially 16–30.

[421] Crossan, *The Cross That Spoke*, 17.

[422] R.E. Brown, 'The *Gospel of Peter* and Canonical Gospel Priority', *NTS* 33 (1987) 330.

more roughly-hewn and less logical version of the same account which is smoothed by the process of transmission.[423] The failure of Crossan to address this point considerably weakens his thesis. In addition to this problem, Brown also catalogues a number of inconsistencies in the narrative which undermine the claim that the *Gospel of Peter* is logically coherent narrative.[424]

For those sceptical of Crossan's reconstruction, the decision to separate these three blocks from a putative early layer is no arbitrary choice. Rather, Crossan appears to have located passages that are obviously dependent on the canonical gospels and declared these to be a later addition. This then allows him to deal with a reduced body of material for which it is more difficult to demonstrate dependence on the four canonical accounts. Yet even with this remaining kernel some of the material that it contains appears more likely to be derivative on canonical accounts than *vice versa*.[425]

Under the heading 'word integration',[426] Crossan advances another argument which he sees as supporting his thesis, but on closer inspection appears to prove precisely the opposite to what he argues. Considering the second of his examples for illustrative purposes, Crossan focuses on the language used to describe the burial location. He states that the 'core difficulty is that the original *Cross Gospel* had used the Greek word ὁ τάφος for the burial place of Jesus while the intracanonical tradition preferred τὸ μνημεῖον or τό μνῆμα for that same place.'[427]

(a) ὁ τάφος:        6.24; 8.31a; 9.36, 37; 10.39; 11.45; 13.55a, 55b
(b) τὸ μνῆμα:       8.30, 31b, 32; 11.44; 12.50, 52
(c) τὸ μνημεῖον:    9.34; 12.51, 53

The fact that each of these three terms occurs in both the independent layers and the dependent material is not seen as problematic.[428]

---

[423] Brown, 'The *Gospel of Peter* and Canonical Gospel Priority', 330.

[424] Brown, 'The *Gospel of Peter* and Canonical Gospel Priority', 334.

[425] Consider the story of the crucified thief who speaks on Jesus' behalf in G.Pet. 4.13 (cf. Lk 23.39–43), where the theological trajectory would appear to favour the removal of the reviling thief in a later version of the story, rather than the introduction of this figure.

[426] Crossan, *The Cross That Spoke*, 24–29.

[427] Crossan, *The Cross That Spoke*, 27.

[428] The small amount of material in the so-called redactional layer contains only one reference to the burial place, using the term μνῆμα at 11.44.

Instead Crossan contends that intentional jumbling up of terminology was part of the redactor's methodological technique.

> The redactor ends up even-handedly with eight cases of ὁ τάφος from the original *Cross Gospel* and nine cases of the intracanonical preference for τὸ μνῆμα or τὸ μνημεῖον. But it is now no longer possible to correlate term and source easily and thus have the former draw attention to the latter.[429]

This appears to be a case of special pleading, for how can Crossan know that the term ὁ τάφος was the preferred and unique way that the hypothesized early source designated the place of burial. Since he no longer has access to that source, and even if it were embedded in the Akhmîm text, the evidence does not support his contention that it is uniquely found in the preserved blocks of the *Cross Gospel*. Moreover, the term τάφος is not unevidenced in the canonical accounts of the burial of Jesus. It is Matthean terminology, Matt 27.61, 64, 66; 28.1. This leads Crossan to speculate about the final redactor's editorial decisions. Rather, if one bases conclusions on the physical evidence of the preserved text, it is possible to observe that the account shows only a similar range of vocabulary as that found in the canonical accounts for referring to Jesus' burial place. Thus it is more likely that the variation in terminology was introduced by the author of the text for stylistic reasons, rather than that the canonical evangelists replaced the term τάφος with either μνῆμα or μνημεῖον, and then later a hypothesized redactor re-integrated these divergent choices in terminology.

Notwithstanding such difficulties, Crossan's theory has been taken up either as it stands or in modified form by a number of scholars. In a series of four articles Arthur Dewey derives the creative impetus for his own work from Crossan's insights. This results in a modified theory of multiple redactional layers in the *Gospel of Peter*.[430] Dewey seeks to take the source-critical analysis a stage further back than Crossan's *Cross Gospel* stage. He argues that behind this *Cross Gospel* source

---

[429] Crossan, *The Cross That Spoke*, 27.

[430] In chronological order these are: A.J. Dewey, 'And an Answer Was Heard from the Cross', *Foundations and Facets Forum* 5.3 (1989) 103–111; '"Time to Murder and a Time to Create": Visions and Revisions in the *Gospel of Peter*', in R. Cameron (ed.) *Semeia* 49 (1990) 101–127; 'Resurrection Texts and the *Gospel of Peter*' *Foundations and Facets Forum* 10.3-4 (1994) 177–196; 'The Passion Narrative of the Gospel of Peter', *Forum* New Series 1.1 (1998) 53–69.

stands a yet earlier source along with a number of stages of redactional
accretions that Dewey claims to be able to separate.

> While the first layer of material is meagre, I would argue that we have
> enough material to conclude that the story of the vindication of the righ-
> teous is both anticipated and acknowledged in the death scene of the
> Lord. I would further suggest that this narrative was originally used to
> come to grips with the probable collision of ideological expectation and
> political failure of Jesus of Nazareth. I have further argued that there
> is a second layer, which expands the story of the righteous one by the
> addition of a miraculous epiphany story. This expansion may well have
> come during the early stages of missionary advancement by the Jesus
> movement.[431]

Further, Dewey posits another two stages of redactional expansion.
The third layer is seen as complicating the basic message of the vindication story of the first layer. Finally, it is suggested a fourth layer
is added after the fall of Jerusalem (the others are earlier than 70 CE).
Consequently, this final layer polarizes the distinction made in the text
between the disciples of the Lord on the one hand and 'the Jews' on
the other. Schematically the material in the various layers is represented by Dewey as follows:

Table 14. Dewey's lines of development for *Gos. Pet.*

| | |
|---|---|
| Original layer | 2.5c–5.15a; 5.16–6.21; 8.28b |
| Story of the vindicated just one | |
| Secondary layer | 8.28a; 8.29b–9.37; 10.39b; 10.40; 11.45 |
| Epiphany story | |
| Tertiary layer | 2.3–4; 6.23b–24 (Joseph frg.); |
| Fragments and redactional elements | 10.41–42 (Cross frg.); 1.1–2; 2.5a,b; |
| | 5.15b; 6.22–23a; 8.29a; 10.38–39a,c; |
| | 10.43; 11.46–49 |
| Final redactional layer | 7.25; 7.26–27; 11.44; 12.50–13.57; |
| (*Gospel of Peter*) | 14.58–60 |

It is interesting to note the similarity between both the final layers in
the different schemas of Crossan and Dewey. They both see the bulk of
this layer comprising of *Gos. Pet.* 12.50–14.60. However, whereas Crossan includes 6.23–24 as part of the final stage, Dewey sees this 'Joseph

---

[431] Dewey, '"Time to Murder and a Time to Create": Visions and Revisions in the
*Gospel of Peter*', 123–124.

fragment' as being added in stage three. He also includes 7.26–27 and
11.44 as elements of the final composition. In effect Crossan would
agree with this, since this material constitutes part of his redactional
preparatory material for the intracanonical materials. The major difference is Dewey's inclusion of 7.25, which Crossan sees as part of
the *Cross Gospel*.

Dewey's reconstruction is accompanied by a detailed discussion
of the various theological perspectives and community settings that
would have brought about these compositional stages. There are also
theological consequences that Dewey sees emerging from his reconstruction of a story of the vindicated suffering one. Namely that the
'presumption of some sort of kernel of historicity for the passion narrative may well be just that.'[432] Such observations are not unique to
discussion of the passion narrative based on the text of the *Gospel
of Peter*. Similar perspectives have also been articulated in relation to
the canonical accounts. One significant difference between Dewey and
Crossan concerns their respective understandings of the material contained in *Gos. Pet.* 12.50–14.60. For Crossan it was the recognition that
this material showed signs of dependence on the Markan material that
led him to suggest a multi-layered compositional theory. By contrast,
Dewey sees no clear signs of direct literary relationship. He states, 'it
is not certain that Peter has used Mark 16:1–8 as its source. Nor can
one say that the reverse is likely. It would seem, then, that an earlier
version of both the Markan and Petrine empty tomb stories may have
existed, since the empty tomb story in Peter has been redacted by the
final editor.'[433] Here Dewey's logic is unpersuasive. If the text of the
*Gospel of Peter* shows clear traces of editorial activity, and a parallel account of the story is known from Mark's gospel with a striking
number of literary points of contact, it seems unnecessary to multiply
hypothetical sources. The most obvious conclusion is that the Akhmîm
text drew upon the Markan account. Dewey admits that, 'when one
removes final redactional elements from the empty tomb story (12:1b,
12.3a), one is left with a format strikingly like Mark 16:1–8 (minus
Mark 16.7).'[434] Yet for Dewey, the reason for resisting the conclusion
of direct dependency appears to stem from the divergences, which he

---

[432] Dewey, 'And an Answer Was Heard from the Cross', 110.
[433] Dewey, 'Resurrection Texts and the *Gospel of Peter*', 191.
[434] Dewey, 'Resurrection Texts and the *Gospel of Peter*', 189–190.

implicitly appears to view as being too large to allow the author of the *Gospel of Peter* to have exhibited such a degree of creativity with the source material. In a subsequent article Dewey further develops his understanding of the structure of the first compositional layer.[435]

Despite Dewey's repeated articulation of his theories of various redactional layers, these ideas have won little support. This is perhaps due to three principal factors. First, the complexity of the solution and the attendant certainty with which it is articulated results in a hypothesis which seems to go beyond the available textual evidence. Secondly, he rejects the very insight that led Crossan to postulate redactional layers namely that while wanting to hold to the notion that the narrative contained primitive traditions, Crossan also recognized the dependence of the text on canonical materials at certain points.[436] Thirdly, the majority of scholars still remain more convinced by the case for dependence on canonical traditions.

Dewey is not the only scholar to have modified Crossan's thesis. One of the more prominent examples of modification is presented in the *Anchor Bible Dictionary* entry on the *Gospel of Peter*. Paul Mirecki makes even more radical claims than those advanced by Crossan. He states, 'The *Gospel of Peter* (= *Gos. Pet.*) was a narrative gospel of the synoptic type which circulated in the mid-1st century under the authority of the name Peter. An earlier form of the gospel probably served as one of the major sources for the canonical gospels.'[437] Thus, for Mirecki, the final version of the *Gospel of Peter* appears to have been in circulation by the middle of the first century, presumably prior to the composition of any of the canonical accounts. Yet, there was also an earlier literary stage which the evangelists drew upon in composing their own narratives. It is uncertain when this primitive form was composed, but according to Mirecki's outline this must have been earlier than 50 CE. The major departure from Crossan's thesis is in suggesting that the final form of the *Gospel of Peter* was completed prior to the composition of the canonical gospels. This is in opposition

---

[435] In this article Dewey deviates from the standard numbering system, by recommencing the verse numbers at one, for each paragraph division thus 2.3c is equivalent to 2.5c in the standard system. This can give the erroneous appearance that he has altered the contents of the base layer. See Dewey, 'The Passion Narrative of the Gospel of Peter', 53–69.

[436] See Crossan's statement of this in 'The Gospel of Peter and the Canonical Gospels: Independence, Dependence, or Both?', *Forum* New Series 1.1 (1998) 1–51.

[437] Mirecki, 'Peter, Gospel of', *ABD* V, 278.

to one of Crossan's most direct statements: 'I agree, of course, that our present Gospel of Peter is dependent on the canonical gospels. That has always been my position.'[438] However, they may agree in broad terms on the date of composition of the source behind the final version of the *Gospel of Peter*. For Crossan appears to agree with Theissen[439] that the passion narrative was formed during the early forties, during the reign of Agrippa I (41–44 CE).[440]

Where do such scholarly debates leave the discussion? At one level Crossan is correct that the *Gospel of Peter* is neither dependent or independent on the canonical accounts – it is both. There are passages which appear to show significant borrowing from the four canonical gospels, while there are others which are totally unrelated. Yet, it is the last category that causes disagreement. Do such otherwise unattested elements evidence a pre-canonical source, independent free-floating traditions integrated to form an expanded narrative, or the redactional creativity of a popularizing author? To answer such questions it is necessary first to look at specific passages that show dependence on the four canonical accounts, and to assess how such evidence of dependence is integrated throughout the text. The method utilized here will consider some of the more striking cases of literary dependence for each of the gospels in canonical order. A more comprehensive discussion of possible cases of dependence is considered in the body of the commentary.

### 9.2. *The Gospel of Matthew*

In his discussion of the literary relationships between the *Gospel of Peter* and individual canonical gospels, Vaganay divides the types of parallels into three classes. These are resemblances which are 'slight' (legères), 'striking' (frappantes), and 'demonstrative' (démonstratives).[441] Vaganay explicitly states that on their own the 'slight resemblances' are inconclusive. Rather, he includes them to build a cumulative case to highlight the thoroughgoing manner in which the author of the *Gospel of Peter* has constructed his own narrative as a pastiche of canonical

---

[438] Crossan, 'The Gospel of Peter and the Canonical Gospels: Independence, Dependence, or Both?', 31.

[439] G. Theissen, *The Gospels in Context* (Edinburgh: T&T Clark, 1992) 198.

[440] Crossan, 'The Gospel of Peter and the Canonical Gospels: Independence, Dependence, or Both?', 39–40.

[441] Vaganay, *L'Évangile de Pierre*, 46–47.

scenes and terminology, albeit with added details and revised theological perspectives.

The purpose of the present discussion is to outline, in relation to each of the four New Testament accounts, what are potentially the most decisive examples of literary dependence. By so doing, it will be argued that the theory which states the *Gospel of Peter* is an independent and early witness to the events of the passion is incorrect. For this reason those points of contact which can at best be classified as 'slight resemblance' will not be explored in any detail. Instead, attention will focus on those parallels that can be classed as being either demonstrative or striking. In effect, this approach privileges the criterion suggested by Köster, which looks for evidence of the use of redactional material.[442] For Köster's criterion to be applicable in this case the most likely direction of dependence must also be debated, for without this step all that one can demonstrate is that a literary relationship exists, not the direction of that relationship.

The case for literary borrowing between the Matthean account and the *Gospel of Peter* is extremely strong. There are repeated examples of material that is present among the canonical gospels only in the Matthew's account, but which is also shared with the *Gospel of Peter*. The story of the guard-at-the-tomb is perhaps the most significant example for a discussion of the relationship between the *Gospel of Peter* and Matthew. Within the context of the *Gospel of Peter* this story represents approximately one-third of the extant text (*Gos. Pet.* 8.[28]29–11.49), with the centurion and soldiers portrayed as primary witnesses to the actual resurrection. By contrast, in the Matthean version the story is much shorter, and there is only one fleeting reference to the presence of guards during the actual removal of the stone from the tomb (cf. Matt 27.62–66; 28.4, 11–15). Probably under the influence of the Matthean structure Vaganay divides his 'demonstrative' evidence into three sections – the guard at the tomb, the resurrection, and the corruption of the guard by the Jewish authorities.[443] The terminological similarities are discussed at length in the commentary sections dealing with *Gos. Pet.* 8.28–11.49 and hence such discussion will not be

---

[442] H. Köster, *Synoptische Überlieferung bei den Apostolischen Vätern*, TU 65 (Berlin: Akademie Verlag, 1957) 3.
[443] Vaganay, *L'Évangile de Pierre*, 50–51.

repeated here. Rather, given that this is an obvious case of some type of literary relationship, the focus is on the nature of that relationship.

In this case there are three possible major explanations: (i) Matthew knew the account in the *Gospel of Peter*; (ii) the *Gospel of Peter* knew the Matthean account; or (iii) a common literary source stands behind both Matthew and the *Gospel of Peter* and was used independently by both authors. Obviously, at a theoretical level these are not the only three possibilities. It is possible that there was an independent account known to both the *Gospel of Peter* and Matthew, but, if the *Gospel of Peter* were the later text, it could also have known the Matthean account as well – thus the use of the guard-at-the-tomb tradition would not be fully independent of the Matthean handling of that tradition. While such an explanation is possible, it will be argued that such a complex solution is not required here.

The case for a common source underlying both accounts has been most forcefully advanced by Raymond Brown. In his initial article dealing with this topic, Brown notes 'there is remarkably little exact verbal identity in word or form.'[444] Consequently, albeit tentatively, he offers the following proposal.

> I would argue strongly that while scholars have discussed the influence of oral tradition on Gospel origins, there has been inadequate consideration of a second orality that must have dominated in the 2nd century when, because of a dearth of copies, most Christians' knowledge of written Gospels was through hearing and an oral communication that combined and confused details.[445]

This comment helpfully provides one possible scenario that led to the inclusions of the additional details contained in the version of the passion presented by the *Gospel of Peter*. However, by the time Brown revisited this question he had moved away from theories of secondary orality, instead preferring the suggestion of an underlying written source shared independently by both accounts. Thus at a later date he states,

> I shall contend that the author of *GPet* drew not only on Matt but on an independent form of the guard-at-the-sepucher story, and in *GPet* 8:28–11:49 the basic story is still found consecutively (even if details in

---

[444] R.E. Brown, 'The *Gospel of Peter* and Canonical Gospel Priority', *NTS* 33 (1987) 333.

[445] Brown, 'The *Gospel of Peter* and Canonical Gospel Priority', 335.

the story are modified by later developments). Matt, however, divided up the guard story to constitute the second episode (27:62–66 before the resurrection) and the fourth episode (28:11–15 after the resurrection) in the burial resurrection narrative.[446]

For Brown this conclusion arises from two features that he discerns from the parallel accounts of this narrative. The first is that the guard story was 'originally a consecutive story', and secondly that 'the story that is preserved in Matt [is] in a less developed form than in GPet'.[447] In support of his first contention, that it was originally a consecutive story, Brown presents 'two observable facts'. The first being the implausibility of the author of the *Gospel of Peter* extracting elements from the interwoven story presented by Matthew to create a consecutive account The second (which is actually just a corollary of the first point) is that the removal of Markan elements leaves a continuous story, thereby showing that the two accounts are not highly integrated.[448]

Taking the last point, it is fully possible to concur with Brown's observation, yet not to support the conclusion he derives from it. For supporters of the two-source theory it is precisely true that Matthew has taken the basic Markan account and supplemented it with additional material, here the guard-at-the-tomb story. Whether this integrated material was purely a Matthean redactional creation, or represented an oral or written source may be debated – probably without resolution. Yet it is unsurprising that Brown observes that a coherent narrative can be constructed with the Markan material removed, since Matthew's purpose is to introduce a new brief narrative into the Markan context. The real issue is whether one believes that the author of the *Gospel of Peter* can have extracted the discrete but related elements from Matthew to create an uninterrupted continuous story, or whether it is necessary to suggest access to a written source utilised indenpently by Matthew. Two factors make the extraction theory more plausible than Brown acknowledges. First, Matthew's own redactional handling of Markan material demonstrates that an ancient author could re-connect broken stories to create a continuous narrative. Mark contains a number of 'sandwich', or intercalated stories. Taking the example of the Markan story of the fig tree (Mk 11.12–14, 20–21),

[446] R.E. Brown, *The Death of the Messiah: From Gethsemane to Grave*, vol 2 (New York: Doubleday, 1994) 1287.

[447] Brown, *The Death of the Messiah*, 1301, 1305.

[448] Brown, *The Death of the Messiah*, 1301.

which is wrapped around the temple cleansing (Mk 11.15–19). Here, it is apparent that Matthew separates the two stories that have been interwoven. He places the temple cleansing first in his own narrative (Matt 21.12–17) and then presents a connected account of the withering of the fig tree (Matt 21.18–22), with the heightened and more spectacular miraculous detail of the instantaneous shrivelling of the tree. Interestingly this is basically the same process that occurs if one views the *Gospel of Peter* as working only with the Matthean account. Two separated blocks of existing tradition, Matt 27.62–66 and Matt 28.11–15, are joined to form a continuous account and the new consecutive story has heightened miraculous elements. The only slight difference is that Matthew had made one reference to the guard story in the central block (Matt 28.4), when he combined the two stories.[449]

A second factor which tells against Brown's proposal is the fact that the *Gospel of Peter* (as it will be argued below) had access to the Markan account, and this shaped his editorial decisions. Mark privileges the story of the women's discovery of the empty tomb, making them the only recorded witnesses to the empty tomb. The author of the *Gospel of Peter*, following the Markan source for the story of the women at the tomb, separates this incident in order to keep distinct the two incidents. Thus he highlights the complicit suppression of the resurrection by the authorities (although they have first hand testimony from the soldiers), in opposition to the experience of the women who are confused witnesses of the empty tomb. In this sense the author of the *Gospel of Peter* had a greater textual motivation for orchestrating such a reconnection of the guard story, than simply tidying-up literary seams in the Matthean narrative. Rather, the motivation for this editorial decision arose from the fact that he had access to the the women at the tomb tradition as a separate block in Mark's gospel.

If recourse to a common underlying source is not compelling, what of the suggestion that the version in the *Gospel of Peter* forms the basis of the Matthean account? Here Brown's next set of observations concerning the primitivity of the version in the Matthean narrative can

---

[449] Brown notes that the 'interweaving rearrangement in Matt's sepulchre/resurrection narrative also means that Matt has departed from Mark, who used the burial as a connective between the crucifixion and the resurrection accounts.' (Brown, *The Death of the Messiah*, 1303). However, he does not explain how this impinges upon understanding the compositional techniques of G.Pet.

helpfully be employed to respond to those suggestions to the contrary.[450] Apart from noting the folkloric aspects of the *Gospel of Peter*, Brown also observes that the 'author had an affinity for the dramatic and the extraordinary.'[451] While acknowledging Sanders' caution against over-simplisitic theological trajectories that see the development of the gospel tradition as a strictly linear progression, such as high Christology being self-evidently later than low Christology (however such things are judged), or heightened miraculous elements are automatically seen as the product of subsequent generations.[452] Nonetheless, when these developments are connected with other theological tendencies that can be more clearly mapped as later developments it is perhaps much more plausible to use such tendencies as indicators of relative temporal sequence of developing traditions. The expanded form that occurs in the *Gospel of Peter* functions as a more developed aetiology to explain how the Jewish leadership managed to suppress the truth of the resurrection. Moreover, it also fills existing holes in the Matthean account by explicitly stating that the guard was Roman (*Gos. Pet.* 8.31), hence their independence is assured, the precautions in securing the tomb are more precisely narrated so that stories of body-snatching could not be entertained (*Gos. Pet.* 8.32–33), the guards witness the actual resurrection scene as Jesus is led forth from the tomb (*Gos. Pet.* 10.38–39) thereby leaving the audience in no doubt concerning the miraculous nature of the event, and Pilate, although convinced by the veracity of the testimony of the guards, is persuaded by the political expedient action proposed by the Jewish leaders (*Gos. Pet.* 11.49). Such a combination of features, coupled with the known and documentable tendency to shift the blame for the crucifixion on to Jewish figures in later texts, means that it is simply not possibly to read the account in the *Gospel of Peter* as the earlier stage of the tradition.

This then leaves the solution that the *Gospel of Peter* had drawn directly upon the Matthean account in formulating its own version of the guard-at-the-tomb story as the most natural and compelling explanation of the evidence. Contrary to Brown, there does not appear to be any need to posit an underlying shared source at this point.[453] Moreover, Crossan's argument that the direction of influence is from

---

[450] Brown, *The Death of the Messiah*, 1305–1309.
[451] Brown, *The Death of the Messiah*, 1307.
[452] Sanders, *The Tendencies of the Synoptic Tradition*, 16.
[453] Brown, *The Death of the Messiah*, 1305–1309.

the *Gospel of Peter* to Matthew simply fails to persuade.[454] His suggestion that Matthew wants Jewish guards but not Jewish authorities at the tomb not only appears contrived, but actually even if this were the case does not prove that Matthew represents a later stage in the development of the tradition.[455] Therefore the Matthean form of the guard-at-the-tomb story represents a more primitive form of this tradition than the form contained in the *Gospel of Peter* and moreover, the expansions to this story contained in the text from Akhmîm can naturally be explained as embellishments to the version of this incident as it appears in Matthew's gospel without recourse to theories of an underlying, but now no longer extant common source.

So far the discussion of the relationship between the *Gospel of Peter* and Matthew has focused upon one incident, the guard-at-the-tomb story. It needs to be remembered that this occupies about one-third of the text of the *Gospel of Peter*, thereby making it a highly significant test case. Yet there are other striking points of contact between these two texts. Although Vaganay sees the report of Pilate's handwashing in Matt 27.24 as highly significant, it must be remembered that no matter how suggestive *Gos. Pet.* 1.1 may be of this being the incident that precedes the opening of the Akhmîm text, the fact that it is not present is extant text means that it cannot legitimately be presented as a literary parallel.[456] More helpful are four parallels that contain details that occur uniquely in Matthew among the canonical accounts. First, Pilate's declaration of innocence (Matt 27.24//*Gos. Pet.* 11.46) although reported in slightly different terms, ἀθῷός εἰμι ἀπὸ τοῦ αἵματος τούτου//ἐγὼ καθαρεύω τοῦ αἵματος τοῦ υἱοῦ τοῦ θεοῦ, appears to be an intentional parallel although the demonstrative pronoun in the Matthean account has been replaced by a more explicit christological title. Also, as Swete first noted, '[i]n Peter the words possibly did not accompany the symbolic washing, but were reserved for this later juncture.'[457] Regardless of whether this saying was reserved for this context or reused to form a doublet in the *Gospel of Peter* it is certain that Swete saw it as directly dependent on Matt 27.24.

A second highly significant shared tradition is the earthquake that accompanies Jesus death. In Matthew's post-death scene he expands

---

[454] Crossan, *The Cross that Spoke*, 276–280.
[455] Crossan, *The Cross that Spoke*, 277.
[456] Vaganay, *L'Évangile de Pierre*, 48.
[457] Swete, *The Akhmîm Fragment*, 20.

upon the Markan tradition of the tearing of the Temple veil by adding three other apocalyptic portents: a miraculous earthquake; split rocks; and the re-animation of the bodies of the dead saints (Matt 27.51b–53). Here it is instructive to look in a little detail at the structure of the two accounts:

ἡ γῆ πᾶσα ἐσείσθη καὶ φόβος μέγας ἐγένετο (Gos. Pet. 6.21b)
ἡ γῆ ἐσείσθη...ἰδόντες τὸν σεισμὸν καὶ τὰ γενόμενα ἐφοβήθησαν σφόδρα (Matt 27.51, 54)

Once again the *Gospel of Peter* appears to compress two parts of the same incident taken over from Matthew's account. After employing a virtually identical opening phrase with the addition of the adjective πᾶς the *Gospel of Peter* brings forward the second part of the Matthean mention of the earthquake which speaks of the fear of the Roman soldiers and makes this a general physiological response of all those present.[458]

The final two significant elements shared between these two texts are the detail that Jesus was laid to rest in the tomb of Joseph of Arimathea (Matt 27.60//*Gos. Pet.* 6.24), and the return of the disciples to Galilee after the passion and resurrection (Matt 28.16//*Gos. Pet.* 14.59). Although these affinities are at a narratival, rather than a terminological level, they nonetheless are striking. In combination with the analysis of the guard-at-the-tomb story, where the priority of the Matthean account was defended, these four further examples lend strong support to the theory that the *Gospel of Peter* knew and consciously employed traditions which among the canonical accounts are contained only in the Gospel of Matthew. The one caveat that can perhaps be added is that although it appears that the author of the *Gospel of Peter* knew of Matthew as a literary source, it may be the case that his compositional method did not involve consulting the parallel in the canonical account in a textual form, but rather via his recollection of the text.[459] Such a process would align with the most plausible explanation of the manner in which Ignatius cites scripture apparently from memory while he is being transported to Rome.[460]

---

[458] Vaganay, *L'Évangile de Pierre*, 48–49.
[459] Cf. Stillman, 'The Gospel of Peter: A Case for Oral-Only Dependency?', 114–120.
[460] Foster, 'The Epistles of Ignatius of Antioch and the Writings that later formed the New Testament', 165, 167.

## 9.3. *The Gospel of Mark*

Finding obvious traces of the Gospel of Mark in subsequent Christian literature is no easy task. There are two reasons for this state of affairs. In large part Mark was superseded by the Matthean account so there was a tendency among early Christian writers to overlook the text as a source for their theological reflections. Secondly, even when Mark is perhaps being cited it is often difficult to be certain that this is in fact the case since his gospel contains so many close parallels with the Matthean account. This makes it virtually impossible to identify which source is being used.[461] Moreover, given the known preponderance of early Christian writers to cite Matthew the sensible default position would be to assume that Matthew, rather than Mark, is being quoted. It is therefore in many ways remarkable that the first text in the Akhmîm codex can be shown to be dependent on Mark with almost virtual certainty.[462] Although reworked at a number of places the account of the visit of the women to the tomb in *Gos. Pet.* 12.50–13.57 shows knowledge of a number of striking Markan redactional features. As has been noted, it was recognition of this fact that led Crossan to abandon an overly simply theory of the priority of the *Gospel of Peter* over the synoptic gospels, and instead to advance the more methodologically sophisticated and defensible notion of a pre-canonical gospel source embedded in the *Gospel of Peter*. He therefore placed the material in *Gos. Pet.* 12.50–13.57 in the category of 'later redactional additions' to the underlying hypothetical Cross Gospel source.[463]

Looking at some of the specific points of contact, the strongest piece of evidence for demonstrable literary dependence stems from the extended verbal parallel that exists between *Gos. Pet.* 12.53 and the question in Mk 16.3, which in the canonical tradition is unique to Mark. The parallel may be set out as follows:

---

[461] As Streeter famously stated, 'Matthew reproduces 90% of the subject matter of Mark in language very largely identical with that of Mark; Luke does the same for rather more than half of Mark.' Streeter, *The Four Gospels*, 151.

[462] In the commentary section on 12.50c there is a comparison between G.Pet. and the list of twelve points that Davies and Allison (*The Gospel According to Saint Matthew*, vol. III, 660) note as differences between the Markan and Matthean accounts. Although G.Pet. does not have a parallel to each of these points, where it does the similarity is with the Markan account.

[463] For a fuller discussion of this see section 7.1 above and Crossan 'The Gospel of Peter and the Canonical Gospels: Independence, Dependence, or Both?', 31.

τίς δὲ ἀποκυλίσει ἡμῖν καὶ τὸν λίθον τὸν τεθέντα ἐπὶ τῆς θύρας τοῦ
μνημείου (*Gos. Pet.* 12.53a)
τίς ἀποκυλίσει ἡμῖν τὸν λίθον ἐκ τῆς θύρας τοῦ μνημείου (Mark
16.3)

There are a few minor differences. The opening five words of the Markan account are reproduced by the *Gospel of Peter*, but with the insertion of two conjunctions. The last four words are identical, although
governed by a different preposition. The most obvious difference
is that the *Gospel of Peter* inserts the participial phrase τὸν τεθέντα
thereby linking this incident back to *Gos. Pet.* 8.32, the point at which
the stone was placed at the entrance of the tomb.

Although Crossan acknowledges that the *Gospel of Peter* is dependent on Mark for the material in 12.50–13.57, he detects multiple
stages in the tradition history of the story of the women at the tomb.
It is this level of specificity in mapping out the steps of the evolving
tradition, along with its reliance on *Secret Mark* as the earliest stage
of that process which leads one to doubt the additional observations
proposed by Crossan and only to trust his assessment that here the
*Gospel of Peter* is dependent upon Mark. Crossan's intial stage of the
tradition history depends on Koester's thesis that *Secret Mark* preceded canonical Mark.[464] Accepting this hypothesis, Crossan states
that 'Mark composed his account in 16:1–8 by using the literary debris
from his destruction of the story of the resurrected youth in *Secret
Mark*.'[465] Unfortunately for Crossan this aspect of his proposal has
been severely weakened by recent studies.[466] This is not only a consequence of detailed refutations of the genuineness of *Secret Mark*,[467] but
also stems from scholars who uphold the authenticity of that text but
see it as being more naturally explained as a later stage in the develop-

---

[464] H. Koester, 'History and Development of Mark's Gospel (From Mark to Secret
Mark and "Canonical" Mark', in B. Corley (ed.), *Colloquy on New Testament Studies:
A Time for Reappraisal and Fresh Approaches* (Macon, GA: Mercer University Press,
1983) 35–57.

[465] Crossan, *The Cross that Spoke*, 284.

[466] For an overview of recent debates see P. Foster, 'Secret Mark: Its Discovery and
the State of Research', *Exp Tim* 117 (2005) 46–52, 64–68.

[467] See the works by S.C. Carlson, *The Gospel Hoax: Morton Smith's Invention of
Secret Mark* (Waco: Baylor, 2006); P. Jeffery, *The Secret Gospel of Mark Unveiled:
Imagined Rituals of Sex, Death and Madness in a Biblical Forgery* (Yale: Yale UP,
2007); and, F. Watson, 'Beyond Suspicion: On the Authorship of the Mar Saba Letter
and the Secret Gospel of Mark', *JTS* 61 (2010) 128–170.

ment of Markan material.[468] This, however, is not the only implausible aspect of Crossan's proposal. It is further suggested that the existing narrative in *Gos. Pet.* 12.50–13.57 is in fact a conflation of material and structural sequence from Mark 16.1–8, coupled with two Johannine themes. These themes are 'fear of the Jews from 19:38, 20.9, and weeping for Jesus from 20:11, 13, 15.'[469] There are two problems with this proposal. First, these 'themes' are not uniquely Johannine, and secondly, there are no clear examples of Johannine language or phraseology in *Gos. Pet.* 12.50–13.57. Once again, Crossan's complex theories of conflation and intercalation fail to convince, primarily because they appear to depend on ideas that cannot be derived from the textual evidence present in the multiple sources that he weaves together to form his theory of the tradition history of this incident. The only aspect that remains convincing is his central premise, that here the *Gospel of Peter* is using Mark 16.1–8 as its basic source.

The parallel between *Gos. Pet.* 12.53a and Mk 16.3 has been discussed above, since it provides extremely strong, if not conclusive evidence for the dependence of the *Gospel of Peter* on the Markan account.[470] This example can be further supplemented by other reasonably clear cases of literary dependence. These are discussed in more detail at their respective points in the commentary. Some of the unique details among the canonical gospels that occur only in the Markan account which are taken up by the *Gospel of Peter* include the hour of crucifixion (Mk 15.25), the astonishment of Pilate in relation to the speed of the death of Jesus (Mk 14.44–45a) and various points of contact with the story of the visit of the women to the tomb (Mk 16.1–8).[471] From this list of parallels it is possible to state that the use of Mark is perhaps the strongest demonstrable case of dependence by the *Gospel of Peter* on any one of the canonical accounts. This is striking give the usual 'invisibility' of Mark among Patristic sources. Such a conclusion should not be seen as calling into question the likelihood of the use of the other canonical accounts by the *Gospel of Peter*, for as

---

[468] S.G. Brown, *Mark's Other Gospel: Rethinking Morton Smith's Controversial Discovery*, ESCJ 15 (Waterloo, Ontario: Wifred Laurier, 2006).

[469] Crossan, *The Cross that Spoke*, 285.

[470] Among those who argue for a first century dating for material in G.Pet. this is recognized not only by Crossan. Dewey also comes to similar conclusions concerning Mark being the source from which G.Pet. derives this incident. See Dewey, 'And an Answer Was Heard from the Cross', 110.

[471] See Vaganay, *L'Évangile de Pierre*, 52–53.

was argued in the previous section the widespread use of Matthew at many points through the *Gospel of Peter* is the best explanation of the origin of a number of the traditions in the text. Rather, this conclusion simply highlights the strength of the claim, based on explicit parallels in extended portions of text, that the *Gospel of Peter* knew and used the Gospel of Mark.

### 9.4. *The Gospel of Luke*

Parallels with the Gospel of Luke in the *Gospel of Peter* are not as frequent as those that exist with either Matthew or Mark. This may lend further support to Gregory's thesis that the reception and use of the Lukan account occurred relatively late in the second century and was not necessarily a particularly widespread phenomenon.[472] Notwithstanding the comparative sparsity of literary parallels with the third gospel, there still exists a variety of striking details that appear to betray knowledge of features unique to the redactional hand of the third evangelist.

In his list of nine items peculiar to the *Gospel of Peter* and Luke, Brown notes that 'Co-crucified are "wrongdoers", one is favourable to Jesus.' This parallel between Luke 23.39–43 and *Gos. Pet.* 4.13–14 strongly suggests knowledge of Luke by the author of the *Gospel of Peter* and also can only be plausibly explained on the assumption that the *Gospel of Peter* was drawing on the Lukan account rather than *vice versa*. The story of the co-crucified reviling Jesus is absent from the Johannine account. Matthew and Mark record that both criminals engaged in the abuse of Jesus, whereas Luke transforms one of these criminals into an advocate for Jesus. This positive figure, in the Lukan account, rebukes his fellow criminal for engaging in abuse and failing to recognize who Jesus really is.[473] Yet again what appears to be happening with the author of the *Gospel of Peter* is not a process of mechanical repetition of existing traditions, but a radical reformulation of existing stories for theological reasons. This is no more or

---

[472] Gregory concludes his discussion of the reception of Luke by stating, 'the point at which *Luke* became recognized as one of the four controlling and authoritative accounts of the life of Jesus, as implied by Tatian in the Diatesseron and testified clearly to by Irenaeus, remains unclear.' A. Gregory, *The Reception of Luke and Acts in the Period before Irenaeus*, WUNT II/169 (Tübingen: Mohr Siebeck, 2003) 298.

[473] See J.A. Fitzmyer, *The Gospel According to Luke X–XXIV* (New York: Doubleday, 1985) 1508–1509.

no less radical than the way Luke had handled the Markan source at this point by re-writing the incident to have one criminal declare the innocence of Jesus. In turn, the author of the *Gospel of Peter* continues this theological trajectory commenced by Luke. He writes out of the account any reference to a reviling thief. Thus the rebuke of the supportive criminal is directed against the Jewish crucifiers of Jesus. If one is to call Luke's use of Mark a case of literary dependence, then the *Gospel of Peter*'s use of the Lukan story is no less an example of the same phenomenon. Brown is nevertheless reticent to describe what the author of the *Gospel of Peter* does with his canonical sources literary dependence. He writes

> I am convinced that one explanation makes better sense of the relationship between *GPet* and the canonical Gospels than any other. I doubt that the author of *GPet* had any written gospel before him, although he was familiar with Matt because he had read it carefully in the past and/or had heard it read several times in community worship on the Lord's Day, so that it gave the dominant shaping to his thought. Most likely he had heard people speak who were familiar with the Gospels of Luke and John – perhaps traveling preachers who rephrased salient stories – so that he knew some of their contents but had little idea of their structure.[474]

The trouble with such a rejection of literary dependence is that it reveals that it is based on a very narrow understanding of that phenomenon. Hence it appears to see literary dependence as occurring only when there is a level of replication of the source that is almost approaching what would more naturally be described as scribal copying. Here Brown appears unable to entertain the idea that the use of a literary text can take in a number of different ways. It can entail the subversion of the meaning of the source text, or it can recast the authoritative source to introduce new ideas and yet get such ideas a wider circulation by attaching to a written authority, or it can simply replicate the exemplar with minimal variation.

Yet Brown shows elsewhere that he considers the Lukan version of this story to be the more primitive form, although he does not feel that this was a direct literary source for the *Gospel of Peter*. Presumably Brown sees this as a further case where the Lukan story has been mediated to the author of the *Gospel of Peter* through a process of

---

[474] Brown, *The Death of the Messiah*, 1334–1335.

secondary orality. Therefore, refuting Crossan's notion that Luke drew on the hypothetical Cross Gospel for this story, Brown asks

> Are we to think that Luke and John read *GPet* 4:13–14, and that Luke excerpted and developed the element of one penitent wrongdoer while John excerpted and developed the element of no leg-breaking, without either giving the slightest indication of being aware of the other element in this two verse passage?[475]

Thus, for Brown the version of the story of the penitent thief in the *Gospel of Peter* is self-evidently later. Furthermore, according to Brown, the *Gospel of Peter*'s version is derived from Luke, but this is not classed as literary dependence since the author shows too much creativity with the source material (though no more than Luke does with Mark). Yet it is precisely this creativity that demonstrates that we are not dealing simply with scribal copying, but rather this creative retelling of the tradition is based upon a known canonical story. Admittedly, this recasting may have been undertaken without the text of Luke before the author of the *Gospel of Peter*, but if the text had been read (or even heard) by the author at some stage previously this is surely a case of what can be broadly understood as a type literary or textual dependence.

Apart from the source critical reasons Brown adduces for rejecting the priority of the *Gospel of Peter* over Luke in this incident of the penitent thief, there is also a theological trajectory which appears to preclude the priority of the *Gospel of Peter*. It seems incomprehensible that the tradition history could have evolved as a story of a single thief who speaks on Jesus behalf, then have been transformed in the Markan account into a story of two reviling thieves (followed in turn by Matthew), and then reworked under the influence of the *Gospel of Peter* into the Lukan version of the story with the mediating position of one the confession of Jesus' innocency from the narrative to introduce two blaspheming figures has been suggested. By contrast, the opposite trajectory not only seems natural but is also similar to other examples of development contained within the canonical gospel tradition. For example, Jesus' theologically problematic response 'why do you call me good?' (Mk 10.18) to the man who addresses him as 'Good teacher', is carefully recast in Matt 19.16–17. Again Crossan's theory is unbelievably complex, and his counter question of why the *Gospel of*

---

[475] Brown, *The Death of the Messiah*, 1333.

Peter 'read the story of the two thieves in Luke 23.32–33b, 39–43 but reduced it to *Gospel of Peter* 4:10b, 13, 14', can surely be explained as a simple way to remove the odium of having a thief speak against Jesus. Thus a potentially negative story is transformed by the author of the *Gospel of Peter* into a ringing endorsement of Jesus' character.

Other points of contact with Luke's gospel include the following examples that lend cumulative weight to the case that the third gospel had made an impact on the author of the *Gospel of Peter*. These include: (i) the relationship between Pilate and Herod Antipas during the trial (*Gos. Pet.* 2.5//Lk 23.12); (ii) mention of the fate of Jerusalem (*Gos. Pet.* 7.25//Lk 23.28–31); (iii) Lament of the Jewish people (*Gos. Pet.* 7.25, 8.28//Lk 23.27, 48); (iv) Jesus described as 'just' δίκαιος (*Gos. Pet.* 8.28//Lk 23.47); (v) Sabbath 'dawning' (*Gos. Pet.* 9.34//Lk 23.54); (vi) returning home of people ὑποστρέφειν (*Gos. Pet.* 14.58//Lk 23.48).[476] Hence although the narrative of the *Gospel of Peter* is not shaped to the same extent by Luke as it is by Matthew, nor are there extended portions of exact verbal correspondence as is the case between the *Gospel of Peter* and Mark, nonetheless it appears certain that the author of the *Gospel of Peter* knew a number of uniquely Lukan redactional incidents or details and either used or recast them for his own narratival and theological purposes.

## 9.5. The Gospel of John

Knowledge of the fourth gospel by the author of the *Gospel of Peter* cannot be demonstrated with any degree of certainty. Vaganay wishes to argue that the *Gospel of Peter* knew the fourth gospel, but to advance this conclusion it is necessary for him to alter his own criteria from those employed for establishing dependence on the synoptic gospels. In particular, the presence of shared text or redactional elements becomes less significant. Yet having made this concession all Vaganay can really conclude is that '[o]ne arrives at the conclusion that our copyist depends upon John in some manner.'[477] Although Brown lists ten points of potential parallel he dismisses these as virtually inconsequential. He comes to the conclusion that '[i]t is virtually inconceivable

---

[476] This list is derived from the one presented by Brown, *The Death of the Messiah*, 1330–1331.

[477] 'On arrive a se convaincre que notre faussaire dépend de Jean en quelque manière.' Vaganay, *L'Évangile de Pierre*, 65.

that the author of *GPet* had John before him and copied so little distinctively Johannine; and it is scarcrely less conceivable that the author
of John had *GPet* as his main source in constructing his PN.'[478] Thus
it needs to be recognized that there is a significant difference between
using a text as a 'main source' and the case of knowing a text such as
the fourth gospel and only using it sparingly. In the latter case it may
not be possible to conclusively demonstrate the form of dependence
between the two texts.

Yet, paradoxically, it is something not contained in the exant portion
of the *Gospel of Peter* that makes knowledge of the fourth gospel by the
*Gospel of Peter* more plausible. The conclusion of the narrative breaks
off mid-sentence at the *Gospel of Peter* 14.60. This final verse has just
set the scene for a post-resurrection incident that is about to take place
beside some unspecified sea. Among the canonical gospels, only in
John do we have a post-resurrection scene that takes place beside the
shores of a body of water (Jn 21.1–23). In the Johannine account the
water is named as the Sea of Tiberias, and like the *Gospel of Peter*
the name of the first disciple in the two admittedly unidentical lists is
given as Simon Peter. While these features are highly suggestive that
the narrative is developing the Johannine story that occurs beside the
Sea of Tiberias, in reality it must be admitted that there is simply not
enough of the story preserved to make this a secure conclusion. This
is especially the case given the tendency of the author of the *Gospel of
Peter* to be extremely creative in his retelling of the passion story.

### 9.6. *The Use of the Canonical Gospels*

To summarise, the following conclusions can be offered. First, the
*Gospel of Peter* appears to be posterior to the canonical gospels where
there are parallel passages. In those case where there is unparalleled
material, there is little reason to suppose that this is due to anything
other than the author's own creativity. Secondly, a strong case can be
mounted for the literary dependence of the *Gospel of Peter* on all three
of the synoptic accounts. However, it is necessary to state that literary
dependence does not equate to slavish copying of sources, or even a
desire to preserve the narratival macrostructure of any one of the synoptic accounts. Rather literary dependence is seen as occurring when

---

[478] Brown, *The Death of the Messiah*, 1331.

an author of a later text recasts the work of an earlier author with which he is familiar even if that text is not lying before the author at the time of writing his own narrative. Notwithstanding this last caveat, the familiarity of the author with so many Matthean traits, although often in new and highly refracted forms, may well mean that this gospel did in fact lay before him as a text to be consulted. Alternatively, the text may have been deeply emblazoned on his mind so that direct consultation was unnecessary. Without knowing the scribal practices of the author it is no longer possible to determine the full set of circumstances, it is only possible to note that the textual imprint of Matthew is stamped across much of the *Gospel of Peter*.

By contrast, the Gospel of Mark makes a less widespread impact across the entire narrative of the *Gospel of Peter*, but the literary parallels that exist show an even great correspondence in shared terminology than was the case with the Matthean parallels. Again, given the level of verbal agreement it is possible that a text of Mark was consulted directly for the composition of *Gos. Pet.* 12.50–13.57. However, this also could have occurred through recall of the literary form of the text. The impact of Luke on the *Gospel of Peter* is most fully demonstrated in the story of the supportive criminal. Here the theological motivation for deleting the reviling thief is apparent and coincides with a trajectory already developed within the third gospel itself. Finally, the closing verse is suggestive, but ultimately inconclusive for showing knowledge of the fourth gospel. If the author of the *Gospel of Peter* did know John then this would be a case where an author demonstrates the use of the fourfold gospel canon.[479] However, uncertainty about use of John means that it is probably best to state that the author of the *Gospel of Peter* knew the three synoptic accounts, and that this can be demonstrated with a strong degree of certainty.

## 10. Christology of the 'Gospel of Peter'

Traditionally an analysis of an author's beliefs concerning the nature of Jesus has been undertaken by investigating the titles that are employed as descriptions of status. One of the classical exponents of

---

[479] On the development of the fourfold gospel canon see T.C. Skeat, 'The Oldest Manuscript of the Four Gospels?' *NTS* 43 (1997) 1–34; Stanton, *Jesus and Gospel*, 63–91.

this approach is Oscar Cullmann. Describing his desire to be analytical in his methodology for deriving the Christological concepts from the New Testament, Cullmann provided the following explanation.

> This does not mean that we shall investigate in turn each New Testament writing with all the different titles that appear in it, but rather that we shall examine in its precise meaning each Christological title for itself as it appears throughout all the New Testament books.[480]

Although privileging this titular approach, Cullmann acknowledges that in some ways it creates a false dichotomy between the person and the work of Christ. He states, 'The New Testament hardly ever speaks of the person of Christ without at the same time speaking of his work.'[481] Thus in discussing the Christology that the *Gospel of Peter* presents, it is necessary to consider both the titles used and the significance it attributes to the work of Christ. Tuckett notes the protest made by a number of scholars against the overuse of titles, but cautions against throwing the proverbial 'baby out with the bath-water'. Thus he comments that, 'we cannot ignore key christological terms or 'titles' completely. In any case, many of these key terms or titles became important in subsequent Christian history when they were adapted and used as key descriptions of who Jesus was.'[482] Therefore, to investigate the Christology of the *Gospel of Peter* it is necessary to consider both the titles used as designations for Jesus, and the actual actions he engages in which are of Christological importance.

## 10.1. ὁ κύριος The Lord

Without doubt the preferred Christological title of the narrator of the *Gospel of Peter* is ὁ κύριος 'the Lord'. The title is used thirteen times in the extant portion of the text.[483] The scribe of this text writes this title utilising the common Christian scribal practice of a *nomen sacrum* on eleven occasions, but twice giving the title in full.[484] This title emerged as a popular designation for Jesus in the earliest stages of the develop-

---

[480] O. Cullmann, *The Christology of the New Testament* (trans. by S.C. Guthrie and C.A.M. Hall; London: SCM, 1959) 6.

[481] Cullmann, *The Christology of the New Testament*, 3.

[482] C.M. Tuckett, *Christology and the New Testament: Jesus and His Earliest Followers* (Edinburgh: EUP, 2001) 11.

[483] The thirteen occurrences of this title are found at G.Pet. 1.2; 2.3 (twice); 3.6; 3.8; 4.10; 5.19; 6.21; 6.24; 12.50 (twice); 14.59; 14.60.

[484] See 3.8 and 6.24.

ment of the movement that engaged in devotion to him in the post-Easer era. This title is widely attested in the genuine Pauline epistles, and appears to have been used at an even earlier stage, if certain pre-Pauline traditions have been correctly identified in the letters of Paul.[485] Bousset asserted that this title could only have originated in Hellenistic circles. He contends that 'it is all the more proved that ὁ κύριος in the religious sense for Jesus is conceivable only on the soil of the Hellenistic communities.'[486] Bousset attempts to dismiss the counter-evidence provided by the *Maranatha* formula of 1 Cor 16.22, by arguing that this may have developed 'not on the soil of the Palestinian primitive community, but in the bilingual region of the Hellenistic communities of Antioch, Damascus, and even Tarsus.'[487] While this special pleading is not convincing, Bousset shows that the κύριος title was not problematic for Hellenistic communities, and it may have in fact resonated with the early Pauline Christians as a subversive counterclaim to the imperial declarations of divinity. As Hurtado notes in relation to κύριος, '[i]t also came to be used for the Roman emperor, more so in the Eastern provinces where traditions of divine kingship were strong and cultic devotion to the living emperor (and not only to the deceased ones) was more acceptable than in the West.'[488] Thus for the author of the *Gospel of Peter* this title had a long heritage in Christian tradition as a primary referent for designating the status of Jesus, and the texts shows that the title can be used in an absolute sense, without qualification. Used in this manner, it may reflect the liturgical practice of the community of which the author may have been part, as the principal way of designating Jesus.

Commenting on the theological import of the term ὁ κύριος in the *Gospel of Peter* is difficult. This is primarily because, unlike Pauline

---

[485] The title κύριος permeates the Pauline tradition of the Eucharistic words (1 Cor 11.23–26). The invocation Maranatha 'Our Lord come', preserved in a transliterated form from the Aramaic μαράνα θά = מרנא תא (1 Cor 16.22) reflects the early application of the title κύριος as a reference for the resurrected Jesus. In the Christological hymn of Phil 2.5–11, the term κύριος is used as part of the climactic confession of v. 11.

[486] W. Bousset, *Kyrios Christos: A History of the Belief in Christ from the Beginnings of Christianity to Irenaeus* (trans. John Steely; Nashville: Abingdon, 1970; German original: Göttingen: Vandenhoeck & Ruprecht, 1913) 128.

[487] Bousset, *Kyrios Christos*, 129.

[488] L.W. Hurtado, *Lord Jesus Christ: Devotion to Jesus in Earliest Christianity* (Grand Rapids, Michigan: Eerdmans, 2003) 109. See also S.R.F. Price, *Rituals and Power: The Roman Imperial Cult in Asia Minor* (Cambridge: CUP, 1984).

traditions, it is not used in a confessional setting (Phil 2.11), nor is it aligned with references God the Father (e.g. Rom 1.7; 1 Cor 1.3; 2 Cor 1.2), nor does it serve as a test of allegiance (Rom 10.9; 1 Cor 12.3). Moreover, in the Pauline epistles Jesus status as Lord results in the gift of eternal life (Rom 6.23). It is also normative practice to invoke the name of the Lord in cultic settings (1 Cor 1.2). Through the lordship of Jesus one is called into fellowship (1 Cor 1.9), and there is an expectation that this dominical figure will return (Phil 3.20; 1 Thess 2.19). In contrast to the rich and varied nuances associated with the title κύριος in the Pauline writings, it cannot be determined whether the *Gospel of Peter* either assumes such understandings, or if such understandings are of little importance since the title functions almost exclusively as a reference or name for the central figure in the narrative (cf. *Gos. Pet.* 1.2; 2.3 etc). However, from the perspective of the narrative, one does see that this title, although used as a name, can be employed to designate the central figure during the trial scene (*Gos. Pet.* 1.2), while he is being crucified (*Gos. Pet.* 5.19),[489] after his death (*Gos. Pet.* 6.21), and to refer to him after the resurrection (14.60). Perhaps the only implication to be drawn from the way the title is employed in the *Gospel of Peter*, apart from its limited use as a name, is that disciples are linked to the Lord, Μαριὰμ ἡ Μαγδαλινὴ μαθήτρια τοῦ κυ (*Gos. Pet.* 12.50) and οἱ δώδεκα μαθηταὶ τοῦ κυ (*Gos. Pet.* 14.59). Head makes the observation that the title κύριος never refers to the resurrected Jesus. He states,

> Interestingly, in the text as we have it, κύριος never applies to the resurrected one. The four occurrences after the resurrection all refer to the pre-resurrected one (v50: 'a woman disciple of the Lord'…'the sepulchre of the Lord'; v59: 'the twelve disciples of the Lord'; and v60: 'Levi…whom the Lord [had called]').

While strictly speaking Head is correct, it is not fully apparent that the text is seeking to make a distinction between pre- and post-resurrection states and even if it were, it does not explain what this distinction might be.[490]

---

[489] See J. Denker, *Die theologiegeschichtliche Stellung des Petrusevangeliums*, Europäische Hochschulschriften 23/36 (Bern: Herbert Lang/Frankfurt: Peter Lange, 1975) 71.

[490] P.M. Head, 'On the Christology of the Gospel of Peter', *VC* 46 (1992) 211.

For Vaganay the author's preference for the title ὁ κύριος reflected the docetic mindset of the text. He suggests that the *Gospel of Peter* intentionally replaces the 'terrestrial' name Jesus with a celestial title Lord to downplay the human nature of Christ.[491] To designate this as a theologically motivated replacement, however, seems to be erroneous. The widespread use of the title ὁ κύριος in both the writings of the New Testament and the early Church shows that this was not a uniquely docetic phenomenon. Furthermore, the title is not used to avoid human attributes, but as a reflection of the Christological piety of the author and his community.

### 10.2. *Son of God*

While the choice of the title ὁ κύριος is perhaps unsurprising as the author's favoured way of referring to Jesus, the titles placed upon the lips of Jesus' opponents when they refer to him are striking. On four occasions Jesus is referred to as 'the Son of God'.[492] The first two instances (*Gos. Pet.* 3.6; 3.9) are placed on the lips of the baying Jewish crowd as it rushes Jesus to the place of his execution. The third occasion when this title is used the author appears to draw upon the positive register of centurion's confession in Mk 15.39 which affirms Jesus' veiled yet true status as 'Son of God'.[493] The final occurrence is neutral. Responding to the centurion's affirmation, Pilate seems to happily pick up the 'Son of God' language, but this is for descriptive rather than confessional purposes.[494]

Treating the first two examples of the 'Son of God' title together, it appears to be the case that the mob is using this title ironically. By addressing Jesus in terms of filial relationship to God and yet acting with complete contempt of that status, the crowd reveals that it views

---

[491] He states, '[e]n docète achevé, le pseudo-Pierre s'ingénie à remplacer cette appellation terrestre par les titres qui font le moins ressortir la nature humaine du Christ.' Vaganay, *L'Évangile de Pierre*, 109.

[492] The four occurrences of the 'Son of God' title are found at G.Pet. 3.6; 3.9; 11.45; 11.46.

[493] Donahue and Harrington comment that in the Markan account the centurion's declaration should be taken as 'a genuine confession of faith that echoes Mark 1:1 ("Jesus Christ, the Son of God") and constitute the climax of the gospel. Only at his death on the cross is the true identity of Jesus as the suffering Messiah and as God's Son revealed.' J.R. Donahue and D.J. Harrington, *The Gospel of Mark*, Sacra Pagina 2 (Collegeville, MN.: Liturgical Press, 2002) 449.

[494] Head, 'On the Christology of the Gospel of Peter', 211.

such a relational title as actually being incorrect or devoid of meaning. Thus calling Jesus 'Son of God' is a means of mocking his claims. Yet there is a second level in the narrative at which these two instances of τὸν υἱὸν τοῦ θυ function ironically. While from the perspective of the crowd the title is self-evidently false and thus they can use it as a taunt, they are blind to the fact that they are abusing the one who actually holds the status which they deny. In the *Gospel of Peter* this second level of irony is not greatly developed, but it does nonetheless appear to be present even if it is left floating for readers to see this implication for themselves. Hence, according to Vaganay, the truth of acclaiming Jesus Son of God is only comprehended at this point by the author and his privileged readers.[495]

The third instance of the 'Son of God' seems to parallel the intent of the centurion's declaration recorded in the synoptic gospels (Matt 27.54; Mk 15.39; cf. Lk 23.47), but it is placed in a different context. In Mark, as Tuckett observes, 'the centurion's confession (15.39) is in response to the actual death of Jesus (v.37).'[496] By contrast, in the *Gospel of Peter* this affirmation is uttered by a Roman centurion only after observing the events of the resurrection. Thus, whereas Mark offers his readers a Christology based on suffering, brokenness and death as the event that allow true perception of Jesus' identity, for the *Gospel of Peter* the basis is the defeat of death as manifest in the resurrection. From this perspective, the Christology of the *Gospel of Peter* is triumphalistic in orientation with the identity of Jesus being revealed to onlookers at the moment of his heavenly vindication, which itself functions as a demonstration of filial relationship with God. Therefore, Jesus is revealed through resurrection to be God's son. Such a perspective is not unique to the *Gospel of Peter*. It is also represented in the Pauline writings with Jesus being understood as having been declared to be Son of God through the resurrection (Rom 1.4). Yet neither in Paul or the *Gospel of Peter* does this demonstration of filial status at the resurrection necessarily need to be understood in an Adoptionist sense. Rather the emphasis appears to fall upon the powerful manifestation of Jesus' status as God's son by the resurrection event. Com-

---

[495] Vaganay states, 'Cette expression «Fils de Dieu» doit s'entendre, suivant les idées de l'évangéliste, d'une véritable filiation. Il est à croire que les bourreaux reprennent sur le mode ironique une déclaration solennelle faite par le Sauveur en face de ses juges.' Vaganay, *L'Évangile de Pierre*, 224.

[496] Tuckett, *Christology and the New Testament*, 115.

menting on the passage in Romans Dunn can state 'the full extent of God's purpose could only be realized through Jesus as Messiah (of Israel) risen from the dead to become the Son of God in power (for all).'[497] Similarly, Fitzmyer stresses that the accent falls on the powerful vindication of status and is not suggesting that a new status was achieved by the resurrection.

> Before the resurrection Jesus Christ was Son of God in the weakness of his human existence; as of the resurrection he is the Son of God established in power and has become such for the vivifying of all human beings.[498]

Although not exhibiting the theological reflection and richness of Romans in relation to this Christological perspective, the *Gospel of Peter* implicitly agrees that the resurrection represented the powerful demonstration of the status of Jesus as Son of God.

The final use of the title is *Gos. Pet.* 11.46 simply has Pilate take up the title used by the centurion in the previous verse. What is striking is the fact that from the perspective of the *Gospel of Peter* there is no need to have the Roman prefect question the appropriateness of the designation. Instead, he continues the conversation utilising the description of the centurion. As Mara comments 'Pilate accepts not only the report of the group, but even the conclusion which is derived and that the group explicitly affirms: υἱὸς ἦν Θεοῦ.'[499]

### 10.3. *King of Israel*

Although the anti-Jewish perspective of the author is both well known and self-evident from the narrative, he seems to distinguish between historic Israel and contemporary Judaism as though they were two separate and unrelated entities. The title 'King of Israel' occurs only twice in the extant portion of the gospel. In the *Gospel of Peter* 3.7, it parallels the mocking use of the title 'Son of God' by the Jewish mob in the previous verse (*Gos. Pet.* 3.6). In the canonical gospels the title 'King of Israel' occurs only four times. The first two instances are the parallel accounts of the crowd reviling Jesus while he is on

---

[497] J.D.G. Dunn, *Romans 1–8* (Dallas: Word, 1988) 14.

[498] J.A. Fitzmyer, *Romans* (New York: Doubleday, 1993) 235.

[499] 'Pilate accepte non seulement le rapport de la commission, mais encore la conclusion qui en dérive et que la commission a explicitement affirmé: υἱὸς ἦν Θεοῦ.' Mara, *Évangile de Pierre*, 194.

the cross. In Matthew the taunt is reported in the following terms. 'He saved others; he cannot save himself. So he is the king of Israel! Let him come down from the cross now, and we will believe in him.' (Matt 27.42). The Markan form is more compact, and also uses the title Christ. 'Let the Christ, the King of Israel, come down now from the cross that we may see and believe.' (Mk 15.32). The mockery in Matthew appears even more pointed. In Mark, the crowd are inviting Jesus to demonstrate his kingly status by coming down from the cross, whereas in the Matthean account, the title is not as closely tied to the request for proof by descent from the cross. Rather, it stands alone, reviling Jesus royal pretensions. In the Matthean narrative the crowd does not actually challenge his status as king,[500] rather they use the title with obvious incredulity. There are only two places in the canonical accounts where the title is used in a positive sense. The first occurs when Nathanael encounters Jesus at the beginning of the fourth gospel, and makes his Christological affirmation by combining two titles: 'Nathanael answered him, Rabbi, you are the Son of God! You are the King of Israel!' (Jn 1.49). The second, also in the fourth gospel, is placed upon the lips of the Palm Sunday crowd as Jesus enters Jerusalem, 'So they took branches of palm trees and went out to meet him, crying, Hosanna! Blessed is he who comes in the name of the Lord, even the King of Israel!' (Jn 12.13)

Unlike this confessional example in Jn 1.49, the first instance of the use of the title 'King of Israel' in *Gos. Pet.* 3.7 aligns with the mocking tone to be found in the account of the crowds at the cross in Matthew and Mark. Prior to the crucifixion Jesus is placed on the judgment seat and the jeering crowd taunt him to 'Judge justly King of Israel' (*Gos. Pet.* 3.7). Although not in a judicial context, this incident seems to parallel the pre-crucifixion mockery of the Roman soldiers, who address Jesus as 'King of the Jews', (Mk 15.18).[501] If that incident were in the author's mind when he created this scene, he has been careful to remove the term 'Jews' from the salutation and instead replace it with what is to him the more acceptable title 'King of Israel'. If corroboration of this anti-Jewish tendency is required, the change from 'Jews' to 'Israel' is even more explicit on the second occasion this title is used in the *Gospel of Peter*. The canonical gospels uniformly record the *titu-*

---

[500] U. Luz, *Matthew 21–28* (Minneapolis: Fortress, 2005) 539.
[501] See Vaganay, *L'Évangile de Pierre*, 226.

*lus* on the cross as reading ὁ βασιλεὺς τῶν Ἰουδαίων 'the King of the Jews' (Matt 27.37; Mark 15.26; Lk 23.38; Jn 19.19). Vaganay suggests that the change is not motivated by anti-Jewish sentiments, instead he argues that '[i]t is rather a memory of the Messianic assertions of Jesus in presence of Herod.[502] While it is not possible to know whether the *Gospel of Peter* contained such messianic affirmations spoken in the presence of Herod, it does, by contrast, contain a clearly heightened anti-Jewish tendency. Thus, it is not possible to agree with Vaganay's explanation of the change at this point. The alteration seems motivated by a desire to distance Jesus from association with the Jews. Hence the author is keen to assert Jesus' kingly pedigree, yet not in relation to the Jewish people, but rather over historic Israel the people of the covenant and not with those who are, at least from the author's perspective, recalcitrant and condemned Jews.

### 10.4. *Saviour of the World*

The penitent thief who speaks out on Jesus' behalf in *Gos. Pet.* 4.13 demonstrates greater Christological perspicacity in this account than in the parallel version in Lk 23.39–43. In the Lukan account, the thief who supports Jesus discloses his Christological understanding in two ways: through dialogue with the reviling thief, and by a direct appeal to be remembered by Jesus when he entered his kingdom. Yet although in Luke's account the words of the first criminal are mocking and cynical,[503] it is, nonetheless, this figure that uses a Christological title to describe Jesus. Obviously the designation ὁ χριστός is not offered as an expression of piety, but of derision since Jesus as the one who claimed messianic status is sharing the fate of condemned criminals. Yet while not repeating the title, the corrective of the penitent criminal shows that he does not deride the claims to messiahship.[504] Moreover, the request to be remembered when Jesus enters his kingdom, shows acceptance of Jesus' royal heritage.

By contrast, since the *Gospel of Peter* excises the reviling criminal from this scene, it needs to find fresh ways for the believing thief to express the basis of his confidence in Jesus. This is done by creating a

---

[502] 'Elle est plutôt un souvenir des affirmations messianiques de Jésus en presence d'Hérode.' Vaganay, *L'Évangile de Pierre*, 226.

[503] J. Nolland, *Luke 18.35–24.53*, WBC 35C (Dallas: Word, 1993) 1152.

[504] Fitzmyer, *Luke X–XXIV*, 1507.

short monologue in which the thief responds not so much to taunts from those in the executing party, but apparently to the action of dividing Jesus' garments. The response consists of three components:

   i. A declaration that he and his co-insurrectionist have committed evil.
   ii. A description of Jesus as 'saviour of men.'
   iii. A rhetorical question underscoring the innocence of Jesus.

The title 'saviour of men', in the theology of the *Gospel of Peter*, appears to be predicated upon a belief that, in contrast to other humans, Jesus had committed no evil. While the term saviour is common in the New Testament, nowhere is there an exact match of the title σωτὴρ τῶν ἀνθρώπων. However, the universalistic outlook of this title is mirrored is three places in the NT with similar title. In the Johannine writings on two occasions the phrase ὁ σωτὴρ τοῦ κόσμου is employed (Jn 4.42; 1 Jn 4.14). Yet the closest parallel is to be found in the deutero-Pauline writings, where Jesus is described as σωτὴρ πάντων ἀνθρώπων (1 Tim 4.10). The only difference is the use of the masculine genitive plural definite article τῶν before ἀνθρώπων instead of the adjective πάντων. In relation to the phrase in 1 Timothy, commentators have noted both the universal scope of salvation expressed by this clause and the existence of parallels to this phrase in Hellenistic texts.[505] While this Christological description in 1 Tim 4.10 is certainly qualified by the words that follow, μάλιστα πιστῶν, it seems inappropriate to read this either as a rejection of an inclusive soteriology,[506] or as proof of a thoroughgoing universalism.[507] Rather the traditional saying that is cited here forms part of the author's doxological reflection on salvific hope.

    Similarly, in *Gos. Pet.* 4.13 there is no carefully thought-out universal perspective behind this title. Rather, it emphatically presents the significance of Jesus not as Jewish messiah alone (nothing could be

---

[505] See I.H. Marshall, *The Pastoral Epistles* (Edinburgh: T&T Clark, 1999) 556. The parallels include the description of Heracles as τῆς γῆς καὶ τῶν ἀνθρώπων σωτήρ (Dio Chrysostom 1.84) and Serapis as κηδεμόνα καὶ σωτῆρα πάντων ἀνθρώπων αὐτάρκα θεόν (Aelius Aristides 45.20K).

[506] G.W. Knight III, *Commentary on the Pastoral Epistles*, NIGNT (Grand Rapids, Michigan: Eerdmans, 1992) 203–204; T.C. Skeat, '"Especially the Parchments": A Note on 2 Timothy iv.13', *JTS* 30 (1979) 173–177.

[507] See M.J. Erickson, *Christian Theology* (Grand Rapids, Michigan: Baker, 1983) 2.834.

further from the mind of the author), but as the figure who is the soteriological key for all humanity.

### 10.5. *Docetic Christology and the* Gospel of Peter

From the time of the first flurry of discussions that accompanied the publication Akhmîm codex scholars have been keen to detect docetic elements in the document's Christology. This has largely been motivated by the belief that the first untitled text in the codex was none other than the *Gospel of Peter* known to Serapion, as described in a story related by Eusebius. In fact, in the portion of Serapion's letter *Concerning the so-called Gospel according to Peter* cited by Eusebius, it is not even clear that this gospel text ever contained any explicitly docetic teachings, rather the concern was that it had been used by docetic groups.

> But we...were enabled by others who studied this very gospel, that is by the successors of those who began it, whom we call Docetae (for most of the ideas belong to their teaching) using [the material supplied] by them, were enabled to go through it and discover that the most part was in accordance with the true teaching of the Saviour, but that some things were added, which also we place below for your benefit. (Eusebius, *H.E.* 6.12.6).[508]

Notwithstanding this apparent distinction made by Serapion, there has been a desire to locate actual docetic proclivities in the gospel. Swete set the agenda for much of the subsequent discussion by cataloguing what he saw as the examples of docetic theology in the text. He listed five examples.

1. The Lord's freedom from pain at the moment of crucifixion.
2. His desertion by His 'Power' at the moment of Death.
3. The representation of His Death as ἀνάληψις.
4. The supernatural height of the Angels and especially the Risen Christ.
5. The personification of the Cross.[509]

Prior to discussing each of these as potential examples of docetism, it is first necessary to attempt some definition of the basic tenets of the docetic outlook.

---

[508] Translation J.E.L. Oulton, *Eusebius, Ecclesiastical History: Books VI–X*, LCL 265 (Cambridge, Mass.: Harvard, 1932) 41–43.

[509] Swete, *The Akhmîm Fragment*, xxxviii.

The description 'docetic' was applied to a number of groups in the early church. These groups, or individuals, did not hold to a uniform or systematic set of beliefs and practices. Rather, these somewhat discrete groups shared some similar features in terms of beliefs centring on their Christological understandings, but they did not necessarily agree with each other in all aspects. Moreover, the label 'δοκεῖν' could be used as a powerful negative label by the proto-orthodox groups. Since its application could stigmatize opponents, and call into question the totality of their beliefs without having to engage in reasoned debate. Because of this multiplicity of differing articulations of 'docetism' in the early church, the phenomenon is perhaps best seen as a theological tendency rather than a clearly defined doctrine. This means that it is only possible to identify broad patterns of commonality rather than demand uniformly articulated understandings of this theological perspective.[510] The initial glimpses of docetism that surface in Christian texts, as reported by opponents to such views, characterize this outlook as either failing to affirm the reality of the humanity of Christ, or unable to accept that he was capable of suffering. This first feature is seen in the Johannine epistles. In 1 Jn 4.7 the ability to make the confession Ἰησοῦν Χριστὸν ἐν σαρκὶ ἐληλυθότα is seen as being the test which differentiates Johannine believers from their docetic opponents. More explicitly in 2 Jn 7 those who are unable to make this confession are labelled as 'the deceiver and antichrist': Ὅτι πολλοὶ πλάνοι ἐξῆλθον εἰς τὸν κόσμον, οἱ μὴ ὁμολογοῦντες Ἰησοῦν Χριστὸν ἐρχόμενον ἐν σαρκί· οὗτός ἐστιν ὁ πλάνος καὶ ὁ ἀντίχριστος. Despite Strecker's contention that 2 Jn 7 describes a different phenomenon from that of 1 Jn 4.2,[511] it appears best to see these descriptions as referring to the same group

---

[510] For further discussion of this point see 'Docetism', in F.L. Cross and E.A. Livingstone, *The Oxford Dictionary of the Christian Church* (3rd ed. rev.; Oxford: OUP, 2005) 496. The article notes, 'In the early Church, a tendency, rather than a formulated and unified doctrine, which considered the humanity and sufferings of the earthly Christ as apparent rather than real.'

[511] In relation to 2 Jn 7, Strecker argues that the present participle ἐρχόμενον is highly significant conveying a future meaning, i.e. Jesus Christ, the one coming in the eschaton. From this Strecker argues that a chiliastic interpretation is involved. However, it is the Johannine community that is chiliastic in its thinking while the secessionists deny that Christ will come in the flesh to inaugurate the thousand year period of messianic reign. Strecker finds corroboration of this thesis in the person of Papias. He states, 'Papias, however, was also a chiliast. This agrees with the fact that he was instructed by John the presbyter.' G. Strecker, *The Johannine Letters* (trans. L. Maloney; Minneapolis: Augsburg Fortress, 1996) 234–235.

of opponents. Thus, the issue at stake would appear to be adherence to belief in the Incarnation. Refusal to accept such a teaching is at the core of what the Johannine author understands by his description of the deceivers who 'do not confess Jesus Christ coming in the flesh.' As Smalley suggests, '[i]n such a case the elder would be describing those of his flock who were inclined to docetism, and who denied that the "flesh" of Jesus was real. Heretics of this kind may well have formed a majority in the Johannine community by this time.'[512] Hence the earliest feature of the docetic tendency that can be identified is a denial of the reality of the humanity of Christ.

The next time the phenomenon of docetism arises in Christian literature occurs in the first quarter of the second-century in the writings of Ignatius of Antioch. He appears to be confronting two sets of opponents,[513] one group with a Judaizing tendency (although probably not ethically Jewish, cf. *Phld.* 6.1)[514] and a second group with docetic proclivities. This docetic set of opponents is mentioned in three epistles, those to the Ephesians, Trallians and Smyrneans. While the first of these letters offers at best only a generalized description of this phenomenon, the other two are more explicit in the descriptions they contain. When writing to the Trallians Ignatius states 'but if, as some who are atheists – that is, unbelievers – say, that he only appeared [δοκεῖν] to suffer, it is they who are the appearance [δοκεῖν]' (*Trall.* 10.1). The same critique of heretics emerges in addressing the Smyrneans. This refutes the notion that Jesus Christ accomplished his redemptive work in appearance or semblance alone (*Smyrn.* 4.2), and Ignatius continues by declaring,

---

[512] S.S. Smalley, *1, 2, 3 John* WBC 51 (Waco, Texas: Word: 1984) 329.

[513] The question of whether Ignatius was combating a single group of opponents or fighting on two-fronts is a highly disputed issue. For recent statements of alternative positions see J.W. Marshall, 'The Objects of Ignatius' Wrath and Jewish Angelic Mediators', *JEH* (2005) 1–23. M. Myllykoski, 'Wild Beasts and Rabid Dogs: The Riddle of the Heretics in the Letters of Ignatius', in Jostein Ådna (ed.), *The Formation of the Early Church* (WUNT 183; Tübingen: Mohr Siebeck, 2005) 341–377.

[514] In his epistle to the Philadelphians, Ignatius includes the rather enigmatic advice that, 'if anybody should interpret Judaism to you, do not listen to him. For it is better to hear Christianity from a man who is circumcised than Judaism from one who is uncircumcised' (*Phld.* 6.1). The possibility of hearing Judaism from an uncircumcised person, suggests that those whom Ignatius describes are not ethnic Jews or even proselytes to the Jewish faith, but rather certain Gentiles who held to a form of Christian faith that promoted Jewish observance without the necessity of circumcision.

> For how does anyone benefit me if he praises me but blasphemes my
> Lord, not confessing that he bore flesh? The one who refuses to say this
> denies him completely, as one who bears a corpse. But I see no point in
> recording their disbelieving names. I do not even want to recall them,
> until they repent concerning the Passion, which is our resurrection.
> (*Smyrn.* 5.2–3)

Employing language reminiscent of that used against the secessionists by the author of 1 John, Ignatius levels against his opponents the
charge that they likewise deny the reality of Christ appearing and
suffering in the flesh. Trebilco, specifically discussing the situation
Ignatius addressed in Ephesus, suggests that 'what Ignatius says about
the *current* threat of docetists as he writes shows that the Johannine
secessionists are still in town, have developed their teaching further in
the docetic direction, and that Ignatius is concerned that they might
continue to gain a hearing.'[515] Furthermore, the suggestion that the
docetists were actively engaged in missionizing is supported by the
presence of similar teachings among the Smyrneans and Trallians, as
well as by the observation that those described in 1 John with such
Christological views had gone into the world and 'the world listens
to them' (1 John 4.5).[516] For Ignatius, those who hold such beliefs are
blasphemers and have no hope in partaking in the resurrection since
by denying the physical suffering of Christ they deny the efficacy of the
redemptive act.[517] Thus the further feature of docetic teaching that is
apparent from the writings of Ignatius is not only there denial of the
incarnation, but the corollary of this, namely that it was impossible for
Christ to undergo suffering.[518]

These two snapshots of early-docetism reveal that the central tenets
of its belief structure, at least from the viewpoint of opponents, revolve
around the affirmation that Christ was not constrained by human
form, but only appeared to be in such a form to human observers.
Yet even here texts such as the *Acts of John* disclose to readers that
at certain times the inner-circle of disciples observed Jesus transcend
the boundaries of human physical limitations, thus demonstrating the

---

[515] P. Trebilco, *The Early Christians in Ephesus from Paul to Ignatius* (Tübingen:
Mohr Siebeck, 2004) 695.

[516] For a fuller explanation of this suggestion see Trebilco, *The Early Christians in
Ephesus from Paul to Ignatius*, 695.

[517] See *Smyrn.* 5.2–3.

[518] For a fuller discussion of Ignatius' opponents see P. Foster, 'The Epistles of Ignatius of Antioch (Part 1)', *Exp Tim* 117 (2006) 487–495.

non-incarnate nature of his form.[519] While docetic belief that Jesus'
human appearance was a mere chimera and that he did not experience
suffering may be fairly normative features of docetism, such beliefs
could also be integrated into wider cosmological understandings. Thus,
for instances, Manichaean teachers married docetic understandings of
the nature of Christ with their radically dualistic perspective on the
universe and humanity.[520] Such variation needs to be fully recognized
when assessing whether the Akhmîm fragment should be adjudged as
being docetic, or not. Thus as Slusser has argued a broad definition of
docetism must be maintained not as a concession to the early church
fathers who 'lumped so many Christologies together...but because
all who they termed docetistic denied that in Jesus Christ the divine
Savior was truly subject of all the human experiences of the historical
man.'[521]

The first point in Swete's list is potentially the most conclusive in
mounting a case for the docetic character of this apocryphon. He suggests that the text depicts the Lord's freedom from pain at the moment
of death. This is no doubt based on the editorial comment that during
the crucifixion Jesus 'was silent as though having no pain', αὐτὸς δὲ
ἐσιώπα ὡς μηδέν πόνον ἔχων (Gos. Pet. 4.10). The construction, however, uses the term ὡς to introduce a simile which describes a counter-
intuitive comparison. Thus the emphasis falls on the fact that, contrary
to what was obviously the case, the Lord endured the pain like one not
experiencing suffering. Here the accent falls on heroic death, rather
than an articulation of docetic Christology. However, Vaganay takes
the grammatical force of the particle as causal.[522] If this were the case,
then the sense would be something along the lines of 'he was silent since
he had no pain.' Apart from the fact that this, if it were true, would
hardly be remarkable, more significantly at the level of the narrative it
does not align with how Jesus is depicted as he undergoes the various
stages of his torments. This is also observed by McCant who states
'[s]uffering is integral to the "Petrine" passion narrative and silence is a
pronounced feature of this narrative, with the Lord speaking only once

---

[519] For a discussion of polymorphic Christology in the *Acts of John* see P.J. Lalleman,
*The Acts of John*, Studies on the Apocryphal Acts of the Apostles (4) (Leuven, Peeters, 1998);
and E. Junod and J.-D. Kaestli, *Acta Iohannis*, Tomus 1: Praefatio – Textus; Tomus 2:
Textus alii – commentaries – indices; CCSA 1–2 (Turnhout: Brepols, 1982).

[520] W.H.C. Frend, *The Rise of Christianity* (Philadelphia: Fortress, 1984) 386.

[521] M. Slusser, 'Docetism: A Historical Definition', *Second Century* 1 (1981) 172.

[522] 'Sans doute ὡς construit avec un participe est causal.' Vaganay, *L'Évangile de
Pierre*, 236.

(GP 5.19a).'[523] Perhaps even more telling is the parallel contained in the *Martyrdom of Polycarp*. Upon being pushed out of the wagon that has transported him to the stadium for martyrdom, Polycarp injures his shin. Yet he does not acknowledge such a wound, rather he walks as one 'whom nothing had hurt' καὶ μὴ ἐπισταφείς ὡς οὐδὲν πεπονθὼς (*M.Pol.* 8.3). Unless one wishes to posit some docetic ontological state for the very human Polycarp, it again seems that the import of this phrase is heroic endurance in the face of pain, not the absence of pain from one who cannot be touched by the material world.[524]

The second point Swete lists is the desertion of 'Power' at the moment of death. This is presumably seen by Swete, and those who have followed him, as paralleling accounts in docetic texts where the divine Christ departs from the human Jesus, thereby leaving a mere fleshly shell to suffer whereas the spiritual being is immune from such torment. Two texts suffice to exemplify this aspect of docetic thought. In the *Acts of John* the eponymous apostle is engaged in conversation with the Lord, who simultaneously appears to the multitudes as though he is being crucified.

> καὶ στὰς ὁ κύριός μου ἐν μέσῳ τοῦ σπηλαίου καὶ φωτίσας με εἶπεν· Ἰωάννη, τῷ κάτω ὄχλῳ ἐν Ἱεροσολύμοις σταυροῦμαι καὶ λόγχαις νύσσομαι καὶ καλάμοις, ὄξος τε καὶ χολὴν ποτίζομαι. σοὶ δὲ λαλῶ καὶ ὃ λαλῶ ἄκουσον.

> And my Lord stood in the middle of the cave, and illuminating me he said, 'John, to the multitude down below in Jerusalem I am being crucified, and being pierced with lances and reeds, and gall and vinegar is being given to me to drink. But to you I am speaking, and pay attention to what I say.' (*AJ* 97.7–10)

Although not totally explicit, the tone of the narrative suggests that what the crowd perceives is a mere semblance.[525] Much more forthright in its portrayal of the avoidance of suffering by the divine Christ is the conversation between Jesus and Peter that takes place during

---

[523] J.W. McCant, 'The Gospel of Peter: Docetism Reconsidered', *NTS* 30 (1984) 261.

[524] G. Buschmann, *Das Martyrium des Polykarp* (Gottingen: Vandenhoeck & Ruprecht, 1998).

[525] For a fuller discussion of this passage see the work of E. Junod and J.-D. Kaestli, *Acta Iohannis*, Tomus 2, 593.

the crucifixion as described in the Coptic *Apocalypse of Peter*.[526] In the
*Apocalypse*, Peter, observing the crucifixion, encounters three Jesus-
like figures.[527] Peter says,

> I saw him [i.e. Jesus] seemingly being seized by them. And I said, "What
> do I see, O Lord, that it is you yourself whom they take, and that you are
> grasping me? Or who is this one, glad and laughing on the tree? And is it
> another one whose feet and hands they are striking?" The Saviour said to
> me, "He whom you saw on the tree, glad and laughing is the living Jesus.
> But the one into whose hands and feet they drive nails is his fleshly part,
> which is the substitute being put to shame, the one who came into being
> in his likeness. But look at him and look at me. (*Apocalypse of Peter* 81,
> Nag Hammadi VII, 3)

Here it is possible to see the text presenting the real Jesus as totally
avoiding the pain and suffering of crucifixion. Instead, a physical form,
which is a mere chimera of the divine being, acts as a substitute and
endures the physical torment.

By contrast, even if the *Gospel of Peter* were depicting the departure
of the divine Christ from the human Jesus, the moment of separation
appears to come at far too late a stage. The point of such separation in
overtly docetic texts is to enable the divine being to avoid the taint of
passible experience. Having such a separation occur at the very end of
the crucifixion fails to deliver what docetic theology sought to promote,
namely the outlook that the divine Christ avoided suffering.[528] Instead,
the cry 'My power, the power, you have left me' (*Gos. Pet.* 5.19) is the
author's attempt to modify the problematic sense of God forsaken-
ness communicated by Jesus in the form of the cry of dereliction as it
is presented in the Matthean and Markan accounts (Matt 27.46; Mk
15.34). Rather, it simply is intended as announcing the moment of
death as the life-force leaves the now dead Jesus. Moreover, it needs to
be remembered that what is left behind, according to the perspective
of the author of the *Gospel of Peter* is not a mere physical shell. For
when the body of the Lord comes in contact with the earth the very

---

[526] This text is not to be confused with the Greek *Apocalypse of Peter* discovered in
the same codex as the *Gospel of Peter* in 1886/1887. The Coptic *Apocalypse of Peter* was
discovered as part of the Nag Hammadi corpus of texts sometime in late 1945.

[527] This point is also made by B. Ehrman, *Peter, Paul and Mary Magdalene: The Followers of Jesus in History and Legend* (Oxford: Oxford University Press, 2006) 46–47.

[528] See M. Slusser, 'Docetism: A Historical Definition', *Second Century* 1 (1981)
163–172.

ground reverberates as testimony the sanctity of the corpse which has been laid in contact with it.

The remaining three items listed by Swete as reflective of docetism require less detailed comment. In each case it is highly questionable whether these features are in any representative of a docetic theology. The suggestion that the representation of Jesus' 'death as ἀνάληψις'[529] is indicative of such an outlook is not compelling. The term ἀναλαμβάνω is used twice in the NT in post-resurrection context which describe the movement of Jesus' body.

Ὁ μὲν οὖν κύριος Ἰησοῦς μετὰ τὸ λαλῆσαι αὐτοῖς ἀνελήμφθη εἰς τὸν οὐρανὸν καὶ ἐκάθισεν ἐκ δεξιῶν τοῦ θεοῦ.

So then the Lord Jesus, after he had spoken to them, was taken up into heaven, and sat down at the right hand of God. (Mk 16.19)

οὗτος ὁ Ἰησοῦς ὁ ἀναλημφθεὶς ἀφ' ὑμῶν εἰς τὸν οὐρανὸν οὕτως ἐλεύσεται ὃν τρόπον ἐθεάσασθε αὐτὸν πορευόμενον εἰς τὸν οὐρανόν.

This Jesus, who was taken up from you into heaven, will come in the same way as you saw him go into heaven. (Acts 1.11b)

Both of these references depict the ascension rather than the moments following Jesus' death on the cross. This would appear to be the basis of Swete's designation of the phrase καὶ εἰπὼν ἀνελήφθη (Gos. Pet. 5.19) as docetic in nature, since it could be seen as transporting the Lord directly to heaven without the experience of the grave. A number of factors tell against taking this brief turn of phrase as a veiled reference to docetic theology. First, as McCant helpfully illustrates, the term Ἀνάληψις can mean death or decease as it does in Ps. Sol. 4.18 (τὸ γῆρας αὐτοῦ εἰς ἀνάληψιν).'[530] Secondly, later scenes in the gospel reveal that the author undoubtedly understood the Lord to be placed in a tomb and his resurrection to be effected by the two men who descend from heaven (Gos. Pet. 9.34–10.42). Thirdly, the author writes at a popular level and is unconcerned about precise distinctions between death or ascension terminology but happily confuses features of different events.[531]

---

[529] Swete, The Akhmîm Fragment, xxxviii.
[530] McCant, 'The Gospel of Peter: Docetism Reconsidered', 266.
[531] As Mara states, 'La confusion des moments est plutôt la compenetration d'un moment dans un autre; l'abandon et la mort deviennent des passages obligatoires,

The final two features listed by Swete have no distinctively docetic resonances, but rather reflect the popularizing trend that is so notable in the *Gospel of Peter*. The supernatural size of the figures which emerge from the tomb and the personification of the cross are depictions that can be found in other texts deemed to be orthodox. In particular 'cross-piety' is a growing phenomenon in late antique and medieval texts.[532] This discussion of the points listed by Swete, and subsequently followed by others, cannot be seen as sustaining the categorization of the text as docetic. The question remains as to how this aligns with Eusebius' testimony that Serapion eventually rejected the text because of such tendencies. First, it needs to be acknowledged that the form of the text we possess may not be the same as that available to Serapion (or for that matter, it needs to be remembered that P.Cair. 10759 may not even be the same text as Serapion's *Gospel of Peter*). However, perhaps a more likely solution may be found in the explanation that Serapion himself on initial inspection of the text at Rhossos did not recognize any docetic features contained within it. Only upon returning to Antioch did some of his advisers inform him that the text had the potential to be used by docetics to promote their teachings. This is a long way short of seeing the text itself as being the product of docetic thinking.

## 10.6. *Polymorphic Christology*

An overlooked feature in the study of early christological understanding is what may be denoted as 'polymorphic Christology'.[533] This term is used to designate the manner in which Jesus is able to appear in differing, or multiple forms. Junod has defined this phenomenon as: 'Polymorphism is a deliberate appearance of somebody in multiple forms; the change in forms is not hidden, on the contrary it is made obvious for the sake of witness.'[534] While it is argued below that it is a case of overdifferentiating to split polymorphy, appearing simultaneously

---

mais ce sont des passages, en vue du retour dont parle Matt. 26:54.' Mara, *Évangile de Pierre*, 220.

[532] See the discussion of G.Pet. 10.39, 42 in the commentary section.

[533] In the classic treatment analyzing views of Jesus in the New Testament, O. Cullmann, *The Christology of the New Testament*, no attention is given to Jesus ability to appear in multiple forms as being part of the Christological reflection contained in these texts.

[534] 'Or la polymorphie est une apparition délibérée de quelqu'un sous plusieurs formes; le changement de formes n'est pas dissimulé, il est au contraire rendu évident

in multiple forms, and metamorphosis, appearing in a changed form, such a separation of these two aspects has been suggested. Lalleman has argued that polymorphy is in fact a subset of the category of metamorphic appearances.

> To put it more exactly, polymorphy is part of the wider concept of metamorphosis or shape shifting, which is the idea that a person or thing (usually a deity) can at any moment assume another form, stature or age...Polymorphy is a metamorphosis of such a kind that the person or deity can be seen differently by different people *at the same time.*[535]

While such precision is not unhelpful, splitting the categories to this extent has the potential to exclude important data from the discussion. For this reason polymorphy will be treated more loosely, and changes of form will be considered alongside simultaneous appearances in multiple form. Methodologically, this is valid since it can be argued that the ability to transform into another state in fact attests that the being has multiple states, or is polymorphous. Yet even more significantly when the evidence from the *Acts of Thomas* is considered, it will be seen that this text uses the term polymorphous, πολύμορφος, to refer not to an appearance in multiple forms, but to describe a change in form, that is what on the above definition would be classified as metamorphosis.[536] This direct textual evidence undercuts the distinction between metamorphosis and polymorphy suggested by Lalleman.

Such polymorphic appearances are reported chiefly, but not exclusively, in post-resurrection contexts. One of the main aspects of such christological formulations is to emphasize that Jesus is not constrained by the material world. This perspective meant that views of Christ that encompassed polymorphism were particularly attractive to docetic or gnostic groups, since it aided their assertions that the substance of Christ was not of the same order as the rest of the material world. Yet, polymorphic understandings of Jesus were also attractive in orthodox writings, often in a more restrained form, especially for describing resurrection encounters, since it was a way of communicating Jesus' transcendence over the realm of death.

---

pour le témoin.' E. Junod, 'Polymorphie du Dieu Sauveur', in J. Ries (ed.), *Gnosticisme et Monde Hellénistique* (Louvain-la Neuve, 1982) 38–46.

[535] P.J. Lalleman, 'Polymorphy of Christ', in J.N. Bremner (ed.), *The Apocryphal Acts of John* (Kampen: Kok Pharos, 1995) 99.

[536] See *Acts of Thomas* 48, 153.

As part of the depiction of the actual moment of resurrection in the *Gospel of Peter*, the body of Jesus is described as having undergone a miraculous transformation.

> 39. καὶ ἐξηγουμένων αὐτῶν ἃ εἶδον πάλιν ὅρασιν ἐξελθόντος ἀπὸ τοῦ τάφου τρεῖς ἄνδρες καὶ τοὺς δύο τὸν ἕνα ὑπορθοῦντας καὶ σταυρὸν ἀκολοθοῦντα αὐτοῖς. 40. καὶ τῶν μὲν δύο τὴν κεφαλὴν χωροῦσαν μέχρι τοῦ οὐρανοῦ, τοῦ δὲ χειραγωγουμένου ὑπ' αὐτῶν ὑπερβαίνουσαν τοὺς οὐρανούς.

> 39. While they were reporting what they had seen, again they saw coming out from the tomb three men, and the two were supporting the one, and a cross following them. 40. And the head of the two reached as far as heaven, but that of the one being led by them surpassed the heavens.[537]

It needs to be acknowledged that the *Gospel of Peter* is theologically an unsophisticated text, and it provides minimal reflection on the heightened miraculous depictions it narrates. Nonetheless, there is an implicit Christology that is communicated through the vision of Jesus and his two attendants having enlarged heads.[538] Again, occurring in a resurrection or post-resurrection context, bodily metamorphosis is used to stress that the raised figure no longer belongs exclusively to the earthly realm. In this scene where resurrection and ascension are compressed, the two attendants, who earlier were described as descending from heaven, form part of a victorious procession returning to their place of origin.[539] The comparison of the relative dimensions of the heads of the three figures is also a primitive way to denote the status of the two men in contrast to that of the one whom they support. While they have cephalic contact with the heavens, the head of the now risen Christ surpasses the heavens. This is not primarily a designation of the

---

[537] The translation is taken from the commentary section.

[538] Bodily metamorphosis is also recorded as happening to figures other than Jesus. In a text rarely cited, *The Gospel of the Twelve Apostles*, apparently dating from the eighth century, in the section relating the 'Revelation of Simeon Kepha', Peter has his body enlarged: 'And Simeon was moved by the Spirit of God: and his appearance and body were enlarged.' See J.R. Harris (ed.), *The Gospel of the Twelve Apostles: Together with the Apocalypses of Each One of Them* (London: CUP, 1900/reprinted, Piscataway, NJ: Gorgias Press, 2002) 31.

[539] As Vaganay observes, 'On s'attend à une resurrection triomphale et voici que le Christ apparait soutenu par ses compagnons.' L. Vaganay, *L'Évangile de Pierre*, 297.

subservience of the two accompanying figures, rather it emphasizes the supremacy of Jesus in the heavens.

Although in some regards Jesus' form resembles that of the two accompanying figures, this should not be understood as an angelomorphic Christology.[540] This categorization is not dismissed for the facile reason that the text of the *Gospel of Peter* refrains from labelling the accompanying figures as 'angels', since they are certainly understood as heavenly envoys.[541] Rather, angelomorphic Christology is not an appropriate designation in this context because the author seeks to distance the central figure from the attendants by the quantitative difference in the body enlargement he experiences in comparison to that of the two heavenly figures. Hence, for the author of this text, what is significant is not Jesus being metamorphized into a form similar to that of his attendants, but rather that the change in physical form denotes the now unbounded nature of his being. Jesus is no longer trapped in the tomb, he has been released from death and raised beyond the constraints of purely physical existence. Therefore, in this context, polymorphism is a vivid way of depicting the interface between the previously earthbound Jesus and his new status in the heavens. So in essence, here the transformation of physical form communicates that Jesus is no longer limited by the force of death. Moreover, by his resurrection and corresponding bodily metamorphosis it is demonstrated that he has been instantiated in the heavenly sphere.

## 11. Conclusions: Possible Dating and Place of Origin

As will be seen from the foregoing discussion a number of alternatives have been suggested for the dating of the archetype that lies behind the first document contained in the Akhmîm codex. The location of the composition of the document is far more problematic, and consequently there has been less discussion surrounding the place of origin

---

[540] The whole question of 'angelomorphic Christology' is contested. Rowland has convincing argued that imagery associated with angelophanies was appropriated into early christological formulations. See C.C. Rowland, 'A Man Clothed in Linen: Daniel 10.6ff. and Jewish Angelology' *JSNT* 24 (1985) 99–110. The assessment and critique offered by K. Sullivan is invaluable, K. Sullivan, *Wrestling with Angels: A Study of the Relationship Between Humans and Angels in Ancient Jewish Literature and the New Testament*, AGJU 55 (Leiden: Brill, 2005) 231–235.

[541] Swete, *The Akhmîm Fragment*, 17.

of this document. This section advances tentative conclusions for each of these questions, which have arisen out of consideration of the internal evidence of the text, external testimony in patristic sources and general tendencies in early Christianity.

## 11.1. *Dating*

It has been apparent in the survey of scholarship and the discussion concerning the literary relationship with canonical gospels and early Christian writers that much diversity of opinion exists in relation to the date of original composition. Perhaps the earliest dating suggested thus far is provided by Mirecki who states that the '*Gospel of Peter*...circulated in the mid-1st century...An earlier form of the gospel probably served as one of the major sources for the canonical gospels.'[542] Precisely how much earlier this early form may be is not stated, but Mirecki's suggestion dates the text to no more than about fifteen years after the events of the crucifixion.

A far more nuanced and reflective statement in support of a first century origin of the major source that is seen as being embedded in the *Gospel of Peter* is articulated in the many works of Crossan on this subject.[543] While he sees the Cross Gospel, which accounts for approximately eighty percent of the material contained in the first document of the Akhmîm codex, as a source independent of the canonical accounts, he nonetheless finds obvious traces of dependence on canonical gospel material in the final form of the *Gospel of Peter*. This is viewed as being due to later redactional reworking of the Cross Gospel. While Crossan does not date this final phase editorial retouching, he nonetheless raises an interesting methodological problem. The issue is at what point is it legitimate to speak of the date of composition of a document that has various stages of redaction and embeds literary sources. Thus, is dating the *Gospel of Peter* to the first century because it contains a Cross Gospel source any more legitimate than arguing Matthew schould be dated to around 70 CE because it incorporates Mark's account? This raises the whole question of when a document that is to some extent a rolling corpus becomes a finished

---

[542] Mirecki, 'Peter, Gospel of', in D.N. Freedman (ed.) *The Anchor Bible Dictionary*, volume 5, 278–281.

[543] Crossan, *The Cross That Spoke*; and Crossan, 'The Gospel of Peter and the Canonical Gospels: Independence, Dependence, or Both?'.

product, and whether it is meaningful to speak of a publication date for such a text. Such issues even more obviously surround the *Gospel of Thomas*.[544] However, it has been argued at some length that the case for the dependence of the canonical gospels upon material embedded in the *Gospel of Peter* is not particularly strong, and in fact the tradition history of the material contained in the *Gospel of Peter* is better explained be suggesting that the first document in the Akhmîm codex is itself dependent on the canonical accounts.

The majority of critical scholarship, despite the challenges raised by Crossan and other, still prefers to locate the text in the second century. Yet even here there is great divergence concerning how early or late it is to be placed. In essence the decision rests upon perceived literary relationships with the writings of individuals such as Justin Martyr,[545] Mileto of Sardis[546] and other second century figures. Interestingly, a recurring phenomenon is the tendency to assume that once a case for literary relationship has been argued that this proves that the *Gospel of Peter* is the source text. Thus, the direction of dependence is rarely argued. Instead it is taken as self-evident that the *Gospel of Peter* is behind the writings where similar traditions are detected. However, apart from this fundamental methodological weakness, the analysis of the parallels from second century texts proved to be at best elusive, and in reality virtually non-existent. This leaves the tradition preserved in Eusebius concerning the late second century, early third century episcopal figure Serapion as the earliest external evidence for a text known as the *Gospel of Peter*. Thus most scholars argue that the text must have been written prior to *circa* 190 CE. While this still remains the most plausible explanation a number of caveats need to be considered. First, it requires that the tradition preserved by Eusebius is accurate. It is the case that at points there is reason to question the transmission of traditions by Eusebius, but there is no particular reason to doubt the information at this point. In fact, the observation that Eusebius' own editorial comments about the *Gospel of Peter* do not fully align with the source he cites actually lends weight to the suggestion that he has transmitted a received tradition accurately, rather than invented mate-

---

[544] A. DeConick, *Recovering the Original* Gospel of Thomas: *A History of the Gospel and its Growth* (LNTS [JSNTS] 286, London: T&T Clark International, A Continuum Imprint, 2005).

[545] Pilhofer, 'Justin und das Petrusevangelium' 60–78.

[546] Perler, 'L'Évangile de Pierre et Méliton de Sardes', 584–590.

rial to support his own theological stance. Secondly, while Serapion refers to the *So-called Gospel of Peter* the text from Akhmîm has no title, so it remains an assumption of modern scholarship that the two texts are identical. Thirdly, it needs to be remembered that the fragment P.Oxy. 2949, which dates to approximately late second to early third century, while showing affinities with P.Cair. 10759 also contains extensive points of deviation. This final point raises the question of whether P.Oxy. 2949 represents an independent tradition that was also shared by the Akhmîm text, or if it evidences a different stage in the evolution of the text discovered interred in the burial site. It is therefore not impossible, although less likely, that the text from Akhmîm is not entirely the same text-form as referred to by Serapion. If that were the case then the dating is a far more open issue and theoretically the text could have been composed at any stage up until shortly prior to the writing of the Akhmîm manuscript perhaps as late as the seventh century.

While this needs to be recognized as a possibility, and scholars have too quickly made the identification between the text mentioned by Serapion and the first document in the Akhmîm codex, that position, nonetheless, still remains the most likely explanation. This being the case, then the *Gospel of Peter* would have been composed prior to the end of the episcopate of Serapion who is usually dates as bishop of Antioch are usually given in there widest extent as 189–211 CE.[547] Scholars have usually favoured placing the reported visit to Rhossos during the last decade of the second century. While the reason for this is not usually stated, it appears to arise from doubts concerning the official succession lists for the Patriarchiate of Antioch which have Serapion in office without a break until Ascelpiades the Confessor, his next known successor, follows as bishop. Many scholars seem to

---

[547] The *ODCC* places the year of Serapion's death in 211, but states, 'Bp. of Antioch from 199' (1495). By contrast Swete, following Lightfoot states 'Serapion's episcopate began between AD 189 and 192: the year of his death is less certain, but he seems to be living during the persecution of the Church by Septimus Severus (AD 202–3).' Swete, *The Akhmîm Fragment*, x. Without comment, Robinson baldly states, 'Serapion was Bishop of Antioch 190–203', Robinson & James, *The Gospel according to Peter, and the Revelation of Peter*, 15. The succession lists for the Patriarchiate of Antioch list Serapion as ascending to episcopal office in 191, following Maximus I and succeeded by Ascelpiades the Confessor in 211. Although various branches of Orthodox Christianity now claim the office of Patriarch of Antioch, their succession lists agree up to various points of division. This does not result is any difference in the dates for Serapion. See: http://sor.cua.edu/Patriarchate/PatriarchsChronList.html

assume that he died around 202–203, as part of the persecutions under Septimus Severus. Again it is possible to speak of only approximate datings. While there is general assent that the *Gospel of Peter* was composed prior to Serapion's ascension to the episcopate, the length of time it must have been in circulation prior to this is highly speculative and ultimately inconclusive. Assumptions about the length of time a document must be in circulation before it can attain status in a community are inconclusive and highly speculative arguments.[548]

Hence in conclusion, based on the assumption that the first document in the Akhmîm codex is a close approximation to the text that Serapion encountered on his visit to Rhossos, the composition of the *So-called Gospel of Peter* took place prior to the end of the second century. In the face of lack of evidence it seems ill-advised to push this dating unnecessarily early in this period, so a date some time in the second half of the second century is perhaps to be preferred. This was still a period in which there was an interest in gospel traditions, and the composition of infancy and other traditions flourished during this period, as it did in the third and subsequent centuries. Thus a date of composition during the period 150–190 CE seems the most sensible suggestion. Without further evidence this range cannot be narrowed or pushed earlier. In fact the apparent lack of knowledge of this text in the writings of the Apostolic Fathers, Justin Martyr or Melito of Sardis means that attempts to date the text to the first half of the second century stand in tension with the surving, but admittedly limited textual evidence of early Christian writers.

## 11.2. *Place of Composition*

While there has been ongoing debate surrounding dating, there has been relatively little discussion of the place of origin of the *Gospel of Peter*. This is in marked distinction to such questions being asked of the canonical gospel, the *Gospel of Thomas* and other early Christian texts. All that can be stated with certainty is that Eusebius believed (probably correctly) that Rhossos was a location were a text known as the *Gospel of Peter* was read, and that several centuries later a text that may be largely identical with the text that Serapion encountered

---

[548] For this type of reasoning see Gardner-Smith, 'The Gospel of Peter', 403. Here he assumes that at least twenty years is require before a document can attain the status of being an authority among a community.

had been buried in a presumably Christian grave at Akhmîm in Upper Egypt. Therefore, it is possible to speak only of two locations as foci of reception for what is probably the same text. While Swete does not explicitly discuss the place of origin, he notes that '[i]t is natural to infer that the circulation of the Gospel before AD 190 was very limited, and probably confined to the party from which it emanated.'[549] This may mean that Swete saw the gospel as being composed in Rhossos itself, or at least not too distant from that location. However, this is not stated explicitly by Swete. Both Vaganay[550] and Harnack[551] discuss the link with Rhossos as a centre of reception, but make no comment concerning the place of composition.

Within the text there is no real clue given as to the place of writing. There are no helpful geographical details that shown a specific awareness of Judean or Galilean topography. In fact this lack of detail may well count against seeing either of these two areas as being the place of composition of the text. The language of the text offers little help. Greek was widely spoken in the Eastern Mediterranean, urban centres in Egypt, and even in Rome. The fact that the canonical gospels were written in Greek (and it has been argued that the *Gospel of Peter* is dependent on these texts and consequently originally composed in Greek as is supported by the surviving text) might account for the choice of language rather than being related to any geographical location.

Perhaps the only possibility other than an absolute guess is that the text first surfaced somewhere near its place where it is first evidenced, in this case either in Rhossos or its environs. This becomes a little more likely the later one places the composition of the text in the second century, since this lessens the time for circulation (however, as has been noted texts could circulately widely in a very short period of time). Also the links between Syrian and Eygptian monasticism are well known from the late third and early fourth century onwards.[552] Thus various sayings of the desert fathers which seem to have a Syrian

---

[549] Swete, *The Akhmîm Fragment*, xi.

[550] Vaganay, *L'Évangile de Pierre*, 1–8.

[551] Harnack, *Bruchstücke des Evangeliums und der Apokalypse des Petrus*, 4–5.

[552] Anson note the almost simultaneous rise of monasticism in the Egyptian and Syrian contexts. 'It appears that there were men leading an ascetic life around Antioch and Beroea, also anchorites and hermits in the mountains, fairly soon after the first eremetical colonies had made their appearance in the Egyptian deserts.' P. Anson, *The Call of the Desert* (London: SPCK, 1964) 37.

provenance are found in Egyptian documents.[553] Perhaps these same communication channels enabled the text of the *Gospel of Peter* to be spread from an original Syrian context to a monastic community based at Akhmîm. This would not only explain the link between the two known centres of reception, but may also explain the knowledge of the text possessed by Origen and Didymus the Blind, who both had contacts with monastic communities during their lives. The former may have had such contacts both in Alexandria and in a Palestinian context, while Didymus operated in an Egyptian context. Such speculations go beyond what is suggested by the available evidence, but they do offer a plausible possibility, even if it remains ultimately unprovable.

---

[553] Benedicta Ward observes, 'In Palestine, Syria and Asia Minor there were also Christians who were involved with the ascetic life in its monastic forms, and some stories and sayings from these areas are occasionally found among the Egyptian sources.' B. Ward, *Wisdom of the Desert Fathers* (Oxford: SLG Press, [new edition] 1985) ix.

TEXT

# THE PHOTOGRAPHS OF P.CAIR. 10759 WITH FACING TRANSCRIPTION

The photographs of P.Cair. 10759 are reproduced here with a transcription of the text on the right-hand facing page. The superscripted numbers in the transcription refer to the text critical notes that can be found in the relevant section of the commentary. The numbering of these text critical notes recommences at one at the beginning of each of the fourteen pericopae into which the text is traditionally divided.

Special thanks must be expressed to Dr. Adam Bülow-Jacobsen (AIP-archive), the photographer of these plates, who gave permission to use these images.

The images are also available online at: http://ipap.csad.ox.ac.uk/GP/GP.html.

*P.Cair.* 10759 f.1v

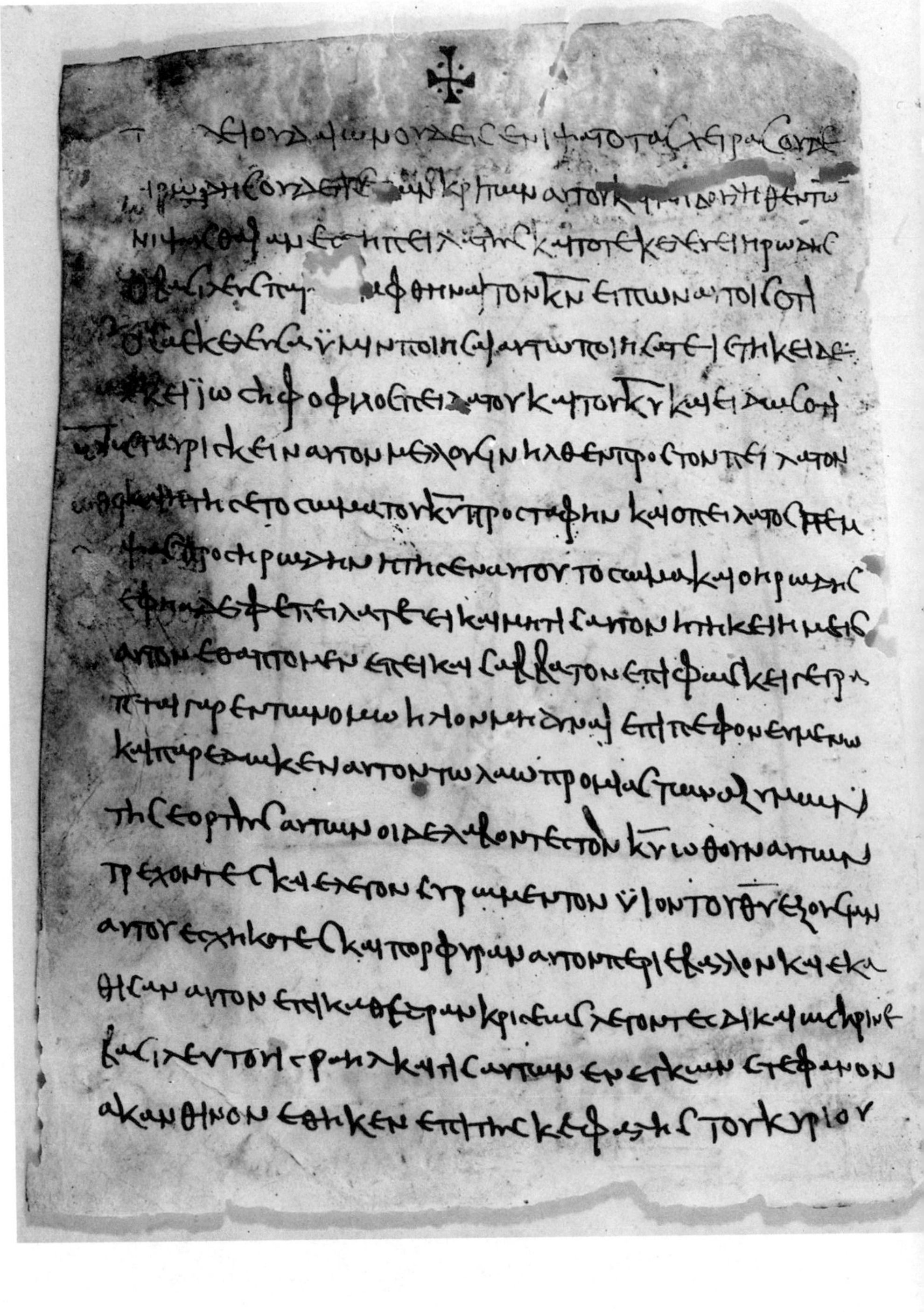

Page 2

1.1. τ[ῶν][1] δὲ Ἰουδαίων οὐδεὶς ἐνίψατο τὰς χεῖρας, οὐδὲ
Ἡρῴδης οὐδ᾽ εἷς[2] [τ]ῶν κριτῶν αὐτοῦ. καὶ[3] [μὴ] βουληθέντω(ν)
νίψασθαι, ἀνέστη Πειλᾶτος. 2. καὶ τότε κελεύει Ἡρῴδης
ὁ βασιλεὺς παρ[αλη]μφθῆναι[4] τὸν κ̅ν̅[5], εἰπὼν αὐτοῖς ὅτι·
5    Ὅσα ἐκέλευσα ὑμῖν[6] ποιῆσαι αὐτῷ, ποιήσατε. 2.3. ἱστήκει[1] δὲ
ἐκεῖ Ἰωσὴφ[2] ὁ φίλος Πειλάτου[3] καὶ τοῦ κ̅υ̅.[4] καὶ εἰδὼς ὅτι
σταυρίσκειν[6] αὐτὸν μέλλουσιν, ἦλθεν πρὸς τὸν Πειλᾶτον
καὶ ἤτησε[8] τὸ σῶμα τοῦ κ̅υ̅ πρὸς ταφήν. 4. καὶ ὁ Πειλᾶτος πέμ
ψας[9] πρὸς Ἡρῴδην ἤτησεν αὐτοῦ τὸ σῶμα. 5. καὶ ὁ Ἡρῴδης
10   ἔφη·[10] ἀδελφὲ Πειλᾶτε, εἰ καὶ μή τις[11] αὐτὸν ἠτήκει, ἡμεῖς
αὐτὸν ἐθάπτομεν, ἐπεὶ καὶ σάββατον[12] ἐπιφώσκει· γέγρα
πται γὰρ ἐν τῷ νόμῳ ἥλιον μὴ δῦναι ἐπὶ πεφονευμένῳ
καὶ παρέδωκεν αὐτὸν τῷ λαῷ πρὸ μιᾶς τῶν ἀζύμων,
τῆς ἑορτῆς αὐτῶν. 3.6. Οἱ δὲ λαβόντες τὸν κ̅υ̅[1,2] ὤθουν αὐτῶν[3]
15   τρέχοντες καὶ[4] ἔλεγον· Σύρωμεν[5] τὸν υἱὸν[6] τοῦ θ̅υ̅,[7] ἐξουσίαν
αὐτοῦ ἐσχηκότες. 7. καὶ πορφύραν αὐτὸν περιέβαλλον[8], καὶ ἐκά
θισαν αὐτὸν ἐπὶ καθέδραν[9] κρίσεως, λέγοντες· Δικαίως κρῖνε,
βασιλεῦ τοῦ Ἰσραήλ. 8. καί τις αὐτῶν ἐνεγκὼν στέφανον
ἀκάνθινον ἔθηκεν ἐπὶ τῆς κεφαλῆς τοῦ κυρίου

*P.Cair.* 10759 f.2r

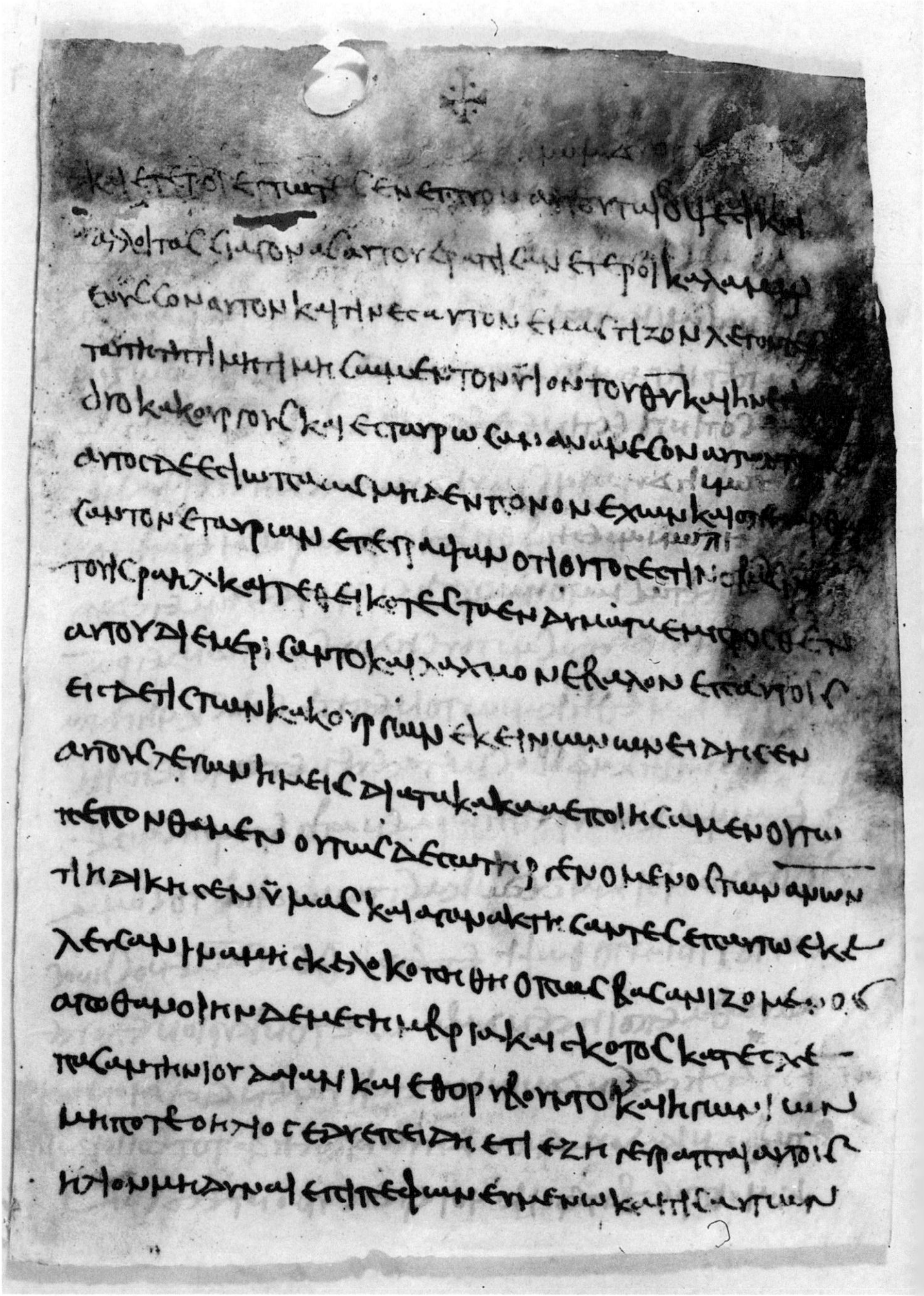

Page 3

9. καὶ ἕτεροι ἑστῶτες¹⁰ ἐνέπτυον αὐτοῦ ταῖ˥¹¹ ὄψεσι, καὶ

ἄλλοι¹² τὰς σιαγόνας αὐτοῦ ἐράπισαν ἕτεροι¹³ καλάμῳ

ἔνυσσον αὐτὸν καί τινες αὐτὸν ἐμάστιζον λέγοντες·

ταύτῃ τῇ τιμῇ τιμήσωμεν τὸν υἱὸν¹⁴ τοῦ θ̅υ̅.¹⁵ 4.10. καὶ¹ ἤνεγκον²

5    δύο³ κακούργους⁴ καὶ ἐσταύρωσαν⁵ ἀνὰ⁶ μέσον αὐτῶν τὸν κ̅ν̅⁷.

αὐτὸς δὲ ἐσιώπα⁸ ὡς μηδέν πόνον ἔχων. 11. καὶ ὅτε⁹ ὤρθω

σαν¹⁰ τὸν σταυρὸν ἐπέγραψαν ὅτι οὗτός ἐστιν ὁ βασιλεὺς¹¹

τοῦ Ἰσραήλ. 12. καὶ τεθεικότες¹² τὰ ἐνδύματα ἔμπροσθεν¹³

αὐτοῦ διεμερίσαντο καὶ λαχμὸν ἔβαλον ἐπ᾽ αὐτοῖς.

10    13. εἷς δέ τις τῶν κακούργων ἐκείνων ὠνείδησεν¹⁴

αὐτοὺς λέγων· Ἡμεῖς διὰ τὰ κακὰ ἃ ἐποιήσαμεν οὕτω

πεπόνθαμεν, οὕτως¹⁵ δὲ σωτὴρ γενόμενος τῶν α̅ν̅ω̅ν̅¹⁶

τί ἠδίκησεν ὑμᾶς; 14. καὶ ἀγανακτήσαντες ἐπ᾽ αὐτῷ ἐκέ

λευσαν ἵνα μὴ σκελοκοπηθῇ¹⁷ ὅπως βασανιζόμενος

15    ἀποθάνοι. 5.15. Ἦν δὲ μεσημβρία, καὶ σκότος κατέσχε(ν)¹

πᾶσαν τὴν Ἰουδαίαν· καὶ ἐθορυβοῦντο καὶ ἠγωνίων

μήποτε ὁ ἥλιος ἔδυ, ἐπειδὴ ἔτι ἔζη· γέγραπται αὐτοῖς

ἥλιον μὴ δῦναι ἐπὶ πεφωνευμένῳ.¹ 16. καί τις αὐτῶν

P.Cair. 10759 f.2v

Page 3

εἶπεν· Ποτίσατε αὐτὸν χολὴν μετὰ ὄξους· καὶ κερά

σαντες ἐπότισαν. 17. καὶ ἐπλήρωσαν πάντα καὶ ἐτε

λείωσαν κατὰ τῆς κεφαλῆς αὐτῶν τὰ ἁμαρτήμα

τα. 18. περιήρχοντο δὲ πολλοὶ μετὰ λύχνων νομίζον

5  τες ὅτι νύξ ἐστιν ἐπέσαντο.[2] 19. καὶ ὁ κ̅ς̅ ἀνεβόησε

λέγων· Ἡ δύναμίς μου ἡ δύναμις κατέλειψάς με

καὶ εἰπὼν ἀνελήφθη. 20. καὶ αὐτός[3] ὥρας διεράγη τὸ

καταπέτασμα τοῦ ναοῦ τῆς Ἰερουσαλὴμ εἰς δύο.

6.21. καὶ τότε ἀπέσπασαν[1] τοὺς ἥλους ἀπὸ τῶν χειρῶ(ν)[2]

10  τοῦ κ̅υ̅[3] καὶ ἔθηκαν[4] αὐτὸν ἐπὶ τῆς γῆς·[5] καὶ ἡ γῆ πᾶ

σα[6] ἐσείσθη καὶ φόβος[7] μέγας ἐγένετο.[8] 22. τότε ἥλιος

ἔλαμψε καὶ εὑρέθη ὥρα ἐνάτη. 23. ἐχάρησαν δὲ

οἱ Ἰουδαῖοι καὶ δεδώκασι[ν][9] τῷ Ἰωσὴφ τὸ σῶμα

αὐτοῦ ἵνα[10] αὐτὸ θάψῃ ἐπειδὴ θεασάμενος ἦν ὅσ

15  α[11] ἀγαθὰ ἐποίησεν. 24. λαβὼν δὲ τὸν κύριον ἔλουσε[12]

καὶ εἴλησε[13] σινδόνιν[14] καὶ εἰσήγαγεν εἰς ἴδιον

τάφον καλούμενον κῆπον Ἰωσήφ. 7.25. τότε οἱ Ἰουδαῖοι[1]

καὶ οἱ πρεσβύτεροι καὶ οἱ ἱερεῖς[2] γνόντες[3] οἷον

*P.Cair.* 10759 f.3f

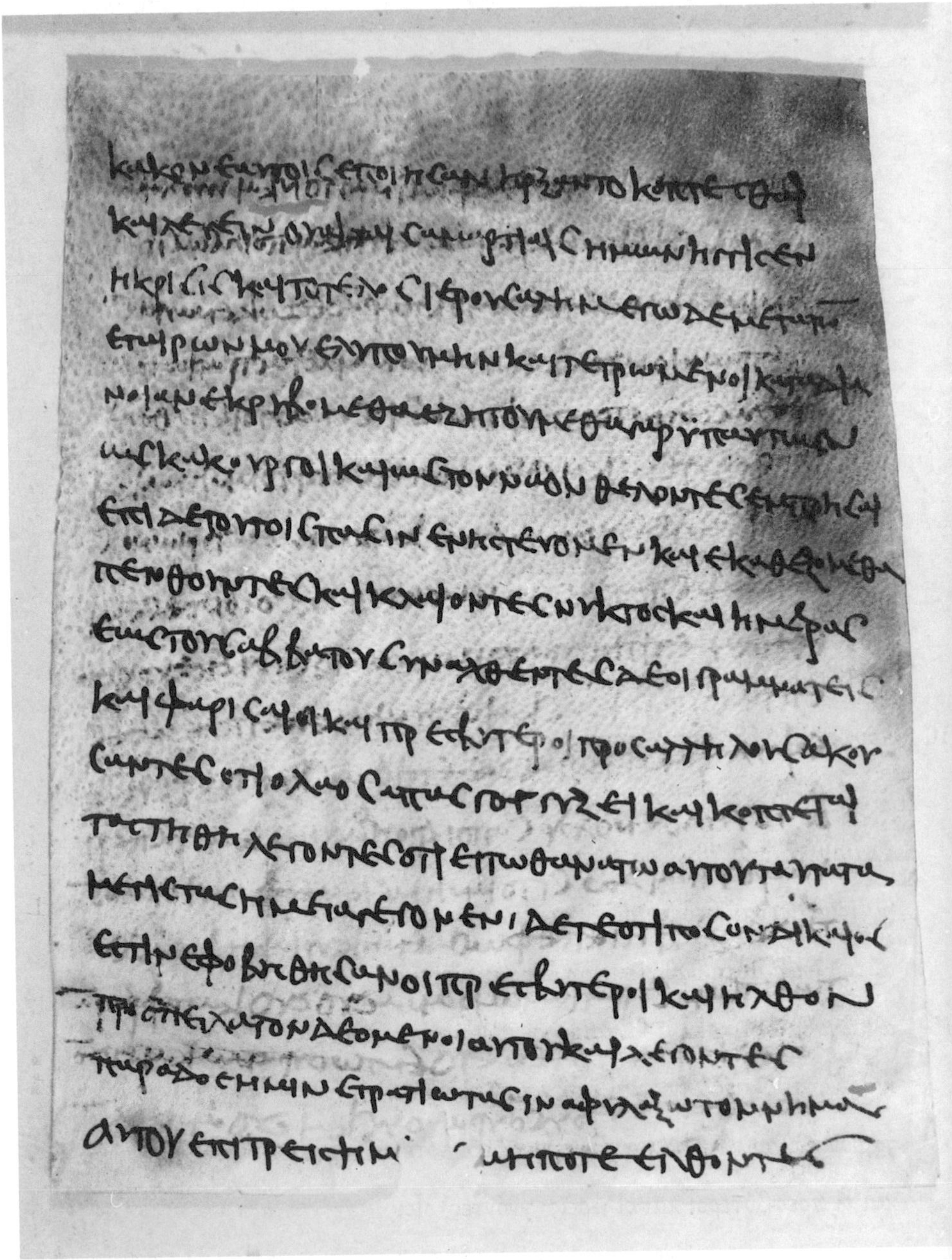

Page 4

κακὸν ἑαυτοῖς ἐποίησαν, ἤρξαντο[4] κόπτεσθαι

καὶ λέγειν· οὐαί ταῖς[5] ἁμαρτίαις ἡμῶν· ἤγγισεν

ἡ κρίσις καὶ τὸ τέλος Ἰερουσαλήμ. 26. ἐγὼ δὲ μετὰ τῶ(ν)[6]

ἑταίρων μου ἐλυπούμην καὶ τετρωμένοι κατὰ διά

5  νοιαν ἐκρυβόμεθα. ἐζητούμεθα γὰρ[7] ὑπ' αὐτῶν

ὡς κακοῦργοι καὶ ὡς τὸν ναὸν θέλοντες ἐμπρῆσαι.[8]

27. ἐπὶ δὲ τούτοις πᾶσιν ἐνηστεύομεν καὶ ἐκαθεζόμεθα[9]

πενθοῦντες καὶ κλαίοντες νυκτὸς καὶ ἡμέρας

ἕως τοῦ σαββάτου. 8.28. συναχθέντες δὲ οἱ γραμματεῖς

10  καὶ Φαρισαῖοι καὶ πρεσβύτεροι πρὸς ἀλλήλους[1] ἀκού

σαντες ὅτι ὁ λαὸς[2] ἅπας[3] γογγύζει καὶ κόπτεται[4]

τὰ στήθη λέγοντες ὅτι, εἰ τῷ θανάτῳ αὐτοῦ ταῦτα τὰ

μέγιστα σημεῖα γέγονεν, ἴδετε ὅτι πόσον δίκαιός

ἐστιν. 29. ἐφοβήθησαν οἱ πρεσβύτεροι καὶ ἦλθον

15  πρὸς Πειλᾶτον δεόμενοι αὐτοῦ καὶ λέγοντες·

30. Παράδος ἡμῖν στρατιώτας, ἵνα φυλάξω[5] τὸ μνῆμα[6]

αὐτοῦ ἐπὶ τρεῖς ἡμ[έρας][7] μήποτε ἐλθόντες

*P.Cair.* 10759 f.3v

οιμαθηταιαυτουκαεφωσιναυτονκαιπολλοι
ολλοσοτεκνεκρωναυεστηκαιποιησωσιν
ημινκακαοδεπειλατοσπυρασεδωκεναυτοισ
πετρωνιοντονκεντυριωναμεταστρατιωτων
φυλασσειντοντραφονκαι συναυτοισηλθον
πρεσβυτεροικαι γραμματεισ επιτομνημακαι
κυλισαντεσλιθονμεγανκατατουκεντυριωνοσ
κυτωνστρατιωτωνομοιπαντεσοιοντεσεκει
εθηκαν επιτηθυρατουμνηματοσκαι επεχρισαν
επτασφραγιδασκαι σκηνηνεκειπηξαντεσ
εφυλαξαντπρωιασδε επεφωσκοντοσσαββατου
ηλθοχλοσαπο ιεροσολυμωνκαιτησπερι
χωρουιναιδωσιτομνημειον εσφραγισμενο
τηδενυκτιηι επεφωσκενηκυριακηφυλασσον
τωντωνστρατιωτωνανα δυοδυοκαταφρουρα
μεγαληφωνη εγενετο εντωουρανωκαιειδο
ανοιχθεντεστουσουρανουσκαι δυοανδρασ

Page 5

οἱ⁸ μαθηταὶ αὐτοῦ κλέψωσιν αὐτὸν καὶ ὑπολάβῃ⁹

ὁ λαὸς ὅτι ἐκ νεκρῶν ἀνέστη, καὶ ποιήσωσιν

ἡμῖν κακά. 31. ὁ δὲ Πειλᾶτος παραδέδωκεν αὐτοῖς

Πετρώνιον τὸν κεντυρίωνα μετὰ στρατιωτῶν¹⁰

5  φυλάσσειν¹¹ τὸν τάφον. καὶ σὺν αὐτοῖς ἦλθον

πρεσβύτεροι καὶ γραμματεῖς ἐπὶ τὸ μνῆμα. 32. καὶ

κυλίσαντες¹² λίθον μέγαν κατὰ¹³ τοῦ κεντυρίωνος

καὶ τῶν στρατιωτῶν ὁμοῦ πάντες οἱ ὄντες ἐκεῖ

ἔθηκαν ἐπὶ τῇ θύρᾳ τοῦ μνήματος. 33. καὶ ἐπέχρεισαν¹⁴

10  ἑπτὰ σφραγῖδας καὶ σκηνὴν ἐκεῖ πήξαντες

ἐφύλαξαν. 9.34. πρωΐας δὲ ἐπιφώσκοντος τοῦ σαβ

βάτου ἦλθεν ὄχλος ἀπὸ Ἰερουσαλὴμ¹ καὶ τῆς περι

χώρου ἵνα ἴδωσι² τὸ μνημεῖον ἐσφραγισμένο(ν)³.

35. τῇ δὲ νυκτὶ ᾗ⁴ ἐπέφωσκεν ἡ⁵ κυριακή, φυλασσόν

15  των τῶν στρατιωτῶν⁶ ἀνὰ δύο⁷ δύο κατὰ φρουρά(ν),⁸

μεγάλη φωνὴ ἐγένετο ἐν τῷ οὐρανῷ. 36. καὶ εἶδο(ν)

ἀνοιχθέντες τοὺς οὐρά[ν]ους⁹ καὶ δύο ἄνδρας

*P.Cair.* 10759 f.4r

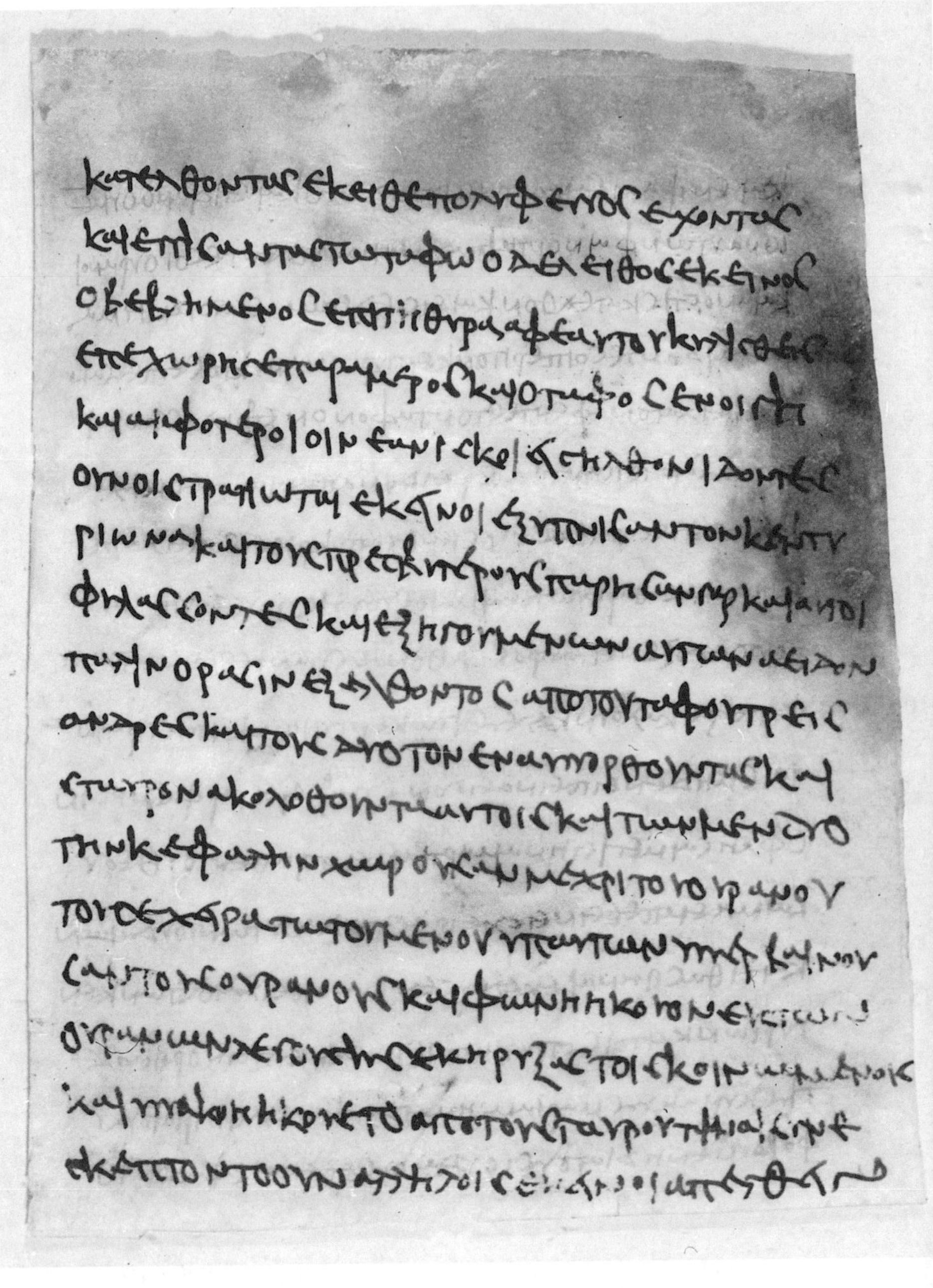

Page 6

κατελθόντας ἐκεῖθε πολὺ φέγγος ἔχοντας

καὶ ἐγγίσαντας¹⁰ τῷ τάφῳ. 37. ὁ δὲ λείθος¹¹ ἐκεῖνος

ὁ βεβλημένος¹² ἐπὶ τῇ θύρᾳ ἀφ' ἑαυτοῦ κυλισθεὶς

ἐπεχώρησε¹³ παρὰ μέρος καὶ ὁ τάφος ἐνοίγη¹⁴

5 καὶ ἀμφότεροι οἱ νεανίσκοι εἰσῆλθον¹⁵. 10.38. ἰδόντες

οὖν οἱ στρατιῶται ἐκεῖνοι¹ ἐξύπνισαν² τὸν κεντυ

ρίωνα καὶ τοὺς πρεσβυτέρους· παρῆσαν γὰρ καὶ αὐτοὶ

φυλάσσοντες. 39. καὶ ἐξηγουμένων αὐτῶν ἃ εἶδον

πάλιν³ ὅρασιν⁴ ἐξελθόντος⁵ ἀπὸ τοῦ τάφου τρεῖς

10 ἄνδρες⁶ καὶ τοὺς δύο τὸν ἕνα ὑπορθοῦντας καὶ

σταυρὸν ἀκολοθοῦντα⁷ αὐτοῖς. 40. καὶ τῶν μὲν δύο

τὴν κεφαλὴν χωροῦσαν μέχρι τοῦ οὐρανοῦ,

τοῦ δὲ χειρατωτουμένου⁸ ὑπ' αὐτῶν ὑπερβαίνου

σαν τοὺς οὐρανούς. 41. καὶ φωνῆ[ς]⁹ ἤκουον ἐκ τῶν

15 οὐρανῶν λεγούσης· ἐκήρυξας τοῖς κοιμωμένοις;¹⁰

42. καὶ ὑπακοὴ ἠκούετο ἀπὸ τοῦ σταυροῦ [ὅ]τι ναί.¹¹ 11.43. συνε

σκέπτοντο οὖν ἀλλήλοις¹ ἐκεῖνοι ἀπελθεῖν

P.Cair. 10759 f.4v

ΚΑΙ ΕΝΦΑΝΙϹΑΝΤΩΝ ΤΑΥΤΩ ΩΠΠΕΙΛΑΤΩ ΚΑΙ ΕΤΙ ΔΙΑΝΟΟΥΜΕ
ΩΝ ΑΥΤΩΝ ΦΑΙΝΟΝΤΑΙ ΠΑΛΙΝ ΑΝΟΙΧΘΕΝΤΕϹ ΟΙ ΟΥΡΑΝΟΙ
ΚΑΙ ΑΝΟϹΤΙϹ ΚΑΤΕΛΘΟΝ ΚΑΙ ΕΙϹ ΕΛΑΥΝ ΕΙϹ ΤΟ ΜΝΗΜΑ
ΤΑΥΤΑ ΙΔΟΝΤΕϹ ΟΠΕΡ ΠΠΟΝ ΚΕΝΤΥΡΩΝ Α ΝΥΚΤΟϹ ΕΠΕΤΕΩΝ
ΠΡΟϹΠΕΙΧΑΤΟΝ ΑΦΕΝΤΕϹ ΤΟΝ ΤΑΦΟΝ ΟΝ ΕΦΥΛΑϹϹΟΝ ΚΑΙ
ΕΞΗΓΗϹΑΝΤΟ ΠΑΝΤΑ ΑΠΕΡ ΕΙΔΟΝ ΑΓΩΝΙΩΝΤΕϹ ΜΕΓΑΛΩϹ
ΛΕΓΟΝΤΕϹ ΑΛΗΘΩϹ ΥΙΟϹ ΗΝ ΘΥ ΑΠΟΚΡΙΘΕΙϹ Ο ΠΕΙΛΑΤΟϹ
ΕΦΗ ΕΓΩ ΚΑΘΑΡΕΥΩ ΤΟΥ ΑΙΜΑΤΟϹ ΤΟΥ ΥΙΟΥ ΤΟΥ ΘΥ ΟΥΜΗΝΔΕ
ΤΟΥΤΟ ΕΔΟΞΕΝ ΕΠΙ ΤΙΤΡΟϹ ΕΛΘΟΝΤΕϹ ΠΑΝΤΕϹ ΕΔΕΟΝΤΟ ΑΥΤΟΥ
ΚΑΙ ΠΑΡΕΚΑΛΟΥΝ ΚΑΙ ΕΝϹΤΩ ΚΕΝΤΥΡΙΩΝ ΚΑΙ ΤΟΙϹ ϹΤΡΑΤ
ΤΑ ϹΙΗΔΕΝ ΕΙΠΕΙΝ Α ΕΙΔΟΝ ϹΥΜΦΕΡΕΙ ΓΑΡ ΦΑϹΙΝ ΗΜΙΝ
ΟΦΛΗϹΑΙ ΜΕΓΙϹΤΗΝ ΑΜΑΡΤΙΑΝ ΕΜΠΡΟϹΘΕΝ ΤΟΥ ΘΥ
ΚΑΙ ΜΗ ΕΜΠΕϹΕΙΝ ΕΙϹ ΧΕΙΡΑϹ ΤΟΥ ΛΑΟΥ ΤΩΝ ΙΟΥΔΑΙΩΝ
ΚΑΙ ΛΙΘΑϹΘΗΝΑΙ ΕΚΕΛΕΥϹΕΝ ΟΥΝ Ο ΠΕΙΛΑΤΟϹ ΤΩΝ ΚΕΝ
ΤΥΡΙΩΝ ΚΑΙ ΤΟΙϹ ϹΤΡΑΤΙΩΤΑΙϹ ΜΗΔΕΝ ΕΙΠΕΙΝ ΟΡΘΟΥ ΔΕ
ΤΗϹ ΚΥΡΙΑΚΗϹ ΜΑΡΙΑ Η ΜΑΓΔΑΛΗΝΗ ΜΑΘΗΤΡΙΑ ΤΟΥ ΚΥ
ΦΟΒΟΥΜΕΝΗ ΔΙΑ ΤΟΥϹ ΙΟΥΔΑΙΟΥϹ ΕΠΕΙΔΗ ΕΦΛΕΓΟΝΤΟ

Page 7

καὶ² ἐνφανίσαι ταῦτα τῷ Πειλάτῳ. 44. καὶ ἔτι διανοουμέ(ν)

ων³ αὐτῶν φαίνονται πάλιν ἀνοιχθέντες οἱ οὐρανοὶ

καὶ α̅ν̅ο̅ς̅ τις κατελθὼν⁴ καὶ εἰσελθὼν εἰς τὸ μνῆμα.

45. ταῦτα ἰδόντες οἱ περὶ τὸν κεντυρωνα⁵ νυκτὸς ἔσπευσαν

5   πρὸς Πειλᾶτον ἀφέντες τὸν τάφον ὃν ἐφύλασσον καὶ

ἐξηγήσαντο πάντα ἅπερ εἶδον ἀπωνιῶντες⁶ μεγάλως

καὶ λέγοντες· ἀληθῶς υἱὸς ἦν θ̅υ̅. 46. ἀποκριθεὶς ὁ Πειλᾶτος

ἔφη· ἐγὼ καθαρεύω τοῦ αἵματος τοῦ υἱοῦ τοῦ θεοῦ⁷ ἡμῖν⁸ δὲ

τοῦτο ἔδοξεν. 47. εἶτα προσελθόντες πάντες ἐδέοντο αὐτοῦ

10  καὶ περεκάλουν⁹ κελεῦσαι τῷ κεντυρίων¹⁰ καὶ τοῖς στρατιώ

ταις μηδὲν¹¹ εἰπεῖν ἃ εἶδον. 48. συμφέρει γάρ, φασίν, ἡμῖν

ὀφλῆσαι μεγίστην ἁμαρτίαν ἔμπροσθεν τοῦ θεοῦ

καὶ μὴ ἐμπεσεῖν εἰς χεῖρας τοῦ λαοῦ τῶν Ἰουδαίων

καὶ λιθασθῆναι. 49. ἐκέλευσεν οὖν ὁ Πειλᾶτος τῶν κεν

15  τυρίων¹² καὶ τοῖς στρατιώταις μηδὲν εἰπεῖν. 12.50. ὀρθοῦ¹ δὲ

τῆς κυριακῆς Μαριὰμ² ἡ Μαγδαλινὴ³ μαθήτρια τοῦ κ̅υ̅⁴

φοβουμένη διὰ τοὺς Ἰουδαίους, ἐπειδὴ ἐφλέγοντο

*P.Cair.* 10759 f.5r

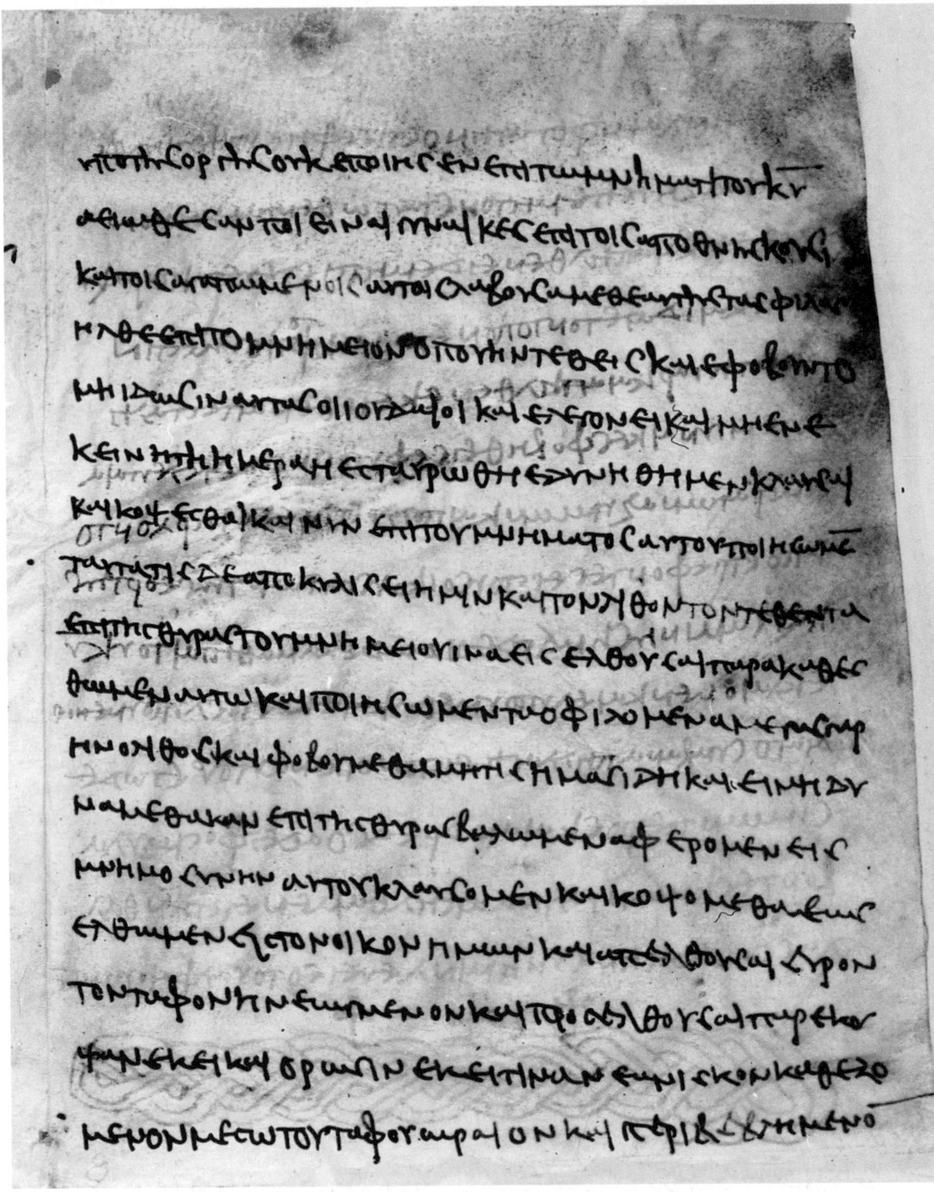

Page 8

ὑπὸ τῆς ὀργῆς, οὐκ ἐποίησεν ἐπὶ τῷ μνήματι τοῦ κ̄ῡ [5]

ἃ εἰώθεσαν ποιεῖν αἱ γυναῖκες ἐπὶ τοῖς ἀποθνήσκουσι

καὶ τοῖς ἀγαπωμένοις αὐταῖς. 51. λαβοῦσα μεθ᾽ ἑαυτῆς τὰς φίλας

ἦλθε ἐπὶ τὸ μνημεῖον ὅπου ἦν τεθείς. 52. καὶ ἐφοβοῦντο

5   μὴ ἴδωσιν αὐτὰς οἱ Ἰουδαῖοι καὶ ἔλεγον· εἰ καὶ μὴ ἐν ἐ

κείνῃ τῇ ἡμέρᾳ ᾗ ἐσταυρώθη ἐδυνήθημεν κλαῦσαι

καὶ κόψεσθαι,[6] καὶ νῦν ἐπὶ τοῦ μνήματος αὐτοῦ ποιήσωμε(ν)[7]

ταῦτα. 53. τίς δὲ ἀποκυλίσει ἡμῖν καὶ τὸν λίθον τὸν τεθέντα

ἐπὶ τῆς θύρας τοῦ μνημείου, ἵνα εἰσελθοῦσαι παρακαθεσ

10  θῶμεν αὐτῷ καὶ ποιήσωμεν τὰ ὀφιλόμενα;[8] 54. μέγας γὰρ

ἦν ὁ λίθος. καὶ φοβούμεθα μή τις ἡμᾶς ἴδῃ. καὶ εἰ μὴ δυ

νάμεθα, κἂν ἐπὶ τῆς θύρας βάλωμεν ἃ φέρομεν εἰς

μνημοσύνην αὐτοῦ, κλαύσομεν καὶ κοψόμεθα[9] ἕως

ἔλθωμεν εἰς τὸν οἶκον ἡμῶν. 13.55. καὶ ἀπελθοῦσαι εὗρον[1]

15  τὸν τάφον ἠνεῳγμένον καὶ προσελθοῦσαι[2] παρέκυ

ψαν ἐκεῖ καὶ ὁρῶσιν ἐκεῖ τινα νεανίσκον καθεζό

μενον μέσῳ τοῦ τάφου ὡραῖον καὶ περιβεβλημένο(ν)[3]

*P.Cair.* 10759 f.5v

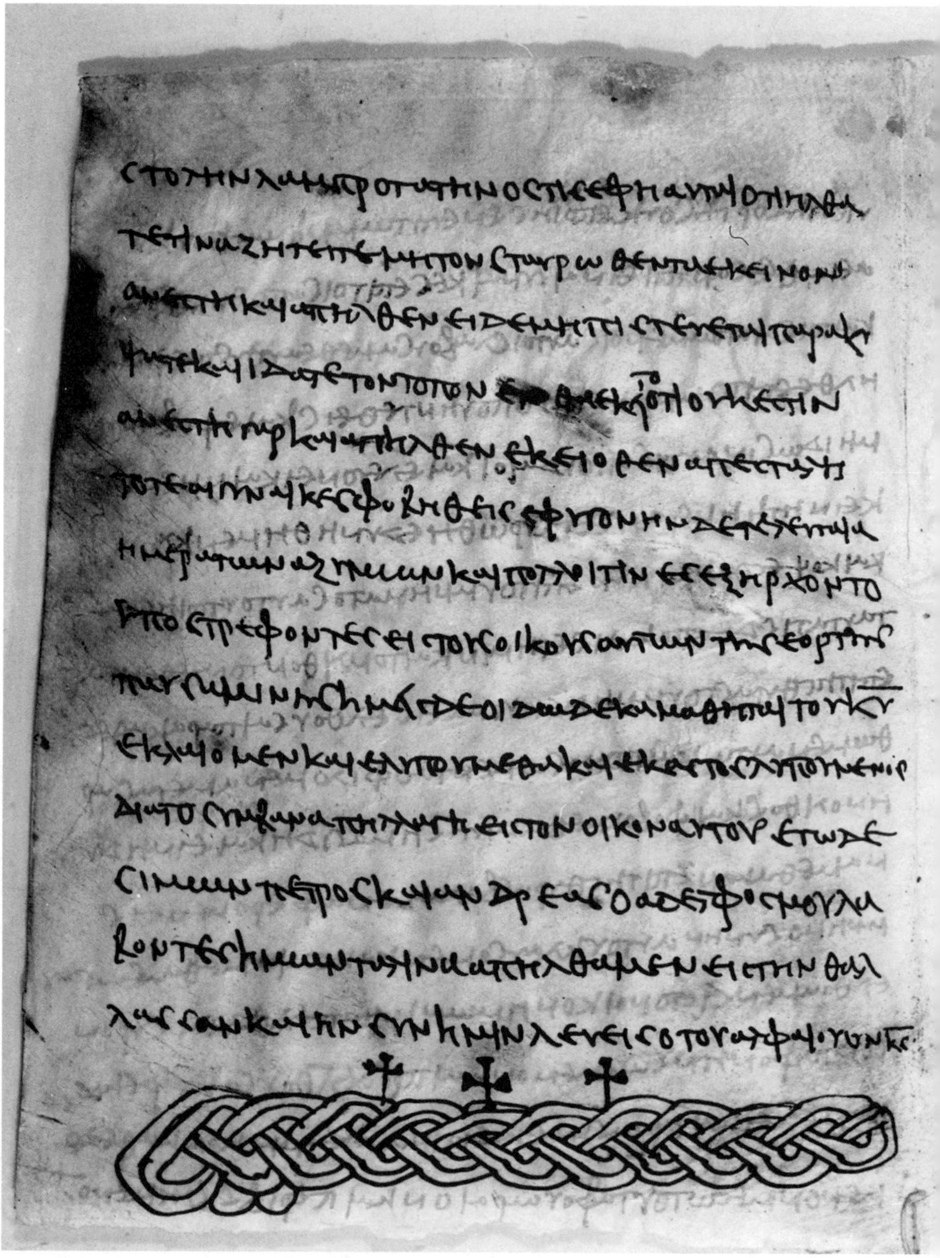

Page 9

στολὴν λαμπροτάτην ὅστις ἔφη αὐταῖ⟨ς⟩[4]· 56. ὅτι[5] ἦλθα

τε; τίνα ζητεῖτε; μὴ τὸν σταυρωθέντα ἐκεῖνον;

[6]ἀνέστη καὶ ἀπῆλθεν. εἰ δὲ μὴ πιστεύετε, παρακύ

ψατε καὶ ἴδατε[7] τὸν τόπον [ἔνθα] ἔκει[8] το [9] ὅτι οὐκ ἔστιν.

5    ἀνέστη γὰρ καὶ ἀπῆλθεν[6] ἐκεῖ ὅθεν ἀπεστάλη.

57. τότε αἱ γυναῖκες φοβηθεῖς⟨αι⟩[10] ἔφυγον. 14.58. ἦν δὲ τελευταία[1]

ἡμέρα τῶν ἀζύμων καὶ πολλοί τινες[2] ἐξήρχοντο

ὑποστρέφοντες εἰς τοὺς οἴκους αὐτῶν τῆς ἑορτῆς

παυσαμίνης.[3] 59. ἡμεῖς δὲ οἱ δώδεκα μαθηταὶ τοῦ κ̅υ̅

10   ἐκλαίομεν καὶ ἐλυπούμεθα καὶ ἕκαστος λυπούμενος

διὰ τὸ συμβὰν ἀπηλλάγη εἰς τὸν οἶκον αὐτοῦ. 60. ἐγὼ δὲ

Σίμων Πέτρος καὶ Ἀνδρέας ὁ ἀδελφός μου λα

βόντες ἡμῶν τὰ λίνα ἀπήλθαμεν εἰς τὴν θάλ

λασσαν[4], καὶ ἦν σὺν ἡμῖν Λευεὶς ὁ τοῦ Ἀλφαίου ὃν κ̅ς̅[5]...

# THE 'GOSPEL OF PETER'
## GREEK TEXT WITH FACING ENGLISH TRANSLATION

In this section English translations of the relevant manuscript evidence for the *Gospel of Peter* are provided. This comprises of three textual items. First, the large Akhmîm fragment which contains nine continuous pages of text. It has been argued that this is potentially the only extant witness to the text referred to by Serapion as 'the so-called Gospel of Peter.' The other two items of textual witness that have been suggested as pertinent to the reconstruction of the text are P.Oxy. 2949 and P.Oxy. 4009. The first, P.Oxy. 2949, has some short snatched of shared terminology, but also some large discrepancies from *Gos. Pet.* 2.3–5a. The fragmentary nature of this text and its limited extent are readily seen. The identification of this text as part of the *Gospel of Peter* is in part motivated by a desire to the text behind the Akhmîm fragment as more securely located in the second century. Although P.Vindob.G 2325 is also sometimes considered relevant to this discussion it is not included here since it has been argued that it is not a textual witness to the *Gospel of Peter*.

The third piece of evidence, P.Oxy. 4009, is even more fragmentary than P.Oxy. 2949 often with only a few letters of a single word preserved on each line. Extensive and speculative reconstruction has led to the suggestion that this text is part of the now otherwise no longer extant section of the *Gospel of Peter*. Part of the motivation for wishing to identify this text as a fragment of the *Gospel of Peter* is that it would then show that the gospel text was not just a Passion account, but in fact recorded events from Jesus' ministry. Unfortunately, to reach this conclusion the text must be reconstructed to such an extent that the strength of the argument is minimal and the reasoning circular.

The style of translation adopted for the Akhmîm fragment has been that of close representation of the Greek text, rather than dynamic equivalence. The Greek of the Akhmîm fragment is not particularly refined and consequently no attempt has been made to render the English translation using a more elevated linguistic or syntactical construction. The repeated use of conjunctions at the beginning of new clauses is a feature of the Greek text, and this has been preserved in the translation. The 'translation' of the two Oxyrhynchus fragments is problematic. This is because no complete sentence or clause is preserved in either of the papyrus texts. At best one can identify individual words, short clusters of words, or occasionally a phrase.

1.1. τ[ῶν] δὲ Ἰουδαίων οὐδεὶς ἐνίψατο τὰς χεῖρας, οὐδὲ Ἡρώδης οὐδ᾽ εἷς [τ]ῶν κριτῶν αὐτοῦ. καὶ [μὴ] βουληθέντω(ν) νίψασθαι, ἀνέστη Πειλᾶτος. 2. καὶ τότε κελεύει Ἡρώδης ὁ βασιλεὺς παρ[αλη]μφθῆναι τὸν κ(ύριο)ν, εἰπὼν αὐτοῖς ὅτι· Ὅσα ἐκέλευσα ὑμῖν ποιῆσαι αὐτῷ, ποιήσατε.

2.3. ἱστήκει δὲ ἐκεῖ Ἰωσὴφ ὁ φίλος Πειλάτου καὶ τοῦ κ(υρίο)υ. καὶ εἰδὼς ὅτι ⁵σταυρίσκειν αὐτὸν μέλλουσιν, ἦλθεν πρὸς τὸν Πειλᾶτον καὶ ᾔτησε τὸ σῶμα τοῦ κ(υρίο)υ πρὸς ταφήν. 4. καὶ ὁ Πειλᾶτος πέμψας πρὸς Ἡρώδην ᾔτησεν αὐτοῦ τὸ σῶμα. 5. καὶ ὁ Ἡρώδης ἔφη ἀδελφὲ Πειλᾶτε, εἰ καὶ μή τις αὐτὸν ᾐτήκει, ἡμεῖς αὐτὸν ἐθάπτομεν, ἐπεὶ καὶ σάββατον ἐπιφώσκει· γέγραπται γὰρ ἐν τῷ νόμῳ ἥλιον μὴ δῦναι ἐπὶ πεφονευμένῳ. καὶ παρέδωκεν αὐτὸν τῷ λαῷ πρὸ μιᾶς τῶν ἀζύμων, τῆς ἑορτῆς αὐτῶν.

3.6. Οἱ δὲ λαβόντες τὸν κ(ύριο)υ ὤθουν αὐτῶν τρέχοντες καὶ ἔλεγον· Σύρωμεν τὸν υἱὸν τοῦ θ(εο)ῦ, ἐξουσίαν αὐτοῦ ἐσχηκότες. 7. καὶ πορφύραν αὐτὸν περιέβαλλον, καὶ ἐκάθισαν αὐτὸν ἐπὶ καθέδραν κρίσεως, λέγοντες· Δικαίως κρῖνε, βασιλεῦ τοῦ Ἰσραήλ. 8. καί τις αὐτῶν ἐνεγκὼν στέφανον ἀκάνθινον ἔθηκεν ἐπὶ τῆς κεφαλῆς τοῦ κυρίου 9. καὶ ἕτεροι ἑστῶτες ἐνέπτυον αὐτοῦ ταῖς ὄψεσι, καὶ ἄλλοι τὰς σιαγόνας αὐτοῦ ἐράπισαν, ἕτεροι καλάμῳ ἔνυσσον αὐτόν, καί τινες αὐτὸν ἐμάστιζον λέγοντες· ταύτῃ τῇ τιμῇ τιμήσωμεν τὸν υἱὸν τοῦ θ(εο)ῦ.

4.10. καὶ ἤνεγκον δύο κακούργους καὶ ἐσταύρωσαν ἀνὰ μέσον αὐτῶν τὸν κ(ύριο)ν. αὐτὸς δὲ ἐσιώπα ὡς μηδέν πόνον ἔχων. 11. καὶ ὅτε ὤρθωσαν τὸν σταῦρον ἐπέγραψαν ὅτι οὗτός ἐστιν ὁ βασιλεὺς τοῦ Ἰσραήλ. 12. καὶ τεθεικότες τὰ ἐνδύματα ἔμπροσθεν αὐτοῦ διεμερίσαντο καὶ λαχμὸν ἔβαλον ἐπ᾽ αὐτοῖς. 13. εἷς δέ τις τῶν κακούργων ἐκείνων ὠνείδησεν αὐτοὺς λέγων· Ἡμεις διὰ τὰ κακὰ ἃ ἐποιήσαμεν οὕτω πεπόνθαμεν, οὕτως δὲ σωτὴρ γενόμενος τῶν ἀν(θρώπ)ων τί ἠδίκησεν ὑμᾶς; 14. καὶ ἀγανακτήσαντες ἐπ᾽ αὐτῷ ἐκέλευσαν ἵνα μὴ σκελοκοπηθῇ ὅπως βασανιζόμενος ἀποθάνοι.

5.15. Ἦν δὲ μεσημβρία, καὶ σκότος κατέσχε(ν) πᾶσαν τὴν Ἰουδαίαν· καὶ ἐθορυβοῦντο καὶ ἠγωνίων μήποτε ὁ ἥλιος ἔδυ, ἐπειδὴ ἔτι ἔζη· γέγραπται αὐτοῖς ἥλιον μὴ δῦναι ἐπὶ πεφωνευμένῳ. 16. καί τις αὐτῶν εἶπεν· Ποτίσατε αὐτὸν χολὴν μετὰ ὄξους· καὶ κεράσαντες ἐπότισαν. 17. καὶ ἐπλήρωσαν πάντα καὶ ἐτελείωσαν κατὰ τῆς κεφαλῆς αὐτῶν τὰ ἁμαρτήματα. 18. περιήρχοντο δὲ πολλοὶ μετὰ λύχνων νομίζοντες ὅτι νύξ ἐστιν ἐπέσαντο.

1.1. but of the Jews no-one washed the hands, nor Herod, nor one of his judges. And when they were not willing to wash, Pilate rose up. 2. And then Herod the king commanding the Lord to be brought, saying to them, 'Whatever I commanded you to do to him, do.'

2.3. And Joseph the friend of Pilate and of the Lord stood there, and seeing that they were about to crucify him, he came to Pilate and asked for the body of the Lord for burial. 4. And Pilate sent to Herod [and] asked for his body. 5. And Herod said, 'Brother Pilate, even if somebody had not asked for him, we would have buried him, since also Sabbath is dawning. For it is written in the law, 'The sun should not set on one who has been put to death.' And he handed him over to the people before the first day of the unleavened bread, their festival.

3.6. So those taking the Lord were pushing him while running along, and they were saying, 'Let us drag the son of God having authority over him.' 7. And they were clothing him in purple and they sat him on the seat of judgment saying, 'Judge justly King of Israel.' 8. And one of them brought a thorn crown and placed it on the head of the Lord. 9. And others who stood by were spitting in his face, and others struck his cheeks, others were piercing him with a reed and some were scourging him saying, 'With this honour let us honour the son of God.'

4.10. And they brought two criminals and crucified the Lord in the middle of them, and he was silent as though having no pain. 11. And when they erected the cross they wrote, 'This is the king of Israel.' 12. And having laid out the clothes before him, they divided [them] and cast lots for them. 13. But one of those criminals rebuked them saying, 'We, because of the evil we did, are suffering thus, but this man who is the saviour of men, how has he wronged you?' 14. And they were angry with him and ordered that the legs not be broken, so that he might die being distressed.

5.15. And it was noon and darkness covered all Judaea. And they were troubled and distressed lest the sun had already set since he was alive. It is written by them, 'The sun is not to set on one who has been put to death.' 16. And one of them said, 'Give him gall with vinegar to drink.' And having mixed it they gave it to him to drink. 17. And they fulfilled all things and they accumulated the sins on their head. 18. And many were going about with lamps, supposing it was night, stumbled.

19. καὶ ὁ κ(ύριο)ς ἀνεβόησε λέγων· Ἡ δύναμίς μου ἡ δύναμις κατέλειψάς με· καὶ εἰπὼν ἀνελήφθη. 20. καὶ αὐτός ὥρας διεράγη τὸ καταπέτασμα τοῦ ναοῦ τῆς Ἰερουσαλὴμ εἰς δύο.

6.21. καὶ τότε ἀπέσπασαν τοὺς ἥλους ἀπὸ τῶν χειρῶ(ν) τοῦ κ(υρίο)υ καὶ ἔθηκαν αὐτὸν ἐπὶ τῆς γῆς καὶ ἡ γῆ πᾶσα ἐσείσθη καὶ φόβος μέγας ἐγένετο. 22. τότε ἥλιος ἔλαμψε καὶ εὑρέθη ὥρα ἐνάτη. 23. ἐχάρησαν δὲ οἱ Ἰουδαῖοι καὶ δεδώκασῖ(ν) τῷ Ἰωσὴφ τὸ σῶμα αὐτοῦ ἵνα αὐτὸ θάψη ἐπειδὴ θεασάμενος ἦν ὅσα ἀγαθὰ ἐποίησεν. 24. λαβὼν δὲ τὸν κύριον ἔλουσε καὶ εἵλησε σινδόνιν[1] καὶ εἰσήγαγεν εἰς ἴδιον τάφον καλούμενον κῆπον Ἰωσήφ.

7.25. τότε οἱ Ἰουδαῖοι καὶ οἱ πρεσβύτεροι καὶ οἱ ἱερεῖς γνόντες οἷον κακὸν ἑαυτοῖς ἐποίησαν, ἤρξαντο κόπτεσθαι καὶ λέγειν· οὐαί ταῖς ἁμαρτίαις ἡμῶν· ἤγγισεν ἡ κρίσις καὶ τὸ τέλος Ἰερουσαλήμ. 26. ἐγὼ δὲ μετὰ τῶ(ν) ἑταίρων μου ἐλυπούμην καὶ τετρωμένοι κατὰ διάνοιαν ἐκρυβόμεθα. ἐζητούμεθα γὰρ ὑπ᾽ αὐτῶν ὡς κακοῦργοι καὶ ὡς τὸν ναὸν θέλοντες ἐμπρῆσαι. 27. ἐπὶ δὲ τούτοις πᾶσιν ἐνηστεύομεν καὶ ἐκαθεζόμεθα πενθοῦντες καὶ κλαίοντες νυκτὸς καὶ ἡμέρας ἕως τοῦ σαββάτου.

8.28. συναχθέντες δὲ οἱ γραμματεῖς καὶ Φαρισαῖοι καὶ πρεσβύτεροι πρὸς ἀλλήλους ἀκούσαντες ὅτι ὁ λαὸς ἅπας γογγύζει καὶ κόπτεται τὰ στήθη λέγοντες ὅτι, εἰ τῷ θανάτῳ αὐτοῦ ταῦτα τὰ μέγιστα σημεῖα γέγονεν, ἴδετε ὅτι πόσον δίκαιός ἐστιν. 29. ἐφοβήθησαν οἱ πρεσβύτεροι καὶ ἦλθον πρὸς Πειλᾶτον δεόμενοι αὐτοῦ καὶ λέγοντες· 30. Παράδος ἡμῖν στρατιώτας, ἵνα φυλάξω τὸ μνῆμα αὐτοῦ ἐπὶ τρεῖς ἡμ[έρας] μήποτε ἐλθόντες οἱ μαθηταὶ αὐτοῦ κλέψωσιν αὐτὸν καὶ ὑπολάβη ὁ λαὸς ὅτι ἐκ νεκρῶν ἀνέστη, καὶ ποιήσωσιν ἡμῖν κακά. 31. ὁ δὲ Πειλᾶτος παραδέδωκεν αὐτοῖς Πετρώνιον τὸν κεντυρίωνα μετὰ στρατιωτῶν φυλάσσειν τὸν τάφον. καὶ σὺν αὐτοῖς ἦλθον πρεσβύτεροι καὶ γραμματεῖς ἐπὶ τὸ μνῆμα. 32. καὶ κυλίσαντες λίθον μέγαν κατὰ τοῦ κεντυρίωνος καὶ τῶν στρατιωτῶν ὁμοῦ πάντες οἱ ὄντες ἐκεῖ ἔθηκαν ἐπὶ τῇ θύρα τοῦ μνήματος. 33. καὶ ἐπέχρεισαν ἑπτὰ σφραγῖδας καὶ σκηνὴν ἐκεῖ πήξαντες ἐφύλαξαν.

9.34. πρωΐας δὲ ἐπιφώσκοντος τοῦ σαββάτου ἦλθεν ὄχλος ἀπὸ Ἰερουσαλὴμ καὶ τῆς περιχώρου ἵνα ἴδωσι τὸ μνημεῖον ἐσφραγισμένο(ν). 35. τῇ δὲ νυκτὶ ᾗ ἐπέφωσκεν ἡ κυριακή, φυλασσόντων τῶν στρατιωτῶν ἀνὰ δύο δύο κατὰ φρουρά(ν), μεγάλη φωνὴ ἐγένετο ἐν τῷ οὐρανῷ.

19. And the Lord cried out saying, 'My power, the power, you have left me.' And saying this he was taken up. 20. And at the same hour the curtain of the temple in Jerusalem was torn in two.

6.21. And then they drew the nails from the hands of the Lord and placed him on the earth, and all the earth was shaken and there was great fear. 22. Then the sun shone and it was found to be the ninth hour. 23. And the Jews rejoiced and gave to Joseph his body that he might bury it, since he had seen all the good things he had done. 24. And taking the Lord he washed and wrapped [him] in a linen cloth and brought [him] into his own tomb called 'Joseph's garden.'

7.25. Then the Jews, and the elders and the priests knowing what evil they had done to themselves, they began to lament and say, 'Woe to our sins, the judgment and the end of Jerusalem is at hand.' 26. But I with my companions was grieved, and being wounded in mind we hid. For we were being sought by them as evildoers and as those wishing to burn the temple. 27. But through all of these things we were fasting and were sitting, mourning and weeping night and day until the Sabbath.

8.28. And the scribes and the Pharisees and the elders gathered together with one another when they heard that all the people grumbled and beat their chests saying, 'if at his death these greatest signs have happened, behold how just he was.' 29. The elders were afraid and came to Pilate petitioning him and saying, 30. 'Give to us soldiers that I may guard his tomb for three days, lest his disciple come and steal him and the people suppose that he is risen from the dead, and they might do evil things to us.' 31. And Pilate gave to them Petronius the centurion with soldiers to guard the tomb. And with them went elders and scribes to the tomb. 32. And having rolled a great stone towards the centurion and the soldiers, where all those who were there set it at the entrance of the tomb. 33. And they spread out seven seals and pitching a tent there, they kept watch.

9.34. Now when the morning of the Sabbath dawned a crowd came from Jerusalem and the surrounding region that they might see the tomb which had been sealed. 35. But during the night in which the Lord's day dawned, while the soldiers were guarding two by two according to post, there was a great voice in the sky.

36. καὶ εἶδο(ν) ἀνοιχθέντας τοὺς οὐρά[ν]ους καὶ δύο ἄνδρας κατελθόντας ἐκεῖθε πολὺ φέγγος ἔχοντας καὶ ἐγγίσαντας τῷ τάφῳ. 37. ὁ δὲ λείθος ἐκεῖνος ὁ βεβλημένος ἐπὶ τῇ θύρᾳ ἀφ᾽ ἑαυτοῦ κυλισθεὶς ἐπεχώρησε παρὰ μέρος καὶ ὁ τάφος ἐνοίγη καὶ ἀμφότεροι οἱ νεανίσκοι εἰσῆλθον.

10.38. ἰδόντες οὖν οἱ στρατιῶται ἐκεῖνοι ἐξύπνισαν τὸν κεντυρίωνα καὶ τοὺς πρεσβυτέρους· παρῆσαν γὰρ καὶ αὐτοὶ φυλάσσοντες. 39. καὶ ἐξηγουμένων αὐτῶν ἃ εἶδον πάλιν ὅρασιν ἐξελθόντος ἀπὸ τοῦ τάφου τρεῖς ἄνδρες καὶ τοὺς δύο τὸν ἕνα ὑπορθοῦντας καὶ σταυρὸν ἀκολοθοῦντα αὐτοῖς. 40. καὶ τῶν μὲν δύο τὴν κεφαλὴν χωροῦσαν μέχρι τοῦ οὐρανοῦ, τοῦ δὲ χειραγωγουμένου ὑπ᾽ αὐτῶν ὑπερβαίνουσαν τοὺς οὐρανούς. 41. καὶ φωνῆ[ς] ἤκουον ἐκ τῶν οὐρανῶν λεγούσης· ἐκήρυξας τοῖς κοιμωμένοις; 42. καὶ ὑπακοὴ ἠκούετο ἀπὸ τοῦ σταυροῦ [ὅ]τι ναί.

11.43. συνεσκέπτοντο οὖν ἀλλήλοις ἐκεῖνοι ἀπελθεῖν καὶ ἐνφανίσαι ταῦτα τῷ Πειλάτῳ. 44. καὶ ἔτι διανοουμέ(ν)ων αὐτῶν φαίνονται πάλιν ἀνοιχθέντες οἱ οὐρανοὶ καὶ ἀν(θρωπ)ός τις κατελθὸν καὶ εἰσελθὸν εἰς τὸ μνῆμα. 45. ταῦτα ἰδόντες οἱ περὶ τὸν κεντυρίωνα νυκτὸς ἔσπευσαν πρὸς Πειλᾶτον ἀφέντες τὸν τάφον ὃν ἐφύλασσον καὶ ἐξηγήσαντο πάντα ἅπερ εἶδον ἀγωνιῶντες μεγάλως καὶ λέγοντες· ἀληθῶς υἱὸς ἦν θ(εο)ῦ. 46. ἀποκριθεὶς ὁ Πειλᾶτος ἔφη· ἐγὼ καθαρεύω τοῦ αἵματος τοῦ υἱοῦ τοῦ θεοῦ ἡμῖν δὲ τοῦτο ἔδοξεν. 47. εἶτα προσελθόντες πάντες ἐδέοντο αὐτοῦ καὶ περεκάλουν κελεῦσαι τῷ κεντυρίωνι καὶ τοῖς στρατιώταις μηδὲν εἰπεῖν ἃ εἶδον. 48. συμφέρει γάρ, φασίν, ἡμῖν ὀφλῆσαι μεγίστην ἁμαρτίαν ἔμπροσθεν τοῦ θεοῦ καὶ μὴ ἐμπεσεῖν εἰς χεῖρας τοῦ λαοῦ τῶν Ἰουδαίων καὶ λιθασθῆναι. 49. ἐκέλευσεν οὖν ὁ Πειλᾶτος τῶν κεντυρίων[11] καὶ τοῖς στρατιώταις μηδὲν εἰπεῖν.

12.50. ὀρθοῦ δὲ τῆς κυριακῆς Μαριὰμ ἡ Μαγδαλινὴ μαθήτρια τοῦ κ(υρίο)υ φοβουμένη διὰ τοὺς Ἰουδαίους, ἐπειδὴ ἐφλέγοντο ὑπὸ τῆς ὀργῆς, οὐκ ἐποίησεν ἐπὶ τῷ μνήματι τοῦ κ(υρίο)υ ἃ εἰώθεσαν ποιεῖν αἱ γυναῖκες ἐπὶ τοῖς ἀποθήσκουσι καὶ τοῖς ἀγαπωμένοις αὐταῖς. 51. λαβοῦσα μεθ᾽ ἑαυτῆς τὰς φίλας ἦλθε ἐπὶ τὸ μνημεῖον ὅπου ἦν τεθείς. 52. καὶ ἐφοβοῦντο μὴ ἴδωσιν αὐτὰς οἱ Ἰουδαῖοι καὶ ἔλεγον· εἰ καὶ μὴ ἐν ἐκείνῃ τῇ ἡμέρᾳ ᾗ ἐσταυρώθη ἐδυνήθημεν κλαῦσαι καὶ κόψεσθαι, καὶ νῦν ἐπὶ τοῦ μνήματος αὐτοῦ ποιήσωμε(ν) ταῦτα. 53. τίς δὲ ἀποκυλίσει ἡμῖν καὶ τὸν λίθον τὸν τεθέντα ἐπὶ τῆς θύρας τοῦ μνημείου, ἵνα εἰσελθοῦσαι παρακαθεσθῶμεν αὐτῷ καὶ ποιήσωμεν τὰ ὀφιλόμενα;

36. And they saw the heavens were being opened, and two men descended from there, having much brightness, and they drew near to the tomb. 37. But that stone which had been placed at the entrance rolled away by itself and made way in part and the tomb was opened and both the young men went in.

10.38. Then those soldiers seeing it awoke the centurion and the elders, for they were present also keeping guard. 39. While they were reporting what they had seen, again they saw coming out from the tomb three men, and the two were supporting the one, and a cross following them. 40. And the head of the two reached as far as heaven, but that of the one being led by them surpassed the heavens. 41. And they were hearing a voice from the heavens saying, 'Have you preached to those who sleep?' 42. And a response was heard from the cross, 'Yes.'

11.43. Then those men together determined with each other to go and report these things to Pilate. 44. And while they were still thinking, again the heavens were seen opening, and a certain man descended and entered into the tomb. 45. Seeing these things those who accompanied the centurion rushed by night to Pilate, leaving the tomb which they were guarding, and related everything which they saw, being greatly distressed and saying, 'Truly this was God's son.' 46. Answering, Pilate said, 'I am clean from the blood of the son of God, and this is recognized by us.' 47. Then they all came, and were beseeching and entreating him to command the centurion and the soldiers to say nothing of what they had seen. 48. 'For it is better', they said, 'for us to incur the liability of a great sin before God, and not to fall into the hands of the people of the Jews and to be stoned.' 49. Therefore, Pilate ordered the centurion and the soldiers to say nothing.

12.50. Now at dawn of the Lord's Day Mary Magdalene, a disciple of the Lord, being afraid because of the Jews, since they were inflamed by rage, had not done at the tomb of the Lord those things which women are accustomed to do over those who have died and for those who are loved by them. 51. Taking the friends with her, she went to the tomb were he had been laid. 52. And they were afraid the Jews might see them and they were saying, 'Since we were not able on the day on which he was crucified to weep and to wail, even now at his tomb let us do these things. 53. But who will roll away for us also the stone that has been placed at the door of the tomb that when we have gone in we might sit beside him and do the things that are necessary.

54. μέγας γὰρ ἦν ὁ λίθος, καὶ φοβούμεθα μή τις ἡμᾶς ἴδη. καὶ εἰ μὴ δυνάμεθα, κἂν ἐπὶ τῆς θύρας βάλωμεν ἃ φέρομεν εἰς μνημοσύνην αὐτοῦ, κλαύσομεν καὶ κοψόμεθα ἕως ἔλθωμεν εἰς τὸν οἶκον ἡμῶν.

13.55. καὶ ἀπελθοῦσαι εὗρον τὸν τάφον ἡνεῳγμένον καὶ προσελθοῦσαι παρέκυψαν ἐκεῖ καὶ ὁρῶσιν ἐκεῖ τινα νεανίσκον καθεζόμενον μέσῳ τοῦ τάφου ὡραῖον καὶ περιβεβλημένο(ν) στολὴν λαμπροτάτην ὅστις ἔφη αὐταῖ〈ς〉 56. τί ἤλθατε; τίνα ζητεῖτε; μὴ τὸν σταυρωθέντα ἐκεῖνον; ἀνέστη καὶ ἀπῆλθεν. εἰ δὲ μὴ πιστεύετε, παρακύψατε καὶ ἴδατε τὸν τόπον [ἔνθα] ἔκ[ει]το ὅτι οὐκ ἔστιν. ἀνέστη γὰρ καὶ ἀπῆλθεν ἐκεῖ ὅθεν ἀπεστάλη. 57. τότε αἱ γυναῖκες φοβηθεῖσ〈αι〉 ἔφυγον.

14.58. ἦν δὲ τελευταία ἡμέρα τῶν ἀζύμων καὶ πολλοί τινες ἐξήρχοντο ὑποστρέφοντες εἰς τοὺς οἴκους αὐτῶν τῆς ἑορτῆς παυσαμίνης. 59. ἡμεῖς δὲ οἱ δώδεκα μαθηταὶ τοῦ κ(υρίο)υ ἐκλαίομεν καὶ ἐλυπούμεθα καὶ ἕκαστος λυπούμενος διὰ τὸ συμβὰν ἀπηλλάγη εἰς τὸν οἶκον αὐτοῦ. 60. ἐγὼ δὲ Σίμων Πέτρος καὶ Ἀνδρέας ὁ ἀδελφός μου λαβόντες ἡμῶν τὰ λίνα ἀπήλθαμεν εἰς τὴν θάλασσαν, καὶ ἦν σὺν ἡμῖν Λευεὶς ὁ τοῦ Ἀλφαίου ὃν κ(ύριο)ς ...

54. For the stone was great, and we are afraid lest somebody sees us. And if we are not able, let us place at the door what we are bringing for his memorial, and we shall weep and wail until we return to our house,'

13.55. And after they set out, they found the tomb had been opened and as they approached they stooped down there and they saw there a certain young man sitting in the midst of the tomb, beautiful and wearing a shining robe who said to them, 56. 'Why did you come? Whom do you seek? Not that one who was crucified? [He has risen and gone...] But if you do not believe, stoop down and see the place from... [the...] [because he is not...]. For he has risen and gone to the place from whence he was sent. 57. Then the women fearing, fled.

14.58. Now it was the last day of the unleavened bread and many people left, returning to their houses, the feast being over. 59. But we, the twelve disciples of the Lord, wept and were saddened, and each being sad because of the event withdrew to his house. 60. But I, Simon Peter, and Andrew my brother, taking our nets went to the sea, and there was with us Levi the son of Alphaeus, whom the Lord...

TRANSCRIPTION AND TRANSLATION OF P.OXY. 2949
AND P.OXY. 4009

*P.Oxy. 2949*

*Fragment 1*

| Line 5 | ὁ φίλος Π[ε]ιλά̣[τ]ο̣υ | the friend of Pilate |
| | ις ὅτι ἐκέλευσεν | that he commanded |
| | ελ]θὼν πρὸς Πειλᾶτο[ν | came to Pilate |
| | ]τὸ̣ σῶμα εἰς ταφὴν [ | the body to a tomb |
| | Ἡρῴδ]ην ἠτησα[το | Herod asked |
| Line 10 | ] ηναι εἰπὼ[ν | ...saying |
| | ]αιτησα [ | asked |
| | ]αὐτὸν [ | him |
| | ] ὅτι α[ | that |

*Fragment 2*

| Line 15 | μου[ | of me |
| | Πειλ[ατ | Pilate |
| | τις α[ὐτὸν | somebody [him] |
| | με̣ν̣ | we ?... |

## P.Oxy. 4009

*Recto*

| Line 1 | ] [ | ? |
|---|---|---|
| | ] ει [ | ? |
| | ] κα [ | ? |
| | ] θερισμος [ | harvest |
| Line 5 | ] αιος ως αι [ | ...as the |
| | ] αι φρονιμ [ | the wise |
| | ] εσεσθε ως [ | be as |
| | ] ον λυκων [ | ...wolves |
| | ] ον εαν ου | ...if not |
| Line 10 | ] μεν | ? |
| | ]λεγει μοι οι | he says to me the |
| | ] ξαντες το | ...the |
| | ] κετι αυτω ου | no longer to him not |
| | ] ποιησ...δι | did |
| Line 15 | ] μειν...ψο | remain? |
| | ] ναπ [ | ? |
| | ] σκαι [ | ? |
| | ] μηκε [ | ? |
| | ] ν [ | ? |
| Line 20 | ] ω [ | ? |
| | ] μει [ | ? |

## P.Oxy. 4009

*Verso*

| Line 1 | ] [ | ? |
| | ] ψε̣ [ | ? |
| | ] υστ̣ [ | ? |
| | ουδε γ[ | but not |
| Line 5 | παρεσχ [ | supply |
| | θοντιμ [ | …honour |
| | κας δια [ | …because |
| | οτι αφ︥ια̣ [ | that… |
| | λαι αμα[ | ? together |
| Line 10 | αυτω ε-κ[ | to him from |
| | μενωγ[ | remaining |
| | νοματ[ | ? |
| | αφεις κ̄ε̄ [ | …Lord |
| | ] ουθ[ | nothing |
| Line 15 | ]μμαι[ | the? |
| | ]πφο̣.[ | ? |
| | ].πη.[ | ? |
| | ] ι̣ν [ | ? |
| | ] ρ̣α̣ι[ | ? |
| Line 20 | ] ν̣ [ | ? |
| | ]. [ | ? |

COMMENTARY

# THE NON-WASHING OF HANDS AND THE INSTRUCTIONS
## OF HEROD ANTIPAS (1.1–2)

1. τ[ῶν]¹ δὲ Ἰουδαίων οὐδεὶς ἐνίψατο τὰς χεῖρας, οὐδὲ Ἡρῴδης οὐδ᾽ εἷς [τ]ῶν² κριτῶν αὐτοῦ. καὶ³ [μὴ] βουληθέντω(ν) νίψασθαι, ἀνέστη Πειλᾶτος. 2. καὶ τότε κελεύει Ἡρῴδης ὁ βασιλεὺς παρ[αλη]μφθῆναι⁴ τὸν $\overline{κν}$⁵, εἰπὼν αὐτοῖς ὅτι· Ὅσα ἐκέλευσα ὑμῖν⁶ ποιῆσαι αὐτῷ, ποιήσατε.

1. but of the Jews no-one washed the hands, nor Herod, nor one of his judges. And when they were not willing to wash, Pilate rose up. 2. And then Herod the king commanding the Lord to be brought, said to them, 'Whatever I commanded you to do to him, do.'

## TEXT CRITICAL NOTES

1. The original heliographic images of the text are of extremely poor quality, especially for the top two lines of the first page of text, as well as the left-hand side of the page.¹ Much clearer images of the text were produced in the early 1980s by Adam Bülow-Jacobsen. These are available either online,² or in the edition by Kraus and Nicklas.³ For convenience, they are also presented as plates in this volume. The initial τ of the first partially visible word can just be read and is followed by white space. From the newer images this does not appear to be a hole in the manuscript, but a section of abraded text.

2. At this point the text is somewhat uncertain. There is a hole that has removed the first letter of the immediately following word. This letter, however, can be reconstructed with a strong degree of certainty as being τ. The reasons for this are twofold. First, the word

---

¹ The original heliographs of the text are reproduced by Lods, L'Évangile et l'Apocalypse de Pierre avec le texte grec du livre d'Hénoch. Text publié en fac-simile, par l'héliogravure d'après les photographies du manuscrit de Gizéh'. A set of photographs of improved quality in comparison to the original heliographs can be found in Gebhardt, *Das Evangelium und die Apokalypse des Petrus. Die neuentdeckten Bruchstücke nach einer Photographie der Handschrift zu Gizéh in Lichtdruck herausgegeben.*

² http://ipap.csad.ox.ac.uk/GP/GP.html

³ Kraus und Nicklas, *Das Petrusevangelium und die Petrusapokalypse*, as plates at the end of the volume. See also, A.E. Bernhard, *Other Early Christian Gospels*, plates 8–16. These are reproduced at a much lighter level of contrast.

is almost certainly the masculine genitive plural form of the article. Second, there appear to be the vestiges of the horizontal crossbar of the τ. The main problem arises with the letters before the hole. After the name Ἡρῴδης, one can read with certainty the letters ουδε the next (two or three?) letters are uncertain due to what appears to be poor formation and possibly the overwriting of existing script. A number of readings have been proposed. Bruston suggested the reading οὐδὲ ἑτέρων.[4] This would then take the final letters of what is commonly reconstructed as a masculine genitive plural form of the article as instead the ending of ἑτέρων. The problems here are: (i) this does not account for the remains of the horizontal cross-bar; and (ii) the descender of the supposed ρ, if of the same shape and length of that of the ρ in the following word κριτῶν, should be visible below the small hole. This is not the case. Furthermore, the letter that is unclear after the visible letters ουδε does not appear to be analogous to any of the forms of the letter τ that occur throughout the text. As another possibility, Hilgenfeld suggests the reading οὐδέ τις.[5] Here again the problem is that of reconstructing the letter τ. Lods[6] and Swete see textual emendation having occurred as the result of the scribe's self-correction. This is seen as involving the reading οὐδ' εἷς[7] being changed to οὐδέ τις. Thus Swete notes, 'εἷς is uncertain: ουδ εις has perhaps been corrected to ουδε τις.'[8] This theory perhaps better explains the apparent overwriting of an existing text, although, if this is the case, the scribe has made a very poor attempt at forming the letter τ in place before the ι. Both Zahn[9] and Vaganay prefer the non-elided form οὐδὲ εἷς, with the latter scholar arguing that both classical and Hellenistic usage prefers a non-elided form and that in the same sentence οὐδέ is not elided before the word Ἡρῴδης.[10]

---

[4] Bruston, 'De quelques texts difficiles de l'Évanglie de Pierre' *Revue des études grecques* (1897) 58–65.

[5] A. Hilgenfeld, 'Das Petrus-Evangelium über Leiden und Auferstehung Jesu' *ZWT* 36 (1893) part 1, 439–454 and 'Das Petrus-Evangelium', part 2, 220–267.

[6] Lods, 'L'Évangile et l'Apocalypse de Pierre avec le texte grec du livre d'Henoch', 219.

[7] Not οὐδὲ εἷς as Vaganay suggests. See Vaganay, *L'Évangile de Pierre*, 202.

[8] Swete, *The Akhmîm Fragment of the Apocryphal Gospel of St Peter*, 1.

[9] Zahn, *Das Evangelium des Petrus*, 8.

[10] Vaganay, *L'Évangile de Pierre*, 202–203.

The fundamental difficulty with this proposal is that the photographs of the manuscript do not show the required two successive epsilons. Since this reconstruction does not adequately account for the letters that can be read or for the amount of space remaining, it is not possible to see the non-elided form as the reading of the text. Thus the elided reading οὐδ᾽ εἷς proposed independently by Harnack[11] and Robinson,[12] and followed by the majority of translations remains the most probable reading. This, however, should probably be taken in conjunction with Swete's attempt to make sense of the overwritten text.

3. There is a tear in the page at this point extending inwards from the right-hand side for about 3.5cm. The tear is not totally continuous, since 6mm in from the right-hand side there is a 3mm wide portion of parchment remaining that adjoins the the first and second lines of text. Fortunately for most of its length the tear occurs between lines. Its slight downward slope (from right to left), however, does obscure the text between the first letter of the καί and the clearly visible ο in βουληθέντων. Traces of the bottoms of the α and the ι of the καί are still visible.

Bouriant reconstructed the text as καὶ [τῶν] βουληθέντων.[13] Although the presence of the article before a participle is common,[14] thereby substantivizing it, the primary problem seems to be with the traces of the final letter before the β in βουληθέντων. If this letter were to be read as ν, comparison with other forms of this letter as it occurs in the word τῶν throughout the manuscript do not appear to match. The scribe writes the letter nu in a majuscule

---

[11] Harnack, *Bruchstücke des Evangeliums und der Apokalypse des Petrus*, 8.

[12] Robinson, *The Gospel according to Peter and the Revelation of Peter: Two Lectures on the Newly Recovered Fragments together with the Greek Texts* (London: C.J. Clay and Sons, 1892) 83.

[13] Bouriant, 'Fragments du texte grec du livre d'Énoch et de quelques écrits attribués à saint Pierre', 137. This was also the reading Swete originally published (*The Apocryphal Gospel of Peter*, 1), but he changed this later in his fuller book *The Akhmîm Fragment of the Apocryphal Gospel of St Peter*, 1.

[14] It is should also be recognised that *koine* Greek allowed for participles to function as nouns without the presence of a definite article, cf. Lk 3.14; Jn 1.24. For a discussion of the topic see F. Blass and A. Debrunner, *A Greek Grammer of the New Testament and other Early Christian Literature* (trans. R.W. Funk, Cambridge: CUP, 1961) §413 'The participle used as a substantive', 212–213.

form, N.[15] Although the visible vertical stroke on the right-hand side could theoretically match the final stroke of the N, what is missing is any trace of the downward sloping diagonal which connects the two vertical strokes. Furthermore, the distance between the end of the word αὐτοῦ and the trace of the β in βουληθέντων is 11mm. The next καί to occur in the text occupies about 7mm with surrounding whitespace, which appears to be the same length of text occupied by the word here. This then leaves 4mm of text to be reconstructed. The clearly readable example of τῶν on this second line of text requires 7–8mm of space. Alternatively, Vaganay presents the text as κ[αὶ μὴ] βουληθέντων.[16] Comparing the μή in line 10 on the first page of text, it can be measured as occupying 4mm of space. Moreover, when one traces over the μή from line 10 and places it over this gap of approximately 4mm in line two there is a near perfect correspondence between the traces of the letters visible and the bottom of the μή from line 10.

4. The missing letters are caused by a hole rather than an abrasion. The right-hand vertical stroke of the μ is still visible. Also the bottom portion of the descender from the μ is visible.

5. This is the first use of a *nomen sacrum* by the scribe in this text. The term κύριος is used thirteen times, eleven of which occur in the contracted abbreviated form with a supralinear crossbar (*Gos. Pet.* 1.2; 2.3 [twice]; 3.6; 4.10; 5.19; 6.21; 12.50 [twice]; 14.59, 60). However, on two occasions κύριος occurs in a non-abbreviated form (*Gos. Pet.* 3.8; 6.24).[17]

6. The scribe employs a diacritical sign over the first letter of the word ὑμῖν. The diacritical mark consists of two dots in a horizontal line over the letter upsilon, and may be termed an umlaut or diæresis. This sign occurs in a total of seven places in this text, three on the first page, one on the second page, one on the fifth page, and two on the seventh. The second is above the iota in the name ἵωσηφ (*Gos. Pet.* 2.3). The third is above the word ὑιον (*Gos. Pet.* 3.6). Three

---

[15] Gebhardt observes that in comparison to the minuscule form of the μ 'Während das μ fast ausgeprägte Minuskelform zeigt, unterscheidet sich das ν oft nur dadurch von dem uncialen N.' Gebhardt, *Das Evangelium und die Apokalypse des Petrus*, 12.

[16] Vaganay, *L'Évangile de Pierre*, 202.

[17] The standard work on the subject is still L. Traube, *Nomina Sacra: Versuch einer Geschichte christlichen Kürzung* (Munich: Beck'sche Verlagsbuchhandlung, 1907). For a more recent discussion of the lack of uniformity in use of *nomina sacra* see C.M. Tuckett, 'Nomina Sacra in Codex E', *JTS* new series 57 (2006) 487–499.

of the remaining four occurrences (*Gos. Pet.* 3.9; 11.45, 46) repeat the form found in *Gos. Pet.* 3.6. The remaining case occurs in *Gos. Pet.* 9.35 where it is used above the feminine article, ἡ. In this case there is no preceding or following vowel. There are two common ways in which the diæresis functions. (i) The 'organic' use, to mark the separation of a sequence of two or more vowels, indicating that they are to be articulated with distinct pronunciation rather than as a diphthong. (ii) The 'inorganic' use, not to separate vowels, but simply to mark an initial vowel.[18] The symbol may have originated as an indication that potential diphthongs are pronounced as separate syllables. This usage is common in a number of early papyrus manuscripts, including the egospel fragment 𝔓[52]. However, it is common practice to write a diæresis on an initial iota or upsilon, even when there is no preceding or following vowel to distinguish.[19] The present example is a case of the organic use, to mark a separation between the preceding alpha and the initial upsilon of ὑμῖν.

## COMMENTARY

**1.1a** τ[ῶν] δὲ Ἰουδαίων οὐδεὶς ἐνίψατο τὰς χεῖρας. The notice about the Jews refusing to wash their hands forms a contrast with the now missing portion of the sentence or storyline, (if there was, as seems most likely, preceding material) introduced by the discontinuity indicator δέ.[20] Moreover, the mention of Pilate without explanation in 1.2 suggests that this character had already been introduced into the narrative. From Matt 27.24 there is a tradition of Pilate washing his hands as a symbolic declaration of innocence. This material is unique to the first gospel. The passage in question states,

ἰδὼν δὲ ὁ Πιλᾶτος ὅτι οὐδὲν ὠφελεῖ ἀλλὰ μᾶλλον θόρυβος γίνεται· λαβὼν ὕδωρ ἀπενίψατο τὰς χεῖρας ἀπέναντι τοῦ ὄχλου λέγων· ἀθῷός εἰμι ἀπὸ τοῦ αἵματος τούτου· ὑμεῖς ὄψεσθε. (Matt 27.24)

---

[18] See E.G. Turner, *Greek Manuscripts of the Ancient World* (2nd ed., rev. and enl., ed. P. Parsons; London: Institute for Classical Studies, 1987) 10.

[19] Turner, *Greek Manuscripts of the Ancient World*, 10.

[20] As discussed in the recent conference presentation by S.E. Porter and M.B. O'Donnell, 'Conjunctions and Levels of Discourse,' New Testament Philology Section, European Association of Biblical Studies Annual Meeting, Budapest, Hungary, 6–9 August 2006.

It is impossible to know for certain if this incident formed the imme-diately foregoing contrast in the Akhmîm text. It is, however, the most plausible suggestion for three reasons. First, Pilate is named in both narratives; second, the washing of hands here in the *Gospel of Peter* during the trial is highly reminiscent of the actions of the Roman Pre-fect, and third, this heightens a theological trajectory introduced in the Matthean account, namely it further implicates the Jews as the instigators of Jesus' crucifixion while simultaneously absolving Pilate. Whether the current text also contained a version of the corporate acknowledgement of responsibility for the death of Jesus which again forms part of the Matthean *Sondergut* cannot be known with any degree of certainty (καὶ ἀποκριθεὶς πᾶς ὁ λαὸς εἶπεν· τὸ αἷμα αὐτοῦ ἐφ' ἡμᾶς καὶ ἐπὶ τὰ τέκνα ἡμῶν Matt 27.25). What can be observed is that the traditions of Pilate washing his hands and the acknowledgement of responsibility for the execution of Jesus at Jewish instigation were known in texts besides Matthew's gospel, although these texts are likely to be dependent upon the Matthean account. In the *Acts of Pilate* 9.4 the following scene in the trial is narrated:

> καὶ λαβὼν ὕδωρ ὁ Πιλᾶτος ἀπενίψατο τὰς χεῖρας αὐτοῦ ἀπέναντι τοῦ ἡλίου λέγων Ἀθῷός εἰμι ἀπὸ τοῦ αἵματος τοῦ δικαίου τούτου· ὑμεῖς ὄψεσθε. πάλιν κράζουσιν οἱ Ἰουδαῖοι ὅτι τὸ αἷμα αὐτοῦ ἐφ' ἡμᾶς καὶ ἐπὶ τὰ τέκνα ἡμῶν (Acts Pil. 9.4b)[21]

It is immediately apparent that there is some form of literary depen-dence between the *Acts of Pilate* and the Gospel of Matthew. The most likely scenario is that here the *Acts of Pilate* is drawing directly on the work of the first evangelist.[22] The actual words of Pilate and the respondents are the same in both texts. The polemic in the *Acts of Pilate* seems to be heightened, referring to the crowd as οἱ Ἰουδαῖοι rather than Matthew's more neutral πᾶς ὁ λαός. Furthermore, the additional detail that Pilate washed his hands ἀπέναντι τοῦ ἡλίου, may indicate a later text expanded with incidental details. Thus it seems best to conclude that the *Gospel of Peter* and the *Acts of Pilate* reflect independent trajectories of this tradition.

---

[21] Tischendorf, *Evangelia Apocrypha*, 230.

[22] Throughout the trial and Passion scene the *Acts of Pilate* seems to be a composite of material drawn from the four canonical gospels, combined with other traditions (perhaps both written and oral) along with creative redactional interpretation of these traditions.

The main verb in this clause occurs in the aorist form ἐνίψατο. Recent studies of verbal aspect have noted that in narrative texts the main function of the aorist indicative form is 'to provide the main-line of narrative proper, outlining the skeletal structure of the story.'[23] Therefore the presence of the aorist indicative in this broken sentence would appear to indicate that the details being narrated are central to the main storyline.

**1.1bα   οὐδὲ Ἡρῴδης.** The member of the Herodian family mentioned here is not specifically identified. The assumed historical setting, however, demands that the text is referring to Herod Antipas, the son of Herod the Great by his marriage to Malthace.[24] Although Antipas was not the offspring of Herod's final marriage, he does appear to have been the youngest of his male children. This is supported by Josephus in two parallel passages.

καὶ βασιλέα μὲν ἀπεδείκυεν Ἀντίπαν ἀμελῶν τῶν πρεσβυτάτων, Ἀρξελάου καὶ Φιλίππου· διαβεβλήκει γὰρ καὶ τούτους Ἀντίπατρος.

He now named Antipas king, passing over his eldest sons, Archelaus and Philip, who had also been the objects of Antipater's calumnies. (*B.J.* 1.646)[25]

εἰς νόσον δὲ ὁ βασιλεὺς ἐμπεσὼν διαθήκας γράφει, τῷ νεωτάτῳ τῶν υἱῶν τὴν βασιλείαν διδοὺς μίσει τῷ πρὸς τόν τε Ἀρξέλαον καὶ Φίλιππον ἐκ τῶν Ἀντιπάτρου διαβολῶν.

But the king fell ill and made a will, giving the kingdom to his youngest son because of his hatred of both Archaleus and Philip, arising from the calumnies of Antipater. (*A.J.* 17.146).[26]

Antipas was appointed by Roman imperial authority as tetrarch of Galilee and Peraea. He continued in this role until being deposed and exiled in the summer of 39 CE. The incident in the *Gospel of Peter*

---

[23] C.R. Campbell, *Basics of Verbal Aspect in Biblical Greek* (Grand Rapids: Zondervans, 2008) 84.

[24] H.W. Hoehner, *Herod Antipas* (SNTSMS 17, Cambridge: CUP, 1972) 10.

[25] Josephus, *The Jewish War* Books I–II, (trans. H. St. J. Thackeray, LCL 203; Bury St Edmunds: Harvard, 1927).

[26] Josephus, *Jewish Antiquities* Books XVIXV–II, (trans. R. Marcus and A. Wikgren, LCL 410; Bury St Edmunds: Harvard, 1963).

needs to be read in light of Lk 23.6ff. where the same member of the Herodian family is in view. In Luke's Gospel the decision made by Pilate to summon Antipas, likewise simply named as 'Herod' (Lk 23.7), is made on the basis of his jurisdiction over Galilee. In relation to the Lukan account Fitzmyer notes,

> The Lucan passion narrative is unique in breaking up the trial of Jesus before Pilate with the insertion of his appearance before Herod Antipas (23:6–12). It is occasioned by Pilate's hearing about the Galilean matrix of Jesus' teaching. Jesus is therefore sent to the Galilean authority, who questions him but gets no answer; accordingly, he treats Jesus with contempt and sends him back to Pilate.[27]

Obviously Fitzmyer's claim concerning the uniqueness of the Lukan narrative is made in terms of the corpus of the four canonical gospels. While the source critical relationship between the *Gospel of Peter* and Luke's gospel is debated, the most probable conjecture is that the latter was the source for the former, or that the tradition of Jesus appearing before Antipas itself draws on an intermediate source that was itself dependent on the third gospel. The fact that the *Gospel of Peter*, which like Luke's account also mentions Antipas in the trial narrative, raises a number of further source critical questions. Discussing the Lukan pericope, Fitzmyer outlines two options. Firstly, he notes, '[t]he episode has often been regarded as a Lucan creation.'[28] He dismisses the reasons that have been put forward for this view. Thus he shows his preference for a second option, namely that 'the evidence does not all point toward Lucan fabrication. The appearance of Jesus before Herod could be just as historical as the Lucan depiction of the morning session of the Sanhedrin interrogation.'[29]

If the first option were correct, this would mean that the composition of the *Gospel of Peter* post-dated that of Luke's Gospel and while dependence on the third gospel in some form would necessarily be this case, this would not exclude a circuitous path of either literary or oral dependence (or even a combination of these). Although one could not necessarily assume direct literary dependence, this would perhaps remain the most plausible explanation. However, the second option,

---

[27] J.A. Fitzmyer, *The Gospel According to Luke X–XXIV* (New York: Doubleday, 1985) 1478.

[28] Fitzmyer, *The Gospel According to Luke X–XXIV*, 1478.

[29] Fitzmyer, *The Gospel According to Luke X–XXIV*, 1479.

which sees the tradition of Antipas' role in the trial as pre-Lukan, does not exclude the possibility that the *Gospel of Peter* was dependent upon Luke. Regardless of the tradition history of the examination before Antipas, it seems highly plausible rather than knowing this incident through an independent oral tradition the *Gospel of Peter* has drawn this incident from Luke's gospel. This is strengthened by the identification of other Lukan features in the *Gospel of Peter* (see introduction 7.4). If this were the case, then the *Gospel of Peter* depends upon an element that is a redactional component in the Lukan account and consequently is a witness to the reception history of the third gospel. This case satisfies Koester's criterion that literary dependence of a text can be identified only when the secondary work draws upon the redactional composition of an earlier author.[30] However, even with this criterion Gregory's caveat needs to be borne in mind.

> Therefore it is possible that a later text which parallels such material might do so because its author had access to such a source rather than because he drew on *Luke* or *Acts*. This difficulty applies to much of *Luke* and to virtually all of *Acts*. It does not render Koester's criterion invalid, for positive indications of the reception of *Luke* that meet this criterion may be accepted as secure, but it does suggest that such results may be obtainable only from a limited selection of material in *Luke-Acts*.[31]

Ultimately, the issue of dependence cannot be decided without consideration of the dating of the *Gospel of Peter*. The later one believes the *Gospel of Peter* to have been composed, the less likely it is that it is drawing on an independent oral tradition, and the more probable dependence becomes on the canonical tradition preserved in the third gospel. Moreover, for those who think that the *Gospel of Peter* (or the Cross Gospel embedded within it) was composed around the middle of the first century CE it is possible that the direction of dependence can be reversed, and Luke can be seen as being dependent on the *Gospel of Peter*, or the tradition behind it. However reference to the presence

---

[30] Köster, *Synoptische Überlieferung bei den Apostolischen Vätern*, 3.

[31] Gregory, *The Reception of Luke and Acts in the Period before Irenaeus*, 14. As Gregory notes elsewhere, 'Koester's weakness may be that his criterion makes it virtually impossible to demonstrate any dependence on a Synoptic Gospel except in passages where the redactional activity of an evangelist may be readily identified.' (A. Gregory and C.M. Tuckett, 'Reflections on Method: What constitutes the use of the Writings that later formed the New Testament in the Apostolic Fathers?', 71).

of Antipas during the trial shows some shared knowledge possessed by
Luke and the *Gospel of Peter.*

**1.1bβ   οὐδ᾽ εἷς τῶν κριτῶν αὐτοῦ.** The antecedent of the phrase
τῶν κριτῶν αὐτοῦ is ambiguous. There are perhaps three possibilities.
The genitive pronoun αὐτοῦ could refer to the immediately preceding
Herod. The second option is that it could denote the no longer extant
character who headed the list of figures who would not wash their
hands. Presumably this missing name was Pilate. The third option does
not take the αὐτοῦ as a possessive genitive, but in an objective genitive
indicating one of the people judging him, that is Jesus. Hence, on this
reading, it is a reference to the one being judged: in the vocabulary
of the *Gospel of Peter* this person is 'the Lord.' Taking these possibilities in reverse order, the identification of the pronoun as denoting
Jesus has been followed by a number of scholars such as Bruston,[32]
Hilgenfeld,[33] Swete,[34] Robinson[35] and Mara.[36] The fullest defence of the
viewpoint is provided by Mara who argues in opposition to Vaganay
(who supports the idea that the pronoun denotes the judges of Herod).
Thus Mara argues that the third peson singular pronoun when used
in the *Gospel of Peter* occurs in an absolute and solemn manner and
is reserved to refer to 'the Lord'.[37] There are, however, two occasions
when the masculine genitive singular form of the pronoun is used
where the reference is obviously not to 'the Lord.' First, in 11.47, after
both Pilate and the Son of God have been named in the preceding
verse, the narrator comments εἶτα προσελθόντες πάντες ἐδέοντο αὐτοῦ
('then they all came asking him'). The person to whom the request is
addressed to command the soldiers to keep silent can only be Pilate.
Mara acknowledges this observing that the request is directed to Pilate
by the Jewish figures.'[38] Similarly, the final clause of 14.59, εἰς τὸν οἶκον

---

[32] Bruston, 'De quelques texts difficiles de l'Évanglie de Pierre', 60.

[33] Hilgenfeld, 'Das Petrus-Evangelium', Part 2, 243.

[34] Swete offers the following translation with the associated comment, '"Nor yet
any one of His judges," *i.e.*, the members of the Sanhedrin who had condemned Him
(Mark xiv. 64).' Swete, *The Akhmîm Fragment of the Apocryphal Gospel of St Peter*, 1.

[35] Although Robinson does not comment on this issue explicitly his translation
makes his interpretation clear through the capitalization of the English translation of
the pronoun, 'nor any one of His judges.' Robinson, *The Gospel according to Peter and
the Revelation of Peter*, 16.

[36] Mara, *Évangile de Pierre*, 73–74.

[37] Mara, *Évangile de Pierre*, 73–74.

[38] Mara, *Évangile de Pierre*, 195.

αὐτοῦ, is a clear designation of an individual member of the Twelve, and in no way is it a reference to the Lord even though the Twelve are described as μαθηταὶ τῆς κυρίου in the same verse. These two examples demonstrate that overarching theories about the pronoun αὐτοῦ being used as a dominical marker simply do not hold. Rather, one must determine the referent of the pronoun on a case by case basis. The case for the pronoun denoting Pilate is weakened by the fact that he is not named in the surviving portion of text. Moreover, such a reference would undermine the outlook of the entire text which is the exoneration of the Romans at the expense of implicating Jewish figures as being fully responsible for the execution of Jesus. Since the central character in the proceedings of the trial is Antipas, it is most obvious to understand τῶν κριτῶν αὐτοῦ as being the judicial officers of the Herodian court. The historical probability of such figures being in attendance with Antipas during a paschal visit to Jerusalem is of no consequence to the author of the *Gospel of Peter*.

**1.1bγ** καὶ [μὴ] βουληθέντων νίψασθαι. Harnack's versification differs at this point, he commences his second verse at this point.[39] Subsequent divisions have continued the first verse as far as the reference to Pilate and then start the second verse with the actions of Herod being described, καὶ τότε…. This latter division is the one followed here, not only because it has been adopted by the majority of commentators, but since it is a much more natural sense division. As discussed in the textual notes, there are a number of problems surrounding the reconstruction of the text. It is not assisted by the poor letter formation in the visible text. The aorist middle infinitive is clearly read on the following line, and is to be understood as a middle of self-interest, referring to the judges refusal to wash themselves. The exact meaning of this clause depends on the letters that occupied the lacuna in the text and the syntactical relationship of the clause to the remainder of the verse. If the masculine plural form of the definite article filled the gap this would mean this sequence would be best understood as a subordinate clause modifying the previous reference to 'the judges'. In this case one would have οὐδ' εἷς [τ]ῶν κριτῶν αὐτοῦ, καὶ [τῶν] βουληθέντων νίψασθαι, 'nor one of his judges, even among those who wished to wash.' If, however, the lacuna were filled with the

---

[39] Harnack, *Bruchstücke des Evangeliums und der Apokalypse des Petrus*, 8.

negative particle μή, then the construction would be best taken as a genitive absolute which introduces the actions of Pilate, the subject of the sentence, as being a direct consequence of the three named parties who refuse to wash their hands. In this case the clause would be co-ordinated with the following element, καὶ [μὴ] βουληθέντων νίψασθαι, ἀνέστη Πειλᾶτος, 'and when they did not wish to wash, Pilate arose.' Following the brief discussion by Murray,[40] a number of commentators accept his suggestion that μή is the preferred reading.[41] Yet, as Murray himself acknowledges, he was not the first to come up with this proposal. He states, 'It is difficult to interpret M. Bouriant's brackets, but if they are meant to indicate illegibility in the MS., it would be tempting to read, as has already been suggested, καὶ μὴ βουληθέντων.'[42] Three points need to be made in reference to this comment. First, it appears that Swete may have been the first to propose this reading.[43] Secondly, Murray states that he has not seen the manuscript, or photographs of it, rather he is working from the published transcription made by Bouriant. Thirdly, the purpose of Murray's article is 'to point out some hitherto unnoticed traces of the use of this document [the *Gospel of Peter*] in early Christian literature.'[44] It must therefore be borne in mind that the reading Murray proposes allows him to find even greater correspondence between this phrase in the *Gospel of Peter* and a passage in Origin's commentary on Matthew. Murray presents the parallels under consideration in the following form.

> (1) "Et ipse quidem se lavit, illi autem *non solum se mundare nolu-erunt* a sanguine Christi, sed etiam super se susceperunt, dicentes: Sanguis ejus super nos, et super filios nostros." – *Orig. in Mat.*, 124.
> Cf. §1. καὶ [τῶν] βουληθέντων νίψασθαι.[45]

By preferring the negative particle in the reading from the *Gospel of Peter*, Murray's case for Origin's knowledge is strengthened (although it still is not highly significant). While this does not exclude reading the negative particle, one needs to be aware of the motivation for Murray's preference.

---

[40] J.O.F. Murray, 'Evangelium Secundum Petrum', *The Expositor* (1893) 50–61.
[41] Vaganay, *L'Évangile de Pierre*, 203.
[42] Murray, 'Evangelium Secundum Petrum', 55.
[43] Swete, *The Akhmîm Fragment of the Apocryphal Gospel of St Peter*, 1.
[44] Murray, 'Evangelium Secundum Petrum', 55.
[45] See Murray, 'Evangelium Secundum Petrum', 55.

Whichever reading is preferred, the emphasis is to accent the perversity of those who would not wash their hands. If the negative is read, this most likely refers to the combined refusal of all three parties, the Jews, Herod and the judges. If, however, the definite article is read, then this focuses on the judges and their dereliction of duty. In the latter case the complicity of the judges is heighten, not only by singling them out, but more significantly the narratives shows that some of this group wished to wash their hands, but for unspecified reasons they did not choose this course of action.

**1.1bδ** ἀνέστη Πειλᾶτος. This is the first explicit mention of Pilate in the narrative. The fact that the name Pilate occurs without explanation or title strengthens the case that this figure had already been mentioned previously, in the now no longer extant portion of the narrative. Historically Pilate was the fifth Roman governor of Judea, and most plausibly he held office between 26–37 CE.[46] Contrary to the designation used by Swete[47] and Mara,[48] the title 'procurator' is historically incorrect. The New Testament evidence is of little help is establishing the correct Roman title for the office held by Pilate. On the occasions it uses a title it opts for 'governor' either in a noun form, ἡγεμών (Matt 27.2, 11, 14, 15, 21, 27; 28.14; Lk 20.20) or a participial form, ἡγεμονεύοντος Lk 3.2. The issue does, however, appear to have been resolved by the discovery in June 1961 of a building inscription at Caesarea contemporary with Pilate's period of office. The inscription reads:

line 1:        TIBERIEVM
line 2: PON]TIVS PILATVS
line 3: PRAEF]ECTVS IVDA

This inscription provides the only extant epigraphical reference to Pilate and refers to him unambiguously as Prefect.[49]

---

[46] H.K. Bond, *Pontius Pilate in History and Interpretation*, SNTSMS 100 (Cambridge: CUP, 1998) 1, fn. 1. Revisionist attempts to re-date this period of office have not proven to be convincing, see D.R. Schwarz, 'Pontius Pilate's Appointment to Office and the Chronology of Antiquities, Books 18–20', in *Studies in the Jewish Background to Christianity* (Tübingen: J.C.B. Mohr [Paul Siebeck], 1992) 182–201.

[47] In passing Swete writes, 'The object is to minimise the sin of the Procurator...' *The Akhmîm Fragment of the Apocryphal Gospel of St Peter*, 1.

[48] Mara states, 'Il se peut que l'auteur ignore quelles étaient les attributions précises d'un *procurateur* romain depuis les réformes d'Auguste...' *Évangile de Pierre*, 79.

[49] The inscription was excavated by a team of Italian archaeologists led by Frova. The original inscription is now housed in the Israel Museum in Jerusalem, although

Within the narrative of the *Gospel of Peter*, the note that 'Pilate arose' forms part of the wider tendency to exonerate Pilate, while simultaneously further implicating the Jews as being responsible for the death of Jesus. Frustrated by the combined intractability of the Jews, Herod and the judges, Pilate withdraws in protest. The tendency to shift the blame from Rome, represented specifically in the person of Pilate, is evidenced in other early Christian literature, most notably the *Acts of Pilate*, where the Roman Prefect consistently rebukes the Jews and repeatedly declares the innocence of Jesus.[50] Swete refers to Acts 26.30 as a text to be compared with the description of Pilate rising up.[51] The text in Acts describes the king (Agrippa II),[52] the governor,[53] Bernice and their entourage rising up in order to signal the end of hearing the testimony of Paul, Ἀνέστη τε ὁ βασιλεὺς καὶ ὁ ἡγεμὼν ἥ τε Βερνίκη καὶ οἱ συγκαθήμενοι αὐτοῖς (Acts 26.30). While both usages of the verb ἀνέστη occur in judicial settings, the similarity is in all probability coincidental, perhaps reflecting normal trial etiquette, rather than being an intentional echoing of the examination of Paul before Agrippa and Festus by the author of the *Gospel of Peter*. The significant point to note is that Pilate, as he is presented in the narrative, has distanced himself from the events that are about to follow. He stands aloof, taking a non-interventionist role, perhaps not completely exonerated because of his inaction, but nonetheless definitely

---

a replica has been placed *in situ* in the theatre in Caesarea Maritima. On the face is a monumental inscription which is part of a larger dedication to Tiberius Caesar which clearly says that it was from 'Pontius Pilate, Prefect of Judea.'

[50] See J.K. Elliott, *The Apocryphal New Testament* rev. ed. (Oxford: OUP, 1999) 169–185.

[51] Swete, *The Akhmîm Fragment of the Apocryphal Gospel of St Peter*, 1.

[52] See D.C. Braund, 'Agrippa', *ABD* vol. 1, 99–100.

[53] Barrett has noted, in relation to the phrase ὁ βασιλεὺς καὶ ὁ ἡγεμών 'The repeated article makes it clear that two persons are intended.' C.K. Barrett, *The Acts of the Apostles*, vol II (ICC; Edinburgh: T&T Clark, 1998), 1172. Although Festus is not explicitly identified as 'the governor' there can be little doubt that this is what is intended. First the term ἡγεμών is used to denote Pilate in the gospels, second, elsewhere in Acts the term has been used to refer unambiguously to the Roman Procurator Felix (Acts 23.24, 26, 33; 24.1, 10), third there is no other figure in Acts 26 to whom the title could be applied apart from Porcius Festus. Although Haenchen does not discuss this point explicitly he uses the titles procurator and governor interchangeably in his comments on Acts 26.30, 32 in reference to Festus. In relation to v. 30 'King and procurator arise...' and discussing v 32 'Agrippa, the authority here, explains to the governor...'. See E. Haenchen, *The Acts of the Apostles: A Commentary* (Oxford: Blackwell, 1971) 690.

not fully complicit in the execution that is to follow in this account of the Passion.

**1.2a   καὶ τότε κελεύει Ἡρῴδης ὁ βασιλεὺς παρ[αλημ]φθῆναι τὸν κύριον.** Herod takes over as the principal character at this point, directing or commanding (κελεύει) the unnamed characters and organising the fate of Jesus. His first order involves bringing (παρ[αλημ] φθῆναι) Jesus to the location where Herod is present. Thus, the narrative implies that Jesus had been absent during the scene where the Jews, Herod, and the judges had refused to wash their hands. The text, as it stands, offers no clues as to where Jesus was being held while this occurred.

Among the Passion traditions preserved in the canonical Gospels, Herod Antipas appears only in the Lukan account. The sequence of events in that context involves:

(a) Pilate sending Jesus to Herod, since he was under Galilean jurisdiction (Lk 23.6–7);
(b) Herod welcoming the opportunity to see Jesus, since he hoped to witness a miracle (Lk 23.8);
(c) The questioning of Jesus by Herod (Lk 23.9);
(d) Vehement accusations being levelled against Jesus by those described as chief priests and scribes (Lk 23.10);
(e) Mocking of Jesus, dressing him in a gorgeous robe and returning him to Pilate (Lk 23.11);
(f) An editorial note about this incident becoming the basis of a friendship between Pilate and Herod (Lk 23.12);
(g) Pilate's comment that implicitly Herod had found Jesus innocent because he sent him back to Pilate (Lk 23.15).

The detail of this structure is not preserved in the extant portion of the Akhmîm text. Moreover, while there was probably an introductory scene bringing Pilate and Herod together, it seems unlikely that it closely paralleled the elements found in Luke's Gospel. Taking the elements in order, it is does not seem possible that Pilate sent Jesus to Herod while remaining in his own location (unnamed in the third gospel),[54] since Pilate is present for the non-washing of hands and

---

[54] Plummer makes the following comments on the location of the Roman trial. 'The Sanhedrin hoped that Pilate would confirm their sentence of death; but Pilate

leaves the recalcitrant combination of Jews, Herod and judges to their own devices. It appears impossible to determine whether the second element was likely to have occurred in the *Gospel of Peter*. With the third element, it is possible that prior to the non-washing of hands that Herod had already interrogated Jesus and that in *Gos. Pet.* 1.2 all that is left is the ordering of the punishment. The accusations of the chief priests and scribes are also absent, and this element may have been dropped or modified in order to shift blame onto Herod. The scene involving the mocking comes later in the narrative. It is undertaken by 'the people' to whom Herod has delivered Jesus for punishment. The Akhmîm text attributes the task of arraigning Jesus with a purple robe and the placing of the crown of thorns to 'the people', whereas in Matthew and Mark it is the Roman soldiers who perform these action. By contrast, in Luke it is Herod, in conjunction with his soldiers, who is said to dress Jesus in gorgeous clothing. Luke's editorial note that Herod and Pilate forged a friendship because of their dealings with Jesus is of course totally inappropriate within the narrative context of the *Gospel of Peter*. Pilate leaves Herod's presence exasperated by his unwillingness to wash his hands. This cannot be reconciled with the note in Luke about establishing a friendship, so presumably this element did not feature in the Akhmîm text. Obviously Pilate's supposition in Luke's Gospel that Herod found Jesus innocent runs counter to the authorial intent in the *Gospel of Peter*, where Pilate alone protests against the corrupt actions of Herod in relation to the trial of Jesus.

At this point in the *Gospel of Peter* the text describes Antipas as ὁ βασιλεὺς. While this may be historically inaccurate it better serves the narrative dynamics, since Herod appears as the a more powerful figure than Pilate with the latter being presented as subservient to the authority of Antipas. Furthermore, the canonical gospels refer to Antipas using the title 'king'. Vaganay suggests that this historically inac-

---

insists on trying the case himself. This he does in his πραιτώριον or palace (Mt. xxvii. 27; Mk. xv. 16; Jn. xviii. 28, 33, xix. 9). But we do not know where this was. A little later than this (Philo, *Leg. ad Gaium*, § 38, ed. Mangey, ii. 589) the Roman governor resided in "Herod's Prætorium," a large palace on the western hill of the city. But Pilate may have used part of the fortress Antonia, the site of which is supposed to be known.' A. Plummer, *A Critical and Exegetical Commentary on the Gospel According to S. Luke*, ICC (4th ed., Edinburgh: T&T Clark, 1901) 519–520. The Gospel of Peter agrees with Luke alone among the canonical in not disclosing the location of Pilate during his meeting with Jesus.

curate use of the term 'king' is a concession to audience expectations.[55] Whether it is correct that the author considered the preferences of his readers in deciding to use the common designation 'king' is uncertain. What can be said with certainty is that the choice of title aligns with usage at points in the synoptic tradition and this may have influenced the decision in this context.

In the Akhmîm text the preferred title for Jesus is ὁ κύριος. This is the most frequent title used to denote Jesus, who is never referred to by name. The term κύριος occurs thirteen times in the manuscript, and apart from the use of a pronoun the author does not employ any other method for the intrusive narrator's designation of Jesus, although the title 'Son of God' is used by Jesus' opponents (Gos. Pet. 3.6, 9; 11.45, 46) and the title 'King of Israel' is used twice, once by his opponents (Gos. Pet. 3.7) and also on the titulus attached to the cross (Gos. Pet. 4.12). This is in contrast to the Gospel of Mark where '[t]he term Lord (kyrios) seems to play a rather insignificant role.'[56] The usage is more akin to Matthew's gospel where the term is reserved for those who form part of the community of faith (cf. Matt 8.2, 6, 8, 21, 25; 9.28; 14.28; 15.22; 16.22, etc.).[57] In the Gospel of Peter the term is used exclusively by the intrusive author, who refers to Jesus in his apparent role as a representative of the perspective held by those who are believers. For Cullmann the title κύριος emerged in the worshipping context of early believers as they brought their prayers before God.[58] He argues that,

> This title rests on two essential element of Heilsgeschichte: (1) Jesus is risen; (2) the fact that the decisive event of the resurrection has already happened but that the eschatological fulfilment has not yet happened does not mean that the Heilsgeschichte has been interrupted.[59]

While it appears likely that the author of the Gospel of Peter was employing the christological title that was pre-eminent in his own worshipping community, and most likely reflected the form of address used to petition the risen Jesus in prayer, there is nothing in the text to suggest that it was consciously being used to affirm the continuity

---

[55] Vaganay, L'Évangile de Pierre, 204.
[56] Tuckett, Christology and the New Testament: Jesus and His Earliest Followers, 110.
[57] Again see Tuckett, Christology and the New Testament, 123–124.
[58] Cullmann, The Christology of the New Testament, 195.
[59] Cullmann, The Christology of the New Testament, 233.

between the salvation historical events of the resurrection and the *parousia*. The centrality of affirming the risen status of Jesus in the *Gospel of Peter* is fully apparent from the space devoted to reporting the resurrection in the narrative.[60] As Hurtado observes the manner in which the 'young man' at the tomb speaks implies a belief in a pre-earthly existence. 'A "young man" from heaven in angelic attire at the empty tomb proclaims Jesus' resurrection and ascent "back to where he was sent," which probably alludes to a belief in Jesus' pre-existence and descent to human existence.'[61] However, it would appear that the Christology of the *Gospel of Peter* is reflecting the title used to address Jesus in the community in which it was written and, moreover, that it saw the title κύριος as an affirmation of Jesus' risen status, yet without necessarily suggesting that the status the title connoted was entirely derivative upon the resurrection event.

**1.2b** εἰπὼν αὐτοῖς ὅτι· Ὅσα ἐκέλευσα ὑμῖν ποιῆσαι αὐτῷ, ποιήσατε. Herod continues directing the action, and specifically takes the dominant role by informing those present to follow his lead by acting in accordance with his commands. The emphasis on the role of Antipas in these proceedings continues to function as a means for shifting the blame from Pilate to the Jews, who are characterized as the minions of the one who commands them. Effectively the narrative detaches Pilate and the Roman authority from the responsibility of the execution, This perspective is maintained through this ideologically and theologically reformulated Passion account.

The formula εἰπὼν αὐτοῖς ὅτι which introduces Herod's words is not common in the extant portion of this text, although there are partial parallels to it. Although the author prefers present participial forms of λέγω to report speech (cf. *Gos. Pet.* 3.7, 9; 4.13; 5.19; 8.28, 29; 11.45), he does use the aorist form of the participle (εἰπών) both here and in 5.19. In 5.19 the aorist seems may be employed both for its verbal aspect and its *Aktionsart* force of denoting a punctiliar past action, since it reports Jesus' completed words immediately prior to his death. However, the use of the aorist participle here (*Gos. Pet.* 1.2b) is less obvious. It may be that in combination with the report of speech by

---

[60] See J. Denker, *Die theologiegeschichtliche Stellung des Petrusevangeliums*, Europäische Hochschulschriften 23/36 (Bern: Herbert Lang/Frankfurt: Peter Lange, 1975).

[61] L.W. Hurtado, *Lord Jesus Christ: Devotion to Jesus in Earliest Christianity* (Grand Rapids, Michigan: Eerdmans, 2003) 445.

Herod 'commanding that the Lord be brought',[62] that it is necessary to anticipate the notice of Herod's complete action of giving instruction. The use of the recitative ὅτι is also not a common feature of the narrative. It is used in *Gos. Pet.* 10.42 to introduce the affirmative answer given by the Cross, but there it occurs without an accompanying verbal form of λέγω.

It remains unclear specifically what Herod required of those to whom he instructs Ὅσα ἐκέλευσα ὑμῖν ποιῆσαι αὐτῷ, ποιήσατε. As Swete suggests, '[t]his order is possibly intended to include the mockery.'[63] This may be construed from both the events that follow and the description in the third gospel, ἐξουθενήσας δὲ αὐτὸν [καὶ] ὁ Ἡρῴδης σὺν τοῖς στρατεύμασιν αὐτοῦ καὶ ἐμπαίξας (Lk 23.11). Yet in all likelihood it contains a more general reference to the range of events that follow, including the mocking, torture, execution, disposal of the body and the attempt to suppress the story of the empty tomb circulating. Thus Herod, the representative leader of the Jews, becomes the figure to whom ultimate responsibility is attached for the various events in the Passion from this point onwards. The aorist verb ἐκέλευσα, suggests that Antipas' action is part of the central line of the narrative, and to carry out those orders and to put them into effect. Again it appears that Antipas is the supreme authority figure in the judicial process and that Pilate has had to begrudgingly acquiesce to his will.

---

[62] See BDF §392.4.
[63] Swete, *The Akhmîm Fragment of the Apocryphal Gospel of St Peter*, 2.

## JOSEPH'S REQUEST AND THE ENSUING EXCHANGE
## BETWEEN PILATE AND HEROD (2.3–5)

3. ἱστήκει¹ δὲ ἐκεῖ Ἰωσὴφ² ὁ φίλος Πειλάτου³ καὶ τοῦ $\overline{\mathrm{κυ}}$.⁴ καὶ εἰδὼς ὅτι ⁵σταυρίσκειν⁶ αὐτὸν μέλλουσιν, ἦλθεν πρὸς τὸν Πειλᾶτον ⁷καὶ ἤτησε⁸ τὸ σῶμα τοῦ $\overline{\mathrm{κυ}}$ πρὸς ταφήν. 4. καὶ ὁ Πειλᾶτος πέμψας⁹ πρὸς Ἡρώδην ἤτησεν αὐτοῦ τὸ σῶμα. 5. καὶ ὁ Ἡρῴδης ἔφη·¹⁰ ἀδελφὲ Πειλᾶτε, εἰ καὶ μή τις¹¹ αὐτὸν ἠτήκει, ἡμεῖς αὐτὸν ἐθάπτομεν, ἐπεὶ καὶ σάββατον¹² ἐπιφώσκει· γέγραπται γὰρ ἐν τῷ νόμῳ ἥλιον μὴ δῦναι ἐπὶ πεφονευμένῳ. καὶ παρέδωκεν αὐτὸν τῷ λαῷ πρὸ μιᾶς τῶν ἀζύμων, τῆς ἑορτῆς αὐτῶν.

3. And Joseph the friend of Pilate and of the Lord stood there, and seeing that they were about to crucify him, he came to Pilate and asked for the body of the Lord for burial. 4. And Pilate sent to Herod [and] asked for his body. 5. And Herod said, 'Brother Pilate, even if somebody had not asked for him, we would have buried him, since also Sabbath is dawning. For it is written in the law, "The sun should not set on one who has been put to death."' And he handed him over to the people before the first day of the unleavened bread, their festival.

### Text Critical Notes

1. The form ἱστήκει is clearly visible in the manuscript. However, in his transcription Bouriant misses the first three letters and cites the word as ἤκει.⁶⁴ This transcription is followed by Harnack,⁶⁵ Robinson⁶⁶ and apparently stands behind the translation of Rendel Harris.⁶⁷ The correct transcription is given by Swete.⁶⁸ While it is not possible to be entirely certain, it appears that this is a correction

---

⁶⁴ Bouriant, 'Fragments du texte grec du livre d'Énoch et de quelques écrits attribués à saint Pierre', 137.

⁶⁵ Harnack, *Bruchstücke des Evangeliums und der Apokalypse des Petrus*, 8.

⁶⁶ *Robinson, The Gospel according to Peter and the Revelation of Peter*, 83.

⁶⁷ No where in his volume does Harris state the source from which he draws the Greek text for his translation. He gives the following English rendering of *Gos. Pet.* 2.3, 'And there was come thither Joseph…' Harris, *A Popular Account of the Newly Recovered Gospel of St Peter*, 43.

⁶⁸ Swete, *The Akhmîm Fragment of the Apocryphal Gospel of St Peter*, 2.

made by Lods. Since the time of this correction, all major editions and commentaries have followed the reading ἱστήκει (see, Vaganay,[69] Mara,[70] Kraus and Nicklas).[71] The form ἱστήκει is an iotacism for εἱστήκει. As is noted in regard to this particular iotacism in BDF §23 'The phonetic leveling of ει and ῑ betrays itself by the *rather frequent* confusion in usage in the early Hellenistic period, in Attic inscriptions from ii BC end, in Egyptian papyri from iii BC mid., the confusion of ει and ῑ is much less frequent.'[72]

2. At this point a diacritical sign is employed in the text above the iota in the name ἰωσηφ. The diæresis was originally used to indicate that the potential diphthong is, in fact, pronounced as two separate syllables. This is the so-called organic use of the diæresis (see text critical note 6 in the previous section).

3. There is a hole in the manuscript effecting only very slightly the bottom portion of the lambda in the name Πειλάτου. However, enough of the letter remains to ensure that the reading is certain.

4. A *nomen sacrum* is used at this point in the text for κύριου, and again later in this verse for the identical abbreviation in the genitive singular case. This is one of the seven most common words abbreviated in Christian texts using contraction (omitting the middle of the word) of letters (rather than 'suspension' found in some non-Christian abbreviations where only the first one or two letters of a word are written) and a supralinear horizontal crossbar above the remaining letters.

5. Examination of the photographs of P.Cair. 10759 for line 7 of the *verso* of the first leaf reveals some extraneous writing prior to what most transcriptions cite as the first word on the line, σταυρίσκειν. The three visible letters are, reading left to right, reflected, or mirror images, of ν̄κ̄ν̄. These are actually the impressions of the final three letters on the facing page, the *recto* of leaf 2, line 5. The dampness that seems to have caused the dark patches on the upper margins of these two pages appears to have acidified the previously set ink and hence caused a reversed printing to the opposite page.

---

[69] Vaganay, *L'Évangile de Pierre*, 210.
[70] Mara, *Évangile de Pierre*, 42.
[71] Kraus und Nicklas, *Das Petrusevangelium und die Petrusapokalypse*, 32.
[72] BDF §23, 13.

6. The form of the verb σταυρίσκω is disputed in some reconstructions. On inspection of the photographs the form σταυρίσκειν is certain. The perceived problem is, as Swete observes, that 'Σταυρίσκειν is unknown to the lexicons; σταυρώσειν has been proposed, but perhaps unnecessarily.'[73] However, it is the very rarity of the infinitive of σταυρόω that makes such orthographical variation more likely. In fact there is a recognized tendency in post-Classical Greek to introduce regular verbal forms in place of contract verbs such as σταυρόω.[74]

7. As with note 5, there are the reflected forms of three letters visible prior to the καί which commences line eight. These are ωθρ, reading left to right, which are the second third and fourth letters of the word ὤρθωσαν, where the ωρθω- occurs at the end of line six and the letters -σαν as the commencement of line seven on the *recto* of leaf 2.

8. The form ἤτησε drops the final ν, since it occurs before a consonant, where the form in line nine (*Gos. Pet.* 2.4) ἤτησεν retains the final ν as it occurs before a vowel.[75] The ligature between the final two letters is also somewhat unusual (but repeated in a similar form on the line below), with the top of the open form sigma descending diagonally to connect to the base of the following epsilon. The result is that the epsilon appears slightly elevated on the line and does little to produce even a roughly bilinear text.

9. The final three letters of πέμψας, which commence line nine, may have vestiges of imprinted writing from the opposite page. In particular the large final ς of πέμψας appears to enclose the remnant of another letter. It is, however, no longer possible to determine this over-printed letter with any degree of certainty although presumably it may be one of the letters of the final word on line seven of the facing page, βασιλε[ὺ]ς.

---

[73] Swete, *The Akhmim Fragment of the Apocryphal Gospel of St Peter*, 2.

[74] See L.R. Palmer, *Grammar of the Post-Ptolemaic Papyri* (London: OUP, 1946) 148.

[75] Although there is a lack of consistency there is an increasing tendency in Greek literature to omit the final ν before a consonant while retaining it before a vowel. As is noted in BDF §20, 12, 'Movable ν appears in Ionic-Attic dialects of the classical period without definite rule...Moreover from the V BC on the tendency to employ ν to avoid hiatus, and therefore to comply with the modern rule which stems from the Byzantine period, betrays itself in an increasing degree. It is very popular in the Hellenistic language, but e.g. in the papyri of the Ptolemaic period (Mayser I¹ 236–40) it is *omitted* often before vowels and *appears* still more often before consonants.'

10. There is a light ink marking that occurs under the α of the αδελφέ. From the photographs, it is not possible to determine whether this is an aberrant pen stroke, and erased letter, or even a partially reflected imprinted letter from the word ἔμπροσθεν on line eight of the facing page. The mark occurs 4mm to the left of the boundary line between the darken region on the page and the lighter region. The lambda of αδελφέ is highly compressed, comprised of two short unconnected penstrokes. Also to be noted, to be found 4mm in from the right edge of this page, before the commencement of this line of text one finds the ο of the word ἔμπροσθεν from the facing page. It is possibly that the mark is a reflected imprint of part of the ο or perhaps also the σ which it touches.

11. The final ς of τις is poorly formed. Instead of the usual large curved shape which is characteristic of this scribe, the letter is compressed and appears to consist of two separate strokes rather than a continuous curve.

12. The letter β although not occurring with great frequency within this text is a letter that occurs with inconsistency in both size and shape. The two examples in σάββατον show some variation, but both vary even more greatly from the examples at the beginning of line eighteen on verso of page one and lines nine and fourteen of the recto of page two.

## COMMENTARY

**2.3aα** ἱστήκει δὲ ἐκεῖ Ἰωσήφ. At this stage in the narrative a new character is introduced into what is presumably the same scene. While the verbal aspect of perfect and pluperfect forms is still an ongoing debate in New Testament linguistics, the pluperfect form (ε)ἱστήκει could plausibly denote a stative aspect.[76] According to Porter the purpose is to signal to readers that there is a new state of affairs that is in view in the narrative.[77] This would fit with the scene shift that is introduced. The location is not clarified apart from the generalised

[76] Campbell, *Basics of Verbal Aspect in Biblical Greek*, 48.

[77] For his initial discussion see S.E. Porter, *Verbal Aspect in the Greek of the New Testament with Reference to Tense and Mood* (Studies in Biblical Greek 1; New York: Peter Land, 1989), and subsequently *Idioms of the Greek New Testament* (2nd ed.; Biblical Languages: Greek 2; Sheffield: Sheffield Academic Press, 1994) 21–22.

ἐκεῖ, which seems to connote the same setting where Herod has been giving his orders. The character, who is known simply by the name Joseph, has apparently been standing and observing what has transpired. According to Swete, Joseph 'had anticipated the sentence.'[78] In terms of the narrative, this is not the only possibility. As was noted in relation to *Gos. Pet.* 1.2, the use of the aorist verb, Ὅσα ἐκέλευσα, in the statement made by Antipas may denote a set of instructions given prior to the point where the text now commences. Thus, Joseph may not have 'anticipated' what was about to transpire, but instead realised with the withdrawal of Pilate, that what Antipas had previously ordered would now certainly be enacted.

### EXCURSUS: THE PORTRAYAL OF JOSEPH OF ARIMATHEA IN THE CANONICAL GOSPELS

From the canonical accounts readers would naturally identify the character named as Joseph in the *Gospel of Peter* with Joseph of Arimathea. This identification would occur both on the basis of the forename and the similarity of the actions of the character as they will emerge. Joseph of Arimathea is named in the passion accounts of all four canonical gospels (Matt 27.57, 59; Mk 15.43, 45; Lk 23. 50–51; Jn 19.38). This multiple attestation makes him a relatively stable element in the tradition surrounding the events of the death of Jesus. In Mark's account nine details are provided about him: (i) he came from Arimathea; (ii) he was a well-respected council member; (iii) he was awaiting the kingdom of God; (iv) he took the bold step of asking Pilate for the body of Jesus (after his death in the Markan sequence); (v) Pilate granted Joseph his request (Mk 15.45); (vi) Joseph wrapped the body in a linen cloth which he had bought; (vii) he took Jesus down from the cross; (viii) laid him in a tomb hewn in rock; and (ix) rolled the stone into place to seal the tomb (Mk 15.46). Matthew tells the incident with a number of different details, as Hagner notes, 'Matthew's pericope is only half as long as Mark's.'[79] There is no reference to either Joseph being a council member or his expectation of the kingdom. Instead he is described as being a rich man, although, in agreement with Mark, his place of origin is described as being Arimathea. His request made to Pilate is not described as requiring him to 'gather courage' τολμήσας (cf. Mk 15.43). Pilate simply grants the request without enquiring if Jesus already was dead.[80] Next Joseph arranges the burial, yet unlike

---

[78] Swete, *The Akhmîm Fragment of the Apocryphal Gospel of St Peter*, 2.

[79] D.A. Hagner, *Matthew 14–28*, WBC 33B (Dallas: Word, 1995), 857.

[80] As Hagner observes, 'The biggest departure from the Markan text involves the omission of Mark 15:44–45a concerning Pilate's inquiry about whether Jesus was in fact dead (omitted also by Luke).' Hagner, *Matthew 14–28*, 857.

Mark he simply takes the body, but not 'down', καθελών, by implication from the cross, he wraps it in a linen cloth – but the detail that he bought this cloth is omitted – although the first gospel additionally states that the shroud was καθαρᾷ. Matthew provides the further detail that the tomb was Joseph's and hewn by his own hand (Matt 27.60). The stone used to seal the tomb is described by adding the adjective μέγαν. Finally Matthew removes Joseph from the scene by addition ἀπῆλθεν.[81]

The Lukan account is even more truncated consisting of only 57 words. It primarily appears to be an abbreviation of the Markan narrative. As Fitzmyer notes, 'Luke has abridged the Marcan account omitting such details as Joseph's courage (Mark 15.43), Pilate's checking on Jesus' death (15:44–45 – as does Matt 27:58), Joseph buying the linen cloth (15.46a), the closing of the tomb (15.46d).'[82] To this list one may also add that there is no note of Pilate agreeing to Joseph's request, this is simply assumed by the Lukan narrative. Only three extra details are provided by Luke. First, in addition to being a member of the council Joseph is described as ἀνὴρ ἀγαθὸς καὶ δίκαιος. (Lk 23:50). This detail, like a number of Luke's character descriptions (cf. Lk 1:6; 2:25, in both cases the term δίκαιος is also used), is designed to impress the integrity of the character upon the audience before outlining an action that is a specific example of the generalised trait.[83] Second, Luke introduces a specific detail that illustrates Joseph's integrity, namely that he did not agree with the decision of the council, οὗτος οὐκ ἦν συγκατατεθειμένος τῇ βουλῇ καὶ τῇ πράξει αὐτῶν (Lk 23.51).[84] Third, at the end of v. 53 Luke states that the tomb had not been previously occupied, οὗ οὐκ ἦν οὐδεὶς οὔπω κείμενος. Matthew provides a similar fact stating the tomb was new, ἐν τῷ καινῷ αὐτοῦ

---

[81] Davies and Allison list five points of significant difference in the Matthean account of Joseph of Arimathea in comparison with Mark. '(i) Matthew's story of the burial is shorter (Mt: 64 words; Mk: 89 words). (ii) In Matthew Joseph is a rich man and a disciple of Jesus. In Mark he is a respected member of the council who is looking for the kingdom of God. (iii) Matthew omits Pilate's amazement at Jesus' quick death and the governor's questioning of the centurion (Mk 15.44–5). (iv) Only in Matthew is the shroud clean, the rock large, and Jesus' tomb new. (v) Mark tells us neither that Joseph owns the tomb nor he himself hewed it out of the rock.' W.D. Davies and D.C. Allison, *The Gospel According to Saint Matthew*, vol. III (Edinburgh: T&T Clark, 1997) 646.

[82] J.A. Fitzmyer, *The Gospel according to Luke X–XXIV*, AB 28A (New York: Doubleday, 1985), 1523.

[83] Green notes that 'Luke is not simply content to speak about Joseph's piety, but goes on to demonstrate it.' J.B. Green, *The Gospel of Luke*, NICNT (Grand Rapids: Michigan: Eerdmans, 1997) 830.

[84] Although the term used in the sense of 'decision' is consistent with other Lukan usages (cf. Lk 7:30; Acts 2:23; 4:28; 5:38; 13:36; [19:1 in Codex Bezae] 20:27; 27:12, 42, the term may also be used to denote a council (see the related term βουλευτής in Lk 23:50). It may be the case that here Luke is stating that Joseph the councillor did not agree with 'the council and their deed' rather than 'their plan and deed'. Alternatively Luke may intended to exploit the ambiguity of the term. (See Green, *The Gospel of Luke*, 829–830).

μνημείῳ, but there is no overlap in vocabulary of these parallel details in the two gospels. This would suggest that the evangelists were either drawing on a free floating tradition perhaps in oral form because of the variation,[85] or had independently added a similar, but nonetheless divergent, redactional detail.[86] The issue is further complicated by the Johannine version which describes the tomb as both new and unused, μνημεῖον καινὸν ἐν ᾧ οὐδέπω οὐδεὶς ἦν τεθειμένος (Jn 19.41). If this tradition was free floating but also in a relatively fixed form it would appear that Matthew has selected the detail that the tomb was new, while Luke mentions that it was unused.

The Johannine description of Joseph of Arimathea is heavily infused with redactional concerns and vocabulary typical of the fourth evangelist. In agreement with Matthew's account Joseph is described as a 'disciple', but the further qualification is added that this discipleship was exercised in secret, ὢν μαθητὴς τοῦ Ἰησοῦ κεκρυμμένος (Jn 19.38). In reference to the description 'a disciple of Jesus', Brown notes that a 'similar designation of Joseph, but in different Greek is found in Matt xxvii 57.'[87] Yet the Greek may perhaps be closer than appears to be the case from Brown's statement. The Matthean description reads as follows, ὃς καὶ αὐτὸς ἐμαθητεύθη τῷ Ἰησοῦ (Matt 27.57). In both cases the same semantic group μαθητεύω is employed, in verbal form Matthew while in nominal form in John, also the name Jesus occurs in both clauses with required case changes. The fourth gospel adds a uniquely Johannine qualification to this description of Joseph's discipleship. As Beasley-Murray states, 'John alone adds, "but a secret one through fear of the Jews."'[88] The detail κεκρυμμένος δὲ διὰ τὸν φόβον τῶν Ἰουδαίων resonates with the reference in Jn 12.42 to believers of significant status who would not confess their faith openly, ἐκ τῶν ἀρχόντων πολλοὶ ἐπίστευσαν εἰς αὐτόν, ἀλλὰ διὰ τοὺς Φαρισαίους οὐχ ὡμολόγουν ἵνα μὴ ἀποσυνάγωγοι γένωνται.[89] There is some sense of negativity surrounding this description of Joseph. Perhaps the perfect passive participle κεκρυμμένος conveys the sense of a past continuous state that no longer holds, i.e. 'but having been secretly.' It is plausible that in terms of the Johannine understanding Joseph's faith becomes publicly manifest through the very action of approaching Pilate.[90] In accordance with

---

[85] In support of this element being due to shared oral tradition see Davies and Allison, *The Gospel According to Saint Matthew*, vol. III, 646.

[86] For the case that the unused or new tomb reference is due to independent editing see C.M. Tuckett, 'On the Relationship between Matthew and Luke', *NTS* 30 (1984) 138–139.

[87] R.E. Brown, *The Gospel according to John XIII–XXI*, AB 29A (New York: Doubleday, 1970), 939.

[88] G.R. Beasley-Murray, *John*, WBC 36 (Waco, Texas: Word, 1987) 358.

[89] Barrett likewise draws attention to Jn 12.42 as mentioning 'secret disciples of rank.' C.K. Barrett, *The Gospel according to St John* (London: SPCK, 1955) 464.

[90] Keener understands the narrative to function in this manner. He states, 'The narrative also presents Joseph's current act as a positive model for discipleship, for, in coming forward to seek Jesus' body, Joseph ceases to be merely a "secret" disciple.' C.S. Keener, *The Gospel of John: A Commentary*, vol. II (Peabody, Mass.: Hendrickson, 2003) 1160.

the synoptic accounts Pilate agrees to Joseph's request and hence he takes possession of the body.

The fourth gospel continues to go its own way in v. 39 by introducing Nicodemus, another secret disciple of rank, who begins to demonstrate his belief in a more public manner by bring the necessary material to prepare the body for burial. According to Jewish custom the body is prepared, in the fourth gospel by Nicodemus and Joseph working together (Jn 19.40). While the note about them both taking the body seems to repeat the end of v. 38,[91] this appears to suit the narratival purpose of the Johannine account in that previously hidden disciples now take active roles. Finally in v. 42 Joseph and Nicodemus lay Jesus in the unused tomb described in the previous verse.

In comparison to Joseph's role in the canonical accounts, two significant features in the Akhmîm text can be noted. First, since unlike the fourth gospel the *Gospel of Peter* does not introduce Nicodemus into the narrative this may lend weight to the suggestion that it is uninfluenced by Johannine tradition at this point.[92] Secondly, the narrative is structured in two parts, the request for the body prior to the burial (*Gos. Pet.* 2.3), followed later by the handing over of the body and the burial after the crucifixion has been described (*Gos. Pet.* 6.23–24). This suspension of the storyline and interruption by the description of the crucifixion functions to distance Joseph from the actions of Antipas and his supporters, while also further emphasizing the positive role of Pilate in seeking an honourable death for the still living Jesus.

**2.3aβ  ὁ φίλος Πειλάτου καὶ τοῦ κͧ̄.** This description is unique to the Akhmîm text although it is likely that the first half of the description, 'the friend of Pilate' is also present in the fragmentary text P.Oxy. 2949. Brown suggests that the portrayal of Joseph as Pilate's friend is not due to independent tradition, but rather derives from reflection on the canonical versions of the incident.[93] For Swete the specific details that triggered this deduction were statements in the gospels about Joseph's social status.[94] The narrative may, however, be

---

[91] Brown, *The Gospel according to John XIII–XXI*, 941.

[92] This will be discussed further in the commentary on 6.24 since both Jn 19.41 and *Gos. Pet.* 6.24 alone share the term κῆπος in the narrative surrounding Joseph's role in the passion.

[93] Brown, *The Gospel according to John XIII–XXI*, 939.

[94] 'His acquaintance with Pilate may have been inferred from his wealth and position (πλούσιος, Mt., εὐσχήμων βουλευτής, Mk.), or from his boldness.' Swete, *The Akhmîm Fragment of the Apocryphal Gospel of St Peter*, 2.

more 'Pilate-centred' at this point. Rather than emphasising Joseph's social standing, the narrative 'sandwiches' Pilate between the references to Joseph and the Lord. This further positions the representative of Roman authority on what for the author is obviously the correct side in this trial, while implicitly alienating Antipas and the Jews by presenting their recalcitrant attitude in rejecting both Roman authority and God's anointed agent.[95] Swete appears to pick up on this point when he observes, 'Pilate is again placed in a favourable light; he is a friend of the Lord's friend.'[96]

Joseph's friendship with the Lord depicts a greater degree of intimacy than that described either by Matthew and John where he is a disciple (and only secretly in the fourth gospel), or as an even more distant figure awaiting the kingdom in Mark and Luke. Vaganay notes his function in the *Gospel of Peter* is not just that of one awaiting the kingdom of God, but is that of a close associate.[97] This level of intimacy appears to heighten the importance of Joseph in comparison to his role in the canonical texts. However, it is impossible to know whether he had appeared earlier in the now no longer extant portion of the *Gospel of Peter*.

**2.3bα** καὶ εἰδὼς ὅτι σταυρίσκειν αὐτὸν μέλλουσιν. As has been discussed, the form σταυρίσκειν is a *hapax legomenon*, occurring nowhere else in all extant Greek literature.[98] While it is obviously the intention of the author to distance figures such as Joseph from Jewish institutions such as the Sanhedrin, it is not necessarily the case that Joseph's knowledge of the sentence of crucifixion came through public rumour, contary to Vaganay.[99] The beginning of this verse introduces Joseph as though he had been present at least observing the preceding scene in the narrative. This may suggest that he had heard the earlier pronouncements made by Antipas, to which the narrative alludes in *Gos. Pet.* 1.2. Thus the term εἰδὼς need not refer to special insight

---

[95] Commenting on the role of Pilate in chapter 2 of the Gospel of Peter, Robinson states, 'We have here incidentally two details helping to exculpate Pilate: Joseph is his 'friend'; Pilate can do nothing without Herod's leave.' Robinson, *The Gospel according to Peter and the Revelation of Peter*, 17.

[96] Swete, *The Akhmîm Fragment of the Apocryphal Gospel of St Peter*, 2.

[97] Vaganay, *L'Évangile de Pierre*, 211.

[98] Robinson, *The Gospel according to Peter and the Revelation of Peter*, 16.

[99] Vaganay, *L'Évangile de Pierre*, 212.

or knowledge of widespread rumour, but rather simply be assuming presence during the pronouncement of Antipas.

The use of μέλλουσιν after a present infinitive is a feature of later Greek, whereas classical usage prefers the future infinitive after forms of μέλλω.[100] This form also conveys the sense of immediacy with which the crucifixion will follow, as well as preparing the audience for the rapid chain of events that are depicted as the narrative leads to the point where it portrays the death of Jesus.

**2.3bβ   ἦλθεν πρὸς τὸν Πειλᾶτον.** Pilate is named for the second time in this verse. Whereas in the Markan account Joseph's approach is described as requiring courage, there is less tension in the *Gospel of Peter*. Pilate has already been described as Joseph's friend, and his actions have shown that he firmly believes Jesus to be innocent. Perhaps the only surprising thing about the request is that Joseph appears to be approaching a person without the requisite power, since the narrative has depicted Pilate's authority as being subservient to that of Antipas.[101] While this will actually been seen to be the case, nonetheless through the ensuing communication between Pilate and Herod the narrative further accentuates the intercessory role that Pilate adopts on behalf of Jesus. Thus, although Pilate is portrayed as being in a subordinate position, he continues to use what authority he possesses to ensure an honourable burial. In the *Gospel of Peter* Joseph's approach to Pilate is described with a simplex verbal form, ἦλθεν. By contrast Mark uses the compound εἰσῆλθεν with the preposition πρὸς following (εἰσῆλθεν πρὸς τὸν Πειλᾶτον, Mk 15.43) whereas Matthew and Luke both make what are probably independent changes, resulting in use of the form προσελθών (Mt 27.58; Lk 23.52). Thus, although the *Gospel of Peter* uses the simplex form ἦλθεν in other respects it is identical to the Markan report of this incident.

---

[100] Vaganay, *L'Évangile de Pierre*, 211. The rarity of the future infinitive in the NT is illustrated by only five occurrences four in Acts (11.28; 23.30; 24.15; 27.10) and one in Hebrews (3.18). See D.B. Wallace, *Greek Grammar: Beyond the Basics* (Grand Rapids: Zondervan, 1996) 567.

[101] Mara observes that this characterisation of roles obviously does not reflect the realities of political system in Palestine during Pilate's term of office. Nonetheless, the apparent purpose is to subordinate the role of Pilate, thereby absolving him of blame. Mara, *Évangile de Pierre*, 79.

**2.3bγ** καὶ ἤτησε τὸ σῶμα τοῦ κ̄ῡ πρὸς ταφήν. This element is paralleled in all four canonical accounts. The synoptics agree in the five word phrase ἠτήσατο τὸ σῶμα τοῦ Ἰησοῦ (Matt 27.58; Mk 15.43; Lk 23.52), with only Mark using the conjunction καί to connect the reference to Pilate with this clause reporting the request. The Johannine version employs a different verb, ἵνα ἄρῃ τὸ σῶμα τοῦ Ἰησοῦ (Jn 19.38).[102] The verb αἰτέω is retained in the *Gospel of Peter*, but in a different form, ἤτησε. Both ἠτήσατο of the synoptics and ἤτησε of the Akhmîm text are third person singular aorist forms. The difference in ending simply represents the tendency in later *koine* Greek to use second aorist endings with first aorist stems. The form ἤτησε is therefore consistent with sixth to ninth century date for the Akhmîm text, but this is also the kind of change that may be made by a scribe copying an exemplar with earlier verbal forms. Hence nothing can be concluded about the date of the exemplar behind the Akhmîm text on the basis of this form.

The Akhmîm text also alters the name Jesus to its preferred Christiological title κυρίου, here written in the normal form of a *nomen sacrum*, κ̄ῡ. It adds the further explanatory detail that Joseph ask for the body for burial, πρὸς ταφήν. This is not totally extraneous, but functions to introduce the ensuing discussion between Pilate and Antipas.

At this point in the narrative, unlike the canonical gospels, Joseph disappears from the narrative only to return later to carry out the burial, resulting from the implied permission he gains as a result of the correspondence between Pilate and Antipas. The words are reminiscent of the εἰς ταφήν of Matt 27.7, although in Matthew the phrase is used in reference to the burial of Judas.[103] Once again there is an echo of a term unique to the first gospel, both ταφή (Matt 27.7) and τάφος (Matt 23.27, 29; 27.61, 64, 66; 28.1) are used by Matthew alone among the canonical gospels. These terms are also favourites in the Akhmîm text (ταφή *Gos. Pet.* 2.3; τάφος *Gos. Pet.* 6.24; 8.31; 9.36f; 10.39; 11.45; 13.55).[104] This reinforces the case for a close literary relationship between Matthew and the *Gospel of Peter*.

---

[102] The Johannine account has no parallel for the approach of Joseph, he is simply present and his first act is that of asking for the body, rather than coming to Pilate as in the synoptic tradition.

[103] Swete, *The Akhmîm Fragment of the Apocryphal Gospel of St Peter*, 2. Also cf. *Acta Pilati* B, xi.

[104] See BDAG, 991–992.

**2.4a** καὶ ὁ Πειλᾶτος πέμψας πρὸς Ἡρῴδην. The narrative brings together again the Roman prefect and Herod, the latter again characterized as the politically more powerful character. Here, however, the contact and ensuing conversation are reported as being indirect, although in the following verse the ploy of communication through an intermediary appears to give way to direct speech as Antipas answers Herod's request. No clue is provided by the author concerning the location to which Joseph went to make his request to Pilate, and the same ambiguity is preserved as the Roman governor sends his request to Herod. The actions which serve to absolve Pilate of blame are of more consequence in the narrative, than are details of geography.[105]

Moreover, the narrative is not interested in describing the precise method of communication adopted by Pilate, whether a written communication, or an oral request announced by a third party employed by Pilate for this purpose. Mara's translation 'by a message'[106] is equally ambiguous even if though it is not a very literal rendering of the Greek. Vaganay's translation may read too much into the underlying Greek, 'And Pilate having an envoy attached to Herod.'[107]

**2.4b** ἤτησεν αὐτοῦ τὸ σῶμα. This description of the request made by Pilate to Herod, echoes the form used to describe the request Joseph made to Pilate. On both occasions the narrative does not give direct speech (or citation of the form of words, if Pilate's request was written), but rather conveys the content of the supplication. The αὐτοῦ clearly refers to Jesus, because the pronoun occurs in the genitive case. If Herod had been intended αἰτέω would take the accusative case.[108] Thus the use of αὐτοῦ following the verb αἰτέω, stands in parallel to the words τοῦ κ̅υ̅ that occur in Joseph's request to Pilate in *Gos. Pet.* 2.3, ἤτησε τὸ σῶμα τοῦ κ̅υ̅ πρὸς ταφήν.

---

[105] Vaganay notes that geography is the last concern of the author, *L'Évangile de Pierre*, 212.

[106] 'par un message' Mara, *Évangile de Pierre*, 43.

[107] Vaganay offers two translations, the more literal rendering of the Greek that occurs in the body of the discussion, and the smoother French rendering which is presented at the head of the right-hand pages. The form, 'Et Pilate, ayant envoyé auprès d'Hérode', is the more literal, although on this occasion the only difference is the replacement of *ayant envoyé* with the preterite *envoya*, which serves to give the narrative a more literary feel. Vaganay, *L'Évangile de Pierre*, 212–213.

[108] See, W. Radl 'αἰτέω' in Horst Balz and Gerhard Schneider (eds.), *Exegetical Dictionary of the New Testament* vol. 1 (Grand Rapids: Michigan: Eerdmans, 1990) 43.

**2.5aα  καὶ ὁ Ἡρῴδης ἔφη.** The response made by Herod is introduced by a typical formula in biblical Greek for reporting direct speech, consisting of three elements: a conjunction (often optional); a reference to the character who is about to make an utterance; and, a verbal form of φημί. Such examples are frequent in the New Testament, ὁ δὲ Πέτρος ἔφη (Mk 14.29) and καὶ ὁ Κορνήλιος ἔφη (Acts 10.30).[109] The verbal form ἔφη, especially in constructions of this type, is a Matthean favourite (ἔφη: Matt: 14 times; Mk: 6 times; Lk: 7 times; Jn: 2 times). Such an introductory formula creates a degree of tension in the narrative. In the previous verse Pilate has sent his message indirectly to Herod, yet here Herod appears to respond directly, as though Pilate were present.[110]

**2.5aβ  ἀδελφὲ Πειλᾶτε.** Such double vocatives are not uncommon in the NT or in other Greek literature. In the prologue to the third gospel, Luke addresses his named dedicatee as κράτιστε Θεόφιλε (Lk 1.3). Nolland observes that κράτιστε 'is an honorific title.'[111] This contrasts with the use of ἀδελφέ, which is a term intimacy or relational proximity – here perhaps presumed or ironic as opposed to signalling actual friendship. The double vocative is a characteristic Lukan construction in the NT (see Acts 13.26; 17.22).[112] The address from Herod to Pilate as 'brother' is, according to Vaganay, both friendly and a formal courtesy.[113] While this general observation may be correct, it is possible that more is being conveyed in the narrative in this instance. Although there is an air of polite respect, this follows the previous interaction between Pilate and Herod where the former withdrew from the presence of Antipas in protest against the perceived injustice of the circumvention of the judicial process. In this sense the term may be understood not so much as indicating the amiability of the relationship between these two figures, rather it highlights the desire on the part of Antipas to be conciliatory towards Pilate and to effect a rapprochement with the representative of Roman authority.

---

[109] Further related examples include, Matt 4.7; 8.8; 13.28; 17.26; 19.21; 26.34; 27.11; Mk 9.12, 38; 10.29.

[110] A. Wabnitz, 'Les fragments de l'évangile et de l'apocalypse de Pierre', *Revue de théologie et des questions religeuses* (1893) 359–360.

[111] J. Nolland, *Luke 1–9:20*, WBC 35A (Dallas: Word, 1989) 10.

[112] See 'Vocative', BDF §146–147.

[113] Vaganay, *L'Évangile de Pierre*, 213. Cf. Josephus, *Ant.*, XII, 2, 2.

**2.5αγ** εἰ καὶ μή τις αὐτὸν ᾐτήκει. The narrative continues relating this incident, which is unknown from the canonical accounts. Herod's speech is framed in a manner that presents an expression for self-justification concerning the morality of his behaviour. There is a degree of incongruence between the action of passing judgment on Jesus and the contrast with the hypothetical events that would have occurred if there had not been a request for the body. Such tension is not exploited by the author, although the readers are perhaps meant to perceive the hypocrisy in Herod's affirmation that he would have treated the corpse with the required deference regardless of Pilate's request. However, it is possible that rather than being motivated by an implicit desire to portray Herod as hypocritical at this point, this tension may simply arise from the authorial desire to organize the additional details so that they are integrated within the broad sequence of events of the Passion Narrative as contained in the canonical accounts. This is no simple task since it requires both re-arrangement and creativity. Having moved the request made by Joseph to Pilate from its position in the canonical accounts after the death of Jesus to a position prior to the crucifixion, the author seeks both to exonerate Pilate as well as to conclude this event before moving on to the depiction of the crucifixion, thereby removing the Roman prefect from any decision making process during the crucifixion.

**2.5αδ** ἡμεῖς αὐτὸν ἐθάπτομεν. As is noted by a number of scholars, this phrase serves to show that Antipas identified himself with the Jews according to the *Gospel of Peter*.[114] The term ἐθάπτομεν is used among the canonical gospels only by Matthew and Luke (although it is also employed in Acts 2.29; 5.6, 9, 10, and 1 Cor 15.4). In Matthew and Luke, however, it is not used in connection with the burial of Jesus (cf. Matt 8.21; 14.12; Lk 9.59f; 16.22).[115] What strikes the reader at this point is the stark antithesis between Herod's punctilious concern for the body in comparison to the lack of integrity in handling the trial. This may reflect part of the narrative's anti-Jewish polemic. This might in turn be influenced by a similar tendency, although in less developed form, drawn from Matthew's gospel (cf. Matt 23.23).

---

[114] Swete, *The Akhmîm Fragment of the Apocryphal Gospel of St Peter*, 2.
[115] Harnack, *Bruchstücke des Evangeliums und der Apokalypse des Petrus*, 24.

**2.5αε ἐπεὶ καὶ σάββατον ἐπιφώσκει.** Any initial impressions the narrative gave that Antipas was motivated out of respect for the dead body are undercut by this clause. It immediately becomes apparent that Herod's concern was halakhic rather than humane, if this is not too much of a false dichotomy. The Torah stipulation provided as the conclusion to this verse will make this point obvious. Here the issue is first alluded to as a worry about the Sabbath dawning. There appear to be resonances with John 19.31, where the prospect of Jesus having to remain on the cross leads the Jews to request Pilate to order Jesus' legs to be broken.

> Οἱ οὖν Ἰουδαῖοι, ἐπεὶ παρασκευὴ ἦν, ἵνα μὴ μείνῃ ἐπὶ τοῦ σταυροῦ τὰ σώματα ἐν τῷ σαββάτῳ, ἦν γὰρ μεγάλη ἡ ἡμέρα ἐκείνου τοῦ σαββάτου, ἠρώτησαν τὸν Πιλᾶτον ἵνα κατεαγῶσιν αὐτῶν τὰ σκέλη καὶ ἀρθῶσιν. (Jn 19.31)

Mara sees the text influenced by Johannine theology in a slightly different manner. She notes that the two accounts prevent Jesus from celebrating Passover, instead he dies at the time of preparation.[116] Her observation, however, may read too much into the narrative. Nowhere does the *Gospel of Peter* identify Jesus as the Passover Lamb dying as the Jews slaughtered their sacrificial animals. Rather, the text appears to operate at a less sophisticated level. It seeks to make Antipas the representative and complicit Jew, and even his concern for the body is shown to be motivated not by compassion, but by ceremonial compliance. While this may not be a fair representation of Jewish religion, it is one that the author presents for polemical purposes.

**2.5βα γέγραπται γὰρ ἐν τῷ νόμῳ ἥλιον μὴ δῦναι ἐπὶ πεφονευμένῳ.** While there are no exact parallels in the NT to the formula employed to introduce this scriptural citation, there are nevertheless a number of examples of citation formulae which combine the verbal form γέγραπται and refer to νόμος. The following are some of the more significant parallels:

| | |
|---|---|
| καθὼς γέγραπται ἐν νόμῳ κυρίου | (Lk 2.23) |
| καὶ ἐν τῷ νόμῳ δὲ τῷ ὑμετέρῳ γέγραπται | (Jn 8.17) |
| ἐν γὰρ τῷ Μωϋσέως νόμῳ γέγραπται | (1 Cor 9.9) |
| ἐν τῷ νόμῳ γέγραπται | (1 Cor 14.21) |

---

[116] Mara, *Évangile de Pierre*, 82.

While a fixed form has not fully developed there are some common elements in these four examples. They include the use of the preposition ἐν, reference to νόμος apparently with preference for the use of the definite article, and the term γέγραπται introducing a citation.[117] The quotation appears to refer back to a stipulation in Deuteronomy, οὐκ ἐπικοιμηθήσεται τὸ σῶμα αὐτοῦ ἐπὶ τοῦ ξύλου ἀλλὰ ταφῇ θάψετε αὐτὸν ἐν τῇ ἡμέρᾳ ἐκείνῃ (Deut 21.23 LXX).[118] Even a cursory comparison shows a lack of close verbal correspondence between the text of Deut 21.23 and the stipulation presented by the author of the *Gospel of Peter*. In fact of the five word form of the ruling used in the Akhmîm text, not even one of these words is found in the text of Deuteronomy. Swete has helped to clarify the basis for the tradition that is cited as 'being written in the law' in *Gos. Pet.* 2.5. First he notes that a parallel occurs in the *Apostolic Constitutions* (v. 14) θάπτεται πρὸ ἡλίου δύσεως. Furthermore, 'Epiphanius (*haer.* 66.79) even cites the Deuteronomic law in this form: ἔλεγεν ὁ νόμος...οὐ μὴ δύνῃ ὁ ἥλιος ἐπ' αὐτῷ...θάψαντες θάψατε αὐτὸν πρὸ δύσεως τοῦ ἡλίου.' This tradition is taken a further stage back by Swete who argues that this 'gloss can be traced to Philo and Josephus; cf. Philo *de spec. legg.* [*sic.*] 28...Jos. *B.J.* iv.5.12.'[119] While the similarities with the *Apostolic Constitutions* and Epiphanius are strong, the parallels with Josephus and Philo are not as certain. It seems likely, therefore, that this tradition drew upon Jewish reflections on Deut 21.23, but was developed in Christian circles into a form that best suited the apologetic agenda.

The term πεφονευμένῳ seems incongruous on the lips of Antipas. This perfect passive particle, which describes the actions about to be undertaken as 'murder', implicitly implies the falsity of the condemnation of Jesus and portrays those who are about to carry out the sentence not as murderers rather than lawful executioners. This accords with Swete's observation that 'πεφονευμένῳ is strangely attributed to Herod, from whom we should have expected κεκρεμασμένῳ or the like; but it agrees with the anti-Judaic tone of the fragment.'[120]

---

[117] For a discussion of the issues surrounding the citation of scripture see C.D. Stanley, *Paul and the Language of Scripture: Citation Technique in the Pauline Epistles and Contemporary Literature*, SNTSMS 74 (Cambridge: CUP, 1992).

[118] The Hebrew text, לֹא־תָלִין נִבְלָתוֹ עַל־הָעֵץ כִּי־קָבוֹר תִּקְבְּרֶנּוּ בַּיּוֹם הַהוּא, has been rendered accurately by the LXX.

[119] Swete, *The Akhmîm Fragment of the Apocryphal Gospel of St Peter*, 3.

[120] Swete, *The Akhmîm Fragment of the Apocryphal Gospel of St Peter*, 3.

**2.5bβ** καὶ παρέδωκεν αὐτὸν τῷ λαῷ πρὸ μιᾶς τῶν ἀζύμων, τῆς ἑορτῆς αὐτῶν. This final comment by the narrator is a transitional unit that leads into the following scene. Swete places this part of the text as the opening line of his third chapter.[121] He is, however, alone in this decision. Robinson presents it at the conclusion to his second paragraph.[122] Similarly, Harnack places the material as the conclusion of v. 5, which represents the conclusion of his first paragraph division.[123]

It does however need to be noted that Harnack does not present the entirety of this comment. Following Bouriant's text,[124] he replicates the transcriptional error of omitting the words καὶ παρέδωκεν αὐτὸν τῷ λαῷ.[125] When Harnack wrote he did not have access to images of the text and was dependent upon Bouriant's transcription alone. After the appearance of Lods' transcription in 1893, those who followed Harnack's system of versification maintained the whole clause as the conclusion to v. 5.[126] The first correction of this error among German scholars appears to have been made by Hilgenfeld. His note pre-dates the appearance of Lods' fresh transcription, and the correction is attributed to Bensly who examined the codex in Egypt.[127] It appears more appropriate to read this clause as the conclusion to the foregoing material not simply because this is the established consensus, but more importantly since this action by Herod is connected to his preceding actions. Moreover the temporal reference σάββατον and πρὸ μιᾶς τῶν ἀζύμων appear to be closely related in the narrative.

This is the final action of Herod in the *Gospel of Peter*. After having handed Jesus over to the people he disappears from the narrative and events unfold without him. As the narrative develops Pilate comes to the fore as the principal authority figure (cf. *Gos. Pet.* 8.31; 11.43, 45, 49). The indefinite group termed ὁ λαός is mentioned here for the first time, and they will be explicitly referred to by that name again (cf. *Gos. Pet.* 8.28, 30; 11.48). In the canonical accounts ὁ λαός is also a significant group. Apart from the infamous reference in Matt 27.25,

---

[121] Swete, *The Akhmîm Fragment of the Apocryphal Gospel of St Peter*, 3.
[122] Robinson, *The Gospel according to Peter and the Revelation of Peter*, 83.
[123] Harnack, *Bruchstücke des Evangeliums und der Apokalypse des Petrus*, 9.
[124] Bouriant, 'Fragments du texte grec du livre d'Énoch et de quelques écrits attribués à saint Pierre', 137.
[125] Harnack, *Bruchstücke des Evangeliums und der Apokalypse des Petrus*, 9.
[126] Hilgenfeld, 'Zu dem Petrus-Evangelium', *ZWT* 36 (1893), 160.
[127] Hilgenfeld, 'Zu dem Petrus-Evangelium', 160.

this group is present in the Lukan Passion narrative, but they form a more neutral group who are either feared by the Jewish authorities (Lk 20.19; 22.2), or who function as passive observers (Lk 23.27, 35). In relation to Lk 23.35, Green notes that 'Importantly "the people" only "stand by, watching," and are segregated from their leaders at this stage of the narrative.'[128] This depiction stands in marked contrast to the role taken by the people in the Akhmîm text, where they are both instigators of mob violence and puppets who carry out the judicial murder sanctioned by Antipas.

While using terminology that is shared with the canonical gospels in reporting the handing-over of Jesus for crucifixion, the *Gospel of Peter* attributes the actions to a different set of characters. Jesus is handed over by Herod to the people, who in turn drag him away to carry out an act of mob-murder, which is reminiscent of the death of Stephen (Acts 7.54, 57). By contrast, the canonical accounts agree in attributing the 'handing-over', παρέδωκεν, to Pilate. Where they differ is in describing the group to whom Jesus was handed over. In the Markan account Jesus is sentenced to crucifixion and given to the soldiers to carry out this punishment (Mk 15.15f).[129] The Matthean account is similar, although the role of the crowd in calling for Jesus' death is heightened (Matt 27.25–26).[130] The Lukan account presents a different version of events. Jesus is delivered up 'to their will', τὸν δὲ Ἰησοῦν παρέδωκεν τῷ θελήματι αὐτῶν (Lk 23.25). The immediate context does not clarify to whom the third person pronoun αὐτῶν refers. The logical antecedent is to be found back in v. 13, where three groups are portrayed as acting in concert, i.e. Πιλᾶτος δὲ συγκαλεσάμενος τοὺς ἀρχιερεῖς καὶ τοὺς ἄρχοντας καὶ τὸν λαὸν. It thus appears that the comment in v. 26, following the handing-over, καὶ ὡς ἀπήγαγον αὐτόν, is to be understood as denoting the combined actions of chief-priests,

---

[128] Green, *The Gospel of Luke*, 820.

[129] As Donahue and Harrington note, 'Just as the chief priests had handed Jesus over to Pilate (see 15:1, 10), now Pilate hands Jesus over to the Roman soldiers.' J.R. Donahue and D.J. Harrington, *The Gospel of Mark*, Sacra Pagina 2 (Collegeville, MN.: Liturgical Press, 2002) 434.

[130] Hagner expresses the Matthean purpose in these verses in the following terms: 'now referred to deliberately as πᾶς ὁ λαός , "all the people" (= Israel; *pace* Kosmala), they readily take upon themselves responsibility for the death of this man.' Hagner, *Matthew 14–28*, 827.

rulers and people.[131] The Johannine account places the blame squarely upon the priestly classes. They alone call for the execution of Jesus and there is no accompanying chorus from the general populace. In Jn 18.35 Pilate informs Jesus that οἱ ἀρχιερεῖς παρέδωκάν σε ἐμοί. The chief priests remain in focus as those who call for and bring about the execution of Jesus. They are explicitly named as those who declare that they 'have no king but Caesar' (Jn 19.15). Then Pilate hands Jesus into their custody τότε οὖν παρέδωκεν αὐτὸν αὐτοῖς ἵνα σταυρωθῇ (Jn 19.16a). In the following part of the verse they take charge of Jesus. This same group appears to be referred to by John as those who crucify Jesus, ὅπου αὐτὸν ἐσταύρωσαν (Jn 19.18). However, there is a tension in the Johannine narrative at this point. As Brown notes,

> By strict sequence the "they" here [19.16b] and in vs. 18 ("they cruci-fied him") should refer to the last mentioned plural subject, namely, the chief priests (vs. 15). However, in 23 it becomes clear that the soldiers (Romans, under Pilate's jurisdiction: vss. 31–32) were the ones who cru-cified Jesus.[132]

Thus, while none of the canonical gospels present the full theological development that occurs in the *Gospel of Peter*, where Pilate is exoner-ated and in his stead Herod and the Jewish people alone are implicated in his execution, there are nonetheless tendencies in that direction. These are most clear in both the Johannine account and Lukan nar-rative. In the former it appears that the theological retelling of the passion, which seeks to blame the chief priests, is not sustained due to editorial fatigue and the more historically accurate details of Jesus crucified by the Romans intrudes into the theologically shaped nar-rative. The reworking is more thorough in Luke's gospel where the chief priests in consort with the rulers and people take Jesus away and crucify him. Yet even though these accounts tend in the direction developed further by the *Gospel of Peter*, they do not totally absolve the Roman authority. Thus as Fitzmyer observes, 'Luke has, however,

---

[131] Fitzmyer concurs was this reading. 'Who is "they"? It cannot refer to Pilate, and though some commentators are inclined to think that the Romans are the sub-ject…this is to miss an important aspect of the Lucan passion narrative. The "they" has to refer to those who "asked for" the release of Barabbas and to whom Pilate handed over Jesus according to "their will" (v. 25). This must include "the chief priests, the leaders, and the people" of v. 13.' Fitzmyer, *The Gospel according to Luke X–XXIV*, 1496.

[132] Brown, *The Gospel according to John XII–XXII*, 898.

not completely exonerated Pilate; he is involved. To appreciate this the contrast with the Akhmîm text, one only has to look at the *Gos. Peter* 1:1–2.'[133]

At this point the narrative also makes a temporal reference to the Passover, πρὸ μιᾶς τῶν ἀζύμων. This aligns more easily with the chronology presented in the fourth gospel where the crucifixion precedes the Passover.[134] The term τὰ ἄζυμα, however, is not used in the Johannine account, but occurs in all three synoptic gospels (Matt 26.17// Mk 14.12//Lk 22.1). The co-ordination of the terms 'unleaven bread' τὰ ἄζυμα and 'festival' ἑορτή also occurs in 1 Esdras:

> καὶ ἠγάγοσαν οἱ υἱοὶ Ισραηλ οἱ εὑρεθέντες ἐν τῷ καιρῷ τούτῳ τὸ πασχα καὶ τὴν ἑορτὴν τῶν ἀζύμων ἡμέρας ἑπτά (1 Esdr 1.17)

Moreover, it is clear from Josephus that this festival of Unleaven Bread is synonymous with the Passover, κατὰ τὸν καιρὸν τῆς τὰ ἀζύμων ἑορτῆς, ἥν πάσχα λέγομεν (*Ant.* 14.21). However, referring to the Passover as τῆς ἑορτῆς αὐτῶν has resonances with the Johannine narrative. In the fourth gospel the Passover is described as ἡ ἑορτὴ τῶν Ἰουδαίων (Jn 6.4).[135] While it is the case that the chronology of the Akhmîm text conforms to that of the fourth gospel, this cannot be seen as providing independent corroboration for such a dating schema. While there may not be direct literary contact between these two texts at this point, it appears either that the *Gospel of Peter* is influenced indirectly by tradition which informed the Johannine tradition, or that there is oral dependence on the fourth gospel,[136] a text which may have been known by the author of the *Gospel of Peter*, wasbut does not appear to have been consulted directly in the composition of his own account at this point.

---

[133] Fitzmyer, *The Gospel according to Luke X–XXIV*, 1492.
[134] Swete, *The Akhmîm Fragment of the Apocryphal Gospel of St Peter*, 3.
[135] Vaganay, *L'Évangile de Pierre*, 216.
[136] See Stillman, 'The Gospel of Peter: A Case for Oral-Only Dependency?', 114–120.

6. Οἱ δὲ λαβόντες τὸν κ̅υ̅[1,2] ὤθουν αὐτῶν[3] τρέχοντες καὶ[4] ἔλεγον· Σύρωμεν[5] τὸν υἱὸν[6] τοῦ θ̅υ̅,[7] ἐξουσίαν αὐτοῦ ἐσχηκότες. 7. καὶ πορφύραν αὐτὸν περιέβαλλον[8], καὶ ἐκάθισαν αὐτὸν ἐπὶ καθέδραν[9] κρίσεως, λέγοντες· Δικαίως κρῖνε, βασιλεῦ τοῦ Ἰσραήλ. 8. καί τις αὐτῶν ἐνεγκὼν στέφανον ἀκάνθινον ἔθηκεν ἐπὶ τῆς κεφαλῆς τοῦ κυρίου 9. καὶ ἕτεροι ἑστῶτες[10] ἐνέπτυον αὐτοῦ ταῖς[11] ὄψεσι, καὶ ἄλλοι[12] τὰς σιαγόνας αὐτοῦ ἐράπισαν, ἕτεροι[13] καλάμῳ ἔνυσσον αὐτὸν καί τινες αὐτὸν ἐμάστιζον λέγοντες· ταύτῃ τῇ τιμῇ τιμήσωμεν τὸν υἱὸν[14] τοῦ θ̅υ̅.[15]

6. So those taking the Lord were pushing him while running along, and they were saying, 'Let us drag the son of God having authority over him.' 7. And they were clothing him in purple and they sat him on the seat of judgment saying, 'Judge justly King of Israel.' 8. And one of them brought a thorn crown and placed it on the head of the Lord. 9. And others who stood by were spitting in his face, and others struck his cheeks, others were piercing him with a reed and some were scourging him saying, 'With this honour let us honour the son of God.'

## TEXT CRITICAL NOTES

1. Although all transcriptions of the text either give the full form κύριον[137] or the abbreviated *nomen sacrum* κ̅υ̅[138] with *supra*linear bar, they all agree in printing the term in the accusative case. This agrees with the preceding accusative masculine singular form of the definite article, thereby producing the correct case agreement. The photograph, however, clearly shows that the *nomen sacrum* consists of two letters, a kappa and an upsilon. This obviously represents the full form κυρίου, a masculine genitive singular which does not agree

---

[137] See Bouriant, 'Fragments du texte grec du livre d'Énoch et de quelques écrits attribués à saint Pierre', 137; Swete, *The Akhmîm Fragment of the Apocryphal Gospel of St Peter*, 3; Harnack, *Bruchstücke des Evangeliums und der Apokalypse des Petrus*, 8; Robinson, *The Gospel according to Peter and the Revelation of Peter*, 83; Vaganay, *L'Évangile de Pierre*, 222; and Mara, *Évangile de Pierre*, 44.

[138] Kraus und Nicklas, *Das Petrusevangelium und die Petrusapokalypse*, 32.

in case with the preceding article. The shape of these two letters that form the *nomen sacrum* is identical to the two previous occurrences of this form, ὁ φίλος Πειλάτου καὶ τοῦ x̄ū (*Gos. Pet.* 2.3αβ) and τὸ σῶμα τοῦ x̄ū (*Gos. Pet.* 2.3bγ). It is, however, markedly different in shape from the accusative singular form παρ[αλημ]φθῆναι τὸν x̄ū (*Gos. Pet.* 1.2a). The reason for this conflict in case endings on the part of the scribe is no longer possible to determine with any degree of certainty. The most plausible explanation is that this confusion in case endings is simply due to an inadvertent scribal error, either on the part of the scribe responsible for the text in P.Cair. 10759, or a scribe who copied the text at some earlier point in its transmission. Alternatively, the scribe responsible for this form may have believed a genitive absolute construction was required. Although in normal classical usage the genitive absolute is limited 'to the sentence where the noun or pronoun to which the participle refers does not appear either as subject or in any other capacity',[139] there is much fluidity in usage in later periods. Even if this were the case, the scribe has made a poor attempt at conforming this clause to such a construction. Moreover as is noted in BDF, if this were the case then this example would fall into the rarest category of (mis)use of the genitive absolute construction. '(4) The harshest and at the same time rarest case is where the 'antecedent' follows as subject.'[140] Since these factors make a genitive absolute construction both a rarity and a misuse, it may be best to conclude that the genitive form κυρίου is simply a scribal blunder.

2. Also of interest is the positioning of the *supra*linear bar. The scribe is not altogether consistent. Here, as well as in the previous use of a *nomen sacrum* (*Gos. Pet.* 2.3bγ), the bar commences to the right of the extended vertical stroke of the kappa, and is positioned at a slightly lower level than the top of that vertical stroke. The first two examples of *nomina sacra* that occur in the text (*Gos. Pet.* 1.2a; 2.3αβ) have a slightly different appearance. In these cases the *supra*linear bar commences to the left of the up-stroke of the kappa and extends above both letters in the abbreviation. This variation does not occur with other abbreviated words; in those cases the bar is above all letters. The variation arises with the term κύριος, because

---

[139] See BDF §423.
[140] See BDF §423.

of the extended vertical stroke of the kappa which is preferred by
this scribe.

3. The form αὐτῶν that occurs in the manuscript in place of αὐτόν
which seems to be required, is probably the result of phonetic variation due to the flattening of the distinction in the pronouncia-
tion between omicron and omega (cf. Rom 5.1). The transcription
made by Lods is the first instance of αὐτῶν being cited as the reading contained in the manuscript.[141] Most editions of the text have
tended to print αὐτόν as originally transcribed by Bouriant,[142] but
the recent critical edition of Nicklas and Kraus notes the variant.[143]
It is impossible to tell whether this is due to dependence on the
transcription made by Bouriant, or whether this variant is considered an orthographical mistake to be corrected without comment.
French scholarship has been consistent in noting the existence of
the form αὐτῶν in the manuscript.[144]

4. Here the middle letter of the καί is extremely poorly formed. This
results in a highly compressed form of the word occupying approximately 5mm of line space. This is in contrast to the 7mm occupied
by the same word on line 6 of the first page. This may need to be
considered in the reconstruction of the reading on line 2.

5. Although the reading σύρωμεν is relatively secure, a number of
alternative readings have been proposed. Presumably the uncertainty has been occasioned by the poorly formed initial sigma.
Unlike the enlarged and rounded form of sigma the scribe uses
in general, written with a single stroke of the pen, here the letter
is much smaller and appears to be formed with two strokes. This,
however, is similar to the shape employed in the initial letter in
the word σάββατον (*Gos. Pet.* 2.5). Alternatives that have been suggested include: εὕρωμεν 'let us find', but there is no cross-stroke in
the first letter as would be required to form an epsilon;[145] σύρομεν
'we are dragging', yet the fourth letter has the three upward strokes

[141] Lods, 'L'Évangile et l'Apocalypse de Pierre avec le texte grec du livre d'Hénoch',
219.
[142] Bouriant, 'Fragments du texte grec du livre d'Énoch et de quelques écrits
attribués à saint Pierre', 137.
[143] Kraus und Nicklas, *Das Petrusevangelium und die Petrusapokalypse*, 32.
[144] See Vaganay, *L'Évangile de Pierre*, 'faute de copiste dans le ms.: αυτων', 222; and
Mara, *Évangile de Pierre*, 44.
[145] Bouriant, 'Fragments du texte grec du livre d'Énoch et de quelques écrits
attribués à saint Pierre', 137.

of omega and cannot be read as an omicron;[146] Other suggestions include σταυρῶμεν 'let us crucify';[147] κυρῶμεν 'let us confirm' or 'decide in favour of';[148] αἴρωμεν 'let us seize';[149] and ἄρωμεν 'let us hale'.[150]

6. This is the third time that the scribe employs a diæresis. It occurs above the initial letter of the word υἱόν. Unlike the occurrence (*Gos. Pet.* 1.2) it is not employed here to indicate the separation of phonemes in a potential diphthong (since the preceding letter here is a consonant and not a vowel). Here it conforms to the so-called inorganic usage of the diæresis which simply marks an initial vowel (see text critical note 6, in the section *Gos. Pet.* 1.1–2).

7. A second *nomen sacrum* occurs at this point in *Gos. Pet.* 3.6. The horizontal bar is raised above both letters, and abbreviates the genitive form θεοῦ. This noun agrees in case with the preceding definite article, unlike the earlier example in this verse.

8. The formation of the double lambda in περιέβαλλον is written in such a way that shorter left to right diagonal stroke of the first lambda is connected to the preceding alpha. Next, what should be the longer downwards left to right diagonal stroke of the first lambda is truncated and at approximately two-thirds of its expected length the pen turns about ninety degrees to form the short stroke of the second lambda. Finally the scribe forms a detached left down to right diagonal stroke to write the long arm of the second lambda. This is a slightly irregular formation of the double lambda which may be important in determining the form of the word βουληθέντω(ν) in *Gos. Pet.* 1.1, where there appears also to be an irregular lambda formation. It is understandable that a number of studies have not distinguished the double lambda or have taken it as a scribal error for the aorist περιέβαλον.[151]

---

[146] Gebhardt, *Das Evangelium und die Apokalypse des Petrus*, 17–18.

[147] J.E. Sandys, *The Academy* (1893) 486.

[148] K. Manchot, 'Die neuen Petrus-Fragmente', *Protestantische Kirchenzeitung* (1893) 6:126–143; 7:160–166; 8:176–183; 9:201–213.

[149] Zahn, *Das Evangelium des Petrus*. Lejay, 'L'Évangile de Pierre' *L'enseignement biblique* (1893) 59–84, 267–270.

[150] H. von Wilamowitz-Möllendorf, 'Conjecturen zu den Petrus-Fragmenten', *Index Scholarum von* Göttingen (1893) 31–33. Harris, *A Popular Account of the Newly Recovered Gospel of St Peter*, 43.

[151] See Mara, *Évangile de Pierre*, 44 and also Vaganay, *L'Évangile de Pierre*, 225. The latter states, 'Περιέβαλον (dans le ms. Faute de copiste : περιέβαλλον).' It is not

9. The letter delta in the word καθέδραν deviates from the scribe's regular form. The delta that appears two words later at the beginning of the word δικαίως exhibits the normal practice of this scribe and of many majuscule manuscripts in general which maintain a triangular shape of approximately equilateral proportions, i.e. Δ. By contrast the delta in καθέδραν is formed by two pen-strokes. Attached to the central horizontal bar of the preceding epsilon is the initial stroke in the shape of a crescent with the nadir of this convex shape at the bottom of the line. This stroke represents both the left-hand diagonal and the base of the regular triangular form. Instead of the sharp right-hand diagonal, the second stroke is almost horizontal across the top of the crescent with a slight right to left ascent. Once again, the poor penmanship of the scribe is fully apparent.[152]

10. Although the three words that commence Gos. Pet. 3.9, καὶ ἕτεροι ἑστῶτες, are faint, it is not accurate to describe then as being invisible[153] In fact from the photographs reproduced by Nicklas and Kraus[154] nearly all letters can be read without any uncertainty. The exceptions are the partially erased head of the rho in the word ἕτεροι and the first sigma in the word ἑστῶτες, and even here the faint outline of the letter can still be recognized. Therefore, the reading as originally transcribed by Bouriant is secure,[155] and should not be classed as a reconstruction.

11. The scribe appears to have corrected his own manuscript at this point by supplying the initially omitted final sigma of the feminine plural dative definite article, by writing it in a superscripted fashion just to the right of the elongated iota and slightly above the omicron of the following word ὄψεσις.

12. There occurs here a further example of the scribal peculiarity of the formation of the double lambda combination. This aligns with the formation in the word περιέβαλλον in Gos. Pet. 3.7.[156]

---

necessarily the case that the imperfect form is a transcriptional error on the part of the scribe of P.Cair. 10759.

[152] For further discussion of this topic see C.H. Roberts, *Greek Literary Hands 350 B.C.–A.D. 400* (Oxford: Clarendon Press, 1955).

[153] See Mara, 'dans le ms. les mots sont illisibles.' Mara, *Évangile de Pierre*, 44.

[154] Kraus und Nicklas, *Das Petrusevangelium und die Petrusapokalypse*, unnumbered page, plate *P.Cair.* 10759 f.2r, the top line of text.

[155] Bouriant, 'Fragments du texte grec du livre d'Énoch et de quelques écrits attribués à saint Pierre', 138.

[156] See text critical note 7 in this section.

13. The word ἕτεροι can be compared to the partially erased form of the identical term which occurs also as the second word in this verse. The continuous stroke between the crossbar of the epsilon and the following rho is the same in both locations. It is also possible to see from the second example that the head of the rho is extremely small and that this could easily fit into the space where the erasure has occurred with the first form of this word in *Gos. Pet.* 3.9.

14. This is the fourth time that the scribe employs a diæresis. It occurs above the initial letter of the word υἱόν. In this case the purpose appears to be to indicate that the potential diphthong is not formed with the following vowel, *i.e.*, the organic usage. This form with diacritical marking is identical to ϋιον in *Gos. Pet.* 3.6. It is interesting that the scribe does not choose to employ the device of a *nomem sacrum* to represent the word υἱός. As Hurtado notes the term υἱός falls into a group of eight words 'which are abbreviated less consistently and appear to have joined the list of sacred terms latest.'[157]

15. In contrast to the term υἱός which two words earlier does not occur as a *nomen sacrum*, the scribe, as is his regular practice, abbreviates the term θεός in the regular pattern of suspension with a *supra*linear bar. While the term θεός was among the group of four words that show the earliest attestation as *nomina sacra*[158] and υἱός which is here unabbreviated is among a later group of words to appear as *nomina sacra*, this cannot be used as a datum for dating this manuscript or the exemplar which laid behind it. First, on palaeographical grounds P.Cair. 10759 is to be dated to a period when all fifteen most common *nomina sacra* were demonstrably in widespread use. Secondly, scribal practice was not consistent, so it is impossible to generalize about scribal habits and then apply those generalizations to an individual manuscript without taking into account its overall epigraphical characteristics. Thirdly, it is impossible to be certain that the scribe of P.Cair. 10759 was accurately copying the forms of *nomina sacra* that occurred in his exemplar, rather than conforming his transcription to his own preferences.

---

[157] L.W. Hurtado, 'The Origin of the *Nomina Sacra*: A Proposal', *JBL* 117 (1998) 655–673, see especially 655–657.

[158] Hurtado, 'The Origin of the *Nomina Sacra*: A Proposal', 655.

## Commentary

**3.6aα Οἱ δὲ λαβόντες τὸν κ̅υ̅.** Judgment under the pretext of lawfully constituted authority appears to give way to an act of mob violence at this point. Although there is no significant point of verbal contact, the scene is reminiscent of the actions of the crowd against Stephen, καὶ ὥρμησαν ὁμοθυμαδὸν ἐπ' αὐτὸν καὶ ἐκβαλόντες ἔξω τῆς πόλεως ἐλιθοβόλουν (Acts 7.57b-58a). Similar acts of group aggression were suffered by other early Christian martyrs. The role of the mob in hunting out Christians appears to have been commonplace in second century Lyons.

> Καὶ πρῶτον μὲν τὰ ἀπὸ τοῦ ὄχλου πανδημεὶ σωρηδὸν ἐπιφερόμενα γενναίως ὑπέμενον, ἐπιβοήσεις καὶ πληγὰς καὶ συρμοὺς καὶ διαρπαγὰς καὶ λίθων βολὰς συγκλείσεις καὶ πάνθ' ὅσα ἠγριωμένῳ πλήθει ὡς πρὸς ἐχθροὺς καὶ πολεμίχους φιλεῖ γίνεσθαι Eusebius (*H.E.* 5.1.7)[159]

> And first, they nobly endured what was inflicted by the mob: hostile shouting and blows and dragging and despoiling and stone throwing and imprisonment, and everything that an enraged mob loves to do to their most hated enemies and foes.[160]

Although not explicitly named in the *Gospel of Peter*, the mob which takes hold of Jesus is to be understood as members of the Jewish populace in Jerusalem. This is apparent from the reference contained in *Gos. Pet.* 2.5 where Antipas hands Jesus over to the people, καὶ παρέδωκεν αὐτὸν τῷ λαῷ. Swete makes a distinction between the terminology used here and that which occurs in the Johannine account. He states, 'The λαός are the subject, for λαβόντες takes up παρέδωκεν – comp. John xix. 16, 17 παρέδωκεν αὐτὸν αὐτοῖς (= τοῖς Ἰουδαίοις, cf. 14)...παρέλαβονουν τὸν Ἰησοῦν.'[161] While the Johannine account refers to 'the Jews' in Jn 19.12, 14, the group to whom Jesus is handed over (19.16) are those

---

[159] The sole source for this text is Eusebius (*H.E.* 5.1.7). In the printed editions it is conveniently presented in H. Musurillo, *Acts of the Christian Martyrs*, vol. 2, Martyrs of Lyons 1.7, (Oxford: OUP, 1972) 62; and K. Lake, *Eusebius: Ecclesiastical History*, Books I–V, LCL 153 (Cambridge, Massachusetts: Harvard University Press, 1926) 408.

[160] The translation does not follow that of either Musurillo, or Lake. Rather it presents a more accurate rendering than the former, and removes the archaic terms used by the latter.

[161] Swete, *The Akhmîm Fragment of the Apocryphal Gospel of St Peter*, 3–4.

named in the previous verse as οἱ ἀρχιερεῖς (Jn 19.15). Thus, in the fourth Gospel Jesus' crucifixion is not an act of group violence, but responsibility is attributed to the calculating schemes of the Jerusalem religious authorities. Furthermore, Swete's distinction between ὁ λαός of *Gos. Pet.* 2.5 and οἱ Ἰουδαῖοι of John 19.12ff. is not a distinction that would have been recognized by the author of the Akhmîm text. Mara notes the different terminology designating the same Jewish subjects as 'them', 'the people' or through reference to ethnic practices 'their festivals'.[162] Harnack concurs with this perspective.[163] Vaganay is perhaps the most unequivocal in his assessment, 'After the τῆς ἑορτῆς αὐτῶν which terminates the preceding verse, οἱ δέ must designate the Jews.'[164]

The action of 'taking the Lord' portrays the overt aggression by a vindictive crowd who have rejected the jurisdiction of Roman justice as exemplified by Pilate. The verb λαμβάνω has a wide semantic range, however, in the present context it is being used negatively to denote the unlawful and violent seizure of Jesus. The action of 'taking' (λαβόντες) Jesus may reflect the usage of a compound form of the verb in the fourth gospel where in the immediate context it first appears that the chief priests are taking Jesus away παρέλαβον οὖν τὸν Ἰησοῦν (Jn 19.16b).[165] In the Matthean account the compound verb form is used to describe the actions of the soldiers τότε οἱ στρατιῶται τοῦ ἡγεμόνος παραλαβόντες τὸν Ἰησοῦν εἰς τὸ πραιτώριον (Matt 27.27a).[166] Here agian the intrusive narrator describes Jesus using his favoured Christological title ὁ κύριος.

**3.6aβ ὤθουν αὐτὸν τρέχοντες.** The verb ὠθέω does not occur in the New Testament, but is used on seven occasions in the LXX (Num 35.20, 22; Job 14.20; Ps 61.3; 117.13; Isa 30.22; and Jer 34.11) to translate one of three Hebrew verbs הדף, דחה, or תקף.[167] The imperfect

---

[162] 'Par οἱ δέ, il semble clair que l'auteur désigne les Juifs, indiqués deux fois au v. 5, par λαῷ, le people qui Jésus est livré, et par αὐτῶν dans τῆς ἑορτῆς αὐτῶν, «leur fete». Mara, *Évangile de Pierre*, 87.

[163] 'Das Jüdische wird als ein fernstehendes behandelt, s.v. ὁ τῆς ἑορτῆς αὐτῶν.' Harnack, *Bruchstücke des Evangeliums und der Apokalypse des Petrus*, 23.

[164] Vaganay, *L'Évangile de Pierre*, 222.

[165] See the discussion on 2.5bβ.

[166] As Vaganay states 'λαβόντες τὸν κύριον peut etre compare aux termes de Mt. (παραλαβόντες τὸν Ἰησοῦν) au debut de la scene de derision.' Vaganay, *L'Évangile de Pierre*, 222.

[167] See Hatch and Redpath, *Concordance to the Septuagint* (2nd ed.; Grand Rapids, Michigan: Baker, 1998) 1492, column 3.

third person plural form ὦθουν indicates continuous action in the past, which here is co-ordinated with the action of the participle τρέχοντες. This syntactically subsequently placed participle indicates a sequence of actions, with ὦθουν being prior to τρέχοντες, with the latter portraying a more proximate action in the narrative. Outside of the LXX the term is also used by other Jewish writer, Philo, *Aet. Mund.* 136; and Josephus, *Bell.* 1.250. The term ὠθέω denotes 'pushing' or 'shoving' and is a verb where syllabic augment before a vowel is missing.[168]

The co-ordinated action is described be the participle τρέχοντες. The verb occurs twenty-one times in the New Testament in various forms.[169] Of these twenty-one occurrences, three occur in 1 Cor 9.24, and these are used to depict the act of running in a stadium. The first of these usages is the only place in the New Testament where the same form of τρέχω is used as occurs here in the *Gospel of Peter*.

Together, the pair of verbs describes the uncontrolled actions of an unruly mob keen to carry out an act of summary justice. One would perhaps expect the narrative to unfold with an uninterrupted sequence leading Jesus to the place of execution. Such, however, is not the case. Rather, Jesus is first arraigned in purple, place on the chair of judgment and then mocked and brutalized by the baying crowd.

**3.6bα** καὶ ἔλεγον· Σύρωμεν τὸν υἱὸν τοῦ θ̄ῡ. The physical actions of the mob are here paralleled by their verbal declaration. The words that are put on their lips depict the crowd speaking in unison, and cohortatively declaring their desire to further mistreat Jesus. The term σύρω is used in the Acts of the Apostles to describe various occasions of persecution or mob violence. It is used to depict the pre-Damascus Road Saul harrying men and women who were believers in Jesus (Acts 8.3). It also describes the violence perpetrated against Paul at Lystra, where Paul is stoned and dragged outside the city by a Jewish reactionary group,[170] being left for dead (14.19).[171] Finally, in Acts, the

---

[168] See BDF §66.2.

[169] See W.F. Moulton & A.S. Geden, *Concordance to the Greek New Testament*, Sixth edition, fully revised, I.H. Marshall (ed.), (London: T&T Clark – A Continuum Imprint, 2002) 1045.

[170] Fitzmyer comments, 'In the Greek text the subject is clearly *Ioudaioi*, who have come the considerable distance from Antioch and Iconium. Now they succeed, whereas at Iconium they only tried to stone the two missionaries.' J.A. Fitzmyer, *The Acts of the Apostles*, Anchor Bible 31 (New York: Doubleday, 1998) 532–533.

[171] Crossan and Reed argue that the cause of the violent Jewish reaction against Paul was due to his missionary strategy of going first to the synagogues not primarily

term is also employed when narrating the hauling of Jason before the city authorities by the Jews in Thessalonica (17.6).[172]

In sources outside the NT the term σύρω, or one of its cognates, is used in a number of martyrdom stories. In the narrative of the Martyrs of Lyons, one of the abuses suffered at the hands of the crowd is συρμούς 'draggings' (H.E. 5.1.7). In the Acts of Philip the term is used repeatedly to describe the reaction of the Proconsul of Hierapolis, in response to the conversion of his wife, Nicanora. First, 'he seized her by the hair of her head, and dragged her along, kicking her.' Then, the public executioners at the command of Nicanora's husband 'dragged them [Philip and his companions] along, leading them to where the proconsul was.' Finally, as part of their torture, after the scourging, the Proconsul orders the following treatment of Philip and his co-workers:

> to be dragged through the streets of the city as far as the gate of their temple. And a great crowd was assembled, so that scarcely any one stayed at home; and they all wondered at their patience, as they were being violently and inhumanly dragged along. (Acts of Philip 15)

The final phrase in this description βιαίως καὶ ἀπανθρώπως συρομένων αὐτῶν, is coupled with adverbs depicting brutal and inhumane behaviour. Justin preserves a tradition that shares certain details with the description of the crowd seizing Jesus:

> καὶ γὰρ (ὡς εἶπεν ὁ προφήτης) διασύροντες αὐτὸν ἐκάθισαν ἐπὶ βήματος καὶ εἶπεν Κρῖνον ἡμῖν. (Justin, Apol. i. 35)

> For, as the prophet said, 'They dragged him and set him on the judgement seat, and said, "Judge for us."' (Justin, Apol. i. 35)

Justin acknowledges his dependence here on the prophetic writings (Isa 58.2). Therefore, this interpretation appears to be due to Justin's reflection on the Isaianic prophecies, and not due to source material contained in a gospel-like text. It appears that the similarity between Justin and the Gospel of Peter at this point is not due to Justin use of the Akhmîm text, rather it is more likely either that both texts were

---

to convert ethnic Jews, but rather to poach the Gentile adherents known as God-fearers. John Dominic Crossan and Jonathan L. Reed, In Search of Paul: How Jesus' Apostle Opposed Rome's Empire with God's Kingdom (London: SPCK, 2005) 32.

[172] Barrett notes, 'The rioters set about dragging (ἔσυρον, imperfect; the word at 8.3; 14.19) Jason and his fellow Christians ἐπὶ τοὺς πολιτάρχας. C.K. Barrett, The Acts of the Apostles, vol. 2, ICC (Edinburgh: T&T Clark, 1998) 814.

independently drawing on traditions that saw the passion foretold by the prophet Isaiah, or that the Akhmîm text was drawing on a tradition which originated with Justin's use of the Isaianic text.

The Christological title that the author places on the lips of the crowd is somewhat surprising. In the synoptic gospels the appellation τὸν υἱὸν τοῦ θεοῦ is used primarily in confessional contexts, or at junctures where Jesus' true status is recognized. Discussing the Markan usage, Tuckett notes, 'Despite then its relatively infrequent occurrence in the Gospel, it seems then that Son of God is of vital significance for Mark as the term most adequately describing who Jesus is.'[173] However in other texts, like this occurrence in the Gospel of Peter, it can also be used in the context of mockery. Those who malign the Matthean Jesus during his crucifixion, challenge him to prove his claim to be 'Son of God' (Matt 27.40, 43).[174] Yet in the present context the sense is slightly different. Although the title is used in the wider setting of mockery, it is not itself explicitly used to mock Jesus.[175] The narrative may, nonetheless, be implicitly building on the Matthean redactional device of having those who oppose Jesus address him as Son of God, but they fail to recognize that such is his true status.

**3.6bβ**  ἐξουσίαν αὐτοῦ ἐσχηκότες. The crowd's unified cry to drag Jesus along is seen as an expression of their authority in this situation. The term ἐξουσία is used in the Johannine exchange between Jesus and Pilate, where the former denies that the authority claim of the latter. Pilate states, οὐκ οἶδας ὅτι ἐξουσίαν ἔχω ἀπολῦσαί σε καὶ ἐξουσίαν ἔχω σταυρῶσαί σε; (Jn 19.10), to which Jesus replies, οὐκ εἶχες ἐξουσίαν κατ᾽ ἐμοῦ οὐδεμίαν εἰ μὴ ἦν δεδομένον σοι ἄνωθεν (Jn 19.11). Here, however, Jesus is not involved in conversation, rather the reference to authority forms part of the mob's desire to demonstrate that they are the possessors of authority through their subjugation of the one they have referred to as the Son of God.

---

[173] Tuckett, *Christology and the New Testament*, 114.

[174] Cullmann dismisses these references from his discussion of the title 'Son of God' because 'neither the high priest nor those who mock him at the cross really believe that Jesus is the Son of God.', Cullmann, *The Christology of the New Testament*, 279.

[175] As Mara observes, 'Ici, le contexte est différent. Il ne s'agit pas d'une interrogation. Le trait n'a pas de parallèle dans les Synoptiques.' Mara, *Évangile de Pierre*, 90.

The grammatical construction is somewhat unusual. Vaganay suggests that the use of an objective genitive without a governing preposition indicates the result of the actions which are yet to be undertaken.[176] As Wallace states, '[t]he genitive substantive functions semantically as the *direct* object of the verbal idea implicit in the head noun.'[177] Here the construction is more complex, since ἐξουσίαν is given in the accusative case indicating that it is the direct object of ἐσχηκότες, while the personal pronoun αὐτοῦ functions as a prepositional phrase without being governed by a preposition. Thus, the claim of the crowd is not to have gained Jesus' own authority in a subjective or possessive sense of the genitive construction, rather they are intent on showing that their own actions demonstrate the authority they have over the one whom they are humiliating in this manner. Understanding the genitive construction in this manner means that the phrase is not to be translated as 'having his authority' as though some transference of power had taken place. Rather it denotes that from the perspective of the crowd, that they have obtained control of him.

**3.7a  καὶ πορφύραν αὐτὸν περιέβαλλον.** Among the canonical gospels Luke is unique in not attributing to the Roman soldiers the act of dressing Jesus in a lavish robe, as part of their mock investiture and homage. Instead, Luke changes the identity of those who carried out these actions from Roman troops to Herod and his soldiers, ἐξουθενήσας δὲ αὐτὸν [καὶ] ὁ Ἡρῴδης σὺν τοῖς στρατεύμασιν αὐτοῦ καὶ ἐμπαίξας περιβαλὼν ἐσθῆτα λαμπρὰν (Lk 23.11). Luke offers a different description of the colour or quality of the robe, describing it as λαμπρός rather than purple. Nonetheless, he does use the verb περιβάλλω to denote the act of placing this garment upon Jesus. For Fitzmyer the term λαμπρός is intentionally used by Luke to symbolize Jesus' innocence. He states, 'There is no suggestion in this Lucan episode that this gorgeous robe has anything to do with Jesus' alleged kingship. That is to read a Markan nuance into it. It is chosen to mock his guiltlessness.'[178]

---

[176] 'Il suffit de signaler, d'une part, avec la construction de ἐξουσία avec un génitif objectif sans l'intermédiaire d'une préposition (cf. *Mc.*, VI, 7; *Jn.*, XVII, 2; *I Cor.*, IX, 12; comme aussi dans les LXX (*Dan.*, V, 4) et les papyrus; au contraire, ἐξουσίαν κατ' ἐμοῦ dans *Jn.*, XIX, 11), d'autre part, le participe remplaçant une préposition causale et l'emploi très juste du parfait pour indiquer que l'état résultant d'une action dure encore.' Vaganay, *L'Évangile de Pierre*, 224.

[177] Wallace, *Greek Grammar: Beyond the Basics*, 116.

[178] Fitzmyer, *The Gospel According to Luke X–XXIV*, 1482.

Yet as Bock mentions this interpretation is contested. He describes two further alternatives. 'It is debated whether λαμπρός (*lampros*) means "white" garment (Grundmann 1963: 425; Oepke, *TDNT* 4:27; Danker 1988: 366), which would make Jesus a king-designate wearing a *toga candida*, or is a reference to a regal purple garb (Klostermann 1929: 233 notes the options).'[179] Of the remaining canonical accounts all three agree that the robe was placed on Jesus by the Roman soldiers as part of their mockery (Matt 27.28; Mk 15.17; Jn 19.2). Mark and John both describe the colour of the garment as purple, using respectively either the noun πορφύρα, or the adjective πορφυροῦς qualifying the noun ἱμάτιον. By contrast, Matthew describes the garment as χλαμύδα κοκκίνην (Matt 27.28). Hagner is perhaps incorrect when he states of this garment that '[t]his was his royal robe.'[180] Although Matthew retains the thorn crown and reed sceptre, the description of the garment as a 'scarlet cloak' appears to move away from royal imagery. As Gundry notes in discussing the change from the Markan wording, 'a truly royal robe becomes an ordinary solidier's mantle.'[181] Davies and Allison corroborate the observation concerning the military nature of the robe, but nonetheless suggest that it continues to function emblematically as a symbol of regal vesture. In relation to the term χλαμύς they observe:

> The word means 'cloak' (cf. 2 Macc 12.35) and here refers to a soldier's cloak (Cf. Plutarch, *Phil.* 11). This probably explains the substitution of = 'scarlet' (cf. Heb 9.19; Rev 17.3-4; 18.12, 16) for Mark's 'purple'. For whereas purple (made from Mediterranean molluscs: Pliny, *N.H.* 9.62.135) was expensive and so firmly associated with wealth and royalty, scarlet (derived from insects) was the colour of the Roman soldier's cloak: thus Jesus is dressed as a Roman soldier...In any case the context requires that the 'cloak', whether scarlet or purple, serve as a mock royal garb, and χλαμύς can refer to a king's mantle.[182]

The terms used to denote the 'putting on' of the garment differ in the canonical accounts, Matt 27.28 περιτίθημι; Mark 15.16 ἐνδιδύσκω; both Lk 23.12 and Jn 19.2 περιβάλλω. This last term is the one preferred by the Akhmîm text to describe the act of dressing Jesus in the purple

---

[179] D.L. Bock, *Luke 9:51-24:53*, ECNT (Grand Rapids, Michigan: Baker, 1996) 1820-1821.

[180] Hagner, *Matthew 14-28*, 831.

[181] R.H. Gundry, *Matthew: A Commentary on His Handbook for a Mixed Church under Persecution* (2nd ed.; Grand Rapids, Michigan: Eerdmans, 1994) 566.

[182] Davies and Allison, *The Gospel According to Saint Matthew*, vol. III, 601-602.

garment, although it must be noted the Luke, John and the *Gospel of Peter* all differ in the form of περιβάλλω that they employ.

This range of similarities and differences leads one to conclude that the *Gospel of Peter* is most heavily influenced by the Johannine narrative at this point, but not necessarily directly dependent upon it. It uses the term περιβάλλω in common with John and Luke, but *contra* Matt and Mark. The garmemt is described as being 'purple' in agreement with John and Mark, although admittedly the Akhmîm text employs the nominal form as does the Markan text and not the adjectival form employed by John. Furthermore, the description that follows with Jesus being placed on the 'judgment-seat' recalls the reference to the βῆμα in the Johannine account of the discussion with Pilate (19.13). Mara concurs with this assessment.[183] While there is debate as to whether Matthew has played down the royal overtones in the robing of Jesus, the *Gospel of Peter* highlights this theme not only by retaining the description of the garment as purple, but even more explicitly through the description of Jesus being mocked as 'King of Israel.'

**3.7b καὶ ἐκάθισαν αὐτὸν ἐπὶ καθέδραν κρίσεως.** Having dressed Jesus in the purple garment, the mob does not rush to the place of execution uninterrupted, first it pauses at what is described a location which is depicted as the καθέδραν κρίσεως. In the Akhmîm text the narrator makes it explicit that Jesus is the one placed on this seat. As the taunts which follow will make clear, this is part of the mocking of Jesus which attempts to parody notions of the Messiah as a judge figure. In the Danielic vision the appearance of the 'one like Son of Man' (Dan 7.13) before the Ancient of Days occurs in a juridical context. A court is constituted, books are opened (7.8), and judgment is passed in favour of the saints (7.22). Yet while the messianic figure is associated with this scene, it is the coming of the Ancient of Days which precipitates the deliberations of the court and the Son of Man figure has no explicit involvement in the judicial aspect of this vision. Expectations of messianic judgment are more pronounced in *1 Enoch.* Although the judgment scene may encapsulate anti-Seleucid sentiment, *1 Enoch* 90 further developed the evolving conceptual framework that

---

[183] Referring to the passage in Jn 19.2 Mara states, 'c'est donc avec lui que *Ev.P.* 7 est le plus ressemblant.' Mara, *Évangile de Pierre*, 94.

envisaged a messianic figure acting as an end-time judge. In the Eno-
chic vision a figure dressed in white opens the sealed books of the Lord
of the Sheep (90.20), then one of seven white figures brings the seventy
shepherds before the Lord and they are condemned (90.22). Here the
figure dressed in white takes a more active role in the judicial process.
As Oegema observes, 'In this case he [the one dressed in white] would
be a representative divine figure or angel, whose role is that of a judge,
but even then he stands for the concept of the Messiah as a latter-
day Judge.'[184] In the Qumran writings there are a number of multi-
dimensional aspects to the messianic expectations held by the group.
Although there is no formal courtroom judgment scene involving the
messianic figures, there is a sense in which the messianic role entails
actively dispensing judgment, often militarily (CD 7.14–21). Similarly
the *Psalms of Solomon* envisage the Messiah actively bringing judgment with the rod of his discipline (Pss. Sol. 18.7).[185] Particularly striking is 11QMelchizedek,[186] where a Melchizedek *redevivis* figure both
dispenses justice and presides over the assembly.[187] Similarly in the
fragmentary text 4Q534, which has been identified as a messianic text,
an unnamed figure appears to be involved in discerning 'the secrets of
all living things' (col 1.8).[188] Themes of eternal justice are also prominent in the *Songs of the Sabbath Sacrifices*, but there are no explicit
messianic links in these texts.

Coupled with this mocking of Jesus as a judge-figure, the narrative
in the *Gospel of Peter* appears to be drawing creative inspiration for
this scene from traditions inherited from the Johannine passion narrative. Following the accusation made by the Johannine chief priests
that Pilate would not be a friend of Caesar if he released Jesus, the
vacillating Pilate oscillates between being guided by the chief-priests
and accepting the testimony of Jesus. Towards the end of this scene

---

[184] G.S. Oegema, *The Anointed and his People: Messianic Expectations from the Maccabees to Bar Kochba*, JSPS 27 (Sheffield: Sheffield Academic Press, 1998) 69.

[185] Oegema, *The Anointed and his People: Messianic Expectations from the Maccabees to Bar Kochba*, 104–105.

[186] Catalogued by number as 11Q13.

[187] See F. García Martínez, E.J.C. Tigchelaar, and A.S. van der Woude, *Manuscripts from Qumran Cave 11 (11Q2–18, 11Q20–30)*, (DJD XXIII; Oxford: Clarendon Press, 1997), 221–242.

[188] J. Starcky, 'Un texte messianique araméen de la grotte 4 de Qumrân', in *École des langues orientales anciennes de l'Institut Catholique de Paris. Mémorial de cinqua-tenaire 1914–1964* (Paris: Bloud et Gay, 1964) 51–66.

Pilate brings Jesus outside, into the presence of his accusers. His actions are described in these words:

ὁ οὖν Πιλᾶτος ἀκούσας τῶν λόγων τούτων ἤγαγεν ἔξω τὸν Ἰησοῦν καὶ ἐκάθισεν ἐπὶ βήματος εἰς τόπον λεγόμενον λιθόστρωτον, Ἑβραϊστὶ δὲ Γαββαθα. (Jn 19.13)

Although most translations and commentaries understand the subject of the phrase ἐκάθισεν ἐπὶ βήματος as being Pilate, it is ambiguous. Lincoln comments of the possible interpretations stating that the 'syntax allows the verb to be taken transitively,... with Jesus as the object, or intransitively, 'he sat', with Pilate doing the sitting.'[189] Lincoln notes that grammatical arguments are ultimately unconvincing, and that intentional ambiguity on the part of the fourth evangelist 'is the least satisfying solution.'[190] Instead he argues, 'if Jesus is seated on the judgment seat, this reads more naturally as a further aspect of Pilate's humiliation of Jesus, which he also employs to mock "the Jews".'[191] This, moreover, would accord with the dramatic irony in the narrative, whereby Pilate is characterized as not being the powerful figure in control of the situation, rather he is just part of the unfolding divine plan.[192] The ambiguity in the narrative is a feature that has not only been recognized by recent modern literary critics. Keener wishes to resist this interpretation on historical grounds. 'Some suppose that Pilate seated Jesus in the judgment seat as part of the mockery (19:13); but this act would have breached Roman protocol so thoroughly that it is inconceivable that Pilate would have done it.'[193] Leaving aside the issue of whether the Johannine account of the passion should be read as an historical commentary on Roman judicial practices, it may simply be noted that Justin Martyr, while living in Rome itself,

---

[189] A.T. Lincoln, *The Gospel according to St John*, BNTC (London: Continuum, 2006) 458, n. 1.

[190] Lincoln, *The Gospel according to St John*, 469.

[191] Lincoln, *The Gospel according to St John*, 469.

[192] Although Brown does not opt for the view that Jesus was the one sitting on the judgment seat, he notes that the context makes it a plausible reading. 'But the strongest argument for this translation stems from its suitability in the framework of Johannine theology. For John, Jesus is the real judge of men, for in condemning him they are judging themselves; therefore, it is fitting for him to be on the judgment seat. Brown, *The Gospel according to John XIII–XXI*, 880.

[193] C.S. Keener, *The Gospel of John: A Commentary*, vol. 2 (Peabody, Mass.: Hendrickson, 2003) 1129.

understood Jesus as the one who had been seated upon the βῆμα (see below, *Apol.* i. 35).

Specifically in relation to Jn 19.13 Robinson comments, 'Archbishop Whately used to translate the words, "and he set Him on the judgement seat" – a perfectly legitimate rendering of the Greek. So it seems Justin Martyr read them: and so too the writer of our Gospel, or the source from which he borrowed.'[194] Swete is more cautious about seeing dependence on the text of the fourth gospel in this detail. He states, '[p]ossibly based on John xix. 13.'[195] He then continues, 'The reference to St John seems to be more direct in Justin *Apol.* i. 35 καὶ γὰρ (ὡς εἶπεν ὁ προφήτης) διασύροντες αὐτὸν ἐκάθισαν ἐπὶ βήματος καὶ εἶπεν Κρῖνον ἡμῖν.'[196] Swete is correct that the retention by Justin of the term βήματος does mean there is more verbal correspondence between Justin and the fourth gospel than exists between the *Gospel of Peter* and the fourth gospel. This, however, does not weaken the case for seeing the Akhmîm text as drawing upon Johannine material ot tradition (although not necessarily directly) at this point, albeit with much redactional creativity.

For Vaganay, the image of sitting Jesus on the καθέδραν κρίσεως is more concerned with the mockery of kingly claims, rather than with the crowd parodying the pretentions to fulfil the role of messianic judge. For this reason he describes the καθέδρα as a 'throne'.[197] Vaganay's case is obviously strengthened by the fact that at the end of this verse Jesus is addressed as 'King of Israel.' Yet it is not necessary to choose between these options. The messianic, royal and judicial images (or varying pairs) exist in various intertestamental texts.[198] This is unsurprising, since the Messiah is often conceived as being of Davidic or Aaronic descent, and more generally a juridical aspect is often combined with both kingly and priestly offices in the ancient Mediterranean or Near-Eastern worlds.

**3.7b** **λέγοντες Δικαίως κρῖνε, βασιλεῦ τοῦ Ἰσραήλ.** The now installed Jesus is derided with the mock request for just judgment.

---

[194] Robinson and James, *The Gospel according to Peter and the Revelation of Peter*, 18.
[195] Swete, *The Akhmîm Fragment of the Apocryphal Gospel of St Peter*, 4.
[196] Swete, *The Akhmîm Fragment of the Apocryphal Gospel of St Peter*, 4.
[197] 'Cette scène du trône n'appartient pas à la tradition évangélique.' Vaganay, *L'Évangile de Pierre*, 225.
[198] See the discussion above on the messiah as a judge-figure.

There are a number of intentional ironies in this taunt. The cry for just judgment stands out in marked contrast to the unjust judicial process to which Jesus has been subjected. There is a failure to realise that Jesus is in fact their true judge, and significantly their actions mean that even as a passive judge, Jesus is condemning them for these deeds. Finally, the title 'King of Israel', used to mock kingly and messianic claims, is in fact given to the one who, in the eyes of the narrator, is the correct recipient of such homage. Theologically, in the NT the adverb δικαίως is used to describe the quality of the judgment given by God. The penitent thief acknowledges that his sentence is just, but also that God will be angered because Jesus has been condemned in an unjust manner, οὐδὲ φοβῇ σὺ τὸν θεόν, ὅτι ἐν τῷ αὐτῷ κρίματι εἶ; καὶ ἡμεῖς μὲν δικαίως, ἄξια γὰρ ὧν ἐπράξαμεν· ἀπολαμβάνομεν οὗτος δὲ οὐδὲν ἄτοπον ἔπραξεν (Lk 23.40b-41). Similarly, in 1 Pet 2.23 Jesus is described at his passion as handing himself over to the the the one who judges justly, παρεδίδου δὲ τῷ κρίνοντι δικαίως.[199] Josephus also presents a similar perspective on entrusting judgment to God.[200]

In the NT Jesus is never called upon to δικαίως κρῖνε. Here it may be seen as further mockery of claims of divine status. Perhaps the closest the NT comes to this idea is when Jesus is called upon to arbitrate in a question of inheritance by an angry sibling, εἶπεν δέ τις ἐκ τοῦ ὄχλου αὐτῷ· διδάσκαλε, εἰπὲ τῷ ἀδελφῷ μου μερίσασθαι μετ᾽ ἐμοῦ τὴν κληρονομίαν. ὁ δὲ εἶπεν αὐτῷ· ἄνθρωπε, τίς με κατέστησεν κριτὴν ἢ μεριστὴν ἐφ᾽ ὑμᾶς; (Lk 12.13-14). Although the verb κρίνω is not used, Jesus is implored with the singular imperative form of εἰπέ. In this context Jesus declines the role as judge, perceiving that the request is motivated by greed (Lk 12.15).[201]

At this point in the *Gospel of Peter* the mob address Jesus as 'king of Israel', βασιλεῦ τοῦ Ἰσραήλ. For the author of this text and his intended readers this title is understood as a correct designation, although those who use it in the narrative do so to mock claims made by, or on behalf

---

[199] Michaels emphasizes that 1 Pet 2.23 highlights Jesus' nonretaliation, and in relation to the description 'the one who judges justly' he notes that this 'corresponds to "the One who judges impartially according to each person's work" in 1:17 and clearly refers to God (cf. also 4:5). J.R. Michaels, *1 Peter*, WBC 49 (Waco, Texas: Word, 1988) 147.

[200] See Jos. *Ant.* 4.33; 7.199.

[201] As Marshall correctly observes, 'Jesus proceeds to address the crowd with a warning against the covetessness which he has detected behind the man's request.' I.H. Marshall, *Commmentary on Luke*, NIGNT (Exeter/Grand Rapids, Michigan: Paternoster/Eerdmanns, 1978) 522.

of Jesus. In this sense the appellation functions in the same manner
as did the title τὸν υἱὸν τοῦ θεοῦ in the previous verse. The Akhmîm
text uses the title βασιλεῦ τοῦ Ἰσραήλ both here and as the inscription on the *titulus* (*Gos. Pet.* 4.11). In the canonical gospels this form
of address is not employed in the passion accounts,[202] instead Jesus
is referred to as βασιλεῦ τῶν Ἰουδαίων (Matt 27.29, 37; Mk 15.18, 26;
Lk 23.38; Jn 18.33; 19.3, 19, 21). Commentators stress that the title
'king of the Jews' would have been understood as politically subversive by Roman authorities. Hence used in a mocking manner by the
Roman soldier and upon the *titulus*, Jesus is jeered as an inconsequential political pretender. Thus France observes, '[i]n mocking the title
which had formed the basis of Jesus' condemnation the soldiers reflect
Pilate's view that he posed no real threat; as members of neighbouring
ethnic groups they found the idea of a Jewish 'king' (and *such* a king)
hilarious.'[203]

The motivation for the Akhmîm text changing the familiar des-
ignation βασιλεῦ τῶν Ἰουδαίων to the less frequent title βασιλεῦ τοῦ
Ἰσραήλ is not hard to perceive. The concern is not that βασιλεῦ τῶν
Ἰουδαίων will be seen as potentially more politically subversive, reflecting the fact that the Jews were a contemporary religio-political force.
Rather, the change is made for far cruder reasons, simply to distance
Jesus from the contemporary reality of his Jewish heritage. Jews are
paradigmatically evil and perverse for the author of the Akhmîm text.
As Brown correctly states, 'This work is quite hostile to the Jews, and
its author may have wished "the Lord" to be given a totally acceptable title.'[204] Thus, Jesus is made king of God's historically chosen covenantal people and not tainted by Jewish association. Vaganay notes
that the correction has no historical basis or motivation.[205] There was,
however, a tendency among the first commentators on the text not to

---

[202] It is used by Nathanael, who himself is described as 'a true Israelite' (Jn 1.47)
and then returns the compliment by acknowledging Jesus as σὺ βασιλεὺς εἶ τοῦ Ἰσραήλ
(Jn 1.49). Brown understands the title to function as identifying both the king of Israel
and his subjects. 'It is Nathanael, the genuine Israelite, who hails him; and therefore "the king of Israel" must be understood as the king of those like Nathanael who
believe.' R.E. Brown, *The Gospel according to John I–XI*, AB 29 (New York: Doubleday,
1966), 87.

[203] R.T. France, *The Gospel of Mark*, NIGNT (Carlisle/Grand Rapids, Michigan:
Paternoster/Eerdmanns, 1978) 202.

[204] Brown, *The Death of the Messiah*, vol. 1, 868.

[205] As he states, the correction 'n'est pas inspirée par le sens historique de l'auteur.'
Vaganay, *L'Évangile de Pierre*, 226.

see this change as being motivated by the anti-Judaic sentiments of the author.[206]

**3.8a  καί τις αὐτῶν ἐνεγκὼν στέφανον ἀκάνθινον.** Among the canonical gospels reference to the crown of thorns is found in Matthew (27.29), Mark (15.17) and John (19.2, 5), but is absent from the Lukan account due to the omission of the whole scene of the mockery by the Roman soldiers. Outside the NT the tradition is widespread. One of the earliest extra-canonical references, admittedly in a slightly convoluted form, is found in the *Epistle of Barnabas*, although the image occurs in a more convoluted form. First *Barnabas* refers to the cursed one being crowned, and then after a brief digression speaks of wool in the midst of thorns.

> καὶ ὅτι τὸν ἐπικατάρατον ἐστεφανωμένον...τί δέ, ὅτι τὸ ἔριον εἰς μέσον τῶν ἀκανθῶν τιθέασιν; (*Barn.* 7.9, 11)

The OT imagery in this passage draws primarily upon the regulations concerning the scapegoat contained in Lev 16.5, 7–10, 20–22, to create a typological understanding of the death of Jesus.[207] As Paget states in regard to *Barn.* 7.6–11, 'This section announces itself as exegesis of the ritual concerned with the two goats. With the exception of vv.6, 9 and 10, B. concentrates on the cursed goat, described in Lev. 16, and associated with Azazel.'[208] In addition, there may also be resonances with the Akedah (Gen 22.1–19), but these are not explicit in the *Epistle of Barnabas*, although the image of the wool (a goat or lamb) in the midst of thorns may be the strongest allusion, depicting the provision of the ram caught by its horns in the thicket as a substitute sacrifice (Gen 22.13). The *Epistle of Barnabas*, like the Akhmîm text, attributes blame

---

[206] A quick scan of the secondary literature shows that the change is either not commented upon, or is seen as a natural change (A. Resch, *Aussercanonischer Paralleltexte zu den Evangelien*, II, *Matthaeus und* Markus, [Leipzig, 1894] 352) or a more honourable title (A. Sabatier, *L'Évangile de Pierre et les évangiles canonique* [Paris, 1893] 14).

[207] Hvalvik observes that, 'Both 7:6–11 and 8:1–6 will demonstrate how rituals from the history of Israel are types of Christ.' R. Hvalvik, *The Struggle for Scripture and Covenant: The Purpose of the Epistle of Barnabas and Jewish-Christian Competition in the Second Century*, WUNT 82 (Tübingen: Mohr Siebeck, 1996) 183.

[208] J.C. Paget, *The Epistle of Barnabas: Outlook and Background*, WUNT 64 (Tübingen: Mohr Siebeck, 1994) 136.

to the Jews for the events that befell Jesus. Prostmeier sees the identity of the subject of the verb τιθέασιν in *Barn.* 7.11 as being the Jews.[209]

By contrast, in the *Gospel of Peter* an individual comes forward, acting on behalf of the crowd and places the crown of thorns on Jesus' head.[210] The term στέφανος when used in a non-metaphorical sense, denotes a wide range of different forms of head-dress that indicate rank, high status or outstanding achievement. Most frequently the term refers to 'a wreath made of foliage or designed to resemble foliage.'[211] In addition to being used to reward athletes and those successful in various competitions, such wreaths were worn to indicate regal or imperial status.[212] The term also described more substantial metallic objects, usually made of gold (cf. Rev 4.4, 10), but the familiarity with wreaths made from foliage in order to distinguish holders of high office, explains the use of a στέφανον ἀκάνθινον as a means of subverting Jesus' kingly pretentions. It perhaps also was used as a device to inflict pain, although Hooker shows that this may not be the only explanation.

> The thorny crown is usually assumed to be an instrument of torture, but it is possible that it was made from the long spines of a date palm, worn with the point of the thorn facing away from the head, and that it was a deliberate caricature of the radiate crown (imitating the rays of the sun-god) with which 'divine' rulers were portrayed on coins of the period.[213]

Once again the emblems of kingly or judicial office are shallowly imitated by those who will bring about the execution of Jesus. As an example of the imperial image that is being parodied by the mock investiture of Jesus it is helpful to compare Suetonius' description of the contemporary emperor Tiberias 'clad in the purple bordered toga and crowned with laurel' (*Tib.* 17.2). In contrast to the canon-

---

[209] 'Die Vokablel bezieht sich also kollectiv auf die Gemeinschaft, in der der Sündenbockritus zum regelmäßigen Vollzug angeordnet ist, die Juden.' F.R. Prostmeier, *Der Barnabasbrief*, KAV (Göttingen: Vandenhoeck & Ruprecht, 1999) 315.

[210] As Swete notes, 'Peter individualizes where the Synoptic Gospels speak generally.' Swete, *The Akhmîm Fragment of the Apocryphal Gospel of St Peter*, 4.

[211] See BDAG, 943.

[212] For a discussion of wreaths as a symbol; of imperial office see A. Papthomas, 'Das agonistische Motiv 1 Kor 9.24ff. im Spiegel zeitgenossischer dokumentarischer Quellen' *NTS* 43 (1997) 223–241. For the background to the use of the term in imperial Rome see 225–233.

[213] M.D. Hooker, *The Gospel according to Saint Mark*, BNTC (London: A&C Black, 1991) 370.

ical accounts there is no mention of the act of weaving or plaiting πλέξαντες of the crown. According to Vaganay this is the result of the author's decision to replace the generalized group action (ἐπέθηκαν, Matt and Jn; περιτιθέασιν. Mk) by an individual figure who acts on behalf of the group, τις αὐτῶν ἐνεγκὼν.[214]

**3.8b** **ἔθηκεν ἐπὶ τῆς κεφαλῆς τοῦ κυρίου.** Here the narrative appears closest to the Matthean account, both in terms of actual wording and in the sequence of putting the robe on Jesus before the crown is placed on his head. John inverts this order with the plaited crown being set on Jesus' head before he is wrapped in the purple robe (Jn 19.2). The Matthean wording ἐπέθηκαν ἐπὶ τῆς κεφαλῆς αὐτοῦ (Matt 27.29) differs from that in the *Gospel of Peter* in two respects. First ἐπιτίθημι, which is a compound verb and third person plural in Matthew, is replaced by a simplex form which is third person singular in the *Gospel of Peter*, and secondly, the pronoun αὐτοῦ is replaced by the favoured Christological title τοῦ κυρίου in the *Gospel of Peter*. The Markan form of this tradition is significantly different, καὶ περιτιθέασιν αὐτῷ πλέξαντες ἀκάνθινον στέφανον (Mk 15.17). Stucturally, this version deviates from the Matthean account and the *Gospel of Peter* by placing the reference to the 'thorny crown' after the the main verb. Moreover, there are deviations in vocabulary. Davies and Allison make the following pertinent observations, 'Mk 15.17 has: "they put (περιτιθέασιν) it on him". Closer is Jn 19.2: ἐπέθηκαν αὐτοῦ τῇ κεφαλῇ. The similarity can be taken as evidence of John's knowledge of Matthew. But the coincidence in wording seems altogether natural: what else does one do with a crown but put it on a head (cf. Gos. Pet. 6.8 [*sic.*])?'[215] While the agreement between the Johannine and Matthean accounts may be due to coincidence, the even more striking similarities between the *Gospel of Peter* and Matthew cannot be explained in the same way. The greater degree of verbal correspondence combined with the similarity in order of the dressing along with redactional changes that are easily accounted for as being due to the Christological perspective of the *Gospel of Peter* makes the case for knowledge of the Matthean narrative by the author of the Akhmîm text the most plausible explanation.

---

[214] Vaganay, *L'Évangile de Pierre*, 226.
[215] Davies and Allison, *The Gospel According to Saint Matthew*, vol. III, 603.

As has been noted, the narrator replaces the Matthean pronoun αὐτοῦ, which refers to Jesus' head, with his preferred Christological title τοῦ κυρίου. In contrast to the four previous occasions when this term was used this example does not employ the format of a *nomen sacrum*. There are thirteen occurrences of κύριος in the Akhmîm text,[216] and only here and at 6.24 is the unabbreviated form employed. It is unnecessary to look for a complicated theory to explain these deviations. The scribe does not exhibit particularly consistent practices, and this appears to be a further example of non-professional scribal habits.[217]

**3.9aα** καὶ ἕτεροι ἑστῶτες ἐνέπτυον αὐτοῦ ταῖς ὄψεσι. Regardless of whether the crown of thorns was itself employed as act of torture or simply functioned as an emblematic mocking of a royal wreath, there can be little doubt that a catalogue of physical violence is provided in v. 9. This may support understanding the crown of thorns as part of the process of scourging, although this function does not remove the possibility that the crown was also used to mock kingly pretentions. The description of the abuses endured by Jesus differs between the various gospel accounts both in content and order. The Akhmîm text contains the fullest account of a single sustained session of mocking, but this appears to be achieved by conflating details from the Jewish (Matt 26.67–68; Mk 14.65; Lk 22.63–65; Jn 18.22–23) and Roman (Matt 27:27–31a; Mk 15.16–20a; Jn 19.2–3) acts of abuse. As Brown postulates,

> GPet seems to have combined echoes of the Jewish and Roman mockeries from the canonical Gospels: The mockery is done by the Jewish people; it is done after a trial in which Herod and Pilate are featured; the contents are much the same as the canonical Roman mockery; and the theme of seating Jesus on a chair of judgment and mocking him to judge justly seems to echo a tradition close to both Matt 27:19 and John 19:13.[218]

While this is true, it need to be further observed that the Matthean account of the Roman mockery serves as the basis for the account in the *Gospel of Peter*, but this is stripped of references to the Romans and recast as the action of an angry Jewish mob. To this end the account

---

[216] See *Gos. Pet.* 1.2; 2.3 (2x); 3.6, 8; 4.10; 5.19; 6.21, 24; 12.50 (2x); 14.59, 60.
[217] Cf. the use of the wrong case ending for κύριος in 3.6.
[218] Brown, *The Death of the Messiah*, vol. 1, 863.

is suffused with additional traditions gleaned from the account of the
Jewish mockery. The Markan account of the Roman mockery lists the
beating on the head with the reed prior to the spitting (Mk 15.19).
This order is inverted in the Matthean narrative, and as Davies and
Allison point out 'Matthew's new order agrees with 26.67',[219] although
the terminology for spitting (Matt 26.67 = ἐνέπτυσαν; Matt 27.30 =
ἐμπτύσαντες) and striking (Matt 26.67 = ἐκολάφισαν; Matt 27.30 =
ἔτυπτον) differs between the two Matthean accounts.

In the *Gospel of Peter* the Matthean order is preferred with the spitting preceding the hitting on the head, but this sequence is interrupted
by the striking of the cheeks. The act of spitting is carried out by a
subset of the crowd, who are described as ἕτεροι ἑστῶτες. The perfect
active participle represents a stative condition in this instance, and this
form is found on five other occasions in the NT (Matt 6.5; 26.73; Acts
5.25; Rev 7.9; 11.4). The participle qualifies the indefinite plural adjective ἕτεροι, denoting an unnamed sub-group from the mob. According
to the narrative various discrete groups of people come forth in turn
to inflict one of the sequence of abuses: first one person approaches
to place the crown of thorns, then others to spit in his face, others to
strike his cheeks and so on.[220] Although the *Gospel of Peter* follows the
Matthean order by commencing the catalogue of abuses with the spitting, the term that is used appears to depend on Mark. Swete categorically states, "Ἐνέπτυον is from Mark xv. 19.'[221] This, however, is not the
only explanation. Apart from drawing upon material from the Roman
abuse scene, the *Gospel of Peter* also conflates this with material from
the list of physical affronts Jesus suffers during the Jewish trial. In particular the next detail in the sequence of events in the *Gospel of Peter*,
the striking of the cheeks, appears to be dependent upon the portrayal
of the Jewish abuse in the Matthean account since both share the term
ἐράπισαν (Matt 27.67). Preceding this detail, both in *Gos. Pet.* 3.9 and
Matt 26.67 there is a description of Jesus being spat upon by his Jewish
accusers. Various verbal forms are used in the different descriptions of
the act of spitting. The form of the verb used in Matt 26.67 is the aorist ἐνέπτυσαν, whereas the imperfect form ἐνέπτυον employed in *Gos.
Pet.* 3.9 and Mk 15.19, while the aorist participle ἐμπτύσαντες is used
in Matt 27.30. Thus it is possible that the reference to spitting is drawn

---

[219] Davies and Allison, *The Gospel According to Saint Matthew*, vol. III, 604.
[220] Vaganay, *L'Évangile de Pierre*, 227.
[221] Swete, *The Akhmîm Fragment of the Apocryphal Gospel of St Peter*, 4.

from one of the Matthean descriptions of this abuse and the change
of tense to the imperfect results in a coincidental agreement with Mk
15.19. The use of the form ἐνέπτυον in *Gos. Pet.* 3.9 may be employed
since the imperfective aspect of the verb creates a more vivd narrative
by depicting the action from inside as it unfolds, while still presenting
a spatial sense of remoteness which is employed since the narrator is
not directly present in the story.[222]

The spittal is described as being directed at αὐτοῦ ταῖς ὄψεσι. The
noun ὄψις[223] is rare in the NT occurring only three times (Jn 7.24;
11.44; Rev 1.16), and this is its only occurrence in the *Gospel of Peter*.[224]
In the Matthean and Markan accounts of the Roman mockery the soldiers are reported as simply spitting on Jesus (ἐμπτύσαντες εἰς αὐτόν/
ἐνέπτυον αὐτῷ respectively) with no mention of his face. Within the
canonical accounts of the Jewish trial the term πρόσωπον is used, for
which ὄψις can function as a synonym. In the Markan account the
use of πρόσωπον is not in connection with the act of spitting, but with
the immediately following act of covering Jesus face before he is subjected to the maltreatment of a blindfolded beating (Mk 14.65). Matthew deletes the reference to the blindfolding and connects the term
πρόσωπον with the act of spitting, ἐνέπτυσαν εἰς τὸ πρόσωπον αὐτοῦ
(Matt 26.67). Here again the Akhmîm text shows greatest affinities
with the Matthean narrative, although the divergence in terminology
may suggest that the author is not composing his text with Matthew's
account directly before him. Swete is categorical in his assessment of
the compositional practice of the author of the *Gospel of Peter*, 'ταῖς
ὄψεσιν corresponds to εἰς τὸ πρόσωπον αὐτοῦ, Matt. xxvi. 67.'[225] The
plural form of the noun, ὄψεσι, which occurs here in the Akhmîm text
can take on a more specific meaning of 'eyes.' Thus BDAG observes,
'Also the pl. αἱ ὄψεις, chiefly the eyes.'[226] The use is well attested in
various Greek texts,[227] but examples are given where the plural retains
the meaning 'face.' Included in this list is a reference to *Gos. Pet.* 3.9:

---

[222] Porter, *Verbal Aspect in the Greek of the New Testament with Reference to Tense and Mood*, 111.

[223] The range of NT meanings is given as 'face, contenance, appearance' in Balz and Schneider (eds.), *Exegetical Dictionary of the New Testament*, vol. 2, 555.

[224] It is also used in the *Apocalypse of Peter* occurring twice in verse 7.

[225] Swete, *The Akhmîm Fragment of the Apocryphal Gospel of St Peter*, 5.

[226] See BDAG, 747.

[227] See in particular Orig., *Contra Celsum* 7.39, 47, where it is used to denote the closing of the visual organs.

'means more gener. *Face* (Jos., Ant. 12, 81; TestReub 5:5; ApcMos 37 ἐπ' ὄψεσι κείμενοι) ἐνέπτυον αὐτοῦ ταῖς ὄψεσι GPt 3:9.[228]

**3.9aβ  καὶ ἄλλοι τὰς σιαγόνας αὐτοῦ ἐράπισαν.** The second abuse inflicted upon Jesus in this catalogue is the slapping or hitting of his cheeks. While in the scene of abuse involving the Roman soldiers Jesus is hit on the head with the reed (Matt 27.30; Mk 15.19), slapping only occurs in during the Jewish trial (Matt 26.67; Mk 14.65). In Matthew's account those who slap Jesus are not clearly identified, but perhaps the most likely antecedent subject in to be found in v. 59, οἱ δὲ ἀρχιερεῖς καὶ τὸ συνέδριον ὅλον. Because of the distance between this explicit subject in v. 59 and the use of the third person plural verb, ἐράπισαν, in v. 67 no strong case can be made for concluding that this same group is still in Matthew's mind. However, this group still remains the most likely identification in the Matthean narrative, since when the high priest addresses a group of people in the third person (v. 66) they are consulted to make a ruling concerning Jesus' fate. This would still seem to be a reference to the ruling caste. As Davies and Allison describe this aspect, 'The high priest, having made his decision, now seeks the consent of the entire Sanhedrin.'[229] Similarly, Harrington states, 'The logic of Matthew's account demands that it was the members of the Sanhedrin who were responsible for the abuse visited upon Jesus.'[230] The Markan narrative differs in the sequencing of event and those to whom various abuses are attributed. Presumably the group who spit, then cover Jesus' head and strike him is the Sanhedrin, then the attendants or underlings, οἱ ὑπηρέται, slap Jesus while leading him away,[231] ῥαπίσμασιν αὐτὸν ἔλαβον (Mk 14.65). The account of the single slap by an individual attendant in the Johannine passion

---

[228] BDAG, 747.

[229] Davies and Allison, *The Gospel According to Saint Matthew*, vol. III, 535.

[230] D.J. Harrington, *The Gospel of Matthew*, Sacra Pagina 1 (Collegeville, MN.: Liturgical Press, 1991) 380.

[231] The rendering of Mk 14.65b is difficult. Swete translates ῥαπίσμασιν αὐτὸν ἔλαβον as '[they] caught him with blows.' H.B. Swete, *The Gospel according to St. Mark*, (3rd ed., London: Macmillan, 1909) 363. Other commentators, such as Lane, render it as 'the officers received him with blows of their hands.' W.L. Lane, *The Gospel of Mark*, NICNT (Grand Rapids, Michigan: Eerdmans, 1974) 529. For a discussion of this problem see V. Taylor, *The Gospel according to St. Mark*, (2nd ed., London: Macmillan, 1966) 571.

narrative is less brutal (Jn 18.22). As Brown comments, 'The slap was more an insult than a physically damaging blow.'[232]

While drawing on a number of these details, most notably from the Matthean account, the *Gospel of Peter* continues to go its own way in recounting the abuses endured by Jesus. First, another sub-group, καὶ ἄλλοι, comes forward from the mob to inflict the second physical abuse. It is not, however, necessarily the case that οἱ δὲ ἐράπισαν in Matt 26.67 denotes a separate group in the same manner that the *Gospel of Peter* delineates subsections of the crowd.[233] Thus it is more likely that in the Matthean account some of those giving the slaps were also involved in the previous torments. The desire to see two separate groups is perhaps a result of the Matthean narrative being read through a Markan lens.[234] Beare's translation of οἱ δέ may capture the implied sense, 'and some of them beat him',[235] that is, some of those who had been involved in the previous acts of mistreatment.

The reference to Jesus' cheeks τὰς σιαγόνας αὐτοῦ is unique to the *Gospel of Peter*. Mara is correct in her observation that the author of wishes to make clear differentiations between the various parts of the body that are mistreated, and in part this is done by describing separate groups responsible for each abuse.[236] Swete suggests possible texts that may have influenced the author's inclusion of a reference to cheeks. Τὰς σιαγόνας may look back to Matt. v. 39 ὅστις σε ῥαπίζει εἰς τὴν δεξιὰν σιαγόνα κ.τ.λ., but more probably rests directly on Isaiah l. 6 τὰς δὲ σιαγόνας μου εἰς ῥαπίσματα [ἔδωκα].'[237] In this case, however, it appears unnecessary to look for literary influence from canonical texts. This is the kind of expansive detail that appeals to the author of the Akhmîm text for the purpose of making the story more graphic and vivid. The term σιαγών, occurs only twice in the NT in the Q saying

---

[232] Brown, *The Gospel according to John XIII–XXI*, 826.

[233] Vaganay argues that 'Marc et Matthieu n'ont raconte ce genre d'outrages que dans la séance chez le grand prêtre et tous deux se servant de κολαφίζειν (cf. Mt., XXVI, 67: οἱ δὲ ἐράπισαν, pour une autre sorte de coups).'Vaganay, *L'Évangile de Pierre*, 228.

[234] This may be the factor which leads Gundry to suggest, 'Matthew's inserting οἱ δέ, "but some," differentiates those who slap Jesus from those who spit in his face and hit him with their fists. Only those who slap him challenge him to prophesy.' Gundry, *Matthew: A Commentary on His Handbook for a Mixed Church under Persecution*, 547.

[235] F.W. Beare, *The Gospel according to Matthew* (Oxford: Blackwell, 1981) 519.

[236] Mara, *Évangile de Pierre*, 102.

[237] Swete, *The Akhmîm Fragment of the Apocryphal Gospel of St Peter*, 5.

concerning turning the other cheek (Matt 5.29//Lk 6.29). There are, however, numerous occurrences in the LXX.[238]

**3.9aγ** ἕτεροι καλάμῳ ἔνυσσον αὐτὸν. The third physical torment in this sequence to which Jesus is subjected, consists of being pricked or pierced with a reed. This obviously draws upon the tradition in the synoptic gospels that the Roman soldiers struck him on the head with a reed (Matt 27.30; Mk 15.19). It is only in the Matthean account that the term κάλαμος is introduced prior to the striking. In Matt 27.29 it is placed in Jesus' right hand as an imitation sceptre. Davies and Allison note. "'Reed' has been brought forward from Mk 15.19, where it strikes Jesus on the head but is not put in his hand.'[239] This Matthean redactional detail is not reproduced in the Akhmîm narrative, instead, like Mark, it is introduced only as a device to inflict pain. As Lane describes the purpose of the reed in the Markan account 'the buffeting and striking of the exhausted prisoner with rods and with the fist was mere brutality.'[240]

Again, in the *Gospel of Peter*, a separate group is depicted as coming forth from the crowd to inflict this next act of physical torment. The abuse is described as piercing him with a reed, καλάμῳ ἔνυσσον αὐτόν. The precise nature of this torment is not explained, nor, unlike the two previous acts of violence, is there any mention of the part of the body affected. For Vaganay this description originates from the synoptic accounts where Jesus is portrayed as being beaten over the head with the reed.[241] While Vaganay is unquestionably correct that there is dependence upon Matt 27.30 and Mk 15.30 at this point, which both depict Jesus being struck on the head by the Roman soldiers with a reed, there is also another canonical tradition that shapes this narrative. In the Gospel of John the piercing of Jesus is recorded as being brought about by the lance thrust into his side which results in the bringing forth of blood and water, ἀλλ' εἷς τῶν στρατιωτῶν λόγχῃ αὐτοῦ τὴν πλευρὰν ἔνυξεν (Jn 19.34). Recording the efflux of blood and

---

[238] See Jdg 15.14, 15, 16, 17, 19; 1 Kgs 22.24; 2 Chr 18.23; Jb 21.5; Ps 31.9; Song 1.10; 5.13; Sir 32.15; Hos 11.4; Mic 5.1; Isa 50.6; Lam 1.2; 3.30; Ezek 29.4.

[239] Davies and Allison, *The Gospel According to Saint Matthew*, vol. III, 603.

[240] Lane, *The Gospel of Mark*, 560.

[241] 'De prime abord on est tenté de croire à une banale correction de la notice des deux synoptiques: καὶ ἔτυπτον αὐτοῦ τὴν κεφαλὴν καλάμῳ, car νύσσω, qui signifie proprement «piquer», a aussi comme τύπτω, le sens dérivé de «frapper».' Vaganay, *L'Évangile de Pierre*, 228.

water may seek to combat Docetic notions within the Johannine community, especially in conjunction with the use of the same imagery in 1 Jn 5.6.[242] Admittedly in the context of John's Gospel that is at best a secondary concern, although undoubtedly the fourth gospel seeks to demonstrate the reality of Jesus' death. While Beasley-Murray argues, 'the soldier could have simply pricked the flesh of Jesus to test whether he was really dead, or more likely, he thrust the spear deep into his side to ensure that he did die',[243] this does not appear to be the most compelling reading given that the previous verse state that the soldiers observed that Jesus was already dead εἶδον ἤδη αὐτὸν τεθνηκότα (Jn 19.33). In the *Gospel of Peter* there is no mention of a spear, probably a Roman *pilum*,[244] since imperial forces are not involved in the abuse. There are also references to the piercing of Jesus in Jn 19.37 and Rev 1.7 which occur without mentioning a lance. The latter, in particular, may have shaped the thinking of the author of the Akhmîm text not only here, but also elsewhere in the narrative. In Rev 1.7 those who pierced Jesus are predicted to wail at his final coming. Such wailing occurs proleptically prior to the resurrection in *Gos. Pet.* 7.25, when 'the Jews, and the elders, and the priests' collectively realize the significance of the apocalyptic signs they experience. This corporate realization continues in 8.28 where the 'whole people' continue their lament. In terms of the choice of verb employed to describe the piercing in Revelation, Aune notes 'The verb ἐξεκέντησαν is used together with the pronoun αὐτόν in Rev 1:7, as well as in John 19.37, where αὐτόν is omitted, though understood.'[245] The verb in the Akhmîm text is νύσσω, which agrees with the verb used in Jn 19.34. The most likely explanation is that the text is the product of a writer who is highly familiar with the canonical accounts, but is composing his narrative in a creative manner without directly consulting those texts which are shaping his thinking at this point.

Standing behind the NT texts that refer to the piercing of Jesus is the reference in Zechariah referring to the prophesied attack on Jerusalem. Following on from the promised outpouring of the spirit, Zech 12.10 announces that the inhabitants of Jerusalem will look on the

---

[242] Keener, *The Gospel of John: A Commentary*, vol. 2, 1152.
[243] Beasley-Murray, *John*, 354.
[244] Brown, *The Death of the Messiah*, vol. 2, 1177.
[245] D.E. Aune, *Revelation 1–5*, WBC 52A (Dallas: Word, 1997) 56.

one they have pierced and weep. The Masoretic and LXX texts read as follows:

Masoretic:    וְהִבִּ֫יטוּ אֵלַ֗י אֵ֥ת אֲשֶׁר־דָּקָֽרוּ

LXX:      καὶ ἐπιβλέψονται πρός με ἀνθ᾽ ὧν κατωρχήσαντο[246]

As can be seen the LXX rendering of דקר by κατορχέομαι 'to dance in triumph over, treat despitefully,' significantly changes the meaning of the passage. The tendencies of the LXX revisions is to render the Hebrew text more accurately:[247] Aquila σὺν ᾧ ἐξεκέντησαν;[248] Symmachus ἔμπροσθεν ἐπεξεκέντησαν;[249] Theodotion ὃν ἐξεκέντησαν.[250] Hence it is not possible to conclude with absolutely certainty whether the third abuse in the series that occurs in the *Gospel of Peter* is due to familiarity with canonical gospels, or with the description in Rev 1.7, or the revisions to the LXX, or the Masoretic text, or even some combination of these traditions. A further possibility is that the author is drawing on a catena of OT *testimonia* sayings, especially since the words at the end of *Gos. Pet.* 3.9 represent a re-working of Zech 11.13. On balance, however, the author's widespread dependence on the passion narratives contained in the canonical gospels throughout his text makes this the most likely source for this detail, although this may have been combined with the text of Rev 1.7 in the mind of the author, since the tradition of piercing is free from the reference to a lance in that text.

There is one further significant parallel that may inform the discussion further. None of the canonical texts associate the κάλαμος as the tool for inflicting this piercing. In the *Acts of John* that association

---

[246] The LXX text is taken from the Rahlfs edition, and is the reading presereved in the majuscule mss A B S.

[247] Fernández Marcos shows that it is no longer possible to see the motivation for such revision as being based in the Jewish-Christian polemic concerning correct interpretation of scripture. He states, 'there are indications of the rejection of the LXX by the Jews prior to the 2nd century CE…Furthermore, there are manuscript witnesses that come from the Jews and are earlier than Christianity, the most surprising of which is the Twelve Prophets scroll from Naḥal Ḥever, which exhibits clear signs correction of the Greek text to fit it to the Hebrew text then current.' N. Fernández Marcos, *The Septuagint in Context: Introduction to the Greek Version of the Bible* (Leiden: Brill, 2000) 109.

[248] This reading is preserved in the Syro-Hexapla. See J. Ziegler, *Septuaginta Vetus Testamentum Graecum*, vol. XIII Duodecim prophetae (Gottingen: Vandenhoeck & Ruprecht, 1984) 319.

[249] Ziegler, *Septuaginta Vetus Testamentum Graecum*, 319.

[250] Ziegler, *Septuaginta Vetus Testamentum Graecum*, 319.

does occur, although the lance is still mentioned, καὶ λόγχαις νύσσομαι καὶ καλάμοις 'and I am being pierced with lances and reeds' (*Acts Jn.* 97.2). The similarities with the text of the *Gospel of Peter* are obvious, although it is not possible to establish whether there is direct dependence, and if so in which direction, or if these text share a common tradition, or if the similarity is due to independent redacrtional reworking. The *Gospel of Peter* is a witness to the fluidity of the traditions surrounding the piercing of Jesus either by lance or with a reed. The Akhmîm text appears to have conflated various traditions to produce a version of events which is congenial to the author's own theological perspective, especially in further implicating the Jews as the perpetrators of Jesus' crucifixion and torture.

**3.9aδ καί τινες αὐτὸν ἐμάστιζον.** The fourth distinct group is referred to as καί τινες. They perform the fourth and final item in the list of the physical abuses inflicted upon Jesus in this verse. The act is described as αὐτὸν ἐμάστιζον and this is the least developed description in the list of torments, whereas the previous abuses have either included a reference to the part of the body which is attacked or of the instrument used to inflict pain. In the NT the verb μαστιγόω occurs with reference to Jesus only four times.[251] Three of these occur in the triple tradition parallel text of the third passion prediction (Matt 20.19//Mk 10.34//Lk 18.33). Hooker notes the more explicit nature of the final prediction. 'As before, the teaching about the Passion is given privately to the Twelve, but this time in far greater detail.'[252] It is interesting that while the third passion announcement predicts the scourging of Jesus, none of the synoptic gospels use the verb μαστιγόω in the passion narratives. This is least surprising in the Lukan account, since the whole Roman abuse scene is deleted. However, this prediction finds its fulfilment in both the Matthean (27.26) and Markan (15.15) accounts by using the verb φραγελλόω.[253] The term φραγελλόω is derived from the Latin *flagello*, 'to whip'; and the term *flagellum*, the diminutive of *flagrum* denoting the instrument used in a scourging, *i.e.* a whip or scourge.[254] As Davies and Allison note, 'The word [μαστιγόω] does

---

[251] See Moulton & Geden, *Concordance to the Greek New Testament*, Sixth edition, 668.

[252] Hooker, *The Gospel according to Saint Mark*, 245.

[253] As Marshall observes, 'cf. Mk 15.15 for fulfilment.' Marshall, *Commmentary on Luke*, 690.

[254] See C.T. Lewis and C. Short, *A Latin Dictionary* (Oxford: Clarendon Press, 1879).

not appear later on, but its equivalent does: φραγελλώσας (27.26).'²⁵⁵ Only the fourth gospel uses the verb μαστιγόω in the passion narrative, τότε οὖν ἔλαβεν ὁ Πιλᾶτος τὸν Ἰησοῦν καὶ ἐμαστίγωσεν (Jn 19.1). In the Johannine narrative the scourging is brought forward in the narrative and is not linked with the sentence of crucifixion. Thus as Brown comments, 'Scourging, instead of being part of the crucifixion punishment (as is the flogging in Mark/Matt), becomes in John a lesser punishment that Pilate hopes will satisfy "the Jews" by causing then to give up on this wretched Jesus.'²⁵⁶ The description in the *Gospel of Peter* has no such benign purpose.

The brutality of a scourging has been well described²⁵⁷ and Swete comments in relation to Jn 19.1 that 'so serious a punishment was kept by the Procurator in his own hands.'²⁵⁸ While this may actually miss the purpose of the scourging in the Johannine narrative, it is the case that the Akhmîm text presents this as the climactic physical torment to be endured by Jesus in this sequence. However, this climax is not necessarily to by thought of in terms of the intensity of the abuses, but in terms of literary arrangement which allows those who scourge Jesus to also utter the immediately following words as part of the mockery.²⁵⁹ Therefore, at a literary level the final brief notice of physical abuse in the series functions to introduce the transition to this direct speech that concludes this verse.

**3.9b** λέγοντες ταύτη τῆ τιμῆ τιμήσωμεν τὸν υἱὸν τοῦ $\overline{\theta υ}$. Those who scorge Jesus are the only group of tormentors to speak. A saying derived from Zech 11.13 is placed on their lips, which is designed to show ironically the low value they place on the life of the one the address as the Son of God. Among the canonical gospels the quotation of Zechariah 11.13 occurs only in Matthew's Gospel,²⁶⁰ in the passion narrative, but in a different context to the one in which it

---

²⁵⁵ Davies and Allison, *The Gospel According to Saint Matthew*, vol. III, 81.
²⁵⁶ Brown, *The Death of the Messiah*, vol. 1, 827.
²⁵⁷ See J.D. Douglas and F.F. Bruce 'Scourging, Scourge', in J.D. Douglas and F.F. Bruce (eds.), *New Bible Dictionary* (2nd ed.; Leicester: IVP, 1982) 1078. Drawings are provided of Roman scourges.
²⁵⁸ Swete, *The Akhmîm Fragment of the Apocryphal Gospel of St Peter*, 5.
²⁵⁹ Vaganay picks up on this arrangement, 'Elle a seulement pour but de terminer la scène de dérision sur une note plus élégante.' Vaganay, *L'Évangile de Pierre*, 229.
²⁶⁰ For an extended discussion of the use of this text by Matthew see, P. Foster, 'The Use of Zechariah in Matthew's Gospel', in C.M. Tuckett (ed.), *The Book of Zechariah and its Influence* (Aldershot: Ashgate, 2003) 65–85; see esp. 77–79.

occurs in the *Gospel of Peter*. In Matthew's account it occurs as part of the aftermath of Judas' remorse (Matt 27.3–5), when the chief priests dispose of the blood money by purchasing a burial field for foreigners (27.6–8). As a redactional comment, Matthew sees this story as a fulfilment of the prophetic text which he cites as, καὶ ἔλαβον τὰ τριάκοντα ἀργύρια, τὴν τιμὴν τοῦ τετιμημένου ὃν ἐτιμήσαντο ἀπὸ υἱῶν Ἰσραήλ. The evangelist attributes this saying to Jeremiah, but the reason for the association is difficult to fathom. 'Perhaps the mention of Jeremiah in the rubric is due to the allegorical story, related in Jer 18–19, referring to the potter's house and earthware vessel, combined with Jer 32:6–25 where Jeremiah purchases the Anathoth field.'[261] This perplexing attribution is not a problem in the *Gospel of Peter* since the saying is not associated with the name of any prophetic figure, nor is it presented as a citation.

The LXX version of Zech 11.13 does not use the term τιμάω or its cognates, which Matthew repeats three times in his rendering of this verse. Instead it goes its own way at this point, but does use cognates of δοκιμάζω twice σκέψαι εἰ δόκιμόν ἐστιν ὃν τρόπον ἐδοκιμάσθην ὑπὲρ αὐτῶν (Zech 11.13b LXX). Thus neither Matt 27.9, nor *Gos. Pet.* 3.9 appears to be dependent on the LXX. The Matthean phrase τὴν τιμὴν τοῦ τετιμημένου reflects the MT אֶדֶר הַיְקָר אֲשֶׁר יָקַרְתִּי.[262] However, the MT only has the term יקר used twice, unlike the triple repetition of τιμάω or its cognates in the Matthean citation. The fact that the Akhmîm text uses the same terminology as Matthean, but only has a double use of the term like the structure of the MT could be due to a number of possibilities. First, the *Gospel of Peter* could have drawn directly on the Matthean account, but abbreviated its triple use of τιμάω language; secondly, it could represent an indepent translation of the MT with coincidental use of τιμάω terminology (however, there is no reason to suppose that the author of the Akhmîm text was familiar with Hebrew); thirdly, both Matthew and the *Gospel of Peter* could be independently drawing on an alternative Greek translation (a Christian catena of OT fulfilment prophecies), which Matthew has expanded with a further repetition of τιμάω, but the *Gospel of Peter* has preserved in its more original form. Of these three options, the second seems the most implausible since there is no reason to attribute

---

[261] Foster, 'The Use of Zechariah in Matthew's Gospel', 77.
[262] Foster, 'The Use of Zechariah in Matthew's Gospel', 78.

facility with the Semitic language to the author of the *Gospel of Peter*. The third possibility would better explain the double use of τιμάω terminology in the *Gospel of Peter*, but its weakness is the lack of concrete evidence for such a collection of proof-texts. The first explanation has the strength that the author of the the the *Gospel of Peter* shows familiarity with Matthew at many points in his narrative, but it is more difficult to explain the closer correspondence with the structure of the MT at this point.[263] If dependence on the Matthean text is the explanation adopted, it becomes necessary to explain the reduced form of the Matthean text as due to the literary reshaping of the story line at this point.[264]

Similar to the use of the Christological title βασιλεῦ τοῦ Ἰσραήλ at the end of *Gos. Pet.* 3.7, the appellation τὸν υἰὸν του θεοῦ is used scornfully by this fourth group of tormentors, who fail to perceive that what they are saying in jest represents a reality beyond their present perception. The title υἰὸν του θεοῦ has also been used previously in this section in *Gos. Pet.* 3.6 where the recalcitrant mob expressed their unified desire to drag Jesus to the place of execution. The tile is used on two further occasions in the Akhmîm text, but the significance is markedly different. In *Gos. Pet.* 11.45 and 46, where first the centurion and his company who were guarding the temple recount to Pilate the miraculous events that have transpired, and as a group they make the confession, ἀληθῶς υἰὸς ἦν θεοῦ. This is followed by Pilate addressing the Jews and declaring his innocence, referring to Jesus as ὁ υἰὸς τοῦ θεοῦ. In both these cases Roman characters accept the title as an accurate description without qualification or any tone of mocking.[265] Thus, the author of the Akhmîm text shows a degree of sophistication in the way Christological titles are deployed, having multi-valence depending on which characters articulate the title, and also reflecting the circumstance in which the title is used.

---

[263] In fact this citation, if dependent upon the canonical gospel tradition is only found in the first gospel. This would be further evidence of the author's dependence on this text, as well as exemplifying the prominence of the Matthean gospel among Patristic and other early Christian writers.

[264] There are, of course, a range of possibilities that could involve combinations of these options. The author of the *Gospel of Peter* could be familiar with the Matthean account, but have dropped the third use of τιμάω language under the influence of the Zechariah text.

[265] As Mara comments, 'Pilate accepte non seulement le rapport de la commission, mais encore la conclusion qui en dérive et que la commission a explicitement affirmé: υἰὸς ἦν θεοῦ.' Mara, *Évangile de Pierre*, 194.

# THE CRUCIFIXION OF THE LORD BETWEEN
# TWO CRIMINALS (4.10–14)

10. καὶ¹ ἤνεγκον² δύο³ κακούργους⁴ καὶ ἐσταύρωσαν⁵ ἀνὰ⁶ μέσον αὐτῶν
τὸν κ̅ν̅⁷. αὐτὸς δὲ ἐσιώπα⁸ ὡς μηδέν πόνον ἔχων. 11. καὶ ὅτε⁹ ὤρθωσαν¹⁰
τὸν σταυρὸν ἐπέγραψαν ὅτι οὗτός ἐστιν ὁ βασιλεὺς¹¹ τοῦ Ἰσραήλ. 12. καὶ
τεθεικότες¹² τὰ ἐνδύματα ἔμπροσθεν¹³ αὐτοῦ διεμερίσαντο καὶ λαχμὸν
ἔβαλον ἐπ᾽ αὐτοῖς. 13. εἷς δέ τις τῶν κακούργων ἐκείνων ὠνείδησεν¹⁴ αὐτοὺς
λέγων Ἡμεῖς διὰ τὰ κακὰ ἃ ἐποιήσαμεν οὕτω πεπόνθαμεν, οὕτως¹⁵ δὲ
σωτὴρ γενόμενος τῶν α̅ν̅ω̅ν̅¹⁶ τί ἠδίκησεν ὑμᾶς; 14. καὶ ἀγανακτήσαντες ἐπ᾽
αὐτῷ ἐκέλευσαν ἵνα μὴ σκελοκοπηθῇ¹⁷ ὅπως βασανιζόμενος ἀποθάνοι.

10. And they brought two criminals and crucified the Lord in the
middle of them, and he was silent as though having no pain. 11. And
when they erected the cross they wrote, 'This is the king of Israel.' 12.
And having laid out the clothes before him, they divided [them] and
cast lots for them. 13. But one of those criminals rebuked them saying,
'We, because of the evil we did, are suffering thus, but this one who
is the saviour of men, how has he wronged you?' 14. And they were
angry with him and ordered that the legs not be broken, so that he
might die being distressed.

## TEXT CRITICAL NOTES

1. The supralinear bar from the *nomen sacrum* θ̅υ̅ which concludes
   *Gos. Pet.* 3.9 over-extends the upsilon, and intersects with apex of
   the vertical stroke of the kappa, the opening letter of the καί that
   commences this verse. It may be the case that the supralinear bar
   and the vertical stroke of the kappa represent a single pen-stroke,
   since there is no apparent break in formation.
2. The endings of lines four to seven on the second page of text are
   the most difficult to discern. This is due to the discolouration of the
   parchment,²⁶⁶ probably due to moisture. From the most recently

---

²⁶⁶ The writing material is parchment (see Bouriant, 'Fragments du texte grec du
livre d'Énoch et de quelques écrits attribués à saint Pierre', 93), not papyrus as Mirecki
suggests (see Mirecki, 'Peter, Gospel of', 279. His initial comment is ambiguous, 'the

available photographs,[267] the word ἤνεγκον is not legible in its entirety. The first four letters can be read, along with the vertical stoke of the fifth letter (kappa). The original heliographic images, presented in the treatments of Lods[268] and the photographic images in the book edited by Gebhardt,[269] revealed less of the line completions than the modern photographs. These images revealed only the initial letter of the word ἤνεγκον. While the more recent photographs means that the reconstruction ἤνεγκον is almost certain, there is a further piece of evidence supplied by the photographs that verifies the reading. Due to the dampness that discoloured the parchment, the set ink became acidified and partially re-liquified. This has resulted in an imprint in mirror image form of the no longer readable letters from the second page of text impressed on the first page. These occur in a slightly raised position to the left of line six. The reverse images of a kappa and omicron can be read, although the final letter still remains uncertain.[270]

3. The initial delta is written in a minuscule style δ rather than the majuscule style Δ which is more common throughout the manuscript. A tendency towards the occasional use of this form has been noted at two earlier points. On the first page of text (f.1v) in line 12 δῦναι and in line 17 καθέδραν the letter delta in both of these words has lost the triangular shape of the majuscule letter formation. Instead those two examples were formed by two pen-strokes, a loop representing both the right to left diagonal and the base of the equilateral triangle, combined with the descending left to right diagonal. By contrast the delta in this example is a single penstroke

---

manuscript is conserved in the papyrus collection of the Cairo Museum.' He goes on, however, to state, 'The strongest evidence which equates the gospel text of the papyri with the *Gos. Pet.* mentioned by Eusebius…is that the voice of the text's narrator-author is identitified in the first person singular as "Simon Peter".' He refers to *Gos. Pet.* 7.26 and 14.60, passages only extant in the Akhmîm text. Thus showing that he is under the misapprehension that P.Cair. 10759 like P.Oxy. 2949 is written on papyrus.

[267] Kraus und Nicklas, *Das Petrusevangelium und die Petrusapokalypse*, plate *P.Cair.* 10759, f.2r, at the rear of the volume.

[268] See the plates in Lods, 'L'Évangile et l'Apocalypse de Pierre avec le texte grec du livre d'Henoch.'

[269] See the plates in Gebhardt, *Das Evangelium und die Apokalypse des Petrus. Die neuentdeckten Bruchstücke nach einer Photographie der Handschrift zu Gizéh in Lichtdruck herausgegeben.*

[270] See Kraus und Nicklas, *Das Petrusevangelium und die Petrusapokalypse*, plate *P.Cair.* 10759, f.1v.

that appears to commence at the top of the loop. The scribe continues in a roughly circular motion, but with a flattened right-hand side resulting in an almost straight line being formed on the upward continuation of the stroke.[271] Thus there is a clear tendency towards the minuscule form of the letter. This mixture of forms is consistent with a seventh to eighth century dating for the manuscript.

4. The scribe provides a further example of his inconsistent tendency to form oversized final sigmas, especially before a following kappa. See the first page of text, page two of the codex, line 16.

5. The final two letters of ἐσταύρωσαν are somewhat poorly formed. The alpha represents a repeated careless trend whereby the scribe fails to close the loop by not attaching it to the descending left to right diagonal. As Gebhart observes, the alpha is in minuscule form throughout,[272] but at certain places the scribe misforms this minuscule shape. The nu demonstrates a tendency towards a cursive style,[273] consisting of a left-hand vertical stroke, and what would be two linear strokes in a strict majuscule hand being replaced a u-shape, with the left-hand arm slanting slightly to serve as the lineal diagonal in majuscule formation.

6. Spacing of the letters is a little unusual here. The first two letters of ἀνά are adjoining, this is followed by a space of only 1mm, then the final α is written in contact with the μ which is the opening letter of the following word.

7. The ending of line five is not as difficult as that of the previous line. The parchment is not as uniformly darkened at this point, moreover, the supralinear bar of the *nomen sacrum* stands out allowing the eye to discern the letters underneath it more readily. Finally, the mirror image of these letters on the facing page is particularly clear.[274]

---

[271] Gebhardt also notes this tendency. 'Neben dieser eckigen uncialen Form findet sich aber nicht selten eine abgerundete cursive…nie, wenn ich nichts übersehe, eine ausgebildete Minuskelform (das δ in δυο III, 5 könnte nur als Ansatz dazu betrachtet werden). Gebhardt, *Das Evangelium und die Apokalypse des Petrus*, 10–11.

[272] 'Das α erscheint nur in der Form der Minuskel.' Gebhardt, *Das Evangelium und die Apokalypse des Petrus*, 10.

[273] This slightly minuscule shape reflects a deviation from the regular scribal habit. As Gebhardt depicts the tendency away from standard practice, 'unterscheidet sich das ν oft nur dadurch von dem uncialen N.' Gebhardt, *Das Evangelium und die Apokalypse des Petrus*, 12.

[274] See Kraus und Nicklas, *Das Petrusevangelium und die Petrusapokalypse*, P.Cair. 10759, f.2r, line 6 and also the reflected image to the left of f.1v, line 7.

8. Again the scribe has produced one of his aberrant letter forms in the word ἐσιώπα. The iota is elongated, measuring 5mm in comparison with a regular length of approximately 3mm. The length of the iota tends to become more pronounced when it is preceded by a letter that has a horizontal upper bar, such as π or τ. The practice is then to make this cross-bar touch the iota about two-thirds of the distance up its height. This often requires lengthening the iota, usually to about 4mm. Here, the top of the preceding sigma has been flattened to give the appearance of a horizontal stroke, and the iota has been lengthened even more so than the scribe's usual habit in such cases.[275]

9. The final epsilon is difficult to read owing to the darkened right-hand edge of the manuscript. There appears to be a smudging or double attempt to write the curved stroke of this letter.

10. A mirror image of the second, third and fourth letters of the word ὤρθωσαν, which stand at the end of the sixth line have been imprinted on the facing page. It may be that such obscured and darkened writing led Bouriant to propose the reading ἐώρθωσαν,[276] followed by Swete in his initial publication.[277] This may be due to the possible double attempt to write the preceding epsilon, as noted above. However, in his book length treatment, after images of the manuscript became available, Swete acknowledged that this reading was incorrect. He states, "Ἐώρθωσαν, if sound, is formed on the analogy of ἐώθουν, ἑώρακα, &c.; but the ε cannot be detected in the heliographic reproduction of the MS.'[278]

11. The word βασιλεύς is particularly obscured by the smudging. The first three letters are legible, as is the final sigma. On this occasion, the reflected image is not particularly clear either, but vestiges of the missing letters can be discerned on the facing page.

12. The letter θ in τεθεικότες is poorly formed. It appears to resemble two conjoined arcs producing a somewhat pointed apex both at the top and bottom of this narrow theta. This is in contrast to the more rounded elliptical shape usually formed by the scribe.

---

[275] Once again, Gebhardt observes this general trend in the scribal formation of the letter iota. 'Das ι erscheint in den verschiedensten Grössen.' Gebhardt, *Das Evangelium und die Apokalypse des Petrus*, 11.

[276] Bouriant, 'Fragments du texte grec du livre d'Énoch et de quelques écrits attribués à saint Pierre', 138.

[277] Swete, *The Apocryphal Gospel of St. Peter*, 2.

[278] Swete, *The Akhmîm Fragment of the Apocryphal Gospel of St Peter*, 6.

13. Although there is still some darkening of the manuscript as far down as the ending of this eighth line, the text has become light enough to enable reading of all letters.

14. The reading of the manuscript ὠνείδησεν appears to be an orthographical variant for ὠνείδισεν.[279]

15. This appears to be an orthographic error on the part of either the scribe or his exemplar for the demonstrative pronoun οὗτος. As Vaganay states, 'οὗτος δέ (mistake of the copyist in the ms.: ουτως).'[280]

16. Discussion of this somewhat unusual *nomen sacrum* occurs in the commentary section.[281]

17. Although emendations have been proposed for σκελοκοπηθῇ: σκελοκοπεῖν by Preuschen[282] and σκελοκοπᾶν by Harnack,[283] the reading is not particularly problematic in choosing to employ a passive subjunctive form at this point.

## Commentary

**4.10aα   καὶ ἤνεγκον δύο κακούργους.** Reference to two other individuals crucified with Jesus is contained in all the canonical gospels. In Mark (15.27), and Matthew (27.38) which closely follows the Markan account, these two characters are depicted as λῃσταί. According to Balz and Schneider the term λῃστής denotes a 'robber' or 'bandit'.[284] It is used elsewhere in the NT metaphorically to characterize those who practice trade in the temple, σπήλαιον λῃστῶν (Matt 21.13//Mk 11.17// Lk 19.46). Jesus uses the term in his address to those arresting him, ὡς ἐπὶ λῃστὴν ἐξήλθατε (Matt 26.55//Mark 14.48//Lk 22.52). Apart from these two examples of shared usage in the triple tradition, Luke

---

[279] See Mara, *Évangile de Pierre*, 46.

[280] Vaganay, *L'Évangile de Pierre*, 241.

[281] See C.M. Tuckett, '"Nomina Sacra": Yes and No?' in J.-M. Auwers and H.J. Jonge (eds.), *The Biblical Canons*, BETL CLXIII (Leuven: Peeters, 2003) 431–458.

[282] E. Preuschen, *Antilegomena, Die Reste die ausserkanonischen Evangelien und Urchristlichen Überlieferungen* (2nd ed., Giessen, 1905).

[283] Harnack, *Bruchstücke des Evangeliums und der Apokalypse des Petrus*, 26. Both Mara (46) and Vaganay (242) refer to Harnack's emended reading. Harnack, however, gives σκελοκοπηθῇ in his text (9) and states that this form is rare (in his notes, 26). In his register of Greek terms he gives σκελοκοπᾶν for v. 14 (75).

[284] Horst Balz and Gerhard Schneider (eds.), *Exegetical Dictionary of the New Testament* vol. 2 (Grand Rapids: Michigan: Eerdmans, 1991) 351.

employs the term in the parable of the Good Samaritan (Lk 10.30, 36),[285] and John pairs it with κλέπτης in the shepherd discourse (Jn 10.1, 8).[286] The fourth gospel describes the two fellow victims of crucifixion as ἄλλους δύο (Jn 19.18). This indefinite reference betrays little interest in the reason for their crucifixion. Among the canonical accounts, Luke alone refers to the pair as κακοῦργοι (Lk 23.32ff.).[287] This shared term, along with the description of the criminal who defends Jesus (again shared by Luke and the *Gospel of Peter*), provides strong evidence for seeing dependence of the Akhmîm text on the third gospel at this point.[288]

As was the case with the list of abuses (*Gos. Pet.* 3.8–9), subjects of verbs (here ἤνεγκον) are not explicitly stated in the immediate context. Within the narrative the last time the group has been explicitly designated is towards the end of *Gos. Pet.* 2.5, where they are described as 'the people' to whom Herod has handed Jesus over. After the cataloguing of a series of actions perpetrated against Jesus by certain subgroups from the crowd (*Gos. Pet.* 3.8–9), for a moment Jesus falls out of focus in the narrative and the crowd simply 'bring' two criminals. No information is provided about either the nature of their wrongdoing, or concerning how the crowd obtained access to these figures.[289] Brown notes one theory that has been postulated, but dismisses it as lacking evidence. 'Since according to Mark there were at this Passover people in prison because of a riot, many scholars have concluded that the two bandits/wrongdoers were from among these; yet no Gospel

---

[285] Discussing the occurrence in the parable of the Good Samaritan, Fitzmyer notes, 'Josephus tells of Essenes who carried on their journeys only arms, precisely as protection against highway robbers – using of the latter the very word *lēstai* that Luke employs here (*J.W.* 2.8,4 § 125; cf. 2.12,2 §228).' Fitzmyer, *The Gospel According to Luke X–XXIV*, 886.

[286] Brown observes that the term ληστής also 'used in the Gospels to refer to guerrilla warriors and revolutionary banditti like Barabbas.' Brown, *The Gospel according to John I–XI*, 385.

[287] Brown proffers the following suggestion to explain the Lukan change in terminology. 'Luke has taken great pains to show that Jesis is *dikaios* ("innocent, just"); yet he is crucified among *kaourgoi* (wrongdoers, malefactors" – a term that Like may have chosen to avoid the political implications of *lēstēs* for his readers in the 80s and 90s after the violence in Judea in the 50s and 60s).' Brown, *The Death of the Messiah*, vol 2, 969.

[288] Apart from the three Lukan usages of κακοῦργος in Lk 23.32–43, the only other place it is used in the NT is in 2 Tim 2.9, μέχρι δεσμῶν ὡς κακοῦργος.

[289] Again the description, with its starkness of detail, aligns with the Lukan account, ἤγοντο δὲ καὶ ἕτεροι κακοῦργοι δύο (Lk 23.32).

promotes this interpretation by vocabulary resemblance.'[290] The case is further weakened for the Akhmîm fragment, since it is impossible to know whether the full narrative contained a reference to the riot mentioned in the Markan account (Mk 15.7). As Mara observes, a different dynamic drives events leading up to Jesus' crucifixion in the Akhmîm text and this results in the omission of a number of details surrounding Jesus' journey after the scourging to the place of execution that are familiar from the canonical gospels.[291] Certain details have been omitted primarily because they would not fit with manner in which the story has been reshaped, but also because they may be seen as ameliorating the brutalization experienced by Jesus at the hand of the Jewish crowd. These details include the role of Simon of Cyrene and the lament of the 'daughter of Jerusalem'.

**4.10aβ** καὶ ἐσταύρωσαν ἀνὰ μέσον αὐτῶν τὸν κν. The focus of the narrative returns quickly to Jesus. The two wrongdoers have been brought into this scene without any background information. Obviously, the concern here is not to tie-up any historically loose ends, but rather to contrast the innocent suffering of Jesus with that of criminals, one of whom demonstrates sufficient perspicacity to recognize the unjust comdemnation to which Jesus is being subjected. As Vaganay notes, the correspondence of this passage is closest to the fourth gospel, ὅπου αὐτὸν ἐσταύρωσαν, καὶ μετ' αὐτοῦ ἄλλους δύο ἐντεῦθεν καὶ ἐντεῦθεν, μέσον δὲ τὸν Ἰησοῦν (Jn 19.18).[292] The Johannine expression stands in marked contrast to the synoptics which all refer to 'one on the right and one on the left' (Matt 27.38//Mk 15.27// Lk 23.33).[293] There are, however, a number of differences between the Akhmîm text and the description given in the fourth gospel. First, the reference to Jesus is replaced with τὸν κύριον, the preferred Christological title of the *Gospel of Peter*. Secondly, the account is compressed, with the middle clause of the Johannine version, καὶ μετ' αὐτοῦ ἄλλους δύο ἐντεῦθεν καὶ ἐντεῦθεν, being at best implied by the phrase ἀνὰ μέσον αὐτῶν. Thirdly, this abbreviation of the tradition has resulted in the

---

[290] Brown, *The Death of the Messiah*, vol. 2, 971.
[291] 'Dans le fragment qui nous est parvenu, des épisodes sont absent: la recontre avec Simon de Cyrene, celle avec «filles de Jérusalem», et, ce que Jean lui-même (19,17) n'a pas omis, la marche vers le Calvaire en portent la Croix.' Mara, *Évangile de Pierre*, 105.
[292] Vaganay, *L'Évangile de Pierre*, 235.
[293] There are slight differences in the Greek, but the similarity is striking.

removal of the two pronominal references to Jesus. In terms of grammatical structure, the pharse ἀνὰ μέσον with a following genitive referent is common in Hellenistic literature.[294]

Equally lacking in detail is the description of the mechanics of the
crucifixion.[295] At this stage in the narrative there has been no description of the cross, no indication of how it happened to be at the place of
execution, nor any description of how Jesus was affixed to the cross. In
this regard the *Gospel of Peter* shows the same characteristic restraint
that appears in the canonical accounts. This is not necessarily reflecting a desire to avoid violent depictions, since aspects of the scourging
are graphically represented, rather it may demonstrate that the details
of execution by crucifixion were sufficiently well known not to require
further explication.[296] The four canonical gospels all use three-word
phrases to describe the actual crucifixion;[297] σταυρώσαντες δὲ αὐτὸν
(Matt 27.35); καὶ σταυροῦσιν αὐτὸν (Mk 15.24); ἐκεῖ ἐσταύρωσαν αὐτὸν
(Lk 23.33); ὅπου αὐτὸν ἐσταύρωσαν (Jn 19.18). John and Luke agree in
employing the third person plural aorist indicative active form of the
verb σταυρόω, and this form is also utiled in the Akhmîm account.

Both graphically and in terms of the development of the narrative
the sufferings of the two criminals become subservient to those of the
central figure in the drama. Their function is a contrastive framing of
Jesus' innocent sufferings. Jesus may die ἀνὰ μέσον αὐτῶν, but he does
not die as one of them. Everything about his death is qualitatively
different. While Mara draws attention to the parallels between this
scene and Isa 53.9a,[298] καὶ δώσω τοὺς πονηροὺς ἀντὶ τῆς ταφῆς αὐτοῦ,
the correspondence is not great. The description in Isaiah appears to
depict a burial rather than a scene of execution, and, moreover, it does
not specifically enumerate two wrongdoers, but instead refers to an

---

[294] Vaganay, *L'Évangile de Pierre*, 235.

[295] For a discussion of crucifixion practices see Brown, *The Death of the Messiah*,
vol 2, 945–952.

[296] Keener also comes to this conclusion in relation to the Johannine account. 'The
Gospel writers require little depiction of the crucifixion (19.18), which was well known
in their world…The full horror of that mode of execution (e.g. Apuleius, *Metam.* 3.9;
6.32; Charito 3.3.12) remained vivid enough in the first century that all four evangelists hurry by the event itself quickly.' Keener, *The Gospel of John: A Commentary*,
vol. II, 1135.

[297] In regard to this brief notice about the crucifixion Brown states, 'All the Gospels are content with this laconic description without entering into gruesome details.'
Brown, *The Gospel according to John XIII–XXI*, 900.

[298] Mara, *Évangile de Pierre*, 106.

indefinite group. The connections with Jesus' burial are even stronger in the next clause from Isa 53.9, καὶ τοὺς πλουσίους ἀντὶ τοῦ θανάτου αὐτοῦ, which may have helped shape the tradition about Jesus being buried in Joseph of Arimathea's sepulchre.

**4.10b  αὐτὸς δὲ ἐσιώπα ὡς μηδέν πόνον ἔχων.** In relation to discussing the Docetic tendencies of the Akhmîm text, this phrase has been of fundamental importance. Among the schedule of five Docetic elements in the *Gospel of Peter*, Swete lists first, because of its chrono-logical sequence in the narrative, 'the Lord's freedom from pain at the moment of Crucifixion.'[299] However other early commentators on this passage noted that a Docetic reading was not the only possibility. Thus Semeria observes:

> v. 10. – The author, speaking of the crucifixion of Christ between two malefactors, says that he remained silent ὡς μηδέν πόνον ἔχων, which can signify: 'because he did not have any pain', – phrase obviously docetist; but one can also translate as: 'as if he did not have any pain', and we return again to orthodoxy, although this observation is not entirely free from some savour of docetism.[300]

In fact Semeria's second option appears to provide the more accurate rendering of the ὡς clause, which makes a simile type comparison, rather than a direct equation between the silence of Jesus and the lack of pain. Thus the comparison is of something that appears to be the case, rather than of something that actually is the case. Despite Seme-ria's astute observation, few have acknowledged the two options he outlined, let alone been willing to argue for the strength of the non-Docetic reading.

The opening part of this phrase relates the remarkable silence of Jesus. This motif is present in the synoptic gospels, albeit in a differ-ent context. The same verbal form, ἐσιώπα, is used in the Matthean and Markan versions of the Jewish trial scene. The Markan account is more emphatic, giving a double description of the silence of Jesus, ὁ δὲ ἐσιώπα καὶ οὐκ ἀπεκρίνατο οὐδέν. (Mk 14.61). The Matthean version

---

[299] Swete, *The Akhmîm Fragment of the Apocryphal Gospel of St Peter*, xxxviii.

[300] 'L'auteur, parlant du Christ crucifié entre deux malfaiteurs, dit qu'il se taisait, ὡς μηδέν πόνον ἔχων, ce qui peut signifier: «parce qu'il n'avait aucune douleur», – phrase évidemment docétiste; mais on peut aussi traduire: «comme s'il n'avait aucune douleur», et nous rentrons ainsi dans l'orthodoxie, bien que cette observation ne laisse pas d'avoir quelque saveur docétiste.' J.B. Semeria, 'L'Évangile de Pierre' *Revue Bib-lique* (1894) 522–560.

preserves only the first element, but does explicitly name Jesus (Matt 26.63). In the fourth gospel the same idea is present in the report of the interaction between Jesus and Pilate, when in response to Pilate's question πόθεν εἶ σύ; the narrator reports, ὁ δὲ Ἰησοῦς ἀπόκρισιν οὐκ ἔδωκεν αὐτῷ (Jn 19.9). Obviously, there is no connection drawn between these passages and Docetic claims (since they do not portray the possibility of Jesus avoiding pain), however, they do illustrate that the silence of Jesus is a recurrent theme in the gospel tradition and that there is no need to *a priori* connect it with Docetic beliefs. Silence in the face of pain appears to draw more upon the concept noble death, both as it occurs in Graeco-Roman and Judaeo-Christian literature. Unflinching suffering in the face of unjust condemnation was highly prized in antiquity. Within the martyrdom literature of the early church, this tendency is exemplified in the account of the martyrdom of Carpus, Papylus and Agathonicê. Describing the death of Papylus the writer of the martyrdom account states:

ἀακρεμασθεὶς δὲ καὶ οὗτος καὶ ξεόμενος ζυγὰς τρεῖς ἤλλαξεν καὶ φωνὴν οὐκ ἔδωκεν, ἀλλ᾽ ὡς γενναῖος ἀθλητὴς ἀπεδέχετο τὸν θυμὸν τοῦ ἀντικειμένου. (*Carpus, Papylus and Agathonicê*, 35).[301]

He too was hung up and scraped and endured three pairs, but did not utter a sound; like a noble athlete he received the angry onslaught of his adversary.[302]

A similar tendency is also found in accounts of noble pagan deaths.[303] Although Socrates remains somewhat garrulous as he approaches death, nonetheless he counsels silence or quietness as the form of conduct that should be adopted by those facing the circumstance of execution.

Socrates alone retained his calmness: 'What is this strange outcry?' he said. 'I sent away the women mainly in order that they might not misbehave in this way, for I have been told that a man should die in peace. Be quiet then, and have patience.' (Plato, *Phaedo*, 66)

---

[301] The text is taken from the edition of Musurillo, *Acts of the Christian Martyrs*, vol. 2, The Martyrdom of Carpus, Papylus and Agathonicê, 26.

[302] The translation is also taken from Musurillo, *Acts of the Christian Martyrs*, vol. 2, The Martyrdom of Carpus, Papylus and Agathonicê, 27.

[303] See A.Y. Collins, 'From Noble Death to Crucified Messiah', *NTS* 40 (1994) 481–503.

Here Socrates' adopts the demeanour expected of those who die nobly, he comforts his friends and counsels a quietistic attitude. To read such features as uniquely docetic is to miss the whole 'noble death' phenomenon which is prominent in the ancient world. Heroic figures dispise death itself, and do not allow the pain of death to gain control of their emotions. This may be part of the wider encratic ideal, attested by Aristotle and other ancient philosophers.

A highly significant parallel to the phrase ὡς μηδέν πόνον ἔχων occurs in the *Martyrdom of Polycarp* 8.3.[304] As Polycarp is pushed out of the wagon transporting him to the stadium to undergo martyrdom, his shin is scraped. In the face of this injury Polycarp strides towards the venue of his impending death. The narrative states that he showed no outward response to his injury: ὡς οὐδὲν πεπονθώς (cf. *H.E.* 4.15.16, οἷς οὐδὲν πεπονθώς). What is being emphasized here is the heroic approach to suffering, which is exemplified by a demeanour that refuses to allow the impact of pain to be shown.[305] Thus, the phrase is to be understood as representing a common feature found in stories describing suffering protagonists who nobly face death without giving their enemies the pleasure of knowing that the inflicted torments are having an effect on the one enduring the pain.

**4.11a** καὶ ὅτε ὤρθωσαν τὸν σταυρόν. In the passion narratives of the canonical gospels the actual raising up or erecting of the cross is not depicted. Both Mark and Matthew move from the unembellished statement that 'they crucified him' to a description of the dividing of the clothes, next after different intervening material (Matt 27.36 and Mk 15.25) they both continue with the description of the inscription on the cross, then finally give reference to the two ληισταί crucified with him. Luke develops the story of the penitent wrongdoer in much greater detail, but likewise has no mention of the setting up of the cross. John also does not offer a description of the mechanics of putting the cross in place, but agrees with the *Gospel of Peter* in describing the inscription on the cross prior to recounting the dividing of

---

[304] This text is also mentioned in the discussion by P.M. Head, 'On the Christology of the Gospel of Peter,' *VC* 46 (1992) 209–224, see esp. 213.

[305] Buschmann also highlights a theological dimension behind this comment, seeing it as an indication of divine oversight: 'Durch Gottes Macht bleibt Polykarp in der Versuchung behütet ὡς οὐδὲν πεπονθώς.' G. Buschmann, *Martyrium Polycarpi – Eine Formkritische Studie* (Berlin: de Gruyter, 1994) 189.

Jesus' garments. Among other non-canonical literature *the Acts of Pilate* show even less interest in the process of Jesus' crucifixion, the two wrongdoers, named as Dysmas and Gestas (*Acts of Pilate* 9.5), are described as being 'hanged up' (*Acts of Pilate* 10.1), but the act of attaching Jesus to the cross or setting his cross in place is not decribed. Brown understands the victim of crucifixion to be set in place in the following manner. 'Criminals were affixed to the crossbeam by being tied or nailed; then the crossbeam was lifted up by forked poles (*furcillae*) and, with the body attached, inserted into the slot in the upright.'[306] Ignatius uses the metaphor of the cross as a machine or crane which lifts believers up to God, διὰ τῆς μηχανῆς Ἰησοῦ Χριστοῦ, ὅς ἐστιν σταυρός (*Eph.* 9.1). However, this metaphor does not describe the physical process by which Jesus would have been set in place upon the cross. Ignatius comes closer to describing an aspect of the crucifixion in his letter to the Smyrnaeans when he describes the reality of the nailing, καθηλωμένον ὑπὲρ ἡμῶν ἐν σαρκί (*Smyrn.* 1.2). Here, however, the reference may be directed against those who denied the reality of the the suffering of Jesus. There is a contrast between the position Ignatius attacks which denies the reality of Jesus suffering on the cross (plausibly some early docetic view), and the depiction in the *Gospel of Peter*, which like Ignatius affirms the reality of the crucifixion being endured by the Lord.

**4.11a** ἐπέγραψαν ὅτι οὗτός ἐστιν ὁ βασιλεὺς τοῦ Ἰσραήλ. The description of the inscription on the *titulus* occurs in all four canonical gospel accounts, but none of the forms of words recorded in those accounts agrees with that presented by the Akhmîm text. The activity of preparing the inscription is described in the *Gospel of Peter* using the term ἐπέγραψαν. None of the canonical gospels use this verb to describe the actual action of writing, and the plural subjects who are not specified in the immediate context must still be the Jewish crowd to whom Jesus was handed over. Thus as Swete observes, '[t]he title is regarded as the work of the Jews (ἐπέγραψαν), not of Pilate.'[307] Obviously this change in identification is not based only on the plural verb, since Matthew uses a plural form, καὶ ἐπέθηκαν ἐπάνω τῆς κεφαλῆς αὐτοῦ (Matt 27.37), but is also required by the wider narrative of the *Gospel of Peter*. In contrast to the Matthean description of the

---

[306] Brown, *The Death of the Messiah*, vol 2, 949.
[307] Swete, *The Akhmîm Fragment of the Apocryphal Gospel of St Peter*, 6.

placement of the titulus, Mark employs a periphrastic construction to describe the inscription having been written ἦν...ἐπιγεγραμμένη (Mk 15.26).[308] Luke's description is locative, decribing the position of the inscription ἦν δὲ καὶ ἐπιγραφὴ ἐπ' αὐτῷ (Lk 23.38).[309] John, like Matthew, uses the verb τίθημι, although this is co-ordinated with a description of the titulus being written ἔγραψεν, but in the singular, since the action is attributed to Pilate alone ἔγραψεν δὲ καὶ τίτλον ὁ Πιλᾶτος καὶ ἔθηκεν (Jn 19.19).[310] Like the Markan account, the Akhmîm text does not strictly state where the titulus was located, only that it had been written. There is no description of it being affixed to the cross. This should not be taken to imply that the Gospel of Peter is envisaging the regular Roman practice of hanging a placard with the charges inscribed around the neck of a condemned person prior to exectution (cf. Suet. Calig. 32.2, Dom. 10.1; Dio Cass. 54.3.6–7, 73.16.5; H.E. 5.1.44). Since the Akhmîm account has already described Jesus being placed on the cross, this is not part of the pre-crucifixion degrading of the condemned victim. Instead, the account assumes the portrayal in the canonical accounts, yet without paralleling all the details contained in those accounts.

The wording on the titulus differs in the canonical gospels as well as in the form it appears in the Gospel of Peter. The variant forms are as follows:

| | |
|---|---|
| Matt 27.37 | οὗτός ἐστιν Ἰησοῦς ὁ βασιλεὺς τῶν Ἰουδαίων. |
| Mk 15.26 | ὁ βασιλεὺς τῶν Ἰουδαίων.[311] |
| Lk 23.38 | ὁ βασιλεὺς τῶν Ἰουδαίων οὗτος. |
| Jn 19.19 | Ἰησοῦς ὁ Ναζωραῖος ὁ βασιλεὺς τῶν Ἰουδαίων. |
| Gos. Pet. 4.11 | οὗτός ἐστιν ὁ βασιλεὺς τοῦ Ἰσραήλ. |

---

[308] Strictly speaking, in the Markan narrative there is nothing that directly connects the titulus with the cross. Thus as France observes, 'Mark does not in fact state where it was ἐπιγεγραμμένη; it is John who says it was placed on the cross, supported by Matthew's statement that it was over Jesus' head.' France, The Gospel of Mark, 645–646.

[309] Gundry correctly notes that the Lukan description 'could also be understood to mean the placard was hung on Jesus himself' rather than above his head. R.H. Gundry, Mark: A Commentary on His Apology for the Cross (Grand Rapids, Michigan: Eerdmans, 1993), 958.

[310] Brown correctly describes the change in narrative dynamics in the fourth gospel when he states, 'John not only develops the inscription into a major episode but changes its import. Pilate writes the title.' (Brown, The Death of the Messiah, vol 2, 964). While Brown is correct that this does not formally contradict the synoptic portrayal, it does result in an ironic reversal, whereby the charge brought against Jesus by his accusers is used in a semi-confessional manner.

[311] Cf. The Acts of Pilate 10.1.

The title ὁ βασιλεύς is common to all five accounts, and this is construed with an explanatory genitive noun clarifying the group over
whom Jesus exercises kingship. The Markan and Lukan forms are
identical apart from the Lukan addition of the demonstrative οὗτος,
at the end of the title. The name 'Jesus' occurs only in Matthew and
John, but in the latter stands in apposition with the term ὁ Ναζωραῖος.
Matthew and the *Gospel of Peter* share the introductory formula οὗτός
ἐστιν, which may suggest that the Matthean form is in the mind of the
author of the Akhmîm account. If it is the case that the *Gospel of Peter*
is drawing on Matthew here, then the two deviations are readily explicable. The deletion of the name Ἰησοῦς fully accords with the non-use
of this name in the narrative, with κύριος being the preferred Christological title. Second the replacement of τῶν Ἰουδαίων with τοῦ Ἰσραήλ
reflects the anti-Jewish sentiments of the narrative, which manifests
itself here by distancing Jesus from that ethnic grouping, but nonetheless associating Jesus with historic Israel, without portraying a link
between the Jews and Israel. Swete argues that the change in title 'is
consistent with its assumed origin.'[312] By this Swete appears to mean
that the title 'king of Israel' is more fitting on the lips of the Jewish
crowd than would be the address 'king of the Jews'. This, however, is
highly questionable and appears to miss the more fundamental reason
for making such an alteration. Vaganay correctly rejects such views
as presented not only be Swete, but also by Stülken[313] and Stocks.[314]
Yet Vaganay's own suggestion represents only a partial reason for this
change. He argues

> By writing these words, the Jewish authorities believed that they were
> simply describing the reason for the judgment. In fact, in a manner simi-
> lar to Caiaphas (Jn. 11. 50f.), they prophesied. Unknowingly, they gave
> testimony to the Messianic royalty of Christ. The ironic inscription is a
> claim to fame. The defamatory titulus proclaims a divine truth.[315]

---

[312] Swete, *The Akhmîm Fragment of the Apocryphal Gospel of St Peter*, 6.
[313] A. Stülken, 'Petrusevangelium' in E. Hennecke (ed.), *Handbuch zu den neutestamentlichen Apokryphen* (Tübingen: J.B.C. Mohr, 1904) 81.
[314] H. Stocks, 'Zum Petrusevangelium', *Neue kirchliche Zeitschrift* 13 (1902) 289.
[315] En écrivant ces quelques mots, les autorités juives ont cru mentionner simplement le motif de la condamnation. En fait, à la manière de Caïphe (*Jn.*, XI, 50 sq.),
elles ont prophétisé. A leur insu, elles ont rendu témoignage à la royauté messianique
du Christ. L'inscription ironique est un titre de gloire. La tablette infamante proclame
une vérité divine. Vaganay, *L'Évangile de Pierre*, 238.

While there is certainly irony, in that the inscription that is intended to deride Jesus actually describes his true identity, there is nothing in the narrative to suggest that one is to read this as an inadvertent fulfilment of prophecy, unlike the intrusive narrator's aside to his audience in Jn 11.50. Nor is there any indication that the title 'king of Israel' is introduced as a messianic claim that the mob supposess it is subverting, while in actual fact the divine status is being established. Although elements of such irony are present, the choice of title represents a much more transparent theological concern. The change is far more plausibly seen as part of the pervasive anti-Jewish sentiment in the narrative. While Mara offers the parallel in Jn 12.13, ὡσαννά· εὐλογημένος ὁ ἐρχόμενος ἐν ὀνόματι κυρίου, [καὶ] ὁ βασιλεὺς τοῦ Ἰσραήλ, as confirming Vaganay's contention that the Jews are unwittingly announcing a messianic prophecy,[316] this still fails to ignore the much simpler explanation. For the author of the *Gospel of Peter* the Jews are unreservedly evil and are the instigators of Jesus' death, who pitilessly mock his true status. From the author's perspective, to label Jesus as king of this recalcitrant people would form a connection which he wishes to resist. However, by contrast, the author conceives of the historic people of the Old Testament, that is Israel, as being a fundamentally different entity. Thus he can comfortably label Jesus as 'king of Israel', but the title 'Jew' is blackened in the narrative to such an extent that it can have no connection with Jesus for the author of this text.

**4.12a καὶ τεθεικότες τὰ ἐνδύματα ἔμπροσθεν αὐτοῦ.** In accord with the order of events contained in the fourth gospel, the *Gospel of Peter* moves from the description of the *titulus* to recount what happened to Jesus' garments. Again the Akhmîm account provides details not found in the canonical story. Neither the synoptic gospels nor John describe the garments as being laid out before Jesus. Vaganay describes this as a 'light' addition to the canonical accounts.[317] Similarly Mara observes, 'The scene of the arrangement of the garments "before him" does not appear in the canonical gospels.'[318] This addition appears to be included for dramatic effect rather than to convey any theologi-

---

[316] Mara, *Évangile de Pierre*, 112.
[317] Vaganay states, 'Légère addition au texte des évangiles canonique.' (Vaganay, *L'Évangile de Pierre*, 238).
[318] 'La scène de la déposition des vêtements «devant lui» n'apparaît pas dans les Évangiles canoniques.' Mara, *Évangile de Pierre*, 112.

cal significance. The implied subject of the verb τεθεικότες remains the Jewish mob, although they have not been explicitly mentioned for some time in the narrative. This lack of explicit identification may have served, perhaps unintentionally, to create ambiguity in the minds of hearers of this text who were familiar with the canonical accounts. It is natural for those familiar with the storyline of the synoptics and John to overlay the indefinite descriptions of the subjects disposing the clothes, with the traditional reference to the Roman soldiers carrying out these actions. While the author of the *Gospel of Peter* remains consistent in his use of indefinite subjects throughout the crucifixion scene, it may not be unnatural for the hearers to 'fatigue' in following the narrative on its own terms and in their thinking to revert to a traditional conception of the subjects contained in other accounts of the passion.[319]

Whereas the term ἱμάτια is used in the canonical gospels (Matt 27.33; Mk 15.25; Lk 23.34; Jn 19.23), the *Gospel of Peter* replaces this with ἐνδύματα. Developing Vaganay's suggestion,[320] Mara argues that this is in order to create a prophetic fulfilment of Ps 21.19, but in an abbreviated form.[321] This theory does not, however, adequately explain the problem that in making this alteration, the terminology actually is shifted away from that of Ps 21.19, whereas one would expect a greater correspondence to be developed. Such correspondence is seen in the fourth gospel where two sets of garments are described in Jn 19.23, in order to align the description with both components of the synonomous parallel contained in Ps 21.19. It is far more likely that the author of the *Gospel of Peter* has recalled the story of the clothes from the synoptic gospels, replaces ἱμάτια with the almost synonomous term ἐνδύματα, and does not recall or retain the Johannine motif of the fulfilment of Ps 21.19.

---

[319] On the theory of narrative fatigue, see M.S. Goodacre, 'Fatigue in the Synoptics', *NTS* 44 (1998) 45–58. Here it is suggested that readers familiar with an alternative version of a narrative can 'fatigue' when following a fresh presentation of a known story. This means that they supply details drawn from outside the narrative frame with which they are directly interacting. This parallels Goodacre's theory that when an author is following a source he can fatigue in the process of consistently changing details to conform to his own theological outlook.

[320] See Vaganay, *L'Évangile de Pierre*, 238–239.

[321] Mara, *Évangile de Pierre*, 114–115.

**4.12b** διεμερίσαντο καὶ λαχμὸν ἔβαλον ἐπ' αὐτοῖς. Here the narrative aligns with details in the canonical accounts, but tells the story in its own terms. As Vaganay observes the same verb, διεμερίσαντο, is employed in the first three gospels.[322] This further supports the suggestion that the *Gospel of Peter* is influenced by the synoptic accounts, and is not following the Johannine concern of the prophetic fulfilment of Ps 21.19. After citing Ps 21.19 LXX (par. 22.18 MT), διεμερίσαντο τὰ ἱμάτιά μου ἑαυτοῖς καὶ ἐπὶ τὸν ἱματισμόν μου ἔβαλον κλῆρον, Justin also preserves a variant account of the division of the garments, οἱ σταυρώσαντες αὐτὸν ἐμέρισαν τὰ ἱμάτια αὐτοῦ ἑαυτοῖς, λαχμὸν βάλλοντες ἕκαστος κατὰ τὴν τοῦ κλήρου ἐπιβολήν, ὅ ἐκλέξασθαι ἐβεβούλητο (*Dial*. 97.3). Here Justin does not use the compound verb διαμερίζω, intead preferring the simplex form μερίζω, however, in common with the canonical accounts he employs the term ἱμάτια to describe the garments. It appears that both Justin and the *Gospel of Peter* have drawn on gospel tradition independently to fashion their own accounts.

Unlike the fourth gospel, the Akhmîm text does not refer to two different sets of garments, the first being dividing among the soldiers while they gamble for the seamless tunic. Instead, in agreement with the synoptic accounts it envisages a process whereby the clothes are divided among the soldiers on the basis of λαχμὸν ἔβαλον. In place of the term λαχμός the synoptics use κλῆρος (βάλλοντες κλῆρον Matt 27.35 and Mk 15.24; ἔβαλον κλήρους Lk 23.34). The term κλῆρος appears to denote a 'lot' of some unspecified type,[323] similarly λαχμός is a non-specific reference to 'an object used as a device for making a decision through sortilege.'[324] Friedrich sees this incident as being in line with Roman practice. 'According to Roman law the executioner was permitted to seize the property of the one executed.'[325] While the canonical gospels prefer the more common term κλῆρος, including the Johannine account in its citation of Ps 21:19 (see Jn 19.24), λαχμός terminology may find its origin in the fourth gospel. The hortatory aorist subjunctive form λάχωμεν (from λαγχάνω) is used in the reported dialogue

---

[322] Vaganay, *L'Évangile de Pierre*, 239.

[323] See the first meaning in BDAG, 'a specially marked object such as a pebble, a piece of pottery, or a stick, used to decide someth.', 548.

[324] BDAG, 587.

[325] See J.H. Friedrick, 'κλῆρος' in Balz and Schneider (eds.), *Exegetical Dictionary of the New Testament*, vol. 2, 299.

between the soldiers to encourage the use of lots to determine who
would possess the seamless tunic. Brown surveys different interpretations of the gambling process involved in the Johaninne account.

> As for what is envisaged, most scholars think something like dice would
> have been thrown. De Waal ("Mora"), however, doubts that the soldiers
> would have so conveniently have brought a *pyrgos* ("dice box") to the
> place of crucifixion. He suggests a *mora* game played by guessing the
> number of outstretched fingers on the opponent's hidden hands. Seem-
> ingly that is how the paraphrase of John by Nonnus of Panopolis (ca.
> 440) understood *lagchanein*: "putting out the fingers of the hand for it
> [the tunic]."[326]

Leaving aside the question of the historicity of the clothes-dividing
incident, it is necessary to see that these early interpretations are as
speculative as their more recent counterparts. Hence all that can be
concluded is that both the canonical accounts and the *Gospel of Peter*
refer to some unknown process of chance by which Jesus' clothes are
allocated among those who crucified him.

**4.13a** εἷς δέ τις τῶν κακούργων ἐκείνων ὠνείδισεν αὐτοὺς
λέγων. The incident depicted in vv. 13–14 is clearly related to the
story of the penitent evildoer, which among the canonical accounts is
unique to Luke's gospel (Lk 23.39–43). There are, however, marked differences which show that the author of the Akhmîm text has reworked
this scene so that it aligns with his own theological proclivities. In
the Lukan narrative the positive assessment of one of the κακοῦργος
emerges only in juxtaposition to the earlier negative taunts of the other
wrongdoer.[327] The author of the *Gospel of Peter* allows no such criticism in his account. The development of this tradition can be traced
through a number of stages.[328] The earliest recoverable stratum is contained in Mk 15.32c which reports καὶ οἱ συνεσταυρωμένοι σὺν αὐτῷ
ὠνείδιζον αὐτόν. Form-critically Luke develops this into a type of pronouncement story, where the saviour articulates a heavenly promise to

---

[326] Brown, *The Death of the Messiah*, vol. 2, 955.

[327] As Fitzmyer states, 'this third taunt becomes a foil for a rebuke from the fellow
criminal.' Fitzmyer, *The Gospel According to Luke X–XXIV*, 1508.

[328] See R. Bultmann, *History of the Synoptic Tradition* (Oxford: Blackwell, 1963)
309–310, who traces the growth in the tradition from the Markan to the Lukan
account, with the tendency towards differentiation and individualization.

a dying figure.[329] In the *Gospel of Peter* a pronouncement is still made, but this time about Jesus rather than by him. This transforms the story into a Christological confession, as well as reinforcing the Lukan declaration of Jesus' innocence by one of the criminals.

The opening words of the Luke pericope, εἷς δὲ τῶν κρεμασθέντων κακούργων (Lk 23.39), are very close to those employed in the *Gospel of Peter*. The difference between the five words that begin the respective accounts is that the *Gospel of Peter* deletes the word denoting the criminal hanging, κρεμασθέντων,[330] and replaces this with the indefinite pronoun τις which is inserted as the third word in the clause. However, there is a more fundamental difference which is not apparent just from a comparison of the introductory clauses of the two accounts, namely that the two authors are referring to different people. In the Lukan narrative these words denote the wrongdoer who mocks Jesus.[331] The Akhmîm text transforms this negative response to Jesus by using the introductory clause to refer to the criminal who is favourable to Jesus, and by having the reviling words directed to those who have crucified Jesus. Luke also introduces the demonstrative pronoun ἐκείνων to remind readers that there is more than one criminal present, however this second figure makes no contribution as the story unfolds. The text continues with the phrase ὠνείδισεν αὐτοὺς λέγων. This prepares for the direct speech which follows, and the choice of verb signals to the audience that the words to be uttered are hostile in nature and, by use of the plural pronoun, that they are directed to a group, either the crowd in general, or those who are involved in gambling for Jesus' clothes. In the Akhmîm account the verb βλασφημέω is replaced by the less specific term ὀνειδίζω. In reference to the Lukan terminology Green notes that

> "To blaspheme" may refer to the casting of insults, but one may hear deeper echoes of a more religious sort, and if Luke were saying that, in denigrating Jesus, this criminal (and with him, perhaps, all those who mock Jesus on the cross) is denigrating the power of God.[332]

---

[329] M. Dibelius, *From Tradition to Gospel* (Cambridge: James Clarke, 1971, trans. of 1933 German edition) 203.

[330] Nolland sees the term κρεμασθέντων as being characteristic of the author of Luke-Acts. 'The clearest Lukan element here is κρεμασθέντων, "hanged" (cf. Acts 5:30; 10:39).' J. Nolland, *Luke 18:35–24.53*, WBC 35C (Dallas: Word, 1993) 1151.

[331] See Bock, *Luke 9:51–24:53*, 1854.

[332] Green, *The Gospel of Luke*, 822.

Such religious overtones are not appropriate in relation to the criminal's mocking of those who have crucified Jesus. This accounts for the change in terminology from βλασφημέω to ὀνειδίζω.

**4.13b ἡμεις διὰ τὰ κακὰ ἃ ἐποιήσαμεν οὕτω πεπόνθαμεν.**
The first part of the wrongdoer's speech is a profession his own guilt and that of the second criminal. From this it should not be assumed that he necessarily had an intimate knowledge of his fellow victim's crime, or that they were partners in crime. Rather this needs to be seen as a literary device, which casts the confession about Jesus' innocence into even sharper relief by showing that the criminal is not just an embittered figure reviling his executioners, but an insightful observer and critic of the injustice that is being perpetrated against Jesus. Yet he is rational enough to recognize that his own punishment is justified. Fitzmyer, discussing the Lukan account, makes a similar point in relation to the criminal's knowledge of Jesus' innocence. 'To ask how the man knew all this about Jesus is to miss the point of the story.'[333] This acknowledgement of the criminals' guilt is modelled on the confession in Lk 23.41, which makes the following observation about their own condemnation, καὶ ἡμεῖς μὲν δικαίως, ἄξια γὰρ ὧν ἐπράξαμεν ἀπολαμβάνομεν. While there is no significant shared terminology, the only common term is ἡμεῖς, the two stories are obviously related. This may suggest an indirect literacy dependence, at least in as far as the author of the Akhmîm narrative may not be sitting with Luke's gospel open before him slavishly copying its text.

**4.13c οὗτος δὲ σωτὴρ γενόμενος τῶν ἀνῶν τί ἠδίκησεν ὑμᾶς;**
In contrast to the negative self-assessmant offered by the criminal, he now challenges his executioners to provide an example of Jesus' wrongdoing that could be used as the basis of his legitimate punishment. Coupled with the rhetorical question, the criminal makes a significant Christological declaration about Jesus, he unabashedly asserts that he is the 'Saviour of men.' Although this exact title is not used in the New Testament, a close parallel is found in the Johannine account of Jesus' encounter with the Samaritan women, where the inhabitants of her village proclaim Jesus to be ὁ σωτὴρ τοῦ κόσμου (Jn 4.42).[334] Such

---

[333] Fitzmyer, *The Gospel According to Luke X–XXIV*, 1508.
[334] Tuckett notes that this title stands as the climactic element in a progression of christological affirmations made about Jesus in John 4. See *Christology and the New Testament*, 158.

universalism may not only reflect a development in early Christian soteriology,[335] but also may be consciously adopted by the author of the *Gospel of Peter* to counter claims of particularism made in relation to Jesus as a Jewish salvific figure. Vaganay rejects the supposition of both von Schubert[336] and Wabnitz[337] that the title ὁ σωτὴρ τοῦ ἀνθρώπων attests gnostic reflections on the soteriological significance of Christ. Swete sees it as possible to understand this title as a development of synoptic tradition and thought. He states, 'in σωτὴρ γενόμενος we have an echo of St Luke's σῶσον σεαυτὸν καὶ ἡμᾶς (v. 39).'[338] However, while Vaganay feels that the contact is not close enough to view this title as a development of Lk 23.39, he argues that this does not necessitate finding gnostic theology behind this title.[339] Although Vaganay is correct to dismiss gnostic influence, Swete's suggestion remains plausible especially when one considers the free approach that is being adopted by the author of the *Gospel of Peter* in reshaping traditions from Lk 23.39–43.

The use of the *nomen sacrum* α̅ν̅ω̅ν̅ is somewhat surprising, since ἀνθρώπων refers to humanity as a whole, rather than a divine figure. Both Roberts[340] and Hurtado[341] place ἄνθρωπος in a second group of *nomina sacra*, which also includes the terms πνεῦμα and σταυρός. Hurtado concurs with Roberts assessment that with these words 'the contracted form is found relatively early and relatively frequently',[342] however, he nuances this statement to present this group of terms as more readily identifiable as a later development. He labels these as 'three additional terms, which appear to be slightly later and less uniformly treated.'[343] The term ἄνθρωπος is particularly problematic, since on a number of occasions it occurs in abbreviated form when

---

[335] In relation to the Johannine title Barrett notes parallels with imperial terminology. 'It [the title σωτήρ] was applied to Roman Emperors, and the full expression σωτὴρ τοῦ κόσμου is very frequently applied in inscriptions to Hadrian.' Barrett, *The Gospel according to St John*, 244.

[336] H. Schubert, *Die Composition des pseudopetrinischen Evangelienfragments* (Berlin: 1893) 28.

[337] A. Wabnitz, 'Les fragments de l'évangile et de l'apocalypse de Pierre', 476–477.

[338] Swete, *The Akhmîm Fragment of the Apocryphal Gospel of St Peter*, 7.

[339] Vaganay, *L'Évangile de Pierre*, 241.

[340] C.H. Roberts, 'Nomina Sacra: Origins and Significance', chap. 2 of his *Manuscript, Society and Belief in Early Christian Egypt* (London: OUP, 1979), 26–48, see esp. 27.

[341] Hurtado, 'The Origin of the *Nomina Sacra*: A Proposal', 655.

[342] Roberts, 'Nomina Sacra: Origins and Significance', 27.

[343] Hurtado, 'The Origin of the *Nomina Sacra*: A Proposal', 655.

it has no sacral function. Apart from the present example, particularly striking is the occurrence in the Greek fragments of the *Gospel of Thomas*, 'My soul is afflicted for the sons of men (ἀνῶν), because they are blind in their hearts and do not see…' (P.Oxy. 1, lines 19–21). As Tuckett quips, 'The context scarcely suggests that the ἄνθρωποι here are regarded as very "sacred"!'[344] Roberts suggests that the origin of the *nomen sacrum* ἄνθρωπος is to be found in the Christological title ὁ υἱὸς τοῦ ἀνθρώπου.[345] Yet Tuckett, citing much helpful evidence, argues that there is 'no clear evidence that the use of ἄνθρωπος in the phrase ὁ υἱὸς τοῦ ἀνθρώπου can be regarded as significant in determining the origin of the practice of abbreviating ἄνθρωπος.'[346] The *Gospel of Peter* is consistent in using a *nomen sacrum* to abbreviate the term ἄνθρωπος. The only other place where the word ἄνθρωπος occurs in the text (*Gos. Pet.* 11.44) it refers to a 'man' who descends from heaven and enters into Jesus' tomb. Here it is also written in contracted form.

Equally striking in the title σωτὴρ τοῦ ἀνῶν is the non-abbreviation of the term σωτήρ. Scholars such as Roberts,[347] Hurtado,[348] and Tuckett[349] agree that this belongs to a wider and later group of terms that enter the scheme at various stages. However the non-use of a *nomen sacrum* at this point cannot be used to date either the Akhmîm manuscript or the exemplar the scribe was following. This is due to empirical observation made by Roberts surrounding the list of eight later terms that 'the contraction is irregular.'[350] Such lack of consistency appears to reflect the preferences of individual scribes, but consequently means that *nomina sacra* cannot be used as a datum for dating manuscripts.

**4.14a** καὶ ἀγανακτήσαντες ἐπ' αὐτῷ. The author informs the audience of two aspects of the response of the belligerent crowd. First insight into its inner attitude is provided, then in the second part of the verse the audience is also informed of how this materializes in

---

[344] Tuckett, '"Nomina Sacra": Yes and No?', 450.

[345] For Roberts this is of fundamental significance. He argues that since the title ὁ υἱὸς τοῦ ἀνθρώπου disappeared relatively soon in Christian devotion this demonstrates that the *nomen sacrum* ἄνθρωπος must have emerged from 'the translations into Greek of Aramaic Gospels or sayings.' Roberts, '*Nomina Sacra*: Origins and Significance', 40.

[346] Tuckett, '"Nomina Sacra": Yes and No?', 451.

[347] Roberts, '*Nomina Sacra*: Origins and Significance', 27.

[348] Hurtado, 'The Origin of the *Nomina Sacra*: A Proposal', 655–657.

[349] Tuckett, '"Nomina Sacra": Yes and No?', 431.

[350] Roberts, '*Nomina Sacra*: Origins and Significance', 27.

a command to prolong the suffering of the outspoken criminal. The term ἀγανακτέω is used seven times in the New Testament to express 'indignation' or 'anger'.[351] In the present context, the term appears to have as its subject a group who have taken control of the events of the crucifixion. Mara suggests that, '[t]he subject of ἀγανακτήσαντες is certainly that which is understood by the pronoun ὑμᾶς of the preceding verse, that is to say "the Jews" considered as the actual instigators of the crucifixion of the Lord.'[352] However, this fails to take into account the fact that the following clause shows that a dominant sub-group has emerged which commands underlings to carry out certain acts, and hence it does not necessarily denote the mob *en masse*.

Vaganay argues that the pronoun αὐτός does not refer to the good criminal, but rather depicts Jesus.[353] This is also the judgment of both Harnack[354] and Völter.[355] If this were the case it would have to be admitted that the author has not signalled the change of subject in a particularly effective manner. In its favour, one may suggests that Jesus has been the sole recipient of Jewish brutality so far in the narrative. On balance, however, the most likely reference still appears to be the immediately preceding subject, namely the criminal who speaks on Jesus' behalf.

**4.14b** ἐκέλευσαν ἵνα μὴ σκελοκοπηθῇ ὅπως βασανιζόμενος ἀποθάνοι. Here there is another reminiscence of a detail from the canonical passion accounts, but again it is transferred to a new context. In the fourth gospel the Jewish leaders ask for the legs of the victims to be broken in order to hasten their deaths (Jn 19.31–33). As the Johannine narrative makes clear, this is not an act of mercy, but emerges from a religious desire to remove the bodies prior to the Sabbath.[356] This request for leg-breaking, which could be construed

---

[351] See BDAG, 5.

[352] 'Le sujet de ἀγανακτήσαντες est certainement celui qui est compris dans le pronom ὑμᾶς du verset précédent, c'est-à-dire les Juifs considérés comme les auteurs matériels de la crucifixion du Seigneur.' Mara, *Évangile de Pierre*, 120.

[353] Vaganay, *L'Évangile de Pierre*, 242.

[354] Harnack, *Bruchstücke des Evangeliums und der Apokalypse des Petrus*, 26.

[355] D. Völter, *Petrusevangelium oder Aegypterevangelium? Eine Frage bezüglich des neuentdeckten Evangeliumfragments* (Tübingen, 1893) 8.

[356] On the practice of breaking the legs of those being crucified see N. Haas, 'Anthropological Observations on the Skeletal Remains from Giv'at ha-Mivtar', *IEJ* 20 (1970) 38–59. Haas reports the case of a skeleton of a crucified man discovered with one fractured leg and the other smashed to pieces.

as a partial act of mercy on the part of the Jews in the fourth gospel, is taken up by the author of the *Gospel of Peter*. Instead of seeking to break the legs to relieve the suffering of the criminal (which might have been the physical result of leg-breaking during a crucifixion), in the narrative this action is not to be taken for precisely the opposite reason. Thus the leaders of the mob single him out for heightened torment, by explicitly denying him any relief that might be afforded by a swift death. In this sense those giving instruction once again demonstrate brutality by prolonging and exacerbating the criminal's pain, ὅπως βασανιζόμενος ἀποθάνοι.

15. Ἦν δὲ μεσημβρία, καὶ σκότος κατέσχε(ν)[1] πᾶσαν τὴν Ἰουδαίαν· καὶ ἐθορυβοῦντο καὶ ἠγωνίων μήποτε ὁ ἥλιος ἔδυ, ἐπειδὴ ἔτι ἔζη· γέγραπται αὐτοῖς ἥλιον μὴ δῦναι ἐπὶ πεφωνευμένῳ.[2] 16. καί τις αὐτῶν εἶπεν· Ποτίσατε αὐτὸν χολὴν μετὰ ὄξους· καὶ κεράσαντες ἐπότισαν. 17. καὶ ἐπλήρωσαν πάντα καὶ ἐτελείωσαν κατὰ τῆς κεφαλῆς αὐτῶν τὰ ἁμαρτήματα. 18. περιήρχοντο δὲ πολλοὶ μετὰ λύχνων νομίζοντες ὅτι νύξ ἐστιν ἐπέσαντο.[3] 19. καὶ ὁ κ̅ς̅ ἀνεβόησε λέγων· Ἡ δύναμίς μου ἡ δύναμις κατέλειψάς με· καὶ εἰπὼν ἀνελήφθη. 20. καὶ αὐτός[4] ὥρας διεράγη τὸ καταπέτασμα τοῦ ναοῦ τῆς Ἰερουσαλὴμ εἰς δύο.

15. And it was noon and darkness covered all Judaea. And they were troubled and distressed lest the sun had already set since he was alive. It is written by them, 'The sun is not to set on one who has been put to death.' 16. And one of them said, 'Give him gall with vinegar to drink.' And having mixed it they gave it to him to drink. 17. And they fulfilled all things and they accumulated the sins on their head. 18. And many were going about with lamps, supposing it was night, stumbled. 19. And the Lord cried out saying, 'My power, the power, you have left me.' And saying this he was taken up. 20. And at the same hour the curtain of the temple in Jerusalem was torn in two.

## TEXT CRITICAL NOTES

1. This is the first of the nine occasions when the scribe omits the movable final ν at the end of the line and marks this with a horizontal bar.[357] In the other eight examples the crossbar is written supralinearly. Here, however, it is written at the same level of the middle crossbar of the epsilon and to the right of the letter. This appears to be due to inconsistent scribal practice.

2. The form written here by the scribe is an orthographic variant of the regular spelling πεφονευμένῳ. Such confusion between short and long vowel sounds is not uncommon in later *koine* manu-

---

357 On the use of the moveable ν see BDF §20, 12–13.

scripts. Caragounis demonstrates the occurrence of this type of scribal error in 𝔓⁶⁶ where, at Jn 5.29, instead of the correct reading ἐκπορεύσονται the scribe writes ἐκπορεύσωνται.[358]

3. The word written by the scribe as ἐπέσαντο, has caused substantial discussion in the various editions of the text. This debate stems from two problems: (i) the text is overwritten by the scribe at this point; and (ii) the form ἐπέσαντο is either orthographically incorrect, or syntactically incomplete. The first problem is commented upon by Kraus and Nicklas who observe, 'The scribe overwrote the original text with ἐπέσ, under the overwritten π can still be seen the remains of an alleged σ, and under the second σ before the αυτο, which was probably added later, an underwritten μ.'[359] Their observation is correct concerning the fact that the text has been overwritten, although it is extremely difficult to reconstruct the underwriting. The result is that the third and fourth letters are oversized, and the middle horizontal stoke of the second epsilon is thinkened to obscure what was written beneath.

The second problem involves determining what the scribe actually meant (or meant to write) when he penned the form ἐπέσαντο. The correct aorist third person plural form of πίπτω is ἐπέσαν, not ἐπέσαντο. This incorrect form has led to various attempts to introduce emendations. Vaganay helpfully organizes the suggestions under three heads:[360]

1. Adding a conjunction and changing the form of the verb.
   (καὶ) νομίζοντες ὅτι νύξ ἐστιν ἀνέπεσαν.

   τότε...                                          von Schubert[361]

   (καὶ) νομίζοντες ὅτι νύξ ἐστιν ἀνεπαύσαντο.  Gebhardt[362]

   νομίζοντες ὅτι νύξ ἐστιν (καὶ) ἀνέπεσαντο.  Lods[363]

---

[358] C.C. Caragounis, *The Development of Greek and the New Testament* (Tübingen: Mohr Siebeck, 2004) 514.

[359] 'Der Schreiber überschrieb ursprünglichen Text mit ἐπές, wobei unter bzw. über π noch Reste eines vermeintlichen σ zu sehen sind und das zweite σ vor αυτο wohl nachträglich (über μ?) zugefügt wurde.' Kraus und Nicklas, *Das Petrusevangelium und die Petrusapokalypse*, 36.

[360] Vaganay, *L'Évangile de Pierre*, 253–254.

[361] H. von Schubert, *Die Composition des pseudopetrinischen Evangelienfragments* (Berlin, 1893).

[362] Gebhardt, *Das Evangelium und die Apokalypse des Petrus*, 43.

[363] Lods, 'L'Évangile et l'Apocalypse de Pierre avec le texte grec du livre d'Hénoch', 220.

νομίζοντες ὅτι νύξ ἐστιν (καὶ) ἐπιέσαντο.            Rauschen[364]

νομίζοντες ὅτι νύξ ἐστιν (καὶ) πταίοντες.           Lejay[365]

2. Changing only the form of the verb.

νομίζοντες ὅτι νύξ ἐστιν ἐξίσταντο.                Redpath[366]

νομίζοντες ὅτι νύξ ἐστιν ἐσπεύσαντο.               Bruston[367]

νομίζοντες ὅτι νύξ ἐστιν ἐνέπεσαν. τότε            Lundborg[368]

νομίζοντες ὅτι νύξ ἐστιν μέση.                     Piccolomini[369]

νομίζοντες ὅτι νύξ ἐστιν αἰσία.                    Hilfenfeld.[370]

3. Adding a joining particle without altering the sense of the verb.

νομίζοντες ὅτι νύξ ἐστιν ἔπεσαν τε                 Robinson[371]

νομίζοντες ὅτι νύξ ἐστιν. τινὲς δὲ ἔπεσαν.         Swete[372]

νομίζοντες ὅτι νύξ ἐστιν. μὴ πέσοιντο.             Bennet[373]

νομίζοντες ὅτι νύξ ἐστιν καὶ ἔπεσαν.               Harnack[374]

It needs to be asked, however, whether any of these emendations is actually necessary. The scribe's 'error' may simply have been to write the aorist third person form of πίπτω with a middle rather than an

---

[364] G. Rauschen, *Florilegium patristicum*, III (2nd ed.; Bonn, 1914) 46f.

[365] Lejay, 'L'Évangile de Pierre', 59–84, 267–270.

[366] H.A. Redpath, 'The Gospel According to Peter', *The Academy* 42.10, (1892) 544. Note Vaganay cites this just as volume 10, which is the part number for the year, not the volume number. Redpath's suggested readings are made in light of the first edition of Swete's pamphlet, *The Apocryphal Gospel of Peter. The Greek Text of the Newly Discovered Fragment* (London: Macmillan and Co., November, 1892). In relation to this prosed emendment Redpath states, 'As a confirmation of this reading, we have later on ἐπίσαντας (p. 12, 1.11) for ἐπιστάντας.' It is not altogether clear how this confirms Redpath's proposal of ἐξίσταντο, beyond showing that on one occasion the scribe omitted a τ following a σ.

[367] C. Bruston, 'De quelques texts difficiles de l'Évangile de Pierre', *Revue des études grecques* (1897) 58–65.

[368] M. Lundborg, *Det sk. Petrusevangeliet ett nyfunnet fragment ur en fornkristlig apocryf* (Lund, 1893).

[369] E. Piccolomini, 'Sul testo dei fragmenti dell' Evangelio e dell' Apocalisse del Pseudo Pietro' in *Rendiconti della Reale Accadem. Dei Lincei, Classe discienzi morali, storichi e filogiche*, tom. VIII, 1899, fasc. 7–8 (Roma, 1899) 389–404.

[370] Hilfenfeld, 'Das Petrus-Evangelium über Leiden und Auferstehung Jesu', Part 2, 235. In his first edition of the text Hilfenfeld suggested the following reconstruction νομίζοντες ὅτι νύξ ἐστιν καὶ ἐπαίσαντο, Part 1, 442.

[371] Robinson and James, *The Gospel according to Peter and the Revelation of Peter*, 84.

[372] Swete comments that 'ἐπέσαντο may have been rewritten: the scribe seems to have written νυξεστινεσ.' Swete, *The Akhmîm Fragment of the Apocryphal Gospel of St Peter*, 9.

[373] E.N. Bennett, 'The Gospel According to Peter', *Classical Review* (1893) 41.

[374] Harnack, *Bruchstücke des Evangeliums und der Apokalypse des Petrus*, 9.

active ending. Such a mistake could have been generated in the scribe's thinking by the future forms of πίπτω which do take middle endings, i.e., πεσοῦμαι. Such an error would reflect the limited abilities of the scribe as demonstrated throughout the manuscript. It may well be the case that his native language was Coptic and that he made, on occasions, errors common to non-native speakers of a language. While it is not impossible that a conjunction such as a καί may have dropped out in the transmission of this text, this is not necessarily the case.

4. The form αὐτός does not agree in gender or case with the following noun ὥρας. The most commonly accepted correction is to change a single letter of αὐτός, thus producing a feminine form αὐτῆς, which then agrees in both case and gender with the following noun ὥρας.[375]

## COMMENTARY

**5.15a  ἦν δὲ μεσημβρία, καὶ σκότος κατέσχε πᾶσαν τὴν Ἰουδαίαν.**
This verse opens with the third temporal reference contained in the narrative. Earlier, through the voice of Antipas, the audience has been informed that 'the Sabbath is drawing on' (*Gos. Pet.* 2.5). This date is further clarified in *Gos. Pet.* 3.6 when the narrator comments that the events occurred 'before the first day of unleavened bread.' Now here the narrator indicates the time of day at which certain events take place, namely around noon, μεσημβρία. This term occurs only twice in the New Testament, both in Acts (8.26; 22.6), but as Swete notes it occurs with the same sense as here in *Gos. Pet.* 5.15.[376] In comparison to the synoptic accounts, μεσημβρία replaces their uniform reference to the sixth hour (Matt 27.45; Mk 15.33; Lk 23.44), although the term ὡσεί introduces a note of approximation into the description, καὶ ἦν ἤδη ὡσεὶ ὥρα ἕκτη.[377] The fourth gospel also contains a reference in its passion account to 'the sixth hour', but this occurs in a different

---

[375] Kraus und Nicklas, *Das Petrusevangelium und die Petrusapokalypse*, 36.

[376] Swete, apparently missing the reference to Acts 8.26, states, 'in the N.T. only in Acts xxii. 6.' Swete, *The Akhmîm Fragment of the Apocryphal Gospel of St Peter*, 7–8.

[377] As Bock observes, 'Luke uses ὡσεί (about) frequently to show approximate time; Luke 3:23; 9:14 (twice), 28; 22:41; cf. Acts 2:15; 3:1; 10:3, 9; 23:23. Bock, *Luke 9:51–24:53*, 1858.

context describing the time when Pilate presented Jesus to the Jews, there using the phrase ἴδε ὁ βασιλεὺς ὑμῶν (Jn 19.14).[378]

The reference to darkness over Judaea is also reminiscent of the synoptic accounts of Jesus' crucifixion. Mark and Luke agree in their description σκότος ἐγένετο ἐφ' ὅλην τὴν γῆν ἕως ὥρας ἐνάτης (Mk 15.33; Lk 23.44), Matthew modifies this only slightly by replacing the two words ἐφ' ὅλην with the phrase ἐπὶ πᾶσαν (Matt 27.45). Although the sense conveyed in the *Gospel of Peter* is the same, there are significant differences. First, in the Akhmîm text the verb κατέχω[379] replaces γίνομαι. Second the geographical reference becomes more explicit, naming Judaea rather than a generalized description of the land. This perhaps suggests a degree of unfamiliarity with the location of the events, which the intrusive narrator clarifies for his audience. Vaganay also suggests that this change may also be motivated by apologetic concerns. In limiting the potentially all encompassing reference ἐφ' ὅλην τὴν γῆν the author may be wishing to demonstrate that this darkness was a judgment on the inhabitants of Judaea alone, and not on the whole earth.[380] Third, the temporal reference that describes the duration of the darkness is omitted at this point, although it will be employed in *Gos. Pet.* 6.22. The author uses the space he creates in the narrative by delaying the announcement of the return of the sun in the ninth hour to describe the events that take place during these three hours, as well as to suffuse the narrative with the sense of gloom that is brought about by the unnatural darkness.

**5.15b** καὶ ἐθορυβοῦντο καὶ ἠγωνίων μήποτε ὁ ἥλιος ἔδυ ἐπειδὴ ἔτι ἔζη. Having described the descent of the darkness on the land of Judaea, the narrative assesses the impact it has on those who are conducting the crucifixion. As the participants in this version of the passion are Jews and not Romans, their concerns and fears centre on religio-legal matters, rather than on the strange phenomenon

---

[378] In relation to the Johannine chronology during the Passion, Barrett notes that the phrase ὥρα ἦν ὡς ἕκτη (Jn 19.14) is 'another conflict with the synoptic gospels.' Barrett, *The Gospel according to St John*, 454.

[379] This verb covers wide semantic range. BDAG lists the current reference under its fifth group of meanings 'to have a place as one's own, *take into one's possession, occupy*' (533). The usage of the verb in Lk 14.9 is also placed in this grouping, Here the sense is that of darkness 'occupying' or 'covering' the geographical space in question.

[380] Vaganay, *L'Évangile de Pierre*, 249.

itself. In the synoptic accounts there is no report of the impact that the darkness had upon those by whom it is experienced.[381] By contrast, the *Gospel of Peter* depicts the twin emotions of fear and distress, ἐθορυβοῦντο καὶ ἠγωνίων. However, as the remainder of the verse makes clear, these emotions do not stem from the unnatural phenomemon itself, but rather that the inability to see the sun will lead to an inadvertent transgression of Torah stipulation. The Torah ruling which is cited at the conclusion of the verse prohibits a corpse to remain on display after sunset. At this point, the narrative employs the imperfect form ἔζη in combination with the adverb ἔτι to make clear to readers that Jesus was still alive at this point. However, it is the crowd which is unable, due to the darkness, to consult the usual solar reference to determine if it had transgressed the law.

Both Mara[382] and Brown draw attention to the verbal similarities that occur between *Gos. Pet.* 5.15 and Amos 8.9. As Brown comments in relation to the expressions μεσημβρία and ὁ ἥλιον ἔδη, these 'words echo the description of the day of the Lord in (the LXX of) Amos 8.9 which, as we have already suggested, may have given rise to the symbolism in Mark.'[383] The Septuagintal passage reads as follows:

> καὶ ἔσται ἐν ἐκείνῃ τῇ ἡμέρᾳ λέγει κύριος ὁ θεός καὶ δύσεται ὁ ἥλιος μεσημβρίας καὶ συσκοτάσει ἐπὶ τῆς γῆς ἐν ἡμέρᾳ τὸ φῶς (Amos 8.9)

Undoubtedly there is a striking range of shared terminology in the second half of this verse which aligns with terms used in *Gos. Pet.* 5.15. Apart from the two elements listed by Brown, one should also consider the σκότος terminology which occurs in a verbal form in Amos and a nominal form in the Akhmîm text. Thus, while Amos 8.9 may have shaped the Markan narrative, it appears that the the imagery from Amos has been exploited to a greater extent and to a more readily identifiable degree in the *Gospel of Peter*. It is no longer possible to determine if the author was responsible for this increased correspondence, or whether he utilised a tradition that had aligned this aspect of the Passion more closely with Amos 8.9.

---

[381] Vaganay comments, 'Cette crainte ressentie per les exécuteurs est un motif inconnu de la tradition évangélique.' *L'Évangile de Pierre*, 250.

[382] Mara, *Évangile de Pierre*, 125.

[383] Brown, *The Death of the Messiah*, vol 2, 1037.

**5.15c** γέγραπται αὐτοῖς ἥλιον μὴ δῦναι ἐπὶ πεφονευμένῳ. The reason for concern about the sun having set is now made fully explicit, if evening had already come those carrying out the execution would contravene the scriptural ruling that is quoted here. Brown notes that only the *Gospel of Peter* cites scripture at this point in the narrative, although such thinking may stand behind the canonical accounts with their depiction of a burial before the start of the Sabbath. He does not feel that the use of a citation of this point can be explained only as a means of providing clarification for Gentile readers.[384] Instead he sees the general anti-Jewish sentiment forming the basis of this addition. 'More likely (and perhaps in addition) it represents an antiJewish implication of Hypocrisy: Those who crucified Jesus were extremely careful about such minutiae as the exact hour of sunset, but they did not hesitate to mock the Son of God (3:9).'[385]

The ruling, which the Akhmîm text cites as scripture, appears to be dependent upon the ordinance contained in Deut 21.22–23a, which prescribes details concerning the disposal of the body of an executed criminal.

> ἐὰν δὲ γένηται ἔν τινι ἁμαρτία κρίμα θανάτου καὶ ἀποθάνῃ καὶ κρεμάσητε αὐτὸν ἐπὶ ξύλου οὐκ ἐπικοιμηθήσεται τὸ σῶμα αὐτοῦ ἐπὶ τοῦ ξύλου ἀλλὰ ταφῇ θάψετε αὐτὸν ἐν τῇ ἡμέρᾳ ἐκείνῃ (Deut 21.22–23a)

It is immediately apparent that although the idea presented by the *Gospel of Peter* is much the same as that found in the Deuteronomic prescription, there are few points of contact in terms of vocabulary. Mara states that the text offers an interpretation that is faithful to idea contained in Deut 21.23, but she does not highlight the divergences in terminology.[386] Brown comments on the similarity in terminology between the citation in *Gos. Pet.* 5.15c and the injunction in Deut 24.15 concerning payment of a day-worker.[387] That text stipulates αὐθημερὸν ἀποδώσεις τὸν μισθὸν αὐτοῦ οὐκ ἐπιδύσεται ὁ ἥλιος ἐπ' αὐτῷ (Deut 24.15 LXX). However, standard terminology depicting the setting sun is not strong enough to support the suggestion that this verse has influenced the citation in *Gos. Pet.* 5.15.

---

[384] Brown, *The Death of the Messiah*, vol 2, 1037.

[385] Brown, *The Death of the Messiah*, vol 2, 1037–1038.

[386] Mara simply states, '*Ev.P.* 15 donne une interprétation fidèle de *Deut*. 21, 23'. Mara, *Évangile de Pierre*, 128.

[387] Brown, *The Death of the Messiah*, vol 2, 1037.

**5.16a** καί τις αὐτῶν εἶπεν· Ποτίσατε αὐτὸν χολὴν μετὰ ὄξους.
The natural flow of the narrative is somewhat interrupted as it breaks
off to describe the actions of indefinite characters. This interruption
does allow the author to further accent the culpability of the people
who carry out these actions. The opening three words καί τις αὐτῶν followed by an aorist verb parallels the structure of the clause employed
in 3.8 to describe the unnamed person who brings the crown of thorns.
Again an individual emerges from the wider crowd both as a representative and also to carry out a specific action, or to speak on behalf
of the mob. The construction is also reminiscent of the one used by
Matthew when recounting the same incident, καὶ εὐθέως δραμὼν εἷς ἐξ
αὐτῶν καὶ λαβὼν σπόγγον πλήσας τε ὄξους (Matt 27.48). The tone used
at this juncture in the *Gospel of Peter* differs from that in the fourth
gospel. In the Johannine account, the offering of the vinegar, ὄξος, is an
an act of compassion in response to Jesus' cry διψῶ (Jn 19.28). However, in the Matthean and Markan narratives there is an air of mockery
in the action. In response to the cry of desolation, which occurs prior
to the offering of a drink in the first two gospels, the one who proffers the wine soaked sponge addresses the onlookers with the somewhat voyeuristic words, ἄφετε ἴδωμεν εἰ ἔρχεται Ἠλίας καθελεῖν αὐτόν
(Mk 15.36). Evans picks up on this note of mockery in the Markan
scene, 'the gesture is part of the mockery that has been going on peri-
odically since the conclusion of the hearing before the ruling priests
(14:65).'[388] By contrast, while Luke states explicitly that the offering
of the drink is an act of mockery, he identifies it as an action carried out by the soldiers and not by those observing the crucifixion,
ἐνέπαιξαν δὲ αὐτῷ καὶ οἱ στρατιῶται προσερχόμενοι, ὄξος προσφέροντες
αὐτῷ (Lk 23.36). Bock thinks that the difference between Luke and the
other synoptic accounts 'may indicate the presence of another source.'[389]
Similarly, Fitzmyer noting that this is the first time that Luke has introduced Roman soldiers into the crucifixion scene states that their presence 'reflects a historical detail, even though Luke has sought to play
down their involvement.'[390] However, he is less clear as to whether he
thinks that it is a historical detail that the soldiers gave the sour wine
to Jesus, or if this is due Lukan redactional reworking of the Markan

---

[388] C.A. Evans, *Mark 8:27–16:20*, WBC 34B (Nashville: Thomas Nelson, 2001) 508.
[389] Bock, *Luke 9:51–24:53*, 1853.
[390] Fitzmyer, *The Gospel According to Luke X–XXIV*, 1505.

account. Two acts of offering a beverage to Jesus on the cross seem unlikely, especially as this would mean that the evangelists have each chosen to report one of these without overlap with the other scene.

Within the *Gospel of Peter* the notice about the drink given to Jesus interrupts the description of the darkness, which occurs either side of this detail (5.15 and 5.18). Moreover, unlike the canonical gospels, the *Gospel of Peter* offers no clues in the narrative context to explain the reason for the provision of a beverage. This is in contrast to the fourth gospel where Jesus declares his thirst (Jn 19.28), or the setting in Matthew and Mark when the drink is offered to what the crowd seem to have assumed was a delirious Jesus crying for Elijah. Yet as Brown observes, '[t]he author of *GPet* kept the Mark/Matt death context for the offering of vinegary wine, but he eliminated the Mark/Matthew awkwardness by eliminating or forgetting the Elijah component.'[391] The fact that the offering of a drink appears in the *Gospel of Peter* as a tradition without context, and also removes the awkwardness of the combination of 'this wine offering with an eschatological reference to Elijah',[392] strongly suggests that the author is working with existing synoptic traditions, but creating a less problematic narrative at one level although this results in a certain degree of disjointedness at times. The author is relying on his audience to overcome any such 'gaps' by use of their existing knowledge of the gospel tradition.

Like the Matthean account (Matt 27.34) the *Gospel of Peter* also mentions 'gall' χολή in connection with the offering of vinegar-wine. In the first gospel this reference occurs immediately prior to the crucifixion, and this drink-mixture is best understood as some kind of sedative to lessen the pain, although it is reported as being refused by Jesus. In the Babylonian Talmud a tradition is preserved that commands, on the basis of the text in Prov 31.6, that a sedative of this kind should be administered. 'When one is led out to execution he is given a goblet of wine containing a grain of francincence, in order to benumb his senses, for it is written, "Give strong drink unto him who is ready to perish, and wine unto the bitter in soul."' (*b. Sanh.* 43a). While Mark 15.23 contains a reference to wine mingled with myrrh ἐδίδουν αὐτῷ ἐσμυρνισμένον οἶνον, in the Matthean account the reference to myrrh is replaced by the term χολή. Davies and Allison

---

[391] Brown, *The Death of the Messiah*, vol 2, 1060.
[392] Brown, *The Death of the Messiah*, vol 2, 1060.

offer two reasons for this alteration. First, 'the removal of myrrh (in Mark either an anodyne or perfume) makes for distance from 2.11.'[393] Second, they adduce a positive reason, namely that the use of the term 'χολή creates an allusion to LXX Ps 68.22.'[394] The Septuagintal text thus contains the combination of wine and gall.

καὶ ἔδωκαν εἰς τὸ βρῶμά μου χολὴν καὶ εἰς τὴν δίψαν μου ἐπότισάν με ὄξος (LXX Ps 68.22).

Brown categorically states, 'this psalm is certainly in mind in Matt and GPet, for both mention gall, the other psalm component beside the vinegary wine.'[395] While Matthew does appear to have intentionally conformed the Markan description to the text in the Psalms, another explanation may be possible in the case of the Akhmîm text. First it has to be acknowledged that the combination χολὴν μετὰ ὄξους that occurs in Gos. Pet. 5.16, unlike the Matthean account, aligns with the more closely with the text of LXX Ps 68.22. However, it is also the case that the author of the Akhmîm text has moved the reference to 'gall' from the pre-crucifixion first offering of drink (a detail deleted in the Gospel of Peter) and instead incorporates it in what in Matthew and Mark is the second offering of a beverage (Matt 27.47//Mk 15.36). Since in the synoptic tradition the reference to vinegar-wine ὄξος is already present in that second scene, it is unnecessary to postulate that the combination was an intentional allusion to the LXX Ps 68.22 on the part of the author of the Gospel of Peter. Moreover, the combination of 'gall and vinegar' is made in the Epistle of Barnabas in the context of the description of Jesus' foreknowledge of the events which were about to befall him.

Ἐπειδὴ ἐμὲ ὑπὲρ ἁμαρτιῶν μέλλοντα τοῦ λαοῦ μου τοῦ καινοῦ προσφέρειν τὴν σάρκα μου μέλλετε ποτίζειν χολὴν μετὰ ὄξους (Barn. 7.5)

'Since you are about to give me gall mixed with vinegar to drink – when I am about to offer my flesh on behalf of the sins of my new people.'[396]

---

[393] Davies and Allison, The Gospel According to Saint Matthew, vol. III, 612.
[394] Davies and Allison, The Gospel According to Saint Matthew, vol. III, 612.
[395] Brown, The Death of the Messiah, vol 2, 1061.
[396] The translation is taken from B. Ehrman, The Apostolic Fathers, vol. II, LCL 25 (Cambridge, Mass.: Harvard University Press, 2003) 37.

Rather, the primary motive appears to be emphasizing the onging mockery and active torment by the crowd. This is achieved by inserting the negative term χολή, which denotes something bitter to the taste or even poisonous. Hence, as Hagner comments in relation to the Matthean usage where there is a more clearly demonstrable desire to align the text with that of the LXX Ps 68.22, 'The wine here is therefore perhaps to be distinguished from the drugged wine, the wine mixed with myrrh (Mark 15.23)…The offering of this wine involves cruelty and mockery consistent with the context of the Ps 69 reference.'[397] Thus in the *Gospel of Peter* the purpose of the drink is to intensify Jesus' suffering.

**5.16b** καὶ κεράσαντες ἐπότισαν. Like the synoptic gospels there is no clear description of Jesus partaking of the liquid mixture that is presented to him. However, in distintion from the canonical tradition the *Gospel of Peter* shows no interest in describing the mechanics of offering a drink to one undergoing crucifixion. There is no description of either the wine soaked sponge, or the stick which is used to elevate it. Presumably this is a further instance when the author expects his audience to draw upon the shared repository of gospel traditions to fill lacunae in the text with well known details.

The syntactical ordering of the aorist participle κερασάντες preceding the main verb ἐπότισαν may be intended to communicate that the former action is concluded prior to that of the main verb commencing. The verb κεράννυμι is rare in the NT occurring only at two points in Revelation (14.10; 18.6).[398] However, it is attested in other early Jewish[399] and Christian literature[400] as well as in other Greek sources.[401] In the present context the aorist participle is based on the variant lexical form κεράω, which is a commonly attested alternative root in classical literature.[402] It is uncertain whether the main verb in the clause, ἐπότισαν, denotes offering the mixture to Jesus to drink, or whether it constitutes the torment of forcing Jesus to drink this mixture. In

---

[397] Here Hagner is using the Masoretic text numbering of the Psalms, rather than that of the LXX. Hagner, *Matthew 14–28*, 835.

[398] See BDAG, 540.

[399] *Bel* 11 (LXX); *PsSol* 8.14; *SibOr* 11, 126.

[400] *Smyrn.* 3.2; Oenomaus, frag. 6 in Eus., *Praep. Ev. 5.*

[401] See LSJ, 940.

[402] For examples of the use of alternative roots, κεράννυμι, κεραννύω, κεραίω, or κεράω, again see LSJ, 940–941.

relation to this term, Vaganay once more detects a reminiscence of LXX Ps 68.22.[403] Again, it is questionable whether the retention of this term is due to the author's independent reflection on the Psalm, or if it is transmitted through the medium of the canonical gospels, or even other early Christian traditions surrounding the passion. Either way, the concept of torment comes to the fore, and the poisonous mixture of gall and vinegar may be understood in the wider narrative as a means to speed Jesus' death,[404] in order to address the concern that he might be hanging on the cross alive when the no longer visible sun had set.

**5.17a   καὶ ἐπλήρωσαν πάντα.** Many commentators have suggested that these words refer both specifically and exclusively to fulfilling the prophecies of Ps 68.22 (LXX).[405] Swete states that this 'fulfilment of Psalm lxix. completed the accomplishment of the Passion prophecies.'[406] Harnack does not comment on this issue, instead simply he judges there to be no parallel with the canonical gospels.[407] However, it may well be the case that the author of the Akhmîm text is not focussing only on the detail of the 'gall and vinegar' as the reference of fulfilment, but on the wider sequence of events that have comprised the torment, including the division of clothes, the pierecing and other details. In relation to these torments and mockeries, at no point has scripture been explicitly cited. Direct quotation has only been introduced in relation to Torah prescriptions about corpse impurity (*Gos. Pet.* 2.5; 5.15). Rather, the central issue appears to be the whole concept of the fulfilment of scripture, which at times in early Christianity appears as a fundamental area of dispute between Christians and Jews making rival claims concerning the divinely sanctioned status of the respective religions.

---

[403] He states, 'Il lui suffit d'avoir retenu le terme même de la prophétie (ἐπότισαν).' Vaganay, *L'Évangile de Pierre*, 252.

[404] Robinson also suggests this to be the case. He states, 'It seems the draught here given was intended to hasten death.' Robinson and James, *The Gospel according to Peter and the Revelation of Peter*, 20.

[405] Mara observes, 'La raison profonde de la mention de ce geste [the offering of the drink of gall and vinegar] semble devoir être cherchée dans le désir de refléter le plus fidèlement possible le *Ps. 68*, auquel il est fait allusion de nouveau dans *Ev.P. 17*.' Mara, *Évangile de Pierre*, 131.

[406] Swete, *The Akhmîm Fragment of the Apocryphal Gospel of St Peter*, 9.

[407] Harnack, *Bruchstücke des Evangeliums und der Apokalypse des Petrus*, 26–27.

**5.17b**   καὶ ἐτελείωσαν κατὰ τῆς κεφαλῆς αὐτῶν τὰ ἁμαρτήματα.
Such 'fulfilment of all things' has negative consequences for those who
degraded Jesus with the series of physical and verbal insults. The narrator describes the catalogue of torments that the mob has perpetrated as
'sins' that are heaped upon those involved in these actions. Although
it is not possible to make a strong case for direct influence, because of
the lack of shared vocabulary and the fact that this is authorial comment rather than reported speech, there are conceptual overlaps with
the cry of the people in the first gospel, καὶ ἀποκριθεὶς πᾶς ὁ λαὸς εἶπεν·
τὸ αἷμα αὐτοῦ ἐφ' ἡμᾶς καὶ ἐπὶ τὰ τέκνα ἡμῶν (Matt 27.25). Swete,
however, sees a stronger link, 'κατὰ τῆς κεφαλῆς probably refers to
Matt. xxvii. 25 ἐφ' ἡμᾶς.'[408] Although, for the reasons outlined above, it
appears impossible to advance a strong case for dependence. The verb
τελειόω has a range of meanings,[409] which tend to be generally positive
in nuance. Here, however, the connotation is negative, and the sense is
that of filling a full measure of sins.[410] This negative aspect is paralleled
in other Christian texts.

> ἵνα κἀκεῖνοι τελειωθῶσιν τοῖς ἁμαρτήμασιν        (*Barn* 14.5)
> ἐπεὶ δὲ πεπλήρωτο μὲν ἡ ἡμετέρα ἀδιδία καὶ τελείως πεφανέρωτο, ὅτι
> ὁ μισθὸς αὐτῆς κόλασις καὶ θάνατος προσεδοκᾶτο    (*Ep. Diog.* 9.2)
> ἐτέλεσαν τν πονηρίαν αὐτῶν                  (*Didasc.* 5.17)

In these instances the term τελειόω, or the related adverb τελείως, is
connected with sin or wickedness. The subject of the verb could be
an indefinite third person group 'they', or it could be taken to be the
plural definite noun τὰ ἁμαρτήματα. While grammatically it is possible
for 'the sins' to be read as a nominative third person subject rather
than an accusative third person plural object, this appears unlikely
since this would mean that the change in subject from the previous
clause καὶ ἐπλήρωσαν πάντα would have been inelegantly introduced
and, furthermore, this would also be in tension with the use of indefinite references to people as subjects in the narrative. Vaganay correctly

---

[408] Swete, *The Akhmîm Fragment of the Apocryphal Gospel of St Peter*, 9.
[409] In BDAG the use of the term is group under three primary semantic heads,
although the second is subdivided into five categories. BDAG, 996.
[410] See BDAG, 996.

rejects Piccolomini's proposal to correct the text in light of Ps 7.17 (LXX) ἐπιστρέψει ὁ πόνος αὐτοῦ εἰς κεφαλὴν αὐτοῦ καὶ ἐπὶ κορυφὴν αὐτοῦ ἡ ἀδικία αὐτοῦ καταβήσεται.[411] Piccolomini reconstructs *Gos. Pet.* 5.17b as ἐτελείωσαν (καὶ) κατὰ τῆς κεφαλῆς (αὐτῶν κατέβησαν) αὐτῶν τὰ ἁμαρτήματα. In opposition to this theory Vaganay astutely states that this theory is 'a little too complicated.'[412] It is interesting to note the recurrent theme in Matt 27.25, *Barn* 14.5 and *Gos. Pet.* 5.17, where the mistreatment and abuse of Jesus results in sin or blood symbolically coming upon members of the Jewish people. Here it is possible to see the early Christian theme that condemnation is visited upon the Jews primarily because of their role in the passion and crucifixion.

**5.18** περιήρχοντο δὲ πολλοὶ μετὰ λύχνων νομίζοντες ὅτι νύξ ἐστιν ἐπέσαντο. With these words the author returns to describing the impact of the unnatural darkness that had descended on Judaea. The opening verb περιέρχομαι denotes an aimless wandering or meandering path that cannot be totally controlled. In a number of manuscripts of Acts 28.13 περιελθόντες is a variant reading of περιελόντες.[413] In this context it describes the path of a ship governed by the wind. Another use of the term also occurs in a variant reading in Acts. At Acts 13.6 the second corrector of Codex Bezae[414] uses the expression καὶ περιελθόντων to depict the unplanned travels of Paul, Barnabas and John Mark on the island of Cyprus. The use in *Gos. Pet.* 5.18 likewise appears to reflect slightly confused meanderings, occasioned by this strange astronomical or meterological phenomenon. Those

---

[411] E. Piccolomini, 'Sul testo dei fragmenti dell' Evangelio e dell' Apocalisse del Pseudo Pietro', 389–404.

[412] Vaganay, *L'Évangile de Pierre*, 252.

[413] The variant περιελθόντες is preserved in the following mss 𝔓⁷⁴ ℵ² A 066. 1739 𝔐 lat sy. The textual support for this reading was deemed strong enough for it to be printed as the preferred reading in NA²⁵. However, in NA²⁶ and NA²⁷ it is relegated to the critical apparatus. The decision has not been taken on the basis of freshly discovered mss evidence. Metzger states that the committee of the UBSGNT preferred this term 'taking the word to be a technical nautical expression of uncertain meaning (it may be a shorter expression for τὰς ἀγκύρας περιελόντες, as in 27.40, "weighing (anchor)," "casting loose"). See B.M. Metzger, *A Textual Commentary on the Greek New Testament* (2nd ed.; Stuttgart: Deutsche Bibelgesellschaft, 1994) 443. It should be noted that codex Bezae is not extant at Acts 28.13.

[414] See the critical apparatus of NA²⁷ (357) and F.J. Foakes Jackson and Kirsopp Lake (eds.), *The Beginnings of Christianity*, Part 1 *The Acts of the Apostles*, Vol. III, J.H. Ropes (ed.), 'The Text' (London: Macmillan, 1926) 117.

involved in the scene of bewilderment are, as is the author's penchant, described in indefinite terms simply as πολλοί. Obviously this term seeks to show that the impact was widespread, but the author offers no further details concerning the composition or identity of this collective group. In part this is due to the fact that this scene is a redactional creation without canonical parallel.[415] Those described as πολλοί respond to the darkness by going about with lamps, μετὰ λύχνων. The author is not interested to explain how lamps where so readily obtained by so many in order to cope with such an unpredictable event. The focus is on the all pervasive darkness plunging the crowd into nighttime conditions, not on the mechanics of explaining how they came to have lamps. In the passion narratives of the canonical gospels artifical light is only described in the night arrest of Jesus described by the fourth evangelist ἔρχεται ἐκεῖ μετὰ φανῶν καὶ λαμπάδων (Jn 18.3). This reference does not stand behind the description of lamps in *Gos. Pet.* 5.18, the terminology differs, it occurs during the arrest scene, not as the crucifixion reaches its climax, and furthermore in the fourth gospel the artificial light is not used in response to unnatural celestial event. This tradition contained in *Gos. Pet.* 5.18 is shared with the non-canonical text the *Anaphora Pilati*, ἐν παντὶ τῷ κόσμῳ λύχνους ἀπὸ ἕκτης ὥρας ἕως ὀψίας (*Anaph. Pilati* B 7). It is not possible to trace the direction of dependence between these two texts, or to tell if they are independently drawing from other tradition, whether oral or written.

The next clause revisits the initial concern that perhaps, unbeknown to the crowd, night had arrived. In fact the text states that many supposed this to be the case, νομίζοντες ὅτι νύξ ἐστιν. Again, this description emphasizes the degree of the darkness.[416] The thick darkness is reminiscent of the penultimate affliction that besets the land of Egypt prior to the Exodus. In Ex 10.21–23 there is a description of a palpable darkness which covers the land for three days. Although this story is not directly exploited in the Akhmîm text, it does show the existence of a wider judgment motif that associates unnatural darkness during what are normally daylight hours as an expression of divine disapproval. In the *Gospel of Peter* this darkness is disorientating, both

---

[415] Harnack, *Bruchstücke des Evangeliums und der Apokalypse des Petrus*, 27.
[416] As Vaganay comments 'Les Juifs prennent des lampes, parce que, à l'intensité des ténèbres, ils croient la nuit arrivée.' Vaganay, *L'Évangile de Pierre*, 253.

physically and mentally. The crowd find it difficult to move around and they are bewildered by what is happening.

The final word in this verse is syntactically difficult, and there have been a number of conjectural emendations suggested to produce a greater degree of connectivity with the foregoing material.[417] Notwithstanding the awkward sentence structure, the meaning that the author seeks to convey through use of the term ἐπέσαντο is clear. The night-like conditions impair the ability of the mob to move around, they are prone to stagger, stumble, or even fall as they wander about. Robinson suggests that this term finds resonances in both the OT and NT. He states, '[f]or ἐπέσαντο, at the end of the sentence…cf. Isa. lix. 10 καὶ πεσοῦνται ἐν μεσημβρίᾳ ὡς ἐν μεσονυκτίῳ. It also seems an echo of Jn. xviii. 3, 6 ἔρχεται [ἐκεῖ] μετὰ φανῶν καὶ λαμπάδων…καὶ ἔπεσαν χαμαί.'[418] The passage from Isaiah is striking because apart from the verb πίπτω, which occurs here in *Gos. Pet.* 5.18, the less common term μεσημβρία is also found in the wider context, being used in the initial description of the darkness in 5.15. By contrast, it is dubious whether an allusion to Jn 18.3, 6 was ever part of the author's intention, since in that context it is not the darkness that causes members of the arresting party to fall prostrate on the ground, but the self-identification of Jesus, which takes on theophanic overtones.

**5.19a  καὶ ὁ κ̄ς̄ ἀνεβόησε λέγων.** In this pericope, to this point, the text has focussed on descriptions of the darkness and the confusion or behaviour of the crowd. The author now re-centres the audience's attentention on 'the Lord', who had fallen into the background while the strange physical phenomenon and its accompanying effects were being described. The opening words of *Gos. Pet.* 5.19 serve to preface the only reported utterance of Jesus in the narrative. In the canonical gospels the so-called 'cry of dereliction' is present only in the first two gospels, in both cases prefaced by a brief editorial introduction. Comparison of the five introductory words in the *Gospel of Peter*, used by the narrator to introduce the cry from the cross, suggest dependence upon the Matthean, rather than the Markan account at

---

[417] See text critical note 3 in this section.
[418] Robinson and James, *The Gospel according to Peter and the Revelation of Peter*, 20, note 1.

this point. There are two reasons to support this suggestion that can be seen by comparing the introductory phrases.

ἀνεβόησεν ὁ Ἰησοῦς φωνῇ μεγάλῃ λέγων     (Matt 27.46)
ἐβόησεν ὁ Ἰησοῦς φωνῇ μεγάλῃ             (Mk 15.34)

First, like the Matthean account, but in distinction from the Markan narrative, the *Gospel of Peter*. uses the compound verb form ἀνεβόησεν rather than the simplex ἐβόησεν.[419] The only difference between the Akhmîm text and Matthean reading at this point is that the former omits the final movable ν. The second agreement between *Gos. Pet.* 5.19a and Matt 27.46 is the use of the present participle λέγων to emphasize the direct speech that immediately follows. In conjunction, these two elements provide a strong case that here the Akhmîm text is drawing upon the narrative as reported in the first gospel. As Gundry notes in relation to Matthew's account, the use of the compound form 'intensifies the cry of Jesus.'[420] Apart from these similarities, there are also two important distinctions. First, as is the wont of the author of this non-canonical text, the name ὁ Ἰησοῦς is replaced with the preferred Christological title ὁ κύριος. Second, the narrative deletes the reference to φωνῇ μεγάλῇ. Thus, while the narrative appears to be following the Matthean form of words at this point, the method of composition is not slavish copying, but creative retelling of the tradition.

**5.19b**  ἡ δύναμίς μου ἡ δύναμις κατέλειψάς με. Perhaps no other phrase in the *Gospel of Peter* has occasioned the volume of discussion that has been generated by these words. Questions have been raised surrounding their supposedly docetic character, their relationship to the cry of dereliction contained in the gospels of both Matthew and Mark, whether an alternative LXX form of Ps 22.1 stands behind this formulation, and debate concerning the reasons for modifying existing tradition. Obviously these issues are not entirely separate, nevertheless such questions are useful in focusing the analysis of these words.

First it should be noted that unlike the canonical accounts, the Akhmîm fragment does not present the saying as *ipsissima verba*

---

[419] It needs to be noted that a few manuscripts of Matt 27.46 contain a reading with the simplex form of the verb ἐβόησεν. These withnesses include B L W 33. 700 *al.*

[420] Gundry, *Matthew: A Commentary on His Handbookfor a Mixed Church under Persecution*, 573.

of Jesus in his original language. Both Matthew and Mark preserve transliterations of what they present as the underlying semitic form employed by Jesus.

| | |
|---|---|
| ηλι ηλι λεμα σαβαχθανι; | (Matt 27.46) |
| ελωι ελωι λεμα σαβαχθανι; | (Mk 15.34) |

The Markan form represents the original Aramaic stratum of this tradition (this observation does not pre-judge the historicity or otherwise of the saying),[421] perhaps influenced by the targumic tradition on Ps 22.1. By contrast, the form of the saying presented as the Matthean text in the printed edition of NA[27] is a mixed form. As Metzger notes, 'the Matthean parallel is partly Hebrew and partly Aramaic.'[422] The scribe of Codex Bezae presents a form of Matt 27.46 that takes the process of Hebraizing the Markan tradition further and renders the saying entirely in Hebrew.[423] Since the Akhmîm text omits any reference to the underlying semitic form, it also deletes the words employed by Matthew (τοῦτ' ἔστιν) and Mark (ὅ ἐστιν μεθερμηνευόμενον) to introduce their respective translations, which for the *Gospel of Peter* would be obviously redundant.

Although agreeing with Brown's suggestion that to characterize the *Gospel of Peter* as docetic is a misnomer,[424] his assessment that '[t]oday, however, this docetic interpretation of GPet has largely been abandoned'[425] is perhaps over-confident, although admittedly the docetic view is not stated with the regularity with which it occurred among the first commenatators on the text. Early interpreters saw the cry in the *Gospel of Peter* as representing the departure of the *logos* from the human man, thus abandoning him to death. Two factors made this interpretation attractive. First it aligned with the Serapion story contained in Eusebius about a docetic gospel that circulated in Peter's name. Second, such a doctrine of abandonment found precedence in

---

[421] Metzger notes that the printed text of UBS[4] and NA[27] reflects a transliteration of Aramaic. He states, 'in the text preferred by the committee the entire saying represents an Aramaic original.' There are a number of significant variants in the mss tradition, which can nearly all be accounted for as either assimilation to the Matthean text or to the Hebrew form of Ps 22.1. B.M. Metzger, *A Textual Commentary on the Greek New Testament* (2nd ed.; Stuttgart: Deutsche Bibelgesellschaft, 1994) 99–100.

[422] Metzger, *A Textual Commentary on the Greek New Testament*, 100.

[423] Metzger, *A Textual Commentary on the Greek New Testament*, 59.

[424] Brown, 'The *Gospel of Peter* and Canonical Gospel Priority', 321–343.

[425] Brown, *The Death of the Messiah*, vol 2, 1056.

Irenaeus description of the teachings of Cerinthus. As McCant states with a slight rhetorical flourish, '[a]t the mere mention of δύναμις, docetism is charged and a full-scale Cerintian gnostic system is presupposed with the descent of the Divine Christ upon Jesus at baptism and his ascent at the death of Jesus.'[426] To gauge the 'fit' between the *Gospel of Peter* and the teachings of Cerinthus it is necessary to consider the description provided by Irenaeus, although the methodological problem of reading the teachings of Cerinthus through the lens of a strident opponent must be borne in mind.

> Cerinthus, again, a man who was educated in the wisdom of the Egyptians, taught that the world was not made by the primary God, but by a certain Power far separated from him, and at a distance from that Principality who is supreme over the universe, and ignorant of him who is above all. He represented Jesus as having not been born of a virgin, but as being the son of Joseph and Mary according to the ordinary course of human generation, while he nevertheless was more righteous, prudent, and wise than other men. Moreover, after his baptism, Christ descended upon him in the form of a dove from the Supreme Ruler, and that then he proclaimed the unknown Father, and performed miracles. But at last Christ departed from Jesus, and that then Jesus suffered and rose again, while Christ remained impassible, inasmuch as he was a spiritual being. (Irenaeus, *Adv. Haer.* 1.26.1)[427]

One can immediately see that many of the ideas that Irenaeus attributes to Cerinthus cannot be compared with data in the Akhmîm fragment since that text says nothing about the mechanism of creation, Jesus' birth, his manner of life, or his baptism. The one comparison that can be made is with events surrounding the Passion. According to Irenaeus, Cerinthus taught that 'Christ' was impassible since he was a spiritual being, consequently 'Christ' departed from the human Jesus leaving him to suffer, although this Jesus rose again. Two fundamental points must be addressed by those who maintain that such ideas are represented in the cry from the cross that occurs in the *Gospel of Peter*. First, if this is the time of departure of the 'Christ' from the human, then, within the framework of the narrative, he has been suffering

---

[426] McCant, 'The Gospel of Peter', 262.
[427] This translation is taken from Robertson-Davies, 'Against the Heresies', *Ante-Nicene Fathers*.

all the abuses and torments of the crucifixion up until to this point. Therefore the text does a very poor job at preserving the impassibility of Christ. Second, according to the *Gospel of Peter* the risen form that emerges from the tomb takes on supernatural proportions. This does not square with the the description of Cerinthus' theology that the man Jesus rose, devoid of the indwelling spiritual being. On the first point McCant additionally notes that the 'death potion' given to Jesus (*Gos. Pet.* 5.16) 'implies suffering.'[428] The second point depends, of course, on how accurately Irenaeus has represented Cerintus' theology, but there can be little doubt that the *Gospel of Peter* does not envisage the re-animation of a mere human being in its description of head 'reaching beyond the heavens' (*Gos. Pet.* 10.40).

Of course the basis for describing a document as docetic is partly a definitional problem, and it appears that often in the early church the term 'docetic' was a convenient charge to cast at those whose opinions one might wish to undermine or even demonize. In one of the few studies that tries to wrestle with the problems of defining docetism, Slusser notes both a narrow and a broad definition.[429] The narrow definition is that put forward by Peter Weigandt in his unpublished doctoral dissertation. He defines the phenomenon as a Christology in which, 'Jesus Christ is presented as the divine saviour who cannot have any contact, however fleeting, with matter.'[430] The broad definition which Slusser prefers is provided by F.C. Baur.[431] It states that Docetism is 'the contention that the human appearance of Christ is mere illusion and has no objective reality.'[432] Regardless of whether one adopts the narrow or the broad definition described by Slusser, it appears that

---

[428] McCant, 'The Gospel of Peter', 262.

[429] M. Slusser, 'Docetism: A Historical Definition', *Second Century* 1 (1986) 163–172.

[430] Peter Weigandt, *Der Doketismus im Urchristentum und in der theologischen Entwicklung des zweiten Jahrhunderts*, 2 vols. (Diss. Heildelberg, 1961), I, 18, '…ein dogmengeschichtlicher Sammelbegriff Doketismus für diesen Zweck ungeeignet ist.'

[431] Slusser provides a fuller translation of Baur's definition than the abbreviated form which he uses for convenience. The fuller form states, 'Either objectivity is denied to the human in Christ, or at least the human is so separated from the divine that there is no personal unity between the two. The first is the purely docetic view, since it holds that Christ was man only in appearance; but the second has this at least in common with genuine Docetism, that it declares the diviy of the Saviour to be mere appearance. For while it distinguishes between Christ and Jesus, takes Jesus for a real human being, and lets him act in visible fashion for human salvation, it is mere illusion if one takes Jesus for the real person of the Saviour, for the genuine subject of saving activity.' Slusser, 'Docetism: A Historical Definition', 171.

[432] F.C. Baur, *Die christliche Gnosis oder die christliche Religions-Philosophie in ihrer geschichtlichen Entwicklumg* (Tübingen, 1835) 258.

the *Gospel of Peter* does not conform to either of these formulations. Nowhere in the portion of narrative preserved in the Akhmîm codex is there an attempt to remove the divine figure from the material world. In fact, the one whom the *Gospel of Peter* repeatedly hails as ὁ κύριος, is inextricably entaggled in the suffering and brutality of the physical world and its inhabitants. Even on the broader definition, there seems to be nothing in the narrative that seeks to soften the reality of suffering, or to separate the experiences of the divine and human aspects.

The relationship between the verbal form of the cry given in the *Gospel of Peter* and the Greek translations provided by Matthew and Mark shows at the same time verbal divergent, but structural similarity.

| | |
|---|---|
| ἡ δύναμίς μου ἡ δύναμις κατέλειψάς με | (*Gos. Pet.* 5.19b) |
| θεέ μου θεέ μου, ἱνατί με ἐγκατέλιπες; | (Matt 27.46) |
| ὁ θεός μου ὁ θεός μου, εἰς τί ἐγκατέλιπές με; | (Mk 15.34) |

Mark's unusual interrogative construction appears to be the result of a literal rendering of the underlying Aramaic.[433] Matthew improves the Greek by introducing a more readily recognizable form of question. The Akhmîm saying is in the form of a statement rather than a question. This observation is significant for understanding how the author of the *Gospel of Peter* has modified the theology of the canonical accounts. Rather than presenting the cry as an outburst of confused bemusement, it is transformed into a declaration of awareness about immediately approaching death, which in distinction from the canonical accounts occurs directly after the cry in the *Gospel of Peter*. By using the verb καταλείπω,[434] instead of ἐγκαταλείπω as in the canonical accounts the intention appears to be to tone down the sense of desertion, and instead make this a notice concerning knowledge of impending death and departure.

If this interpretation is correct, it means that in the present context δύναμις is not being used as a circumlocution for θεός.[435] Some who

---

[433] See M. Zerwick and M. Grosvenor, *A Grammatical Analysis of the Greek New Testament* (4th ed.; Rome: Pontifical Biblical Institute, 1993) 163.

[434] While it is not impossible for καταλείπω to take on the meaning of 'abandonment' or 'desertion' (cf. M.Pol. 17.2 ἀγνοοῦντες, ὅτι οὔτε τὸν Χριστόν ποτε καταλιπεῖν δυνησόμεθα) this meaning far less frequent than the sense 'to leave'. See BDAG, 520–521.

[435] This view is advocated by F.F. Bruce, who suggests, 'Behind the repeated words "my power" may be some awareness that the root meaning of the Hebrew 'el (God) in Ps 22:1 and so quoted in Mt 27:46 is 'power'. F.F. Bruce, *Jesus and Christian Ori-*

hold this view have suggested that this finds support in Aquila's revision of the LXX of Ps 21.2, where the Hebrew אֵלִי is rendered using ἰσχυρός. Thus Brown suggests that:

> In the 2d cent. AD, contemporary with GPet, as part of a Jewish attempt to produce a Greek translation faithful to the Hebrew, Aquila rendered Ps 22.2 as "my stong one [ischyre], my strong one," a translation which Eusebius thought could be more elogently rendered, "My strength" (Demonstratio evangelica 10.8.30; GCS 23.476).[436]

As Brown goes on to describe, this thesis requires the author of the Gospel of Peter to know which Psalm the gospel writers were citing, but without being able to recall their form of words. Instead the author replaced them with the form more familiar to him from Aquila's revision of the LXX. Regardless of what one makes of the likelihood of this proposal, there is an even more fundamental problem. The form that occurs in the Akhmîm text does not utilise Aquilia's choice of terminology ἰσχυρός, but uses the term δύναμις, which at best is only a partial synonym.

This lack of fit with any of the circumlocutions that are used for 'God' in translations of Ps 22.1, coupled with the fact that the Gospel of Peter places this saying in the form of a statement immediately prior to the description of Jesus 'being taken up', lends weight to the interpretation suggested here. Namely, that it reveals an awareness on the part of Jesus that his life-force is on the point of leaving him. Moreover, such a theological re-interpretation would be attractive to the author of the Gospel of Peter since it minimizes any discomfort felt at seeing a confused and abandoned Jesus expressing his despair while he hung on the cross.[437] This is a theological problem that Luke and John have solved by omission. The author of the Gospel of Peter addresses this same crux, but finds an alterative solution.

---

gins outside the New Testament (London: Hodder and Stoughton, 1974) 156. McCant is even more direct, 'It is possible to understand GP's use of Power in a way that was familiar both in Jewish and early Christian circles as a circumlocution for God.' McCant, 'The Gospel of Peter', 263.

[436] Brown, The Death of the Messiah, vol 2, 1058.

[437] For a fuller discussion of this point see P. Foster, 'Passion Traditions in the Gospel of Peter', in A. Merkt and T. Nicklas (eds.), The Reception and Development of Early Christian Passion Traditions, WUNT (Tübingen: Mohr Siebeck, 2010) 49–70; here esp. section 3.5, 62–63.

**5.19c** καὶ εἰπὼν ἀνελήφθη. In the first two gospels the sequence of events following the cry of dereliction is the offer of the vinegar-wine on a sponge, followed by a second cry, with death occurring at this point. Since the *Gospel of Peter* has reversed the order of the offering of drink and the first cry, a second act of shouting from the cross is redundant, although the narrative has merged elements surrounding the two cries of the canonical gospels into a single event. While the form of words in the *Gospel of Peter* reflects that of the first cry in Matthew and Mark, it functions as a death cry, as does the second cry in the first two gospels. The four canonical gospels describe the death of Jesus in different terms: ἀφῆκεν τὸ πνεῦμα (Matt 27.50);[438] ἐξέπνευσεν (Mk 15.37);[439] ἐξέπνευσεν (Lk 23.46);[440] καὶ κλίνας τὴν κεφαλὴν παρέδωκεν τὸ πνεῦμα (Jn 19.30).[441]

Unlike the canonical accounts, which in varying degrees report the death of Jesus as being precipitated by actions of Jesus usually of an involuntary nature, in the *Gospel of Peter* the Lord recognizes his approaching death and then he is taken up. Again, as Brown notes, there is here 'no docetism as if the real Jesus who was only spiritual went away, leaving an appearance of a body (for in 6:21–24 Jesus' body still has the power to make the earth shake).'[442] Rather the form of words chosen to describe the death aligns with the cry from the cross. Jesus has declared that he feels his life-force ebbing away, and the narrator informs the audience that at this point Jesus was taken up. Here the passive form ἀνελήφθη may characterised from a theological perspective as a 'divine passive'. This does not represent a form which is grammatically different from other passive forms. Rather, it alludes to the agency of the deity, while refraining from naming that figure

---

[438] Davies and Allison observe that 'Matthew's verb emphasizes the voluntary nature of Jesus' death (a theme so important in John and the Fathers): he returns his life or spirit (not the Holy Spirit) to the God who gave it. Davies and Allison, *The Gospel According to Saint Matthew*, vol. III, 628.

[439] France notes that the second and third gospels share the shortest notice of the death. 'All four gospels describe Jesus' actual death in πνεῦμα language, though in varying forms. ἐκπνέω, used by Mark and Luke, and offers even less scope than the πνεῦμα phrases of Matthew and Johm for reading into the scene any reference to the Holy Spirit. France, *The Gospel of Mark*, 655.

[440] Nolland observes that the term ἐξέπνευσεν 'is a standard Greek way of speaking about dying.' Nolland, *Luke 18:35–24.53*, 1158.

[441] For Schnackenburg the παρέδωκεν represents 'a conscious act…a self-offering to the Father.' R. Schnackenburg, *The Gospel according to St. John*, vol. 3 (London: Burns and Oates, 1982), 285.

[442] Brown, *The Death of the Messiah*, vol 2, 1081.

directly. Admittedly, in the narrative the use of the term ἀνελήφθη may potentially result in some confusion between the language of death and ascension. If this is the case, then it appears to stem from lack of authorial skill rather than a conscious desire to introduce a fresh theological understanding.

**5.20**  καὶ αὐτῆς ὥρας διεράγη τὸ καταπέτασμα τοῦ ναοῦ τῆς Ἰερουσαλὴμ εἰς δύο. The rending of the temple veil is a detail that the *Gospel of Peter* shares in common with the synoptic accounts.

καὶ ἰδοὺ τὸ καταπέτασμα τοῦ ναοῦ ἐσχίσθη ἀπ'
   ἄνωθεν ἕως κάτω εἰς δύο                              (Matt 27.51a)
καὶ τὸ καταπέτασμα τοῦ ναοῦ ἐσχίσθη εἰς δύο ἀπ'
   ἄνωθεν ἕως κάτω                                     (Mk 15.38)
ἐσχίσθη δὲ τὸ καταπέτασμα τοῦ ναοῦ μέσον          (Lk 23.45)

The Matthean and Markan accounts show great similarity between themselves. The only divergence is that Matthew has inserted the word ἰδού and moved the phrase εἰς δύο to the end of the clause. In relation to the first alteration, Davies and Allison see this as a stylistic change 'to introduce the following sequence of dramatic events.'[443] Although obviously retelling the same event, the *Gospel of Peter* does so in strikingly different terms. Luke is unique in placing the rending of the veil prior to the death of Jesus, connecting it more with the other mysterious phenomenon of the darkening of the sun. For Brown, the Lukan motivation for moving this tradition was indeed to associate it with the already ominous portent of the eclipse of the sun. In this way Luke ensures that tearing of the curtain does not diminish the optimism that permeates the post-death narrative.[444]

In comparion with these synoptic descriptions, the Akhmîm narrative first opens with a chronological reference which makes explicit what is implicit in the Matthean and Markan accounts, namely the contemporaneous events of the death of Jesus and the splitting of the curtain. Mara sees an apocalyptic element here, highlighting the intervention of God at a precise point in history.[445] Second, a different term

---

[443] Davies and Allison, *The Gospel According to Saint Matthew*, vol. III, 630.
[444] Brown, *The Death of the Messiah*, vol 2, 1103.
[445] Mara states that ὥρα 'désigne, dans l'apocalyptique judaïque, un moment précis de l'histoire du salut, le moment de l'intervention divine à la fin des temps.' Mara, *Évangile de Pierre*, 145.

is used to describe the rending of the veil. The *Gospel of Peter* employs the verb διὰ(ρ)ρήγνυμι, which is used less frequently in the NT than σχίζω, but may also be used to denotes an equally violent action. The narrator also adds to the reference to the temple the geographical detail τῆς Ἱερουσαλήμ. As Swete quite plausibly suggests, this 'is one of several indications that the fragment was written outside Palestine, or at all events for non-Palestinian readers.'[446] Finally, the detail of the direction of the tear, top to bottom, is omitted. This is included in Matthew and Mark to indicate divine fiat, but the significance is either missed by the author of the text, or if, as may be the case, the *Gospel of Peter* is composed from memory of the canonical accounts, then this detail has simply been forgotten.

---

[446] Swete, *The Akhmîm Fragment of the Apocryphal Gospel of St Peter*, 10.

# REMOVAL OF THE BODY FROM THE
## CROSS AND BURIAL (6.21–24)

21. καὶ τότε ἀπέσπασαν¹ τοὺς ἥλους ἀπὸ τῶν χειρῶ(ν)² τοῦ κυ̅³ καὶ ἔθηκαν⁴ αὐτὸν ἐπὶ τῆς γῆς·⁵ καὶ ἡ γῆ πᾶσα⁶ ἐσείσθη καὶ φόβος⁷ μέγας ἐγένετο.⁸ 22. τότε ἥλιος ἔλαμψε καὶ εὑρέθη ὥρα ἐνάτη. 23. ἐχάρησαν δὲ οἱ Ἰουδαῖοι καὶ δεδώκασῖ[ν]⁹ τῷ Ἰωσὴφ τὸ σῶμα αὐτοῦ ἵνα¹⁰ αὐτὸ θάψῃ ἐπειδὴ θεασάμενος ἦν ὅσα¹¹ ἀγαθὰ ἐποίησεν. 24. λαβὼν δὲ τὸν κύριον ἔλουσε¹² καὶ εἴλησε¹³ σινδόνιν¹⁴ καὶ εἰσήγαγεν εἰς ἴδιον τάφον καλούμενον κῆπον Ἰωσήφ.

21. And then they drew the nails from the hands of the Lord and placed him on the earth, and all the earth was shaken and there was great fear. 22. Then the sun shone and it was found to be the ninth hour. 23. And the Jews rejoiced and gave to Joseph his body that he might bury it, since he had seen all the good things he had done. 24. And taking the Lord he washed and wrapped [him] in a linen cloth and brought [him] into his own tomb called 'Joseph's garden.'

## TEXT CRITICAL NOTES

1. Formation of the two sigmas in ἀπέσπασαν is not consistent. The height of the first (approximately 2mm) is slightly lower than the cross bar of the following π. By comparison the second is double the height (approximately 4mm), with the top arching above the following α. Such disparity in size is not uncommon in this text, especially in the formation of the enlarged final ς. This exaggerated form is less frequent in the middle of words, but there are other examples apart from this instance, e.g. βασιλεῦ *Gos. Pet.* 3.7. Much of this variation is noted by Gebhardt.⁴⁴⁷

2. The movable ν has been omitted at the end of the word χειρῶ[ν], which occurs at the end of the ninth line on the third page of text. This cannot, however, be explained on the basis of lack of space, since lines eight and ten extend further to the right than line nine.

---

⁴⁴⁷ Gebhardt, *Das Evangelium und die Apokalypse des Petrus*, 13.

The omission of the final ν is marked by a supralinear stroke which commences over the ω, but is offset to the right. Hence it covers the right-hand half of the ω and the space where the movable ν would have occurred if it were retained. In relation to the supralinear bar employed written in *nomina sacra* Roberts states, 'The purpose of the system was demonstrably not to save either space or the scribe's time; a free space is often left around the abbreviation and the time saved by writing a four-letter word in two letters would be occupied in drawing the line.'[448] Obviously, here there is even less potential to save time by replacing a single letter with a supralinear stroke.[449] Conforming to usual practice, the movable ν is omitted before a consonant, and hence does contravene the convention of retaining it before a following vowel.[450]

3. The scribe follows his more frequent practice of employing a *nomen sacrum* to abbreviate the word κύριος (eleven times out of thirteen usages of this term). It should be noted that later in this paragraph (6.24) the second of the two examples of unabbreviated forms of κύριος occurs (see also 3.8). This is a further example of the lack of consistency on the part of the scribe, indicating, as does the poor quality of the handwriting, that he was not a professional scribe.[451]

4. The first three letters of the word ἔθηκαν appear to be connected by a single stroke that forms the middle stroke of both the ε and θ, as well as the horizontal top part of the η that follows. The circular part of the θ is formed by two non-touching arcs forming the left-hand and right-hand halves of the letter. It appears that these arcs may well have been written after the elongated stroke connecting the first three letters was penned.

5. The scribe forms a small letter γ both here and elsewhere in his text. Gebhardt notes, 'das γ ragt nur wenig unter die Zeile; esist oben oft abgerundet und dann einem σ ähnlich (z. B. III, 9 in κακουργων, VIII, 8 in εγω).'[452]

---

[448]  Roberts, '*Nomina Sacra*: Origins and Significance', 27.

[449]  On the use of abbreviations in non-Christian Greek manuscripts, ostraca and inscriptions see Kathleen McNamee, *Abbreviations in Greek Literary Papyri and Ostraca* (BaspSup 3; Chico, CA: Scholars Pres, 1981).

[450]  See BDF §20.

[451]  See the discussion dealing with *Gos. Pet.* 3.8.

[452]  Gebhardt, *Das Evangelium und die Apokalypse des Petrus*, 10.

6. An unusual word division occurs with πᾶσα at the end of line ten and beginning of line eleven. The scribe has split this short word after the second letter, rather than writing it in its entirety on line eleven. This is in contrast to line seventeen on the same page (7.25), where the final two letters of Ἰουδαῖοι have been written in reduced size to fit them into the end of the line.

7. In forming the two examples of the letter o in the word φόβος, the scribe has reduced their size to the extent that the first has become almost a dot with no white-space in the centre, while the second is slightly larger, but encloses only a minimal area of white-space. This is not without precedence. Towards the end of line four of the same page the second o in the word νομίζοντες (5.18) is dot-like appearance. There are further examples in the final line of the same page. This contrasts with the large forms of this letter which enclose significant white space. Gebhardt notes this lack of consistency. 'Das o, welches oft gross und missgestaltet ist (z. B. VI, 16 εγενετο, XIX, 7 in εκυλιοντο), schrumpft nicht selten, und zwar ohne ersichtlichen Grund, zu einem schwarzen Punkte zusammen (z. B. IV, 11 in φοβοσ, XVIII, 12 in ακοιμητω).'[453]

8. Debate has surrounded the reading of the final letter of ἐγένετο. Kraus and Nicklas state 'εγενετο: Schreiber überschreib einen Buchstaben (ε oder ω?) am Worende mit o.'[454] While there is uncertainity in this letter form, this may be due to misformation rather than overwriting. If it is a case of overwriting, then the underwritten letter is more likely to be ε.

9. With the perfect form δεδώκασι the movable ν is omitted. Again this follows the general rule of such omissions only being possible before a following consonant. However, unlike χειρῶ[ν] which occurs at the end of a line (6.21), there is no supralinear stroke above the omitted ν.[455]

10. The manuscript reading ιυι is correctly understood by scholars as an orthographical error in place of the proposed emendation ἵνα. This correction not only replaces the non-existent word ιυι, but

---

[453] Gebhardt, *Das Evangelium und die Apokalypse des Petrus*, 12.
[454] Kraus und Nicklas, *Das Petrusevangelium und die Petrusapokalypse*, 36.
[455] See note 2 above.

is adopted by a range of scholars including, Bouriant,[456] Swete,[457] Harnack,[458] Gebhardt,[459] Vaganay,[460] Mara,[461] Kraus and Nicklas.[462] However, Lods who main purpose is to correct Bouriant's transcription prints ινι without comment.[463]

11. Again (cf. note 6) the scribe produces an unusual word break. The word ὅσα is divided with the first two letters occurring at the end of line 14, with the final letter α commencing line 15.

12. Here the scribe further demonstrates his continued preference for omitting the movable final ν prior to a consonant.

13. Two points need to be noted in regard to the verbal form εἴλησε. First it is yet another example of the omission of the movable ν. Second, Harnack,[464] Gebhardt[465] and Klostermann[466] suggest a conjectural emendation to the text. In place of εἴλησε, they offer the reading ἐνείλησε as a correction to the text. The basis for the proposed correction stems from the use of the compound form in the synoptic gospels: ἐνείλησε (Mk 15.46) and ἐνετύλιξεν (Matt 27.59; Lk 23.53). Gebhardt states, 'Zu ἐνείλησε v. 24 vgl. Mc 15,46. Das von mehreren Herausgebern beibehaltene εἴλησε wird nirdgends, soviel ich sehe, durch Beispiele belegt.'[467] In their edition, Kraus and Nicklas print εἴλησε with a rough breathing (i.e. εἵλησε) instead of the correct smooth breathing.[468]

---

[456] Bouriant prints the reading ἵνα without comment or footnote. Bouriant, 'Fragments du texte grec du livre d'Énoch et de quelques écrits attribués à saint Pierre', 139.

[457] Swete prints the form and reference '5 ινι.' Swete, *The Akhmîm Fragment of the Apocryphal Gospel of St Peter*, 11.

[458] Harnack does not note any difference between his printed form ἵνα and the mss reading. Harnack, *Bruchstücke des Evangeliums und der Apokalypse des Petrus*, 10.

[459] Gebhardt prints ἵνα without mentioning the reading of the ms. Gebhardt, *Das Evangelium und die Apokalypse des Petrus*, 44.

[460] Vaganay concludes, 'faute de copiste dans le ms.: ινι' Vaganay, *L'Évangile de Pierre*, 265.

[461] Mara, without discussion, states, ' ἵνα: ινι ms.' Mara, *Évangile de Pierre*, 50.

[462] Kraus und Nicklas simply note, 'Ms: ινι;'Kraus und Nicklas, *Das Petrusevangelium und die Petrusapokalypse*, 36.

[463] Lods, 'L'Évangile et l'Apocalypse de Pierre avec le texte grec du livre d'Hénoch', 220.

[464] Harnack, *Bruchstücke des Evangeliums und der Apokalypse des Petrus*, 28.

[465] Gebhardt, *Das Evangelium und die Apokalypse des Petrus*, 23, 44.

[466] Klostermann, *Apocrypha I: Reste des Petrusevangeliums, der Petrusapokalypse und des Kerygma Petri*.

[467] Gebhardt, *Das Evangelium und die Apokalypse des Petrus*, 23.

[468] Kraus und Nicklas, *Das Petrusevangelium und die Petrusapokalypse*, 36, line 16.

14. There is an orthographical error with the term σινδόνιν. Commentators have corrected this to σινδόνι, the dative singular form. It is also possible that the dative plural σινδῶσιν was intended, although preference for the singular is based upon the usage in the canonical gospels (Matt 27.59; Mk 15.46; Lk 23.53).

## COMMENTARY

**6.21aα  καὶ τότε ἀπέσπασαν τοὺς ἥλους ἀπὸ τῶν χειρῶ[ν] τοῦ κ̄ῡ.** In a similar fashion to Matthew's gospel (Matt 27.51b-53), the *Gospel of Peter* follows the notice concerning the rending of the curtain with a sequence of events that accompanied that sign. There is, however, little overlap in the content of these two accounts, nor any other canonical parallel to the events described in 6.21–22.

The canonical gospels pass over the details of physically removing the corpse from the cross. Yet in describing this process, the Akhmîm narrative mentions the nails, ἥλους, for the first time. Until this point the audience has not been informed how Jesus was attached to the cross, simply that he was crucified (4.10). Both Semeria[469] and Mara[470] consider the description of the extraction of the nails as further evidence that the account is not Docetic in nature. Although there is no explicit description of the means of affixing Jesus to the cross in the canonical gospels, there are implied references amongst early Christian writers.

> ἀληθῶς ἐπὶ Ποντίου Πιλάτου καὶ Ἡρώδου τετράρχου καθηλωμένον ὑπὲρ ἡμῶν ἐν σαρκί (*Smyrn.* 1.2)

> Truly, in the time of Pontius Pilate and Herod the Tetrarch, he was nailed on our behalf in the flesh.

Similarly, the author of the *Epistle of Barnabas*, citing Ps 22.20 as prophecy, makes the following reference to 'nailing':

> λέγει γὰρ ὁ προφητεύων ἐπ' αὐτῷ· Φεῖσαί μου τῆς ψυχῆς ἀπὸ Ῥομφαίας, καὶ Καθήλωσόν μου τὰς σάρκας, ὅτι πονηρευομένων συναγωγὴ ἐπανέστησάν μοι. (*Barn.* 5.13)

---

[469] Semeria, 'L'Évangile de Pierre', see in particular the discussion on 534–539.

[470] Mara states, 'L'épisode de l'extraction des clous des mains du Seigneur est, de toute évidence, un passage qui n'est pas docète.' Mara, *Évangile de Pierre*, 142.

> For the one who prophesied about him said, 'Spare my life from
> the sword' and 'Nail my flesh, because an assembly of evildoers
> has risen up against me.'

Within the canonical gospel tradition, the sole reference to the nails
occurs when, according to the fourth gospel, Thomas describes the
nature of proof he requires to accept the report given by the other
disciples that they had encountered the risen Jesus, ἐὰν μὴ ἴδω ἐν ταῖς
χερσὶν αὐτοῦ τὸν τύπον τῶν ἥλων καὶ βάλω τὸν δάκτυλόν μου εἰς τὸν τύπον
τῶν ἥλων (Jn 20.25). As Barrett perceptively states, 'Thomas required
the grossest and most palpable evidence that the body he knew to have
been killed in a specific manner had indeed been reanimated.'[471] Like
the Johannine narrative, the *Gospel of Peter* only refers to the nails
is connection with the hands of Jesus, ἀπὸ τῶν χειρῶν τοῦ κυρίου. It
is unlikely that the Akhmîm text is preserving independent historical tradition here, although some roughly contemporary accounts of
crucifixion describe the nailing through the wrists and the tying of the
feet. In contrast, the tradition of the nailing of the hands and feet can
be traced back at least as early as Justin, although his account may be
shaped by the apologetic desire to make the events of the crucifixion
better correspond to the text of Ps 22.16 (LXX Ps 21.17), which he
views as a prophetic text.

> ὅτε γάρ ἐσταύρωσαν αὐτὸν ἐμπήσσοντες τοὺς ἥλους τὰς χεῖρας καὶ
> τοὺς πόδας αὐτοῦ ὤρυξαν (Justin, *Dial*. 97.3)

> For when they crucified Him, driving in the nails, they pierced
> His hands and feet.

Again, in this description of the ongoing rough treatment of the now
lifeless body the author of the *Gospel of Peter* employs his preferred
Christological title, 'the Lord', to refer to Jesus.

**6.21aβ   καὶ ἔθηκαν αὐτὸν ἐπὶ τῆς γῆς.** Grammatically the pronoun αὐτόν could refer either to the Lord or to the cross. If it were a
reference to inanimate body, deserted by the Lord one would expect
the neuter form of the pronoun, αὐτό, (cf. 6.23b) However, it is almost
certain from the context that the narrative is using the pronoun to

---

[471] Barrett, *The Gospel according to St John*, 476.

refer to the Lord in his deceased form.[472] First, Jesus' body has just been detached from the cross. While there is no description of whether this occurred while the cross was still erect, or if the cross had been laid down in order to remove the corpse, the lack of description of the cross militate against a reference to it in the present clause. If Jesus' body was detached from an erect cross, logically it must be the now freed body that requires a resting place, alternatively, if the body was removed from a cross that had already been lowered, then it had already been placed on the ground prior to the extraction of the nails. Perhaps more significantly, in the following clause it appears more likely that the ground trembles when the body of the Lord comes into contact with it, for the cross had been embedded in the earth throughout the crucifixion. As will be reinforced in v. 23, the unnamed subjects who place the body on the ground are still a subset of the Jewish crowd who have conducted all the events of the crucifixion.

**6.21bα** καὶ ἡ γῆ πᾶσα ἐσείσθη. The post-crucifixion shaking of the earth is also recorded in Matthew's gospel. In the first gospel it occurs immediately after the rending of the Temple curtain, and initiates a series of three eschatological signs not elsewhere depicted among the canonical gospels. Davies and Allison make the source-critical judgment that the incidents contained in Matt 27.51b–53 'preserve pre-Matthean tradition.'[473] Although no explicit link is stated by the Matthean narrator, the series of signs, torn curtain, earthquake, split rocks, and the re-animation of dead corpses, are to be understood as portents that accompany the death of Jesus, and prefigure the eschatological age, or perhaps more accurately they function to collapse the eschatological event horizon into the very moment of Jesus' death, thereby revealing that this is a key moment in salvation history.[474] The phenomenon described in the *Gospel of Peter* does not appear to reflect the same degree of theological sophistication. Brown notes that

---

[472] Vaganay favours this option referring to 'le contact du corps du Christ avec le sol.' Vaganay, *L'Évangile de Pierre*, 260.

[473] Davies and Allison, *The Gospel According to Saint Matthew*, vol. III, 608, see also 629.

[474] As Riches comments, 'The eschatological signs of the shaking earth, the splitting of the rocks and the resurrection of the saints (whether before or after Jesus' resurrection) indicate that Jesus' death on Golgotha inaugurates a new world.' J.K. Riches, *Conflicting Mythologies: Identity Formation in the Gospels of Matthew and Mark* (Edinburgh: T&T Clark, 2000), 237, n. 14.

the *Gospel of Peter* echoes only one of the three traditions contained in special Matthean material, and consequently argues that '[t]his fact strengthens my view that in part *GPet* is a folk-gospel.'[475] Since the *Gospel of Peter* derives little, if any, theological insight from this detail it appears that Brown's assessment is indeed correct,[476] and the report of the shaking of the earth appears rather to function narratologically as a prelude to the expression of fear that is noted as the conclusion of this verse. Although the point is not developed in the account, the way even the earth itself trembles when it comes in contact with the sacred body of the Lord, speaks strongly against docetic interpretations of the narrative at this point, or as a whole.[477]

**6.21bβ** **καὶ φόβος μέγας ἐγένετο.** Such a manifestation of fear, expressed in phenomenological terms, rather than being directly linked to a particular group, serves to highlight the all pervasive and impersonal nature of this fear. The attitude of apprehension which attended the unnatural darkening of the sun (*Gos. Pet.* 5.15), intensifies into a deeper sense of foreboding as a consequence of the even more proximate geophysical occurrence. The link between seismic activity and fear occurs in the Matthean account, ὁ δὲ ἑκατόνταρχος καὶ οἱ μετ᾽ αὐτοῦ τηροῦντες τὸν Ἰησοῦν ἰδόντες τὸν σεισμὸν καὶ τὰ γενόμενα ἐφοβήθησαν σφόδρα (Matt 27.54). In the first gospel such fear is linked to the Roman guards, whereas the *Gospel of Peter* has not identified those who were possessed by fear. In part, this is due to the generalized occurrence of fear, but also because the Jewish crowd remain the central perpetraters of the crucifixion.

**6.22** **τότε ἥλιος ἔλαμψε καὶ εὑρέθη ὥρα ἐνάτη.** At this juncture in the narrative the sun again becomes visible. By solar observation the time can be determined as being the ninth hour. Reference to the ninth hour occurs in the passion narratives of all three synoptic gospels. Matthew and Mark each refer to the ninth hour on two occa-

---

[475] Brown, *The Death of the Messiah*, vol 2, 1118.

[476] Mara's attempt to find a theological agenda behind this incident seems somewhat forced. She argues in relation to the author's intention that, 'il propose, sous forme de récit, un discours théologique. C'est la présentation du Κύριος, de tout ce qu'il est, de tout ce qu'il a fait et fera.' Mara, *Évangile de Pierre*, 142.

[477] As Vaganay convincingly observes, 'le corps de Jésus n'est pas une simple apparence, un vain fantôme, puisque, même après le départ de la δύναμις, il conserve encore un pouvoir surnaturel.' Vaganay, *L'Évangile de Pierre*, 260.

sions during the crucifixion (Matt 27.45, 46; Mk 15.33, 34), Luke only once (Lk 23.44). The second reference made by Matthew and Mark is in connection with the timing of the cry of dereliction. The author of the *Gospel of Peter* has substantially reworked that tradition, and in the process has omitted this second notice about the ninth hour from his account. The earlier temporal note is shared by the three synoptic accounts (Matt 27.45; Mk 15.33; Lk 23.44). Although there are divergences in wording all three describe the darkness that commenced at the sixth hour and follow this by informing the audience that it lifted at the ninth hour. The Akhmîm narrative splits this tradition into two pieces, and thereby accentuates the level of suspense in the narrative by not immediately resolving the problem of the engulfing darkness, and in fact adds to the concern by depicting in folkloric terms further details surrounding the darkness (*Gos. Pet.* 5.18). As has already been noted in the discussion on *Gos. Pet.* 5.15, there the numerical reference to ἔκτης ὥρας (Matt 27.45) is replaced by the synonymous temporal term μεσημβρία (*Gos. Pet.* 5.15). Having given a sense of the time that has elapsed, the author now utilised the second half of the synoptic tradition by making reference to the ὥρα ἐνάτη. Although as Mara correctly observes, 'in contrast to the synoptics, the ninth hour in the *Gospel of Peter* does not signify the end of the darkness, but the moment when the sun begins to shine.'[478] While strictly this is accurate, there is no distinction in the narrative between the end of the darkness and the appearance of the sun. However, this distinction is part of Mara's attempt to load the term ὥρα with eschatological significance. She suggests that

> Thus this banal 'hour', following on in the the text from the deposition of the body, is at the same time a manifestation of the Parousia, which undoubtedly wishes to recall for the reader the conclusion of the mission of the Κύριος.[479]

However, in opposition to this view, the use of ὥρα appears to be derived from the occurrence in the underlying synoptic tradition where it is a simple temporal referent. This is the most likely explanation of its use in the *Gospel of Peter*, especially when this is seen in the light of the

---

[478] Mara, *Évangile de Pierre*, 143.

[479] 'Ainsi ce «banal» ὥρα, suivi, dans le texte, de la déposition du corps qui est en même temps une manifestation de la Parousie, veut sans doute rappeler au lecteur la conclusion de la mission du Κύριος.' Mara, *Évangile de Pierre*, 146.

fact that the Akhmîm narrative omits the eschatological elements that are present in the unique Matthean signs that accompany the rending of the Temple veil (Matt 27.51–53). Hence it is unlikely that the term carries as much eschatological significance as Mara proposes.

**6.23a** ἐχάρησαν δὲ οἱ Ἰουδαῖοι. Explicit reference to the Jews is made here for the second time, the first time being the second complete word in the opening line of the fragment. Their presence in the narrative has not been absent despite lack of use of the appellation οἱ Ἰουδαῖοι. Instead, the author has increased the involvement of the Jews in the Passion, in the form of the angry mob which carries out summary justice. The cause of rejoicing for the Jews is not stated explicitly. There are at least three possibilities which are not necessarily mutually exclusive. In terms of the narrative structure, the joy follows the description of the reappearance of the sun. Mara favours this as the basis of the gladness.[480] Vaganay suggests a more deep seated cause of relief, namely that the sun shows that the Jews had not inadvertently violated the law.[481] Vaganay, however, rejects one possible cause that should not be overlooked. He states in relation to a possible cause of rejoicing that 'it is not the success of their intentioned homicide.'[482] This possibility should not be totally rejected, especially in light of the tension and uncertainty that pervades the execution. The Jews address the Lord both as Son of God (*Gos. Pet.* 3.6; 3.9) and King of Israel (*Gos. Pet.* 4.11). While there is no doubt a large degree of mockery is intended by the use of such titles, there is also an underlying degree of apprehension that is generated in the lack of their certitude surrounding the true identity of Jesus, which is no doubt heightened by the supernatural signs of displeasure during the crucifixion. His death, however, may in part provide convincing proof that such Christological titles were misapplied. Hence it is possible to associate the sense of joy with a certain vindication on the part of the Jews that the execution was of a false claimant of the religio-political titles Son of God and King of Israel. However, there can be little doubt that the primary reference of the joy is that the appearance of the sun, which reveals to

---

[480] 'Le joie des Juifs provenant de ce que le soleil brille et que l'harmonie du monde est revenue.' Mara, *Évangile de Pierre*, 146.

[481] Vaganay, *L'Évangile de Pierre*, 261.

[482] 'Ce n'est pas le succès de leur dessein homicide.' Vaganay, *L'Évangile de Pierre*, 261.

those characters who have expressed concern previously about transgression of the law, that they have not in fact been guilty of violating
Torah stipulations.

**6.23b** καὶ δεδώκασῖν τῷ Ἰωσὴφ τὸ σῶμα αὐτοῦ ἵνα αὐτὸ
θάψῃ. As Brown writes, 'GPet represents only the beginning of a
florid Joseph legend.'[483] Unlike the fourth gospel, there is no connection between Joseph of Arimethea and Nicodemus (Jn 19.38–40).[484]
Although the narrative does not explain how the Jews knew that
Joseph should bury the body, the open communication between Pilate
and Antipas, apparently sent via an intermediary (Gos. Pet. 2.4), may
have, in the mind of the author, resulted in their awareness of this
detail.[485] Alternatively, this could simply be an unresolved tension in
the storyline. The final part of this verse provides another reason for
the handing over of the body to Joseph. It reports that it was a consequence of Joseph having witnessed the 'good works' performed by
Jesus. This raises its own problems to be addressed in the following
paragraph.

Again, little background information concerning Joseph is provided
in this part of the narrative, making it appear likely that Joseph had
been introduced in an earlier, now no longer extant section of the text.
The narrative appears to place greater distance between Joseph and
the Jews than occurs in the canonical tradition, where he is described
as being a member of the Sanhedrin (Mk 15.43; Lk 23.50). Moreover,
there is no fear in his demeanour, which is in contrast with the canonical tradition where he requires courage to overcome his apprehension (cf. Mk 14.43; Jn 19.38). In omitting any description of fear, or
connection with the Sanhedrin, the *Gospel of Peter* agrees with the
Matthean account in down-playing the Jewishness of this character,
and instead, again aligning with the first gospel, presents him as an
exemplary disciple. Brown sees this trend even more accentuated
in the *Gospel of Peter* than in Matthew, because of the omission of
the geographical connection of Arimathea. 'Indeed, since he is not

---

[483] Brown, *The Death of the Messiah*, vol 2, 1233.

[484] As Beasley-Murray observes in relation to the appearance of Nicodemus in the
burial account, '[h]is introductioninto the Passion tradition of the Johannine churches
will have been due to the evangelist.' Beasley-Murray, *John*, 359.

[485] See Vaganay who suggests, 'c'est simplement l'exécution de l'order implicite
d'Hérode (v. 5).' Vaganay, *L'Évangile de Pierre*, 265.

identified as "from Arimathea" and is a friend of Pilate, readers of the extant *GPet* fragment would not even know he was a Jew, unless they recognized "Joseph" as a characteristically Jewish name.'[486]

The verb δεδώκασῖ[ν] is a perfect form that is used with an past reference. Perfect forms are often employed in this manner, here McKay and Porter provide an extended discussions concerning the interplay between perfect and aorist indicative forms.[487] The representatives of the Jewish crowd again take control of the unfolding events, after their sense of fear had been transformed into renewed rejoicing. Without any hint of malice, the body is simple passed to Joseph for the obvious, but also explicitly mentioned task of burial. If anything, there is a sense of urgency, which might be motivated a desire to perform the necessary funerary prior to dusk in order to comply with the stipulation contained in Deut 21.22–23, which has been a source of concern to the Jews.[488]

**6.23c   ἐπειδὴ θεασάμενος ἦν ὅσα ἀγαθὰ ἐποίησεν.** This final clause is enigmatic, both in terms of its connection with the previous material and also in terms of its wider links with what may have stood in the presumably now no longer preserved sections of this gospel account. There appears to be contained in this detail an underlying assumption that Joseph had witnessed the 'good things' performed by Jesus. The relative pronoun ὅσα in its plural form can function as a term of encompassment, hence the translation 'all'.[489] Precisely what is being denoted by ἀγαθά is unclear. Perhaps the most likely possibility is to see it as a reference to miracles performed by Jesus, although this is problematic. The difficulty with this interpretation is that there is no miracle tradition associated with Jesus in the preserved portion of the Akhmîm text, so such a supposition is based upon reliance on the wider Jesus tradition. In the canonical gospels the term ἀγαθά is

---

[486] Brown, *The Death of the Messiah*, vol 2, 1232.

[487] K.L. McKay, 'The Use of the Ancient Greek Perfect down to the End of the Second Century' *Bulletin of the Institute of Classical Studies* 12 (1965) 1–21. K.L. McKay, 'On the Perfect and Other Aspects in New Testament Greek' *NovT* 23 (1981) 289–329. S.E. Porter, 'Keeping up with Recent Studies: 17. Greek Language and Linguistics' *Exp Times* 103 (1991–92) 202–07. Also commenting on the use the perfect for the aorist, BDF observes that 'there are scattered traces of the late use of the perfect in narrative.' See BDF §343.

[488] On this, see Brown, *The Death of the Messiah*, vol 2, 1233.

[489] See BDAG, 725–727.

not used to refer to miracles, instead it describes the good gifts given by fathers (Matt 7.11; Lk 11.13); the generic speaking or bringing forth of 'good things' (Matt 12.33, 34); the quality of possessions judged to be of value (Matt 12.18, 19; 16.25); and the quality of behaviour which results in some entering into resurrection life (Jn 5.29). Notwithstanding the lack of a precedent, it is difficult to see what else ἀγαθά can be denoting in the present context apart from Jesus' miracles. Although the term ἀγαθά is not utilised in this sense in the canonical gospels, this suggestion may gain supported from the reference in Jn 11.45, that states that many believed in Jesus θεασάμενοι ἃ ἐποίησεν. The event that stands behind this report is the miraculous raising of Lazarus and the defeat of the powers of death. Barrett notes that '[m]iracles in John regularly lead either to faith, or to the reverse of faith.'[490] Swete suggests that in 'their lightheartedness the Scribes and Priests indulge themselves in heartless banter at the expense of Joseph.'[491] It is not necessarily the case that the mocking tone attributed to the Scribes and Priests by Swete is actually part of this passage. Although it appears bizarre that the Jewish crowd hands the body over to Joseph because of the qualification that he witnessed the miracles, this may only seem strange if the narrator is working with consistent characterization and narratival logic. Rather, this tension arises precisely because the author does not do this. Instead he imposes his own perspectives on characters even when such outlooks are at odds with those characters' portrayal in the story. This creates a somewhat confused and illogical storyline, but this reflects the limited skills of the writer.

**6.24a** λαβὼν δὲ τὸν κύριον ἔλουσε καὶ εἴλησε σινδόνιν. The activities outlined here in preparing the body for burial have partial counterparts in the canonical tradition. While all four canonical gospels know of the tradition surrounding wrapping Jesus in a linen cloth (Matt 27.56; Mk 15.46; Lk 23.53; Jn 19.40), none of them records a tradition of washing the body prior to burial. The closest that any of the canonical accounts comes to this is the Johannine redactional detail which describes the application of spices to the corpse by Nicodemus and Joseph (Jn 19.40). Brown, however, states that the washing of the corpse accords with Jewish burial practices. 'In burying, the Jews did

---

[490] Barrett, *The Gospel according to St John*, 337.
[491] Swete, *The Akhmîm Fragment of the Apocryphal Gospel of St Peter*, 11.

not eviscerate the cadaver, as did the Egyptians in mummification. Rather the Jews simply washed the body, anointed it with oil and clothed it.'[492]

As in v. 21 the corpse is still referred to as ὁ κύριος, showing that the author still reverences the dead body. As Mara comments, 'the body of Jesus abandoned by the δύναμις is still always the Κύριος.'[493] Following the bidding of the Jews, Joseph removes the body from the scene of the crucifixion to an unnamed location to carry out the requisite preparations. The washing of Jesus' body prior to burial may well be historically correct, but it does not follow that the author of the Akhmîm text had access to extra-canonical tradition at this point. Rather, what he has assumed on the basis of his contemporary experience of burial customs may accurately reflect the preaparations made to ready the corpse for burial. During the first century, and subsequent periods in Jewish history, washing of the corpse was an integral component of the burial rites.

> As signs of respect and honor, prior to burial, the corpse was watched over (shemirah) and washed (teharah). This washing was not out of concern for cultic cleanness (a corpse is intrinsically unclean and renders unclean all who touch or are shadowed by it) but was viewed as a continuation of the hygiene that applied when the individual lived. Prior to burial, the body was dressed in shrouds made of plain linen.[494]

The fact that the Gospel of Peter employs a simplex verb form εἴλησε, rather than the compound forms used by the synoptics (ἐνείλησε: Mk 15.46; and ἐνετύλιξεν: Matt 27.59; Lk 23.53) should be seen as a stylistic trait.[495] The orthographical error with the form σινδόνιν has been mentioned in the textual notes. If the Gospel of Peter is following the synoptic tradition then a dative singular form σινδόνι is to be preferred. If this is not the case, a dative plural form σινδῶσιν is equally possible. This may gain further support from the use of the plural in certain LXX passages (Jdg 14.12; Prov 31.24), although these occurrences do not denote funeral shrouds.

---

[492] Brown, The Gospel according to John XIII–XXI, 941.

[493] Mara, Évangile de Pierre, 148.

[494] 'Burial' in J. Neusner and W.S. Green (eds.), Dictionary of Judaism in the Biblical Period (Peabody, Mass.: Hendrickson, 1996) 104.

[495] Mara observes this tendency, mentioning 'le préférence connu de Ev.P. pour formes simples.' Mara, Évangile de Pierre, 148.

**6.24b** καὶ εἰσήγαγεν εἰς ἴδιον τάφον καλούμενον κῆπον
Ἰωσήφ. There are two possible ways to interpret this clause. First, and
perhaps most likely given the storyline of the canonical accounts, the
verb εἰσήγαγεν refers to the act of bringing Jesus' body into the tomb.
It then becomes necessary to supply a direct object αὐτόν 'him'. This
is also necessary with the co-ordinated verbal pair in the preceding
clause, ἔλουσε καὶ εἴλησε. While most translations adopt this alternative, without supplying an object for the verb εἰσήγαγεν the text simply
reports Joseph entering his own tomb, without reference to the body
being brought to that place. No doubt the desire to supply the object
is motivated by improving the sense and under the influence of the
synoptic tradition (καὶ ἔθηκεν αὐτὸ[ν] Matt 27.60; Mk 15.46; Lk 23.53).
In the fourth gospel the body is taken to the tomb by an unspecified
group of people, ἔθηκαν τὸν Ἰησοῦν (Jn 19.42). If the movement of the
corpse is not being described, then the narrative at this point is interested in identifying the tomb.

There is a double association with Joseph and the burial place, it is
his own tomb and it is located in a garden that bears his name. Swete's
comment that 'Peter's καλούμενον κῆπον κ.λ.ω. may have arisen from a
desire to convey the impression of independent knowledge'[496] perhaps
attributes to much sophistication to the author of the text. Rather,
the report in Matthew's gospel (Matt 27.57) that Joseph was a rich
man, may stand behind this desire to link both tomb and garden with
his name.

---

[496] Swete, *The Akhmîm Fragment of the Apocryphal Gospel of St Peter*, 12.

# REACTIONS OF JEWISH GROUPS AND
# THE COMPANIONS (7.25–27)

25. τότε οἱ Ἰουδαῖοι¹ καὶ οἱ πρεσβύτεροι καὶ οἱ ἱερεῖς² γνόντες³ οἷον κακὸν ἑαυτοῖς ἐποίησαν, ἤρξαντο⁴ κόπτεσθαι καὶ λέγειν· οὐαί ταῖς⁵ ἁμαρτίαις ἡμῶν· ἤγγισεν ἡ κρίσις καὶ τὸ τέλος Ἰερουσαλήμ. 26. ἐγὼ δὲ μετὰ τῶ(ν)⁶ ἑταίρων μου ἐλυπούμην καὶ τετρωμένοι κατὰ διάνοιαν ἐκρυβόμεθα. ἐζητούμεθα γὰρ⁷ ὑπ' αὐτῶν ὡς κακοῦργοι καὶ ὡς τὸν ναὸν θέλοντες ἐμπρῆσαι.⁸ 27. ἐπὶ δὲ τούτοις πᾶσιν ἐνηστεύομεν καὶ ἐκαθεζόμεθα⁹ πενθοῦντες καὶ κλαίοντες νυκτὸς καὶ ἡμέρας ἕως τοῦ σαββάτου.

25. Then the Jews, and the elders and the priests knowing what evil they had done to themselves, they began to lament and say, 'Woe to our sins, the judgment and the end of Jerusalem is at hand.' 26. But I with my companions was grieved, and being wounded in mind we hid. For we were being sought by them as evildoers and as those wishing to burn the temple. 27. But through all of these things we were fasting and were sitting, mourning and weeping night and day until the Sabbath.

## Text Critical Notes

1. The word Ἰουδαῖοι, which occurs at the end of the second last line of the third page of text is the completion of the longest line of text on that page. This results in the the final two letter being compressed, the o is dot-like with no visible enclosed white-space, and the ι is much reduced in height, measuring only 2mm in comparison to the usual length of 4–5mm.
2. The script actually reads οιερεις instead of οιιερεις (as in the emended text above), hence omitting an iota towards the beginning of this sequence of letters. Kraus and Nicklas note 'Ms: ο ιερεις',[497] but there is better reason to divide the letters as οι ερεις, which although still a mistake is more easily explained both in terms of the physical features of the manuscript as well as trends in scribal habits.

---

[497] Kraus und Nicklas, *Das Petrusevangelium und die Petrusapokalypse*, 36.

First, examination of the photographs reveals that the iota stands in closer proximity to the preceding omicron (1mm space), than to the following epsilon (2mm space). Although spacing between words is not maintained with great consistency by the scribe of P.Cair. 10759, he does often, although admittedly erratically, leave larger spaces at the end of words. Second, although itacism was more common with scribes in late antiquity, there is at times a tendency to make changes with other initial vowel combinations.[498] Here, however, the error is most likely due to haplography, that is accidentally omitting one of the two iotas.

3. The scribe continues his habit of poor and inconsistent formation of the letter γ in the word γνόντες. Gebhardt has noted the poor formation of the γ.[499]

4. Underneath the word κακόν, which commences the first line of the fourth page of text there is reflected writing impressed from the facing page. The reflected writing slopes upward in relation to the text written on the fourth page. The result is that whereas it was beneath the text at the beginning of the line it intersects with the text towards the end of the word ἐποίησαν and throughout much of the word ἤρξαντο. Consequently this, in combination with the darkening at the top of the page, obscures much of the term ἤρξαντο. The uncertain letters, marked with the customary dot beneath them, are ηρξαντο. Of the remaining letters, the final two (το) are clearly visible, the ρ is recognizable from the downward stoke and the ξ, although written on a dark portion of the page can be readily discerned. With the aid of magnification, the main shape of the initial η can be made out. The other two letters (αν) are poorly formed, and appear to be obscured more by the darkness of the page than the imprinted reflected writing.

5. Here again reflected writing obscures the text. Although the word οὐαί is partially affected all letters can be determined. The scribe's habit of writing oversized iotas actually assists here in reading the final letter of οὐαί. The next word ταῖς suffers to a greater degree. Again an enlarged iota is visible, and offers some assistance in marking the position of the previous letter. However, the initial

---

[498] For a general discussion of shifts in vowels during the evolution of the Greek language see BDF §22–28. For a much more detailed analysis see Caragounis, *The Development of Greek and the New Testament*, 489–502.

[499] Gebhardt, *Das Evangelium und die Apokalypse des Petrus*, 10.

τ has the shape of an amorphous ink-blot, although the crossbar stroke is legible.

6. This is third of nine examples in the manuscript where the scribe uses a supralinear stoke, usually offset to the right to varying degrees, to indicate the omission of a final letter. As Kraus and Nicklas observe 'Ms: τῶ.'[500] In all nine cases the letter is the movable ν. As with the previous example in 6.21, this seems to have become a stylistic convention rather than being necessitated by a lack of space.[501]

7. The scribe's difficulty with the formation of the letter γ continues here. The opening letter of the word γάρ is almost 'invisible', consiting of a single vertical stroke joining the preceding and following alphas.[502]

8. The letter ρ in the word ἐμπρῆσαι is heavily obstructed by the darkening of the manuscript. Although the vertical stroke appears shorter than other examples of this letter, thus making identification even more problematic, the arc forming the righthand loop of the letter is partially visible, thus assisting the reading of the letter in this case.

9. An unusual aspect of the formation of the final letter of the word ἐκαθεζόμεθα is the elongated diagonally sloping tail. This results in the penstroke running to the edge of the page of the manuscript. This appears to be the only example in this text where the scribe has written to the extremity of the page. Other elongated tails on the letter α at the end of a line also occur in lines 12 and 16 on this page, but those penstrokes do not intersect with the edge of the page.

## Commentary

**7.25a** τότε οἱ Ἰουδαῖοι καὶ οἱ πρεσβύτεροι καὶ οἱ ἱερεῖς γνόντες οἷον κακὸν ἑαυτοῖς ἐποίησαν. The material contained in *Gos. Pet.* 7.25–27 is not closely paralleled in any of the canonical accounts. The conjunction τότε can either denote a logical, or a sequential

---

[500] Kraus und Nicklas, *Das Petrusevangelium und die Petrusapokalypse*, 38.
[501] See BDF §20.
[502] See Gebhardt, *Das Evangelium und die Apokalypse des Petrus*, 10.

chronological connection.[503] These alternatives are not necessarily mutually exclusive, and this overlap in use appears to be intended here. The τότε is sequential in that it indicates a temporal progression, but it is also consequential, since the reaction it introduces is predicated upon observation of the miraculous portents which have accompanied the crucifixion of Jesus.[504]

The combination of the three groups, Jews, elders and priests, is unattested elsewhere in the narrative. In fact this is the only reference to a priestly caste in the text. The other groups do have multiple references: οἱ Ἰουδαῖοι 6 times (Gos. Pet. 1.1; 6.23; 7.25; 11.48; 12.50, 52); οἱ πρεσβύτεροι 5 times (Gos. Pet. 7.25; 8.28, 29, 31; 10.38). Apart from this example the term οἱ Ἰουδαῖοι is used in conjunction with other subjects only in 1.1, where their non-washing of hands is connected with both Herod and the judges. By contrast, οἱ πρεσβύτεροι are linked with scribes and Pharisees (8.28); scribes alone (8.31); and the centurion, who is unnamed in the immediate context (10.38). The combination of the three groups is not an attempt to allot the blame to the leaders. Rather, the generalized reference to 'the Jews' linked with the two leadership groups appears to demonstrate that the author attributed blame for the crucifixion to all eschalons of Jewish society.[505]

Psychological analysis is provided by the author of the text. He informs the audience that the three parties became aware that their actions were calamitous for themselves. This is a further example of the rapid mood swings that are portrayed among Jesus' persecutors. First, in response to the onset of darkness the crowd becomes ἐθορυβοῦντος καὶ ἠγωνίων (Gos. Pet. 5.15). Second, the sense of apprehension is noted again when the ground convulses καὶ φόβος μέγας ἐγένετο (Gos. Pet. 6.21). Third, almost immediately after this with the return of the sun there is a sense of emotional relief which the author

---

[503] The use of the conjunction τότε is similar to the Matthean usage. In relation to the occurrence in the first gospel Black states, 'Τότε may function either on the levelof discourse structure, for example, marking paragraphs within as an episode, or at a more local level, marking the use of a theologically significant lexical form or a climactic point within a pericope.' S. Black, Sentence Conjunctions in the Gospel of Matthew: καί, δέ, τότε, γάρ, οὖν and Asyndeton in Narrative Discourse, JSNTSMS 216 (London: Sheffield Academic Press, 2002) 253. See also A.H. McNeile, 'Τότε in St Mattew', JTS 12 (1911) 127–128.

[504] See Gos. Pet. 6.21.

[505] As Mara states, 'Notre auteur emploie l'expression τότε οἱ Ἰουδαῖοι pour designer toute la nation a partir du nom de la region palestinienne (Ἰουδαία).' Mara, Évangile de Pierre, 150.

describes as joy, ἐχάρησαν δὲ οἱ Ἰουδαῖοι (*Gos. Pet.* 6.23). Fourth, here the narrative introduces a sense of foreboding as the three groups in concert become aware of the consequences of there actions. Unlike the preceding three references to emotions which were linked to certain physical phenomena, here there is no description of the catalyst that has evoked this awareness among these groups. As Vaganay observes, such questions of cause or details about the extent of remorse are of no interest to the author, rather he uses the description for apologetic purposes in order to further characterize the Jews in a negative manner.[506]

**7.25b** ἤρξαντο κόπτεσθαι καὶ λέγειν· οὐαί ταῖς ἁμαρτίαις ἡμῶν· ἤγγισεν ἡ κρίσις καὶ τὸ τέλος Ἰερουσαλήμ. Recognition of the evil brought upon themselves is accompanied by the twin elements of breast-beating and a corresponding saying. The action is reminiscent of the uniquely Lukan account of the response of the multitudes, θεωρήσαντες τὰ γενόμενα, τύπτοντες τὰ στήθη ὑπέστρεφον (Lk 23.48). While there are no direct verbal parallels, the similarity in the scenes depicted make the possibility of non-literary dependence likely. Both accounts place the event after the crucifixion, it is a collective action, and follows a description of insight gained by the crowds into the significance of the events that have transpired. However, there are important differences that can be accounted as due to the redactional concerns of the *Gospel of Peter*. Among them, as Vaganay states, '[t]he third Evangelist speaks simply of the populace: καὶ πάντες... ὄχλοι. It is the ordinary crowd of executions.'[507] Whereas, here the author of the *Gospel of Peter* specifies the three groups which form the crowd. Unlike the generalized dportrayal of lament in Luke, the description in the *Gospel of Peter* emphasizes that these groups were major protagonists in bringing about the execution. Moreover, their mourning is motivated by self-interest, not by the injustice of the events that have occurred. The language of lament κόπτω is common in the NT (cf. Matt 24.30; Rev 1.8; 18.9), and choosing this in place of Luke's τύπτοντες τὰ στήθη may reflect the tendency in orally transmitted narratives to replace less familiar terminology with that in wider circulation. One of the most significant features of the 'beating of breasts' motif in the

---

[506] See Vaganay, *L'Évangile de Pierre*, 268.
[507] Vaganay, *L'Évangile de Pierre*, 268.

*Gospel of Peter* is its repetition in 8.28 where it is carried out by ὁ λαὸς ἅπας. As will be discussed in relation to the *Gospel of Peter* 8.28, the verbal parallels are even closer to Lk 23.48, which suggests that the author may have created a doublet out of that tradition.

The words of lament, perhaps like similar NT predictions,[508] represent a *vaticinum ex eventu*. The lack of detail surrounding the destruction of Jerusalem, in contrast to the Lukan prediction (Lk 21.20–24),[509] should not be taken as an indication of the primitivitity of the tradition preserved here as Crossan would urge. He comments, 'I see nothing in *Gospel of Peter* 7.25 that demands a date after the fall of Jerusalem or an experience of that destruction.'[510] While Crossan is careful to avoid the positive corollary, that this passage demands a date prior to the destruction, this is the clear thesis of his study. In response it should be noted that the portion of the *Gospel of Peter* that is preserved does not contain a parallel to Mk 13, so it is unclear how the prediction may have been handled in its entirety, second, this summary statement may well allude to a fuller prophetic account of the fate of Jerusalem given earlier in the now non-extant portion of the narrative, and third, in the present context the focus is upon the apprehension of the Jews and their leaders.

The saying comprises of two elements admission of sin and recognition of the eventual fate of Jerusalem. Brown feels that these twin elements explain why the Jews, elders and priests beat their chests. He states that this is 'because by their sins they have made inevitable God's wrathful judgment and the end of Jerusalem, and thus they have done wrong to themselves.'[511] Although the narrative does not explicitly outline this causal chain, nevertheless it does seem to be present by implication. The term οὐαί which opens this saying is often used to commence laments or warnings,[512] and this appears to be the predominant use in the 46 instances in the NT (cf. Matt 11.21; 18.7; Mk

---

[508] For the debate on whether Mk 13 reveals a knowledge of the events surround the destruction of the temple in 70 C.E. see the standard commentaries as well as G.R. Beasley-Murray, *Jesus and the Last Days* (Peabody, Mass.: Hendrickson, 1993).

[509] Bultmann saw the redactional changes to Mk 13 introduced by Luke as intended to produce a better fit with the actual events that took place. 'In chapter 21 Luke has attempted several corrections of apocalyptic prophecies in Mk. 13, partly under the influence of historical events (21²⁰⁻²⁴). Bultmann, *History of the Synoptic Tradition*, 127.

[510] Crossan, *The Cross That Spoke*, 257.

[511] Brown, *The Death of the Messiah*, vol. 2, 1190.

[512] On this see 'οὐαί' in EDNT, vol. 2, 540.

14.21; Lk 6.26). Apart from one instance in the Pauline corpus (1 Cor 9.16) and one in Jude 11, the term is used only in the synoptic gospels and Revelation. In the latter, apart from its usual sense as an interjection, it can also function as a noun ἡ οὐαὶ ἡ μία ἀπῆλθεν· ἰδοὺ ἔρχεται ἔτι δύο οὐαὶ μετὰ ταῦτα (Rev 9.12). The admission of sin is somewhat surprising, although there are some similarities with the declaration made by Judas in Matt 27.4, ἥμαρτον παραδοὺς αἷμα ἀθῷον. Unlike the declaration made by Judas, there is no remorse or repentance for involvement in the death of Jesus.[513] Although the saying has no parallel in the Greek manuscript tradition of the NT, the versional witness to the Old Latin, Codex Sangermanensis (g[1]),[514] preserves a saying that is akin to it: uae nobis[515] quae facta sunt hodie propter peccata nostra, appropinquauit enim desolation Hierusalem (Lk 23.48). This may lend some further weight to the suggestion that the author of the *Gospel of Peter* shows some awareness of an alternative form of Luke's gospel. This tradition is also preserved by the *Diatessaron* as far as it can be reconstructed through the commentary of Ephrem, in the *Doctrine of Addai*, as well as in Syriac versional manuscripts, i.e. sy[c s].[516] It is also possible that this tradition came to the author of the *Gospel of Peter* independently of any form of Luke's gospel.

**7.26a**   ἐγὼ δέ μετὰ τῶν ἑταίρων μου ἐλυπούμην καὶ τετ-ρωμένοι κατὰ διάνοιαν ἐκρυβόμεθα. Here the implied narrator surfaces for the first time in this extant portion of the text. The first person narrative is maintained throughout vv. 26–27, but does not resurface again until the final two verses of this text, where Peter is explicitly identified as the first person narrator. Once again, there is no direct

---

[513] In fact Brown distinguishes between this group and the '*repentant* Jews' of (8.28b). See Brown, *The Death of the Messiah*, vol. 2, 1190.

[514] Codex Sangermanensis (g[1]) is a manuscript of the gospels, housed in the National Library in Paris, and dating to the eighth or ninth centuries, making it roughly contemporaneous with the Akhmîm text. See NA[27], 714. Although g[1] is classified as an Old Latin text, it is important to be aware of the cross-fertilization of readings contained in the Vulgate tradition. See K. Aland and B. Aland, *The Text of the New Testament*, 187.

[515] At this point the text reads vobis. This scribal error has been rectified and is not reproduced in the form of the text printed above.

[516] For an extended discussion of the witnesses to this reading see Vaganay, *L'Évangile de Pierre*, 269–271. For a brief discussion of the problems in reconstructing the text of the *Diatessaron* see P. Foster, 'Tatian', *Exp Times* 120 (2008) 105–118, esp. 110–114.

parallel with material in the canonical accounts, but the whole account is reminiscent of a scene in the fourth gospel. According to the Johannine account, during the evening of the first day of week following the resurrection the disciples congregate behind shut doors because of fear of the Jews: οὔσης οὖν ὀψίας τῇ ἡμέρᾳ ἐκείνῃ τῇ μιᾷ σαββάτων καὶ τῶν θυρῶν κεκλεισμένων ὅπου ἦσαν οἱ μαθηταὶ διὰ τὸν φόβον τῶν Ἰουδαίων (Jn 20.19). In this case, the points of contact are suggestive rather than conclusive of any theories of direct borrowing from the fourth gospel. In fact the time of gathering of the disciples is different in the two accounts. In the *Gospel of Peter* it occurs on the day of crucifixion, whereas in John's gospel it occurs on the evening of the day of resurrection. Vaganay suggests that possibly both Jn 20.19 and other Johannine traditions as shaping the narrative at this point.[517] His degree of hesitancy is fully understandable, since there is a lack of explicit overlap in terms of vocabulary, yet this is characteristic of the way in which the author freely rewrites existing traditions for his own polemical and apologetic purposes.

The term ἑταῖρος is rare in both the NT and Patristic literature. In the NT it is a Matthean term used on three occasions: to address the servant who questions the master's generosity in paying equally all workers a denarius (Matt 20.13); as an appellation to the person that attends the wedding feast incorrectly attired (Matt 22.12); and, as the form Jesus adopts to address Judas when he betrays him (Matt 26.50). In the first two instances it takes on the common classical and Hellenistic use for addressing a person whose name one does not know.[518] It also occurs as a variant reading in 𝔓⁷⁵ for ἕτεροι (Lk 23.32). Although

---

[517] 'Beaucoup de commentateurs y voient une influence johannique (*Jn.*, VIII, 59; XII, 36; XIX, 38; XX, 19, 26). C'est possible.' Vaganay, *L'Évangile de Pierre*, 272.

[518] See BDAG, 398.

[519] Although the reading ἑταῖροι is not listed among the apparatus of variants in NA²⁷ (or discussed in the standard commentaries), presumably because it was seen as an itacism rather than a theologically motivated alteration, it may not be a mere orthographic change. There is some instability in the word order in this text with the majority of manuscripts reversing the order of the words κακοῦργοι and δύο in the phrase ἕτεροι κακοῦργοι δύο to avoid any implication that Jesus was classed as an evildoer. Although NA²⁷ lists 𝔓⁷⁵ as supporting the printed reading, in actual fact it reads ἑταῖροι κακοῦργοι δύο. This also resolves any possibility of Jesus being identified with the κακοῦργοι. See Victor Martin and Rodolphe Kasser, *Papyrus Bodmer XIV: Evangile de Luc chap. 3–24* (Cologny-Geneva: Bibliotheca Bodmeriana) 141. Note that this variant is not recorded in P. Comfort and D. Barrett, *The Complete Text of the Earliest New Testament Manuscripts* (Grand Rapids, Michigan: Baker, 1999) 552, even though they present a transcription of 𝔓⁷⁵.

the choice of terminology may be influenced by Matthean usage, it carries a different nuance, denoting a set of fellow companions whose names are known to the first person narrator (cf. *Gos. Pet.* 14.60). Joint emotions of mourning and disoriented senses are presented as the motivation for concealment. This information is not contained in the canonical accounts. John alone describes the disciples furtive gathering, with the reason for secrecy being given as 'fear of the Jews' διὰ τὸν φόβον τῶν Ἰουδαίων (Jn 20.19). This aspect is recounted in the second half of *Gos. Pet.* 7.26, but the extra reason given in the first part of the verse stems from the twin feelings of bereavement and incomprehension concerning the events that have transpired. Commenting on the expression τετρωμένοι κατὰ διάνοιαν Vaganay makes the following observation. 'the formula is not in the gospel-style. One often meets it however in the LXX: τιτρώσκεσθαι τὴν διάνοιαν (*II Mac.*, III, 16; cf. Diodore de Sicile, XVII, 112: τετρωμένος τήν ψυχήν).'[520] This is reflective of the creative manner in which the author of the *Gospel of Peter* expands gospel traditions in popularizing ways. Here the term ἐλυπούμην is employed to describe the grief of Peter and his fellow disciples. Interestingly, when λυπέω is used in the canonical accounts in passion and resurrection narratives, it is employed in contexts where the disciples, or specifically Peter, are present. During the Last Supper, the disciples become grieved in response to Jesus' declaration that one of them would betray him (Matt 26.22//Mk 14.19). In Gethsemane, Jesus becomes grieved λυπεῖσθαι in the presence of Peter and the two sons of Zebedee (Matt 26.37). In the Johannine scene which is often understood as the rehabilitation of Peter reversing his threefold denial,[521] Peter becomes grieved ἐλυπήθη when asked for the third time whether he loves Jesus (Jn 21.17). However, the fact that the author of the Akhmîm text uses the same term in the Passion context with a similar set of characters may be purely coinicidental. Alternatively, it may show that the language of the canonical portrayals of the disciples had permeated his thinking to such an extent that he automatically

---

[520] Vaganay, *L'Évangile de Pierre*, 271.

[521] As Brown states, 'Most commentators have found in Jesus' thrice-repeated question "Do you love me?" and in Peter's threefold "You know that I love you" a symbolic undoing of Peter's threefold denial of Jesus. Consequently, they have seen in 15–17 Peter's rehabilitation to discipleship after his fall.' Brown, *The Gospel according to John XIII–XXI*, 1111.

employed it as the most apt way to describe the emotions of the disciples on this occasion.

**7.26b** ἐζητούμεθα γὰρ ὑπ᾽ αὐτῶν ὡς κακοῦργοι καὶ ὡς τὸν ναὸν θέλοντες ἐμπρῆσαι. Once again the narrative presents readers with a detail that has a vague connection with the canonical accounts, but significantly develops that tradition in order to add colour and fresh insight into the details surrounding the events of the crucifixion and resurrection. As Mara states, 'The detail of the apostles hidden because of fear of the Jews and treated like criminals…finds some resonances with the Johannine account, notably in Jn 20.19.'[522] The term κακοῦργοι has been employed in the narrative to designate the two fellow victims of crucifixion (*Gos. Pet.* 4.10, 13). Regardless of whether the term has overtones of political anarchy, it is fully transparent that such a charge can result in death by crucifixion as the penalty. The impression is conveyed of an active search to seek out the disciples, this vivid detail heightens both the tension and colour of the story in a manner that does not occur in the canonical versions.[523] The pursuers, designated by the pronominal phrase ὑπ᾽ αὐτῶν, can be understood generally as the Jews (which is the sense assumed by Vaganay), or in the immediate context it may designate actions undertaken by the triad of groups mentioned in 7.25, which may designate that the search is instigated primarily by leadership figures among the Jews. However, it was suggested in the comments on *Gos. Pet.* 7.25a, that the combination of groups is intended as an inclusive designation of all the Jews, who are stigmatized by the author as being responsible for the crucifixion.

The reference to burning the Temple is significant and may give a partial clue to the dating of the text. Such a connection between the Temple and 'burning' as its means of destruction is unknown in the NT.[524] References to Temple destruction in the NT use more generalized verbs, καταλύω (Matt 26.61; 27.40; Mk 14.58) or λύω (Jn 2.19). By contrast, as Vaganay argues that 'the verb "to set fire to" (ἐμπρῆσαι)

---

[522] Mara, *Évangile de Pierre*, 156.
[523] Thus Vaganay comments that '[l]a crainte des Douze est on ne peut mieux fondée et n'a rien de répréhensible, car les Juifs sont a leur porsuite.' Vaganay, *L'Évangile de Pierre*, 272.
[524] See Mara, *Évangile de Pierre*, 155.

shows that the author remembers the catastrophe of the year 70.'[525]
Fire is prominent is Josephus' description of the destruction of Jerusalem. He notes that is some instances the streams of blood extinguished
fires (Bell. 6.406) and that eventually flames overtook the whole city,
φλεγομένοις δ ἐπανέτειλεν Ἱεροσολύμοις ἡμέρα Γορπιαίου μηνὸς ὀγδόη
(Bell. 6.407).[526] Moreover, accusations are brought against the Jews of
Antioch for having devised a plan to burn the whole city (Bell. 7.47),
with those accused being put to death by burning. When later fire
destroyed the market square of Antioch the Jews are again seen as
arsonists (Bell. 7.54–56). This can also be seen as reflecting the accusations made against Christians in Rome as being involved in incendiary
activity during the fire that broke out in the Neronic period. Tacitus
writes that for the purpose of deflecting reports that Nero himself had
ordered the conflagration, the Christians were accused of starting the
fire: ergo abolendo rumori Nero subdidit reos et quaesitissimis poenis
adfecit quos per flagitia invisos vulgus Christianos appellabat (Tacitus,
Ann. 15.44).[527] In relation to the connection with the fire in Rome,
Vaganay acknowledges that there is some relationship here between
the charge of arson and the most widespread accusation brought
against Christians during the first persecutions in Rome.[528] However,
what all of these partial parallels are lacking is a clear reference to
the Temple, instead they describe the destruction of all Jerusalem by
fire, or link Christians with the practice or arson, but each of these
examples fail to have the combination of connections found in the
present text where followers of Jesus are being accused of plotting to
destroy the Temple with fire.

**7.27a** ἐπὶ δὲ τούτοις πᾶσιν ἐνηστεύομεν. The reference to fasting may be an explicit attempt to produce fulfilment of the prediction
uttered by Jesus in the synoptic accounts, that his followers would

---

[525] Vaganay, L'Évangile de Pierre, 272.

[526] 'And the dawn of the eighth day of the month Gorpiaeus broke upon Jerusalem
in flames.' H. St. J. Thackery, Josephus: The Jewish War, LCL 210 (Cambridge, Mass.:
Harvard, 1928) 297.

[527] 'Consequently, to get rid of the report, Nero fastened the guilt and inflicted the
most exquisite tortures on a class hated for their abominations, called Christians by
the populace' (Tacitus, Ann. 15.44).

[528] 'Tout au plus pourrait-on admettre que cette accusation d'incendie n'est pas
sans rapport avec les calumnies le plus ordinairement répandues contre les chrétiens
pendant les premières persécutions.' Vaganay, L'Évangile de Pierre, 272.

fast when the bridegroom was taken away (Matt 9.15//Mk 2.19–20// Lk 5.34–35).[529] By contrast, Mara argues that the inspiration for this passage is to be found in a rabbinic development of ascetic practices.[530] Yet given the author's antipathy towards Jewish practices this may not be altogether likely. Swete's translation, 'to add to our troubles we were keeping fast',[531] seems to miss the point of the verse. The act of fasting is not portrayed as an additional burden, but an indicator of the spiritual sincerity of the disciples who try to fathom the significance of the events and open themselves to being recipients of divine communication through such an activity. Perhaps a better paraphrased translation would be 'in the face of all of these things, we were fasting.'

**7.27b καὶ ἐκαθεζόμεθα πενθοῦντες καὶ κλαίοντες νυκτὸς καὶ ἡμέρας ἕως τοῦ σαββάτου.** Two further acts are described which accompany the fasting. The actions of mourning and weeping, coupled with the reference to fasting are typical features of lamentation in response to death. The combination of mourning and weeping seems to be a stock hendiadys to denote lamentation. As Vaganay notes 'the terms which he employs all have the air of a cliché.'[532] This pairing occurs numerous times in the NT (Mk 16.10; Lk 6.25; Jam 4.9; Rev 18.11). The posture of sitting ἐκαθεζόμεθα is also described in lament scenes. Hagar sits as she mourns the approaching death of her weeping son Ishmael καὶ ἐκάθισεν ἀπέναντι αὐτοῦ ἀναβοῆσαν δὲ τὸ παιδίον ἔκλαυσεν (Gen 21.16). In Job, sitting is also adopted as the posture of lament (Job 2.8, 13; 29.25).

The author's concern to indicate the time-frame of events comes to the fore with the temporal note νυκτὸς καὶ ἡμέρας ἕως τοῦ σαββάτου. The genitive case is employed to indicate the duration of the actions of fasting, mourning and weeping. This description also has the narratival function of filling the gap that exists in the canonical accounts between the crucifixion and resurrection by depicting the ongoing piety of the disciples who engage in proper lament, as opposed to those responsible for the crucifixion, who exhibit self-interest and plot against the followers of Jesus. Debates surrounding this reference as a

---

[529] For a discussion of the possibility that the Markan material is responding to a controversy over fasting in the early church see Guelich, *Mark 1–8.26*, 106–117.

[530] Mara, *Évangile de Pierre*, 156.

[531] Swete, *The Akhmîm Fragment of the Apocryphal Gospel of St Peter*, 13.

[532] Vaganay, *L'Évangile de Pierre*, 273.

contribution to the Quartodeciman controversy appear to be foreign to the actual narrative.[533] If such were the intention of the passage it would have to be concluded that it fails miserably in communicating its preferred solution. Furthermore, Vaganay's discuss of whether the term ἕως is inclusive or exclusive of the Sabbath seems to miss the narrative intention.[534] The author is not describing actual history, or using the preposition to clarify duration of periods of fasting, instead it is part of the characterization of the disciples in the interim period between the death of Jesus and his resurrection, denoting them in stylized fashion as adopting the correct behaviour for mourners. Admittedly Eusebius notes that Irenaeus stated that the controversy was not only about the date of Easter, but also concerned the length of the fasting period which accompanied it.

> οὐδὲ γὰρ μόνον περὶ τῆς ἡμέρας ἐστὶν ἡ ἀμφισβήτησις, ἀλλὰ καὶ περὶ τοῦ εἴδους αὐτοῦ τῆς νηστείας. οἱ μὲν γὰρ οἴονται μίαν ἡμέραν δεῖν αὐτοὺς νηστεύειν, οἱ δὲ δύο, οἱ δὲ καὶ πλείονας, οἱ δὲ τεσσαράκοντα ὥρας ἡμερίας τε καὶ νυκτερινὰς συμμετροῦσιν τὴν ἡμέραν αὐτῶν. (Eusebius, *H.E.* 5.24.12)

> For the controversy is not only about the day, but also about the actual character of the fast; for some think that they ought to fastone day, others two, others even more, some count their day as forty hours, day and night.

While fasting may well have been a significant aspect of the Quartodeciman controversy, the reference to fasting in *Gos. Pet.* 7.27 does not mean that this protracted debate is in view in the present context.

---

[533] See Zahn, *Das Evangelium des Petrus*, 20, n. 2, and Vaganay, *L'Évangile de Pierre*, 273.

[534] Vaganay, *L'Évangile de Pierre*, 273–275.

## SECURING THE SEPULCHRE (8.28–33)

28. συναχθέντες δὲ οἱ γραμματεῖς καὶ Φαρισαῖοι καὶ πρεσβύτεροι πρὸς ἀλλήλους¹ ἀκούσαντες ὅτι ὁ λαὸς² ἅπας³ γογγύζει καὶ κόπτεται⁴ τὰ στήθη λέγοντες ὅτι, εἰ τῷ θανάτῳ αὐτοῦ ταῦτα τὰ μέγιστα σημεῖα γέγονεν, ἴδετε ὅτι πόσον δίκαιός ἐστιν. 29. ἐφοβήθησαν οἱ πρεσβύτεροι καὶ ἦλθον πρὸς Πειλᾶτον δεόμενοι αὐτοῦ καὶ λέγοντες· 30. Παράδος ἡμῖν στρατιώτας, ἵνα φυλάξω⁵ τὸ μνῆμα⁶ αὐτοῦ ἐπὶ τρεῖς ἡμ[έρας]⁷ μήποτε ἐλθόντες οἱ⁸ μαθηταὶ αὐτοῦ κλέψωσιν αὐτὸν καὶ ὑπολάβῃ⁹ ὁ λαὸς ὅτι ἐκ νεκρῶν ἀνέστη, καὶ ποιήσωσιν ἡμῖν κακά. 31. ὁ δὲ Πειλᾶτος παραδέδωκεν αὐτοῖς Πετρώνιον τὸν κεντυρίωνα μετὰ στρατιωτῶν¹⁰ φυλάσσειν¹¹ τὸν τάφον. καὶ σὺν αὐτοῖς ἦλθον πρεσβύτεροι καὶ γραμματεῖς ἐπὶ τὸ μνῆμα. 32. καὶ κυλίσαντες¹² λίθον μέγαν κατὰ¹³ τοῦ κεντυρίωνος καὶ τῶν στρατιωτῶν ὁμοῦ πάντες οἱ ὄντες ἐκεῖ ἔθηκαν ἐπὶ τῇ θύρᾳ τοῦ μνήματος. 33. καὶ ἐπέχρεισαν¹⁴ ἑπτὰ σφραγῖδας καὶ σκηνὴν ἐκεῖ πήξαντες ἐφύλαξαν.

28. And the scribes and the Pharisees and the elders gathered together with one another when they heard that all the people grumbled and beat their chests saying, 'if at his death these greatest signs have happened, behold how just he was.' 29. The elders were afraid and came to Pilate petitioning him and saying, 'Give to us soldiers that I may guard his tomb for three days, lest his disciple come and steal him and the people suppose that he is risen from the dead, and they might do evil things to us.' 31. And Pilate gave to them Petronius the centurion with soldiers to guard the tomb. And with them went elders and scribes to the tomb. 32. And having rolled a great stone towards the centurion and the soldiers, where all those who were there set it at the entrance of the tomb. 33. And they spread out seven seals and pitching a tent there, they kept watch.

### Text Critical Notes

1. The scribe shows yet another variation in forming the double lambda combination. This is perhaps one of the more successful attempts in terms of legibility, since both letters are nearly identical in shape. The right-hand leg is almost perpendicular to the left-hand leg which is only slightly askew from the vertical. The result

is that the right-hand stroke descends only a little below horizontal at the vertex where the two legs join.

2. The formation of the letter α is most irregular in this line. Gebhardt notes the generalized tendency in forming this letter: 'The α appears only in the minuscule form; it is smaller than the other letters, usually open at the top, occasionally only a point with a checkmark as part of it.'[535] A number of these features are present in this case, but it is less 'point-like' than some example of the α contained on this line. In λαός the letter is both minuscule and small, yet it is written in an open fashion and not as a single point with a tail.

3. By contrast with the preceding α in the word λαός and the second occurrence in this word ἅπας, the initial α is like a fullstop with a tail.[536]

4. This is perhaps the most idiosyncratic form of the varying styles of the letter α shown on this line. It follows an enlarged τ contained in the word κόπτεται, the vertical stroke measures 4mm. By contrast the first τ in κόπτεται is only 2mm tall. The α is written in a raised position, the topmost part level with the enlarged τ, but the α measuring only 1mm in height. It is, however, written as an open letter and not as a point.

5. The verbal form φυλάξω, a first person singular aorist subjunctive, is corrected by most commentators in one of two ways. The more prevalent emendation is to the form φυλάξωμεν, thereby making it a first person plural subjunctive. This reading is adopted by Harnack, Swete, Mara, and Kraus and Nicklas among others.[537] Another option that has been suggested is when the form is modified to a third person plural aorist subjunctive, φυλάξωσιν. This emendation is proposed by Robinson, Zahn and Vaganay.[538] Bouriant and Lods

---

[535] 'Das α erscheint nur in das Form der Minuskei; es ist kleiner als die anderen Buchstaben, gewöhnlich oben offen, zuweilen nur ein Punkt mit einem Häkchen daran.' Gebhardt, *Das Evangelium und die Apokalypse des Petrus*, 10.

[536] Again see the fuller comments of Gebhardt on the formation of the letter α; *Das Evangelium und die Apokalypse des Petrus*, 10.

[537] Harnack, *Bruchstücke des Evangeliums und der Apokalypse des Petrus*, 10; Swete, *The Akhmîm Fragment of the Apocryphal Gospel of St Peter*, 14; Mara, *Évangile de Pierre*, 54; Kraus und Nicklas, *Das Petrusevangelium und die Petrusapokalypse*, 39.

[538] Robinson and James, *The Gospel according to Peter and the Revelation of Peter*, 85; Hilgenfeld, 'Das Petrus-Evangelium über Leiden und Auferstehung Jesu', Part 1, 442; Vaganay, *L'Évangile de Pierre*, 280.

are happy to retain the form written in the manuscript.[539] While the form written in the manuscript creates a tension with the preceding reference to a first person plural group, παράδος ἡμῖν, it is certainly not an impossible reading. It requires one to see an unmarked transition from a plural group reference to an unnamed spokesperson, thus using a self-reference in the singular. While this may be less than elegant in stylistic terms, the quality of the narrative suggests that one should not be surprised by such inconsistencies. As the form φυλάξω occurs mid-line in an undamaged portion of the text and preserves a form that is both grammatically possible, which can be understood in its narrative context, it is perhaps best to retain that form without modification.

6. There is a small horizontal hole in the page above the tail of the final elongated α. The hole extends for 3mm, but is never wider than 1mm. It does not obstruct the text.

7. There is a significant hole located in the centre of the bottom line of text resulting in the loss of final four letters of the word ἡμ[έρας]. A fraction of the uppermost part of the final ς is preserved, but otherwise the final four letters are completely lost. Nonetheless, the context makes the reconstruction virtually certain.

8. The *verso* of page three commences with this word. This page is one of the least damaged pages in terms of darkening, however, a hole at the bottom line of this page results in the loss of a single letter.

9. The combination of the initial υ with π results in an unusual formation of the second letter. The π does not have the conventional clearly drawn horizontal crossbar, but this stroke is undulating, surmounted astride two thick and short vertical strokes. This form of the letter π appears to occur in other words that commence with υπ-.[540] While this is a feature that is replicated, cf. ὑπορθοῦντας (*Gos. Pet.* 10.39), ὑπερβαίνουσαν (*Gos. Pet.* 10.40) and ὑπακοη, (*Gos. Pet.* 10.42), it does not occur consistently throughout the manuscript. For examples where the π is formed conventionally after the letter υ cf. ὑπο (*Gos. Pet.* 7.26; 10.40; 12.50) and ὑποστρέφω (*Gos. Pet.* 14.58).

---

[539] Bouriant, 'Fragments du texte grec du livre d'Énoch et de quelques écrits attribués à saint Pierre', 139; Lods, *L'Évangile et l'Apocalypse de Pierre avec le texte grec du livre d'Henoch*, 221.

[540] Gebhardt, *Das Evangelium und die Apokalypse des Petrus*, 13.

10. In reading στρατιωτον the manuscript reads a morphologically impossible form, but this can be seen as arising due to the phonological confusion between omicron and omega. This should be corrected to the plural form στρατιωτῶν on the basis of the correct form that is utilised in the following verse, and the introduction of soldiers as a plural subject *Gos. Pet.* 8.30. This correction is made in most editions of the Greek text, e.g. Robinson,[541] Harnack,[542] Swete,[543] Vaganay,[544] Mara,[545] and Kraus and Nicklas.[546] However, Bouriant retains the form in the manscript without comment, although the omicron in the ending is printed in a smaller font than the rest of the word.[547] Yet it appears that he attempts to produce the force of this otherwise unknown singular form by translating it as 'avec une troupe pour garder le tombeau.[548]

11. Letter formation is again poor for the combination of the second, third and forth characters, υλα, of the word φυλάσσειν. The right-hand stroke of the upsilon is connected, apparently without lifting the pen, to the short left-hand stroke of the lambda. The resultant shape looks similar to the way in which the scribe forms the letter η. The right-hand diagonal stroke of the lambda is shorter than usual and connects with the head of a point-like alpha in a most unconventional manner, even by the standards of this highly irregular scribe.

12. Here the υλ combination occurs in the word κυλίσαντες. Similarly to the previous note where this sequence of letter is discussed, there is again little separation between these two letters and the following iota. This shows the scribe's tendency towards a cursive form of script.

---

[541] Robinson and James, *The Gospel according to Peter and the Revelation of Peter*, 85.

[542] Harnack, *Bruchstücke des Evangeliums und der Apokalypse des Petrus*, 10.

[543] Swete, *The Akhmîm Fragment of the Apocryphal Gospel of St Peter*, 15.

[544] Vaganay, *L'Évangile de Pierre*, 284.

[545] Mara, *Évangile de Pierre*, 54.

[546] Kraus und Nicklas, *Das Petrusevangelium und die Petrusapokalypse*, 40.

[547] Bouriant, 'Fragments du texte grec du livre d'Énoch et de quelques écrits attribués à saint Pierre', 139.

[548] Bouriant, 'Fragments du texte grec du livre d'Énoch et de quelques écrits attribués à saint Pierre', 139.

13. The word κατά is emended to μετά by various scholars including Harnack,[549] Robinson,[550] Gebhardt,[551] Semeria,[552] Vaganay,[553]
Mara,[554] and Kraus and Nicklas.[555] The problem stems from the
fact that the κατά appears to require the unacceptable sense of
the stone being rolled against the soldiers. Although this concern
is only partially articulated explicitly by Vaganay who sees the
force of κατά as being foreign to the narrative: 'the context does
not seem favourable to this interpretation.'[556] Swete translates the
preposition in two different ways. In his continuous translation
he simply renders the phrase as 'away from the centurion and
the soldiers.'[557] However in his notes accompanying the Greek
text, Swete writes, Κατὰ τοῦ κ. καὶ τῶν στρ. 'to exclude the Centurion and soldiers,' who might be bribed to deliver the body to
the disciples. The watch of course is not cogniznt of this purpose.'[558]
Another, perhaps simpler, option is to consider the wider semantic
range of the preposition κατά. According BDAG when it governs
the genitive case one of its main usages is as a 'marker of extension
or orientation in space or specific area.'[559] One example cited 'Od.
9.330 κ. σπείους "into the depths of the cave" '[560] is instructive since
it involves both motion and descent. The use of the preposition in

[549] Harnack simple notes 'κατὰ ego μετὰ'. See *Bruchstücke des Evangeliums und der
Apokalypse des Petrus*, 10.

[550] Apparently independent of Harnack, Robinson makes the same emendation,
listed in the notes without comment. Robinson and James, *The Gospel according to
Peter and the Revelation of Peter*, 85.

[551] Gebhardt notes his dependence on Harnack for this correction. Gebhardt, *Das
Evangelium und die Apokalypse des Petrus*, 44.

[552] Semeria prints μετά, but notes that the reading of the codex is κατά. Semeria,
'L'Évangile de Pierre', 528.

[553] Vaganay has an extended discussion of this emendation where he observes, 'Le
ms. Porte κατα. Certains critiques (Swete, p. 16; Cassels, p. 85) conservent cette leçon
et traduisent «contre le centurion et les soldats»…Le context ne semble guère favourable à cette interprétation…C'est pourquoi nous avons adopté la rectification μετά
proposée par Harnack.' Vaganay, *L'Évangile de Pierre*, 285.

[554] Mara, following Vaganay, lists the opposing points of Swete and Cassels on the
one hand against that represented by Harnack. Mara, *Évangile de Pierre*, 54.

[555] Kraus und Nicklas simply list the emendment. See, *Das Petrusevangelium und
die Petrusapokalypse*, 40.

[556] Vaganay, *L'Évangile de Pierre*, 285.

[557] Swete, *The Akhmîm Fragment of the Apocryphal Gospel of St Peter*, 26.

[558] Swete, *The Akhmîm Fragment of the Apocryphal Gospel of St Peter*, 15.

[559] BDAG, 511.

[560] BDAG, 511.

the present context could function similarly, with the stone moved towards the soldiers and down into the mouth of the tomb. As is noted in LSJ the semantic range of the term developed: 'later, *towards* a point' (cf. Hdn. 6.7.8; Luc. *Rh.Pr.* 9).[561]

14. The orthographical variant ἐπέχρεισαν is corrected to ἐπέχρισαν, the standard lexical form, by the majority of commentators either without comment (cf. Swete);[562] or with little comment (cf. Harnack;[563] Nicklas and Kraus;[564] Vaganay).[565] This itacism is best taken as variation rather than error.[566]

## COMMENTARY

**8.28a** συναχθέντες δὲ οἱ γραμματεῖς καὶ Φαρισαῖοι καὶ πρεσβύτεροι πρὸς ἀλλήλους. In this continuing sequence of post-crucifixion events there is an assembling of members from various Jewish groups. The verbal form συναχθέντες occurs only once in the canonical gospels, also in the context of post-crucifixion plotting by Jewish authorities. It is employed in Matt 28.12 after the disappearance of the body to describe a meeting between the chief priests and the elders to conceal the resurrection by supplanting it with an account of the theft of the body. Brown argues that it is the Matthean redactor who is responsible for interweaving a women-at-the-tomb story into an already existing guard-at-the-sepulcher narrative, he does not see this as decisive in establishing the priority of the *Gospel of Peter*.[567] Furthermore, rejecting simple models of the literary dependence of the *Gospel of Peter* on the canonical gospels, he suggests that prior to its appropriation by the author of the *Gospel of Peter* 'the guard-at-the-sepulcher story had continued to develop in extraGospel narration and become a longer and more elaborate composition.'[568] It is not impossible that the story originated in the Matthean community, and the evangelist reworked such traditions into his own narrative. The primary reason for Brown rejecting the priority of the *Gospel of*

---

[561] LSJ, 883.

[562] Swete, *The Akhmîm Fragment of the Apocryphal Gospel of St Peter*, 15.

[563] Harnack, *Bruchstücke des Evangeliums und der Apokalypse des Petrus*, 10.

[564] Kraus und Nicklas, *Das Petrusevangelium und die Petrusapokalypse*, 40.

[565] Vaganay, *L'Évangile de Pierre*, 285.

[566] As BDF §23 notes, 'The phonetic levelling of ει and ι˜ betrays itself by the *rather frequent* confusion in usage.'

[567] Brown, *The Death of the Messiah*, vol. 2, 1305.

[568] Brown, *The Death of the Messiah*, vol. 2, 1306.

*Peter* and instead arguing that the narrative drew upon a pre-existing source at this point is due both to the expanded form of the story that it preserves, yet while at the same time it presents a connected narrative. As he comments,

> when one compares the Matthean account of the guard at the sepulchre that is some ten verses in length with the twenty-two-verse account in *GPet* (over one-third the length of the total *GPet* PN!), one notices that no other part of the *GPet* passion or resurrection account has been expanded so extensively by comparison with a corresponding canonical scene.[569]

Moreover, it is noted that Codex Bobiensis has an alternative version of this incident inserted between Mk 16.3 and 16.4. Notwithstanding this creative solution to the source critical problem, there is nothing inherently implausible or even less likely in the suggestion that the author of the Akhmîm text reconnected the interwoven stories from Matthew's account to create separate narratives dealing with the guards at the tomb and the visit by the women. Such rejoing of material to create continuous accounts is most clearly demonstrated in Matthew's handling of the Markan intercalated incident of the cleansing of the temple (Matt 21.12–17//Mk 11.15–19) framed by the two parts of the story of the cursing of the fig tree (cf. Matt 21.18–22//Mk 11.12–14, 20–21). Here the first evangelist appears to miss the narratival purpose of Mark and undoes the linkage which shows that one story is to be interpreted in the light of the other, thereby removing the hermeneutically more developed textual structure.[570]

At this point in the narrative, the gathering that is described is the result of a confluence of three groups. This meeting of οἱ γραμματεῖς καὶ Φαρισαῖοι καὶ πρεσβύτεροι is reminiscent of the meeting between the chief priests and elders in a similar scene in Matthew's account (Matt 28.11–12). Such a threefold combination does not occur anywhere in the New Testament. The term Φαρισαῖοι occurs in the plural eighty-six times in the New Testament, and this group is regularly paired with other factions, although by far the most common occurrence of this group is without connection with other groups. This phenomenon is most easily appreciated if the usages of the plural term Φαρισαῖοι within the gospels and Acts are tabulated.

---

[569] Brown, *The Death of the Messiah*, vol. 2, 1306.
[570] For more discussion of this point see section 7.2 in the introduction.

Table 15. The use of the term Φαρισαῖοι in the New Testament

| | |
|---|---|
| Φαρισαῖοι | Matt 9.11, 14, 34; 12.2, 14, 24; 15.2; 19.3, 22.15, 34,[571] 41; Mk 2.24; 8.11; 10.2; Lk 6.2, 7.36, 11.39, 42, 43; 12.1; 13.31; 14.1; 16.14; 17.20; 19.39; Jn 1.24; 3.1; 4.1; 7.47; 8.13; 9.13, 15, 16, 40; 11.46; 12.19, 42; Acts 15.5; 23.26 (twice).[572] |

| | |
|---|---|
| Φαρισαῖοι + γραμματεῖς | Matt 15.1; Mk 7.1, 5; Lk 5.30; 15.2. |
| γραμματεῖς + Φαρισαῖοι | Matt 5.20; 12.38; 23.2, 13, 15, 23, 25, 27, 29; Lk 5.21; 6.7; 11.53; Jn 8.3. |
| οἱ γραμματεῖς τῶν Φαρισαῖοι | Mk 2.16; Acts 23.9. |
| οἱ μαθηταὶ τῶν Φαρισαῖοι | Mk 2.18 |
| ἀρχιερεῖς + Φαρισαῖοι | Matt 21.45; 27.62; Jn 7.32, 45; 11.47, 57, 18.3. |
| Φαρισαῖοι + Σαδδουκαῖοι | Matt 3.7; 16.1, 6, 11, 12; Acts 23.7, 8. |
| μαθηταὶ Ἰωάννου + Φαρισαῖοι | Mk 2.18; Lk 5.33. |
| Φαρισαῖοι + Ἡρῳδιανοί | Mk 3.6; 12.13. |
| Φαρισαῖοι + Ἰουδαῖοι | Mk 7.3. |
| Φαρισαῖοι + Ἡρώδης | Mk 8.15 |
| Φαρισαῖοι + νομοδιδάσκαλοι | Lk 5.17. |
| Φαρισαῖοι + νομικοί | Lk 7.30; 14.3. |
| ἄρχοντες + Φαρισαῖοι | Jn 7.48. |

From this data a number of salient features can be noted. First, although paired with γραμματεῖς on eighteen occasions, this never occurs in conjunction with a third group. The order γραμματεῖς καὶ Φαρισαῖοι occurs thirteen of those eighteen times, although seven of these occur in Matt 23 where probably a heightened polemic acts as the trigger for this combination rather than an historically accurate depiction. The term Φαρισαῖοι never occurs in combination with πρεσβύτεροι. Pharisees are only mentioned in connection with the Passion Narratives on two occasions (Matt 27.62; Jn 18.3) and their involvement in the trial of Jesus appears to be historically dubious, with their presence

---

[571] The classification of the reference could be disputed because since the Sadducees are also mentioned in this verse. However, the Sadducees are not acting in combination with the Pharisees, but they function as a discrete unit. Οἱ δὲ Φαρισαῖοι ἀκούσαντες ὅτι ἐφίμωσεν τοὺς Σαδδουκαίους συνήχθησαν ἐπὶ τὸ αὐτό (Matt 22.34).

[572] With the first reference in Acts 23.26, like Matt 22.34 (see note 535 above), the Sadducees are mentioned, but distinguished from the Pharisees.

being inserted to further blacken this group. Harrington notes in general, 'That they [the Pharisees] would have joined the chief priests on the Sabbath for such embassy to Pilate is unlikely from a historical perspective.'[573] If the embassy is historically unlikely, the actual presence of the Pharisees as a significant political force is at least equally problematic.[574] Brown goes even further in his assessment of the role of the Pharisees 'who appear only here in the Matthean PN. In other words, this story about the guard at the sepulchre violated the traditional (and even historical) rememberance that the Pharisees were not active in the death of Jesus.'[575] However, on a literary level, if the reference to οἱ ἀρχιερεῖς καὶ οἱ Φαρισαῖοι (Matt 27.62) is taken in conjunction with the appearance of πρεσβύτεροι (Matt 28.12), this may explain the basis for the threefold combination of groups here (Gos. Pet. 8.28). However, it does need to be acknowledged that the ἀρχιερεῖς, mentioned in Matt 28.11, would then have been omitted.

Strictly speaking the phrase πρὸς ἀλλήλους is redundant, as the verb συναχθέντες already implies a coming together. However, such redundancy functions to allow a certain emphasis to fall on the common purpose that exists in this gathering. The narrative stresses the collectivity of action attributed to those deemed to be the enemies of the person who has just been crucified and his followers.

**8.28b** ἀκούσαντες ὅτι ὁ λαὸς ἅπας γογγύζει καὶ κόπτεται τὰ στήθη. The verb of aural perception discloses the motivation for the gathering, namely that the people are grumbling and beating their chests. The term ὁ λαός is used with a different nuance to its occurrence in Gos. Pet. 2.5. There it denoted the hostile mob to whom Pilate handed over Jesus for execution. From this generalized group came forth various individuals and sub-groups that inflicted torments upon Jesus. Swete notes this altered role for the crowd when he states in relation to the gathering of scribes, Pharisees and elders that 'Peter adds a new reason for these fears – the changed attitude of the populace.'[576]

---

[573] Harrington, The Gospel of Matthew, 405.

[574] See also the comments of Allen on the role of the Pharisees in the first gospel. W.C. Allen, Gospel according to Saint Matthew, ICC (2nd ed.; Edinburgh: T&T Clark, 1907) lxxviii–lxxix.

[575] Brown, The Death of the Messiah, vol. 2, 1289.

[576] Swete, The Akhmîm Fragment of the Apocryphal Gospel of St Peter, 14.

This more neutral role, tending towards a positive recognition of the identity of Jesus as 'Son of God', is maintained in the other two usages of this term in *Gos. Pet.* 8.30 and 11.47. Although Swete characterizes this change as intentional on the part of the author of the Akhmîm text, this may be attributing too much subtlety to the writer.[577] Rather, it may well be the case that this represents an example of what Goodacre has characterized 'editorial fatigue' on the part of an author consulting source material.[578] Goodacre defines editorial fatigue in the following way.

> Editorial fatigue is a phenomenon that will inevitably occur when a writer is heavily dependent on another's work. In telling the same story as his predecessor, a writer makes changes in the early stages which he is unable to sustain throughout...They are interesting because they can betray an author's hand, most particularly revealing to us the identity of his sources.[579]

In creating the scene involving the first mention of ὁ λαός (*Gos. Pet.* 2.5) the author is not constrained by canonical Gospel sources. When, however, the narrative depicts the fears of the three leadership groups because of the negative reactions of the people, this detail is quarried from accounts in Luke and John although it is reconfigured in *Gos. Pet.* 8.28. The description of the crowds returning home beating their chests is drawn from Luke 23.48, καὶ πάντες οἱ συμπαραγενόμενοι ὄχλοι ἐπὶ τὴν θεωρίαν ταύτην, θεωρήσαντες τὰ γενόμενα, τύπτοντες τὰ στήθη ὑπέστρεφον. Also from a non-Passion context the author appears to have been influenced by the reference to the Pharisees hearing the crowds whispering about Jesus in John 7.32, ἤκουσαν οἱ Φαρισαῖοι τοῦ ὄχλου γογγύζοντος περὶ αὐτοῦ ταῦτα. Although the term ὄχλος, shared by the canonical accounts in these passages, is replaced by λαός, the author's more favoured term,[580] nonetheless the neutral or even slightly positive nuance is carried over, replacing the negative depiction of λαός in *Gos. Pet.* 2.5.

In the NT there are only two references to στῆθος in a context where the chest is struck to demonstrate lament, mourning or grief (Lk 18.13; 23.48). In both of these examples the verb used to denote the act of

---

[577] See again Swete, *The Akhmîm Fragment of the Apocryphal Gospel of St Peter*, 14.
[578] Goodacre, 'Fatigue in the Synoptics', 45–58.
[579] Goodacre, 'Fatigue in the Synoptics', 46.
[580] The author of the Akhmîm text uses the term λαός on four occasions (*Gos. Pet.* 2.5; 8.28, 30; 11.47. By comparison ὄχλος occurs only once (*Gos. Pet.* 9.34).

striking the chest is τύπτω. By contrast, here the verb used is κόπτω (*Gos. Pet.* 8.28).This term is a lexical favourite of the author, who employs it on four occasions, *Gos. Pet.* 7.25; 8.28; 12.52, 54, whereas τύπτω is not used in the extant portion of the Akhmîm text. While the term κόπτω can denote mourning in general, it can refer to the specific act of striking one's chest as a manifestation of lamentation.[581] Also the term γογγύζω has a wide range of meaning. Unlike John 7.32 where the people in the crowd are whispering so their conversations are not overheard by the authorities, here the term is employed with its more common nuance of 'grumbling' or 'complaining'.[582] Such angst is directed against the leaders, whom the people now recognizes as having executed a religiously significant figure, although the narrative does not allow them to make the christological affirmation which the soldiers pronounce later in the narrative (*Gos. Pet.* 11.45).

**8.28c** λέγοντες ὅτι, εἰ τῷ θανάτῳ αὐτοῦ ταῦτα τὰ μέγιστα σημεῖα γέγονεν. Accompanying the grumbling and chest beating, the narrator makes explicit the reason that the people have come to oppose the actions of their rulers. In line with the flow of the story, they recall the miraculous portents that attended the death of Jesus. In particular, in terms of the narrative, one is to think of the three signs that have been described, the darkness that covered Judaea, the tearing of the veil, and the quaking of the ground (*Gos. Pet.* 5.15, 20; 6.21). Vaganay notes a thematic connection between this passage and the function of the events surrounding the crucifixion in Luke. Thus he states, 'Precisely in Lk 23.47–48, these same signs brought about the repentance of the populace (θεωρήσαντες τὰ γενόμενα) and motivated the profession of faith in the centurion (ἰδὼν…τὸ γενόμενον).'[583] Although the term σημεῖα in its plural form is a highly significant Johannine term (Jn 2.11, 23; 3.2; 4.48; 6.2, 14,[584] 26; 7.31; 9.16; 11.47; 12.37; 20.30), the

---

[581] See EDNT, vol 2, 308. 'Mid. *Hit oneself* (on the breast as a sign of mourning)/ mourn greatly (e.g., Aeschylus *Pers.* 683; Plato *Phd.* 60d; LXX; Josephus *Ant.* vii.41).

[582] The primary range of meaning in BDAG is 'to express oneself in low tones of disapprobation, *grumble, murmur*' (204). A range of biblical and extra-biblical citations are given in support of this semantic domain. By contrast the secondary meaning 'to express oneself in low tones of affirmation, *speak secretly, whisper*' is only evidenced, according to BDAG, by the usage in Jn 7.32.

[583] Vaganay, *L'Évangile de Pierre*, 280.

[584] The plural form σημεῖα occurs in 𝔓⁷⁵ B 091 *pc* a, the singular σημεῖον is read by other manuscripts.

plural does occur in the synoptic gospels to describe the miracles of Jesus. The closest parallel to the phrase μέγιστα σημεῖα, which occurs here in the Akhmîm text is σημεῖα μεγάλα (Matt 24.24; Lk 21.11). However, whereas Matthew and Luke employ the basic form of the adjective, the *Gospel of Peter* qualifies σημεῖα with the superlative form, μέγιστα (cf. 2 Pet 1.4).

**8.28d** ἴδετε ὅτι πόσον δίκαιός ἐστιν. Famously, Luke alters the centurion's declaration at the cross from ἀληθῶς οὗτος ὁ ἄνθρωπος υἱὸς θεοῦ ἦν (Mk 15.39) to ὄντως ὁ ἄνθρωπος οὗτος δίκαιος ἦν (Lk 23.37). Fitzmyer's conjecture that here 'Luke has chosen not to follow Mark, but rather a tradition from "L."'[585], may not be the most natural explanation of this alteration. Rather, Green has noticed that Luke, on a number occasions, identifies Jesus with the Suffering Servant of deutero-Isaiah. He draws attention to, 'the comparable use of "righteous" in conjunction with Jesus' death in Acts 3.13–14, in a co-text where the allusion to Isa 52:13–53:12 is indisputable.'[586] Hence, he concludes, 'Luke has brought into close proximity the dual identification of Jesus as Messiah and Servant, so as to articulate the suffering role of the Messiah.'[587] Thus, it is most likely that the term δίκαιος is taken over by the author of the Akhmîm text from the third gospel, rather than being dependent on a putative source, which both he and Luke utilised independently.

Whereas the centurion's cry in Luke's gospel appears to be primarily an acknowledgement of the innocence of Jesus, the term δίκαιος may carry more theological significance in the present context when placed on the lips of 'the people.' Coupled with recognition of the miraculous signs that accompanied his death as being divine attestation of status, the crowd now, at least in part, share in the recognition of status. Thus contrary to Vaganay, this is not simply a 'proclamation of the innocence of the Saviour',[588] but tends towards a christological outlook that acknowledges that the crucified figure is also the righteous one of God (cf. Acts 3.13–14).

---

[585] Fitzmyer, *The Gospel According to Luke X–XXIV*, 1520.
[586] Green, *The Gospel of Luke*, 827.
[587] Green, *The Gospel of Luke*, 827.
[588] Vaganay, *L'Évangile de Pierre*, 280.

**8.29** ἐφοβήθησαν οἱ πρεσβύτεροι καὶ ἦλθον πρὸς Πειλᾶτον δεόμενοι αὐτοῦ καὶ λέγοντες. Curiously, Pilate is presented as a figure with far greater authority in the post-crucifixion events without any explanation of the tension this causes in literary terms when compared to his limited power in the earlier scene involving Antipas (*Gos. Pet.* 1.1–2.5). Obviously narratival consistency is subservient to theological interest, and the author's concern is to exonerate Pilate while shifting blame to Jewish opponents. The triple group of subjects at the beginning of *Gos. Pet.* 8.28 is replaced here by the single grouping, οἱ πρεσβύτεροι. This should not be taken as implying that only one group makes the approach to Pilate, rather it is a literary simplification that avoids cumbersome repetition, which seeks to represent the three previously named groups by the most general of the terms employed earlier. This is the first use of the verb φοβέομαι in the Akhmîm text, but the term is used on subsequent occasions to explain this emotion as the motivating factor behind various actions that are taken (see *Gos. Pet.* 12.50, 52, 54; 13.57).

It is at this point that the author re-introduces Pilate into the narrative. There is no explanation of the decision to call upon Pilate, apparently it requires no clarification, presumably because the audience is familiar with the Matthean form of the story which is being expanded in this narrative. Events are reported in a matter-of-fact manner.[589] Here the attitude of the leaders towards Pilate is one of deference, as indicated by the participle δεόμενοι (the middle form is probably denoting the aspect of self-interest in the request). This is a redactional element that the narrator adds to the Matthean storyline, which simply reports that the chief-priests and Pharisees came πρὸς Πιλᾶτον λέγοντες· κύριε…(Matt 27.62–63). It is possible that the use of δεόμενοι αὐτοῦ should be seen as an intentional replacement for the Matthean form of address to Pilate, κύριε. In relation to the Matthean account, Brown observes, 'Matt 27:63 has the Jewish authorities address the prefect as "Lord," a politeness never attested in previous encounters in the PN.'[590] Since the term κύριος is the favoured christological term in the *Gospel of Peter* for referring to Jesus, it would be unsurprising if this was in fact the reason why it had not been taken over from the

---

[589] Thus Mara comments, 'Arrivés chez Pilate, ils prièrent de leur donner des soldats pour surveiller la tombeau.' Mara, *Évangile de Pierre*, 166.
[590] Brown, *The Death of the Messiah*, vol. 2, 1290.

Matthean account. It is reserved by the author of the Akhmîm text exclusively for Jesus, and hence he finds an alternative way to express the deference shown to Pilate.

**8.30a** παράδος ἡμῖν στρατιώτας, ἵνα φυλάξω τὸ μνῆμα αὐτοῦ ἐπὶ τρεῖς ἡμέρας. The request consists of two parts: the provision of soldiers and an indication of the time they will be required to guard the tomb. Here the speech is much shorter than the Matthean parallel, and moreover, it introduces a 'continuity' problem by failing to explain the significance of the three day period. By abbreviating the narrative at this point, the author assumes that auditors of his narrative will supply the pre-knowledge from the Matthean account to make sense of the three-day period, or alternatively, perhaps the significance of this period was mentioned at an earlier point in the narrative. The expansive features that appear later in the Akhmîm version of the guard-at-the-tomb story make it *a priori* unlikely that Matthew has used the *Gospel of Peter* as a source, and resolved any supposedly perceived literary difficulty by explaining the time period (ἐμνήσθημεν ὅτι ἐκεῖνος ὁ πλάνος εἶπεν ἔτι ζῶν· μετὰ τρεῖς ἡμέρας ἐγείρομαι, Matt 27.63). This detail is much more likely to have been omitted by the *Gospel of Peter* because of the description of Jesus as ἐκεῖνος ὁ πλάνος.

The request is succinct, παράδος ἡμῖν στρατιώτας. The narrative simply seeks to move the required characters into place so there can be multiple witnesses to the stupendous events that will be described as accompanying the resurrection. Swete draws attention to the fact that this is the first mention of a Roman military force in the text.[591] While a Roman presence has been removed from the previous scenes involving the torture and execution of Jesus, it is now required as a reliable witness to the veracity of the resurrection. For this reason the author has the Jewish leaders beseech the impartial Pilate to provide the soldiers, who in narratival terms will perform the more significant role of reliable witnesses.

In text-critical note 5 in this section the range of proposed emendations to the form φυλάξω were noted. It was argued that it is possible to retain the first person singular form (as written in the manuscript)

---

[591] 'στρατιώτας] The first mention in the fragment of the Roman soldiers. No part has been assigned to them either in the mockery or at the Crucifixion.' Swete, *The Akhmîm Fragment of the Apocryphal Gospel of St Peter*, 14.

without introducing an intolerable tension into the text. If either this form, or the more popular emendation φυλάξωμεν is read, then the Jewish authorities see themselves as primarily responsible for guarding the tomb although they need Roman manpower to assist them. By contrast, if the alternative conjecture φυλάξωσιν is read, then there is a total handing over of the securing of the sepulchre to the Romans. While this would not be impossible, the desire to implicate the Jewish leaders in the cover-up of the true explanation of events (*Gos. Pet.* 11.48–49) somewhat militates against this reading. Hence it is more likely that a first person form of the verb φυλάσσω was indeed the reading of the text.[592] In describing the burial place the term employed here is μνῆμα. This is the first of its six occurrences in the narrative (*Gos. Pet.* 8.30, 31, 32; 11.44; 12.50, 52), however, the author is happy to alternate between this term and τάφος without communicating any obvious sense of a change of meaning (for τάφος see *Gos. Pet.* 6.24; 8.31 9.36, 37; 10.39; 11.45; 13.55 [2 times]). Although Matthew prefers the form μνημεῖον to μνῆμα, nonetheless he alternates between μνημεῖον (in the passion narrative 5 times: Matt 27.52, 53 60[twice]; 28.8 and τάφος (in the passion narrative 4 times: Matt 27.61, 64, 66; 28.1). Thus, in general, the Akhmîm text follows the interchangability of terms evidenced in the Matthean account.

The phrase ἐπὶ τρεῖς ἡμέρας, as already mentioned, denotes an unexplained period of time in the narrative. This contrasts with the Matthean account where the significance of this period is explicitly explained for Pilate, and consequently for all who read or hear the story as presented by the first gospel (Matt 27.63–64). There may be a tension between the temporal designations in the first gospel with Matt 27.63 reporting Jesus to have claimed μετὰ τρεῖς ἡμέρας ἐγείρομαι, and the request in the following verse for guards to be posted by Pilate ἕως τῆς τρίτης ἡμέρας (Matt 27.64). Thus, Davies and Allison comment, "'Until the third day" appears to contradict v.63: if Jesus prophesied resurrection 'after three days', having a guard up to and including the third day would be insufficient.'[593] Although the later synoptic evangelists show some sensitivity to this issue, as evidenced by the modifications made to the temporal indicators to the Markan passion predictions

---

[592] *Contra* Vaganay who suggests that 'De fait, les soldats romains comptent parmi les principaux gardiens du tombeau.' Vaganay, *L'Évangile de Pierre*, 282.
[593] Davies and Allison, *The Gospel According to Saint Matthew*, vol. III, 654.

(Mk 8.31;[594] 9.31;[595] 10.34[596]),[597] it appears inappropriate to expect strict logical consistency. By contrast, the *Gospel of Peter* offers a third form of this indication of time, ἐπὶ τρεῖς ἡμέρας. This formulation appears appears to stand closest to the ἕως τῆς τρίτης ἡμέρας of Matt 27.64, although its preference is for cardinal rather than ordinal enumeration of the days.

**8.30b** μήποτε ἐλθόντες οἱ μαθηταὶ αὐτοῦ κλέψωσιν αὐτὸν. Still following the sequence of the Matthean storyline (Matt 27.64b) the *Gospel of Peter* next relates the concern that the disciples will steal the body to create the deception that Jesus had in fact risen from the dead. Among the canonical accounts this detail is unique to the first gospel, with Matthew narrating the same concern utilizing identical words (cf. Matt 27.64b). This exact correspondence forms an extended sequence of seven words shared by the two accounts. Since this clause is not present in the other canonical gospels the case for direct literary dependence between the two accounts at this point is extremely strong. As it has been argued elsewhere there is a noticeable tendency in the Akhmîm text to heighten miraculous elements in the text, to show a more developed anti-Jewish outlook and to expand legendary details. Such theological trajectories suggest in general that the *Gospel of Peter* is posterior to the canonical accounts. Thus, the direction of literary dependence in this case is most plausibly seen as being that of the *Gospel of Peter* having taken over this phrase from the Matthean account. Although not presenting verbatim agreement, Justin's interlocutor Trypho appears to know this story and draws upon it to refute claims concerning the resurrection of Jesus, 'but his disciples stole him by night from the tomb' (Justin, *Dial.* 108).[598]

Like Matthew, the *Gospel of Peter* emphasizes the fact that the disciples of Jesus were not present at the tomb as direct witnesses to the

---

[594] Cf. Matt 16.21//Mk 8.31//Lk 9.22.

[595] Cf. Matt 17.23//Mk 9.31.

[596] Cf. Matt 20.19//Mk 10.34//Lk 18.33.

[597] Hagner argues in relation to Matt 16.21 that 'Matthew substitutes, "on the third day to be raised to life" (Luke 9:22 agrees with this change, against Mark), for Mark's less accurate, "after three days to rise again," probably reflecting the more precise language of the kerygma and liturgy of the church (cf. 1 Cor 15:4, including the passive use of the verb).' Hagner, *Matthew 14–28*, 477.

[598] See the edition by Marcovich, *Apologiae pro Christianis – Dialogus cem Tryphone* 255.

process of resurrection. Davies and Allison note that 'tomb robbery was common' and there exists inscriptional evidence illustrating 'the customary use of maledictions against violation of tombs.'[599] However, through the disciples not being present at the tomb and the description of the miraculous events that accompany the opening of the tomb, the author makes clear that no mundane explanation can account for this case of an empty tomb. Whereas Matthew revisits the story of the stolen body (Matt 28.13),[600] the *Gospel of Peter* has Pilate (acting perhaps in his one deceptive act) command the soldiers to say nothing. In this way, the Akhmîm text appears to unpick, or miss, the irony that exists in the Matthean story whereby the Jewish leaders are forced to circulate the false story which they imagined might transpire in reality.

**8.30c    καὶ ὑπολάβῃ ὁ λαὸς ὅτι ἐκ νεκρῶν ἀνέστη, καὶ ποιήσωσιν ἡμῖν κακά.** Structurally, the sequence follows that in Matthew's gospel after narrating the possibility of the disciples stealing the body. There is a report of the anticipated reactions coupled with a comment concerning the consequences of the people's reaction. Thus Vaganay observes, 'The first concern is not foreign to the text of Matthew...Our copiest expresses only one more explicit reason.'[601] However, there are important differences in content. In Matthew it is the disciples who are seen as being likely to announce to the people that ἠγέρθη ἀπὸ τῶν νεκρῶν (Matt 27.64c). This contrasts with the *Gospel of Peter* where the people formulate their own supposition concerning the resurrection. The verb used to describe resurrection is ἐγείρω in Matthew's account, but the *Gospel of Peter* uses ἀνίστημι. This terminology reflects the preferred usage of the *Gospel of Peter* with ἀνίστημι being use four times (1.1; 8.30. 13.56 twice), and ἐγείρω never employed. Vaganay notes that the formula ἀνεστῆναι ἐκ νεκρῶν is used to anticipate the resurrection in Mk 9.9–10.[602] This similarity with the Markan formulation appears to be coincidental, being brought about by the author changing the Matthean terminology to his favoured form, which Mark also used in another context.

---

[599] Davies and Allison, *The Gospel According to Saint Matthew*, vol. III, 654.

[600] Hagner states, '[t]he reference to the disciples steaing the body reflects the very story the Jewish authorities themselves later find it necessary to invent (cf. 28:13).' Hagner, *Matthew 14–28*, 862.

[601] Vaganay, *L'Évangile de Pierre*, 283.

[602] Vaganay states, 'Quant à la formule ἀνεστῆναι ἐκ νεκρῶν, à propos de résurrection de Jésus, cf. Mc., IX, 9–10.' Vaganay, *L'Évangile de Pierre*, 283.

Once again, there is a heightening of the negative attitude exhibited towards the Jewish authorities. Their concern, as it is described in Matthew 27.64, is that a more pernicious religious misunderstanding will circulate among the people, καὶ ἔσται ἡ ἐσχάτη πλάνη χείρων τῆς πρώτης. By comparison, in the Akhmîm text the leaders are motivated by self-protection rather than concern to guard the people from falsehood, καὶ ποιήσωσιν ἡμῖν κακά. The precise nature of the evil things that will be done to the leaders is not made explicit, but readers have already seen a detailed account of how the crowd could treat an individual whom they despised.

**8.31a** ὁ δὲ Πειλᾶτος παραδέδωκεν αὐτοῖς Πετρώνιον τὸν κεντυρίωνα μετὰ στρατιωτῶν φυλάσσειν τὸν τάφον. Pilate acquiesces to wishes of the Jewish leaders and provides a detachment of soldiers to secure the tomb. Unlike the account in the first gospel there is no speech reported from Pilate (cf. Matt 27.65, ἔφη αὐτοῖς ὁ Πιλᾶτος· ἔχετε κουστωδίαν· ὑπάγετε ἀσφαλίσασθε ὡς οἴδατε), instead the narrator simply reports the compliance of the senior Roman official with the request. The narrative also supplies the name of the centurion, Petronius. The presence of the named centurion in this account is a feature not present in the canonical accounts. While increased detail is often seen as a general tendency in later traditions, the opposite tendency can also occur.[603] Matthew and Luke both delete the names of Alexander and Rufus who are mentioned as being sons of Simon (Matt 27.32// Mk 15.21//Lk 23.26). Hooker argues that 'Alexander and Rufus were presumably known to Mark's readers (by name if not in person).'[604] In relation to the third gospel Nolland suggests that, 'Simon's family links are omitted, since they will have no significance for Luke's intended audience.'[605] The addition of the name of Petronius is more likely to be an invention, either by the author of the *Gospel of Peter*, or some other extra-canonical tradent, due to a fascination for detail in the development of the tradition, rather than the preservation of a historical detail unknown in the canonical accounts.[606] One significant piece

---

[603] E.P. Sanders, *The Tendencies of the Synoptic Tradition* (SNTSMS 9; Cambridge: CUP, 1969) see chapter 3, 'Increasing detail as a possible tendency or the tradition', 88–189.

[604] Hooker, *The Gospel according to Saint Mark*, 372.

[605] Nolland, *Luke 18:35–24.53*, 1136.

[606] In relation to the naming of Petronius Bauckham states '[f]or a tendency to name previously unnamed characters there is a little more evidence in extracanoni-

of information in support of this is the variation that occurs in relation to the names associated with centurions in the Passion story. In the *Acts of Pilate* the name of the centurion at the cross is Longinus.[607] It may appear unnecessary to equate the two figures, for there would have been more than one centurion garrisoned in Jerusalem during the Passover. However, Robinson counters the argument that separate historical details are being described by noting 'but we shall see presently that the words attributed in our Gospels to the centurion at the cross are here assigned to the centurion at the Sepulchre.'[608] Thus, the whole scene is best understood as a literary fabrication created from existing canonical material coupled with redactional creativity.

Petronius is described as being a centurion, κεντυρίων. This rank is often equated to that of a non-commissioned officer is current military structures, such as a sergeant. This comparison perhaps obscures some of the significant differences. A Roman cohort was made up of six centuries each commanded by a centurion. 'The centurions were soldiers of many years' experience, normally promoted from the ranks.'[609] Moreover, as Keppie states, 'Centurions were paid at much higher rates, and could become wealthy men.'[610] Yet at times the lowly legionaries were mistreated by corrupt and abusive centurions.[611] Such details, however, appear to have little importance in the Akhmîm narrative. Rather, what is important from the perspective of the author of the *Gospel of Peter* is that the Roman presence at the tomb provides

---

cal Gospels and traditions, though even here it is notably scarce in the earlier texts.' R.J. Bauckham, *Jesus and the Eyewitnesses: The Gospels as Eyewitness Testimony* (Grand Rapids, Michigam: Eerdmans, 2006) 43. However, Bauckham's conclusion is not entirely neutral, since he wishes to marginalise the phenomenon of previously unnamed figures being named, since this undermines his wider thesis that named characters in individual gospel narratives may have been eyewitnesses who could verify the events narrated in the gospel accounts.

[607] The name Longinus occurs in *Acts of Pilate* 16.7 both in the Greek A and Greek B recensions of the text, where he is named as the soldier who pierced Jesus' side. In Greek B (11.1) Longinus is named as the centurion who declares 'Truly this was a son of God'. See Elliott (ed.), *The Apocryphal New Testament*, 164–185; and C. Tischendorf, *Evangelia Apocrypha* (2nd ed.; Leipzig, 1876) 210–432.

[608] Robinson and James, *The Gospel according to Peter and the Revelation of Peter*, 23–24.

[609] L. Keppie, 'The army and the navy', in A.K. Bowman, E. Champlin and A. Lintott (eds.), *The Cambridge Ancient History*, 2nd ed.; Vol. X: The Augustan Empire, 43 B.C. – A.D. 69 (Cambridge: CUP, 1996) 372.

[610] Keppie, 'The army and the navy', 378.

[611] Tacitus, *Ann.* 1.17ff, 78.

independent and reliable verification of the events surrounding the resurrection.

The size of the detachment of soldiers is not specified. In the 13th century Syriac text, *Book of the Bee*, the size of the squad is given along with the names of the individuals, although it is noted that there is dispute over the number of soldiers present: '[they] were five, and these are their names, Issachar, Gad, Matthias, Barnabas, and Simon; but other say they were fifteen, three centurions and their Roman and Jewish soldiers.'[612] The names provided in this text are striking because of their apparently Jewish, rather than Roman character. As the text elucidates the Matthean version of the guard-at-the-tomb story, it may adopt the interpretation of Matt 27.65, ἔχετε χουστωδίαν· ὑπάγετε ἀσφαλίσασθε ὡς οἴδατε, as a refusal of Pilate to comply with the request. Thus this reading understands Pilate as telling the Jewish leaders to use their own guard to secure the sepulchre. Luz notes that this dominant Western interpretative tradition 'began with the Vulgate ("habetis") and understood Pilate's answer as a refusal: You already have your own guards, the temple police; use them!'[613] A number of factors tell against this interpretation. First, the the term χουστωδία is a Latin loanword; second, when the group is described in 28.12 the term used is στρατιῶται 'soldiers' it should be noted that this is the usual term employed to denote the ranks of the Roman military (cf. Matt 27.27); third, the group guarding the tomb are answerable to Pilate, not the Jewish leadership, in Matt 28.11.[614] Hence the tradition of reading Pilate's reply as indicating non-compliance with the request should be seen as part of a tendency to exonerate Pilate from blame by distancing him from the events of the crucifixion. It is interesting that while the Akhmîm text share the general tendency to portray a 'blameless' Pilate, nevertheless, in this specific detail it retains the understanding that the troops were in fact Roman, and that Pilate complies with the request of the Jewish leadership. This is presumably because the *Gospel of Peter* finds it more theologically important to have neutral Roman witnesses present at the resurrection. A Roman guard also seems to be envisaged in one of the fragments of the *Gospel*

---

[612] See B.M. Metzger, 'Names for the Nameless in the New Testament', in P. Granfield and J.A. Jungmann (eds.), *Kyriakon: Festschrift for J. Quasten* (2 vols.; Munster: Aschendorff, 1970) vol. 1, 79–95, see esp. 95.

[613] Luz, *Matthew 21–28*, 588, fn 27.

[614] Hagner makes similar observations. See Hagner, *Matthew 14–28*, 863.

*of the Nazarenes* which preserves a variant tradition of Matt 27.65, 'And he delivered to them armed men that they might sit over against the cave and guard it day and night.'[615] Thus the *Gospel of Peter* follows Matthew in having Pilate provide the Jewish authorities with a detachment of soldiers of unspecified strength to guard the tomb. It provides the additional detail that the name of the centurion in charge of the party was Petronius.

**8.31b** καὶ σὺν αὐτοῖς ἦλθον πρεσβύτεροι καὶ γραμματεῖς ἐπὶ τὸ μνῆμα. Here the text makes explicit the identification of a group somewhat ambiguously described by the nominative masculine plural form of the aorist passive participle in Matt 27.66, οἱ δὲ πορευθέντες. The Akhmîm text replaces this form of the verb πορεύομαι, with the third person aorist form of ἔρχομαι, and then lists the subjects as πρεσβύτεροι καὶ γραμματεῖς. Again, the *Gospel of Peter* has correctly understood the Matthean text, since in the first gospel the group that is described as going to the tomb, employ the guards to seal the tomb, σφραγίσαντες τὸν λίθον μετὰ τῆς κουστωδίας. Thus, the guards form a distinct group (although perhaps not totally discrete) from those who are described by the participle πορευθέντες. Nolland adopts the same line of reasoning when he concludes, '[w]e should rather think of the guard as the means by which the Jerusalem leaders "went and secured the tomb".'[616] Here the text mentions two groups, the soldiers using the dative plural pronoun αὐτοῖς, and the Jewish leaders explicitly mentioned with the pairing πρεσβύτεροι καὶ γραμματεῖς. Therefore the *Gospel of Peter* does not maintain the threefold designation of the leadership which it introduced in *Gos. Pet.* 8.28, οἱ γραμματεῖς καὶ Φαρισαῖοι καὶ πρεσβύτεροι. Instead, in *Gos. Pet.* 8.31b, the Pharisees are dropped. Interestingly, the Pharisees only occur in the *Gospel of Peter* at 8.28. While many commentators on Matt 27.62 doubt the historical accuracy of the presence of the Pharisees during the Passion and resurrection events,[617] it is to be strongly doubted that the author of the

---

[615] See, W. Schneemelcher, *New Testament Apocrypha*, vol. I: Gospels and Related Writings (Louisville: WJK, 1991) 162, fragment 22.

[616] J. Nolland, *The Gospel of Matthew*, NICGT (Grand Rapids, MI: Eerdmans, 2005) 1239.

[617] See Luz, *Matthew 21–28*, 587–588; Allen, *Gospel according to Saint Matthew*, lxxviii-lxxix. By contrast Davies and Allison may be more open to the possibility of the historical reliability of the presence of the Pharisees at this point. 'This is the only mention of the Pharisees in the synoptic passion accounts – a fact explained only by

Akhmîm text has intentionally deleted the reference to the Pharisees in order to improve the historical veracity of the narrative, or even for any theological reason. If the omission is at all intentional, it appears that literary economy would be the sole motivation.[618]

Thus together this somewhat motely group of Roman troops and representative Jewish leaders head for the tomb to prevent the possible theft of the body by the disciples. Here the author switches the terminology used to depict the burial place employing μνῆμα, in place of τάφος, which occurred earlier in this verse. No great significance should be attributed to this alteration. In this pericope (*Gos. Pet.* 8.28–33) τάφος is used only in v. 31a, whereas μνῆμα occurs three times. For a fuller treatment see the discussion at 8.30a.

**8.32a   καὶ κυλίσαντες λίθον μέγαν κατὰ τοῦ κεντυρίωνος καὶ τῶν στρατιωτῶν.** This verse describes the collective act of moving the stone into place to close the sepulchre. There is considerable deviation from the account of the rolling of the stone to seal the tomb, which occurs in only two of the canonical gospels.[619] Both Matthew and Mark agree that Joseph of Arimathea was solely responsible for taking the body of Jesus, wrapping it in a linen sheet, placing the body in the tomb, and single-handedly rolling the stone into place (Matt 27.59–60//Mk 15.45–46).[620] In the Matthean account the actions of Joseph, including the sealing of the tomb, take place before the Jewish leaders request a guard to be set at the tomb. The Akhmîm account reverses this sequence, since it involves the Roman soldiers in the act of burial. This reversal of events, resulting in the active involvement of the Roman military in the burial, should be seen as part of the author's purpose to provide a validation of the placement of the body in the tomb prior to the miraculous resurrection that the narrative reports. Not only is the guard present at the empty tomb, moreover,

---

the influence of historical memory.' Davies and Allison, *The Gospel According to Saint Matthew*, vol. III, 653.

[618] As Vaganay observes, 'Il ne convient pas, d'ailleurs, d'attacher grande importance à la mention spéciale des anciens et des scribes ainsi qu'à l'exclusion des pharisiens (cf. v. 28). L'auteur veut uniquement nous laisser entendre que les principaux chefs de la nation vont prendre une part active à la fermeture du tombeau.' Vaganay, *L'Évangile de Pierre*, 284.

[619] Although it should be noted that the text of Codex Bezae expands the Lukan account to incorporate a reference to the stone, ἐπεθηκεν τῷ μνημειῷ λίθον ὃν μόγις εἴκοσι ἐκύλιον (Codex D, Lk 23.53).

[620] Brown, *The Death of the Messiah*, vol. 2, 1296.

they can attest to the presence of the body in the sepulchre prior to the act of sealing the grave-site. While it is not explicitly stated, the value of Roman testimony is more highly prized than that of their Jewish counterparts.

The Matthean and Markan accounts both have differences and agreements among themselves and with the *Gospel of Peter* A synoptic comparison of the accounts is useful in illustrating this:

Matt 27.60       καὶ προσκυλίσας λίθον μέγαν τῇ θύρᾳ τοῦ μνημείου ἀπῆλθεν.

Mark 15.46      καὶ προσεκύλισεν λίθον ἐπὶ τὴν θύραν τοῦ μνημείου.

Gos. Pet. 8.32    καὶ κυλίσαντες λίθον μέγαν...ἐπὶ τῇ θύρᾳ τοῦ μνήματος.

It immediately becomes apparent that Matthew and Mark agree against the Akhmîm text in reading the compound verb form προσκυλίω and using the term μνημεῖον to denote the tomb rather than the related form μνῆμα employed in the *Gospel of Peter*. The *Gospel of Peter* has three important agreements with the Matthean version that are not shared with the Markan account: (i) although it does not employ the compound verb, it agrees with Matthew in using an aorist participle form, rather than the indicative form in Mark; (ii) in agreement with Matthew, it qualifies the noun λίθον with the adjective μέγαν;[621] and (iii) it uses the dative case in describing the location of the stone at the door, τῇ θύρᾳ. In relation to the second point, Porter notes, '[i]n the *Gospel of Peter*, adjectival modifiers preceding or following their head-term are not as frequent as one might expect...approximately 60% of the instances have the modifier preceding the head-term, a ratio very similar to that found in the letters of Paul.'[622] The one significant agreement that the *Gospel of Peter* shares with Mark against Matthew is the common use of the preposition ἐπί. The fact that both the Markan and Akhmîm text omit the final Matthew word, ἀπῆλθεν, is not particularly striking. Based on the Two Document Hypothesis, this can be understood as a Matthean addition to the Markan text,

---

[621] Swete notes that the description of the stone as 'great' does occur later in the Markan narrative, '(μέγας σφόδρα, Mark xvi. 4)'. Swete, *The Akhmîm Fragment of the Apocryphal Gospel of St Peter*, 15.

[622] S.E. Porter, 'The Greek of the Gospel of Peter: Implications for Syntax and Discourse Study', in Merkt and Nicklas (eds.), *The Reception and Development of Early Christian Passion Traditions*, 77–90, here 80.

which the *Gospel of Peter* has, independent of the Markan text form, decided not to take-over from the first gospel.

Far greater detail is provided in terms of the mechanics of moving the stone into place in the Akhmîm version of the story. As has been discussed earlier,[623] many commentators have proposed the conjectural emendation of the preposition word κατά to μετά. It has been argued that such a correction is unnecessary, since the text makes sense as it stands. What appears to be envisaged is the Jewish party rolling the stone towards the soldiers, who stand in front of the stone and steady it as it moves down into place at the mouth of the tomb. Thus a collaborative enterprise is being described, wherein the two group act together to postion the large stone.

**8.32b** ὁμοῦ πάντες οἱ ὄντες ἐκεῖ ἔθηκαν ἐπὶ τῇ θύρᾳ τοῦ μνήματος. The opening phrase in this clause, ὁμοῦ πάντες οἱ ὄντες ἐκεῖ, appears to be somewhat redundant. Its purpose is to reiterate the corporate involvement of the various parties present, thereby showing that the stone could not be easily moved. Thus Vaganay comments, 'the stone is so large that the efforts of all persons present are required in order to move it.'[624] Having expanded the central part of this verse to make explicit the role of a different set of subjects from those referred to in the canonical accounts, the author returns to the wording contained in the Markan and Matthean storyline (Matt 27.60//Mk 15.46). Thus, the Akhmîm narrative continues its pattern of intertwining the familiar and the innovative in its re-telling of the Passion and post-crucifixion events. With the final clause the preposition ἐπί aligns with the Markan account (but is probably not directly dependent upon it), the dative case is used in τῇ θύρᾳ, here in agreement with Matthew, and finally the *Gospel of Peter* deviates from both the Markan and Matthean usage of τοῦ μνημείου preferring the related form τοῦ μνήματος. These forms are interchangeable in canonical texts, classical literature and throughout the Hellenistic and later periods.[625]

**8.33** καὶ ἐπέχρεισαν ἑπτὰ σφραγῖδας καὶ σκηνὴν ἐκεῖ πήξαντες ἐφύλαξαν. Three precautionary actions are described, which are insti-

---

[623] See text crirtical note 13.
[624] Vaganay, *L'Évangile de Pierre*, 285.
[625] For details see *BDAG* 654–655; *LSJ* 1139, although μνῆμα is probably the more ancient form, or at least more widely used in the earlier period.

tuted to make secure the burial site in order to protect it from tampering. These are the setting of seven seals, the rupturing of which would
show that the stone had been moved and subsequently replaced; the
pitching of a tent, to maintain an ongoing presence during the three-
day period; and, a vigilant guarding of the site. The Matthean account
of the guard-at-the-tomb story attests the sealing of the tomb, although
it does not enumerate seven seals. By implication it supports the ongoing presence of guards, since their fearful reaction at the appearance
of the angel of the Lord is narrated (Matt 28.4). There is, however,
no mention of a tent being pitched at the site. In Matt 27.66, the
third person plural subjects who seal the tomb refers at least to the
guards sent by Pilate, but may also include members of the Jewish
leadership in a supervisory role, which may have avoided working on
the Sabbath. Discussing the nature of the seal placed on the tomb
Brown states,

> In both Matt and *GPet* the implication is that wax was put on the stone
> in such a way that opening the tomb would break the wax, and in the
> wax an imprint of a seal was made. A special element in *GPet* is that
> there were seven seals. The number seven is commonly symbolic in the
> Bible, but it is difficult to be certain whether the seven is just part of the
> folkloric imagination or has special symbolism.[626]

The verb πήγνυμι used to describe the act of setting up the tent, is used
in the NT only once, in Heb 8.2 in connection with the 'true tent' set
up in heaven by the Lord. The verb is, however, commonly used in
the wider literature of the period to denote erecting a physical tent. In
the *Protevangelium of James*, Joachim, the father of Mary, went into the
wilderness and 'there pitched [ἔπηξεν] his tent and fasted forty days
and forty nights' (1.4). Here, in Akhmîm narrative, the notice about
the tent underscores the continued presence and vigilance of the
guard. The *Gospel of Peter* account excludes the possibility that there
was at any point an opportunity for the followers of Jesus to despoil
the tomb of the body.

   In terms of a *Traditiongeschichtliche* trajectory, it is implausible
to account for these elements as representing an earlier phase of the
tradition than that narrated in the Matthean account. The obviously
folkloric quality of these elements, coupled with the apologetic motivation for introducing them, speaks strongly of these details being later

---

[626] Brown, *The Death of the Messiah*, vol. 2, 1296.

accretions. Surprisingly, even at this point where such folkloric details are perhaps most clearly identified, Crossan does not categorize these elements as part of the later redactional strand that he argues has been added to the *Cross Gospel* to form the *Gospel of Peter.*[627] Instead he argues that the

> *Cross Gospel* describes a proper situation with a tent for those who were not actually on watch. A later literary benefit of that description will be to offset any idea that the soldiers were simply dreaming. Those who were on actual watch in *Gospel of Peter* 9:35 will have to awaken the others in 10:38.[628]

It is uncertain what Crossan means by a 'proper situation', whether this denotes an historical occurrence, or if it describes an event that was plausible on the initial literary level. He seems to assume, on his assumption of Matthean dependence on the *Cross Gospel*, that the reason for deleting this detail about the tent is that it left open the possibility that instead of keeping watch the guards 'were simply dreaming.' Such reasoning is frankly far from convincing and seems to smack of special pleading. Crossan argues that Matthew's theological slant in rewriting the story of the guards is an 'attempt to change the *Cross Gospel's* consistent combination of Jewish authorities and Roman guards into one in which the Jewish authorities are not at the tomb, and Jewish, and not Roman, guards are.'[629]

Even if this were the case (it has been argued that Pilate grants a guard in Matt 27.65, and that this guard is answerable to Pilate, Matt 28.14), it is still not convincing that either the seven seals or the pitching of a tent were so uniquely Roman activities that Matthew would have felt constrained to delete these details. Thus, the most plausible explanation is that the account in the first gospel (or a source behind that account, if one chooses to adopt the suggestion of Brown[630]) represents a more primitive form of the guard-at-the-tomb story, and this has been embellished by the *Gospel of Peter* through the inclusion of details which serve the apologetic function of excluding explanations of non-permanent survellience, sleeping guards, or tampering with the tomb.

---

[627] Crossan, *The Cross That Spoke: The Origins of the Passion Narrative*, 16–30, in particular 17–20.

[628] Crossan, *The Cross That Spoke: The Origins of the Passion Narrative*, 273.

[629] Crossan, *The Cross That Spoke: The Origins of the Passion Narrative*, 278.

[630] As is stated according to the solution preferred by Brown. See Brown, *The Death of the Messiah*, vol. 2, 1299–1313.

34. πρωΐας δὲ ἐπιφώσκοντος τοῦ σαββάτου ἦλθεν ὄχλος ἀπὸ Ἰερουσαλὴμ[1] καὶ τῆς περιχώρου ἵνα ἴδωσι[2] τὸ μνημεῖον ἐσφραγισμένο(ν)[3]. 35. τῇ δὲ νυκτὶ ᾖ[4] ἐπέφωσκεν ἡ[5] κυριακή, φυλασσόντων τῶν στρατιωτῶν[6] ἀνὰ δύο[7] δύο κατὰ φρουρά(ν),[8] μεγάλη φωνὴ ἐγένετο ἐν τῷ οὐρανῷ. 36. καὶ εἶδο(ν) ἀνοιχθέντας τοὺς οὐρά[ν]ους[9] καὶ δύο ἄνδρας κατελθόντας ἐκεῖθε πολὺ φέγγος ἔχοντας καὶ ἐγγίσαντας[10] τῷ τάφῳ. 37. ὁ δὲ λείθος[11] ἐκεῖνος ὁ βεβλημένος[12] ἐπὶ τῇ θύρᾳ ἀφ' ἑαυτοῦ κυλισθεὶς ἐπεχώρησε[13] παρὰ μέρος καὶ ὁ τάφος ἐνοίγη[14] καὶ ἀμφότεροι οἱ νεανίσκοι εἰσῆλθον[15].

34. Now when the morning of the Sabbath dawned a crowd came from Jerusalem and the surrounding region that they might see the tomb which had been sealed. 35. But during the night in which the Lord's day dawned, while the soldiers were guarding two by two according to post, there was a great voice in the sky. 36. And they saw the heavens were being opened, and two men descended from there, having much brightness, and they drew near to the tomb. 37. But that stone which had been placed at the entrance rolled away by itself and made way in part and the tomb was opened and both the young men went in.

## TEXT CRITICAL NOTES

1. The noun Ἰερουσαλὴμ has a number of scribal anomalies. The initial letter iota stands closer to the preceding final letter of the word ἀπό, than it does to the following letter epsilon. In part, this is caused by the unusual conjunction of the second and third letters. The mid-stroke of the elevated and mis-shapened epsilon is extended to form the arc of the letter rho. The exact order of pen strokes is hard to determine. It appears that intead of a single curve to form the epsilon, the scribe has first written two oblique, but nonetheless generally linear strokes to form the body of the epsilon, presumably with the longer stroke written first. Next it appears that the vertical line of the rho has been written. Then lastly the crossbar of the epsilon which as a continuous stroke forms the arc of the rho is added. This results in an ususal compression of letters and non-standard ligatures between them. Nothwithstanding these aberrant features,

Gebhardt's general observations about the formation of the letter rho hold in this case: 'The ρ frequently shows a small downward curvature, most often to the left than to the right.[631]

2. As in note 1, the initial letter, an iota, is connected to the preceding letter, and is then followed by a slight break that distances it from the following letters. There is a second larger break in the word ἴδωσι occurring between third and fourth letters which measures approximately 2mm. As is common, this third person plural form is written without the movable ν at the end.

3. The form ἐσφραγισμένο̄, which stands at the end of line thirteen of the *verso* of page three, employs the supralinear stroke to indicate the omission of the final ν. Kraus and Nicklas note '13 Ms: ἐσφραγισμένο̄'[632] in place of their printed form ἐσφραγισμένον. On the movable ν, see the standard Greek Grammars.[633]

4. The feminine dative relative pronoun is written with an iota adscript, rather than the now standard iota subscript as printed above. This appears to be the only place in the manuscript where an adscript is employed, even when the feminine dative relative pronoun is used elsewhere (cf. ᾗ *Gos. Pet.* 12.52). There is, however, one place in the manuscript where the subscript form is written by the scribe, this occurs with the masculine dative singular definite article, τῷ (*Gos. Pet.* 11.47). Citing the observation of Strabo, BDF notes the widespread tendency to ignore the iota in either adscript or subscript form. 'According to the Strabo (14, p. 648: πολλοὶ γὰρ χωρὶς τοῦ ι γράφουσι τὰς δοτικὰς καὶ ἐκβάλλουσι δὲ τὸ ἔθος φυσικὴν αἰτίαν οὐκ ἔχον), many omitted the ι even in the dative where rules were easily given, and so it is omitted for the most part in the older NT MSS.'[634]

5. A diacritical sign is used above the feminine definite article, ἡ, in the form of a diæresis, here to indicate a separation of the ἡ from both the preceding and following letters, although there is no possibility of a potential diphthong since both those letters are consonants. This is the so-called 'inorganic' use, employed not to separate vowels, but simply to mark an initial vowel.[635]

---

[631] Gebhardt, *Das Evangelium und die Apokalypse des Petrus*, 13.
[632] Kraus und Nicklas, *Das Petrusevangelium und die Petrusapokalypse*, 40.
[633] For example, BDF §20, 12–13.
[634] BDF §26.
[635] Other occurrences in this text can be found at *Gos. Pet.* 1.2, ὑμῖν; 3.6, υἱόν.

6. An interesting ligature occurs in the word στρατιωτῶν, where the crossbar of the second letter τ continues to become the hook of the following ρ (cf. note 1 above). The vertical stroke of the ρ is parallel to that of the preceding τ, but starts slightly lower and does not ascend to quite the same height, thus not connecting with the crossbar of the τ.

7. The delta here follows the more rounded form that the scribe writes on certain occasions, in comparison to the more traditional triangular form of the letter which is used with greater frequency. This phenomenon of alternating between a traditional majuscule form and a form that has obvious minuscule tendencies is noted by Gebhardt.[636]

8. Like the ending of the form ἐσφραγισμένō (see text-critical note 3, above), φρουρᾱ, which also stands at the end of a line is written without the final ν. This omission is indicated by a supralinear stroke.

9. There is a tear in the manuscript which obscures only the letter ν in the word οὐρά[ν]ους. As the writing on the *recto* of page three continued closer to the bottom of the page more text was obscured on the *recto* side.[637]

10. The double gamma letter formation could easily be misread for the letter π. The scribe is not as careful in the formation of this combination as was the case three words earlier where in the word φέγγος the double gamma is given a more pronounced undulating top, which distinguishes it from the flattened top in this case which results in the similarity with the π. In fact a number of scholars have adopted the reading ἐπιστάντας, the aorist active nominative masculine plural participle of ἐφίστημι, meaning 'to stand near' or 'to draw near.'[638] This reading is supported by Robinson.[639] Bouriant reads the text as ἐπίσαντας, and translates this with the reflexive verb *se poser*, which would appear to imply that he took the correct Greek form to be ἐπιστάντας.[640] The suggestion

---

[636] Gebhardt, *Das Evangelium und die Apokalypse des Petrus*, 10–11.

[637] See text-critical note 7, in the section on *Gos. Pet.* 8.28–33.

[638] See BDAG, 418–419.

[639] In his notes Robinson gives the actual reading as 'ἐπίσαντας' Robinson and James, *The Gospel according to Peter and the Revelation of Peter*, 86.

[640] Bouriant, 'Fragments du texte grec du livre d'Énoch et de quelques écrits attribués à saint Pierre', 140.

ἐπιστάντας is problematic because the word written in the text lacks the required fifth letter τ. It is much more likely that the correct form is indeed ἐγγίσαντας, and early transcriptions confused the double gamma with the letter π.

11. Itacism is the cause of the occurrence of the form λεῖθος in place of the more regular orthography, λίθος. BDF notes tendency of replacement of 'ει for ῖ to distinguish it from ι.'[641] It is not, however, necessary to follow the conclusion that is drawn from this concerning the editing of ancient manuscripts. 'Consequently, the only possible procedure for an editor of the NT is, of course, to carry through Attic spelling without any regard to the MSS.'[642] Vaganay states, 'ὁ δὲ λίθος (mistake of the copiest in the manuscript.: λεῖθος).'[643] It may be somewhat harsh to categorize this as a 'mistake' rather than recognizing it as an orthographical variant in a fluid language without strict controls on grammar and spelling.

12. In the word βεβλημένος the lambda is partially abraded. What remains visible is the top left-hand descending part of the long stroke and the bottom left-hand ascending part of the short stroke.

13. The form ἐπεχώρησε is written with the movable ν omitted.[644] There appears to be little system in the scribe's practice throughout the manuscript.

14. The augment used in the form ἐνοίγη does not correspond to the rules laid out in scholastic handbooks. One would expect the aorist passive third person singular form to be written as ἠνοίγη, showing the lengthening of α to η. Again the confusion may arise due to the phonological interchange between ε and η. This reflects the freedom with which these rules were applied and perhaps also the scribe's lack of formal training.

15. The ligature between the ε and ι in the word εἰσῆλθον produces an irregular letter shape for the initial ε in this word. This non-standard letter formation is evidenced at other points in the manuscript (cf. εκεῖνοι *Gos. Pet.* 10.38).

---

[641] BDF §23.
[642] BDF §23.
[643] Vaganay, *L'Évangile de Pierre*, 295.
[644] BDF §20.

## COMMENTARY

**9.34a** πρωΐας δὲ ἐπιφώσκοντος τοῦ σαββάτου. This genitive absolute construct relates the temporal details necessary to situate the unusual coming of the crowd to inspect the burial site. Again the narrative reveals the author's interest in locating the time at which certain events occur. Such fabricated temporal specificity may be a mechanism the author employs in an attempt to provide the narrative with an air of historical authenticity. The construction is reminiscent of the opening clause in Matt 28.1, which recounts the visit of Mary Magdalene and the other Mary to the sepulchre, ὀψὲ δὲ σαββάτων, τῇ ἐπιφωσκούσῃ εἰς μίαν σαββάτων. Whereas Matthew uses this phrase to jump to the events that took place on the day after the Sabbath, the *Gospel of Peter* retains the Matthean language but employs it to describe the gathering of the crowds on the Sabbath. This is a detail unknown in the canonical accounts. The feminine noun πρωΐα occurs only twice in the NT, Matt 27.1 and Jn 21.4.[645] In relation to the Johannine usage which occurs in a post-resurrection setting, Barrett notes that 'Elsewhere in John (18.28; 20.1; cf. 1.41) the indeclinable form πρωΐ is used.'[646] By contrast, in Matthew the term is used to introduce events that transpire on the morning of the crucifixion, πρωΐας δὲ γενομένης (Matt 27.1). Davies and Allison comment that 'Matthew's expression creates an *inclusio* with v. 57 (ὀψίας δὲ γενομένης; cf. 26.20) the day dawns with the Jewish leaders handing Jesus over to Pilate; it sets with Pilate handing Jesus' body over to Joseph of Arimathea.'[647] In the *Gospel of Peter* in terms of location in the narrative there is a slightly stronger parallel with Matt 28.1, although the term πρωΐας is not used in the same context. However, in term of syntactical and lexical parallels there are more points of contact with Matt 27.1, where the term πρωΐας also is utilised in a genitive absolute construction. This may suggest that the author of the Akhmîm narrative is influenced by Matthean language at this point, but may not be consulting the text directly. Also of significance are points of contact internal to the narrative of the Akhmîm text. At *Gos. Pet.* 2.5 Antipas refers in anticipation to the Sabbath dawning, ἐπεὶ καὶ σάββατον ἐπιφώσκει. The second

---

[645] See Moulton and Geden, *Concordance to the Greek New Testament*, 954.
[646] Barrett, *The Gospel according to St John*, 482.
[647] Davies and Allison, *The Gospel According to Saint Matthew*, vol. III, 654.

and third occurrences of the verb ἐπιφώσκω in *Gos. Pet.* 9.34, 35, are where the dawning of 'the Sabbath' and of 'the Lord's day' respectively are described.[648]

**9.34b** ἦλθεν ὄχλος ἀπὸ Ἰερουσαλὴμ καὶ τῆς περιχώρου. Here the storyline of the Akhmîm text introduces a detail that is not disclosed in the canonical accounts, namely the visit of the crowd to the burial site on the morning of the Sabbath day which intervened between the crucifixion and the day of resurrection. Whether this visit is intended to be viewed as an act of corporate piety or group fascination in light of the miraculous events that accompanied the crucifixion (according to this narrative) is unclear. The two options, however, are not entirely mutually exclusive. The crowd that visits the tomb is described as coming from Jerusalem and the surrounding area. The co-ordination of the terms 'Jerusalem' (although in the alternative form Ἱεροσόλυμα) and περίχωρος occurs only once in the NT, at Matt 3.5: τότε ἐξεπορεύετο πρὸς αὐτὸν Ἱεροσόλυμα καὶ πᾶσα ἡ Ἰουδαία καὶ πᾶσα ἡ περίχωρος τοῦ Ἰορδάνου. Here, however, the sense is different, with περίχωρος indicating the area surrounding the river Jordan, not the region near Jerusalem. Vaganay notes that during the great pilgrimage festival large numbers of people resided in the outlying area surrounding Jerusalem. However, he rejects this historical detail as being the basis for the reference to a crowd assembling from the city and its hinterland.[649]

Moreover, Vaganay is suspicious that the group is delimited to the inhabitants of Jerusalem and the environs, because of the restrictions on Sabbath day journeys. 'It should not be asked whether this walk was respecting the Sabbath limit, *Act.*, I, 12 (cf. Strack-Billerbeck, II, pp. 590–594).'[650] While this may indeed be correct, and the intention may be to demonstrate the widespread, but nonetheless localized, fascination with the figure of Jesus, the concern over the legitimate extent of travel on the Sabbath was a perennial concern in Jewish writings both during the Second Temple period and after its destruction. The Qumran sectarians legislated that on the Sabbath one was 'not to walk more than one thousand cubits outside the city' (CD 10.21). The legis-

---

[648] On the use of ἐπιφώσκω see Robinson and James, *The Gospel according to Peter and the Revelation of Peter*, 24, n. 2.

[649] Vaganay, *L'Évangile de Pierre*, 287.

[650] Vaganay, *L'Évangile de Pierre*, 287.

lation in the Temple Scroll which imposes the purity standards of the sanctuary on the whole of Jerusalem, instructed that defecation and urination should not take place within three thousand cubits of the city (11QT$^a$ 46.13–16). On the Sabbath this would have caused more than an uncomfortable textual tension.[651] Rabbinic discussion contained in the Mishnah attest to a slightly more liberal attitude with a limit of two thousand cubits being permitted (*m.Erub.* 4.3–8).[652] Yet the obviously anti-Judaic perspective of the *Gospel of Peter* makes it extremely unlikely that such restrictions played any part in the author's formulation of the text. This is especially likely to be the case when one considers the manner in which the author explicitly portrays the halakhic concern of the people over the timing of Jesus' death before the setting of the sun. In that case he emphasized the punctilious observance of the law in contrast to the exercise of true justice. Here the journey is reported as an incidental detail with no further significance attached.

**9.34c** ἵνα ἴδωσι τὸ μνημεῖον ἐσφραγισμένο. Voyeurism alone does not appear to be the motivation behind the crowd visiting the tomb. Their attraction to the site appears to be motivated, at least in terms of the preceding events in the narrative, as an ongoing part of the corporate act of morning that was described in *Gos. Pet.* 8.28. Another significant element that should not be overlooked is the way this extended group of witnesses function to increase the circle which can validate the veracity of a sealed and guarded tomb containing the corpse of Jesus. A third motivation may be the expectation of seeing further examples of the divine fiat. Already the death of Jesus has resulted in the rending of the Temple curtain, the darkening of the heavens and the quaking of the earth. Such phenomena may be part of the reason why the author depicts a gathering crowd. While these three suggestions may be plausible authorial perspectives that legitimate the inclusion of this new detail of the congregating crowd, the narrative simply states that the motivation was to see the tomb, yet it does not explicitly state why this grave-site was such a source of fascination. Obviously it is bound up with the significance of the body in the sep-

---

[651] J.C. Vanderkam, *The Dead Sea Scrolls Today* (London/Grand Rapids, MI.: SPCK/Eerdmans, 1994) 86–87.

[652] The Mishnaic text helpfully discusses the meaning of these restrictions if one is engaged in travelling on board a ship on a Sabbath (*m.Erub.* 4.1–2), or inadvertently asleep in a wagon when Sabbath falls (*m.Erub.* 4.5).

ulchre, but the text offers no help beyond that observation. Swete gives a popularizing interpretation of what transpired. 'The rumor that the tomb was sealed and guarded had reached the city and the suburbs during the night, and early on the Sabbath morning the crowds came to see it.'[653] This explanation does not have a basis in the narrative, and appears to depend on a perception of what is historically plausible, rather than recognizing the detail as an authorial invention that should be explained on the basis of clues within the narrative.

**9.35a** τῇ δὲ νυκτὶ ᾗ ἐπέφωσκεν ἡ κυριακή. Having given a fleeting glimpse of the events of the Sabbath that intervened between the crucifixion and the resurrection, the author introduces another temporal clause to indicate the further passage of time. Unlike Matt 28.1, which describes the second day after the crucifixion as εἰς μίαν σαββάτων 'on the first day of the week', the Akhmîm text replaces this with the substantivized adjective ἡ κυριακή. This is obviously a recognizable temporal reference. As Bauckham states in relation to the use of κυριακή both here and in 12.50, 'it is clear that κυριακή is already an accepted technical term and refers to a day.'[654] Yet, as he further observes, it is not possible from the usage in the *Gospel of Peter* to make a decision whether this term is referring specifically to the resurrection day, or is a more general reference to any Sunday as the Lord's day.[655] Consideration of the wider usage in early Christian texts needs to be considered in order to see if clarification is possible.

The adjective κυριακός is found only twice in the NT. In what is the earliest documentable Christian use, Paul refers to the communal meal in Corinth as κυριακὸν δεῖπνον. Here the adjective does not have a temporal sense, and may in fact be a conscious attempt to apply the terminology of the imperial office to the ritual practices of the early Christians. The non-Christian application of the term, usually found in inscriptional texts or papyri, according to LSJ occurs 'usu. *of the Roman Emperor*.'[656] This aligns with the claim advanced by Crossan and Reed that Paul's choice of terminology was an intentional attempt

---

[653] Swete, *The Akhmîm Fragment of the Apocryphal Gospel of St Peter*, 16.

[654] R.J. Bauckham, 'The Lord's Day', in D.A. Carson (ed.), *From Sabbath to Lord's Day: A Biblical, Historical and Theological Investigation* (Grand Rapids, MI.: Zonderan, 1982), 229.

[655] Bauckham, 'The Lord's Day', 229.

[656] For examples of κυριακός in connection with the Emperor see LSJ, 1013, section II under the head-word.

to subvert the Roman cult and imperial ideology.[657] The second, later usage in the NT is to be found in Rev 1.10. In that context it clearly functions as a temporal term, where John, while situated on the isle of Patmos, is caught up in the spirit and sees a vision. These events are recorded as having taken place ἐν τῇ κυριακῇ ἡμέρᾳ, 'on the Lord's Day.' The majority of commentators on this passage argue that here the sense is general designate a 'Sunday' rather than a specific reference to Easter day.[658] Furthermore, Aune dismisses the suggestion that the reference in Revelation means Easter day. He states, '[t]hough many of the early Christian references to ἡ κυριακή (ἡμέρα) *could* refer either to Sunday or Easter (*Did* 14.1; Ign. *Magn.* 9.1; *Gos. Pet.* 35, 50), some clearly refer to Sunday (*Acts Pet.* 29; *Acts Paul* 7 "And Paul cried out to God on the Sabbath as the Lord's day drew near").'[659] He understands the reference in Rev 1.10 as referring to Sunday in general. Further it is noted even with references in the first group that such texts are associated with areas where the Quartodeciman practice of celebrating Easter on 14 Nisan predominated, thus problematizeing the view that the term κυριακή refers specifically to the resurrection day and not just Sundays in general.[660]

The documented occurrences from before the second half of the second century may not even be as potentially ambiguous as Aune suggested.

> κατὰ κυριακὴν δὲ κυρίου συναχθέντες κλάσατε ἄρτον... (*Did.* 14.1)

The κατά here appears to have distributive force, 'Each Lord's day when you have gathered together, break bread...' Thus, the most natural way to understand this instruction concerning habitual practice is as a reference to the weekly Sunday meetings of believers. As Nieder-wimmer argues, 'The Didacist wants to speak about confession and

---

[657] Crossan and Reed state the central thesis of their study as being their 'insistence that Paul opposed Rome with Christ against Caesar, not because that empire was particularly unjust or oppressive, but because he questioned *the normalcy of civilization itself*, since civilization had always been imperial, that is, unjust and oppressive.' Crossan and Reed, *In Search of Paul: How Jesus' Apostle Opposed Rome's Empire with God's Kingdom*, x–xi.

[658] G.K. Beale, *The Book of Revelation*, NIGTC (Grand Rapids, MI/Carlisle: Eerdmans/Paternoster, 2005) 203.

[659] Aune, *Revelation 1–5*, 84.

[660] Aune, *Revelation 1–5*, 84.

the purity of sacrifices, and for that purpose he places the reader in the time of the Sunday worship service.'[661] The use of the term κυριακή by Ignatius in his *Epistle to the Magnesians* 9.1, is perhaps susceptible of being undertood as a reference to another day apart from a Sunday. He writes, μηκέτι σαββατίζοντες, ἀλλὰ κατὰ κυριακὴν ζῶντες, 'no longer be Sabbath observers, but live according to the Lord's day.' It is, however, most natural to see Ignatius calling for the replacement of the Jewish weekly festival, with that weekly event which is observed by Christians. This makes even more sense if, as appears to be the most natural way to read the epistles. In his corpus of seven letters Ignatius is responding to two groups of opponents, however in *Magnesians* it is those with Jewish proclivities who are being opposed.[662] Thus while the possibility exists of reading κυριακή as a reference to a specific day such as the Resurrection day, the more natural way of understanding those texts from before the second half of the second century which preserve the term is as witnessing to the continuing trend of using κυριακή as a technical term for 'Sunday'. Thus it is best to concur with Bauckham's assessment that

> The evidence from the *second half* of the second century is therefore consistent and unambiguous. The most obvious conclusion is that this usage continues the earlier usage attested in the *Didache*, Ignatius and the *Gospel of Peter*, which would therefore also refer to Sunday.[663]

Significantly, claims that the usage in texts from the first half of the second century is ambiguous may in fact in part be giving too much credence to the less plausible line of interpretation.

**9.35b** φυλασσόντων τῶν στρατιωτῶν ἀνὰ δύο δύο κατὰ φρουρά(ν). Absent from the canonical tradition, the *Gospel of Peter* provides more elaborate details about the process of guarding the tomb. The account relates that the soldiers took watch in pairs. For Swete this leads to a calculation of the number of military personnel who were present at the scene according to the Akhmîm account. He states,

---

[661] K. Niederwimmer, *The Didache*, Hermeneia (Minneapolis: Fortress, 1998) 194–195.

[662] P. Foster, 'The Epistles of Ignatius', (Part 1), *Exp Times* 117 (2006) 487–495; (Part 2) *Exp Times* 117 (2006) 1–11.

[663] Bauckham, 'The Lord's Day', 330.

The κουστωδία consists of eight men and the centurion. In Acts xii. 4 there are sixteen (τέσσαρσιν τετραδίοις), but eight of the whole number are required to guard the prisoner's person (6); here it is enough to provide two sentaries at the door for each watch.[664]

It is, however, questionable whether the calculus that Swete employs is applicable to the current situation. It appears to be dependent on the understanding that the period was divided into four watches. While this may even be historically accurate, it needs to be bourne in mind that this detail is a redactional expansion of the tradition, and the report of the guard taking turns two-by-two is not motivated by a desire to import accurate historical details into the narrative, but rather it functions as part of the motif of validating the miraculous.

The expression ἀνὰ δύο δύο, two-by-two, has an exact parallel in the preamble to the Lukan mission charge given to the seventy(-two), in the version of that verse preserved in Codex Vaticanus and a number of other manuscripts (Lk 10.1).[665] Without the preposition ἀνά the repeated numeral δύο δύο is also found in the preamble to the Markan charge to the Twelve (Mk 6.7). While there is probably no direct literary dependence between either Lk 10.1 or Mk 6.7 and this passage in *Gos. Pet.* 9.35 (although there may be some dependence between Mk 6.7 and Lk 10.1),[666] the usage in the canonical gospels shows that this was a stardard way to denote pairs of people performing an activity together. Thus Vaganay is correct in his assessment that δύο δύο is not due to dittography. As he argues,

> The distributive sense is expressed in classical and helenistic Greek, sometimes by ἀνά or κατά with the cardinal number (Mk 6.40), sometimes by the simple repetition of the cardinal number (Mk 6.7). But in *koine* Greek one sometimes finds these two constructions joined together ἀνὰ δύο δύο (*Acts of Philip*, ch. 142, II, 2, p. 79; cf. Lk 10.1 in B Θ, etc.), κατὰ δύο δύο (P.Oxy., VI, 886, 19). This manner of reinforcing the expression is frequent in popular speech.[667]

---

[664] Swete, *The Akhmîm Fragment of the Apocryphal Gospel of St Peter*, 16.

[665] This reading is preserved in the following manuscripts: B K Θ *f*[13] 565. *l*2211 *al* sy[h]; Eus.

[666] The two canonical passages Mk 6.7 and Lk 10.1 may constitute a Mark-Q overlap. In *The Critical Edition of Q* the editors ask 'Is Luke's δύο δύο in Q or from Mark?' See Robinson, Hoffmann & Kloppenborg (eds.), *The Critical Edition of Q*, Hermeneia, 159, note 9. Tuckett classifies the mission charge (Mk 6.7–13//Q 10.1–16) as one of the Mark-Q overlaps, C.M. Tuckett, *Q and the History of Early Christianity* (Edinburgh: T&T Clark, 1996) 31.

[667] Vaganay, *L'Évangile de Pierre*, 292.

All these additional details ensure that for the readers of this narrative there can be no doubt that the tomb is securely guarded by alert soldiers. The phrase κατὰ φρουράν designates order and vigilance in carrying the assigned task. Hence the author emphasizes the attention to duty in order to make the accusation of theft of the body by the disciples untenable. Once again the apologetic intent is further heightened in the narrative.

**9.35c** μεγάλη φωνὴ ἐγένετο ἐν τῷ οὐρανῷ. Voices from heaven are not an uncommon element in biblical narrative, yet in the canonical accounts such a type of theophanic manifestation is remarkably absent from the Passion accounts. In many ways the first portent that accompanies the opening of the tomb in the Matthean account may be considered more physically spectacular, ἰδοὺ σεισμὸς ἐγένετο μέγας (Matt 28.2). This is the second earthquake in the Matthean account, and although all synoptic gospels contain apocalyptic predictions of calamitious seismic activity (Matt 24.7//Mk 13.8//Lk 21.11), Matthew is the only canonical evangelist who reports earth tremors in connection with his retilling of the passion narrative. This is in part due to the fact that for Matthean the events surrounding the crucifixion and resurrection are of apocalyptic significance, representing the in-breaking of a new age, and consequently may be seen as a partial fulfilment of the prophecy announced in Matt 24.7.[668] Assessing the eschatological elements present specifically in Matt 27.51b-53, Allison comments that this 'passage preserves one more trace of the early church's conviction that the end of Jesus could be depicted as though it marked the eschatological turning point.'[669] The decision in the Akhmîm text to drop the second Matthean earthquake should not, however, be seen as an intentional lessening of apocalyptic motifs. As the remainder of the resurrection scene will demonstrate nothing could be further from the author's intent.

In this passage there is a striking narratival gap, for while the author describes the occurrence of the voice, the audience is not told what

---

[668] Commenting on Matt 27.51b, Hagner alludes to the connection between Matt 24.7 and the earthquake events that took place during the passion. 'Earthquakes are particularly important apocalyptic portents for Matthew (see 24:7; 28.2; for the OT background, cf. Isa 24.19, 29; Jer 10:10; Amos 8:8; and many other texts).' Hagner, *Matthew 14–28*, 849.

[669] D.C. Allison, *The End of the Ages Has Come: An early Interpretation of the Passion and Resurrection of Jesus* (Philadelphia: Fortress, 1985) 46.

precisely was spoken by the voice. Mara may be correct that the omission of this detail is due to the author wanting to relate the even more spectacular events which follow.[670] It is possible that the term φωνή might not be referring to an articulate and intelligible 'voice' but to an indeterminate sound. Against this line of interpretation, it should be noted that when the author uses the term φωνή in *Gos. Pet.* 10.42, it is unquestionably 'a voice', since articulate speech is reported. In fact although BDAG gives as its first range of semantic meanings the following translational alternatives 'an auditory effect, *sound, tone, noise*',[671] it is the second semantic domain which represents the more extensive usage of the term: 'a faculty of utterance, *voice.*'[672]

Perhaps more significantly, in the canonical gospels when the term φωνή is stated as coming from heaven or the clouds, it is always accompanied with an intelligible utterance (cf. Matt 3.17; 17.5; Mk 1.11; 9.7; Lk 3.22, 9.35; Jn 12.28). Such voices occur in the synoptic gospels either at the baptism or transfiguration, and in the Johannine account after the arrival of the Greeks (Jn 12.20) At that point in the fourth gospel, Jesus launches into a monologue that culminates in a call for the Father's name to be glorified (Jn 12.28). In the same verse, in a scene which Brown notes is 'so parallel to the agony in the garden',[673] an affirming voice comes from heaven declaring that the Father's name is glorified, presumably because of Jesus' obedience to the task before him. Thus, here the *Gospel of Peter* deviates from this pattern of the utterance being reported, instead it simply states, using the terminology found in the canonical accounts, that a voice was heard. Such theophanic utterances find significant parallels in the rabbinic discussions concerning the *bat qol*, (literally: 'daughter of a voice'). In these *corpora* of literature such speech from-on-high functions as 'a heavenly or divine voice that conveys God's judgment or will to individuals or groups.'[674] The discussion of this phenomenon is widespread in rabbinic texts, which seek to clarify its status in relation to scriptural revelation.[675] It is unlikely, however, that such rabbinic

---

[670] Mara, *Évangile de Pierre*, 173.

[671] BDAG, 1071.

[672] BDAG, 1071–1072.

[673] Brown, *The Gospel according to John I–XI*, 475.

[674] See Neusner and Green, *Dictionary of Judaism in the Biblical Period: 450 B.C.E. to 600 C.E.*, 83.

[675] See *m.Abot* 6.2; *b.B.Bat.* 73.b; 85b; *Mak.* 23b; *'Erub.* 54b; *Šabb.* 33b; 88a; *Soṭah* 33a; *p.Ber.* 1.3 §4; *Pe'ah* 1.1, §15; *Soṭah* 7.5, §5; *Pesiq. Rab. Kah.* 15.4; *Lev. Rab.* 19.5–6;

traditions are informing the understanding of the 'voice form heaven' that is presented here in the Akhmîm text. Rather, it appears that the author either expects the audience to fill-in the content of the voice from the known declarations that accompanied the baptism and transfiguration scene, which are declarations concerning Jesus' status, or else, the content of the declaration is unimportant, since the author wishes to quickly press on in the narrative to depict the arrival of the two men who come down from heaven.

**9.36a** καὶ εἶδον ἀνοιχθέτας τοὺς ουράνους καὶ δύο ἄνδρας κατελθόντας ἐκεῖθε. Accompanying the voice from above, the heavens are rent asunder and two figures described as being ἀνήρ descend. The combination of the voice, the opening of the heavens and the description of the descent of a being from heaven makes this passage replete with points of contact with the scene of the baptism of Jesus (cf. Matt 3.17–18//Lk 3.21–22). As it is impossible to know whether the *Gospel of Peter* contained an account of the baptism it would only be speculation to assume that this scene is a carefully balanced parallel to an earlier baptismal scene at the Jordan. The opening of the heavens signals a moment of interface between the divine and earthly realms, with an apocalyptic unveiling transpiring. The open heaven is a metaphor used in Revelation καὶ ἰδοὺ θύρα ἠνεῳγμένη ἐν τῷ οὐρανῷ (Rev 4.1) which allows John privileged access to the divine sphere.[676] It is striking that in Rev 4.1 the notion of heaven being opened is combined with a voice, which although sounding like a trumpet, is nonetheless comprehensible and addresses John, καὶ ἡ φωνὴ ἡ πρώτη ἣν ἤκουσα ὡς σάλπιγγος λαλούσης μετ' ἐμοῦ λέγων· ἀνάβα ὧδε, καὶ δείξω σοι ἃ δεῖ γενέσθαι μετὰ ταῦτα (Rev 4.1b).

The two figures that descend are identified as being ἄνδρας 'men'. Commenting on the appearance of these two figures, Brown includes a parenthetic comment concerning their designation: 'two men (angels

---

Lam. Rab. proem 2, 23; Lam. Rab. 1.16, §50; Ruth Rab. 6.4; Eccl. Rab. 7.12, §1; Song Rab. 8.9, §3; Pesiq. Rab Kah. 11.16; Tg. Neof. 1 on Gen 22.10; 27.33; 28.25; Num 21.6; Tg. Ps.-J. on Gen 38.26; Num 21.6; Deut 28.15; 34.5.

[676] Aune comments that 'Parallels in ancient literature suggest that the image of the open door in heaven is appropriate for introducing divine revelation, particularly in the form of an epiphany.' Aune, *Revelation 1–5*, 280. See also C.C. Rowland, *The Open Heaven: A Study of Apocalyptic in Judaism and Early Christianity* (New York: Crossroad, 1982) 78.

have male attributes in Jewish thought).'[677] While this statement is correct it perhaps has to be expanded. In his detailed studied on angels in ancient Jewish literature and in the New Testament, Sullivan draws the following conclusion.

> the evidence supports an understanding for the literature of the period that sees the authors as envisioning God, angels and human beings that for the most part existed in separate spheres, the earthly and heavenly. Angels mediated between these two realms and, though they often *appeared* as human beings and regularly *interacted* with them, they were nevertheless *distinct* from them.[678]

Furthermore, specifically in reference to the description of the 'two men' mentioned here, Sullivan comments that '[t]he *Gos. Pet.* seems to have synthesized the canonical gospels, calling them "two men" from heaven, who are then revealed to be "angels."'[679]

Here a strong case can made for the use of distinctive Lukan language inserted into the wider context of the Matthean narrative, albeit with large amounts of authorial creativity. Luke does not describe the figures as 'angels', nor does he relate their descent from heaven. However, among the synoptic accounts the third gospel alone describes two figures who encounter those going to the tomb to anoint the body, ἰδοὺ ἄνδρες δύο ἐπέστησαν αὐταῖς (Lk 24.4). Mark reports one young man, νεανίσκος, stitting in the tomb on the arrival of the women (Mk 16.5). Matthew describes the descent of a single angel from heaven ἄγγελος γὰρ κυρίου καταβὰς ἐξ οὐρανοῦ (Matt 28.2), who later engages the women in conversation. In the Johannine narrative the women also meet two figures, explicitly described as angels, θεωρεῖ δύο ἀγγέλους ἐν λευκοῖς (Jn 20.12). Bock argues that the 'two men appear to reflect a two-witness motif (Deut 19:15).'[680] This would suit the wider purpose of the *Gospel of Peter* with its desire to validate a miraculous explanation for the empty tomb, yet in this instance the reference to the 'two men' has probably been taken over from the Lukan tradition without any 'witness motif' being in the mind of the author of the *Gospel of*

---

[677] Brown, *The Death of the Messiah*, vol. 2, 1297.

[678] K.P. Sullivan, *Wrestling with Angels: A Study of the Relationship between Angels and Humans in Ancient Jewish Literature and the New Testament*, AGJU 55 (Leiden: Brill, 2004) 236. See also Sullivan's more recent work on this topic, 'Sexuality and Gender of Angels' in April D. DeConick (ed.), *Paradise Now: Essays on Early Jewish and Christian Mysticism*, SBLSS 11 (Atlanta: SBL, 2006) 211–228.

[679] Sullivan, *Wrestling with Angels*, 71.

[680] Bock, *Luke 9:51–24:53*, 1890.

*Peter*. Unlike Luke, who later calls these men 'angels' (Lk 24.23), such a designation is never applied to these figures in the *Gospel of Peter*, although the Markan designation νεανίσκος is used in the following verse (*Gos. Pet.* 9.37) in the plural to describe them as 'young men'. Notwithstanding the retiscence of the author to label these figures as 'angels', their descent from heaven, their shining appearance (*Gos. Pet* 9.36b) and their gigantic appearance (*Gos. Pet.* 10.40) makes it fully apparent that they cannot be classed as normal human beings. The similarities of this scene with the transfiguration account has led to the suggestion that Elijah and Moses are the two figure who descend to the tomb, especially since the text refrains from using the term 'angel' to describe these figures.[681] That specially favoured humans could take on the roles of intermediaries between heaven and earth is not unknown in second temple Jewish apocryphal literature. However, since this identification with Elijah and Moses is not made in the narrative, and it broadly follows the canonical accounts, which likewise do not make this connection, the suggestion is probably best resisted.

**9.36b** πολὺ φέγγος ἔχοντας καὶ ἐγγίσαντας τῷ τάφῳ. All four canonical accounts contain descriptions of the apparel of the human or angelic figures they describe at the tomb. In Matthew, Mark and John it is the whiteness of the clothing that is described (Matt 28.3b; Mk 16.5; Jn 20.12). By contrast, in Luke it is the dazzling nature of the raiment that attracts comment ἐν ἐσθῆτι ἀστραπτούσῃ (Lk 24.4). Yet while Matthew describes the clothing as being white, he describes the physical appearance of the angel as dazzling ἦν δὲ ἡ εἰδέα αὐτοῦ ὡς ἀστραπή (Matt 28.3a). The account in the *Gospel of Peter* does not describe the clothing of the two men, but like Matthew (although not overlapping in vocabulary) pictures the appearance of these two figures as 'having much brightness', πολὺ φέγγος ἔχοντας.

In the Matthean account the rolling away of the stone (Matt 28.2) takes place before the appearance of the angel is described (Matt 28.3). In the Akhmîm text this is reversed, with the description of the men preceding their approach towards the tomb. Such an approach towards the tomb is narrated only in the first gospel employing the

---

[681] Vaganay states that this view is attributed to E. Nestlé by Harnack. 'Nestle (dans Harnack, p. 67) pense a Moise et a Elie, vu que nulle part dans notre fragment on ne parle des anges (ἄγγελος).' Vaganay, *L'Évangile de Pierre*, 294.

participle προσελθών. (Matt 28.2), where it comes before the description of the angel rolling the stone away from the entrance of the tomb. The account in the Akhmîm narrative is much more expansive, stating καὶ ἐγγίσαντας τῷ τάφῳ. In one sense, the approach in the *Gospel of Peter* is only in the direction of the tomb, since it is important for the narrative to emphasize that the opening of the tomb is automated by divine fiat, and not through the efforts of these two figures from heaven. Such deviations from the Matthean narrative are made to emphasize miraculous elements in the sequence of events.[682] The role of the two men will become clear in the next pericope.

**9.37a  ὁ δὲ λίθος ἐκεῖνος ὁ βεβλημένος ἐπὶ τῇ θύρᾳ ἀφ᾽ ἑαυτοῦ κυλισθείς**. It would perhaps be a mistake to classify the form βεβλημένος as a 'divine passive'. Instead, it is perhaps more accurate to note that at this juncture in the narrative objects understood to be inanimate find the ability to animate themselves. This is true here of the stone, and later of the cross (*Gos. Pet.* 10.40, 42). This appears as a familiar motif in folkloric literature where objects or animals are granted powers to attest to, or take part in, the divine plan. In the OT the story of Balaam's ass aligns with this genre (Num 22.28), where the donkey is not so much the passive instrument of God, but is granted the power of speech to articulate its own perspective on the events. Similarly here, the stone rolls away ἀφ᾽ ἑαυτου 'by itself', both to allow the two men from heaven to enter and to permit the release of the one entombed.

This description of a self-animated stone is an element not found in the synoptic accounts. Mark, Luke and John agree that those who go to the tomb (three named women, Mk 16.1; unnamed women from Galilee, Lk 23.55; Mary alone, Jn 20.1) simply discover the stone has been rolled away. There is no explanation accounting for the mechanics of that phenomenon. By contrast, Matthew provides the description that the angel recently arrived from heaven, went over to the stone and physically rolled it away from the entrance of the tomb, ἀπεκύλισεν τὸν λίθον καὶ ἐκάθητο ἐπάνω αὐτοῦ (Matt 28.2). Luz explains this deviation from the other canonical accounts in the following manner.

---

[682] 'Le pseudo-Pierre va d'ailleurs s'écarter de Matthieu tout aussitôt.' Vaganay, *L'Évangile de Pierre*, 295.

What is important for Matthew is that in the resurrection of Jesus God himself acted with clear, visible and traceable consequences. That is why he has the angel descend from heaven, shake the earth, and open the tomb. He creates a powerful sign, unmistakeable for all, including the guards, that God is at work here. However, he has no interest in describing the resurrection. He speaks only of the angel, who afterward rolls the stone away from the tomb. He does this not to enable Jesus gloriously to come out of the tomb but to frustrate the strategy of the Jewish leaders and to enable the women to see the tomb.[683]

It will be important to bear this explanation in mind when considering how the Akhmîm text tells the story of the resurrection.

In marked contrast, in the *Gospel of Peter* the two man who descend from heaven approach the tomb, but make no physical contact with it. The narrator's decision to restrain the heavenly figures from making contact with the stone that seals the burial place is motivated by a desire to emphasize the miraculous manner in which the tomb automatically opens, ἀφ᾽ ἑαυτοῦ. Swete notes what, in the NT, is perhaps the closest parallel to this account, Acts 12.10. In this passge an angel leads Peter out of prison, and as they come to the outermost gate it opens automatically, ἥτις αὐτομάτη ἠνοίγη αὐτοῖς. The self-opening door is a striking parallel because like the stone that rolls away by itself this happens 'although an angel is present to whom the task might have been assigned.'[684] Stories of self opening doors are common is ancient Jewish and Hellenistic literature.[685] Self-opening tombs are less common, although Matthew has already narrated such occurrences, with the tombs of the saints being opened (Matt 27.52–53).

**9.37b** ἐπεχώρησε παρὰ μέρος καὶ ὁ τάφος ἐνοίγη. As was noted in text-critical note fourteen, the aorist passive form ἐνοίγη is not written with the common lengthened augment, i.e. ἠνοίγη. This may provide evidence that the text was dictated to a scribe at some stage in its transmission history, during a period when the aural distinction between ε and η had been lost.[686] Perhaps more problematic is the verb ἐπεχώρησε.

---

[683] Luz, *Matthew 21–28*, 595–596.

[684] Swete, *The Akhmîm Fragment of the Apocryphal Gospel of St Peter*, 17.

[685] For instance see, Homer, Iliad 5.747; Vergil, Aeneid 6.81; Ovid, *Metamorphoses* 3.699–700; Tacitus, *Hist.* V.13; Dio Cassius, 60.35.1; Josephus, *Bell.* 6.293; *b.Yoma* 39b; *y.Yoma* 43c.

[686] Alternatively, this failure to follow standard practice may reflect localized orthographical practice, or the abilities of the scribe who introduced this form.

Many commentators have expressed disquiet over the appropriateness of the meaning of this term in its present context. This is because, as Vaganay notes, 'ἐπιχωρέω not only means "to advance towards" but also "to be withdrawn".'[687] While BDAG attests only the meaning 'move over (towards)',[688] a much fuller semantic range is illustrated in LSJ including the antithetical possibilities 'come towards, join one as an ally Th.4.107' and 'to go against, attack, Id. [= Xenophon] An. 1.2.17.'[689] Although 'movement towards' is one of the primary senses of the term the fact that it can also denote the sense of 'movement away' means that the alternative proposals of ὑπεχώρησε by Robinson,[690] and ἀπαχώρησε by both Harnack[691] and Gebherdt[692] are unnecessary.

The Greek expression that παρὰ μέρος accompanies the verb ἐπεχώρησε is often overlooked in translations, or not given its most natural meaning. Kraus and Nicklas render the clause ἐπεχώρησε παρὰ μέρος as the stone 'moved sideways',[693] Robinson describes the stone as 'departing to one side'[694] and Brown gives the translation 'went a distance to the side.'[695] In the NT the term μέρος occurs forty-two times, but never in conjunction with the preposition παρά. The tendency to understand it as sideways motion is based to passages such as Jn 21.6 τὰ δεξιὰ μέρη τοῦ πλοίου, 'the right side of the boat.' The usage in Gos. Pet. 9.37, however, seems more closely aligned with those examples where it is employed with a preposition. Examples include expressions such as ἐκ μέρους, which Paul uses repeatedly to designate the partial or incomplete aspect of some matter (1 Cor 12.27; 13.9 [2 times], 10, 12). Discussing the term Nebe argues that

Μέρος, meaning "part, portion," has roots in Indo-European (s)mer-, "remember, recall, worry about" (cf Frisk, Worterbuch II, 212). This

---

[687] Vaganay, L'Évangile de Pierre, 295.

[688] BDAG, 387.

[689] LSJ, 674.

[690] Without discussion Robinson notes, 'fors. Leg. ὑπεχώρησε'. Robinson and James, The Gospel according to Peter and the Revelation of Peter, 86.

[691] Harnack acknowledges his dependence on Gebhardt and Blass, 'ἀπαχώρησε, corr. Gebhardt, Blass.' Harnack, Bruchstücke des Evangeliums und der Apokalypse des Petrus, 11.

[692] Gebhardt shows awareness of Robinson's conjecture, 'ἐπεχώρησε cod., ὑπεχώρησε Robinson'. Gebhardt, Das Evangelium und die Apokalypse des Petrus, 45.

[693] Kraus und Nicklas, Das Petrusevangelium und die Petrusapokalypse, 51.

[694] Robinson and James, The Gospel according to Peter and the Revelation of Peter, 24.

[695] Brown, The Death of the Messiah, vol. 2, 1320.

meaning developed in Greek literature in various ways, and this is also the case in the NT. Here μέρος is, first of all, quantitatively and concretely *part/portion, piece* of a possession, an inheritance, fish clothing, etc. (e.g. Luke 15:12; 24:42). Then it came to mean in a derived way *part/portion/place* (Matt 24:51; John 13:8), *side* (John 21:6), *member* (? Eph 4:16), not *party* (Acts 23:9), *branch* of a business (Acts 19:7), *matter/concern/relationship* (2 Cor 3:10; 9:3). In prep. phrases or used adverbially it has the quantitative meaning *partly* (Rom 15:15; 1 Cor 11:18, subst. in 1 Cor 13:10) or *individually* (1 Cor 12:27).[696]

When used in wider Greek literature the expression παρὰ μέρος regularly denotes sequence, i.e. 'in turn' (Plu. *Fab.* 10; Ant. *Lib.* 30.1; Nicom. *Ar.* 1.8.10), but can also give the sense of 'in part/partially' (Alciphr. 3.66). This leads to understand the phrase in the present context as referring to the partial rolling away of the stone.[697] This suits the purpose of the narrative, since this is not to be seen as an incomplete miracle, but rather functions as a device to obscure the dramatic events that take place in the tomb. While the reality of the resurrection is observed when the figures emerge from the sepulchre, the mechanics cannot be seen or described.

The author emphasizes that this was the moment when the unsealing of the sepulchre took place. Thus the clause καὶ ὁ τάφος ἠνοίγη highlights that the tomb had remained secure until this point. Vaganay offers another possible motive for mentioning the opening of the tomb. 'The *Gospel of Peter* itself mentions the opening of the tomb, because it has special reasons for making the two divine envoys enter into it.'[698] It is quite probably that these two explanations are complimentary.

**9.37c   καὶ ἀμφότεροι οἱ νεανίσκοι εἰσῆλθον.** Entrance of these young men or heavenly visitors into the tomb is not described in the canonical accounts. In Mark and John figures are discovered already in the tomb by those visiting the burial place. According to the Markan account the women find one young man sitting to the right of where the body had been placed (Mk 16.5). In the fourth gospel Mary, who waits outside the tomb, on inspection discovers two angels sitting at the place where the head and feet of the body had lain (Jn 20.11–12).

---

[696] Nebe, 'μέρος, ους, τό' in EDNT, vol. 2, 409.
[697] Swete is one of the few translators who adopts this sense. He renders the clause as 'and [the stone] made way in part.' Swete, *The Akhmîm Fragment of the Apocryphal Gospel of St Peter*, 27.
[698] Vaganay, *L'Évangile de Pierre*, 295–296.

In Luke's version of this story, after the women have entered the tomb, two men suddenly appear next to them (Lk 24.4). In Matthew, although the angel does not enter the tomb, he invites the women to go inside (Matt 28.6). The first gospel, however, does not describe whether the women entered the sepulchre after the angel's bidding. Consequently it is unknown whether Matthew envisaged that the angel accompanied the women into the place of burial.

As was noted earlier, the use of the term οἱ νεανίσκοι picks up the Markan depiction of these of these visitors, εἶδον νεανίσκον καθήμενον ἐν τοῖς δεξιοῖς (Mk 16.5). This is one of the points in the Akhmîm narrative where a good case can be made for dependence on a uniquely Markan element. France argues that the Markan use of νεανίσκος is not employed to make a connection with the young man who runs away naked in Mk 14.51–52. Rather he sees the Markan usage in the following terms: 'It seems that Mark is doing what Luke does on a number of occasions, using human language to describe the form in which an angel is seen by human witnesses (Lk. 24:4 with 23; Acts 1:10; 10:30; cf. Tob. 5:5, 7, 10 where Tobias addresses the angel as νεανίσκε because he does not recognize him as an angel and sees only a young man).'[699] Maybe for a similar reason the author of the Akhmîm text refrains from using the term ἄγγελος.

---

[699] France, *The Gospel of Mark*, 679.

# THREE GIGANTIC MEN EMERGE
## FROM THE TOMB (10.38–42)

38. ἰδόντες οὖν οἱ στρατιῶται ἐκεῖνοι¹ ἐξύπνισαν² τὸν κεντυρίωνα καὶ τοὺς πρεσβυτέρους· παρῆσαν γὰρ καὶ αὐτοὶ φυλάσσοντες. 39. καὶ ἐξηγουμένων αὐτῶν ἃ εἶδον πάλιν³ ὅρασιν⁴ ἐξελθόντος⁵ ἀπὸ τοῦ τάφου τρεῖς ἄνδρες⁶ καὶ τοὺς δύο τὸν ἕνα ὑπορθοῦντας καὶ σταυρὸν ἀκολοθοῦντα⁷ αὐτοῖς. 40. καὶ τῶν μὲν δύο τὴν κεφαλὴν χωροῦσαν μέχρι τοῦ οὐρανοῦ, τοῦ δὲ χειρατωτουμένου⁸ ὑπ᾽ αὐτῶν ὑπερβαίνουσαν τοὺς οὐρανούς. 41. καὶ φωνῆ[ς]⁹ ἤκουον ἐκ τῶν οὐρανῶν λεγούσης· ἐκήρυξας τοῖς κοιμωμένοις;¹⁰ 42. καὶ ὑπακοὴ ἠκούετο ἀπὸ τοῦ σταυροῦ [ὅ]τι ναί.¹¹

38. Then those soldiers seeing it awoke the centurion and the elders, for they were present also keeping guard. 39. While they were reporting what they had seen, again they saw coming out from the tomb three men, and the two were supporting the one, and a cross following them. 40. And the head of the two reached as far as heaven, but that of the one being led by them surpassed the heavens. 41. And they were hearing a voice from the heavens saying, 'Have you preached to those who sleep?' 42. And a response was heard from the cross, 'Yes.'

## TEXT CRITICAL NOTES

1. Formation of the letter epsilon deteriorates at a number of places around this section of the text. The ligature between the ε and ι in the word εκεῖνοι, produces an irregular letter shape for the second ε in this word. Such an irregularity was noted on the previous line with the word εἰσῆλθον,⁷⁰⁰ where the first two letters have a similar ε-ι combination. The resultant omission of the central crossbar of the epsilon is noted by Gebhardt.⁷⁰¹

---

⁷⁰⁰ See text-critical note 15, in the previous section, *Gos. Pet.* 9.34–37.
⁷⁰¹ 'In der Verbindung ει stellt meist der nach unten geneigte Mittelstrich des ε das ι dar (z. B. VII, 5 in εισηλθον, VII, 6 in εκεινοι, VII, 17 in απελθειν) oder das ι setzt sich in stumpfem Winkel an den verkürzten Mittelstrich an (z. B. in εισ IX, 14).' Gebhardt, *Das Evangelium und die Apokalypse des Petrus*, 11.

2. Although not in combination with an ι, the ε that commences the word ἐξύπνισαν is also poorly formed with the middle stroke being formed from the upper stroke of the letter ξ that follows.

3. From the photograph of page 4 *recto*, there appears to be a small round hole in the manuscript that only slightly obscures part of the word πάλιν. This occurs where the bottom right hand foot of the long stoke of the lambda intersects the iota.

4. In the manuscript the form ὄρασιν appears in place of what should presumably should have been written, ὁρῶσιν. This emendation is proposed by the vast majority of scholars who have presented a critical edition of the text, such as Harnack,[702] Swete,[703] Robinson,[704] Hilgenfeld,[705] although Boriant simply transcribes the text without suggesting any correction.[706] Lods, likewise, offers an uncorrected transcription without any note at this point.[707] Presumably this error is the result of preserving the α in the ending of the verb ὁράω, and not introducing the vowel change required in the third person plural present form ὁρῶσιν.

5. Again the form ἐξελθόντος contained in the manuscript appears to be erroneously written in place of ἐξελθόντας. This is emended by the same list of scholars who correct the the reading ὄρασιν in the previous note. Also see the corrected text of Kraus and Nicklas.[708] The poor formation of the second epsilon in the word should be mentioned. The letter consists of three strokes: a roughly vertical line of approximately 2mm in length; an oblique stroke of about 2mm, decending left to right, making an angel of approximately 20° with the horizontal, and touching the base of the vertical stroke at about half way along its length; finally there is a stroke made from

---

[702] Harnack note the concatenation of emendments that are required in this verse to introduce the correct grammatical forms, '12sq. ὄρασιν ἐξελθόντος…ἄνδρες.' Harnack, *Bruchstücke des Evangeliums und der Apokalypse des Petrus*, 11.

[703] Swete, *The Akhmîm Fragment of the Apocryphal Gospel of St Peter*, 17.

[704] Robinson and James, *The Gospel according to Peter and the Revelation of Peter*, 86.

[705] Hilgenfeld derives his corrections from the work of Harnack. Hilgenfeld, 'Das Petrus-Evangelium über Leiden und Auferstehung Jesu', Part 1, 443; and 'Das Petrus-Evangelium', part 2, 237.

[706] Bouriant, 'Fragments du texte grec du livre d'Énoch et de quelques écrits attribués à saint Pierre', 140.

[707] Lods, 'L'Évangile et l'Apocalypse de Pierre avec le texte grec du livre d'Hénoch', 222.

[708] Kraus und Nicklas, *Das Petrusevangelium und die Petrusapokalypse*, 42.

the middle of the vertical stroke, 3mm in length, descending left to right but at a slightly sharper angel to the horizontal, maybe 25°, this turns after the 3mm to form a line of 1.5mm in length which is the short leg of the adjacent lambda and is unconnected to the other stroke of that letter. This is another example of the scribe's highly aberrant formation of the letter epsilon.[709]

6. Instead of ἄνδρες the accusative plural form ἄνδρας should be read. This error may have occurred under the influence of the numeral τρεῖς, which has the same form in the nominative and accusative cases. The scribe may have taken it as a nominative and hence made the word that follows agree with his mistaken identification of the case.

7. There is an orthographical error here. Instead of ἀκολοθοῦντα the text should contain an additional letter, upsilon, i.e. ἀκολουθοῦντα.

8. Apart from the transcriptions of Bouriant and Lods, there is uniformity of opinion that the form χειρατωτουμένου should read χειραγωγουμένου.[710] Bouriant struggled with the text at this point splitting it in the following manner 'χεῖρα τῷ τουμένου', but remaining unsure what to make of this word division in his translation 'de la main......indiquaient(?)'[711] Lods correctly transcribed the text as χειρατωτουμενου, but gave no note of what he understood by this form.[712]

9. Where the manuscript reads φωνή the grammatically required form is φωνῆς. The nominative is unacceptable because it is not the subject of the verb, and the genitive case is taken by this verb of perception when the object is animate, whereas 'impersonal objects are usually acc[usative].'[713] This correction is made by nearly all

---

[709] See notes 1 and 2 in this section.

[710] For example, see Harnack, *Bruchstücke des Evangeliums und der Apokalypse des Petrus*, 8; Gebhardt, *Das Evangelium und die Apokalypse des Petrus*, 45; Robinson and James, *The Gospel according to Peter and the Revelation of Peter*, 86; Swete, *The Akhmîm Fragment of the Apocryphal Gospel of St Peter*, 19; Kraus und Nicklas, *Das Petrusevangelium und die Petrusapokalypse*, 42.

[711] Bouriant, 'Fragments du texte grec du livre d'Énoch et de quelques écrits attribués à saint Pierre', 140.

[712] Lods, 'L'Évangile et l'Apocalypse de Pierre avec le texte grec du livre d'Hénoch', 222.

[713] See, G. Schneider 'ἀκούω', in EDNT, vol. 1, 53. Also BDF §173.

scholars: e.g. Robinson,[714] Harnack,[715] Swete,[716] Vaganay,[717] Mara,[718] and Kraus and Nicklas,[719] although the need to correct the text is not noted in the transcriptions of Bouriant[720] or Lods.[721]

10. Many commentators transcribe the form as κοινωμένοις, with the fourth letter being read as ν rather than the required μ. The text is then amended to read κοιμωμέννοις. For example see the textual note recorded by Kraus and Nicklas.[722] While this is certainly possible, it should be noted that the only difference between the scribe's formation of these letters is the final vertical stroke that often serves as a ligature. Here the scribe does not connect the μ to the following letter. The erratic letter formation by the scribe has been well documented throughout the text-critical notes.[723] Thus it may be better to see that the form κοιμωμέννοις was written by the scribe, albeit with an aberrant μ lacking the final vertical stroke.

11. The last five letter (if that is how many letters are written) of v. 42 create what is perhaps the most significant textual problem in the manuscript. The most likely transcription is τιναι. The second letter is problematic. There is the upward vertical stroke measuring 5mm in length, which is within the range of sizes adopted by the scribe in forming the letter iota. However, what complicates this reading is the curving ligature which joins the right hand side of the crossbar of the tau to the third letter nu in the sequence. This has the partial appearance of an upsilon, ψ. The scribe regularly forms the letter psi in this manner, although it is usually smaller

---

[714] Robinson and James, *The Gospel according to Peter and the Revelation of Peter*, 86.

[715] Harnack, *Bruchstücke des Evangeliums und der Apokalypse des Petrus*, 11.

[716] Swete, *The Akhmîm Fragment of the Apocryphal Gospel of St Peter*, 19.

[717] Vaganay, *L'Évangile de Pierre*, 301.

[718] Mara corrects this without note. Mara, *Évangile de Pierre*, 58.

[719] Kraus und Nicklas, *Das Petrusevangelium und die Petrusapokalypse*, 42.

[720] Bouriant, 'Fragments du texte grec du livre d'Énoch et de quelques écrits attribués à saint Pierre', 140.

[721] Lods, 'L'Évangile et l'Apocalypse de Pierre avec le texte grec du livre d'Hénoch', 222.

[722] Kraus und Nicklas, *Das Petrusevangelium und die Petrusapokalypse*, 42, note on line 15 of f. 4r.

[723] As Gebhardt comments, 'Während das μ fast ausgeprägte Minuskelform zeigt, unterscheidet sich das ν oft nur dadurch von dem uncialen N, dass es rechts unten abgerundet ist, nähert sich aber auch nicht selten einer der älteren Minuskel geläufigen Form.' Gebhardt, *Das Evangelium und die Apokalypse des Petrus*, 12.

in size (cf. ἐνίψατο, *Gos. Pet.* 1.1).[724] The problem is that an intial
τ followed by a ψ appears to produce an impossible combination. For this reason the stroke joining the first and third letters
appears to be one of the scribes many aberrations. This leaves the
transcription, τιναι. This must be divided, or emended, to produce
a possible reading. Simple division as τι ναι results in two well
known Greek words, regardless of whether the τι is an interrogative or an indefinite pronoun. The problem is whether this a grammatically permissible combination. A survey of extant Greek texts
reveals no occurrence of this word sequence. A possible reading
that only requires the emendation of a single letter is τὸ ναί. This
has the advantage of being well attested in biblical and extra-biblical texts (cf. Ammonius Phil., In Int. p. 199, 21; 2 Cor 1.17). This
reading is supported by Lührmann,[725] and Swete had originally
conjectured this solution,[726] although he later altered his thinking.[727]
Gebhardt followed Swete's original proposal.[728] The solution Swete
later adopted was not his own proposal, but was put forward by
Robinson,[729] Harnack,[730] Lods,[731] and Zahn.[732] It appears that the
reading ὅτι ναί supported by these four scholars was suggested
independently at least by the first two. The majority of those who
have subsequently written on the text have adopted this solution.
Its main advantages are that it does not require altering the most
likely transcription of the five letters in question, and although it
requires the introduction of an initial letter, it has already been
noted that the scribe omits letters in other words. The disadvan-
tage is that the scribe nowhere else has omitted the initial letter of a word. In terms of meaning either of the two conjectural

---

[724] See Gebhardt, *Das Evangelium und die Apokalypse des Petrus*, 13.

[725] D. Lührmann, *Fragmente Apokryph Gewordener Evangelien: In Griechischer und Lateinischer Sprache* (Marburg: N.G. Elwert, 2000) 89.

[726] Swete, *The Apocryphal Gospel of St Peter: The Greek Text of the Newly Discovered Fragment* 4.

[727] Swete, *The Akhmîm Fragment of the Apocryphal Gospel of St Peter*, 19.

[728] Gebhardt, *Das Evangelium und die Apokalypse des Petrus*, 45.

[729] Robinson and James, *The Gospel according to Peter and the Revelation of Peter*, 86.

[730] Harnack, *Bruchstücke des Evangeliums und der Apokalypse des Petrus*, 11.

[731] See both Lods, 'L'Évangile et l'Apocalypse de Pierre avec le texte grec du livre d'Hénoch', 222; and, A. Lods, *Evangelii secundum Petrum et Petri Apocalypseos quae supersunt* (Paris; Ernest Leroux, 1892).

[732] Zahn, *Das Evangelium des Petrus*.

emendation τὸ ναί or ὅτι ναί, produce the same sense, namely that the cross responds in the affirmative to the question. There is little to favour one suggestion over the other, although perhaps in its favour the reading ὅτι ναί means that the existing text does not require alteration, just supplementation by the addition of a single letter.

## COMMENTARY

**10.38a** ἰδόντες οὖν οἱ στρατιῶται εκεῖνοι ἐξύπνισαν τὸν κεντυρίωνα καὶ τοὺς πρεσβυτέρους. The focus of the narrative falls again on those guarding the tomb. In line with the theological concern to validate the resurrection as a divine event and not a deception perpetrated by the disciples, the story relates that the soldiers on duty saw the two men enter into the tomb. It then quickly assembles a larger group who function as witnesses to the startling events that follow.

The demonstrative pronoun εκεῖνοι obviously refers to the soldiers who were at that moment guarding the tomb when the descent of the two figures from heaven took place. The decisive action of the guards on duty contrasts notably with the account in Matt 28.4. Vaganay notes that although the guards are still fearful, nonetheless they are able to absorb what is happening and to report it to their superiors.[733] The fearful trembling of the Matthean account, which renders the guards ὡς νεκροί (as dead men), presumably refers to a certain immobility. Such a notion would not be consonant with the need of the Akhmîm narrative to quickly assemble a large and varied group of witnesses to attest the veracity of the living figure who emerges from the tomb with the two men who entered. Luz perhaps overplays the theological significance of the guards being rendered as dead men in the Matthean account. Describing the events of the resurrection he argues that 'For the guards they are deadly; for the women they become, through the angels word, a source of joy.'[734] This reading is perhaps too laden with

---

[733] 'Chez *Mt.*, XXVIII, 4, on insiste sur la frayeur toute naturelle des guardiens devant l'apparition céleste (cf. *Ap.*, I, 17). Dans notre apocryphe, la garde ne semble pas le moins du monde terrifiée. Elle a tout vu et, fidèle a la consigne, elle se dispose à prévenir ses chefs.' Vaganay, *L'Évangile de Pierre*, 296.

[734] Luz, *Matthew 21–28*, 596.

theological meaning, especially in seeing reactions to resurrection as causing either mortification or revivification. Rather Davies and Allison appear correct in seeing the response of the Matthean guards as stereotypical for describing encounters with divine beings. They state, 'The response of the Roman guards has many parallels, for fear is what people feel in the presence of an other-wordly being.'[735]

In the *Gospel of Peter* the duty-guards immediately rouse the centurion and, as the audience now learn for certain (since there was some earlier ambiguity cf. *Gos. Pet.* 8.31, 33[736]), that the Jewish elders had in fact remained stationed alongside the Roman military personnel throughout the night. Yet even here the elders are mentioned as an addendum, or maybe afterthought. For once again after this brief appearance they disappear from the narrative, and there is no further reference to sub-groups or leadership parties among the Jewish people. Instead this differentiation is lost, and 'the Jews', when mentioned, are described in terms that are unified, collective and pejorative (*Gos. Pet.* 11.48; 12.50, 52). The term ἐξύπνισαν is the usual word used to refer to waking somebody from sleep, and although it can be used metaphorically to refer to restoring a person to life (cf. Jn 11.11) in the extant portion of the Akhmîm text it is used only here of the physical act of rousing fellow soldiers.

**10.38b** παρῆσαν γὰρ καὶ αὐτοὶ φυλάσσοντες. Here the story makes explicit the reason for the presence of the elders, namely to add another layer of security to the surveillance of the tomb. The verb πάρειμι denotes presence. BDAG distinguishes between two broad semantic domains: 'presence' used either of persons or impersonable objects; or the sense of being 'available for use, *at one's disposal*'.[737] With the latter being a much less frequent usage of the verb πάρειμι. Here it is obviously the first sense that is intended. Having re-introduced

---

[735] They offer the following texts in supporet of this conclusion, 'Dan 10.7–9, 16; Lk 24.5; Gos. Pet. 13.57; 2 En. 1.7.' Davies and Allison, *The Gospel According to Saint Matthew*, vol. III, 666.

[736] In *Gos. Pet.* 8.31 the 'elders and the scribes' accompany the soldiers to the burial site. By the time the narrative describes the third person plural actions in v. 33, it appears this refers to only the Roman military as those affixing the seals, pitching the tent and keeping watch. However, at no stage have the Jewish elders and scribes been reported as leaving the scene. They have just faded from the narrative without explanation and re-materialize in the same manner.

[737] BDAG, 773–774.

the elders after a period of absence from the narrative (last mentioned *Gos. Pet.* 8.31), the author justifies their reappearance in two ways. First he asserts their continued presence by using the verb πάρειμι. Second, he moves on to describe the reason for that presence.

That reason is explicitly given as involvement in the process of guarding the tomb. Why this should be necessary is not stated, was there a perception that the Romans could be bribed to allow the theft of the body, or that they might be derelict in their duties, or perhaps the narrator simply wanted the Jewish elders present at the resurrection to illustrate how recalcitrant they had become in refusing to accept divine revelation and affirmation of Jesus as God's messiah and son? A number of these factors may be combined in the narrator's mind, yet he does not explicitly disclose his reason for shaping the narrative by including the elders at this point. Vaganay's caution at this point against expecting a strict progression in the storyline is well heeded.[738] Again to emphasize that it is indeed the οἱ πρεσβύτεροι who are involved in guarding (φυλάσσοντες) the tomb the author employs the third person plural pronoun αὐτοί.

**10.39a** καὶ ἐξηγουμένων αὐτῶν ἃ εἶδον. After viewing the descent of the two men from heaven, the self-animated partial rolling away of the stone, and the entrance of the two men into the sepulchre, the sentries relate these events, presumable to the senior Roman officer present, but perhaps in the hearing of the other soldiers and the elders. This clause is presented as a genitive absolute construction, and as Vaganay observes the subject 'is the same one as that of the main clause (ὁρῶσιν), a usage which is not rare in *koiné*.'[739] In the Matthean narrative such an account of a report is absent, since the soldiers upon recovering their senses return to the city and inform the chief priests of the events that happen, ἐλθόντες εἰς τὴν πόλιν ἀπήγγειλαν τοῖς ἀρχιερεῦσιν ἅπαντα τὰ γενόμενα (Matt 28.11). In between the two scenes in Matt 28 that describe the guards (28.4 and 28.11–15) Matthew intersperses a conversation between the women and the angel, prior to the women encountering Jesus on the way back to the disciples. This scene is delayed in the Akhmîm text until 13.55–57, where

---

[738] 'C'est trop exiger de notre faussaire que lui demander une suite logique dans la description.' Vaganay, *L'Évangile de Pierre*, 296.

[739] Vaganay, *L'Évangile de Pierre*, 297.

it is related without any encounter with the risen Jesus. As will be discussed later, the material in *Gos. Pet.* 13.55–57 aligns more closely with the Markan version of events (cf. Mk 16.4–8). The Akhmîm narrative simplifies these events by keeping separate the story of the guard-at-the-tomb and the events surrounding the women at the tomb.

**10.39b** πάλιν ὁρῶσιν ἐξελθόντας ἀπὸ τοῦ τάφου τρεῖς ἄνδρας καὶ τοὺς δύο τὸν ἕνα ὑπορθοῦντας. Strictly speaking, the πάλιν does not logically fit the observation of three men coming out of the tomb, since previously there were not three men this is the first occasion when three figures have come out of the tomb, and there is also now a much enlarged group of witnesses, many of whom saw none of the earlier events. Such an understanding would, however, demand too high a standard of consistency from this narrative. Instead the adverb πάλιν is relating the opportunity to view another miraculous event. The subject of the verb ὁρῶσιν consists of the guards who witnessed the two man entering the tomb, their fellow soldiers whom they have now roused, and the Jewish elders present at the site.

Mara notes a literary device employed by the author at this point, whereby the soldiers become the lens through which events are mediated to the readers, or hearers, of this narrative. She states,

> In v. 39, in effect, the event is not recounted directly, but it is retold through the experience of the soldiers until all the official witnesses (soldiers, centurion and elders) see them also, 'three men leaving the sepulchre'; then it becomes direct testimony to the event.[740]

At this point the witnesses now observe three men emerging from the tomb. Although the image of three men leaving the tomb is not present in any of the canonical gospels, the identity of the third figure who emerges from the sepulchre is not a surprise for those who know any form or tradition of the resurrection tradition. The novelty is derived through the additional elements added to the basic narrative.[741]

The description of 'the two' supporting 'the one', immediately leads readers to unambiguously identify the two figures as the same men

---

[740] Mara, *Évangile de Pierre*, 180.

[741] Commenting on the novelty of the account, Vaganay states, 'On est frappé par le caractère énigmatique de cette description. Le pseudo-Pierre a sans doute dessein de piquer la curiosité en évitant toute dénomination pour les protagonists de son tableau vivant. Il laisse au lecteur le soin de les reconnaître et de percer le mystère.' Vaganay, *L'Évangile de Pierre*, 297.

who entered the tomb in the previous verse. The action they are performing for the other figure is described using the Greek verb ὑπορθόω. Vaganay notes that 'ὑπορθόω is extremely rare.'[742] BDAG's full entry for this term is as follows, 'ὑπορθόω (Sym.; Dositheus, Ars Gramm. 76, 1 p. 102) to assist in standing upright, *support* τινά *someone* GPt 10:39.'[743] Under the headword ὕπορθος LSJ gives the following meanings and references '-όω, *prop up, support*, Sm.*Ps.* 43(44).19, Sch.D Od. 8.66, Dosith. p. 435K.'[744]

**10.39c  καὶ σταυρὸν ἀκολουθοῦντα αὐτοῖς.** If there is one aspect of its narrative for which the Akhmîm text is famous, it is surely that of a walking, talking cross. To describe this as an embellishment to the tradition would be to understate this innovative addition. Nonetheless, it should be remembered that such a response from a supposedly inanimate object is not unprecedented in the narrative. The stone rolled away from the tomb automatically when the two men approached (*Gos. Pet.* 6.21), and the ground responded to the placement of the body of the Lord upon its surface by tremoring (*Gos. Pet.* 9.37). The cross is described as ἀκολουθοῦντα 'following', what precisely this was meant to evoke in readers imaginations in uncertain. Perhaps the image is that of the cross floating at some height above the ground behind the three men, alternatively perhaps this is a picture of a cross walking to the ground in some manner. Such details are of no interest to the narrator, neither is there any explanation of how the cross came to be inside the sepulchre. What the narrative does seem to reflect is an increasing trend toward certain forms of 'cross-piety' that emerged maybe at some stage in the second century, and this has remained as a feature of certain strands of Christianity at various times.[745] In the Ethiopic *Apocalypse of Peter* 1, the cross precedes

---

[742] Vaganay, *L'Évangile de Pierre*, 297.

[743] BDAG, 1040.

[744] LSJ, 1893.

[745] One of the more recent examples of 'cross-piety' originated during the so-called 'Caste War' in Yucatan, Mexico when the indigineous Mayan people opposed their Spanish overlords. As a result of the war there were outbreaks of various diseases which the Mayans had not developed immunity to withstand. Those who escaped travelled to Quintana Roo, reorganized themselves into a new homeland and brought with them artefacts which they had integrated as part of their own religious expression. One of the most important towns to grow both politically and religiously during this period of reorganization was Chan Santa Cruz, today called Carrillo Puerto. It was here that the cult of the 'Talking Cross' was established. In 1850 this 'Talking Cross'

Jesus at his Second Coming, 'but as the lightning that shineth from the east unto the west, so will I come upon the clouds of heaven with a great host in my majesty; with my cross going before my face will I come in my majesty.' The same image occurs in both the Ethiopic and Coptic versions of the *Epistula Apostolorum* 16.[746] Ignatius attributes an ongoing significance to the cross, as a crane which carries believers up to Christ (*Eph.* 9.1).[747] Justin argues that the symbol of the cross is embedded or imprinted throughout creation. One of the examples he cites is an attempt to show that cross-symbolism distinguishes humanity from other creatures. 'And the human form differs from that of the irrational animals in nothing else than in its being erect and having the hands extended, and having on the face extending from the forehead what is called the nose, through which there is respiration for the living creature; and this shows no other form than that of the cross' (Justin, *1 Apol.* 55)[748] In the *Epistle of Barnabas* the cross is closely linked to baptism (11.8), and is seen as being typologically referenced in 4 Ezra 4.33; 5.5.[749] At a later period Constantine's vision of the cross prior to the battle of the Milvian Bridge is described as a key moment in his own Christian piety (Eusebius, *Life of Constantine*, 28). Despite this increased fascination with the cross, it must be acknowledged that the specific attributes that the Akhmîm text describes, walking (and later talking), are not typical of the other forms of cross-devotion exemplified in patristic texts.

**10.40a** καὶ τῶν μὲν δύο τὴν κεφαλὴν χωροῦσαν μέχρι τοῦ οὐρανοῦ. In comparison to the canonical accounts accounts, new features of the story are presented to the audience. Although the two men initially mentioned in *Gos. Pet.* 9.36 were noted for their miraculous descent from heaven and the radiance that emanated from them, nothing unususal was mentioned about the proportions of their body.

---

issued a proclamation. Today the cult of the talking-cross persists as a symbol of Mayan national identy, and pilgrimages is undertaken to various shrines of the Mayan talking cross. For more detail this report see: http://www.famsi.org/reports/96072/grammar/section34.htm (27th December 2007).

[746] See Schneemelcher, *New Testament Apocrypha*, vol. 1: Gospels and Related Writings, 258.

[747] See Ehrman (trans.), *The Apostolic Fathers*, vol. 1, 228–229.

[748] See Marcovich (ed.), *Iustini Martyris: Apologiae pro Christianis, Dialogus cum Tryphone*, 110.

[749] Ehrman (trans.), *The Apostolic Fathers*, vol. 1, 54–55, 56–57.

In this context a transformation has taken place, which is apparent to those viewing events as the men leave the tomb. The heads of the two men are described as reaching up to heaven. It is uncertain whether this means that from the shoulders down their bodies remained normal size and only their heads underwent the enlargement, or if the entire physical form was proportiately increased, but the author chose only to mention the fact that the heads were reaching to heaven. Mara suggests that there is a theological motivation for depicting the two men in this manner, which transcends the desire for the spectacular in this narrative. 'The gigantic dimensions of the three persons and especially of the Κύριος, do not have in this context simply a spectacular value but an ontological one: as in Rev 10.1–3, the size is an indication of their authority both in heaven and on earth.'[750] However, in the context of Rev 10.1–3 the mediatory role of the angel between heaven and earth is indicated by motion between the two locations, not through enlarged body dimension that simultaneous occupies both spheres. More significantly Vaganay observes that the portrayal of colossal angels at the resurrection is a motif that can be found in other apocryphal texts.[751] In the Pilate cycle, the text known as the *Anaphora Pilati* provides the report of the Roman prefect to Tiberius. Here Pilate verifies the events of the resurrection, including the appearance of mythic men declaring that Jesus is risen:

> And as lightening flashes come forth in a storm, so there were seen men, lofty in stature, and surpassing in glory, a countless host, crying out, and there voice was heard as that of exceedingly loud thunder, Jesus that was crucified is risen again: come up from Hades ye that were enslaved in subtereaneous recesses of Hades. (*Anaph. Pil.* A. 9).[752]

The phrase describing the stature of Jesus differs slightly in the two recensions of this text. In the A form, the innumerable group of men are described as οὕτως ἄνδρες ἐφαίνοντο ὑψηλοὶ ἐν στολῇ (thus men were seen, lofty in stature), whereas the B form describes the figures as οὕτως ἄνδρες ὑψηλοί τινες κοσμήσεως στολῆς … ἐφαίνοντο ἐν τῷ ἀέρι). Reflection on the polymorphic features of Jesus in both pre- and post-

---

[750] Mara, *Évangile de Pierre*, 183.

[751] Vaganay, *L'Évangile de Pierre*, 300.

[752] This translation is taken from B.H. Cowper, *The Apocryphal Gospels and Other Documents Relating to the History of Christ* (6th ed. London: David Nutt, 1897) 404.

resurrection scenes are not uncommon in early Christian literature of the second and third centuries.[753]

The singular form of κεφαλή should not be seen as necessarily being due to grammatical inaccuracy on the part the scribe, in failing to speak of 'heads' in the plural. Rather, the sense of the genitive appears to be distributive, i.e. 'the head of [each of] the two', even though usually this would be indicated through the use of a preposition.[754] The verb χωρέω, here occurring as a present active participle, feminine accusative singular agreeing with the noun κεφαλή, has the meing of movement by extension. This in the present context it means 'to make movement from one place or position to another, *go, go out/away*, reach'[755] (cf. *Eph.* 16.2; *Mag.* 5.1; *Ep.Diog.* 8.2). The preposition μέχρι with the genitive denote the extent or limit of an object, here the height to which the heads of the men attain. This limitation on the already astounding height of the bodies, becomes important for making the comparison in the following clause.

**10.40b** τοῦ δὲ χειραγωγουμένου ὑπ' αὐτῶν ὑπερβαίνουσαν τοὺς οὐρανούς. If the readers were struck by the size of the angels, the resurrected Lord is described as possessing 'supereminent height.'[756] At this stage the third figure is being referred to using circumlocutions, 'the one being led'. It is uncertain whether this indirect reference is intended to shroud the identity of the third person, or if it is an act of piety. which reverences the risen Lord by not pronouncing his name. These two aspects may been in the author's mind simultaneously. This genitive absolute construction that is used in the opening part of this half-verse aligns with classical usage, 'where the noun or pronoun to which the participle refers does not appear either as subject or in any other capacity.'[757] This genitive absolute clause which appears in the first half of the verse is the last reference to the two men who are leading the third. Their departure from the scene is not narrated. The action described by the participle χειραγωγουμένου, i.e. 'being led

---

[753] Foster, 'Polymorphic Christology: Its Origins and Development in Early Christianity', 1–34.

[754] The two prepositions that are used distributively in the NT are κατά and ἀνά. See C.F.D. Moule, *An Idiom-Book of New Testament Greek* (2nd ed.; Cambridge: CUP, 1959) 59f., 66f.

[755] BDAG, 1094.

[756] Swete, *The Akhmîm Fragment of the Apocryphal Gospel of St Peter*, 18.

[757] BDF §423.

by hand', does not necessarily denote frailty on the part of the one being led, although it may on occasion describe a condition of dependency on others. In the NT on the three occasions this term is used in Acts, twice it refers to Paul's Damascus Road experience and once to the magician Elymas (Acts 13.11). In each of these three instances, it depicts a blinded person being led by his companions.[758] Similarly, in the two usages in the LXX, it refers to blind Samson (Jdg 16.26, Codex Alexandrinus) and to Tobit who no longer needs to be led by hand since his sight has been restored (Tob 11.16, Codex Sinaiticus). Despite the exclusive use by biblical texts in connecting the term χειραγωγέω with blindness, wider usage in Greek literature shows that this is not always the case (cf. Hdn 4.2.8; Plu. *Cleom.* 38; Luc. *Tim.* 32).[759] Moreover, there is nothing in the resurrection account in the Akhmîm text to suggest that the risen Lord has been left blind. Perhaps here it is better to see it as a more servile act, whereby the heavenly beings lead the risen Lord to the new realm in which he is to be installed.

The excessive height of the two men is now surpassed by that of the third person, whose head reaches beyond the heaven. Obviously the chief purpose of this description is to show the superiority of this third figure to emerge from the tomb in comparison to the two men that entered. Again, Mara argues that such enlargement is a way of denoting authority.[760] While this is undoubtedly the case, there appears to be a more developed tendency to represent transformation of appearance as showing that a person has the ability to communicate both with, or move between, the heavenly and earthly realms. In Jewish pseudipigraphical literature this tendency is already apparent. In relation to the figure of Jesus there is a growing trajectory of a polymorphic Christology which finds its origin in at least partial form in the canonical gospels. In resurrection scenes, the body of the risen Christ is able to miraculously materialize in locked rooms (Jn 20.19, 26). Also on the Emmaus Road Jesus is not recognized by those who knew him, although in this case it appears that the visual perception of the observers was obscured, rather than an alteration in the form of the

---

[758] In Acts 9.8 and 22.11 participial forms of the verb χειραγωγέω are used, whereas in Acts 13.11 the nominal form χειραγωγούς is employed.

[759] For further references in classical sources where the term is used without connection to blindness see LSJ, 1984.

[760] She states 'Sa stature exprime les dimensions réelles d'un personage dont l'autorité embrasse le ciel et la terre.' Mara, *Évangile de Pierre*, 183.

risen Lord (Lk 24.16). The version of the encounter between the risen
Jesus and two travelling figure recorded in the Longer ending of Mark,
which is likely to be a reworking of the Emmaus Road scene from
Lk 24,[761] is even more explicit about the altered state of the physical form of Jesus.[762] The text states that μετὰ δὲ ταῦτα δυσὶν ἐξ αὐτῶν
περιπατοῦσιν ἐφανερώθη ἐν ἑτέρᾳ μορφῇ (Mk 16.12). The accounts of the
transfiguration all refer to Jesus' changed form (Matt 17.2; Mk 9.2–3;
Lk 9.29), and interestingly during this altered state Jesus is attended
by two men from heaven.[763] More striking parallels exist outside the
canonical tradition. The *Acts of Peter*, in a context where the apostle
describes his own understanding of the transfiguration, precedes that
description with an understanding of the incarnation that views it as
God changing form: 'God was moved by his mercy to show himself
in another form and in the likeness of man' (*Acts Pet.* 20). Later in
the same text there is a more vivid example of Jesus being seen on the
same occasion in a various forms. This occurs in a post-resurrection
setting which like the Johannine appearance is set in a room. In this
context Peter is with a group of widows, among whom are certain
blind women who are made to see by the bright light. After the event
Peter questions the widows concerning what they have seen:

> And as we lay there, only those widows stood up which were
> blind; and the bright light which appeared unto us entered into
> their eyes and made them to see. Unto whom Peter said: Tell us
> what ye saw. And they said: We saw an old man of such comeli-
> ness as we are not able to declare to thee; but others said: We
> saw a young man; and others: We saw a boy touching our eyes
> delicately, and so were our eyes opened. Peter therefore magni-
> fied the Lord, saying: Thou only art the Lord God, and of what

---

[761] Evans affirms this conclusion when he states, 'We have here a clear allusion to
the story of the two disciples walking on the road to Emmaus (Lk 24:13–35). Evans,
*Mark 8:27–16:20*, 548.

[762] Again see Foster, 'Polymorphic Christology: Its Origins and Development in
Early Christianity' 1–34.

[763] Although the theory is not supported here, for those who wish to suggest that
the transfiguration narrative is a displaced resurrection story (see Bultmann, *History
of the Synoptic Tradition*, 259–261), it might be helpful to see this story as a parallel
development of the underlying account of the appearance of the two men from heaven
here and the figures of Elijah and Moses being part of the transfiguration scene. Such
a link would allow the base tradition to be connected with a resurrection scene. This
suggestion is not followed here, since it is argued that the 'two men from heaven' in
the Akhmîm narrative does not originate in an independent tradition, but is rather
the redactional reworking of the canonical appearance accounts of (young) men, or
angels.

lips have we need to give thee due praise? and how can we give thee thanks according to thy mercy? Therefore, brethren, as I told you but a little while since, God that is constant is greater than our thoughts, even as we have learned of these aged widows, how that they beheld the Lord in various forms. (*Acts Pet.* 21)

In this context it may be that perceptions have been altered, rather than the form of the post-resurrection Lord. Yet what is significant is that the divine transcendence of human thought is demonstrated through the ability of the Lord to be perceived in a variety of forms.

Recounting traditions which may at points be related to those in the *Acts of Peter*, the *Acts of John* also presents a polymorphic Christology. In a miraculous vision reminiscent of that experienced by the blind widows, Jesus, standing on the shore, appears to two his disciples, the brothers James and John, in a variety of forms. James first sees Jesus as a child, Johns sees a man 'who is handsome, fair and cheerful looking'. Then Jesus appears to the pair again. To John he is 'rather bald-headed but with a thick flowing beard', whereas James sees 'a young man whose beard was just beginning' (*Acts John* 88–89). The version of the transfiguration in the *Acts of John* portrays a Jesus changed in body size, but here his form is not enlarged, but diminished. On approaching Jesus during the mystical experience on the mountain, John states, 'he appeared as a small man' (*Acts John* 91). Bodily metamorphosis is also recorded as happening to figures other than Jesus. In a text rarely cited, *The Gospel of the Twelve Apostles*, apparently dating from the eighth century, in the section relating the 'Revelation of Simeon Kepha', Peter has his body enlarged: 'And Simeon was moved by the Spirit of God: and his appearance and body were enlarged.'[764] These texts evidence a diverse and ongoing tradition of representing Jesus (and other significant figures) and having polymorphic bodies. This ability is often linked to post-resurrection or revelatory events, in which the heavenly reality is related to inhabitants of the earth.

**10.41a** καὶ φωνῆς ἤκουον ἐκ τῶν οὐρανῶν λεγούσης. This is second occasion in the narrative when a voice from heaven has been heard. On the previous occasion (*Gos. Pet.* 9.35) the voice accompanied the arrival of the two men from heaven, although in that case the actual words of the voice were not recorded. Here, in the second

---

[764] Harris (ed.), *The Gospel of the Twelve Apostles: Together with the Apocalypses of Each One of Them*, 31.

half of the verse, the content of that voice is revealed to the readers of the text. There are a number of differences in the constructions used to announce heavenly voices. In *Gos. Pet.* 9.35, the structure, μεγάλη φωνὴ ἐγένετο ἐν τῷ οὐρανῷ, makes φωνή the subject of the clause, whereas here it is in the genitive case, being a voice heard by the Roman centurion, guards and Jewish elders, as well as, of course, the three men leaving the tomb and the cross. In the first instance the noun φωνή is qualified by an the adjective μεγάλη, here no qualitative description of the voice is provided. Furthermore, the origin of the voice is described slightly differently. The preposition ἐν in the first instance, appears to describe a voice that was spoken in the heavenly realm and its reverberations could by heard by those below, whereas here the preposition ἐκ here denotes a voice spoken from the heavens down to the earth. Nonetheless, it appears that in both cases the voice is communication from God with heavenly beings, and humans are simply permitted to eavesdrop. Thus in the first instance communication may occur in heaven, the aural echoes of which are heard below, but not the actual content. This may explain the non-disclosure of the contents of the message on that occasion. Consequently, because the actual words are able to be heard by the witnessing party on this occasion, this clause also contains the participle λεγούσης, which functions in a manner similar to a ὅτι recitative to introduce direct speech. Vaganay comments on the wider purpose of such voices-from-heaven in the biblical text. He suggests, 'it is the contemporary way used in Scripture to indicate a word from the heavenly Father.'[765]

**10.41b** ἐκήρυξας τοῖς κοιμωμένοις; The act of preaching to those who are asleep, aligns with the tradition of the 'harrowing of hell', which became important in early Christian writings, as well as in the art and writings of the medieval period. Vaganay confidently asserts that it is this tradition that is being depicted here. 'Without any doubt it denotes the mission of Christ to hell.'[766] Later, more developed descriptions attest an ongoing curiosity to explain the work of Christ in the period between his death and resurrection. It appears to have been uncongenial to suggest a period of suspension of consciousness

---

[765] Vaganay, *L'Évangile de Pierre*, 301.
[766] Vaganay, *L'Évangile de Pierre*, 301.

or 'soul-sleep'. Instead the intervening time is depicted as a period of evangelistic activity.

The verb κηρύσσω occurs sixty-one times in the NT, it can be co-ordinated specifically with the noun εὐαγγέλιον (Matt 4.23; 9.35; 24.14; 26.13; Mk 1.14; 13.10, 14.9; 16.15; Gal 2.2; Col 1.23; 1 Thess 2.9).[767] Although the term εὐαγγέλιον is not expilcitly used here, or elsewhere, in the Akhmîm narrative, the close connection of this term as the content of the proclamation, with the verb κηρύσσω may lead to the supposition that it was 'the gospel' that was announced to those who were sleeping, although the content of the gospel message is not explained. In the NT when the group is described to whom the preaching is being directed, the preferred construction is κηρύσσω+εἰς+acusative (cf. Mk 1.39; Lk 4.44; 1 Thess 2.9). By comparision κηρύσσω with a dative construction occurs only in the Longer Ending of Mark's Gospel (Mk 16.15). This appears to represent a more general shift in *koine* Greek from the second century onwards.

The verb κηρύσσω has a connection with the 'harrowing of hell' tradition from its earliest stage of development in the NT. In 1 Pet 3.19 the event is described as an act of proclamation καὶ τοῖς ἐν φυλακῇ πνεύμασιν πορευθεὶς ἐκήρυξεν. As Merk observes, in this case 'it remains open whether it was for the purpose of repentance or judgment; or Christ proclaimed his victory to the most distant places of the cosmic scene, even (καί) to the "Spirits".'[768] By not employing the reference to 'spirits' or 'prison' contained in the passage from 1 Peter, the Akhmîm account moves its understanding of this event further away from a link with the fate of the antediluvian narrative of Gen 6.1–4, which in second temple Jewish literature was, as Kelly comments, 'avidly dwelt upon and richly embroidered (e.g. 1 Enoch x–xvi; xxi; Apoc. Bar. lvi. 12f.; Jub v.6; 6QD ii.18–21; 1QGn Apoc. ii. 1; 16).[769] In relation to 1 Pet 3.19, the identity of the spirits kept in prison has been relentlessly debated.[770] The connection with the 'days of Noah' in the following

---

[767] See Moulton & Geden, *Concordance to the Greek New Testament*, Sixth edition, 583–584.

[768] Merk, in EDNT, vol. 2, 291.

[769] J.N.D. Kelly, *The Epistles of Peter and Jude*, BNTC (London: A&C Black, 1969) 154.

[770] Achtemeier lists a range of suggestions. He rejects the interpretation that humans are the imprisoned spirits, instead he argues the angelic beings of Gen 6.1–6 who engaged in sexual relations with human women are the beings who are held captive in prison. P.J. Achtemeier, *1 Peter*, Hermeneia (Minneapolis: Fortress, 1996) 254–256.

verse (1 Pet 3.20) opens up that historical horizon as the hermeneutical tool for understanding the meaning in the epistle.[771] The description in the Akhmîm text of those receiving proclamation does not describe them as either 'spirits' or as being 'in prison'. So unless it is argued that such pre-understandings were *de rigueur* part of the 'harrowing of hell' tradition, there is no *a priori* reason to suspect that the Jewish background of Gen 6.1–6 is informing the thinking of the author in his fleeting reference to this tradition.

In fact a second line of interpretation emerges in the NT which may account for the dominant early Christian and medieval understanding that the preaching was made to dead human beings. In 1 Pet 4.6 the text depicts the gospel as being preached to the dead, καὶ νεκροῖς εὐηγγελίσθη. Although a divide developed in Christian thinking between those who understood νεκροί as the 'spiritually dead',[772] and those who took it as some type of post-mortem opportunity to evangelize, the unified tradition of early interpreters was that it referred to human beings. Moreover, in Eph 4.8–10 there is another attempt to account for what happened to Jesus between death and resurrection. Like the two references to this tradition in 1 Peter, this passage is extremely problematic. In fact, in reference to Eph 4.8 Muddiman states, 'This and the next two verses of Ephesians are possibly the most difficult in the whole letter.'[773] Notwithstanding the difficulties raised by this loose citation of material from Ps 68, along with the gloss offered by the explanation contained in Eph 4.9–10, a number of general conclusions can be supported. If the descent mentioned in Eph 4.9 is to the underworld as seems likely, καὶ κατέβη εἰς τὰ κατώτερα [μέρη] τῆς γῆς, and not descent from heaven to earth at incarnation, then there are important parallels with the tradition in 1 Pet 3.19.[774] Importantly, the language of victory procession seems to figure in the image of leading forth prisoners captive ᾐχμαλώτευσεν αἰχμαλωσίαν, although

---

[771] Although rejecting the interpretation that the 'spirits' were the angels of Gen 6.1–4, nevertheless, Goppelt connects the event with same broad period. He states, '"The spirits in prison" are, therefore, the souls of the flood generation preserved in a place of punishment.' L. Goppelt, *A Commentary on 1 Peter* (Grand Rapids, MI: Eerdmans, 1993) 259.

[772] Bigg notes that the interpretation 'spiritually dead' was favoured by, among others, Augustine, Cyril, Bede Erasmus, and Luther. See C. Bigg, *The Epistles of St. Peter and St. Jude*, ICC (Edinburgh: T&T Clark, 1910) 171.

[773] J. Muddiman, *The Epistle to the Ephesians*, BNTC (London: Continuum, 2001) 187.

[774] E. Best, *Ephesians*, ICC (Edinburgh: T&T Clark, 1998) 383–386.

this is not exploited in the interpretive gloss. Many of the medieval depictions of this scene show Christ leading forth those trapped in Hades, although here the identity of the captives is not explained in the Ephesians passage.

What these biblical references show is that the Akhmîm text can be situated in the broad stream of reflections on these NT passages that deal with the descent of Christ into the underworld in the period between his crucifixion and resurrection. This interpretative tradition can be shown to be active from the second century onwards. Although Ignatius is cited by Vaganay as early representative of the descent into hell tradition,[775] the passage in question, which describes the dead prophets being made alive by Christ, does not place this enlivening as taking place between the death and resurrection, although it is a consequence of the resurrection. Neither is the netherworld mentioned.

πῶς ἡμεῖς δυνησόμεθα ζῆσαι χωρὶς αὐτοῦ, οὗ καὶ οἱ προφῆται μαθηταὶ ὄντες τῷ πνεύματι ὡς διδάσκαλον αὐτὸν προσεδόκων; καὶ διὰ τοῦτο, ὃν δικαίως ἀνέμενον, παρὼν ἤγειρεν αὐτοὺς ἐκ νεκρῶν. (*Mag.* 9.2)

How then are we able to live apart from him? Even the prophets who were his disciples in the spirit awaited him as their teacher. And for this reason, the one they righteously expected raised them from the dead when he arrived. (*Mag.* 9.2)[776]

Discussing passages contained in the LXX which he accuses Jews as having removed, Justin lists without discussion the following passage. 'And again, from the sayings of the same Jeremiah these have been cut out: "The Lord God remembered his dead people of Israel who lay in the graves; and he descended to preach to them his own salvation."' (Justin, *Dial.* 72.4). Although ambiguities remain, there are obviously clearer links here with the tradition of descent into hell to preach to the dead, than in the writings of Ignatius. Irenaeus appears to cite the same passage as Justin, but attributes it to Isaiah (Irenaeus. *Adv. Haer.* 3.22.4). However, by the time of Irenaeus this tradition had become prominent in Christian thinking: 'It was for this reason, too,

---

[775] Vaganay has a slight error in his reference. The passage is not the non-existent *Mag.* 9.3, but 9.2. Vaganay, *L'Évangile de Pierre*, 301.

[776] The English translation is taken from Ehrman (trans.), *The Apostolic Fathers*, vol. 1, 251.

that the Lord descended into the regions beneath the earth, preaching his advent there also, and the remission of sins received by those who believe in him.' (Irenaeus. *Adv. Haer.* 4.27.2). For Irenaeus, the discussion of this topic is an important counter to the claims attributed to Marcion which 'denied salvation to the patriarchs of old, teaching that when Christ descended to them in the lower regions they feared a trick and rejected him.'[777] Thus, at least in part, the early interest in reflection on the descent into hell may have been occasioned by a desire to refute Marcionite readings that used this event as an attempt to create a further separation between the creator God of the Old Testament, and the supreme God of the new dispensation, rather than from intrinsic interest in the subject. However, fascination with the 'descent into hell' soon appeared to take on an independent focus of interest without reference to the original polemical context in which the discussion first evolved. The idea appears in the writings of many other prominent early theologians (Clement of Alexandria, *Strom.* 2.9; Tertullian, *De anima* 55; Origen, *Contra Celsum* 2.43) and eventually in staccato form became embedded in the creeds of the church, καθελθόντα εἰς τὰ κατώτατα (Apostles' Creed).

Among the non-canonical gospels, it is given most prominence in the *Gospel of Nicodemus* 17–29.[778] In that text, the Lord releases all the righteous from the power of Hades. They are led forth by Adam, the progenitor of sin, who is given the sign of the cross on his forehead (and in one of the Latin versions, on the heads of all the saints who accompanied him; Latin A, 8.2), and thus leads the company of the righteous into heaven. In English medieval piety the term 'harrowing' is first evidenced around A.D. 1000 as a term denoting the description of Christ's plundering of hell, in the sermons of Ælfric.[779] Middle English drama was fascinated with the 'harrowing of hell' and 'the four great cycles of English mystery plays each devote to it a separate scene.'[780] In this highly developed Medieval form of the tradition, the 'harrowing' denotes Christ's post-crucifixion expedition to hell when

---

[777] C.E. Hill, *From the Lost Teaching of Polycarp: Identifying Irenaeus' Apostolic Presbyter and the Author of* Ad Diognetum (Tübingen: Mohr Siebeck, 2006) 30.

[778] Perhaps the most convenient English translation of the various recensions of the text is to be found in Elliott (ed.), *The Apocryphal New Testament*, 185–204.

[779] See 'harrow' in the *Oxford English Dictionary*.

[780] See 'Harrowing of Hell' in the *Catholic Encyclopedia*, http://www.newadvent.org/cathen/07143d.htm (17 Dec 2005).

he liberates the righteous who had been held captive since the beginning of the world.

The Akhmîm text removes all reference to imprisonment, or Jewish mythology about ensnared angelic spirits. Instead it asks a simple question about the completion of the act of preaching to those who sleep, κοιμωμέννοις. The description of such individuals as 'being asleep' creates the expectation that they need to be roused, and this must be seen as the function of the proclamation, to awaken such individuals from the slumber which has befallen them. The other expectation given to readers is that the central figure will respond to this heavenly question. On this occasion, the author, will defy such expectations with a stikingly discordant note.

**10.42** καὶ ὑπακοὴ ἠκούετο ἀπὸ τοῦ σταυροῦ ὅτι ναί. With the first three words, καὶ ὑπακοὴ ἠκούετο ('and a reply was heard'), the author delays the shock for the audience of the response being uttered by the cross. The presence of the cross in depictions of the descent into hades occurs most vividly in the *Gospel of Nicodemus*,[781] although there is a tendency for the tradition to be expanded in the various recensions of the text. In the Greek tradition of Christ's descent to hell, he simply blesses Adam with the sign of the cross; in the Latin A recension, Adam as spokesperson for the saints asks the Lord to set up the cross in Hades as the sign of victory, whereupon the Lord makes the sign of the cross on Adam and all the saints; finally, in the Latin B recension, the physical cross is planted in Hades as a perpetual victory sign.

| | |
|---|---|
| Greek Tradition: | 'the Saviour blessed Adam with the sign of the cross on his forehead.' *Gos. Nic.* 8(24).2.[782] |
| Latin A: | '"O Lord, set the sign of the victory of your cross in Hades that death may no more have dominion." And the Lord stretching forth his hand, made the sign of the cross on Adam and on all his saints…' *Gos. Nic.* 8(24).2.[783] |

---

[781] The text is also known as the *Acts of Pilate*. As Elliott comments, 'Both of these titles are fairly late and are taken from the introductions to be found in some medieval Latin manuscripts.' Elliott (ed.), *The Apocryphal New Testament*, 164.

[782] Elliott (ed.), *The Apocryphal New Testament*, 189.

[783] Elliott (ed.), *The Apocryphal New Testament*, 195.

Latin B: 'Then all the saints of God asked the Lord to leave as a sign of victory the sign of his holy cross in the underworld that its most impious officers might not retain as an offender any one whom the Lord had absolved. And so it was done. And the Lord set his cross in the midst of Hades and it is the sign of victory which will remain to eternity.' Gos. Nic. 10(26).1.[784]

Also in this tale of Christ's descent into hell, the penitent thief crucified with Jesus turns up carrying his cross claiming admittance to paradise on the basis of the promise made to him by Jesus. He is instructed to wait a little until Adam and the now released band of saints arrive and then they can enter together. Such elements evidence the type of spiritual reflection that evolved around the symbol of the cross, even if these stories do not themselves attest a self-animated cross.

The term ὑπακοή although most widely meaning 'obedience', is also attested elsewhere communicating the same sense as it does here, 'reply'. BDAG provides only one example of this use apart from Gos. Pet. 10.42, which is to be found in Pla, Soph. 217d.[785] Swete cites an example from Methodias, conviv. x virg. 208, but the exact term ὑπακοή is not explicitly used. Instead the passage employs the infinitive, ὑπακούειν.[786] This same semantic range of the verb ὑπακούω and the noun ὑπακοή is more fully illustrated in Lampe's A Greek Patristic Lexicon.[787] In particular, in liturgical context the term denotes responsive obedience.[788]

To describe a speaking cross as an embellishment to the canonical tradition (which it is) is certainly an understatement. The fact that the cross is both self-animated and able to talk demonstrates the suspension of the natural order. Thus, the whole scene is portrayed as counter-intuitive and dumbfounding to the senses, in order to emphasize the enormity of the miraculous in these events. Thus Vaganay rightly rejects the mechanistic explanation of some writers that the response

---

[784] Elliott (ed.), The Apocryphal New Testament, 203.
[785] See BDAG, 1028.
[786] Swete, The Akhmîm Fragment of the Apocryphal Gospel of St Peter, 19.
[787] Lampe (ed.), A Patristic Greek Lexicon, 1432–1433.
[788] For more on this see Vaganay, L'Évangile de Pierre, 303.

had to come form the cross because the head of Jesus was above the heavens. Instead he states,

> In the portrayal of the descent into hell, more than once the cross has been made to play an active role, in the way of an animated being. There is nothing at all surprising if, according to the *Gospel of Peter*, the cross which a few moments earlier walked, starts speaking. Since it had accompanied Christ during his sojourn among the dead, it is not strange that its testimony is called upon.[789]

Thus Vaganay suggests that the author expects his readers to be familiar with the place of the cross in story of the harrowing of hell, and its active role in that setting prepares the audience for its ability to vocalize a reply in response to the voice that asks about the preaching to those who are dead.[790] If correct, such a suggestion would lead to one of two conclusions: either the tradition of an active role for the cross in the accounts of the descent into hell is quite an early element, or the text of the *Gospel of Peter* is later than supposed. The one word reply does not represent an overly talkative cross! Rather the cross appears to declare that the preaching to the dead has occurred and in an emblematic manner the cross was instrumental in the process of declaring the victory of Christ to those who had been slumbering.

---

[789] 'Dans le tableau de la descente aux enfers, on lui a fait jouer plus d'une fois un rôle actif, à la façon d'un être animé. Rien d'étonnant si, chez le pseudo-Pierre, la croix, qui tout à l'heure marchait, se met à parler. Puisqu'elle avait accompagné le Christ au séjour des morts, il n'est pas étrange qu'on invoque son témoignage.' Vaganay, *L'Évangile de Pierre*, 303.

[790] See Vaganay, *L'Évangile de Pierre*, 303.

43. συνεσκέπτοντο οὖν ἀλλήλοις[1] ἐκεῖνοι ἀπελθεῖν καὶ[2] ἐνφανίσαι ταῦτα τῷ Πειλάτῳ. 44. καὶ ἔτι διανοουμέ(ν)ων[3] αὐτῶν φαίνονται πάλιν ἀνοιχθέντες οἱ οὐρανοὶ καὶ α̅υ̅ο̅ς̅ τις κατελθὼν[4] καὶ εἰσελθὼν εἰς τὸ μνῆμα. 45. ταῦτα ἰδόντες οἱ περὶ τὸν κεντυρωνα[5] νυκτὸς ἔσπευσαν πρὸς Πειλᾶτον ἀφέντες τὸν τάφον ὃν ἐφύλασσον καὶ ἐξηγήσαντο πάντα ἅπερ εἶδον ἀπωνιῶντες[6] μεγάλως καὶ λέγοντες· ἀληθῶς υἱὸς ἦν θ̅υ̅. 46. ἀποκριθεὶς ὁ Πειλᾶτος ἔφη· ἐγὼ καθαρεύω τοῦ αἵματος τοῦ υἱοῦ τοῦ θεοῦ[7] ἡμῖν[8] δὲ τοῦτο ἔδοξεν. 47. εἶτα προσελθόντες πάντες ἐδέοντο αὐτοῦ καὶ περεκάλουν[9] κελεῦσαι τῷ κεντυρίων[10] καὶ τοῖς στρατιώταις μηδὲν[11] εἰπεῖν ἃ εἶδον. 48. συμφέρει γάρ, φασίν, ἡμῖν ὀφλῆσαι μεγίστην ἁμαρτίαν ἔμπροσθεν τοῦ θεοῦ καὶ μὴ ἐμπεσεῖν εἰς χεῖρας τοῦ λαοῦ τῶν Ἰουδαίων καὶ λιθασθῆναι. 49. ἐκέλευσεν οὖν ὁ Πειλᾶτος τῶν κεντυρίων[12] καὶ τοῖς στρατιώταις μηδὲν εἰπεῖν.

43. Then those men together determined with each other to go and report these things to Pilate. 44. And while they were still thinking, again the heavens were seen opening, and a certain man descended and entered into the tomb. 45. Seeing these things those who accompanied the centurion rushed by night to Pilate, leaving the tomb which they were guarding, and related everything which they saw, being greatly distressed and saying, 'Truly this was God's son.' 46. Answering, Pilate said, 'I am clean from the blood of the son of God, and this is recognized by us.' 47. Then they all came, and were beseeching and entreating him to command the centurion and the soldiers to say nothing of what they had seen. 48. 'For it is better', they said, 'for us to incur the liability of a great sin before God, and not to fall into the hands of the people of the Jews and to be stoned.' 49. Therefore, Pilate ordered the centurion and the soldiers to say nothing.

## TEXT CRITICAL NOTES

1. The scribe's erratic formation of the double lambda combination has been observed previously. The first attempt to form the λλ sequence in the word μέλλουσιν (Gos. Pet. 2.3) is perhaps the most successful representation of these letters. However, there is a marked deterioriation exhibited with περιέβαλλον (Gos. Pet. 3.7), which led a

number of scholars to miss one of the lambdas, and to postulate an aorist rather than imperfect form. Here in *Gos. Pet.* 11.43, the form is written with an even lower degree of legibility due to the ligature with the following eta,[791] and the the pen becoming blunt is another factor. Other examples of the double lambda combination occur at *Gos. Pet.* 8.28; 14.59, 60. The first of these examples is only slightly superior to the combination at *Gos. Pet.* 11.43; at *Gos. Pet.* 14.59 the legibility is much improved; the final example is unique with the initial lambda being the last letter on a line, and the second lambda being the first letter on the foillowing line.

2. The καὶ is the first word on *verso* of the fourth leaf of the text. On completion of the previous page, the nib of the pen has either been re-cut, or a new sharper pen has been used. It was the habit of scribes to resharpen the nibs of their writing implements with a knife carried as part of the standard tool kit. Usually the pen was formed from a hard reed pen (Latin: *calamus* Greek: κάλαμος) with the point split into two equal parts in such a way as to form a nib.[792] Cribiore describes the scribal practice of pen sharpening.

> The Greeks adopted the reed pen from the ancient Egyptians, but whereas in pharonic Egypt thinner reeds were used (their ends were frayed to function as brushes), in Greco-Roman times reeds were thicker, pointed, and split, with the shape of medieval quills. They could be resharpened many times until they became short stumps, and sometimes the life of a pen was prolonged by sticking a piece of wood into its end.[793]

That such sharpening has taken place in the Akhmîm codex is evident from the vastly improved clarity of penstokes from this point onwards. These more refined letter strokes remain throughout the rest of manuscript.

3. Here the scribe misuses the familiar practice of writing a word with the final ν omittied, especially when the word occurs at the end of a

---

[791] Gebhardt notes the tendency for the bottom half of the longer leg of the lambda to become horizontal when connected to a following eta. See Gebhardt, *Das Evangelium und die Apokalypse des Petrus*, 12.

[792] A. Lemaire, 'Writing and Writing Materials', in D.N. Freedman (ed.), *The Anchor Bible Dictionary*, vol. 6, 1003–1004.

[793] R. Cribiore, *Gymnastics of the Mind: Greek Education in Hellenistic and Roman Egypt* (Princeton, N.J./ Oxford: Princeton University Press, 2001) 157–159; and *Writing, Teachers, and Students in Graeco-Roman Egypt* (Atlanta, Ga.: Scolars Press, 1996).

line.[794] Here he omits the third last letter διανοουμέ[ν]ων, because it occurs at a line ending (line 1, page 4 *verso*) rather than being the final letter of the word. Instead he writes the epsilon with a 5mm supralinear stroke which extends beyond the width of the letter to the right hand side. On each of the eight other occasions the scribe omits a final ν he does so correctly, with the final letter of a word at a line ending. See, line 2, page 1 *verso* (*Gos. Pet.* 1.1); line 9, page 2 *verso* (*Gos. Pet.* 6.21); line 3, page 3 *recto* (*Gos. Pet.* 7.26); line 13, page 3 *verso* (*Gos. Pet.* 9.34); line 15, page 3 *verso* (*Gos. Pet.* 9.35); line 16, page 3 *verso* (*Gos. Pet.* 9.36); line 2, page 5 *recto* (*Gos. Pet.* 12.52); line 2, page 5 *recto* (*Gos. Pet.* 13.55).

4. The scribe mistakenly writes κατελθόν with the ending of the aorist nominative neuter singular participle instead of the required aorist nominative neuter singular participle, κατελθών. The second last letter should be an omega, but the scribe writes omicron. This may suggest one of two possible factors in the copying process. Possibly, the text may have been dictated to the scribe, and he did not distinguish the sound, thereby writing the incorrect ending -ον. However, on seeing the form he had written κατελθόν, he did not replicate the mistake with the following participle εἰσελθών. Alternatively, the text may have been written in a period when the aural distinction in sounds between omega and omicron had been lost. Since, however, this lack of distinction may have begun prior to the Christian era, it offers little help for dating the text. Caragounis argues that 'From the third century B.C. on O and Ω interchange very frequently, which implies that if there had ever been any distinctions between them originally, these letters had now become equivalent.'[795] Caragounis documents this with papyrological evidence spanning from the third century B.C.E. to the beginning of the second century C.E.[796]

5. There is an orthographical error at this point with the iota omitted from the word κεντυρίωνα, which appears in the manuscript as κεντυρωνα.[797]

---

[794] See BDF §20.

[795] Caragounis, *The Development of Greek and the New Testament*, 373.

[796] Caragounis, *The Development of Greek and the New Testament*, 373–374, fn 101.

[797] This is noted by, among others, Kraus and Nicklas, *Das Petrusevangelium und die Petrusapokalypse*, 44.

6. Another orthographical error occurs here with the scribe writing ἀπωνιῶντες for ἀγωνιῶντες. Vaganay states, 'ἀγωνιῶντες (a mistake of the copiest in the ms.: ἀπωνιῶντες; cf. v. 15).'[798] At a number of places the letter γ is replaced by an incorrect π. This may be due to the similarity in shape as exemplified in the scribe's letter formation.

7. For no obviously apparent reason the scribe choses not to employ a *nomen sacrum* for the word θεοῦ in this verse, although he did so with the identical term in the previous line. Rather than attempting to discern some system to the scribe's use of *nomina sacra*, it is best to conclude that he is inconsistent in this practice.

8. The reading ἡμῖν is replaced by the conjectural emendation ὑμῖν by the following scholars: Robinson,[799] Swete,[800] Gebhardt,[801] Harnack,[802] Vaganay,[803] Mara,[804] and Kraus and Nicklas.[805] This change is usually introduced without discussion, and seems to be based upon exegetical decisions rather than upon text-critical judgments. However, it needs to be remembered that these two words were identical in pronunciation (as in Modern Greek) and this could have led to confusion. Vaganay alone offers a fleeting insight into his reasoning, 'ὑμῖν (in the ms. Mistake of the copiest ἡμῖν) δέ corresponds to ἐγώ which precedes.'[806] If the δέ is given adversative force then ὑμῖν may be the more natural reading. If, however, it is conjunctive, then the reading ἡμῖν is not impossible. In fact it may even be preferable. Since a satisfactory meaning can be derived from the text without emendation, it appears best in this context to allow this reading to stand. Moreover, as was argued in relation to the reading φυλάξω (*Gos. Pet.* 8.30), the scribe does not always give the 'expected' subject in his constructions.

---

[798] Vaganay, *L'Évangile de Pierre*, 310.
[799] Robinson and James, *The Gospel according to Peter and the Revelation of Peter*, 87.
[800] Swete, *The Akhmîm Fragment of the Apocryphal Gospel of St Peter*, 21.
[801] Gebhardt, *Das Evangelium und die Apokalypse des Petrus*, 46.
[802] Harnack, *Bruchstücke des Evangeliums und der Apokalypse des Petrus*, 11.
[803] Vaganay, *L'Évangile de Pierre*, 311.
[804] Mara, *Évangile de Pierre*, 60.
[805] Kraus und Nicklas, *Das Petrusevangelium und die Petrusapokalypse*, 42.
[806] Vaganay, *L'Évangile de Pierre*, 311.

9. A further orthographical error is made with the form written as περεκάλουν instead of the correct form παρεκάλουν.[807] Although not explicitly stated, Vaganay appears to be suggesting that the scribe misread the conjunction + compound verb (καὶ παρεκάλουν) as a compound conjunction + verb (καίπερ ἐκάλουν). The difficult with the conjunction καίπερ 'although', is that it does not appear to be suitable for the context, since it must be closely co-ordinated with the preceding verb ἐδέοντο.

10. Whereas the manuscript reads κεντυρίων, the correct dative form is κεντυρίωνι. This is the second of three errors the scribe makes with the word κεντυρίων in this section (*Gos. Pet.* 11.43–49). See also notes 5 and 12.

11. Strictly speaking the term μηδέν, as it occurs here, in the accusative case is grammatically incorrect. This is due to the neuter plural relative pronoun ἅ that follows, which would require the dative form μηδένι, which would then produce a reading meaning 'to say to nobody what they had seen.'[808] This emendment has been preferred by a number of commentators including Zahn[809] and Vaganay.[810] Alternatively it is possible to emend the relative pronoun ἅ to ὧν, resulting in the reading μηδὲν εἰπεῖν ὧν εἶδον, 'to say nothing of what they had seen.' This proposal was suggested to Harnack by Blass.[811] However, both of these proposals place on the scribe a level of grammatical exactitude which appears foreign both to his own abilities and the level of precision found in many other texts of late antiquity. Thus it is best to concur with Swete's observation, 'For μηδέν it has been proposed to read μηδένι, but the change is perhaps unnecessary.'[812]

12. The form τῶν κεντυρίων is problematic. It comprises of the genitive plural definite article accompanied by the nominative singular form κεντυρίων, which is a Latin loanword. The orthography of this loanword shows much variation. LSJ list three possibilities, 'κεντορίων... OGI 196 (Philae): – also κεντουρίων, Lyd.Mag.1.9;

[807] Vaganay states, 'faute de copiste dans le ms.: καιπερεκαλουν'. Vaganay, *L'Évangile de Pierre*, 312.

[808] Brown, *The Death of the Messiah*, vol. 2, 1320.

[809] Zahn, *Das Evangelium des Petrus*.

[810] Vaganay, *L'Évangile de Pierre*, 312.

[811] Harnack, *Bruchstücke des Evangeliums und der Apokalypse des Petrus*, 11.

[812] Swete, *The Akhmîm Fragment of the Apocryphal Gospel of St Peter*, 21.

κεντυρίων, *Ev.Marc*.15.39.'[813] Lampe attests the second and third variations in the Patristic period with κεντουρίων, also being found in Steph.Diac,*v.Steph.* (M.100.11156C).[814] It is noted that in the NT the word is used 'only in Mark 15:39, 44, 45 (ἑκατόνταρχος/ ἑκατόνταρχης in Matthew and Luke) of the Roman leader who stood before the crucified Jesus... [It] also appears as a loanword in rabbinic texts.'[815] Most commentators have suggested emending the text to τῷ κεντυρίωνι,[816] since consistently in the narrative and most recently in this pericope in v. 45 only one centurion has been present, the officer in charge of the soldiers stationed at the tomb. This requires altering the genitive plural definite article to a dative singular form, and also changing the nominative singular noun to a dative singular form. The change to dative forms is made more natural by the observation that the co-ordinated object τοῖς στρατιώταις occurs in the dative. Once this alteration is made, then the accompanying definite article must be placed in the singular form. This explanation is far more plausible than assuming that the author is referring to an unreported assembly of a plurality of centurions. Moreover, an appreciation of the scribal habits throughout the manuscript provides no reason to suppose that the scribe was incapable of this confusion of cases, and the number of persons represented by various endings. This provides further evidence for limited facility in Greek, perhaps by an author whose native language was Coptic.

## COMMENTARY

**11.43 συνεσκέπτοντο οὖν ἀλλήλοις ἐκεῖνοι ἀπελθεῖν καὶ ἐνφανίσαι ταῦτα τῷ Πειλάτῳ.** Two compound verbs are employed to describe the actions of the group of witnesses at the tomb. The first, συσκέπτοντο, depicts the cognitive decision made by those present to go to Pilate. Very few texts attest the use of this term, although interestingly it does occur in the Greek revision of the Psalter by Symmachus

---

[813] LSJ, 938.
[814] Lampe (ed.), *A Patristic Greek Lexicon*, 744.
[815] EDNT, vol. 2, 283.
[816] See for instance Swete, *The Akhmîm Fragment of the Apocryphal Gospel of St Peter*, 21; Vaganay, *L'Évangile de Pierre*, 314; Kraus und Nicklas, *Das Petrusevangelium und die Petrusapokalypse*, 44.

(Ps 2.2; 30.14).[817] It is noteworthy to observe that this is not the only occasion when the Akhmîm text shares rare terminology with Symmachus' version of the Psalms. Also, in *Gos. Pet.* 10.39, the even rarer verb ὑπορθόω occurs in LXX σ Ps 43(44).19. Other instances of the verb συσκέπτομαι occur in the writings of the third century C.E. historian Herodian (1.17.7), the philosophical writings of the third to fourth century Iamblichus (Protr. 21.31), in Justin's *Dialogue* (46.2), [818] and a reference in the writings of Josephus (*B.J.* 1.46). The use in Josephus is unique in not giving any colaborative force to the prefix συν-. Referring to the examination by Archelaus of the documents written by Alexander the verb is used in the following manner: καὶ καθ' ἕκαστον ἐφιστὰς κεφάλαιον συνεσκέπτετο (*B.J.* 1.25).[819] This determination of the character of the documents does not involve any other party apart from Archaleus. By contrast, although a literary device, Justin invites Trypho to consider with him whether it is incumbant on Christians to observe all the Mosaic insitiutions: Κἀγὼ πάλιν· Συσκεψώμεθα κἀκεῖνό εἰ ἔνεστιν ἔλεγον φυλάσσειν τὰ διὰ Μωϋσέυς διαταχθέντα ἅπαντα νῦν (*Dial.* 46.2).[820] The hortatory subjunctive is a rhetorical invitation to join with the author in reconsidering the subject before the two parties. Thus prior to the second century there is no evidence for the use of the term συσκέπτομαι to denote a co-operative act of considering a matter together. In fact Josephus provides the only evidence for the use of this term prior to the mid second century, and the example drawn from his writings shows a different nuance of meaning.

The second compound verb is the form ἐνφανίσαι, which in both Ptolemaic and Byzantine documents is the standard word for reporting to an official or laying a complaint with a magistrate. It can be used in a revelatory sense (Heb 9.24), and can convey self-disclosure

---

[817] The chronology of Symmachus' writings is hard to determine. Arguments suggesting that evidence of Symmachian readings can be found in Origen's commentaries of *c.* 230 C.E. are now difficult to sustain. Nonetheless, it remains likely that his work on the revision of the LXX occurred sometime not long after the beginning of the third century. See N. Fernández Marcos, *The Septuagint in Context: Introduction to the Greek Versions of the Bible* (Leiden: Brill, 2000) 123; and G. Mercati, *L'eta di Simmaco l'interprete e S. Epifanio ossia se Simmaco tradusse in Greco la Bibba sotto M. Aurelio il filosofo* (Modena, 1892 = *ST* (1937), 20–92).

[818] See BDAG, 978.

[819] For the text see Thackeray (ed.), *Josephus: The Jewish War,* Books I–II, LCL 203, 237.

[820] Marcovich (ed.), *Iustini Martyris: Apologiae pro Christianis, Dialogus cum Tryphone,* 144.

in certain contexts (cf. Matt 27.53; Jn 14.22). Here, however, its use aligns more closely with that in Acts, where it describes passing on of information or presenting evidence (Acts 23.15, 22; 24.1; 25.2, 15). This latter range of meanings is the sense most widely attested in secular hellenistic literature.[821]

At this point the narrative moves towards picking up the storyline as it is related in the Matthean account, although this version is replete with embellishments and additions. Here the Akhmîm text envisages a consultation between the Roman forces and the Jewish elders. While neither group of characters is explicitly mentioned in the immediate context, nonetheless, despite the interruptions of the visions, the readers are still expected to see the triad of centurion, legionaries and Jewish elders as constituting the party of observers.[822] The determination which is arrived at, to go to Pilate, continues to highlight a certain tension in the narrative over the source of ultimate authority in Jerusalem, at least as envisaged by the author. It is unclear if the decision to report the events to Pilate is a result of the soldiers following the natural chain of command, or results from a desire to avoid communicating this news to Antipas, or, as is probably most likely, due to the role of Pilate in the canonical guards-at-the-tomb story.

**11.44a** καὶ ἔτι διανοουμένων αὐτῶν. This genitive absolute construction now places the the actions of the observers in a subsidiary position to the main action which will involve another character in the remaining portion of the verse. Structurally, Vaganay sees this clause, and presumably *Gos. Pet.* 11.43, as delineating, for literary purposes, a space between the second and third visions. 'Evidently, this secret meeting is only an interlude to separate the last two visions.'[823] There may be more to this notice than a desire to distinguish miraculous events. The simultaneity of action also functions to signal to the audience the rapidity with which events unfold, and thus it communicates a sense of the bewilderment experienced by the witnesses to those things that transpired on the first Easter morning.

---

[821] See BDAG, 326.

[822] Thus, as Vaganay describes the literary intent, 'Le pseudo-Pierre, lui, imagine une délibération commune auprès du tombeau, parce que les principaux des Juifs y sont déjà rassembles avec la garde païenne.' Vaganay, *L'Évangile de Pierre*, 304.

[823] 'A l'évidence, ce conciliabule n'est qu'un intermède pour séparer les deux dernières visions.' Vaganay, *L'Évangile de Pierre*, 304.

**11.44b**  φαίνονται πάλιν ἀνοιχθέντες οἱ οὐρανοί. As has been noted,[824] the opening of the heavens is a familiar motif in Jewish apocalyptic literature and it signals a moment of dramatic divine disclosure. Thus the interaction between the heavenly and earthly realms signals the importance of the revelatory events that take place at the tomb. Mara sees this passage as part of the intentional transition the author makes to move this narrative back to events in the synoptic accounts. 'As for the new "opening of the skies" and the descent of new a person, it is the means by which our author returns to Synoptic in order to endorse the testimony of the women, by confirming it by that of this constituted commission.'[825] It is noted in BDF that the construction φαίνονται in conjunction with the following participles is common in classical Greek.[826]

**11.44c**  καὶ ἄ̅ν̅ο̅ς̅ τις κατελθὼν καὶ εἰσελθὼν εἰς τὸ μνῆμα. This clause sets up the necessary presence of the single man from heaven, who will encounter the women when they enter the tomb in *Gos. Pet.* 13.55–56. In the later context this figure, following Markan terminology will be described as a νεανίσκος (Mk 16.5). Here, however, the term employed to describe this single figure is ἄνθρωπος. This is different to the choice of terminology in *Gos. Pet.* 9.36, where the two heavenly figures are described as ἄνδρας. The reason for this choice of terms, and the variation between usage is not obvious. In the first visionary scene (*Gos. Pet.* 9.36–37) the narrative most closely follows the Matthean account (Matt 28.2–3), but the author rejects Matthew's description of the heavenly figure as an ἄγγελος, instead describing the now pair of characters as ἄνδρας. Similarly, here, in relating the preparatory details for a later scene which will follow the Markan account, the author at the point eschews the terminology of the second evangelist, νεανίσκος. (although it will be taken up later) and replaces it again with more androcentric language, ἄνθρωπος. Perhaps the reason is to convey the faulty perceptions of the onlookers, rather than to give the privileged perspective of the readers.

---

[824] See the comments on *Gos. Pet.* 9.36.

[825] 'Quant à la nouvelle «ouverture des cieux» et à la descente d'un nouveau personnage, c'est la manière de notre auteur pour revenir aux Synoptiques et pour avaliser le témoignage des femmes, en le confirmant par celui de la commission constituée.' Mara, *Évangile de Pierre*, 191.

[826] BDF §441.3.

The use of the *nomen sacrum* $\overline{\alpha\nu o\varsigma}$ for ἄνθρωπος is interesting in that it applies a form usually reserved for some kind of divine epithet.[827] While it may be possible to argue that the form is being employed since the 'man' in question is a heavenly being, such an explanation is unnecessary since *nomina sacra* are not infrequently used in contexts where the name is not applied to a hallowed being.[828] In fact, already in the Akhmîm text the scribe has used the form $\overline{\alpha\nu\omega\nu}$, in the phrase οὗτος δὲ σωτὴρ γενόμενος τῶν $\overline{\alpha\nu\omega\nu}$ (*Gos. Pet.* 4.13c), to denote humans saved by the the Lord.[829]

Regardless of what exactly the use of this *nomen sacrum* connotes for the author in this context, and here it may be little more than an abbreviation, the figure who descends from heaven on this occasion is certainly to be thought of by the audience as being more than a mere human. The supernatural phenomenon of polymorphic beings descending from and re-ascending to the heavenly realm in the previous scene has created the expectation that this is no mere man.[830] The author's goal is not that of harmonizing the canonical accounts that describe either one (so Matthew and Mark) or two figures (so Luke and John). Instead, the two separate scenes are an important feature of the way the author shapes his narrative. Describing the the different number of figures present in each epiphany of heavenly beings, Vaganay states, 'It is because two people were necessary to constitute the escort of Christ, while only one is enough, as in Mark, to receive the holy women.'[831] Without any explanation given, this newly arrived figure steps into the empty tomb for what at this stage of the story appears to be no apparent purpose. Thus, this final appearance of a heavenly being provides the impetus for the witnesses to hastily depart to Pilate, as well as preparing for the later scene where the women will converse with this man from heaven.

---

[827] Hurtado, 'The Origin of the *Nomina Sacra*: A Proposal', 655–673, in particular see the concluding remarks 671–673.

[828] Tucket notes the amusing example in *G.Thom.* 28, 'My soul became afflicted for the sons of men…', where the usage is anything but sacred. Tuckett, '"Nomina Sacra": Yes and No?', 450.

[829] See the discussion of *Gos. Pet.* 4.13c in this commentary.

[830] Vaganay, *L'Évangile de Pierre*, 304–305.

[831] C'est uniquement parce que deux personages étaient nécessaire pour constituer l'escorte du Christ, tandis qu'un seul suffit, comme dans Marc, à recevoir les saintes femmes. Vaganay, *L'Évangile de Pierre*, 305.

**11.45a** ταῦτα ἰδόντες οἱ περὶ τὸν κεντυρίωνα νυκτὸς
ἔσπευσαν πρὸς Πειλᾶτον. According to the omniscient narrator
the third vision, the appearance of the one man from heaven, is the
event which is determinative in bringing the onlookers' discussion to a
close and causing them to swiftly report what has transpired to Pilate.
The demonstrative pronoun is best understood as referring to what
has just been seen in the third manifestation of heavenly figures and
not as a reference to the sequence of three visions. The reason for
this conclusion is that it is this final epiphanic event that motivates
the onlookers to proceed immediately to Pilate, whereas the previous
events had only led to a discussion about the appropriate course of
action. Thus, the third appearance precipitates the speedy resolution to
go without any further delay to the Roman prefect. Among those who
witness these happenings the centurion is seen by the narrator as the
central figure, and the others involved are only described by reference
to the central character, οἱ περὶ τὸν κεντυρίωνα.

Again, as is his wont,[832] the author provides a temporal indicator.
The genitive form νυκτός indicates time during which an event occurs.[833]
There is, however, a question concerning whether νυκτός qualifies the
clause οἱ περὶ τὸν κεντυρίωνα, 'those who were with the centurion during the night', or the aorist verb ἔσπευσαν, 'they swiftly went by night'.
Grammatically, either is possible. In favour of the second alternative is
the use of νυκτός in Matt 28.13, οἱ μαθηταὶ αὐτοῦ νυκτὸς ἐλθόντες 'his
disciples came during the night'. Since Matt 28.13 is part of the guard-
at-the-tomb story, it might be the basis for the use of νυκτός at this
point in the Akhmîm codex. Neither the fact that the Matthean use of
νυκτός referred to the disciples, nor the observation that this tradition
has already been used in the Akhmîm narrative (*Gos. Pet.* 8.30), militate against this detail being the basis for the temporal frame adopted
here.[834] In favour of reading νυκτός as qualifing οἱ περὶ τὸν κεντυρίωνα,

---

[832] Other places where temporal references are provided include: the Sabbath drawing on' (*Gos. Pet.* 2.5); a reference to 'midday' (*Gos. Pet.* 5.15); the phrase 'at the same
hour' (*Gos. Pet.* 5.20); 'the ninth hour' (*Gos. Pet.* 6.22); 'until the Sabbath' (*Gos. Pet.*
7.27); 'morning of the Sabbath' (*Gos. Pet.* 9.34); 'Lord's day' (*Gos. Pet.* 9.35); 'dawn
of the Lord's day' (*Gos. Pet.* 9.50); 'the last day of the unleavened bread' (*Gos. Pet.*
14.58).

[833] BDF §186.2; Moule, *An Idiom-Book of New Testament Greek*, 39.

[834] Vaganay argues that 'Ce n'est pas une allusion à Mt., XXVIII, 13 (contre von
Schubert, p. 113); c'est une conséquence de la donnée chronologique insinuée par
l'auteur touchant la résurrection (cf. v. 35).' Vaganay, *L'Évangile de Pierre*, 310. How-

it can be noted that in Matt 14.25 (par. Mk 6.28), the temporal genitive qualifies the preceding nominative clause and not the following verb τετάρτῃ δὲ φυλακῇ τῆς νυκτὸς ἦλθεν, 'during the fourth watch of the night, he came'. Although this is possible, the second possibility mentioned above remains the preferred option since the dawn will be noted at *Gos. Pet.* 12.50, and the emphasis appears to fall upon the fact that the events are so momentous that it was considered to be imperative to wake Pilate immediately.

**11.45b** ἀφέντες τὸν τάφον ὂν ἐφύλασσον. Formally, this detail appears to be redundant in the narrative. Its main purpose appears to be emphatic, in that it highlights the fact that the tomb is now left unguarded since the whole party, presumably because of fear, departs from the burial place. Consequently the Roman troops decided to quit the site and report to Pilate. This note is also preparatory to the events that will transpire in vv. 50–57, since it allows the women unhindered access to the tomb. Vaganay suggests that there is one further factor in the inclusion of this detail, namely that for the final time the author wished to stress the fact that up until this point the tomb had been securely guarded. 'Until this moment the guards have supervised the tomb: an idea particularly important to our evangelist and one which he has repeated on every occasion possible (cf. vv. 30, 31, 33, 35, 38).'[835]

**11.45c** καὶ ἐξηγήσαντο πάντα ἅπερ εἶδον. In the Matthean account the report is made by those guarding the tomb to the the Jewish authorities, ἀπήγγειλαν τοῖς ἀρχιερεῦσιν ἅπαντα τὰ γενόμενα (Matt 28.11). Although there are broad similarities in that the appointed guards leave the tomb to make a report of events, the dissimilarities are perhaps even more striking. In the Matthean account the report is made to a different authority, with Pilate being intentionally left out of the deliberations. This is because in the first gospel the report appears to be made to the Jewish authorities out of fear that Pilate will find the soldiers guilty of some dereliction of duty. Furthermore, an almost entirely different vocabulary is employed to describe this detail.

---

ever, Vaganay sets an unnecessary exclusive dichotomy between allusion and chronological cosequence. Both could be contributory factors at this point.

[835] Vaganay, *L'Évangile de Pierre*, 310.

As a partial point of similarity, Luz feels that already in the Matthean account the narrative is shaped in such a way as to blacken the Jewish leaders.

> That the Roman soldiers go to the chief priests rather than to Pilate is not surprising for the readers, because Pilate had put the guards under their authority. It is at any rate clear to them from the passion narrative that it is they who are the actual actors of evil rather than Pilate, who was involved only as a secondary actor.[836]

In both the Matthean narrative and the Akhmîm account the contents of the report made by the guards is not recounted. Hagner, commenting on the Matthean phrase ἄπαντα τὰ γενόμενα, notes that it 'raises the question of how much they had in fact witnessed before they lapsed into unconsciousness.'[837] Most commentators who have discussed this issue have concluded that the events recollected included the earthquake, the descent and appearance of the angel, and the rolling away of the stone.[838] Since the onlookers remained conscious in the account contained in the Akhmîm narrative, there is no reason to doubt that the notice of the report is intended to convey to the audience anything less than the expectation of full disclosure of the events to Pilate. In fact, the change in terminology from τὰ γενόμενα to εἶδον, places more emphasis on the observers as eye-witnesses.

**11.45d** ἀγωνιῶντες μεγάλως καὶ λέγοντες· ἀληθῶς υἱὸς ἦν ϑυ. While the content of the report is not related to the audience, the author does portray both the demeanour of those who had come from the tomb and the implication they themselves drew from the events they had just witnessed. At this point the Jewish elders who were part of the group of witnesses at the tomb appear to have disappeared from the narrative, and the report is presented as an intra-Roman affair with the centurion and legionaries speaking directly to Pilate. Thus, at the beginning of this verse, the expression οἱ περὶ τὸν κεντυρίωνα 'those who were with the centurion' (*Gos. Pet.* 11.45a), is probably meant to indicate a separation of the Roman forces from the Jewish elders.

The disposition of those conveying the report is described as being ἀγωνιῶντες μεγάλως, 'greatly troubled'. In the Matthean account the

---

[836] Luz, *Matthew 21–28*, 609–610.
[837] Hagner, *Matthew 14–28*, 876.
[838] Nolland, *The Gospel of Matthew*, 1255; Hagner, *Matthew 14–28*, 876.

emotional turmoil of the guards takes place as the miraculous events actually occur, and by the time the soldiers present their report they are apparently composed (Matt 28.4, 11–15). In the Akhmîm text the sequence of emotions is reversed. At the tomb the soldiers are presented as passive observers, here they are depicted as agitated. This change of disposition is not related to appearing before Pilate, but is a consequence of their exposure to the vitually incomprehensible events they have just witnessed. The result is that they have become disquited in their senses, but perhaps not to the degree that Matthew reports the impact on the guards while at they tomb, where they were rendered as 'dead men' (Matt 28.4).[839]

Furthermore, the author reports, through direct speech, the implication that the guards draw from the events they have recently observed. They make the christologically significant declaration ἀληθῶς υἱὸς ἦν $\overline{θυ}$ 'truly this was God's son'. This is a close, but not exact, parallel to the confession made by the centurion at the cross in the canonical accounts (Matt 27.54//Mk 15.39). The wording in the Akhmîm text is closer to the Matthean version ἀληθῶς θεοῦ υἱὸς ἦν οὗτος, rather than the Markan form (ἀληθῶς οὗτος ὁ ἄνθρωπος υἱὸς θεοῦ ἦν) since it follows the first gospel in omits the words ὁ ἄνθρωπος from Mark. Also in both Matthew and the Akhmîm account this declaration is introduced by the participle λέγοντες, whereas Mark employs the aorist form εἶπεν. Again it can be concluded that at this point the author is drawing upon the version of this tradition as it occurs in the first gospel. Of more significance is the redactional decision to remove this declaration from the context where it is uttered at the moment of Jesus' death and to locate after the resurrection. This appears to result in a more triumphalistic Christology than that intended by Mark, through his placement of the confession at what may appear to those without the eyes of faith to be the nadir of belief. Tuckett brings out the radical, even discordant, nature of Mark's Christology. Describing this authorial intention, Tuckett states that Mark 'writes his story to show what he regards as the true significance of words that can be spoken. Jesus is the Christ, the Son of God. But the nature of kingship, sonship and of divinity, are all given a stark new meaning by Mark's story,

---

[839] Davies and Allison comment on the wider use of the motif of ineffectual guards in Jewish and Christian literature, where they have been rendered insensible by an encounter with the divine. Davies and Allison, *The Gospel According to Saint Matthew*, vol. III, 666.

especially by his account of Jesus' death on the cross.'[840] While such an articulation of Christology may have been pedagogically and pastorally attuned to the needs of the Markan community in its own liminal situation,[841] it was not an understanding that suited the purposes of the author of the *Gospel of Peter*. Nor is there any indication that in the present context that the declaration of Jesus as 'son of God' was to be understood as a subversion of Imperial cultic ideology, with the centurion confessing something of Jesus that a loyal and pious Roman citizen should only attribute to the emperor.

**11.46a** ἀποκριθεὶς ὁ Πειλᾶτος ἔφη· ἐγὼ καθαρεύω τοῦ αἵματος τοῦ υἱοῦ τοῦ θεοῦ. Pilate does not question the usage of the title 'son of God' by the centurion, instead he appropriates it in his own declaration of innocence. No comment is offered concerning the veracity of the report given by the soldiers. An unsurprised Pilate has placed on his lips a declaration of his own blameworthiness. This is something the narrator has been doing on Pilate's behalf throughout this passion account. While one cannot be sure whether the Akhmîm account contained in its now no longer extant section the infamous blood-guilt cry of the people (Matt 27.25), this verse appear to be such an intentional foil to that tradition. Even if it did not explicitly feature in this narrative, it may well have been featuring in the author's thinking. The other Matthean tradition that may be the counterpart of Pilate's innocence is the self-declaration by Judas of his own guilt, ἥμαρτον παραδοὺς αἷμα ἀθῷον, 'I have sinned by betraying innocent blood' (Matt 27.4).

The words of Pilate at this point parallel the statement made by the Roman prefect in Matt 27.24, ἀθῷός εἰμι ἀπὸ τοῦ αἵματος τούτου. Swete is perhaps correct in his surmise that in 'Peter the words possibly did not accompany the symbolic washing, but were reserved for this later juncture.'[842] That the narrative contained Pilate's hand-washing is perhaps the most secure conjecture concerning the contents of the lost portion of the text.[843] The other possibility besides Swete's conjecture that the saying had been 'reserved', is that it had been repeated making

[840] Tuckett, *Christology and the New Testament*, 116.
[841] See the comments of Marcus on Mark as a persecuted group. J. Marcus, *Mark 1–8* AB 27 (New York: Doubleday, 2000) 28–29.
[842] Swete, *The Akhmîm Fragment of the Apocryphal Gospel of St Peter*, 20.
[843] See the discussion of *Gos. Pet.* 1.1.

an *inclusio* in the text. Either way, again the accent falls on the innocence of Pilate. Although the version of the saying in the *Gospel of Peter*
is close to the Matthean narrative there are changes. Vaganay suggests
that part of the motivation may have been to remove a problematic
semitic construction. 'The author replaces the Hebrew turn of phrase
ἀθῷός ἀπό by the Classical καθαρεύω, unknown by both the LXX and
the NT.'[844] Moreover, the reference to Jesus in the Matthean scene by
the use of the demonstrative τούτου, is replaced by the christologically
rich title τοῦ υἱοῦ τοῦ θεοῦ. Thus Pilate not only confesses his own
innocence, but that innocence is predicated on his non-involvement
in the murder of the one now known to be the son of God. For Mara,
Pilate's use of the title with the article, in contradistinction to the way
it was used in the previous verse, is theologically significant. She states,
'the definite article before υἱός indicates that he is the Son of God the
Father.'[845] While Mara may be correct that for the author the title was
loaded with the understanding of filial relationship with the Father,
it is questionable whether this is to be derived by the presence of the
definite article in this v. 46. Thus the absence of the definite article
in v. 46, notwithstanding Mara's suggested distinction between non-
articular and articular use in the fourth gospel (Jn 1.34, 49; *contra* Jn
11.27), is probably of no great significance.[846]

**11.46b**  ἡμῖν δὲ τοῦτο ἔδοξεν. Pilate's concluding remark is enigmatic. Brown, who also adopts the emendation ὑμῖν for the pronoun
ἡμῖν, glosses the translation as 'but it was to you that this appeared (the
thing to do).'[847] Thus, according to Brown, Pilate's declaration is used
by the author as a further opportunity to emphasize that the blame
rests squarely upon the Jewish authorities, and that he is not complicit in their guilt. 'Pilate's reaction…points out that they [the Jewish
authorities] were the ones primarily responsible for death ("blood")
of him whose standing they now grudgingly acknowledge.'[848] Vaganay
makes a similar suggestion, arguing that the narrative context did not
make it possible for the author to preserve the Matthean ending to
the declaration of innocence, ὑμεῖς ὄψεσθε (Matt 27.24). Therefore, the

---

[844] Vaganay, *L'Évangile de Pierre*, 311.
[845] Mara, *Évangile de Pierre*, 195.
[846] Mara, *Évangile de Pierre*, 195.
[847] Brown, *The Death of the Messiah*, vol. 2, 1320.
[848] Brown, *The Death of the Messiah*, vol. 2, 1299.

tradition is rewritten at this point and 'instead of interrogating the Jews, the Roman magistrate brings to mind their judgment which they carried out.'[849]

There are a number of difficulties with either of these interpretations. First, the Jewish leaders are not explicitly present in this scene at this point. It is not until the following verse that their entrance is announced εἶτα προσελθόντες πάντες, 'Then they all came...' (Gos. Pet. 11.47).[850] Second, the interpretations of Vaganay and Brown require both the additional gloss and the proposed conjectural emendation to be made, in order to produce the meaning they propose. However, these difficulties can be avoided if the comment ἡμῖν δὲ τοῦτο ἔδοξεν is seen as an intra-Roman statement whereby Pilate addresses his soldiers. The phrase 'and thus it appeared to us' is not necessarily Pilate speaking cohortatively of his innocence, assuming an appeal for solidarity in the sense that he would be articulating his desire for the soldiers support of his declaration of guiltlessness. Rather, it can be understood as proclaiming the shared Christological recognition, that 'the Lord' is now understood by both Pilate and his troops to be 'the Son of God.' Thus, the narrative implies that the Romans are willing to publicly confess the very insight which Jewish authorities are attempting to covertly suppress.

**11.47a  εἶτα προσελθόντες πάντες.** At this juncture in the story a transition occurs with the entrance of the figures representing the interests of the Jewish leadership. That the unnamed characters are to be understood as Jewish leadership figures is not only required by consideration of the immediate context, but also because of the links with Gos. Pet. 8.28–29, where the tripartite group of scribes, Pharisees and elders fear the reaction of the people, and the elders come to Pilate to gain support in taking preventative measures to suppress a popular uprising against the leadership. Again, as will become apparent, motivated by fear of the people (Gos. Pet. 11.48) the Jewish authorities approach Pilate to seek protection. The adverb εἶτα is used to mark a temporal sequence in the narrative, it signals the point in time at which this new development occurs in relation to the previous chain

---

[849] Vaganay, L'Évangile de Pierre, 311.

[850] Curiously, Vaganay acknowledges this in his comments on Gos. Pet. 11.47, but does not see this as marking a tension with his interpretation in this verse. Vaganay, L'Évangile de Pierre, 312.

of events being described.⁸⁵¹ Vaganay argues that the adjective πάντες signifies that the group comprised not only of the guards, but now prominent Jewish leaders have arrived on the scene.⁸⁵² While this is true, it is perhaps not the primary purpose of πάντες to mark the group's mixed composition of soldiers and Jewish leaders; rather the magnitude of the perceived problem require a mass delegation be made to Pilate.

**11.47b ἐδέοντο αὐτοῦ καὶ παρεκάλουν κελεῦσαι τῷ κεντυρίωνι καὶ τοῖς στρατιώταις μηδὲν εἰπεῖν ἃ εἶδον.** In the Matthean account the guards are embroiled in the plans to conceal the truth, and Pilate has no part to play in the decision making process. The soldiers are portrayed as being corrupt, taking money to suppress the truth (Matt 28.11–15). All of these elements are absent from the version of events outlined in *Gos. Pet.* 11.47–49. Instead a meeting between Pilate and the leadership takes place in which the soldiers are discussed, but offer no input. The degree of subservience exhibited during this second visit appears to be intensified. At the first meeting the elders' verbal approach is described as δεόμενοι αὐτοῦ καὶ λέγοντες (*Gos. Pet.* 8.29). Here the combination of δέομαι and παρακαλέω creates a heighten sense of imploring Pilate to rescue them from an otherwise untenable situation. The use of the imperfect ἐδέοντο here, appears to be used with the same force as the present participle δεόμενοι in *Gos. Pet.* 8.29. The imperfective aspect of both verbs may be employed to emphasize the 'insider' perspective that the narrator is providing to his audience. Alternatively, the variation may simply reflect common Greek usage.⁸⁵³

Having described the demeanour adopted in approaching Pilate, the author next communicates the content of their request, specifically that the soldiers who observed the events at the tomb should be

---

⁸⁵¹ This temporal meaning is noted in the EDNT, vol. 1, 402. '(a) Temporal: *then, next* (Mark 4:17; 8:25; Luke 8.12; John 13:5; 19:27; 20:27; Jas 1:15).'

⁸⁵² Vaganay, *L'Évangile de Pierre*, 312.

⁸⁵³ The preference for the imperfect with verbs of request or demand is noted in BDF §328. 'Certain verbs by virtue of their special meaning prefer to some extent a form which denotes incomplete action. If an action is complete in itself, but the achievement of a second action, towards which the first points, is to be resented as unaccomplished or still outside the scope of the assertion, then the first takes the imperfect.' More succinctly Vaganay states, 'l'imparfait remplace souvent l'aoriste avec les verbes de demande.' Vaganay, *L'Évangile de Pierre*, 312.

commanded not to communicate what happened. Thus, as is also the case in Matthew's account, an explanation is provided to answer the potential rejection of Christian claims concerning the veracity of the resurrection as witnessed by neutral onlookers. In Matthew it is the result of the bribery and corruption of the guards, here it is due to the official suppression of the truth, instigated by the Jewish leadership. The account provided by Origen is obviously dependent on Matthew, and does not draw upon the form of the tradition contained in the Akhmîm text, since it recalls that the guards were to actively circulate the story of the theft of the body, and that they received payment for their complicity with the Jewish leaders. Thus, responding to Celsus, Origen asserts that certain people (understood to be the Jewish leaders) persuaded the soldiers to propagate the false story of body-snatching by the disciples.

> Their action was akin to that of those individuals who won over those soldiers of the guard at the tomb who were eyewitnesses of the resurrection from the dead, and reported it, and persuaded them by the giving of money and saying to them: 'Say that his disciples stole him at night while we slept. And if this come to the governor's ears we will persuade him and rid you of fear. (Origen, *Contra Celsum*, 1.51)[854]

Here, the soldiers remain unimpeachable, they are not involved in the subterfuge of the Jewish leadership and consequently the veracity of their account of the events at the tomb and Christological confession they made become, for the author's readers, pristine insights into the significance of what has transpired. By contrast, the narrative casts the Jewish leaders as only interested in their own self-preservation. This is noted by Vaganay when he observes, 'the Jewish leaders implore Pilate to silence the guard and to support their request, which they have put forward for the most serious personal reasons.'[855]

**11.48a** συμφέρει γάρ, φασίν, ἡμῖν ὀφλῆσαι μεγίστην ἁμαρτίαν ἔμπροσθεν τοῦ θεοῦ. Although context and content differ, nonetheless, there are here resonances with the declaration of Caiaphas, 'that it is better for one man to die...' (Jn 11.50a). In terms of overlapping

---

[854] See Chadwick, *Origen: Contra Celsum*, 48.
[855] Vaganay, *L'Évangile de Pierre*, 312–313.

vocabulary in the first half of Jn 11.50 and *Gos. Pet.* 11.48 the term συμφέρει is shared, and in the second half of each of these verses the identical form τοῦ λαοῦ is present. While the latter in particular is not unusual terminology, it needs also to be remembered that both verses present Jewish authority figures giving counsel to take the expedient course of action at the cost of justice or truth. Obviously in no way can *Gos. Pet.* 11.48 be considered a citation of Jn 11.50, however, the parallels that do exist may suggest that the Akhmîm narrative has been informed at some level by the Johannine account of the speech of Caiaphas to the Sanhedrian. This observation aligns with the manner in which it has been observed that the author of this text weaves together stories, language and allusions from the canonical accounts to produce his own narrative.

Swete baulks at accepting the natural reading of this verse. He expostulates, 'But Peter can hardly mean to charge the Jews with the impiety of regarding a violent death as a greater evil than the extreme displeasure of God.'[856] While at a historical level Swete is correct that a pious first century Jew would have considered God's displeasure as a fate worse than a violent death, this text is not concerned with presenting historical reality. It is a literary invention that seeks to cast the Jewish authorities in the worst light possible, and it appears that what Swete declares as the impossible reading of the text is, in fact, precisely what the author intended his audience to understand. Namely that the Jewish leaders had become so perverted in their understanding of the divine purpose, that they were willing to abandon any piety or reverence towards God in order to maintain their status in the religious institution. As Robinson comments at this point,

> The hatred of the writer to the Jews, which stands in striking contrast to the just and measured terms of our Evangelists, is nowhere more marked than in the keen satire of this passage. Pilate once more is freed as far as possible from blame.[857]

While it is not necessary to concur with Robinson that the canonical accounts offer a 'just and measured' portrayal of the Jews, it is certainly the case that in the Akhmîm narrative the Jews are depicted in a manner that is less just and less measured than that of the canonical

---

[856] Swete, *The Akhmîm Fragment of the Apocryphal Gospel of St Peter*, 21.
[857] Robinson & James, *The Gospel according to Peter and the Revelation of Peter*, 27–28.

gospels. Thus the narrative again appears to reflect a later period in Church history when there had been an intensification of anti-Jewish sentiments as the Christian movement flourished in gentile circles. Yet even within the Akhmîm account there is a significant differentiation at this point between the Jewish leadership and the Jewish people. The former group fears the response of the latter, who are anticipated as responding violently if they become aware of the fact that their leaders have crucified God's now vindicated son.

Although not explicitly stated in the narrative, the great sin (μεγίστην ἁμαρτίαν) is the suppression of the truth of the resurrection as it is understood by the early Christians. This entails not only silencing those who could attest the physical reality of the event, but more significantly it is viewed as an attempt to interfere with the divine and revelation, namely that the resurrection attests that Jesus is the Son of God. Mara also understands the 'sin' in the following manner: 'This sin is not only the execution of Jesus, but the uninterrupted opposition to the salvific value of the Pascal event.'[858] However, the sin which the leaders are determined to commit is depicted not as a crime against those whose potential faith is thwarted, but as an offence involving God. Perhaps the expression ἔμπροσθεν τοῦ θεοῦ describes not so much a sin against God, but the fact that they acknowledge their covert plan will be judged by God alone and not by the people as a whole.

**11.48b** καὶ μὴ ἐμπεσεῖν εἰς χεῖρας τοῦ λαοῦ τῶν Ἰουδαίων καὶ λιθασθῆναι. While the first half of the verse depicts the guilt that the leaders are willing to accrue, the second half outlines the fate they hope to avoid through their planned deception. The phrase 'to fall into the hand of...' is proverbial in the Old Testament for times of tribulation, affliction or judgment. Thus the sense of being delivered or falling into the hands of ones adversaries results in utter destruction (cf. Zech 11.6). The fate of falling into the hand of the Lord is, however, not necessarily quite as universally a metaphor for destruction.[859] In fact David can opt for the fate of being judged by God ('let me now

---

[858] Mara, Évangile de Pierre, 195.

[859] McCarter argues that 'the use of the expression "the hand of Yahweh,"...is a standard biblical way of referring to plague (1 Sam 5:6; etc.), with extensive Near Eastern parallels.' P. Kyle McCarter, II Samuel, Anchor Bible 9 (New York: Doubleday, 1984) 511. This contrasts with the view of Hertzberg that the expression is ambiguous and could refer to any of the three punishments, especially the first and third. H.W. Hertzberg, I & II Samuel, OTL (London: SCM, 1964) 413.

fall into the hands of the Lord') rather than men in relation to his sin concerning the census, because he appreciates that God's character is merciful whereas human adversaries are not (2 Sam 24.14//1 Chron 21.13, but cf. Heb 10.31). In fact there is a striking thematic reversal of attitude when one considers David's action in contrast to that exhibited by the Jewish leadership. Commenting on the Davidic response to the choice of one of three devastating punishments, Japhet observes, '[t]he words of David do full justice to his image as manifested throughout the book of Samuel: a man who holds direct discourse with God, and whose faith is the motivating force of his personality.'[860] As represented in the LXX there are noticeable overlaps in language between the account of David's decision and the reasoning of the leadership party in this context.

καὶ εἶπεν Δαυιδ πρὸς Γαδ στενά μοι πάντοθεν σφόδρα ἐστίν ἐμπεσοῦμαι δὴ ἐν χειρὶ κυρίου ὅτι πολλοὶ οἱ οἰκτιρμοὶ αὐτοῦ σφόδρα εἰς δὲ χεῖρας ἀνθρώπου οὐ μὴ ἐμπέσω καὶ ἐξελέξατο ἑαυτῷ Δαυιδ τὸν θάνατον (LXX 2 Sam 24.14)

While it must be noted that the divergences outweigh the similarities, and only the terms ἐμπίπτω and χείρ are shared, the whole thought of falling into the hands of man or God produces significant commonality of thought. Although it is highly unlikely that the author had this passage in mind, sentiments like this and wider reflections from the second temple period on the nature of God may, in part, shape the text at this point.

The expression ὁ λαὸς τῶν Ἰουδαίων is unusual in the mouths of fellow Jews. Consequently Vaganay states in relation to this phrase that 'ὁ λαὸς τῶν Ἰουδαίων is unknown on the lips of notable Jews;' however he continues by explaining this expression in the following manner, 'it is only a pleonasm, one that could not be more shocking.'[861] While he is correct about the rarity of the phrase on Jewish lips, his explanation that it is simply a pleonasm appears unconvincing. Instead, the intention appears to create some distance between the leaders and the wider populace by representing the groups as discrete entities. This allows the portrayal of self-interested hierarchical élite in contrast to the

---

[860] S. Japhet, *I & II Chronicles*, OTL (Louisville, Kentucky: Westminster/John Knox Press, 1993) 382.

[861] Vaganay , *L'Évangile de Pierre*, 313.

general mass of Jews who are equally deceived, but perhaps not culpable to the same degree as the rulers. The narrative finally clarifies what 'falling into the hands of the Jewish people' will involve for the leaders. The consecutive infinitive clause καὶ λιθασθῆναι, reflects the common Jewish method of execution, stoning. In Acts 5.26, the temple officers collect the apostle for questioning by the leaders. The light-handed approach they adopt is said to be out of fear of mob violence which could lead to stoning, ἐφοβοῦντο γὰρ τὸν λαὸν μὴ λιθασθῶσιν (Acts 5.26).

**11.49** ἐκέλευσεν οὖν ὁ Πειλᾶτος τῷ κεντυρίωνι καὶ τοῖς στρατιώταις μηδὲν εἰπεῖν. In the Matthean account the decision to say nothing is made by the bribed guards alone (Matt 28.14–15). Throughout the Akhmîm account, leaders play a much more prominent role. Thus in a similar manner to the Jewish leaders planning to deceive the populace, Pilate decides for his now voiceless soldiers that they must keep silence. This is the most negative action that Pilate takes in the extant portion of the narrative. Vaganay notes the contrast this creates with the Matthean narrative, since here Pilate alone is responsible for the silence imposed on the soldiers.[862] Commentators have tried to account for Pilate's decision at this point in different ways. Mara suggests that it is due to the vacillation of Pilate as he is both the supreme authority, but allows himself to become an instrument for the machinations of others.[863] Alternatively, Vaganay suggests that Pilate takes the politically expedient course to protect against a popular uprising.[864] Both of these explanations make the mistake of trying to account for the description of Pilate's actions as though they were historical. It needs to be remembered that the characterization of Pilate and this scene are literary creations of the author of the text. There is, however, one historical reality which must be explained, namely the fact that the 'truth' of the resurrection was not accepted by the majority of the Jewish people. Instead an account of body-snatching by the disciples became the way that the empty tomb was explained by those who did not accept the Christian message. The author does the best he can to explain why the story of the resurrection never emerged in

---

[862] Vaganay, *L'Évangile de Pierre*, 314.
[863] Mara, *Évangile de Pierre*, 196.
[864] Vaganay, *L'Évangile de Pierre*, 314.

a more widespread manner despite the array of witnesses, and yet at the same time he seeks to exonerate Pilate. These competing interests, at a literary level, are solved by a Prefect who both confesses that the resurrection attests that Jesus is the Son of God, but at the same time in this moment of unaccountable frailty acquiesces to the request of the Jewish authorities and becomes a subservient figure. There is no attempt to resolve this tension. The author offers no explanation of political or emotional factors that led to this course of action, and to try to insert such factors into the text is mere speculation.

In text critical note 12, the case has already been made that the reading of the manuscript τῶν κεντυρίων is both grammatically impossible and, if the dative plural were correct, it would not correspond to the single centurion named in the narrative. For this reason the reading is emended to τῷ κεντυρίωνι. In clauses that use the verb κελεύω the typical construction has the verb 'foll. by the aor. inf., which indicates the action to be carried out; the person who receives the order is in the acc.'[865] Here the aorist infinite εἰπεῖν is given at the end of the sentence, but those receiving the command are placed in the dative case. The use of the dative case is, however, frequently attested with κελεύω, in place of εἰς + accusative.[866] The explicit combination of centurion and soldiers as recipients of this command ensures all witnesses to the events at the tomb are silenced. The Roman military figures are now given a direct order not to reveal what happened and the Jewish witnesses maintain silence out of fear of the populace.[867] With this complete media black-out on reporting the events that occurred, the author does not explain to his audience how he is able to relate this version of events. Is this simply the prerogative of an omniscient narrator, the product of divine revelation, the result of a breaking of silence by one of the observers, or do such questions rob this narrative of the impact it was intended to create for its audience?

---

[865] BDAG, 538.

[866] Again see BDAG, 538.

[867] Vaganay notes that it is easy to be drawn into the narratively constructed world of the *Gospel of Peter* and to forget that the official character of this meeting is so strikingly different from the Matthean account of an *ad hoc* meeting, where pecuniary reward sways decisions. Vaganay, *L'Évangile de Pierre*, 314.

## THE WOMEN'S DISCUSSION AS THEY JOURNEY
## TO THE TOMB (12.50–54)

50. ὀρθοῦ[1] δὲ τῆς κυριακῆς Μαριὰμ[2] ἡ Μαγδαλινὴ[3] μαθήτρια τοῦ κ̅υ̅[4] φοβουμένη διὰ τοὺς Ἰουδαίους, ἐπειδὴ ἐφλέγοντο ὑπὸ τῆς ὀργῆς, οὐκ ἐποίησεν ἐπὶ τῷ μνήματι τοῦ κ̅υ̅[5] ἃ εἰώθεσαν ποιεῖν αἱ γυναῖκες ἐπὶ τοῖς ἀποθνήσκουσι καὶ τοῖς ἀγαπωμένοις αὐταῖς. 51. λαβοῦσα μεθ' ἑαυτῆς τὰς φίλας ἦλθε ἐπὶ τὸ μνημεῖον ὅπου ἦν τεθείς. 52. καὶ ἐφοβοῦντο μὴ ἴδωσιν αὐτὰς οἱ Ἰουδαῖοι καὶ ἔλεγον· εἰ καὶ μὴ ἐν ἐκείνῃ τῇ ἡμέρᾳ ᾗ ἐσταυρώθη ἐδυνήθημεν κλαῦσαι καὶ κόψεσθαι,[6] καὶ νῦν ἐπὶ τοῦ μνήματος αὐτοῦ ποιήσωμε(ν)[7] ταῦτα. 53. τίς δὲ ἀποκυλίσει ἡμῖν καὶ τὸν λίθον τὸν τεθέντα ἐπὶ τῆς θύρας τοῦ μνημείου, ἵνα εἰσελθοῦσαι παρακαθεσθῶμεν αὐτῷ καὶ ποιήσωμεν τὰ ὀφιλόμενα;[8] 54. μέγας γὰρ ἦν ὁ λίθος, καὶ φοβούμεθα μή τις ἡμᾶς ἴδῃ. καὶ εἰ μὴ δυνάμεθα, κἂν ἐπὶ τῆς θύρας βάλωμεν ἃ φέρομεν εἰς μνημοσύνην αὐτοῦ, κλαύσομεν καὶ κοψόμεθα[9] ἕως ἔλθωμεν εἰς τὸν οἶκον ἡμῶν.

50. Now at dawn of the Lord's Day Mary Magdalene, a disciple of the Lord, being afraid because of the Jews, since they were inflamed by rage, had not done at the tomb of the Lord those things which women are accustomed to do over those who have died and for those who are loved by them. 51. Taking the friends with her, she went to the tomb were he had been laid. 52. And they were afraid the Jews might see them and they were saying, 'Since we were not able on the day on which he was crucified to weep and to wail, even now at his tomb let us do these things. 53. But who will roll away for us also the stone that has been placed at the door of the tomb that when we have gone in we might sit beside him and do the things that are necessary. 54. For the stone was great, and we are afraid lest somebody sees us. And if we are not able, let us place at the door what we are bringing for his memorial, and we shall weep and wail until we return to our house.'

### Text Critical Notes

1. An orthographical error is present here with the manuscript reading ὀρθοῦ, as given above, instead of the standard spelling ὄρθρου. While the adjective ὀρθός is a common word in extant Greek

literature,[868] three factors tell against it being the correct reading here. First, the form ὀρθοῦ is either a masculine or neuter genitive singular adjective, and it is problematic that it occurs here either in an unsubstantivized form, or without a noun in agreement. Second, the meaning of ὀρθός, 'straight, upright, correct',[869] does not make sense in this context. Third, and perhaps most significant, the term ὄρθρου occurs in the parallel account of the women's visit to the tomb in the gospel of Luke: τῇ δὲ μιᾷ τῶν σαββάτων ὄρθρου βαθέως ἐπὶ τὸ μνῆμα ἦλθον (Lk 24.1). Fitzmyer comments that the expression ὄρθρου βαθέως is 'the Lucan substitute for the Marcan λίαν πρωΐ... ἀνατείλαντος τοῦ ἡλίου'.[870]

2. Kraus and Nicklas note the presence of what appears to be an apostrophe in the manuscript after the name 'Mary'. In their notes on line sixteen of the *verso* of page four, they state, 'Ms with apostrophe: μαριαμ'.'[871] There is little doubt that the penstroke after the second mu in the name μαριαμ does have the hook-like appearance of an apostrophe. The function of this marking, if the penstroke is intentional, is uncertain. The possibility that this is simply an aberrant mark on the page should not be ruled out, especially given the standards exemplified by the scribe elsewhere in the production of this manuscript.

3. The spelling Μαγδαλινή that occurs here in place of the form Μαγδαληνή that occurs in modern lexicons should not be understood as an orthographical error, but rather seen as representing non-standardized spelling practices. Vaganay notes that this form is witnessed in a number of late manuscripts in the text of Jn 20.1 and Lk 24.10.[872] This appears to represent the widespread phenomenon of the flattening of distinctions between the pronunciation of vowels.[873] Caragounis, although generally wary of the use of the term 'itacism' to describe the change in pronunciation from Classical to Hellenistic Greek would, however, allow the use of the term in this case. He states, 'the so-called *itacism* explains only the confusion of

---

[868] LSJ, 1249.

[869] EDNT, vol. 2, 531.

[870] Fitzmyer, *The Gospel According to Luke X–XXIV*, 1544.

[871] Kraus und Nicklas, *Das Petrusevangelium und die Petrusapokalypse*, 44.

[872] Vaganay states, 'Μαγδαληνη, comme dans certains mss. tardifs de *Jn* XX, 1 de *Lc.*, XXIV, 10.' Vaganay, *L'Évangile de Pierre*, 319.

[873] BDF §22.

the i-sound vowels and diphthongs, although strictly, it should be used only of the η being pronounced in the same way as the ι.'[874]

4. This is the eighth time, out of eleven occurrences in the manuscript, that the scribe has used a *nomen sacrum* for the title κύριος as it occurs in its various cases. There are only two places in the text where the term is written in its full form, *Gos. Pet.* 3.8; 6.24. The term κύριος is one of 'the four earliest attested and most consistently rendered words' to be written using a *nomen sacrum*.[875]

5. The form κ̄ῡ, the *nomen sacrum* for the title κυρίου, occurs here for the second time in this verse.

6. A minor orthographical variation occurs here with the scribe writing κόψεσθαι, instead of the standard form κόψασθαι.[876] The cause of the error is easily explicable. The scribe has attached the present middle infinitive ending – εσθαι, to an aorist stem which in the middle infinitive requires the ending – ασθαι.[877]

7. Here, at the end of a line, the scribe writes ποιήσωμε without the final movable ν. This is a regular scribal practice in *koine* manuscripts.[878]

8. The orthographical variant ὀφιλόμενα occurs in place of the lexically correct form ὀφειλόμενα. Such a change is a classical reduction of the distinction in vowel sounds due to itacism. The confusion between ει and ι rightly falls into the category of itacism.[879]

9. An emendation to the co-ordinated future verbs κλαύσομεν καὶ κοψόμεθα has been proposed by Harnack.[880] Instead of the reading κλαύσωμεν καὶ κοψώμεθα, he suggests that these should be taken as subjunctives, in line with the following subjunctive form ἔλθωμεν. Although Harnack reserves this conjecture for his notes,[881] rather than printing it in the text, it has been adopted by Vaganay as the

---

[874] Caragounis, *The Development of Greek and the New Testament*, 500.

[875] Hurtado, 'The Origin of the *Nomina Sacra*: A Proposal', 655.

[876] Cf. Kraus und Nicklas, *Das Petrusevangelium und die Petrusapokalypse*, 46.

[877] For a convenient table of infinitive forms see S.M. Baugh, *A New Testament Greek Primer* (Phillipsburg, NJ.: Presbyterian and Reformed Publishing Company, 1995) 140; also Wallace, *Greek Grammar: Beyond the Basics*, 587–611.

[878] BDF §20.

[879] See note 3 above and the discussion in Caragounis, *The Development of Greek and the New Testament*, 500.

[880] Harnack, *Bruchstücke des Evangeliums und der Apokalypse des Petrus*, 12.

[881] The notes at the bottom of the page state, 'Fort. καὶ κλαύσωμεν καὶ κοψώμεθα.' Harnack, *Bruchstücke des Evangeliums und der Apokalypse des Petrus*, 12.

correct reading in the body of the text that he presents.[882] The reason Vaganay gives for adopting this reading is 'because it introduces into the sentence a certain regularity (cf. earlier: βάλωμεν).'[883] While it is undoubtedly correct that stylistically this alteration is grammatically preferable, this seems to attribute a level of regularity to the text which may in fact be foreign to it. Moreover, it seems to overlook the fact that the subjunctive and future forms could be used interchangeably in certain contexts in later Greek.[884] For this reason the reading preserved in the manuscript is far from being impossibly problematic, and thus should be retained without any emendation.

## COMMENTARY

**12.50a** ὄρθρου δὲ τῆς κυριακῆς Μαριὰμ ἡ Μαγδαλινὴ μαθήτρια τοῦ κυ. Two identifications are made here, one a temporal reference, the other the introduction of a new character. The author frequently gives indications of the time-frame of events in the narrative. This creates a sense of pace, makes the events appear more vivid, and the apparent ability to precisely locate what is reported gives the account a greater sense of reality. In the New Testament, the term ὄρθρος appears to be distinctive Lukan terminology. It occurs at Lk 24.1, the strongest parallel to *Gos. Pet.* 12.50; at Acts 5.21 reporting the apostles arriving early in the morning at Temple; and, the related adjective ὀρθριναί is found at Lk 24.22, where on the road to Emmaus the travellers recount the experience of the women at the tomb on the resurrection morning. In fact the only occurrence outside Lukan writings in what has become part of the canonical form of the New Testament is in the floating tradition of the *pericope adulterae*, where Jesus' arrival in the temple precincts is related, ὄρθρου δὲ πάλιν παρεγένετο εἰς τὸ ἱερὸν (Jn 8.2). This passage has many connections with Luke's gospel. It is found after Lk 21.38 in certain minuscule manuscripts ($f^{13}$),[885] and as Barrett notes specifically in regard to Jn 8.2 '[t]his verse contains several

---

[882] Vaganay, *L'Évangile de Pierre*, 324.

[883] Vaganay, *L'Évangile de Pierre*, 325.

[884] The variant readings at 1 Cor 15.49 and Heb 6.3 attest confusion over future indicative and aorist subjunctive forms. See Caragounis, *The Development of Greek and the New Testament*, 544–546.

[885] Metzger, *A Textual Commentary on the Greek New Testament*, 188–189.

points of contact with the Lucan writings.'[886] Thus, if the author of the *Gospel of Peter* is following the canonical accounts of the visit of the women to the tomb, as appears likely, then his narrative may have been influenced by the Lukan wording at this point.[887]

The term κυριακή is used here in the Akhmîm narrative for the second time. On the previous occasion it was used to denote the pre-dawn hours when the soldiers were guarding the tomb and the two men descended from heaven and led the third figure out of the sepulchre (*Gos. Pet.* 9.35). As was argued in that context,[888] κυριακή does not function as a specific reference to the resurrection day, but it has by this stage become a Christian technical term denoting the first day of the week.[889] Having related the events that transpired prior to dawn in *Gos. Pet.* 9.35–10.42, here the author, after the intervening account of the consultation with Pilate, begins to move the focus back to the tomb.

The manner in which Mary Magdalene is introduced suggests that she may not have previously featured in the narrative. Apart from her name, the audience is informed that she is 'a disciple of the Lord' μαθήτια τοῦ κυ, as though this was previously undisclosed knowledge. Debate has surrounded the question of the extent of the text prior to its mutilated mid-sentence commencement in the Akhmîm text. However, the fact that Mary Magdalene appears to be introduced here for the first time cannot be construed as evidence that the full extent of the narrative was only the passion account. In Matthew, Mark, and John, a Mary also called Magdalene, appears for the first time standing at the foot of the cross (Matt 27.56//Mk 15.40//Jn 19.25). Then in each of these canonical accounts she appears for the second time during the visit to the tomb (Matt 28.1//Mk 16.1//Jn 20.1), a scene which parallels *Gos. Pet.* 12.50–13.57. In fact, it is only in Luke's gospel that she makes an earlier appearance, when she is first introduced as the women from whom seven demons had been cast out, Μαρία ἡ καλουμένη Μαγδαληνή, ἀφ᾽ ἧς δαιμόνια ἑπτὰ ἐξεληλύθει (Lk 8.2).[890]

---

[886] Barrett, *The Gospel according to St John*, 492.

[887] Vaganay likewise judges that the Akhmîm text is drawing upon the third gospel at this point. 'Quant à l'expression ὄρθρου, qui se rencontre dans le passage parallèle de Luc (XXIV, 1).' Vaganay, *L'Évangile de Pierre*, 319.

[888] See the extended discussion in the comments on this term at 9.35a.

[889] Again, see the discussion in Bauckham, 'The Lord's Day', 229.

[890] In relation to the early introduction of Mary Magdalene in the Lukan account Fitzmyer comments, 'Introduced here [Lk 8.2], she foreshadows 23.49; 24.10, where

The name Μαριάμ was extremely common among Jewish women.[891] In her prosopographical study of Jewish names evidenced in the period 330 BCE–200 CE, Tal Ilan demonstrates that far fewer women's names are documented than those of males.[892] This is perhaps unsurprising when one considers the dominant patriarchal orientation of Jewish society in this period. What is more striking is the frequency with which the most common names occur. Ilan enumerates 317 named females in this period,[893] the ten most common names account for 245 of these individuals, or 77.29% (to 4 sig. figs.).[894] The most common name, Μαριάμ, is possessed by 80 of these 317 individuals, or 25.24% (to 4 sig. figs.).[895] So it is suggested by this sample of names that during this period just over one in every four women in Palestine was named Μαριάμ. Ilan's table of the ten most frequent names out of the sample of 317 females is reproduced here:[896]

Table 16. The ten most popular Jewish female names in the period 330 BCE–200 CE

| Ranking | Name | Number of occurrences |
|---------|------|----------------------|
| 1. | Miriam | 80 |
| 2. | Salome | 63 |
| 3. | Shelamzion | 25 |
| 4. | Martha | 20 |
| =5. | Joanna | 12 |
| =5. | Shipra | 12 |
| 7. | Berenice | 10 |
| 8. | Sarah | 9 |
| =9. | Imma | 7 |
| =9. | Mara | 7 |

she becomes a witness to the crucifixion and empty tomb.' Fitzmyer, *The Gospel According to Luke I–IX*, 697.

[891] Plummer argues that the high frequency with which the name is used explains the necessity of the qualifier Μαγδαλινή. Plummer, *A Critical and Exegetical Commentary on the Gospel According to S. Luke*, 215.

[892] Ilan documents 110 different female names in this period, in comparison with a total of 721 different male names. T. Ilan, *Lexicon of Jewish Names in Late Antiquity: Part 1 Palestine 330 BCE–200 CE*, TSAJ 91 (Tübingen: Mohr Siebeck 2002) 55, table 4.

[893] Ilan, *Lexicon of Jewish Names in Late Antiquity*, 55, table 4.

[894] Ilan, *Lexicon of Jewish Names in Late Antiquity*, 57, table 8.

[895] Ilan, *Lexicon of Jewish Names in Late Antiquity*, 57, table 8.

[896] The table is slightly modified in form to improve the presentation of the data.

This data supports the contention made by Plummer, that Mary is such a common name that the additional identifier ἡ Μαγδαλινή is required to distinguish this Mary from the other figures named Mary in early Christian tradition.

The name ἡ Μαγδαλινη has most commonly been seen by scholars as denoting the town of origin of this Mary. Bock, following a long line of scholarship on this term, states, 'The name Μαγδαλανή (Magdalene) suggests that she was from the region of Magdala, a small town on the Sea of Galilee's western shore about three miles north of Tiberias.'[897] As Strange notes the town of Magdala is 'generally identified with Migdal Nûnnaya of the Talmud ('Tower of Fish,' b.Pesaḥ. 46b), which lies approximately one mile N of Tiberias.'[898] The confusion of its distance from Tiberias appears to stem from conflicting traditions in the Babylonian and Palestinian Talmuds, with the former placing it three and three-quarter miles north of Tiberias, and the latter only one mile north of the same location. The context and additional information in parallel passages in the Babylonian Talmud perhaps suggests that the distance given in the Palestinian Talmud is less trustworthy.[899] The town appears to have been an important centre for fishing in the Roman period.[900] Apart from the geographical identification Mary Magdalene is also described as 'a disciple of the Lord' μαθήτρια τοῦ κυρίου. Although some translators have emphasized that she is 'a female disciple',[901] however, the narrative is not interested in her gender, but rather that her relationship to the Lord is that of disciple. The reason a feminine form is used simply reflects the structure of the Greek language. The significance of the term disciple, either here in its feminine for or elsewhere in its masculine form (Gos. Pet. 8.30; 14.59) is simply assumed. The feminine form, μαθήτρια, which here stands in appostion to the name Μαριὰμ ἡ Μαγδαλινή, is rare in the NT. It occurs only once, ἐν Ἰόππῃ δέ τις ἦν μαθήτρια ὀνόματι Ταβιθά (Acts 9.36).

---

[897] D.L. Bock, Luke 1.1–9:50, ECNT (Grand Rapids, Michigan: Baker, 1994) 713.

[898] J.F. Strange, 'Magdala', in ABD, vol. 4, 464.

[899] See the online version of the Catholic Encyclopedia, (http://www.newadvent.org/cathen/09523a.htm).

[900] Strange, 'Magdala', 464.

[901] For instance see, Swete, The Akhmîm Fragment of the Apocryphal Gospel of St Peter, 21, 27; Kraus und Nicklas, Das Petrusevangelium und die Petrusapokalypse, 52.

**12.50b** φοβουμένη διὰ τοὺς Ἰουδαίους, ἐπειδὴ ἐφλέγοντο ὑπὸ τῆς ὀργῆς. Whereas the canonical accounts attribute the delay in attending to the body as being caused by the observance of the Sabbath, here the author states that the women had not come previously because of fear of the Jews. This rewriting simultaneously distances the women from their historical Jewish heritage, and makes the Jews appear more loathsome since they are depicted as a potential threat to pious women going about their funerary duties. The motif of concealment and apprehension being exhibited by the followers of Jesus has already emerged in the narrative. After the events of the crucifixion, the disciples hide themselves out of fear of the Jews (*Gos. Pet.* 7.26).[902] In that context the first person narrator explains that he and his componions were being sought as potential temple arsonists. Here the image of fire is also used, but as a metaphor of the fierce rage being exhibited by the Jews.

Although the narrative contained in *Gos. Pet.* 12.50–13.57 most closely follows the Markan sequence of the visit of the women to the tomb (Mk 16.1–8),[903] both the fear of the Jews and the rulers burning rage are new elements in this account in comparison to that of the canonical gospels. The introduction of this material is structurally cumbersome, even if its general sense is fairly clear. A somewhat exasperated Vaganay described this clause in the following manner. 'We have here the beginning of a long and obscure parenthesis, which has exercised the patience of commentators.'[904] The structural confusion appears more severe because there are probably two parenthetical comments, not just one. The first is the rage of the Jews, the second the note about the inability to fulfil the funerary rites at an early time. Structurally this may be respresented as:

| | |
|---|---|
| Main narrative: | 50. Now at dawn of the Lord's Day Mary Magdalene, a disciple of the Lord, |
| Parenthetical comment 1: | being afraid because of the Jews, since they were inflamed by rage, |

---

[902] This connection has also been noted by Vaganay. 'Ce thème de la crainte des Juifs semble chez le pseudi-Pierre comme une sorte de passé-partout (cf. v. 26).' Vaganay, *L'Évangile de Pierre*, 320.

[903] As Mara observes, 'Dans ces versets 50–57 de notre fragment on remarque une progression de récit semblable à celle de *Mc* (16, 1–8).' Mara, *Évangile de Pierre*, 198.

[904] Vaganay, *L'Évangile de Pierre*, 320.

| Parenthetical comment 2: | had not done at the tomb of the Lord those things which women are permitted to do over those who have died and for those who are loved by them, |
| Resumption of Main narrative: | 51. taking the female friends with her... |

While certain scholars have proposed various emendments to make the flow of thought less disjunctive,[905] such steps are unnecessary, especially once it is realized that these parenthetical comments are included not for stylistic purposes, but instead are used by the author as a logical necessity to explain the delay in attending to the corpse. This new explanation becomes more pressing since the author has excluded the canonical explanation of the women observing the Sabbath. Thus it might be best to be guided by the examples of both Harnack[906] and Swete who do not adopt the recourse of altering the text. As Swete states, 'The sentence is overweighted, and has fallen into grammatical confusion. I have followed Harnack's example in the provisional use of brackets, which makes it possible to construe the sentence without emendation.'[907]

**12.50c** οὐκ ἐποίησεν ἐπὶ τῷ μνήματι τοῦ κυρίου ἃ εἰώθεσαν ποιεῖν αἱ γυναῖκες ἐπὶ τοῖς ἀποθνήσκουσι καὶ τοῖς ἀγαπωμέ νοις αὐταῖς. Ancient cultures around the Eastern Mediterranean often assigned women the duty of preparing bodies for burial. Antigone ignores Creon's order to leave the corpse of her brother Polyneices exposed as carion for wild animals (Soph. *Ant.* 21–39). This is obviously both an act of piety and familial responsibility, but interesting it is a woman who carries out the burial. Antigone recalls that Creon has pronounced the death penalty by stoning on any who fail to observe the order whether they be, 'noble-minded or the corrupt daughter of a noble line' (Soph. *Ant.* 39). Again the use of the term 'daughter'

---

[905] For example, Robinson inserts the word ἥτις before the parenthetical clause, to produces a relative clause subordinated to the main clause. Robinson and James, *The Gospel according to Peter and the Revelation of Peter*, 87.

[906] Harnack, *Bruchstücke des Evangeliums und der Apokalypse des Petrus*, 12, 15, 30.

[907] Swete, *The Akhmîm Fragment of the Apocryphal Gospel of St Peter*, 21.

further evidences the female role in the burial customs of this culture. Furthermore, it should be noted that the proleptic embalming per- formed for Jesus is carried out by a woman (Matt 26.6–13; Mk 14.3–9; Lk 7.36–50; Jn 12.1–8).[908]

Having related the enraged state of the Jewish leaders, Mary's act of piety in coming to the tomb on the first Easter morning cannot be con- strued as an act of delayance, but rather it becomes an act of bravery with such potentially dangerous forces seeking to interfere with those who wish to honour the corpse of the executed man. Precisely what the necessary requirements were for burial preparation are not articu- lated here, although Vaganay is almost certainly correct when he states that it involved 'washing of the corpse, accompanied by anointings with oil.'[909] The narrative also points to the fact that the preparation of the corpse for burial is to take place at the tomb. This aligns with the actions of the women in the synoptic accounts where they are explic- itly reported as taking their spices to the sepulchre (Mk 16.1–2; Lk 24.1). In the Johannine account the preparation and burial of the body is carried out by Joseph of Arimathea and Nicodemus (Jn 19.38–39). The preparation of the body takes place prior to entombment, but the process of washing and embalming take place on site, since the garden in which Jesus was crucified is also conveniently the location of the unused tomb (Jn 19.41). As Beasley-Murray observes, 'Our evangelist [John] alone mentions that there was a garden in the place where Jesus was crucified; accordingly the place where Jesus died was the place of his burial and the scene of the manifestation of his resurrection.'[910] The desire to locate crucifixion, burial and resurrection in the same loca- tion in the Johannine account might serve the apologetic purpose of rebutting the claim that there had been confusion over the site of the tomb, since all events take place in the same location.

Interestingly Matthew drops the detail about the women taking spices to the tomb (cf. Matt 28.1), so consequently in the first gospel no reason is given for the visit to the place of burial by the two Marys. Davies and Allison provide a list of differences between the Markan and Matthean accounts of the visit of the women to the tomb. By comparing the Akhmîm narrative to this list and making observations

---

[908] Vaganay, *L'Évangile de Pierre*, 321.
[909] Vaganay, *L'Évangile de Pierre*, 320.
[910] Beasley-Murray, *John*, 360.

about parallels in the Lukan account, it appears that the story in the *Gospel of Peter* is a weaving together of elements familiar from the synoptic accounts, but that the base story is here drawn from the Markan narrative. Davies and Allison offer the following comparisons:

> The major differences over against Mk 16.1–8 may be enumerated as follows: (i) Three women (so Mark) are now two (Salome is not in Matthew). (ii) The two chronological notices in Mk 16.1 and 2 ('when the Sabbath was past', 'very early on the first day of the week')' which refers to two different things (the buying of spices and the visit to the tomb), are seemingly combined in Matthew and refer only to the visit. (iii) Matthew omits the purchase of spices (Mk 16.1). (iv) He also neglects the woman's question about rolling back the stone (Mk 16.3). (v) Only in Mark do the women plainly enter the tomb. (vi) The appearance of a young man in white (so Mark) is in Matthew a glorious angelophany with apocalyptic details (28.2–4). (vii) Jesus is 'the Nazarene' in Mk 16.6; contrast Mt 28.5. (viii) The angel's 'as he told you' is associated in Matthew not with prophecy about Galilee (so Mk 16.7) but with the resurrection predictions. (ix) Matthew reduces the command to 'tell his disciples and Peter' (Mk 16.7) to 'tell his disciples' (28.7). (x) Mark's conclusion that the women said nothing to anyone, for they were afraid, is replaced by a notice of obedience: they 'ran to tell his disciples'. (xi) The appearance of the risen Jesus in Mt 28.9–10 has no Markan parallel. (xii) So too the legend about the guard (Mt 28.11–15).[911]

Comparing each of these points in turn reveals the heavy (but not exclusive) use of the Markan account by the author of the Akhmîm narrative in shaping his own narrative.

i.  Although the number of women is not explicitly stated, Mary Magalene takes 'friends' with her when visiting the sepulchre. This must result in party of at least three women, but definitely not the two women of Matt 28.1. Luke refers to the women who had come from Galilee. This is a larger group including Mary Magdalene, Joanna, Susanna and 'many other women' (cf. Lk 8.2–3).

ii. The Akhmîm account retains two chronological notices to describe the events with the guard at the tomb before sunrise (*Gos. Pet.* 9.34; cf. 11.45), and the visit of the women to the tomb at dawn (*Gos. Pet.* 12.50). The use of these temporal notices, however, involves a substantial re-writing of the canonical tradition.

---

[911] Davies and Allison, *The Gospel According to Saint Matthew*, vol. III, 660.

iii. As has been noted, although the Akhmîm narrative does not explicitly mention spices it retains the Markan understanding that the women were going to the tomb to prepare the body for burial.

iv. Extremely significant for determining source critical relationships is the question about rolling back the stone, which among the canonical accounts occurs only in Mk 16.3, but is also present in this non-canonical account contained in *Gos. Pet.* 12.53.

v. In Mk 16.5 and Lk 24.3 the women are described as going into (εἰσελθοῦσαι) the tomb. The Akhmîm text appears to preserve the same idea, although it employs a different compound verb προσελθοῦσαι. While Swete translates this verb as describing motion towards, but not entrance into the tomb, 'and they came near',[912] this appears unnecessary. Instead those translations that describe entrance appear to better reflect the intended meaning of the author.[913]

vi. Here there is strong evidence that the Akhmîm narrative is conflating at least two sources, since it includes both the Matthean theophanic account of figures descending from heaven (Matt 28.2–4//*Gos. Pet.* 9.36) and the Markan description of the young man sitting in the tomb (Mk 16.5).

vii. The Akhmîm text deviates from both forms of title used in the first two canonical gospels, i.e., in Matthew, 'Jesus' (Matt 28.5), and in Mark, 'Jesus the Nazarene' (Mk 16.6). Instead it uses the term 'crucified one' τὸν ἐσταυρωθέντα (*Gos. Pet.* 13.56) alone without qualification, which is comparable to the way both Matthew and Mark use τὸν ἐσταυρωμένον (Matt 28.5; Mk 16.6).

viii. This narrative does not preserve a phrase parallel to the Matthean καθὼς εἶπεν (Matt 28.6) or Mark's καθὼς εἶπεν ὑμῖν (Mk 16.7). Hence this cannot be used to determine the sources being employed in this pericope.

ix. Likewise, the narrative does not share with the canonical accounts a commission to report these events to the disciples.

x. The response of the women who 'feared and fled' (*Gos. Pet.* 13.57), aligns more closely with the conclusion of the Markan account than with any of the other canonical accounts.

---

[912] Swete, *The Akhmîm Fragment of the Apocryphal Gospel of St Peter*, 27.
[913] Cf. Kraus und Nicklas, *Das Petrusevangelium und die Petrusapokalypse*, 53.

xi. The encounter with the risen Jesus in Matt 28.9–10 is absent in both the Markan account and the Akhmîm version of events.

xii. The Akhmîm text knows the story of the guards-at-the-tomb. Although it expands on this story, it keeps this material discrete from the narrative of the women's visit to the tomb. Thus stylistically *Gos. Pet.* 12.50–13.57 aligns more closely with the somewhat reserved version of the events of the first Easter morning contained in Mark's gospel, rather than evidencing the mixed form of the Matthean account with its legendary accretions and obviously apologetic perspective (Matt 28.2–4, 11–15).[914]

This short discussion illustrates that the Akhmîm text knows elements of the resurrection account which among the canonical gospels are only found in the Markan narrative (ii, iv, x). Moreover, it conflates parallel accounts to form its own narrative (vi). Thus it appears that the Akhmîm account uses the Markan version of the story of the women visiting the tomb as its major source and framework for its own recasting of this narrative, but at the same time freely modifies the tradition and includes elements from the other canonical accounts of this incident.

The narrative speaks of the need for the women to undertake the duties customarily performed by females to prepare corpses, ἃ εἰώθεσαν ποιεῖν αἱ γυναῖκες. As a specific description of these funerary rites is not provided, it is impossible to say whether the author is presupposing a different set of burial rites to those carried out in a Jewish context. Notwithstanding specific variations, it may be the case that some process of removing the blood from the body and scenting it with perfume would constitute the main activities.[915] The author also informs the audience that these rites carried out by women were performed for those with whom they had a special connection. The relationship is presented in terms of love, τοῖς ἀγαπωμένοις αὐταῖς. Most naturally this would appear to presume a bond of kinship, friendship or other intimate relationship. Intertextual links have been suggested between this passage and texts in the OT. Swete suggested that there was an echo of Zech 12.10 (LXX), καὶ κόψονται ἐπ᾽ αὐτὸν κοπετὸν ὡς ἐπ᾽ ἀγαπητόν.[916]

---

[914] See Bultmann, *History of the Synoptic Tradition*, 285–287.
[915] Cf. Str.-B., vol. II, 52–53.
[916] Swete, *The Akhmîm Fragment of the Apocryphal Gospel of St Peter*, 22.

Alternative Harris suggested a link with Amos 8.10 (LXX) ὡς πένθος ἀγαπητοῦ.⁹¹⁷ Such putative connections are extremely slight, and it is doubted whether any firm basis for establishing an intention textual allusion can be presented. It thus appears that the author is presenting the women in the customary pious role of attending their beloved dead, but he does not explicitly explain the basis of the relationship between the women and Jesus, although Mary Magdalene has been described as a disciple of the Lord.

**12.51a  λαβοῦσα μεθ᾽ ἑαυτῆς τὰς φίλας.** After the two asides about the delay due to fear of the Jews and the need to carry out the burial rites, the central thread of the story is resumed with a description of Mary taking along other women to the tomb. This detail is presented both because of the dependence on the tradition as it occurs in the Markan and parallel versions of this incident, and also for the apologetic purpose of establishing a larger group of witnesses to the empty tomb and the words of the man sitting inside the sepulchre. Grammatically, the aorist particle refers back to Mary Magdalene whose role as chief protagonist in the group is further emphasized both through her instigation of the trip to the tomb and through the use of the reflexive pronoun, ἑαυτῆς. Thus, here the reflexive 'is used to maintain the identity of the person speaking or acting.'⁹¹⁸

Those whom Mary takes to the tomb with her are designated as 'the friends' τὰς φίλας. The context does not clarify if this friendship is understood as being with Mary Magdalene or with Jesus. Perhaps this is an unnecessary choice since the author is depicting a circle of friendship. The specific identity of the members of this wider circle is not provided. If, as has been argued, the Akhmîm text is drawing upon canonical traditions, then the parallel accounts may determine the most likely figures the author has in mind. At this point the author may expect readers to fill this gap in the narrative with their own preknowledge derived from the canonical accounts, which supply the identities of these women. This list of named women present in the canonical passion narrative can be tabulated along with Luke's group

---

⁹¹⁷ J.R. Harris, 'The Structure of the Gospel of Peter', *The Contemporary Review* (1883) 212–236; see especially 224.
⁹¹⁸ Cf. Matt 18.4; 19.12; 23.12; Gal 1.4; 2.20; Rev 2.2. See EDNT, vol. 1, 368.

Table 17. Groups of women associates of Jesus in the canonical accounts

| Passage | Designation of the women |
| --- | --- |
| Matt 27.56 | Mary Magdalene, Mary the mother of James and Joseph, and the mother of the sons of Zebedee |
| Matt 27.61, 28.1 | Mary Magdalene and the other Mary |
| Mk 15.40 | Mary Magdalene, Mary the mother of James the less and Joses, and Salome |
| Mk 15.47, 16.1 | Mary Magdalene, Mary the mother of James, and Salome |
| Lk 23.55 | The women who had come from Galilee |
| Lk 24.10 | Mary Magdalene, Joanna,[919] and Mary the mother of James |
| Lk 8.2–3 | Mary Magdalene, Joanna the wife of Chuza Herod's steward, and Susanna |
| Jn 19.25 | Jesus' mother Mary, her sister, Mary the wife of Clopas, and Mary of Magdala |
| Jn 20.1 | Mary Magdalene |
| Jn 11.1ff. | Mary and Martha |

of women supporters that the evangelist describes during the ministry of Jesus.

From this information it is easy to see that Mary Magdalene in a constant feature in all accounts of the resurrection morning. The names of the other women are more variable although in the synoptic accounts of the visit to the tomb a second women named Mary is invariable present, and this women is identified as 'the mother of James' by both Mark (Mk 16.1) and Luke (Lk 24.10). It is therefore most likely that along with Mary Magdalene, the Akhmîm narrative is assuming a similar group of women to that depicted in the various synoptic versions of this incident. As in the synoptic accounts where 'the women have a unique qualification as witnesses to the empty tomb',[920] so also in the Akhmîm narrative their major function will be to enlarge the circle of witnesses to the empty tomb and resurrection events.

**12.51b** ἦλθε ἐπὶ τὸ μνημεῖον ὅπου ἦν τεθείς. This half-verse comprises of two parts, the notice of the commencement of the journey to the tomb, and the clarifying note that the tomb to which Mary was

[919] For an extensive discussion on Joanna see R. Bauckham, *Gospel Women: Studies of the Named Women in the Gospels* (London: T&T Clark – a Continuum Imprint, 2002) 109–203.

[920] Bauckham, *Gospel Women*, 277.

going was indeed the one where the Lord had been laid. The central interest in Mary Magdalene is highlighted in the use of a third person singular verb. Although a group of women have been introduced, the other figures in the narrative are ancilliary to the central character and her actions subsume those of the others who have no independence at this point, although their collective voice will be heard as the story evolves. The use of the third person singular form ἦλθεν is also feature of the Matthean account, ἦλθεν Μαριὰμ ἡ Μαγδαληνὴ καὶ ἡ ἄλλη Μαρία θεωρῆσαι τὸν τάφον (Matt 28.1). In the first gospel the construction is grammatically correct, since the singular form qualifies the action of Mary Magdalene, and the reference to the 'the other Mary' is added as an after-thought. This coincidence between the verbal forms in Matthew and the Akhmîm narrative should not be seen as a sign of direct dependence, rather independently the authors of these texts have introduced the singular verbal form into the respective re-castings of the Markan story.

In the synoptic tradition the possibility of mis-identification of the burial site as the source of claim of an empty tomb is ruled out. This is achieved by making the women present at the entombment on the day of crucifixion (Matt 27.61; Mk 15.47; Lk 23.55). In relation to the Mark account Donahue and Harrington note of the women that '[h]aving witnessed Jesus' death, they also witness his burial and so on Easter morning they did not go to the wrong tomb.'[921] Moreover, a certain textual unevenness in the Markan account led Taylor to suggest that the 'reference to the women who beheld where Jesus was laid (xv. 47) is appended and does not belong to the narrative proper; it may even be the original introduction to the story of the Empty Tomb.'[922] If this is correct, then this detail was probably added to the tradition at a very early stage for apologetic purposes. Having omitted this detail the Akhmîm story must find another way to protect against the charge that the women visited the wrong tomb. It achieves this by bald assertion, namely that the women went to the correct tomb 'where the body had been laid'. Von Schubert suggested that the final three words of this verse were constructed out of existing synoptic material. He noted that ποῦ (ὅπου in D) is used in the context of the burial story in Mk 15.47,

---

[921] Donahue and Harrington, *The Gospel of Mark*, 455.
[922] Taylor, *The Gospel according to St. Mark*, 602.

and that τεθείς occurs in the Lukan burial account (Lk 23.55).[923] Such an atomistic redactional method, however, does not seem to reflect the generally 'broad brush' approach the author adopts in utilizing source material. Instead it appears the phrase has been formulated to emphasize the fact that it was the tomb of Jesus that was discovered to be empty.

**12.52a** καὶ ἐφοβοῦντο μὴ ἴδωσιν αὐτὰς οἱ Ἰουδαῖοι. This is the second time in this pericope that the fear of the Jews by female characters is registered (cf. *Gos. Pet.* 12.50b). Here the fear is corporate, rather than the emotion of a single character, Mary Magdalene. Thus, the visit at dawn is not only motivated by a desire to carry out the burial rites at the first opportunity, but the half-light is also consonant with the desire to approach the tomb in a covert manner. For Swete, the author's insight into the fear expressed by the women is something he deduced from the chronology of the visit. In relation to the fear he states, 'This seems to be an inference from ὄρθρου βαθέως – they came at break of day before sunrise, in order to escape observation.'[924] Yet such fear at this juncture on the part of the women is without parallel in the canonical accounts. It is, rather part of the redactional contribution of the author which seeks to cast the Jews in the worst possible light. As Mara observes, 'the fear of the women in the face of the Jews reappears, something absolutely unknown in the New Testament.'[925] By contrast, in the synoptic accounts the women express their piety by attending to the funeral rites at the first opportunity after the Sabbath. Since the author of the Akhmîm narrative does not particularly wish to stress the observance of this weekly Jewish festival, he relates in its place this reason for the delay in attending to the corpse.[926]

**12.52b** καὶ ἔλεγον εἰ καὶ μὴ ἐν ἐκείνῃ τῇ ἡμέρᾳ ᾗ ἐσταυρώθη ἐδυνήθημεν κλαῦσαι καὶ κόψεσθαι. Having reported the anxiety of the women, the author narrates a stylized sample of their conversation as they journey towards the place of burial. The καὶ ἔλεγον used

---

[923] von Schubert, *The Gospel of St Peter with Synoptical Tables,*

[924] Swete, *The Akhmîm Fragment of the Apocryphal Gospel of St Peter,* 22.

[925] Mara, *Évangile de Pierre,* 201.

[926] As Vaganay observes, 'Nous sommes loin des évangiles canonique où elles n'ont aucune peur des Juifs et où leur démarche est inspirée par leur seule piété impatiente.' Vaganay, *L'Évangile de Pierre,* 322.

to introduce the speech of the women may well by taken over from Mk 16.3, where it is used to raise the issue about gaining access to the sealed sepulchre. The same question will be stated in this narrative, although the author inserts a fresh element in the narrative between the Markan phrase καὶ ἔλεγον and the question, τίς ἀποκυλίσει ἡμῖν τὸν λίθον ἐκ τῆς θύρας τοῦ μνημείου; (Mk 16.3). Instead, the author continues to absolve the women of any possible accusation of tardiness. The women openly acknowledge those circumstances which prohibited them from mourning appropriately on the crucifixion day. Consequently, even though the danger has not fully abated, they have now determined to perform the required rituals at the first possible opportunity. As Vaganay notes, the construction used here reflects classical Greek,[927] and introduces a concessive proposition, namely since a certain set of circumstances intervened previously ('since we were unable...'), now the women have adopted the present course of action ('let us now do these things...'). Thus the author is keen to show that while the actions of the women have been constrained by the anticipated reprisals of the Jews against any who attempt to mourn Jesus, nonetheless the women are determined to honour his body by carrying out the required funerary customs, albeit with the exercise of due caution. Thus, as Mara presents the authorial intent, '[t]he author highlights one point: the goal of the women is to do what they could not do before: to weep and to fulfil the funeral ceremonies.'[928]

The description of 'weeping and wailing', κλαῦσαι καὶ κόψεσθαι, reflects highly standardized and stylized language of mourning. This stereotypical combination of terms can also be found in Lk 8.52 and Rev 18.9.[929] In the Lukan passage, the two terms occur together to describe the mourning activities of the crowd who are gathered because of the death of Jairus' daughter, ἔκλαιον δὲ πάντες καὶ ἐκόπτοντο αὐτήν (Lk 8.52). In relation to this passage Fitzmyer comments that the verb κόπτειν 'can be used in the middle voice in the sense of 'mourning', see Josephus *Ant.* 13.15,5 §399.'[930]

**12.52c** καὶ νῦν ἐπὶ τοῦ μνήματος αὐτοῦ ποιήσωμεν ταῦτα. Two stylistic features deserve mention. First, the subjunctive ποιήσωμεν is

---

[927] See Vaganay, *L'Évangile de Pierre*, 322 and BDF §372.
[928] Mara, *Évangile de Pierre*, 201.
[929] Vaganay, *L'Évangile de Pierre*, 322.
[930] Fitzmyer, *The Gospel According to Luke I–IX*, 749.

used cohortatively. The plural subjects, the women, who were depicted as speaking with one accord using the verb ἔλεγον, again collectively declare their intention to perform the preparations for the body. Second, the author continues to vary the Greek terminology used to refer to the tomb, μνῆμα (*Gos. Pet.* 8.30, 31, 32; 11.44; 12.50, 52) and μνημεῖον (*Gos. Pet.* 9.34; 12.51, 53). There is no difference in meaning between these terms and the variation simply appears to be a device to avoid repetition. The presence of the subjunctive ποιήσωμεν has led to the conjectural emendation of καί to κἄν.[931] Yet Vaganay is surely correct that this is unnecessary and the subjunctive can stand in a clause introduced by καί.[932] This verse emphasizes the fact that the women are going to the tomb to perform the funeral rites. This is a point that the author has been labouring throughout the first three verses of this pericope. First, the determination of Mary Magdalene is introduced, then the narrative explains the delay in terms of fear of the Jews, finally he has the women assert what is portrayed as their brave determination to reverence the body despite the perceived threat from the Jewish authorities.

**12.53a** τίς δὲ ἀποκυλίσει ἡμῖν καὶ τὸν λίθον τὸν τεθέντα ἐπὶ τῆς θύρας τοῦ μνημείου. The question that forms the first half of this verse is a slightly expanded version of the same question that in the canonical tradition is found only in the Markan account, τίς ἀποκυλίσει ἡμῖν τὸν λίθον ἐκ τῆς θύρας τοῦ μνημείου (Mk 16.3). The opening five words of the Markan version have only been slightly modified through the insertion of two conjunctions, the δέ before the opening verb, and the somewhat redundant καί before reference to the stone. The last four words of each version are identical. The major difference is that the author of the Akhmîm narrative has replaced the Markan preposition ἐκ with the phrase τὸν τεθέντα ἐπί. The inclusion of the substantivized nominal perfect participle and the use of a different preposition do not materially affect the meaning of the passage, at best the alteration emphasizes that the placing of the stone was an event at some distance in the past.

---

[931] Harnack attributes this correction to Blass. See Harnack, *Bruchstücke des Evangeliums und der Apokalypse des Petrus*, 12.

[932] 'Le subjonctif ποιήσωμεν n'est pas amené par κἄν; il marque seulement l'exhortation.' Vaganay, *L'Évangile de Pierre*, 322.

According to Evans, in Mark's gospel the question about moving the stone is occasioned by the fact that, [b]ecause of the early hour, the women likely assume that no one will be available to assist them.'[933] While this element may not be totally absent from the account in the Akhmîm account, it does appear to be motivated by the expectation that any present might well be hostile to their intention, rather than suggesting a lack of available help. In the Markan version the women have 'no expectation of finding it [the tomb] open, so he enables us to share their surprise.'[934] While the open tomb will still be an unexpected discovery for the both the women and the readers of Mark's account, those who hear the version of the story in the *Gospel of Peter* have already been provided with an account of the miraculous unsealing of the sepulchre.

**12.53b** ἵνα εἰσελθοῦσαι παρακαθεσθῶμεν αὐτῷ καὶ ποιήσωμεν τὰ ὀφειλόμενα. Another noticeable contact with the Markan narrative is the delay of the editorial notice that 'the stone was large' (*Gos. Pet.* 12.54), which in many ways would fit better in this immediate context. Different material intervenes in the two contexts. In Mark's story after asking about the need for assistance in moving the stone, the women immediately 'look up' and see the stone rolled back. By contrast, the Akhmîm text postpones such a discovery by the women and thus allows their journey and conversation to continue further. The aorist participle εἰσελθοῦσαι may be carried over from the Markan narrative.[935] In that context it indicates the actual act of entering the tomb, whereas here, in combination with the principal verb in the subjunctive mood it indicates an aspiration on the part of the women.

The author relates that the desire of the women to enter the tomb is generated by two factors. First, they wish to sit beside the body. This is a detail absent from the synoptic parallels to this scene. Vaganay describes the women's intention in the following terms. 'They intend

[933] Evans, *Mark 8:27–16:20*, 535.

[934] Hooker, *The Gospel according to Saint Mark*, 384.

[935] Vaganay notes that compound for occurs in the following manuscripts ℵ A B C etc. Vaganay, *L'Évangile de Pierre*, 322. However according to the textual apparatus in NA²⁷ the simplex form ἐλθοῦσαι is read by B and 2427. Consultation of the facsimile of Codex Vaticanus verifies that the simplex form is indeed the reading of the manuscript. See Bibliorum sacrorum Graecorum *Codex Vaticanus* B (Roma: Istituto poligrafico e Zecca dello Stato, 1999).

to sit down very close to the corpse of their beloved friend in order to give free vent to their tears.'[936] While this interpretation may present more of the motivation and psychological disposition of the women than is actually knowable from the narrative, it perhaps aligns with the practices of mourning that occur in various contemporary ancient cultures. Swete suggested that the desire of the women to sit besides the body of Jesus draws upon the tradition in Lk 10.39 where Mary sits beside the feet of the Lord, Μαριάμ...παρακαθεσθεῖσα πρὸς τοὺς πόδας τοῦ κυρίου.[937] It is, however, more likely that the notion of sitting beside the corpse of Jesus is drawn from the second parallel Swete mentions, Jn 20.12. In that context two angels are seen seated where the body had been lain in the tomb, δύο ἀγγέλους...καθεζομένους, ἕνα πρὸς τῇ κεφαλῇ καὶ ἕνα πρὸς τοῖς ποσίν, ὅπου ἔκειτο τὸ σῶμα τοῦ Ἰησοῦ.[938] Alternatively, the scribe may have inserted a cultural custom with which he was familiar into the context of his re-telling of the story.

The second reason that is presented for the women wishing to gain access to the sepulchre is in order that they might perform the funeral rites of preparation of the body. This is now the third occasion that the scribe has communicated that the women were making this perilous trip to attend to the corpse.

| Gos. Pet. 12.50 | Μαριὰμ ἡ Μαγδαλινή...οὐκ ἐποίησεν ἐπὶ τῷ μνήματι τοῦ κυρίου ἃ εἰώθεσαν ποιεῖν αἱ γυναῖκες. |
|---|---|
| Gos. Pet. 12.52 | καὶ νῦν ἐπὶ τοῦ μνήματος αὐτοῦ ποιήσωμε ταῦτα. |
| Gos. Pet. 12.53 | καὶ ποιήωσμεν τὰ ὀφειλόμενα. |

On the first occasion the intrusive narrator explains Mary Magdalene's previous lack of opportunity to perform these ritual requirements. The next two occasions, are cohortative declarations of intent made by the women signalling their purpose in visiting the burial site. This belaboured repetition emphasizes the womens' piety, but ironically they will find that they are unable to complete their self-appointed task, but not for the reason they have anticipated.

---

[936] 'Elles projettent de s'asseoir tout près du corps de leur Bien-aimé pour donner libre cours à leur larmes.' Vaganay, L'Évangile de Pierre, 323.

[937] Swete, The Akhmîm Fragment of the Apocryphal Gospel of St Peter, 22.

[938] Again see Swete, The Akhmîm Fragment of the Apocryphal Gospel of St Peter, 22.

**12.54a**  μέγας γὰρ ἦν ὁ λίθος. καὶ φοβούμεθα μή τις ἡμᾶς ἴδῃ.
The group speech of the women continues. Again the narrative presents a parallel to a detail found only in the Markan narrative – namely, a description of the size of the stone. In the account contained in the second Gospel the description of the size of the stone is provided by the narrator after he relates the detail that the women saw it had been moved out of position. He then comments, ἦν γὰρ μέγας σφόδρα (Mk 16.4). Since the Akhmîm narrative does not reproduce here the detail Mark gives immediately before this added notice, ἀποκεκύλισται ὁ λίθος, (Mk 16.4) it is required to make the subject of the verb ἦν explicit. This accounts for the slightly different form of wording at this point, although dependence on the Markan narrative is not to be doubted. As Vaganay states at this point, 'The literary dependence of the writer of this apocryphal text upon Mark is undeniable.'[939] In relation to the Markan account, Gundry notes that the 'added statement, "for it was extremely large," does not give the reason why the women found the stone already rolled away; for its extremely large size would explain rather why the should *not* have found already it rolled away.'[940] While this is logically correct, Mark's point is to emphasize that this is not the act of human forces. Such difficulties are overcome in the Akhmîm account, since the women have not yet seen the moved stone. It would be wrong to conclude, however, that this tidying up of the perceived logical difficulty was intended by the author. Rather, it is a by-product of his decision to create a more detailed conversation scene on the journey to the tomb.

Apart for drawing attention to the largeness of the stone as an inhibiting factor, the women also articulate their fear yet again. The desire to remain unobserved results in a course of action being discussed in the rest of this verse if quick access to the tomb is not possible. Although the fear is expressed using a verb in the present tense, thereby expressing the current emotional state of the women, the worry about being observed is a hypothetical concern and consequently utilises a subjunctive construction.[941] The indefinite pronoun τις is used to designate the unknown observer whom the women fear. Although the

---

[939] 'La dépendance littéraire de l'écrivain apocryphe vis-à-vis de Marc est indéniable.' Vaganay, *L'Évangile de Pierre*, 323.

[940] Gundry, *Mark: A Commentary on His Apology for the Cross*, 990.

[941] In this context the usage aligns with 'the subjunctive denoting that which may be the outcome of the present situation under certain circumstances.' See BDF §363.

specific identity of this person obviously cannot be known, as the narrative has already made clear, the fear is that this person is one of 'the Jews'. Sounding again the note of the women's fear, the author makes this repetition into almost a refrain throughout this pericope.[942]

> Gos. Pet. 12.50     Μαριὰμ ἡ Μαγδαλινή...φοβουμένη διὰ τοὺς
>                     Ἰουδαίους.
> Gos. Pet. 12.52     καὶ ἐφοβοῦντο μὴ ἴδωσιν αὐτὰς οἱ Ἰουδαῖοι.
> Gos. Pet. 12.53     καὶ φοβούμεθα μή τις ἡμᾶς ἴδη.

Thus in the first two instances of this repeated theme, 'the Jews' are explicitly mentioned. By contrast, on the third occasion the indefinite pronoun is use to designate a hypothetical individual, but the narrative has been set up in such a manner as to create the perception that this is either an antagonistic Jew himself, or some kind of quisling ready to report the presence of the women to the Jewish leadership.

**12.54b   καὶ εἰ μὴ δυνάμεθα, κἂν ἐπὶ τῆς θύρας βάλωμεν ἃ φέρομεν εἰς μνημοσύνην αὐτοῦ.** This clause outlines the first part of the women's proposed action, if circumstances prevent them from gaining entry to the sepulchre. Mara splits the actions of mourning and preparing the body, arguing that the primary concern was with carrying out a lament for the Lord. She basis this argument on the fact that the women are willing to leave the things they bring with them at the door. Thus Mara states that this clause, 'demonstrates that the women in the first instance went in order to weep and to beat their breasts, and secondarily to bring something.'[943] In many ways Mara has created a false dichotomy. It is dubious whether the narrative places more significance on the weeping than it does on the burial preparations. For the author these are all part of a single funeral ritual. The narrative instead creates an air of realism in the women's expectations and plans for the eventuality of finding the teomb inaccessible. From the women's perspective, this sets up an element of surprise in the plot, which the audience is able to anticipate since it already knows that the stone has been moved from the entrance to the tomb.

The hortatory aorist subjunctive βάλωμεν is used to communicate the corporate decision to leave what they have brought with them at

---

[942] Vaganay, L'Évangile de Pierre, 324.
[943] Mara, Évangile de Pierre, 201.

the entrance to the sepulchre if it is sealed. An exact description of the items in question is not given, but for those who are already familiar with the canonical versions of this story there are certain expectations concerning those things being carried by this group. Most significant at this point is the description in the Markan narrative, which the author heavily quarries to form his own version of the story. In the second gospel the women are described as bearing the items required for embalming the body, ἠγόρασαν ἀρώματα ἵνα ἐλθοῦσαι ἀλείψωσιν αὐτόν (Mk 16.1). Therefore, in relation to the Markan description, Gundry argues that the evangelist is attempting to present the burial as a royal act. He argues that oil not aromatics were customary in Jewish burial, whereas 'aromatics carry a royal or otherwise dignified association when used in reference to death and burial.'[944] France rebuts this interpretation, instead arguing that although the Jewish practice was not to embalm in the technical Egyptian sense, 'aromatic spices and ointment (cf. Lk. 23.56: ἀρώματα καὶ μύρα) were used as a mark of respect and perhaps to keep the corpse fresh for as long as possible.'[945] Since the author of the Akhmîm text does not reproduce the description of the elements as consisting of ἀρώματα, even if Gundry were correct about royal associations, these are not being drawn upon here. Rather, in line with France's interpretation, the things the women bring are intended to provide the corpse with an honourable and dignified burial.

**12.54c** κλαύσομεν καὶ κοψόμεθα ἕως ἔλθωμεν εἰς τὸν οἶκον ἡμῶν. As has been argued in the text-critical notes, the future indicative forms should be retained, and there is no reason to emend the text to produce subjunctive forms throughout.[946] The combination of the verbs κλαίω and κόπτω has already occurred in this pericope (cf. κλαῦσαι καὶ κόψεσθαι Gos. Pet. 12.52). It was noted in the discussion of that verse that this is stereotypical language of mourning. The weeping and wailing is, therefore, not the result of failure to gain entry to the tomb. Rather, it arises as part of the necessary social ritual to be carried out over a corpse. The women determine to at least perform this aspect of the ritual on their journey home, if entry into the sepulchre

---

[944] Gundry, *Mark: A Commentary on His Apology for the Cross*, 989.
[945] France, *The Gospel of Mark*, 677.
[946] See text critical note 9 in this section.

proves impossible. Thus, as Vaganay observes, 'The women will not satisfy themselves by placing the offerings at the entrance, they will weep on their return journey.'[947] Hence a secondary plan is devised which will allow a partial fulfilment of the funerary rites in the likely event (at least from the point of view of the women) that access to the tomb will be prevented. While there are many close points of contact with the Markan parallel throughout *Gos. Pet.* 12.50–54, the author of the Akhmîm text also introduces several expansions to the Markan source material especially through the repetition of key phrases and themes.

---

[947] 'Les femmes ne se contenteront pas de placer les offrandes à la porte; elles pleureront sur le chemin du retour.' Vaganay, *L'Évangile de Pierre*, 324.

## THE WOMEN ENCOUNTER THE YOUNG MAN
## IN THE TOMB (13.55–57)

55. καὶ ἀπελθοῦσαι εὗρον¹ τὸν τάφον ἠνεῳγμένον καὶ προσελθοῦσαι² παρέκυψαν ἐκεῖ καὶ ὁρῶσιν ἐκεῖ τινα νεανίσκον καθεζόμενον μέσῳ τοῦ τάφου ὡραῖον καὶ περιβεβλημένο(ν)³ στολὴν λαμπροτάτην ὅστις ἔφη αὐταῖ⟨ς⟩⁴ 56. ὅτι⁵ ἤλθατε; τίνα ζητεῖτε; μὴ τὸν σταυρωθέντα ἐκεῖνον; ⁶ἀνέστη καὶ ἀπῆλθεν. εἰ δὲ μὴ πιστεύετε, παρακύψατε καὶ ἴδατε⁷ τὸν τόπον [ἔνθα] ἐκ[ει]⁸ ᵗᵒ ⁹ ὅτι οὐκ ἔστιν. ἀνέστη γὰρ καὶ ἀπῆλθεν⁶ ἐκεῖ ὅθεν ἀπεστάλη. 57. τότε αἱ γυναῖκες φοβηθεῖς⟨αι⟩¹⁰ ἔφυγον.

55. And after they set out, they found the tomb had been opened and as they approached they stooped down there and they saw there a certain young man sitting in the midst of the tomb, beautiful and wearing a shining robe who said to them, 56. 'Why did you come? Whom do you seek? Not that one who was crucified? [He has risen and gone...] But if you do not believe, stoop down and see the place from... [the...] [because he is not...]. For he has risen and gone to the place from whence he was sent. 57. Then the women fearing, fled.

### TEXT CRITICAL NOTES

1. Here the initial letter of εὗρον is formed using two oblique strokes that form an angle of approximately ninety degrees. The shorter stroke forming the stylized base of the letter measures 3mm and slopes downwards from left to right. The second stroke, only slightly longer at approximately 3.5mm, commences at a point 1mm along the previous stroke and rises from left to right. There is a ligature from the following upsilon which may be intended to function as the crossbar of the epsilon. Although not as pronounced in the very square shape that occur here, this same general epsilon formation is to be found at *Gos. Pet.* 9.34[948] and 10.39.[949] Gebhardt has also

---

[948] See text critical note 1 in section 9, *Gos. Pet.* 9.34–37.
[949] See text critical note 5 in section 10, *Gos. Pet.* 10.38–42.

note the irregularity in the formation of this letter at various points throughout the manuscript.[950]

2. This is a second instance of irregular epsilon formation. Here the crossbar is clearly present as a ligature that links to the short leg of the following lambda. The same phenomenon occurs earlier in the text at *Gos. Pet.* 10.39 in the word ἐξελθόντος.[951]

3. A supralinear stroke is written over the omicron and extending to the right of the letter to indicate the omission of the final ν. This is the longest supralinear stroke the scribe has written to indicate a final ν. It measures 10mm in length and only terminates because it reaches the edge of the page.[952]

4. Here one would expect to find feminine dative plural form of the third person pronoun, αὐταῖς. Instead the manuscript reads αὐταί, the feminine nominative form. This appears to be due to the omission of the final sigma. This reading is complicated by the textual problem that occurs with the following word. On this, see note 5 below.

5. At this point, the majority of editions of the Greek text read τί instead of ὅτι,[953] understanding the initial two words of the verse as the first in a series of questions, i.e., τί ἤλθατε; The final word of *Gos. Pet.* 13.55 and the initial word of of *Gos. Pet.* 13.56 give the following letter combination, αυταιοτι.[954] It appears that the final sigma of αὐταῖς (see note 4 above) may have been incorrectly transcribed at some stage in the chain of copying. The omicron written by the scribe of this manuscript is well formed, and presumably he understands it a the initial letter of a ὅτι recititive, introducing the direct speech that follows. Perhaps the reason this emendation is so widely accepted, apart from its intrinsic plausibility, is that it

---

[950] Gebhardt, *Das Evangelium und die Apokalypse des Petrus*, 13.

[951] Text critical note 5 in section 10.

[952] This feature is also noted by Kraus und Nicklas, *Das Petrusevangelium und die Petrusapokalypse*, 46.

[953] For instance see Swete, *The Akhmîm Fragment of the Apocryphal Gospel of St Peter*, 23; without comment Harnack makes this correction, Harnack, *Bruchstücke des Evangeliums und der Apokalypse des Petrus*, 12; also without comment Robinson and James, *The Gospel according to Peter and the Revelation of Peter*, 88; Vaganay, *L'Évangile de Pierre*, 328.

[954] See Kraus und Nicklas, *Das Petrusevangelium und die Petrusapokalypse*, 48.

was introduced by Bouriant in the *editio princeps*.[955] In fact the only edition which reproduces αὐταί ὅτι in the main body of its text is the strict transcription prepared by Lods.[956]

6. The two superscripted number sixes in the text bracket a section where there is a major textual problem, which includes the spurious letters το (marked as eight). Two almost identical phrases occur in this verse, first ἀνέστη καὶ ἀπῆλθεν, then the slightly longer form ἀνέστη γὰρ καὶ ἀπῆλθεν. Also it needs to be noted that after the occurrence of the word ἐκ the text becomes particularly confused. The other feature to observe is that the letter that precedes both instances of the phrase ἀνέστη καὶ ἀπῆλθεν is an ν. It may then be the case that the jumbled text is the result of a combination of homoioteleuton (similar endings)[957] and dittography (repetition of words or phrases).[958] The exemplar from which the scribe was copying may have read something like the following.

> ... ἐκεῖνον;
> εἰ δὲ μὴ πιστεύετε, παρακύψατε καὶ ἴδετε τὸν τόπον ἔκειτο...ὅτι οὐκ ἔστιν.
> ἀνέστη γὰρ καὶ ἀπῆλθεν[6] ἐκεῖ ὅθεν ἀπεστάλη

After copying ἐκεῖνον the scribe's eye may have slipped down to the similar ending on the line below (or even two lines below, if the stichometry of the Akhmîm text is any guide). This resulted in the copying of the phrase ἀνέστη [γὰρ] καὶ ἀπῆλθεν immediately after the ἐκεῖνον. Quickly realizing this mistake, the scribe resumed the text of the line that had been inadvertently omitted. But when he completed the word τόπον the text would not run smoothly, so the scribe clumsily erased the mistaken word ἔνθα, and attempted to modify the text to compensate for the error. This all went wrong, and the scribe gave up, and instead recommenced with the phrase ἀνέστη γὰρ καὶ ἀπῆλθεν. This resulted in the following text:

[955] Bouriant, 'Fragments du texte grec du livre d'Énoch et de quelques écrits attribués à saint Pierre', 141.

[956] Lods, 'L'Évangile et l'Apocalypse de Pierre avec le texte grec du livre d'Hénoch', 223.

[957] For a discussion of the phenomenon of homoioteleuton, see Aland and Aland, *The Text of the New Testament*, 237, 242, 285.

[958] Dittography is discussed in Aland and Aland, *The Text of the New Testament*, 283–284.

...μὴ τὸν σταυρωθέντα ἐκεῖνον;
ἀνέστη καὶ ἀπῆλθεν. εἰ δὲ μὴ πιστεύετε, παρακύ-
ψατε καὶ ἴδετε τὸν τόπον [ἔνθα] ἔκει<sup>το</sup> ὅτι οὐκ ἔστιν.
ἀνέστη γὰρ καὶ ἀπῆλθεν⁶ ἐκεῖ ὅθεν ἀπεστάλη.

As part of the attempt to correct the text the scribe commenced inserting a superscripted phrase, but when he had written the initial two letters, το, he discarded this remedy. This has resulted in a reading where
one can see the cause of a number of the errors, but it is impossible to
reconstruct with any confidence the underlying text.

7. There appears to be an orthographical error here which has
   resulted in attaching a first aorist ending -ατε, where a second
   aorist form is required -ετε.[959]
8. The word which occurs here is represented in all editions of the
   Greek text either as ἔκει[960] or ἔκειτο.[961] While the first two letters
   are clear, the next two are highly aberrant especially in comparison with the same four letters of ἐκεῖ that are written on the line
   immediately below, or the example two line above in the word
   ἐκεῖνον. In fact the third and fourth letters may not be letters at
   all, but may be an insertion mark pointing to the superscripted
   το. Perhaps the reason some have preferred the reading ἔκειτο is
   because the word occurs in the parallel passage in Matt 28.6. It
   must be stated again that certainty is not possible here because of
   the the highly corrupt and poorly written state of the text at this
   point.
9. For a discussion of the problematic letters το see note six above,
   where this is assessed in conjunction with the wider textual issues
   which impinge upon this verse.
10. Here the form φοβηθεῖς (aorist passive participle nominative mas-
    culine singular) does not agree in gender or number with the sub-
    ject of the verb, αἱ γυναῖκες (feminine plural). The simplest solution
    is to emend the text by adding the letters αι, thereby changing the
    form to φοβηθεῖσαι (aorist passive participle nominative feminine

---

[959] For a fuller discussion of this phenomenon see BDF §§80–83.
[960] For instance see See Kraus und Nicklas, *Das Petrusevangelium und die Petrus-apokalypse*, 48.
[961] Swete, *The Akhmîm Fragment of the Apocryphal Gospel of St Peter*, 23; Robinson and James, *The Gospel according to Peter and the Revelation of Peter*, 88; Vaganay, *L'Évangile de Pierre*, 328.

plural). This solution has been proposed by almost all of scholars, including most recently Kraus and Nicklas.[962] Although Bouriant simply transcribed the reading preserved in the manuscript, scholars such as Harnack, Robinson and Swete all emended the text to read φοβηθεῖσαι.

## COMMENTARY

**13.55a  καὶ ἀπελθοῦσαι εὗρον τὸν τάφον ἠνεῳγμένον καὶ προσελθοῦσαι παρέκυψαν ἐκεῖ.** The second scene in the story of the women's journey to the tomb commences with their arrival at the burial site. Here, the aorist particle functions adverbially (cf. the simplex form ἐλθοῦσαι in Mk 16.1). Its sequential placement before εὗρον portrays action that occurred before the time of the main verb.[963] Thus, the author communicates a certain time lapse between the conversation that was reported in the previous pericope and the arrival which is described at this point. Having moved the women to the burial site, the discovery of the open tomb is the first observation that is made by the women. Thus, immediately the concerns of gaining access to the tomb which had been articulated by the women as they made their journey are shown to have been irrelevant. Although the canonical gospels do not contain the phrase καί ἀπελθοῦσαι, since they do not have such a developed account of the women's departure and journey, the aorist verb form εὗρον is found in Lk 24.2, εὗρον δὲ τὸν λίθον ἀποκεκυλισμένον ἀπὸ τοῦ μνημείου.[964] It is debatable whether this shared term can be seen as suggesting dependence on the Lukan narrative at this point, since it is both a common term and the natural language of discovery. Moreover, since there are no other connections with the Lukan account in this phrase, it is perhaps best to see this single shared word as being coincidental. It is also noticeable that none of the canonical accounts speaks of 'the tomb having been opened' τὸν τάφον ἠνεῳγμενον. Instead they prefer to describe the phenomenon in terms of the stone having rolled away (Matt 28.2; Mk 16.4; Lk 24.2;

---

[962] Kraus und Nicklas, *Das Petrusevangelium und die Petrusapokalypse*, 48.

[963] Porter, *Verbal Aspect in the Greek of the New Testament with Reference to Tense and Mood*, 111.

[964] This parallel to Lukan account is noted by Swete. See Swete, *The Akhmîm Fragment of the Apocryphal Gospel of St Peter*, 22–23.

Jn 20.1).[965] This may in part be due to the fact that the rolling away of the stone has been narrated at an earlier point (*Gos. Pet.* 9.37),[966] and the language is varied here for stylistic reasons. However, it may simply be due to the author's preference for the verb ἀνοίγω (*Gos. Pet.* 9.36, 37; 11.44; 13.55).

The second half of this clause announces the act of the women entering the tomb. Structurally it mirrors the first part of the verse, the conjunction καί followed by an aorist nominative plural participle co-ordinated with an aorist indicative plural verb. For the author this is a convenient way to express to related actions. The verb προσέρχομαι is used in one other place in this narrative, to describe the scene when the Jewish leaders come to Pilate to request that he orders the soldiers to keep quiet about the events of the resurrection εἶτα προσελθόντες πάντες ἐδέοντο αὐτοῦ (*Gos. Pet.* 11.47). There is a difference of interpretation here among commentators as to whether the verb describes only 'drawing near' to the tomb, or actual 'entering into' the burial place. Swete's translation shows that he favours the first alternative, 'and they came near and stooped down to look in there.'[967] Thus he renders the participle as 'they came near'. Also he understands the women to be peering into the tomb from outside. Vaganay offers the same interpretation in his French translation: 's'étant approchées, elles se penchèrent pour y regarder' ['upon approaching, they stoop down to look'].[968] He also explicitly states, 'The women do not enter, all they do is stoop down.'[969] It should also be observed that the choice of compound verb deviates from the compound form εἰσέρχομαι found in the Markan and Lukan accounts of the entry into the tomb (Mk 16.5; Lk 24.3). The distinction between the preposition πρός denoting movement 'towards', and εἰς describing motion 'into', should probably be preserved here. For the author of the Akhmîm text this distinction seems to be based upon the biblical usage, especially the preponderance of the term as found in the first gospel. Matthew repeatedly reserves

---

[965] In Matthew this is not a discovery, so much as it is an observation of the act of the angel physically rolling the stone away from the mouth of the sepulchre.

[966] Yet even here the parallelism is not perfect. The synotical gospels employ the compound verb ἀποκυλίω to describe the phenomenon, where in *Gos. Pet.* 9.37 the simplex form κυλίω is used. Although when the women discuss the difficulty in rolling the stone away they use the compound form ἀποκυλίω (*Gos. Pet.* 12.53).

[967] Swete, *The Akhmîm Fragment of the Apocryphal Gospel of St Peter*, 27.

[968] Vaganay, *L'Évangile de Pierre*, 327.

[969] Vaganay, *L'Évangile de Pierre*, 326.

the term for approach to or towards a person or location, while using other forms to represent motion into a location. A particularly significant example is found in Matt 8.5 where the two compound verbs προσέρχομαι and εἰσέρχομαι occur in the same verse.

The act of stooping down, also reflects a picture of the women peering into the tomb, but not actually entering into the burial chamber. The term παράκυπτω occurs five times in the NT, three of these in connection with observers stooping down to look into the tomb on the first Easter morning (Lk 24.12; Jn 20.5, 11). From this it may supposed that the burial chamber was at least partially subterranean, able to be viewed from above by looking down through the entrance. This is possible in conjunction with the form of loculi tombs hewn into the hillsides around Jerusalem.[970]

**13.55b   καὶ ὁρῶσιν ἐκεῖ τινα νεανίσκον καθεζόμενον μέσῳ τοῦ τάφου.** The open tomb was not a surprise for the audience of this narrative, since unlike the women they had been privileged with the authorial description of the rolling away of the stone. Similarly, the presence of the young man inside the tomb has already been anticipated for the readers by the author. During the deliberations of the witnesses at the tomb, after the gigantic figures disappear from the story, a 'man' descends and enters the tomb (*Gos. Pet.* 11.44).[971] His role has not been stated to this point, but it now appears that his narrative function is to engage the women in conversation. However, even if this detail had not been announced earlier in the narrative, the audience may still have expected such a figure to be present if they were familiar with the canonical tradition. While there is a concatenation of canonical terminology throughout this pericope, again the closest parallels are with Mark's gospel. Matthew has nobody inside the tomb, instead he has a single angel descend from heaven (Matt 28.2). Luke has two men in dazzling garments appear to the women only after they had entered the tomb, ἄνδρες δύο ἐπέστησαν αὐταῖς ἐν ἐσθῆτι ἀστραπτούσῃ (Lk 24.4).[972] In the Johannine account the tomb is

---

[970] Rachael Hachlili, 'Burials', *ABD* vol. 1, 789–791.

[971] In relation to the young man in the Akhmîm text Brown states, 'Presumably he was the one whom the women found when they came to the tomb.' Brown, *The Gospel according to John XIII–XXI*, 989.

[972] Fitzmyer observes that 'in the Lucan summary of this episode in v. 23, the "two men" will become "angels."' Fitzmyer, *The Gospel According to Luke X–XXIV*, 1545.

initially devoid of people or heavenly beings (Jn 20.5–7), but on her second visit to the burial site Mary Magdalene does later encounter two angels sitting at the head and the foot of where the body had been positioned (Jn 20.12). Mark, in common with the Akhmîm text, has the women discover a single figure, termed νεανίσκος, who is sitting (καθήμενον Mk 16.5//καθεζόμενον Gos. Pet. 13.55) inside the tomb, with an accompanying description of the attire of this being. There is no need to draw too great a distinction between these terms that designate the 'sitting' posture. The word used is Akhmîm text καθέζομαι (only seven times in the NT), is less common than the parallel term κάθημαι in the Markan narrative, which occurs ninety-two times in the NT. The more common term κάθημαι also has the meaning of enthronement associated with it in the NT.[973] This sense, however, is not part of the Markan narrative.

The detail provided in the Akhmîm narrative about the location where the man was sitting, μέσῳ τοῦ τάφου, deviates from the Markan description ἐν τοῖς δεξιοῖς (Mk 16.5), and the Johannine portrayal of the two angelic figures ἕνα πρὸς τῇ κεφαλῇ καὶ ἕνα πρὸς τοῖς ποσίν (Jn 20.12). While it has been suggested that the Markan phrase ἐν τοῖς δεξιοῖς (at the right) 'may suggest that authority to speak for the risen Christ has been delegated to this young man',[974] or that this 'makes the young man represent Christ',[975] it is difficult to see any theological motivation for the author of the Gospel of Peter in making this alteration. Rather it appears to be made for its purely graphic visual impact. Thus Vaganay suggests, 'It is not necessary to seek mysterious reasons for this change. The women who remained outside can see only the central part of the sepulchre.'[976]

**13.55c** ὡραῖον καὶ περιβεβλημένον στολὴν λαμπροτάτην ὅστις ἔφη αὐταῖς. While this being is described as a νεανίσκος, the description of him (and the mode of his manifestation in Gos. Pet. 11.44) suggests anything but an earthly figure. The descriptions of heavenly beings in the canonical accounts centre on luminosity of garments or general appearance. Here a new element is introduced. As Mara notes, 'In biblical literature the adjective ὡραῖος is never associated

---

[973] EDNT, vol. 2, 222–224.
[974] Evans, Mark 8:27–16:20, 536.
[975] Gundry, Mark: A Commentary on His Apology for the Cross, 990.
[976] Vaganay, L'Évangile de Pierre, 327.

with νεανίσκος, whereas such an association is frequent in Classical literature.'[977] This adjective does not occur with great frequency in the NT (four times only: Matt 23.27; Acts 3.2, 10; Rom 10.15), and it denotes the quality of attractiveness, in the sense of being 'beautiful, fair, lovely, pleasant'.[978] Without example, Vaganay notes that ὡραῖος is often used in connection with the term νεανίσκος.[979] This may be seen as exemplifying a homo-erotic idealization of the young male form, but such connections are not necessarily always the basis of the link. However, it is also noted that the adjective 'never refers to angels in the language of the bible.'[980]

Having described the physical beauty of the young man, the author, in line with canonical traditions, depicts the shining clothing that he is wearing, albeit with a different selection of vocabulary. The verbal aspect of the perfect form περιβεβλημένον denotes the state of 'being clothed', here with a στολὴν λαμπροτάτην. In Matthew's account the simile 'white as snow' is employed presumably as a indicator of purity and connection with the heavenly realm, ὁ ἔνδυμα αὐτοῦ λευκὸν ὡς χιών (Matt 28.3). By contrast, Luke relates the dazzling quality of the garments ἐν ἐσθῆτι ἀστραπτούσῃ (Lk 24.4). Like Matthew, John uses an adjective alone to describe the apparel of the two angels, ἐν λευκοῖς (Jn 20.12). Once again, the phraseology chosen by the author of the Akhmîm account aligns most closely with that of Mark's gospel, περιβεβλημένον στολὴν λευκήν (Mk 16.5). It shares the same perfect participle περιβεβλημένον to denote the state of being dressed, it describes the garment as a στολή, and uses a single adjective to qualify the noun. The one difference is in the choice of adjective. In place of the Markan description of 'whiteness' λευκός, this is replaced by a description of the luminous quality of the clothing, λαμπροτάτος. Once again, there is an apparent literary dependence between the Markan account and that story contained in the Akhmîm text. However, the depiction of the garment becomes more spectacular in the latter, by drawing upon Luke's presentation of radiant, or light-infused clothing. Therefore, the direction of dependence appears to be that of the Akhmîm text drawing upon Mark's version of the pericope, but heightening the supernatural phenomenon by following the precedent suggested

[977] Mara, Évangile de Pierre, 206.
[978] BDAG, 1103.
[979] Vaganay, L'Évangile de Pierre, 327.
[980] Vaganay, L'Évangile de Pierre, 327.

by Luke. Vaganay notes that the term λαμπρός 'serves to underline the surpassing brilliance of the supernatural apparition.'[981]

The verse concludes with a formulaic introduction to the speech which follows between the young man and the women in the next two verses, ὅστις ἔφη αὐταῖς. The verse division is perhaps unhelpful and this introduction would be better included with the speech that takes place in the following verse, as is the case with the Mark speech formula in Mk 16.6, ὁ δὲ λέγει αὐταῖς. The use of the relative indefinite pronoun (often in place of the relative pronoun ὅς) is, as BDF notes, a feature that is found with increased frequency in *koine* Greek.[982]

**13.56a** τί ἤλθατε; τίνα ζητεῖτε; μὴ τὸν σταυρωθέντα ἐκεῖνον;.
This verse opens with a series of three unanswered questions addressed by the young man to the group of women. The first question, comprising of a neuter singular interrogative pronoun with an aorist second person plural verb, enquires concerning the motivation of the women in coming to the burial place. The use of the neuter singular interrogative pronoun is the standard manner of asking questions beginning with 'why' in Hellenistic Greek.[983] This first question has no parallel in the canonical tradition, and is most plausibly understood as being a redactional addition of the author of this text. Vaganay sees this as a general introductory question which precedes that the two more specific enquiries that follow.[984] It is debatable, however, whether this question shows any real difference in specificity or generality from the two questions that come after it. The reason for coming to the tomb, would require a more complex answer than the second question, which would be answered with just a name, or the last question which is rhetorical and demands no answer. The accent that emerges from this sequence of unanswered questions is the absurdity, at least from the point of view of the young man, in the women coming to the tomb. His interrogative tone questions their perception, since they have not realized beforehand that the tomb would be empty.

The second question, τίνα ζητεῖτε, finds parallels in the canonical gospels. In Mk 16.6 the same verb is used in conversation between the young man and the women, but not as part of a question. However, in

---

[981] Vaganay, *L'Évangile de Pierre*, 327.
[982] See BDF §293.3.
[983] BDF §299.4.
[984] Vaganay, *L'Évangile de Pierre*, 328.

the synoptic accounts it forms part of a statement made by the male figure explaining why the tomb is empty Ἰησοῦν ζητεῖτε τὸν Ναζαρηνὸν (cf. Matt 28.5; Lk 24.5). John is the only one of the canonical gospels to use the verb ζητέω in this context as part of an interrogative clause, τίνα ζητεῖς; (Jn 20.15).[985] The only difference being that since the fourth gospel has Mary Magdalene present at this stage without accompanying women, this results in the singular verbal form being used, rather than plural form of the verb as in the *Gospel of Peter*. Here the text, which follows in general the Markan outline of the story of the women at the tomb, has introduced a Johannine element to form the series of three questions, but it must modified that element from the fourth gospel to make it grammatically consistent with a plural group of women. It is also important to realize, as in the fourth gospel, the second question directs attention away from the women themselves and instead focuses on Jesus.[986]

The third and final question in this sequence finds no parallel in the fourth gospel, but does align with the description of Jesus as 'the crucified one' τὸν ἐσταυρωμένον (Matt 28.5//Mk 16.6). In the Akhmîm text this description has been transformed into a question μὴ τὸν σταυρωθέντα ἐκεῖνον. The question is largely rhetorical with the tone being an incredulous declaration that the women surely cannot be expecting to find the one who had been crucified present in the tomb. The aorist passive participle σταυρωθέντα indicates perhaps not only an action which was completed in the past, but also may communicate the fact that this state of 'being crucified' is now over.[987]

**13.56b\***     [ἀνέστη καὶ ἀπῆλθεν]. It has been suggested in text critical note that these words, which occur again later in the verse are not original to the text, but have been replicated here due to a scribal error. This phrase will be commented upon when it occurs further on the narrative.[988]

---

[985] In terms of the macronarrative of the fourth gospel Lincoln notes that the question τίνα ζητεῖς 'recalls the similar one that had been Jesus' first words in this Gospel's narrative.' Lincoln, *The Gospel according to St John*, 493.

[986] See A.J. Köstenberger, *John*, BECNT (Grand Rapids: Baker, 2004) 568.

[987] Further on this, see Vaganay, *L'Évangile de Pierre*, 328.

[988] See text critical notes 6–8 in this section for an extended didcussion of the corrupt nature of the text at this point.

**13.56b**  εἰ δὲ μὴ πιστεύετε, παρακύψατε καὶ ἴδετε τὸν τόπον
ἔκ[ει]το…ὅτι οὐκ ἔστιν. Here the young man offers the women the
opportunity to confirm his claims. Yet this is no neutral invitation, it
challenges their level of belief. If they doubt the veracity of his words,
they can inspect the empty tomb for themselves. In certain respects the
narrator has undone the logic of the Markan narrative. In the second
gospel, the young man first tells the women that Jesus has been risen,
that he is no longer present in the tomb, and invites them to inspect
the empty tomb (Mk 16.6). By comparison, the author of this reworked
account of the women-at-the-tomb story, has not communicated the
fact of the resurrection or the empty tomb to this female party. Instead
he gently upbraids their possible unbelief, εἰ δὲ μὴ πιστεύετε. Strictly
in terms of the internal logic of this narrative it is unclear what the
women are meant to believe at this point. However, this story does not
stand on its own. The hearers are meant to draw upon their repository
of understanding which is based on the canonical versions to fill-in
such inconsistencies. Thus again, there is evidence that the author is
working with the pre-existing canonical versions of the story to form
his own recast narrative. Logically, the invitation to inspect the tomb
is also unnecessary, since on their arrival the women stooped down
and looked inside the tomb (*Gos. Pet.* 13.55). Mara notes that there are
verbal correspondences between these words and the story of doubt-
ing Thomas in Jn 20.25–29.[989] This is seen as being coincidental rather
than intentional.

The invitation to view the resting-place of Jesus is found in both the
Matthean and Mark accounts. Here, the language draws more heavily
on the form presented in the first gospel.

| Matt 28.6 | δεῦτε ἴδετε τὸν τόπον ὅπου ἔκειτο |
| Mk 16.6 | ἴδε ὁ τόπος ὅπου ἔθηκαν αὐτόν |
| *Gos. Pet.* 13.57 | καὶ ἴδετε τὸν τόπον [ἔνθα] ἔκ[ει]το |

Matthew and the Akhmîm text agree in the verbal forms they preserve
in this clause.[990] Syntactically the forms agree, and even the expunged
term in *Gos. Pet.* 13.57, suggests this this may have been deleted
because of its deviation from the known word ὅπου.

---

[989] Mara, *Évangile de Pierre*, 206.
[990] Admittedly this depends on reading the superscripted letters το as the continuation of the preceding four letters. On this see text critical note 8.

Having either accidently omitted or intentionally delayed the declaration made by the young man that the body was not present in the tomb, the author now includes this piece of information which is vital for the women. The phrase, ὅτι οὐκ ἔστιν, although probably textually corrupt, is now a somewhat truncated version of the declaration made by the young man to the women οὐκ ἔστιν ὧδε in each of the synoptics concerning the fact that Jesus has been raised. There are slight differences in arrangement in each of those accounts:

Matt 28.6    οὐκ ἔστιν ὧδε, ἠγέρθη γὰρ καθὼς εἶπεν
Mark 16.6    ἠγέρθη, οὐκ ἔστιν ὧδε
Luke 24.6    οὐκ ἔστιν ὧδε, ἀλλὰ ἠγέρθη

The minor agreement between Matthew and Luke in placing the clause οὐκ ἔστιν ὧδε before the verb ἠγέρθη is not an indication of their mutual dependence. Rather, it is the kind of grammatical improvement that one would expect the narratives to make independently. Vaganay observes that the author 'takes up again use of the synoptics which he had let fall earlier'[991] This results in a clause that appears incomplete and out of place. Of the various suggestions to amend the text, Robinson's proposal to instate the word ὧδε at the end of the clause appears the most natural.[992] This may be a likely reconstruction since it is not particularly intrusive, and it also draws upon the synoptic form, which is the base text being used to construct this narrative.

**13.56c** ἀνέστη γὰρ καὶ ἀπῆλθεν ἐκεῖ ὅθεν ἀπεστάλη. The text becomes more certain at this point. The opening clause, ἀνέστη γὰρ καὶ ἀπῆλθεν, combines both resurrection and ascension motifs. Mara argues that this combination 'marks the existential union, for the author, between the resurrection and the ascension, as in Jn 20.17.'[993] It is unclear exactly how this is an 'existential union', and it may be better to speak of a tendency to collapse the temporal distance between these events, in contrast to the portrayal in Matthew and Luke-Acts. Suggestions that this combination of resurrection and ascension reflects a Gnostic tendency, presumably on the basis that resurrection form cannot be contaminated by contact with the material world,

---

[991] Vaganay, L'Évangile de Pierre, 329.
[992] In a note, Robinson suggests '5 ἔστιν] forsitan addendum ὧδε.' Robinson and James, The Gospel according to Peter and the Revelation of Peter, 88.
[993] Mara, Évangile de Pierre, 207.

appears somewhat tenuous.[994] Rather the reason for the report in this form is simply because the audience is already aware that, along with the two supporting figures, the Lord has already returned to the heavenly realm.[995]

Similarly, the young man's final comment, ἐκεῖ ὅθεν ἀπεστάλη, need not be seen as encompassing a Gnostic conception of the descent of the divine *logos* on the human Jesus at baptism (or some other point) only to return to the Father at this later point. As has already been argued, any attempt to link the Christology of the Akhmîm fragment with Gnostic or docetic conceptions, struggle to adequately account for the reality of the suffering on the cross, the fact that the corpse is still a divine entity which causes the earth to quake and that there would be no need for such a body to be resurrected (albeit in its gargantuan form). The notion of Jesus as the divine envoy sent from the Father, who will return to the place from which he was sent, has strong resonances with the Christology of the fourth gospel. This return to the Father is a theme that is announced throughout the fourth gospel, although it perhaps finds its fullest articulation in the second half of the gospel, particularly in the farewell discourses. In Jn 8.14, having declared knowledge of his origin, Jesus also states that he is aware of where he is going, καὶ ποῦ ὑπάγω. The omniscient narrator announces Jesus' self-knowledge of return to the Father, εἰδὼς ὁ Ἰησοῦς ὅτι ἦλθεν αὐτοῦ ἡ ὥρα ἵνα μεταβῇ ἐκ τοῦ κόσμου τούτου πρὸς τὸν πατέρα (Jn 13.1). This same theme is articulated directly by Jesus in Jn 16.28.[996] While such Christological affirmations may partially inform Gnostic understandings of the return of the *logos* to the Father, it is not automatically the case that such language must be classified as Gnostic (unless one wishes to concede that the fourth gospel itself is a Gnostic or Docetic text).[997] Therefore, the ideas of 'return to the Father' or the

---

[994] H. Stocks, 'Zum Petrusevangelium', *Neue Kirckliche Zeitschrift* 13 (1902) 27; 14 (1903) 511–542.

[995] Swete suggests that at this point the narrative is looking back to the exit from the tomb described in chapter 9. Swete, *The Akhmîm Fragment of the Apocryphal Gospel of St Peter*, 23.

[996] Other instances in the fourth gospel where Jesus speaks of return to the Father include Jn 14.12, 28; 16.7; 17.11, 13. For a discussion of this aspect of Johannine Christology see W.R.G. Loader, *The Christology of the Fourth Gospel: Structure and Issues*, BET 23 (2nd rev ed; Frankfurt: Peter Lang, 1992) 81–82.

[997] While the formulations in the fourth gospel may have been congenial to the development of docetic or gnostic theology, the situation in the First Epistle of John

'pre-existence of Christ' are not in themselves proof of the Gnostic or heterodox character of this text.

**13.57** τότε αἱ γυναῖκες φοβηθεῖσαι ἔφυγον. Dependence on the synoptic tradition is once more in evidence. Most notably in the final verse of the shortest form of the Markan narrative the verbs φεύγω and φοβέομαι are combined to describe the response of the women to their encounter with the young man. As in the Markan account, no explicit cause of the fear is provided. However, in contrast to the Markan where the emphasis falls on the fear not only through the verb φοβέομαι, but also by use of the phrase τρόμος καὶ ἔκστασις, here the stress is on the action of fleeing. Although the reason for this fear is not explicitly stated, in relation to the Markan narrative Hooker suggests that 'the reaction of the women is entirely natural...this is precisely how many other characters in the story have reacted up to this point when confronted with the power of God.'[998] Also in relation to the shortest textual form of the Markan narrative, Gilfillan Upton notes the effect of disarray the words of the young man have on the women. She notes that the 'perlocutionary effect of shock and disbelief, for both the women and the audience, is achieved by the use of a series of emotional words.'[999] To a large extent, the motif of shock and the devastating impact on the emotions of the women is downplayed in the *Gospel of Peter* through the omission of some of the more emotionally laden terms from the Markan narrative and by letting the accent fall on the flight rather than the fear.

At this point both the women and the young man disappear from the narrative. Since the extant portion of this text is fast drawing to a close, the change of scene in the next pericope does not allow speculation concerning any further role for these characters in this narrative. Also, it is perhaps not possible to state with any certainty with which form of Mark's gospel the author of the Akhmîm account may have been most familiar. The abruptness of the ending to the material in

---

demonstrates that there were a number of members in the Johannine community who wished to hold on to the formulations of the fourth evangelist, yet without following the docetic tendencies of those who had left the group.

[998] Hooker, *The Gospel according to Saint Mark*, 245.

[999] B. Gilfillan Upton, *Hearing Mark's Endings: Listening to Ancient Popular Texts Through Speech Act Theory*, BINS 79 (Leiden: Brill, 2006) 150.

*Gos. Pet.* 13.55–57, coupled with the clear dependence on the Markan narrative through the women-at-the-tomb story, does, however, suggest that the author may have been drawing from the form of text which ended at Mark 16.8a.[1000]

---

[1000] For recent studies on the ending of Mark's gospel see W.R. Farmer, *The Last Twelve Verses of Mark*, SNTSMS 25 (Cambridge: CUP, 1974); J.A. Kelhoffer, *Miracle and Mission: The Authentication of Missionaries and their Message in the Longer Ending of Mark*, WUNT 112 (Tübingen: Mohr Siebeck, 2000); Gilfillan Upton, *Hearing Mark's Endings*.

# THE DEPARTURE OF THE DISCIPLES AND CROWDS
## FROM JERUSALEM (14.58–60)

58. ἦν δὲ τελευταία¹ ἡμέρα τῶν ἀζύμων καὶ πολλοί τινες² ἐξήρχοντο ὑποστρέφοντες εἰς τοὺς οἴκους αὐτῶν τῆς ἑορτῆς παυσαμίνης.³ 59. ἡμεῖς δὲ οἱ δώδεκα μαθηταὶ τοῦ κ̅υ̅ ἐκλαίομεν καὶ ἐλυπούμεθα καὶ ἕκαστος λυπούμενος διὰ τὸ συμβὰν ἀπηλλάγη εἰς τὸν οἶκον αὐτοῦ. 60. ἐγὼ δὲ Σίμων Πέτρος καὶ Ἀνδρέας ὁ ἀδελφός μου λαβόντες ἡμῶν τὰ λίνα ἀπήλθαμεν εἰς τὴν θάλασσαν⁴, καὶ ἦν σὺν ἡμῖν Λευείς ὁ τοῦ Ἀλφαίου ὃν κ̅ς̅⁵...

58. Now it was the last day of the unleavened bread and many people left, returning to their houses, the feast being over. 59. But we, the twelve disciples of the Lord, wept and were saddened, and each being sad because of the event withdrew to his house. 60. But I, Simon Peter, and Andrew my brother, taking our nets went to the sea, and there was with us Levi the son of Alphaeus, whom the Lord...

## Text Critical Notes

1. Irregular letter formation is apparent in this word due to the ligature between the first and second letters. The top horizontal stroke of the τ descends on the right-hand side, forming an angel of depression of approximately 40° to the horizontal. This becomes the base of the following ε.[1001] The result is that the second letter is slightly raised in comparison to the rest of the letters. This word also represents the scribe's tendency towards cursive writing.
2. There is somewhat confusing inconsistency in letter spacing at this point. The final ι of πολλοί stands closer to the intial letter of τινες, than it does to the penultimate letter of πολλοί. Furthermore, there is a gap of 2mm between the third and fourth letters of τινες, whereas there is no significant spacing between the final ς and the initial ε of ἐξήρχοντο which follows.
3. There is an orthographical error in the ending of the form παυσαμίνης, which presumably should read παυσαμένης. This is

---

[1001] See the comments on the formation of the letter ε in Gebhardt, *Das Evangelium und die Apokalypse des Petrus*, 11.

noted by Swete[1002] and Vaganay. The latter simply states 'παυσαμένης (in the ms. mistake for: παυσαμινης).'[1003] This is another example of an aberrant form due to an itacism. This phenomenon has already been discussed in the commentary,[1004] and Caragounis provides a detailed examination of this confusion in vowels.[1005]

4. An orthographical variant occurs here. Instead of the standard spelling θάλασσαν, the scribe writes this word with a double lambda, i.e. θάλλασσαν. This error is noted by most editions of the Greek text,[1006] or commentaries based upon the Greek of the Akhmîm text.[1007] Robinson corrects the text to the standard lexical form without any comment.[1008]

5. This final use of the title κύριος, which occurs thirteen times in the narrative, presents an otherwise unattested feature. Here the word occurs anarthorously, where on every other occasion it has been preceded by the definite article.[1009] This has led most commentators to suggest the conjectural emendation of inserting a definite article before the noun. Although Swete does not correct the text, he does note that both Robinson and Zahn make such a correction.[1010]

## COMMENTARY

**14.58a** ἦν δὲ τελευταία ἡμέρα τῶν ἀζύμων. The author's fondness for temporal markers throughout the narrative has been noted. This is the last such indication that is provided in the extant portion of text. The period of time that has elapsed between the previous scene and this one may be the largest temporal transition in the text, however, there are two differing understandings of what this temporal notice is representing for the author. The first possibility is that

---

[1002] Swete, *The Akhmîm Fragment of the Apocryphal Gospel of St Peter*, 23.

[1003] Vaganay, *L'Évangile de Pierre*, 337.

[1004] See text critical note 3 in the section dealing with *Gos. Pet.* 12.50, 54.

[1005] Caragounis, *The Development of Greek and the New Testament*, 500.

[1006] See Swete, *The Akhmîm Fragment of the Apocryphal Gospel of St Peter*, 24; Kraus und Nicklas, *Das Petrusevangelium und die Petrusapokalypse*, 48.

[1007] Vaganay, *L'Évangile de Pierre*, 339; Mara, *Évangile de Pierre*, 66.

[1008] Robinson and James, *The Gospel according to Peter and the Revelation of Peter*, 88.

[1009] Vaganay also observes this phenomenon, 'Le mot κύριος a d'ailleurs toujours [except here!] l'article dans notre fragment.' Vaganay, *L'Évangile de Pierre*, 340.

[1010] Swete, *The Akhmîm Fragment of the Apocryphal Gospel of St Peter*, 24.

the author is aware of the accurate details of Jewish cultic festivals and hence understands the full period of eight days of celebrations to have elapsed between the commence of Passover and the details of this scene. Previous events were described as taking place on the morning of the Lord's day ὀρθοῦ δὲ τῆς κυριακῆς (*Gos. Pet.* 12.50). The narrative, if it is attuned to such matters, appears to assume a Johannine chronology in *Gos. Pet.* 2.5,[1011] where it is stated that Jesus was handed over prior to the first day of the festival of unleavened bread. The festival of unleavened bread, which began on the day after the Passover, 'was a related seven-day holiday that also commemorated the exodus from Egypt.'[1012] Thus the execution of Jesus, according to the time frame presumed by the Akhmîm account, would have taken place on the fourteenth of Nisan. This being the case, according to the chronology supplied here, the festival of unleavened bread would have commenced on a Sabbath and ended on the following Friday. The description of all the people quitting Jerusalem on that day, would then be necessitated by the desire to leave Jerusalem after the final corporate gathering in order to arrive home prior to the commencement of the Sabbath, when travel was not possible. Taking this view of the span of the entire narrative, Vaganay states, 'The beginning of this new pericope transports us without transition from the morning of Passover to the "last day of the festival of Unleavened Bread".'[1013] Likewise, Mara concurs with this assessment. She states, 'The author transports us to a week after Passover.'[1014] However, this reconstruction does not resolve all the difficulties inherent in this chronological scheme.

If the last day of unleaven bread denotes events five days after 'the Lord's day', when the women encountered the young man at the tomb, then it becomes necessary to postulate that the disciples gained no knowledge of the resurrection of Jesus during this period. This is precisely what Vaganay suggests, 'The author supposes that, during this lapse of time, the apostles remained in Jerusalem in the sadness caused by the loss of the Master and also, without any doubt, in the ignorance

---

[1011] See Swete, *The Akhmîm Fragment of the Apocryphal Gospel of St Peter*, xxv.

[1012] J.C. Vanderkam, *An Introduction to Early Judaism* (Grand Rapids, Michigan: Eerdmans, 2001) 204.

[1013] Vaganay, *L'Évangile de Pierre*, 331.

[1014] In a footnote, Mara, comments that this temporal scheme has been adopted by Harnack, Schubert, Swete and Stülken, although she is most heavily dependent on Vaganay for the details of this hypothesis. Mara, *Évangile de Pierre*, 209.

of resurrection.'[1015] Not only does this appear counter-intuitive, it also goes against the storylines of the Matthean, Lukan and Johannine accounts with the women reporting what had transpired to the apostles. For this reason Lods suggested that the author of the Akhmîm text is misinformed in his understanding of the duration of the Jewish festival of the unleavened bread and perceives it as ending on the day of resurrection.[1016] This would result in this next scene taking place on the same day as the women's encounter with the young man at the tomb. While the temporal delay presupposed by the first option appears somewhat forced, it is admittedly not impossible, and caution should be exhibited since the conclusion of the narrative is unknown. However, it must also be remembered that the author has closely followed the Markan account of the women-at-the-tomb. Although he has not reproduced the note about the women's silence, καὶ οὐδενὶ οὐδὲν εἶπαν (Mk 16.8), which is one of the concluding editorial comments in the shortest form of gospel. If this were in his mind it would potentially explain why the disciples remained ignorant of the events of the resurrection for an extended period of time.

There are difficulties with either interpretation, and these problems are exacerbated by the fact that the narrative cuts out before any encounter between members of the twelve and the risen Lord take place. It might be best to lean towards taking the narrative at face-value and understanding a longer, rather than shorter temporal division between these scenes. Yet even if one adopts this course, perhaps a greater recognition needs to be given to the provisionality of this decision. This is especially the case since the author shows a decided lack of interest in the Jewish customs and institutions of Jesus' day, and instead seeks to blacken the Jews in his presentation of the events contained in the narrative.

**14.58b** καὶ πολλοί τινες ἐξήρχοντο ὑποστρέφοντες εἰς τοὺς οἴκους αὐτῶν. Here the narrative supplies transitional background information, that allows for a scene change from the city of Jerusalem to what is in *Gos. Pet.* 14.60 an undisclosed location beside an unnamed

---

[1015] Vaganay, *L'Évangile de Pierre*, 331.

[1016] The opinion of Lods is recorded by Swete, 'M. Lods, believing that Peter is still moving among Christian ideas, understands him to refer to Sunday, Nisan 16, Easter Day. No reference is given recording where Lods idea can be found. See Swete, *The Akhmîm Fragment of the Apocryphal Gospel of St Peter*, xxvi.

'sea'. Mara comments that 'many pious Jews, who remained until the end of the festival of Unleavened Bread, are now on the point of returning to their homes.'[1017] The *Gospel of Peter*, however, does not characterize these Jews as being pious, instead it provides a neutral account of their leaving Jerusalem simply as a scene-change device. In fact the term 'Jew' is not employed to describe these people. The author instead uses the expression πολλοί τινες which communicates both the size and indefinite nature of the group involved in the mass exodus from Jerusalem.[1018] Vaganay notes that this expression, which is not biblical in style, is used to denote multiplicity.[1019] It finds a parallel in the writings of Justin Martyr, καὶ πολλοί τινες καὶ πολλαὶ ἑξηκοντοῦται καὶ ἑβδομηκοντοῦται (Justin, *First Apol.* 15.6).[1020] Here the expression occurs in a different setting, describing the sexual continence of many Christian men and women who have never committed adultery and who have attained their sixtieth or seventieth year. It has also been noted that the imperfect form ἐξήρχοντο denotes an action that is likely to have taken place over a protracted period of time.[1021] The Temple Scroll offers the following prescriptions for behaviour on the final day of the festival of unleaven bread. 'The seventh day there will be a solemn assembly for YHWH. On it you will do no menial work.' (11QT 17.15–16).[1022] It is not possible to tell whether the ruling to perform no menial work on the final day, was unique to the Qumran community, or if it reflected wider practice. Philo may attest that certain prohibitions such as the one listed in 11QT were more widely in force. He states, 'Two days out of the seven, the first and the last are declared holy' (Philo, *Spec. Leg.* 2.28). This would suggest that if the injunction against menial work was widely recognized, then the whole endeavour of packing up and leaving Jerusalem on this day becomes historically problematic.

The notice about returning home formally stands as a corollary to the fact that the crowds have departed Jerusalem. The participle

---

[1017] Mara, *Évangile de Pierre*, 209.

[1018] On the size of the gathering of people in Jerusalem see Josephus, *B.J.* 6.420–421, although his figures may be exaggerated, and the calculation he provides is in error.

[1019] Vaganay, *L'Évangile de Pierre*, 336.

[1020] Marcovich (ed.), *Iustini Martyris: Apologiae pro Christianis, Dialogus cum Tryphone*, 54.

[1021] Vaganay, *L'Évangile de Pierre*, 336.

[1022] See F. Garcia Martinez, *The Dead Sea Scrolls Translated: The Qumran Texts in English* (2nd ed.; Leiden/Grand Rapids: Brill/Eerdmans, 1996) 157.

ὑποστρέφοντες denotes an action in progress from the perspective of the author.[1023] This creates an air of simultaneity with the happenings described in the final two verses. The phrase εἰς τοὺς οἴκους αὐτῶν finds an exact parallel in Lk 16.4 in the story of the shrewd steward.[1024] This, however, appears to be purely coincidental and the extremely common nature of these words, coupled with the totally different settings, means that no case for literary dependency can be suggested here. The function of this description of the general populace returning home, is to be able to introduce the parallel action of the disciples in returning to their places of abode as described in *Gos. Pet.* 14.59.

**14.58c** τῆς ἑορτῆς παυσαμένης. This subordinate clause emphisizes the fact that the festival was now finished. The term ἑορτῆς has been used previously in *Gos. Pet.* 2.5 as a way of designating the actual day of Passover. The acting of returning home at the completion of a festival is reminiscent of the infancy story in Lk 2.43–44, which describes the abortive return journey made in caravan by Mary and Joseph.[1025] The verb παύω denotes the completion or termination of an event.[1026] The main emphasis is to signal the close of events in Jerusalem.

**14.59a** ἡμεῖς δὲ οἱ δώδεκα μαθηταὶ τοῦ κ̅υ̅ ἐκλαίομεν καὶ ἐλυπούμεθα. For the second time in the text the presence of a first person narrator becomes apparent. The previous occurrence was in *Gos. Pet.* 7.26, where the first person narrator reports his action and those of his companions in concealing themselves from the Jewish authorities. In a similar vein, here the text returns to first person narration, relating the emotional turmoil experienced by Jesus' companions. The numerical label, οἱ δώδεκα, is used throughout the NT and early Christian literature to refer to a close group of associates who formed the nucleus of the initial stage of the Jesus movement.

---

[1023] Vaganay, *L'Évangile de Pierre*, 336.

[1024] It has been observed that the basis of the steward's plan is built upon the notion of reciprocity that existed in the Graeco-Roman world. (L.T. Johnson, *The Gospel of Luke*, Sacra Pagina 3 (Collegeville, Liturgical Press, 1991) 244. The majority of dwellings were probably primitive one room structures.

[1025] Swete, *The Akhmîm Fragment of the Apocryphal Gospel of St Peter*, 24.

[1026] See BDAG, 790.

As Holtz comments, 'Δώδεκα has its greatest significance in the NT in reference to a fixed group of disciples, whose formation the Gospels attribute to Jesus and who seem to be known in the oldest tradition simply by the designation οἱ δώδεκα.'[1027] Here the narrative expands on the simple designation by adding the additional referent 'disciples' to produce the phrase οἱ δώδεκα μαθηταί as the term used to represent the inner-band of followers. Although Holtz describes the 'fixed' nature of this group, the fluidity in the lists of names preserved in the Gospels suggests that while many of the participants in this group were permanent members,[1028] nonetheless even in this group there appears to have been some variation in constituents.[1029]

Table 18. The lists of the Twelve in the Synoptic Gospels[1030]

| Matt 10.2–5 | Mk 3.16–19 | Lk 6.14–16 |
| --- | --- | --- |
| Simon called Peter | Simon Peter | Simon named Peter |
| Andrew | James | Andrew |
| James | John (the sons of thunder) | James |
| John | Andrew | John |
| Philip | Philip | Philip |
| Bartholomew | Bartholomew | Bartholomew |
| Thomas | Matthew | Matthew |
| Matthew the tax collector | Thomas | Thomas |
| James the son of Alphaeus | James the son of Alphaeus | James the son of Alphaeus |
| Thaddaeus | Thaddaeus | Simon the Zealot |
| Simon the Cananean | Simon the Cananean | Judas the son of James |
| Judas Iscariot | Judas Iscariot | Judas Iscariot |

---

[1027] T. Holtz, 'Δώδεκα', in EDNT, vol. 1, 362.
[1028] See Matt 10.2–5; Mk 3.14–19; Lk 6.14–16.
[1029] R.F. Collins, 'Twelve, The', ABD 6, 671.
[1030] On this whole isse see C.K. Barrett, The Signs of an Apostle (London: Epworth, 1970).

The main difference, apart from ordering and explanatory comments, is Luke's replacement of the name Thaddaeus by Judas, designated as 'son of James' in distinction from Judas Iscariot.[1031]

The term δώδεκα also contains rich salvation-history overtones, drawing upon the heritage of the twelve tribes and twelve patriarchs of Israel as founding figures for the covenant-people. In this sense the appointment of the twelve exploits such a heritage either as an attempt to reformulate the socio-religious understanding of the chosen people, or as a subversion of the claim that Israel possessed a unique relationship with God. While this explains the origin and significance of the term in the initial stages of the Jesus-movement, in the Akhmîm text it is just part of the nomenclature to denote this close band of Jesus' followers.

Not only is the designation δώδεκα qualified by the label μαθηταί 'disciples', furthermore, the author of this texts makes explicit their relationship to a leader by appending the phrase τοῦ x̄ū. The *nomen sacrum* is employed to represent the narrator's preferred terminology for referring to Jesus.[1032] The use of the term 'the twelve' raises an interesting question about the non-extant portion of the narrative concerning the fate of Judas Iscariot. Does the retention of δώδεκα mean that his suicide (Matt 27.5), or untimely end (Acts 1.18) has not been narrated and thus the author can still correctly speak of twelve disciples? Cassels argues that this designation demonstrates that the author is ignorant of the fate of Judas.[1033] He argues that,

> Supposing this statement to be deliberately made, and we have no reason whatever from anything in the rest of the fragment to doubt it, this completely excludes the whole of the story of a betrayal of his master by Judas Iscariot...If the point be considered on the mere ground of historical probability, there is every reason to consider that the betrayal by Judas is a later product of the 'evolved gnosis.'[1034]

---

[1031] In Acts 1.13 a list of eleven names (minus the now dead Judas Iscariot) is recorded. Unsurprisingly this follows the form of names of the earlier Lukan list in Lk 6.14–16, including the description of Simon as 'the zealot'. The order of names is, however, different: Peter, John, James, Andrew, Philip, Thomas, Bartholomew, Matthew, James son of Alphaeus, Simon the Zealot, and Judas son of James.

[1032] As is noted elsewhere, the trem κύριος occurs thirteen times, eleven of which are written using a *nomen sacrum*.

[1033] Cassels, *The Gospel according to Peter: a study by the author of 'Supernatural Religion'*, 104.

[1034] Cassels, *The Gospel according to Peter: a study by the author of 'Supernatural Religion'*, 104.

Despite the certainty with which Cassels mounts his case, the logic he adduces is not necessarily compelling. While on a number of occasions the canonical gospels and Acts speak carefully about the eleven, οἱ ἕνδεκα (Matt 28.16; [Mk 16.14]; Lk 24.9, 33; Acts 1.26; 2.14),[1035] thus demonstrating a knowledge of the demise of Judas, this is not maintained consistently. While most sensitivity to this issue is shown in the Lukan writings, at points the term δώδεκα continues to be used without any sense of embarrassment. This is not because the authors are unfamiliar with the death of Judas, but rather because it has become a technical way of depicting the inner band of Jesus' followers, without concern for its strict numerical accuracy. Perhaps the most stiking occurrence of this is in the fourth gospel where Thomas, in a post-crucifixion scene, is designated as being on of the twelve Θωμᾶς δὲ εἷς ἐκ τῶν δώδεκα (Jn 20.5). In relation to this passage Keener notes that, '"the twelve" remain a defined group, even without Judas.'[1036] Although here it must be acknowledged that the Johannine narrative does not mention the demise of Judas. Similarly, in a resurrection appearance, Jesus is described as being seen by the twelve in the Pauline writings (1 Cor 15.5). Interestingly, in the passage which reads καὶ ὅτι ὤφθη Κηφᾷ εἶτα τοῖς δώδεκα, a number of manuscripts read ἕνδεκα in place of δώδεκα. Those manuscripts which preserve this reading have chiefly the so-called Western text form, D* F G 330 464* it vg sy^hmg goth, thus showing a significantly narrower range of attestation than exists for the reading δώδεκα. Metzger sees the reading ἕνδεκα as a 'pedantic correction.'[1037] Thiselton also notes that 'Since Judas was no longer present, some of the Fathers speculated that Twelve must have included Matthias (i.e. Origen, Chrysostom, Eusebius, Theophylact, and Photius; in the post-reformation period, Bengel).'[1038] Thus he concludes that 'the Twelve became a formal title for the corporate apostolic witness of those who had also followed Jesus during his earthly life, and who therefore underlined the continuity of witness to the One who was both crucified

---

[1035] Strictly speaking, this last reference to 'the eleven' refers to the now reformulated band of twelve disciples, since Matthias has been added to the number, and the eleven are mentioned alongside Peter, thus making a total of twelve, σταθεὶς δὲ ὁ Πέτρος σὺν τοῖς ἕνδεκα.

[1036] Keener, *The Gospel of John: A Commentary*, vol. II, 1208.

[1037] Metzger, *A Textual Commentary on the Greek New Testament*, 500.

[1038] A.C. Thiselton, *The First Epistle to the Corinthians*, NIGNT (Grand Rapids, Michigan/Carlisle: Eerdmans/Paternoster, 2000) 1204.

and raised.'[1039] In this same vein, the *Gospel of Peter* uses the term δώδεκα in a formulaic sense to designate the foundational core group of followers of Jesus, and this term cannot be used to determine the ignorance, or otherwise, of the text in relation to the death of Judas Iscariot.

Assembled together, the disciples are depicted as engaged in a corporate act of mourning and grief, ἐκλαίομεν καὶ ἐλυπούμεθα. For Vaganay there is an intentional contrast between the festal emotions of the departing throng (*Gos. Pet.* 14.58), and the downcast demeanour of the disciples expressed here.[1040] If such a contrast were the intention of the author, he does not go out of his way to communicate this in an explicit manner to his audience. The expression of emotions by co-ordinated pairs of terms is also a feature of the narrative at other points, πενθοῦντες καὶ κλαίοντες (*Gos. Pet.*, 7.27) and κλαῦσαι καὶ κόψεσθαι/κλαύσομεν καὶ κοψόμεθα (*Gos. Pet.* 12.52, 54).[1041] Vaganay speculates that the author does not include fasting as part of the process of lamentation, since the early church ceased its own fast after the paschal week. Thus he states that the author, 'also intentionally omits, the ἐνηστεύομεν of verse 27, because there is no fast in the Church during the Easter week.'[1042] There is, however, little to connect the text as being ætiologically a mirror of early church practice. Instead, this scene is both a flashback to the last occasion when the readers encountered the disciples in the narrative (*Gos. Pet.* 7.26–27), and also an opportunity to progress the story by reporting the dispersal of this assembled group in the following clause.

**14.59b** καὶ ἕκαστος λυπούμενος διὰ τὸ συμβὰν ἀπηλλάγη εἰς τὸν οἶκον αὐτοῦ. The author next describes the departure of the disciples, still in a state of mourning, which takes place concurrently with the festal crowds quitting Jerusalem. The corporate nature of the disciples' period of lament is now replaced by an emphasis on the individual figures returning to their homes. According to the author, the motivation for the return of the disciples to their homes is the experi-

---

[1039] Thiselton, *The First Epistle to the Corinthians*, 1205.
[1040] Vaganay, *L'Évangile de Pierre*, 337.
[1041] See Vaganay, *L'Évangile de Pierre*, 337.
[1042] 'Il omet aussi, et cela avec intention, le ἐνηστεύομεν du verset 27, parce qu'il n'y a pas de jeûne dans l'Église pendant la semaine de Pâques.' Vaganay, *L'Évangile de Pierre*, 337.

ence of sadness in relation to the event that had transpired. The logic is not particularly compelling. Why should sadness lead to departure specifically at this point (or for that matter at any other time)? However, logical explanations are not the primary concern. This description functions more as a device of scene-change, allowing the action to continue outside Jerusalem with the disciples transported to the new location of the story. The singular noun συμβάν used to describe the totality of events does not find exact parallel in the canonical gospels, although there might be a slight verbal echo in the Emmaus Road story of Lk 24.14, περὶ πάντων τῶν συμβεβηκότων τούτων.

The verb ἀπηλλάγη used to describe the departure of the disciples is rare in the NT, occurring only three times.[1043] While it has the meaning in a strong sense of being 'set free' or 'released',[1044] it can also denote the intransitive meaning 'to go away, *leave, depart*.'[1045] It is the latter sense that is intended here. The place of destination is stated imprecisely as εἰς τὸν οἶκον αὐτοῦ. Obviously, part of the reason for the lack of specificity is the fact that there were multiple destinations involved. Yet, as Vaganay notes, geographical imprecision is a feature of this narrative: 'as always the reader must supply the insufficient geographical indications.'[1046] Although nowhere stated in the extant portion of the narrative, commentators, no doubt under the influence of the canonical tradition contained in the Matthean and Mark accounts, have assumed that this destination was Galilee. Matthew and Mark both present a pre-Passion announcement made by Jesus where he declares μετὰ δὲ τὸ ἐγερθῆναί με προάξω ὑμᾶς εἰς τὴν Γαλιλαίαν (Matt 26.32; cf. Mk 14.28). This is reiterated three times in the final chapter of the first gospel (Matt 28.7, 10, 16). This appears to be a Matthean expansion of a tradition preserved in his Markan source material, προάγει ὑμᾶς εἰς τὴν Γαλιλαίαν ἐκεῖ αὐτὸν ὄψεσθε (Mk 16.7). Thus Cassels concludes, 'Simon Peter, and at least some of the disciples, must have gone into Galilee without any vision of the risen Jesus.'[1047]

---

[1043] Lk 12.58; Acts 19.12; Heb 2.15.
[1044] EDNT, vol. 1, 114.
[1045] BDAG, 96.
[1046] Vaganay, *L'Évangile de Pierre*, 338.
[1047] Cassels, *The Gospel according to Peter: a study by the author of 'Supernatural Religion'*, 105.

**14.60a** ἐγὼ δὲ Σίμων Πέτρος καὶ Ἀνδρέας ὁ ἀδελφός μου. The most prominent member of the Twelve is mentioned first here along with his brother Andrew. Thus, finally, the putative identity of the first person narrator of this mutilated text becomes apparent. It may well be the case that Peter's function as narrator had already been revealed to readers in the now no-longer extant portion of the text. The prominence of Peter among the disciples, both historically and at a literary level in the canonical accounts, appears to be beyond dispute. Notwithstanding this observation, leadership among the first generation of post-resurrection Christians appears to have been a fluid rather than a formal arrangement, and the role of James, the brother of the Lord, as leader of the Jerusalem church (cf. Acts 15.13f) must be factored into any discussion of early Christian leadership. Cullmann's suggestion that Peter left his position of local leader in Jerusalem, being replaced by James, to exercise universal influence on the Church, seems to impose a more rigorous hierarchical structure on the fledgling movement than actually was the case. It may be the case that Peter's decision to engage in a peripatetic mission left a leadership vacuum in Jerusalem which was filled by James. Yet we know nothing of James' rise to prominence (although other non-canonical texts testify to that prominence. *G.Thom.* 12). What is, however, apparent is that according to Acts 15, Peter is subservient to James in relation to rulings about the nature of the mission to Gentiles.[1048] Thus, having mentioned οἱ δώδεκα in the previous verse, the author of the *Gospel of Peter* continues this narrative by referring to the member of that group who is always listed first in the lists of the Twelve.

Andrew is named in the NT on only thirteen occasions.[1049] In comparison the name of his more prominent sibling occurs approximately one hundred and fifty-nine times.[1050] On all but one of these thirteen occasions he is linked with Peter, either by being explicated called his brother, or by being placed in a list of names usually headed by Peter. The sole exception is in Jn 12.22, where the name Andrew occurs

---

[1048] For more discussion on this topic from multiple perspectives see R.E. Brown, K.P. Donfried, J. Reumann (eds.), *Peter in the New Testament* (Minneapolis/New York: Augsburg/Paulist, 1973) especially 39–56.

[1049] Matt 4.18; 10.2; Mk 1.16, 29; 3.18; 13.3; Lk 6.14; Jn 1.40, 44; 6.8; 12.22 (2 times); Acts 1.13.

[1050] The reason only an approximate number can be given is due to the occurrence of textual variants alternating between the names, Peter, Simon, Simon Peter, and Cephas. Also the name 'Peter' is found in the Short Ending of Mark's gospel.

twice. In that context he is closely connected with Philip, who consults with Andrew before they both approach Jesus. In this present context in the *Gospel of Peter* Andrew is mentioned in connection with his brother, who explicitly in his role as narrator of this account describes in the first person voice the relationship that exists between himself and Andrew.

**14.60b** λαβόντες ἡμῶν τὰ λίνα ἀπήλθαμεν εἰς τὴν θάλ[λ]ασσαν. Having named himself as Peter and also given the name of Andrew, the first named character continues his narration of events by describing their actions after having left Jerusalem. The narrative depicts the brothers returning to their work as fisherman, which readers of the canonical accounts know to have been their trade prior to becoming disciples of Jesus (Mk 1.16–18). The word used to refer to the fishing tackle taken by the brothers, λίνον, is not used in conjunction with angling terminology on either of the two occasions it occurs in the NT (Matt 12.20; Rev 15.6), where it denotes a lamp-wick in Matt 12.20 and a linen garment in Rev 15.6. These are the two primary meanings in the NT period and earlier.[1051] However, the term λίνον does have the third semantic meaning of 'fish-net'. As Vaganay observes, 'The word, traditional for designating an instrument of fishing, line or net, is never, taken in this sense, in the N.T. where it is so often a question of nets (δίκτυον).'[1052] A variant reading in Mk 1.18 found in the eleventh century minuscule manuscript 700 of the gospels, replaces δίκτυα with λίνα.[1053]

Again, there is a lack of geographic precision in specifying the body of water to which the brothers went. This may be part of the general tendency in this narrative not to provide the specifics of location,[1054] or it may reflect the multiple names for the body of water in Galilee which was fished by the disciples: 'the sea of Galilee' (Matt 4.18;

---

[1051] See the first two meanings listed in BDAG, 596.

[1052] Vaganay, *L'Évangile de Pierre*, 339.

[1053] The Alands class 700 as a category III manuscript, which is described as having 'a distinctive character with an independent text, usually important for establishing the original text, but particularly important for the history of the text.' Specifically in relation to 700 they provide the following description: '700 e, eleventh, pch. London: British Library, Egerton 2610.' Aland and Aland, *The Text of the New Testament*, 106, 133.

[1054] See the comments on *Gos. Pet.* 14.59b.

Mk 1.16); Lake Gennesaret (Lk 5.1); 'the sea of Tiberias' (Jn 21.1).[1055]
Once again, the canonical accounts appear to be resources on which
the author of the *Gospel of Peter* expects his readers to draw to fill in
the gaps he has left in his own account.

**14.60c** καὶ ἦν σὺν ἡμῖν Λευείς ὁ τοῦ Ἀλφαίου ὃν κ̅ς̅. This final
incomplete sentence names a further disciple, presumably a member
of the Twelve, who here is known both by his name Λευείς, and his
filial relationship to his named father, ὁ τοῦ Ἀλφαίου. The name Levi
does not occur in the lists of the Twelve contained in either the synoptics or Acts. In the Markan narrative mention is made of a Levi,
son of Alphaeus, a tax-collector, who entertained Jesus at a meal in his
house (Mk 2.14–15). Porter makes the following observations about
this figure.

> Because Levi is not mentioned in Luke's (6.13–16; Acts 1.13) or Mark's
> lists of disciples, but a James the son of Alphaeus is mentioned at Mark
> 3.18, some texts list James at Mark 2.14…Levi is unknown in Matthew's
> Gospel, although a story is recounted of a disciple who is called to follow
> Jesus in the same manner (9:9) and who is mentioned as a tax collec-
> tor in Matthew's list of disciples (10:2–4, esp. 3). The question naturally
> arises whether this is the same man in all three gospel accounts.[1056]

Opinion has been divided as to the correct answer to that question. As
early as Origen, the evidence was seen as representing two distinct figures. In his refutation of Celsus' accusation that Jesus' followers were a
motley and unsavoury band of tax-collectors and sailors, Origen writes,
'I grant that the Levi also who followed Jesus was a tax-collector; but
he was not of the number of the apostles, except according to one of
the copies of the gospel according to Mark' (Origen, *Cont. Cel.* 1.62).[1057]
Evidence for the use of double names in the Semitic context has been
documented by those who wish to argue for the identitical nature of
the bearer of these two names.[1058] It must be conceded that in this context of the *Gospel of Peter* the author understands Levi to be one of the
Twelve. This may suggest that the writer of the text was familiar with a
similar form of Mark's gospel as the one mentioned by Origen which
appears to have replaced the name James with that of Levi in the list

---

[1055] Vaganay, *L'Évangile de Pierre*, 339.
[1056] S.E. Porter, 'Levi (person)', *ABD* 4, 295.
[1057] Chadwick, *Origen: Contra Celsum*, 57.
[1058] Porter, 'Levi (person)', *ABD* 4, 295.

of the Twelve in Mark 3.18. No extant manuscripts, however, preserve the reading Levi in place of James at Mark 3.18, although the opposite phenomenon is found where the name Levi is replaced by James at Mark 2.14 in the following manuscripts: D Θ *f*[13] 565 it.[1059]

This Levi, who apparently according to the narrative is a member of the Twelve, accompanies Peter and Andrew on their return to the fishing business. The construction which describes the filial relationship Λευεὶς ὁ τοῦ Ἀλφαίου, name of subject + definite article (agreeing with case of the name) + genitive definite article + name of father (in genitive), is a standard way of identifying a character by the father's name as well as his own. This construction occurs a number of times in the NT, in particular in the various lists of the Twelve, e.g. Ἰάκωβος ὁ τοῦ Ζεβεδαίου (Matt 10.2). The final incomplete clause ὃν $\overline{κς}$, would appear to be about to introduce a past event which linked Levi and the Lord. Although it is necessary to be cognizant of the fact that the author introduces several fresh features into his narrative not recounted in the canonical accounts, the only suggestion that can be advanced as to the nature of this past contact is the story of the call of Levi and the subsequent meal in his house (Mk 2.14–15). Out of the thirteen occurrences of the term κύριος in this text, this is the only occasion it is used without a preceding definite article.[1060] Again it is speculation to attempt to guess how the narrative develops in this scene, but it may not be totally unreasonable to suggest that having located Peter, Andrew and Levi beside a sea away from Jerusalem, that the narrative is about to offer a reworked resurrection appearance of Jesus to the disciples which may well parallel that known from Jn 21.1–23. However, it is impossible to have any confidence about which element were preserved, the miraculous draught of fish, the meal Jesus prepares on the shore, the rehabilitation of Peter (Jn 21.15–17), or even the prediction concerning Peter's manner of death (Jn 21.18–19). While the details remain vague, even this fragmentary introduction to the story strengthens the case for knowledge of the fourth gospel by the author of the *Gospel of Peter*.[1061]

---

[1059] For comments on this weakly attested reading see Metzger, *A Textual Commentary on the Greek New Testament*, 66.

[1060] See text critical note 5 in this section.

[1061] See Vaganay, *L'Évangile de Pierre*, 339.

# BIBLIOGRAPHY

## Works Dealing with the 'Gospel of Peter'

Badham, F.P. 'The Origin of the Peter-Gospel' *The Academy* 54 (1893) 91–93, 111.
Bauckham, R.J. 'The Study of Gospel Traditions Outside the Canonical Gospels: Problems and Prospects', in D. Wenham (ed.), *Gospel Perspectives*, Volume 5: *The Jesus Tradition Outside the Gospels* (Sheffield: JSOT Press, 1985) 369–403.
Bennett, E.N. 'The Gospel According to Peter', *Classical Review* (1893) 40–42.
Bernard, J.H. 'The Gospel of Peter and Dionysius of Alexandria' *The Academy* 54 (1893) 275.
Bernhard, A.E. *Other Early Christian Gospels: A Critical Edition of the Surviving Greek Manuscripts*, LNTS (JSNTS) 315 (London: T&T Clark – A Continuum Imprint, 2006).
Beyschlag, K. 'Das Petrusevangelium', in Beyschlag, *Die verborgene Überlieferung von Christus* (Munich and Hamburg: Siebenstern Taschenbuch, 1969) 27–64.
Bouriant, U. 'Fragments du texte grec du livre d'Énoch et de quelques écrits attribués à saint Pierre', dans *Mémoires publiés par les membres de la Mission archéologique française au Caire* (t. IX, fasc. 1; Paris: Ernest Leroux 1892) 93–147.
Brown, R.E. 'The Gospel of Peter and Canonical Gospel Priority', *NTS* 33 (1987) 321–343.
——. *The Death of the Messiah: From Gethsemane to the Grave* (2 vols., ABRL; New York: Doubleday, 1994) see esp. vol. 2, appendix 1, 1317–1349.
Bruston, C. 'De quelques textes difficiles de l'Évanglie de Pierre' *Revue des études grecques* (1897) 58–65.
Cambe, M. 'Les récits de la Passion en relation avec différents textes du 2ᵉ siècle', *Foi et Vie* 81 (1982) 12–24.
Cameron, R. 'The Apocryphal Jesus and Christian Origins', *Semeia* 49 (1990) 1–176.
Cassels, W.R. *The Gospel according to Peter: a study by the author of 'Supernatural Religion'*, (London: Longman, Green and Co., 1894).
Cavallo, G. and Maehler, H. *Greek Bookhands of the Early Byzantine Period A.D. 300–800*, BICS.S 47 (London: University of London, Institute of Classical Studies, 1987) 75.
Charlesworth, J.H. 'Research on the New Testament Apocrypha and Pseudepigrapha', *ANRW* II.25.5 (Berlin: de Gruyter, 1988) 3919–68, esp. 3934–40 ("The Gospel of Peter and the Passion Narrative").
Coles, R.A. '2949. Fragments of an Apocryphal Gospel(?)', in G.M. Browne (ed.), *The Oxyrhynchus Papyri*, vol 41 (Cambridge: CUP, 1972), 15–16.
Crossan, J.D. *Four Other Gospels: Shadows on the Contours of Canon* (New York: Harper & Row, 1985; repr. Sonoma: Polebridge, 1992) 85–127.
——. 'The Cross that Spoke: The Earliest Narrative of the Passion and Resurrection', *Forum* 3 (1987) 3–22.
——. *The Cross that Spoke: The Origins of the Passion Narrative* (San Francisco: Harper & Row, 1988).
——. 'Thoughts on Two Extracanonical Gospels,' *Semeia* 49 (1990) 155–68.
——. 'The Gospel of Peter and the Canonical Gospels: Independence, Dependence, or Both?' *Forum* New series 1,1 (1998) 7–51.
——. 'The *Gospel of Peter* and the Canonical Gospels', in T.J. Kraus and T. Nicklas, *Das Evangelium nach Petrus: Text, Kontexte, Intertexte* (Berlin: de Gruyter, 2007) 117–134.

Czachesz, I. 'The Gospel of Peter and the Apocryphal Acts of the Apostles: Using Cognitive Science to Reconstruct Gospel Traditions', in T.J. Kraus and T. Nicklas, *Das Evangelium nach Petrus: Text, Kontexte, Intertexte* (Berlin: de Gruyter, 2007) 245–261.

Denker, J. *Die theologiegeschichtliche Stellung des Petrusevangeliums*, Europäische Hochschulschriften 23/36 (Bern: Herbert Lang/Frankfurt: Peter Lange, 1975).

Denomme-Rust, D.B. 'The Gospel of Peter: Illustrated Theology', *Bible Today* 27 (1989) 147–52.

Dewey, A.J. '"Time to Murder and Create": Visions and Revisions in the Gospel of Peter', *Semeia* 49 (1990) 101–127.

——. 'The Gospel of Peter' in R.J. Miller (ed.), *The Complete Gospels* (rev ed.; Santa Rosa, Cal.: Polebridge, 1994) 399–407.

——. 'Resurrection Texts in the Gospel of Peter', *Forum* 10/3–4 (1994) 177–96.

——. 'Four Visions and a Funeral: Resurrection in the Gospel of Peter', *Journal of Higher Criticism* 2/2 (1995) 33–51.

——. 'The Passion Narrative of the Gospel of Peter: Redaction and Interpretation', *Forum* 1/1 (1998) 53–69.

Dibelius, M. 'Die alttestamentliche Motive in der Leidensgeschichte des Petrus- und Johannes-Evangeliums', in M. Dibelius, *Botschaft und Geschichte*, vol. 1 (ed. G. Bornkamm; Tübingen: Mohr Siebeck, 1953) 221–47. [originally published in 1918].

Ehrman, B.D. *Lost Christianities: The Battles for Scripture and the Faiths We Never Knew* (Oxford: OUP, 2003).

——. *Lost Scriptures: Books that did not make it into the New Testament* (Oxford: OUP, 2003).

Elliott, J.K. (ed.) *The Apocryphal New Testament* rev. ed. (Oxford: OUP, 1999).

Evans, C.A. 'Jesus in the Agrapha and Apocryphal Gospels', with James H. Charlesworth, in C.A. Evans and B.D. Chilton (eds.), *Studying the Historical Jesus: Evaluations of the State of Current Research* (NTTS 19; Leiden: Brill, 1994) 479–533, esp. 503–14.

——. *Life of Jesus Research: An Annotated Bibliography* (NTTS 24; Leiden: Brill, 1996) 263–66.

——. *Fabricating Jesus: How Modern Scholars Distort the Gospels* (Downers Grove: InterVarsity Press, 2006) 79–85, 256–58 (notes).

——. 'The Apocryphal Jesus: Assessing the Possibilities and Problems', in C.A. Evans and E. Tov (eds.), *Exploring the Origins of the Bible: Canon Formation in Historical, Literary, and Theological Perspective* (Acadia Studies in Bible and Theology; Grand Rapids: Baker Academic, 2008) 147–72, esp. 158–63.

Finegan, J. *Hidden Records of the Life of Jesus* (Philadelphia and Boston: Pilgrim Press, 1969) 231–35.

Foster, P. 'Are there any Early Fragments of the so-called Gospel of Peter?' *NTS* 52 (2006) 1–28.

——. 'The Disputed Early Fragments of the so-called Gospel of Peter – Once Again', *NovT* 49 (2007) 402–6.

——. 'Is there a Relationship between the Writings of Justin Martyr and the Gospel of Peter?' in S. Paris and P. Foster (eds.), *Justin and his Worlds* (Minneapolis: Fortress, 2007).

——. 'The Discovery and Initial Reaction to the So-called Gospel of Peter', in T.J. Kraus and T. Nicklas, *Das Evangelium nach Petrus: Text, Kontexte, Intertexte* (Berlin: Walter de Gruyter, 2007) 9–30.

——. 'The Gospel of Peter', *Exp Tim* 118 (2007) 318–25.

——. 'The Gospel of Peter,' in P. Foster (ed.), *The Non-Canonical Gospels* (London and New York: T & T Clark, 2008) 30–42.

——. *The Apocryphal Gospels: A Very Short Introduction* (Oxford: OUP, 2009) esp. 87–101.

——. 'Passion Traditions in the Gospel of Peter', in A. Merkt & T. Nicklas (eds.), *The Reception and Development of Early Christian Passion Traditions*, WUNT (Tübingen: Mohr Siebeck, 2010) 49–70.

——. 'P.Oxy. 2949 – Its Transcription and Significance: A Response to Thomas Wayment', *JBL* 129 (2010) 173–176.

——. 'The Gospel of Peter: Issues in Contemporary Scholarship', *CBR* (2010) forthcoming.

Fuchs, A. *Die griechischen Apokryphen zum Neuen Testament*. Bd. 1: *Das Petrusevangelium*, Studien zum Neuen Testament und seiner Umwelt B/2 (Freistadt: Linz 1978).

Gardner-Smith, P. ΈΠΙΦΩΣΚΕΙΝ', *JTS* 27 (1926) 179–181.

——. 'The Gospel of Peter', *JTS* 27 (1926) 255–271.

——. 'The Date of the Gospel of Peter', *JTS* 27 (1926) 401–407.

Gebhardt, O. von, *Das Evangelium und die Apokalypse des Petrus. Die neuentdeckten Bruchstücke nach einer Photographie der Handschrift zu Gizéh in Lichtdruck herausgegeben* (Leipzig, 1893).

Green, J.B. 'The Gospel of Peter: Source for a Pre-canonical Passion Narrative?', *ZNW* 78 (1987) 293–301.

Harnack, A. *Bruchstücke des Evangeliums und der Apokalypse des Petrus* (TU IX, 2, J.C. Hinrichs: Leipzig 1893).

Harnack, A. and Schürer, E. *TLZ* 17 (1892) 609–14; 18 (1893) 33–37.

Harnack, A. and von Schubert, H. 'Das Petrus-evangelium', *TLZ* 19 (1894) 9–18.

Harris, J.R. *A Popular Account of the Newly Recovered Gospel of St Peter* (London: Hodder and Stoughton, 1893).

——. 'The Structure of the Gospel of Peter', *The Contemporary Review* (1883) 212–236.

Head, P. 'On the Christology of the Gospel of Peter', *Vigiliae Christianae* 46 (1992) 209–224.

Heen, E. 'Unraveling Gospel History', *Harvard Divinity Bulletin* 21 (1990) 16.

Hilgenfeld, A. 'Das Petrus-Evangelium über Leiden und Auferstehung Jesu', *ZWT* 36 (1893) part I, 439–454;

——. 'Zu dem Petrus-Evangelium', *ZWT* 36 (1893) part II, 160.

——. 'Das Petrus-Evangelium', *ZWT* 36 (1893) part II, 220–267.

James, M. R. *The Apocryphal New Testament* (Oxford: Clarendon, 1924; corrected ed., 1953) 13–14, 90–94.

Johnson, B.A. 'Empty Tomb Tradition in the Gospel of Peter' Harvard University dissertation (1965).

——. 'The Gospel of Peter: Between Apocalypse and Romance', *Studia Patristica* 16 (1985) 170–174.

Junod, E. 'Eusèbe de Césarée, Sérapion d'Antioche et l'Evangile de Pierre: D'un Evangile à un Pseudépigraphe', *Rivista di Storia e Letteratura Religiosa* 24 (1988) 3–16.

Karavidopoulos, J. 'To Apokrypho Euangelio Petrou', *Deltion Biblikon Meleton* 21/2 (1992) 59–64 [Greek].

Karmann, T.R. 'Die Paschahomilie des Melito von Sardes und das Petrusevangelium', in T.J. Kraus and T. Nicklas, *Das Evangelium nach Petrus: Text, Kontexte, Intertexte* (Berlin: de Gruyter, 2007) 215–235.

Kirk, A. 'Examining Priorities: Another Look at the Gospel of Peter's Relationship to the New Testament Gospels', *NTS* 40 (1994) 572–595.

Klauck, H.-J. *Apocryphal Gospels: An Introduction* (London and New York: T & T Clark, 2003) 82–88.

Klijn, A.F.J. 'Het Evangelie van Petrus en de Westerse Tekst', *Nederlands Theologisch Tijdschrift* 15 (1961) 264–269.

Klostermann, E. *Apocrypha I, Reste des Petrusevangeliums, der Petrusapocalypse und des Kerygma Petri* (3rd ed., Berlin, 1933).

Koester, H. *Ancient Christian Gospels: Their History and Development* (London: SCM/ Philadelphia: TPI, 1990).
——. 'Apocryphal and Canonical Gospels', *HTR* 73 (1980) 105–30.
Kraus, T.J. 'Petrus und das Ostrakon *van Haelst* 741', *ZAC* 7 (2003) 203–211.
Kraus, T.J. and Nicklas, T. *Das Petrusevangelium and die Petrusapokalypse: Die Griechischen Fragmente mit deutscher und englisher Übersetzung* (Berlin: Walter de Gruyter, 2004).
Kraus, T.J. and Walter de Nicklas, T. (eds.) *Das Evangelium nach Petrus: Text, Kontexte, Intertexte* (Berlin: Gruyter, 2007).
Lambiasi, F. 'I criteri d'autenticà storica dei vangeli applicati ad un apocrifo: il Vangelo di Pietro', *BeO* 18 (1976) 151–160.
Lapham, F. *An Introduction to the New Testament Apocrypha* (London/New York: T&T Clark, A Continuum International Imprint, 2003) 89–94.
Lejay, J. 'L'Évangile de Pierre' *Ruvue des Études Grecques* (1893) 59–84, 267–270.
Lods, A. *Evangelii secundum Petrum et Petri Apocalypseos quae supersunt* (Paris; Ernest Leroux, 1892).
——. 'L'Évangile et l'Apocalypse de Pierre avec le texte grec du livre d'Hénoch. Text publié en fac-similé, par l'héliogravure d'après les photographies du manuscript de Gizéh' dans *Mémoires publiés par les membres de la Mission archéologique française au Caire* (t. IX, fasc. 3; Paris: Ernest Leroux 1893) 217–231, 322–335.
——. *L'Évangile et l'Apocalypse de Pierre publiés pour la première fois d'après les photographies du manuscrit de Gizéh* (Paris: Ernest Leroux, 1893).
Lührmann, D. 'POx 2949: EvPt 3–5 in einer Handschrift des 2ten/3ten Jahrhunderts' *ZNW* 77 (1981) 216–226.
——. 'Ein neues Fragment des Petrus-evangeliums', in C. Foucant (ed.), *The Synoptic Gospels. Source Criticism and the New Literary Criticism* (BETL 110; Louvain: Peeters, 1993), 579–581.
——. 'POx 4009: Ein neues Fragment des Petrusevangeliums?', *NovT* 35 (1993), 390–410.
——. *Fragmente Apokryph Gewordener Evangelien: In Griechischer und Lateinischer Sprache* (Marburg: N.G. Elwert, 2000).
——. 'Petrus als Evangelist – ein Bemerkenswertes Ostrakon', *NovT* 43 (2001), 348–367.
——. 'Kann es wirklich keine frühe Handschrift des Petrusevangeliums gebens? Corrigenda zu einem Aufsatz von Paul Foster," *NovT* 48 (2006) 379–83.
Lührmann, D. and Parsons, P.J. '4009. Gospel of Peter?' in Parsons et al. (eds.), *The Oxyrhynchus Papyri* (vol. 60; London: Egypt Exploration Society, 1993) 1–5 (+ pl. I).
Lundborg, M. *Det sk. Petrusevangeliet ett nyfunnet fragment ur en fornkristlig apocryf* (Lund, 1893).
Mara, M.G. *Évangile de Pierre: Introduction, Texte Critique, Traduction, Commentaire et Index* (Sources Chrétiennes 201; Paris: Les Éditions du Cerf, 1973).
McCant, J.W. 'The Gospel of Peter: Doceticism Reconsidered', *NTS* 30 (1984) 258–273.
Manchot, K. 'Die neuen Petrus-Fragmente', *Protestantische Kirchenzeitung* (1893) 6:126–143; 7:160–166; 8:176–183; 9:201–213.
Manen, W.C. van *Het Evangilie van Petrus, tekst en vertaling* (Leyde, 1893).
Meunier, C. *L'Évangile selon saint Pierre, traduction française avec notes* (Boulogne: Sociéte Typographique & lithographique, 1893).
Mirecki, P.A. 'Peter, Gospel of', in D.N. Freedman (ed.) *The Anchor Bible Dictionary*, volume 5, (New York: Doubleday, 1992) 278–281.
Murray, J.O.F. 'Evangelium Secundum Petrum', *The Expositor* (1893) 50–61.
Myllykoski, M. 'The Sinful Woman in the *Gospel of Peter*: Reconstructing the Other Side of P.Oxy. 4009', *NTS* 55 (2009) 105–115.
——. 'Tears of Repentance or Tears of Gratitude? P.Oxy. 4009, the Gospel of Peter and the Western Text of Luke 7.45–49', *NTS* 55 (2009) 380–389.

Neirynck, F. 'The Apocryphal Gospels and the Gospel of Mark', in J.-M. Sevrin (ed.), *The New Testament in Early Christianity* (BETL 86; Leuven: Peeters, 1989) 123-175).

Nicklas, T. 'Die "Juden" im Petrusevangelium (PCair 10759): ein Testfall', *NTS* 47 (2001) 206-221.

——. 'Erzähler und Charakter zugleich: zur literarischen Funktion des "Petrus" in dem nach ihm benannten Evangelienfragment', *VC* 55 (2001) 318-326.

——. 'Ein 'neutestamentliches Apokryphon'? Zum umstrittenen Kanonbezug des sog. Petrusevangeliums', *VC* 56 (2002) 260-72.

Orbe, A. 'La Muerte de Jesús en la Economía Valentiniana', *Gregorianum* 40 (1959) 467-499, 636-670.

Osiek, C. 'The Women at the Tomb: What are they Doing There?' *Ex Auditu* 9 (1993) 97-107.

Paulsen, H. 'Das Kerygma Petri und die urchristlichem Apolgetik', *ZKG* 88 (1977) 1-37.

Perler, O. 'L'Evangile de Pierre et Méliton de Sardes', *RB* 71 (1964) 584-590.

Piccolomini, E. 'Sul testo dei fragmenti dell' Evangelio e dell' Apocalisse del Pseudo Pietro' in *Rendiconti della Reale Accadem. Dei Lincei, Classe discienzi morali, storichi e filogiche*, tom. VIII, 1899, fasc. 7-8 (Roma, 1899) 389-404.

Pick, B. *Paralipomena: Remains of Gospels and Sayings of Christ* (Chicago: Open Court, 1908). 'The Gospel of Peter', 40-52.

Pilhofer, P. 'Justin und das Petrusevangelium', *ZNW* 81 (1990) 60-78.

Porter, S.E. 'The Greek of the Gospel of Peter: Implications for Syntax and Discourse Study', in A. Merkt and T. Nicklas (eds.), *The Reception and Development of Early Christian Passion Traditions*, WUNT (Tübingen: Mohr Siebeck, 2010) 77-90.

Preuschen, E. *Antilegomena, Die Reste der ausserkanonischen Evangelien und urchristlichen Überlieferungen* (2nd ed., Giessen, 1905).

Prieur, J.M. 'La Croix Vivante dans la literature chrétienne du IIᵉ siècle', *Revue d'Histoire et de Philosophie Religieuses* 79 (1999) 435-444.

Quarles, C.L. 'The Gospel of Peter: A Pre-Canonical Resurrection Narrative?', in R.B. Stewart (ed.), *The Resurrection of Jesus: John Dominic Crossan and N.T. Wright in Dialogue* (Minneapolis: Fortress Press, 2006) 106-20.

Redpath, H.A. 'The Gospel According to Peter', *The Academy* 42.10, (1892) 544.

Roberts, A. and Donaldson, J. (eds.) *The Ante-Nicene Fathers* (10 vols., Edinburgh: T & T Clark, 1898; repr. Grand Rapids: Eerdmans, 1989) 10:3-31.

Robinson, J.A. and James, M.R. *The Gospel according to Peter, and the Revelation of Peter: Two Lectures on the Newly Recovered Fragments together with the Greek Texts* (London: C.J. Clay and Sons, 1892).

Rodríguez Ruiz, M., 'El evangelo de Pedro un desafío a los evangelios canónicos' Estudios Bíblicos 46 (1988) 497-526.

Sabatier, A. *L'Évangile de Pierre et les évangiles canonique* (Paris: Imprimerie Nationale, 1893).

Sandys, J.E. *The Academy* (1893) 486.

Santos Otero, A. de *Los Evangelios Apócrifos* (Segunda edicion, La Editorial Catolica: Madrid, 1956).

Schaeffer, S.E. 'The Guard at the Tomb (Gos Pet 8:28-11:49 and Matt 27:62-66; 28:2-4, 11-16): a Case of Intertextuality?' *SBLSP* 30 (1991) 499-507.

Schenk, W. 'Das "Matthäusevangelium" als Petrusevangelium', *BZ* 27 (1983) 58-80.

Schneemelcher, W. (ed.). *New Testament Apocrypha. Volume One: Gospels and Related Writings* (rev. ed., Cambridge: James Clarke; Louisville: Westminster/John Knox Press, 1991) 216-27.

Schubert, H. von *Die Composition des pseudopetrinischen Evangelienfragments* (Berlin: 1893).

——. *Das Petrusevangelium, Synoptische Tabelle nebst Übersetzung und Kritischem Apparat* (1893). Eng. trans. By J. Macpherson, *The Gospel of Peter with Synoptical Tables and translation and critical apparatus* (T&T Clark: Edinburgh, 1893).

Semeria, J.B. 'L'Évangile de Pierre', *Revue biblique* (1894) 522,-560, esp. 541–542.

Smyth, E.C. 'The Newly Recovered Gospel of St Peter with a full account of the same', *Andover Review* 19 (1893) 262–266.

Smyth, K. 'The Guard at the Tomb', Heythrop Journal 2 (1961) 157–159.

Soards, M.L. 'Oral tradition before, in, and outside the canonical Passion narratives', in H. Wansborough (ed.), *Jesus and the Oral Gospel Tradition* (JSNTSS 64; Sheffield: JSOT, 1991) 334–350.

Soden, H. von 'Das Petrus Evangelium und die kanonischen Evangelien', ZThK 3 (1893) 52–92.

Stanton, V.H. 'The Gospel of Peter, its early history and character considered in relation to the history of the recognition in the Church of the canonical gospels', *JTS* 2 (1900) 1–25.

Stillman, M.K. 'The Gospel of Peter: A Case for Oral-Only Dependency?', *Ephemerides Theologicae Lovanienses*, 73 no. 1 (1997) 114–120.

Stocks, H. 'Zum Petrusevangelium', *Neue kirchliche Zeitschrift* 13 (1902) 276–314; 14 (1903) 511–542.

——. 'Quellen zur Rekonstruktion des Petrus-evangeliums, ZKG 34 (1913) 1–57.

Stülcken, A. 'Petrusevangelium' in E. Hennecke (ed.), *Handbuch zu den neutestamentlichen Apokryphen* (Tübingen: J.B.C. Mohr, 1904) 72–88.

Swete, H.B. *The Apocryphal Gospel of Peter: The Greek Text of the Newly Discovered Fragment* (1st ed. London 1892; 2nd ed., London, 1893).

——. *The Akhmîm Fragment of the Apocryphal Gospel of St Peter* (London, 1893).

——. 'The Gospels in the Second Century', *The Interpreter* 4 (1907) 138–55.

Treat, J.C. 'The Two Manuscript Witness to the Gospel of Peter', *SBLSP* 29 (1990) 391–399.

Turner, C.H. 'The Gospel of Peter' *JTS* 14 (1913) 161–195.

Tyler, T, '"The Lord" in the Gospel of Peter' *The Academy* 54 (1893) 94, 275.

Vaganay, L. *L'Évangile de Pierre*, Études Biblique (Paris: Gabalda, 1st ed. 1929/2nd ed. 1930).

van Haelst, J. *Catalogue des papyrus littéraires juifs et chrétiens* (Paris: Publication de la Sorbonne, 1976), 597, no. 598.

Verheyden, J. 'Silent Witness: Mary Magdalene and the Women at the Tomb in the Gospel of Peter', in R. Bieringer, V. Koperski and B. Lataite (eds), *Resurrection in the New Testament*, BETL 165 (Leuven: Peeters, 2002) 457–482.

Völter, D. *Petrusevangelium oder Aegypterevangelium? Eine Frage bezuglich des neuentdeckten Evangeliumfragments* (Tübingen, 1893) 8; see the expanded version of this argument in *ZNW* 5 (1905) 368–372.

Wabnitz, A. 'Les fragments de l'évangile et de l'apocalypse de Pierre', *Revue de théologie et des questions religieuses* (1893) 280–294, 353–370, 474–487.

Wayment, T.A. 'A Reexamination of the Text of *P.Oxy.* 2949', *JBL* 128 (2009) 375–382.

Wilamowitz-Möllendorf, H. von, 'Conjecturen zu den Petrus-Fragmenten', *Index Scholarum von* Göttingen (1893) 31–33.

Wright, D.F. 'Apocryphal Gospels: "The Unknown Gospel" (Pap Egerton 2) and the Gospel of Peter', in D.W. Wenham (ed.), *Jesus Tradition Outside the Gospels* (Sheffield: JSOT Press, 1984) 207–232.

——. 'Papyrus Egerton 2 (the Unknown Gospel) – part of the Gospel of Peter', *Second Century* 5 (1985–1986) 129–150.

Zahn, T. *Das Evangelium des Petrus* (Erlangen und Leipzig, 1893).

## OTHER WORKS

Achtemeier, P.J. *1 Peter*, Hermeneia (Minneapolis: Fortress, 1996).

Aland, K. and Aland, B. *The Text of the New Testament* (2nd ed.; Grand Rapids, Michigan: Eerdmans, 1989).

Allen, W.C. *Gospel according to Saint Matthew*, ICC (2nd ed.; Edinburgh: T&T Clark, 1907).

Allison, D.C. *The End of the Ages Has Come: An early Interpretation of the Passion and Resurrection of Jesus* (Philadelphia: Fortress, 1985).

Aune, D. *Revelation 1–5*, WBC 52A (Dallas: Word, 1997).

Baillet, J. 'Le papyrus mathématique d'Akhmîm', in *Mémoires publiés par les membres de la Mission archéologique française au Caire* (t. IX, fasc. 1; Paris 1892) 1–90.

Balz, H. and Schneider G. (eds.) *Exegetical Dictionary of the New Testament*, 3 vols. (Grand Rapids: Michigan: Eerdmans, 1990–1993).

Barrett, C.K. *The Signs of an Apostle* (London: Epworth, 1970).

——. *The Gospel according to St John* (2nd ed., London: SPCK, 1978).

——. *The Acts of the Apostles*, vol II (ICC; Edinburgh: T&T Clark, 1998).

Bauckham, R.J. 'The Lord's Day', in D.A. Carson (ed.), *From Sabbath to Lord's Day: A Biblical, Historical and Theological Investigation* (Grand Rapids, Michigan: Zonderan, 1982).

——. *Gospel Women: Studies of the Named Women in the Gospels* (London: T&T Clark – a Continuum Imprint, 2002).

——. *Jesus and the Eyewitnesses: The Gospels as Eyewitness Testimony* (Grand Rapids, Michigam: Eerdmans, 2006)

Baugh, S.M. *A New Testament Greek Primer* (Phillipsburg, NJ: P&R Publishing, 1995).

Baur, F.C. *Die christliche Gnosis oder die christliche Religions-Philosophie in ihrer geschichtlichen Entwicklumg* (Tübingen, 1835).

Beale, G.K. *The Book of Revelation*, NIGTC (Grand Rapids, MI/Carlisle: Eerdmans/Paternoster, 2005).

Beare, F.W. *The Gospel according to Matthew* (Oxford: Blackwell, 1981).

Beasley-Murray, G.R. *John*, WBC 36 (Waco, Texas: Word, 1987).

——. *Jesus and the Last Days* (Peabody, Mass.: Hendrickson, 1993).

Bigg, C. *The Epistles of St. Peter and St. Jude*, ICC (Edinburgh: T&T Clark, 1910).

Black, S. *Sentence Conjunctions in the Gospel of Matthew: καί, δέ, τότε, γάρ, οὖν and Asyndeton in Narrative Discourse*, JSNTSMS 216 (London: Sheffield Academic Press, 2002).

Blass, F. and Debrunner, A. *A Greek Grammer of the New Testament and other Early Christian Literature* (trans. R.W. Funk, Cambridge: CUP, 1961).

Bock, D.L. *Luke 1:1–9:50*, vol. 1 & *Luke 9:51–24:53*, vol. 2, ECNT (Grand Rapids, Michigan: Baker, 1994, 1996).

Bond, H.K. *Pontius Pilate in History and Interpretation*, SNTSMS 100 (Cambridge: CUP, 1998).

Bousset, W. *Kyrios Christos: A History of the Belief in Christ from the Beginnings of Christianity to Irenaeus* (trans. John Steely; Nashville: Abingdon, 1970; German original: Göttingen: Vandenhoeck & Ruprecht, 1913).

Braund, D.C. 'Agrippa', *ABD* vol. 1, 99–100.

Brown, R.E. *The Gospel according to John*, 2 vols. AB 29, 29A (New York: Doubleday, 1966, 1970).

Brown, R.E., Donfried, K.P. and Reumann J. (eds.) *Peter in the New Testament* (Minneapolis/New York: Augsburg/Paulist, 1973).

Bruce, F.F. *Jesus and Christian Origins outside the New Testament* (London: Hodder & Stoughton, 1974).

Bultmann, R. *History of the Synoptic Tradition* (eng. trans. Oxford: Blackwell, 1963).

Buschmann, G. *Das Martyrium des Polykarp* (Gottingen : Vandenhoeck & Ruprecht, 1998).

Cartlidge, D.R. and Dungan, D.L. *Documents for the Study of the Gospels* (Philadelphia: Fortress, 1980) 83–86.

Campbell, C.R. *Basics of Verbal Aspect in Biblical Greek* (Grand Rapids: Zondervans, 2008).

Caragounis, C.C. *The Development of Greek and the New Testament*, WUNT 167 (Tübingen: Mohr Siebeck, 2004).

Chadwick, H. *Origin: Contra Celsum*, (2nd ed.; Cambridge: CUP, 1965).

Collins, A.Y. 'From Noble Death to Crucified Messiah', *NTS* 40 (1994) 481–503.

Collins, R.F. 'Twelve, The', *ABD* 6, 671.

Comfort, P. and Barrett, D., Best, E. *The Complete Text of the Earliest New Testament Manuscripts* (Grand Rapids, Michigan: Baker, 1999).

——. *Ephesians*, ICC (Edinburgh: T&T Clark, 1998).

Cowper, B.H. *The Apocryphal Gospels and Other Documents Relating to the History of Christ* (6th ed. London: David Nutt, 1897).

Cribiore, R. *Writing, Teachers, and Students in Graeco-Roman Egypt* (Atlanta, Ga.: Scolars Press, 1996).

——. *Gymnastics of the Mind: Greek education in Hellenistic and Roman Egypt* (Princeton, N.J./Oxford: Princeton University Press, 2001).

Crossan, J.D. and Reed, J.L. *In Search of Paul: How Jesus' Apostle Opposed Rome's Empire with God's Kingdom* (London: SPCK, 2005).

Cullmann, O. *The Christology of the New Testament* (trans. By S.C. Guthrie and C.A.M. Hall; London: SCM, 1959).

Davies, J.G. 'The Origins of Docetism', *Studia Patristica* 6 (1962) 13–35.

Davies W.D. and Allison D.C. *The Gospel According to Saint Matthew*, ICC, vol. III (Edinburgh: T&T Clark, 1997).

DeConick, A. *Recovering the Original* Gospel of Thomas:*A History of the Gospel and its Growth* (LNTS [JSNTS] 286, London: T&T Clark International, A Continuum Imprint, 2005).

Dibelius, M. *From Tradition to Gospel* (Cambridge: James Clarke, 1971, trans. of 1934 German edition).

Donahue, J.R. and Harrington, D.J. *The Gospel of Mark*, Sacra Pagina 2 (Collegeville, MN.: Liturgical Press, 2002).

Douglas J.D. and Bruce, F.F. 'Scourging, Scourge', in J.D. Douglas and F.F. Bruce (eds.), *New Bible Dictionary* (2nd ed.; Leicester: IVP, 1982).

Dunn, J.D.G. *Romans 1–8* (Dallas: Word, 1988).

Ehrman, B. *Peter, Paul and Mary Magdalene: The Followers of Jesus in History and Legend* (Oxford: Oxford University Press, 2006).

Evans, C.A. *Mark 8:27–16:20*, WBC 34B (Nashville: Thomas Nelson, 2001).

Farmer, W.R. *The Last Twelve Verses of Mark*, SNTSMS 25 (Cambridge: CUP, 1974).

Fitzmyer, J.A. *The Gospel According to Luke*, AB 28 & 28A, 2 vols. (New York: Doubleday, 1981, 1985).

——. *Romans* (New York: Doubleday, 1993).

——. *The Acts of the Apostles*, AB 31 (New York: Doubleday, 1998).

Foakes Jackson, F.J. and Lake, K. (eds.) *The Beginnings of Christianity*, Part 1 *The Acts of the Apostles*, Vol III J.H. Ropes (ed.), 'The Text' (London: Macmillan, 1926) 117.

Foster, P. 'The Use of Zechariah in Matthew's Gospel', in C.M. Tuckett (ed.), *The Book of Zechariah and its Influence* (Aldershot: Ashgate, 2003) 65–85.

——. 'Polymorphic Christology: Its Origins and Development in Early Christianity' *JTS* 58 (2007) 1–34.

——. 'Tatian', *Exp Times* 120 (2008) 105–118.

France, R.T. *The Gospel of Mark*, NIGNT (Carlisle/Grand Rapids, Michigan: Paternoster/ Eerdmanns, 1978).

Friedrick, J.H. 'κλῆρος' in Balz and Schneider (eds.), *Exegetical Dictionary of the New Testament*, vol. 2, 299.

Gilfillan Upton, B. *Hearing Mark's Endings: Listening to Ancient Popular Texts Through Speech Act Theory*, BINS 79 (Leiden: Brill, 2006).

Goodacre, M.S. 'Fatigue in the Synoptics', *NTS* 44 (1998) 45–58.

Goppelt, L. *A Commentary on 1 Peter* (Grand Rapids, MI: Eerdmans, 1993).

Green, J.B. *The Gospel of Luke*, NICNT (Grand Rapids, Michigan: Eerdmans, 1997).

Gregory, A. *The Reception of Luke and Acts in the Period before Irenaeus* (Tübingen: Mohr-Siebeck, 2003).

Gregory, A. and Tuckett, C.M. *The Reception of the New Testament in the Apostolic Fathers* (Oxford: OUP, 2005).

Gregory, A. and Tuckett, C.M. 'Reflections on Method: What constitutes the use of the Writings that later formed the New Testament in the Apostolic Fathers?', in A. Gregory and C.M. Tuckett (eds.), *The Reception of the New Testament in the Apostolic Fathers* (Oxford: OUP, 2005) 61–82.

Guelich, R.A. *Mark 1–8.26*, WBC 34A (Dallas: Word, 1989).

Gundry, R.H. *Matthew: A Commentary on His Handbook for a Mixed Church under Persecution* (2nd ed.; Grand Rapids, Michigan: Eerdmans, 1994).

Hachlili, R. 'Burials', *ABD* vol. 1, 789–791.

Haenchen, E. *The Acts of the Apostles: A Commentary* (Oxford: Blackwell, 1971).

Hagner, D.A. *Matthew 14–28*, WBC 33B (Dallas: Word, 1995).

Harrington, D.J. *The Gospel of Matthew*, Sacra Pagina 1 (Collegeville, MN.: Liturgical Press, 1991).

Harris J.R. (ed.), *The Gospel of the Twelve Apostles: Together with the Apocalypses of Each One of Them* (London: CUP, 1900/reprinted, Piscataway, NJ: Gorgias Press, 2002).

Hertzberg, H.W. *I & II Samuel*, OTL (London: SCM, 1964).

Hill, C.E. *From the Lost Teaching of Polycarp: Identifying Irenaeus' Apostolic Presbyter and the Author of* Ad Diognetum (Tübingen: Mohr Siebeck, 2006).

Hoehner, H.W. *Herod Antipas* (SNTSMS 17, Cambridge: CUP, 1972) 10.

Hooker, M.D. *The Gospel according to Saint Mark*, BNTC (London: A&C Black, 1991).

Hurtado, L.W. 'The Origin of the *Nomina Sacra*: A Proposal', *JBL* 117(1998) 655–673.

——. *Lord Jesus Christ: Devotion to Jesus in Earliest Christianity* (Grand Rapids, Michigan: Eerdmans, 2003).

Hvalvik, R. *The Struggle for Scripture and Covenant: The Purpose of the Epistle of Barnabas and Jewish-Christian Competition in the Second Century*, WUNT 82 (Tübingen: Mohr Siebeck, 1996).

Ilan, T. *Lexicon of Jewish Names in Late Antiquity: Part 1 Palestine 330 BCE–200 CE*, TSAJ 91 (Tübingen: Mohr Siebeck 2002).

Japhet, S. *I & II Chronicles*, OTL (Louisville, Kentucky: Westminster/John Knox Press, 1993).

Junod, E. and Kaestli, J.-D. *Acta Iohannis*, Tomus 1: Praefatio – Textus; Tomus 2: Textus alii – commentaries – indices; CCSA 1–2 (Turnhout: Brepols, 1982).

Keener, C.S. *The Gospel of John: A Commentary*, 2 vols. (Peabody: Hendrickson, 2003).

Kelhoffer, J.A. *Miracle and Mission: The Authentication of Missionaries and their Message in the Longer Ending of Mark*, WUNT 112 (Tübingen: Mohr Siebeck, 2000).

Kelly, J.N.D. *The Epistles of Peter and Jude*, BNTC (London: A&C Black, 1969).

Keppie, L. 'The army and the navy', in A.K. Bowman, E. Champlin & A. Lintott (eds.), *The Cambridge Ancient History*, 2nd ed.; Vol. X: The Augustan Empire, 43 B.C.–A.D. 69 (Cambridge: CUP, 1996) 372.

Köstenberger, A.J. *John*, BECNT (Grand Rapids: Baker, 2004).

Köster, H. *Synoptische Uberlieferung bei den Apostolischen Vatern*, TU 65 (Berlin: Akademie Verlag, 1957).

Kraus, T.J. *Ad fontes: Original Manuscripts and Their Significance for Studying Early Christianity: Selected Essays* (Texts and Editions for New Testament Study 3; Leiden: Brill, 2007).

Kraus, T., Kruger, M. *Gospel Fragments: Oxford Early Christian Gospel Texts.* (Oxford and New and Nicklas, T. (eds) York: OUP, 2009).

Lake, K. *Eusebius: Ecclesiastical History*, Books I–V, LCL 153 (Cambridge, Massachusetts: Harvard University Press, 1926).

Lampe, G.W.H. *A Patristic Greek Lexicon* (Oxford: OUP, 1961).

Lane, W.L. *The Gospel of Mark*, NICNT (Grand Rapids, Michigan: Eerdmans, 1974).

Lemaire, A. 'Writing and Writing Materials', in D.N. Freedman (ed.), *The Anchor Bible Dictionary*, vol. 6, 1003–1004.

Lincoln, A.T. *The Gospel according to St John*, BNTC (London: Continuum, 2006).

Loader, W.R.G. *The Christology of the Fourth Gospel: Structure and Issues*, BET 23 (2nd rev ed; Frankfurt: Peter Lang, 1992).

Luz, U. *Matthew 21–28* (Minneapolis: Fortress, 2005).

Manson, T.W. 'The Life of Jesus: A Study of the Available Materials', *BJRL* 27 (1942–43) 323–37.

Marcos, N.F. *The Septuagint in Context: Introduction to the Greek Version of the Bible* (Leiden: Brill, 2000).

Marcovich, M. *Apologiae pro Christianis – Dialogus cem Tryphone* (combined edition; Berlin/New York: Walter de Gruyter, 2005).

Marshall, I.H. *Commentary on Luke*, NIGNT (Exeter/Grand Rapids, Michigan: Paternoster/Eerdmanns, 1978).

Martin, V. and Kasser, R. *Papyrus Bodmer XIV: Evangile de Luc chap. 3–24* (Cologny-Geneva: Bibliotheca Bodmeriana).

Martínez, F.G. *The Dead Sea Scrolls Translated: The Qumran Texts in English* (2nd ed.; Leiden/Grand Rapids: Brill/Eerdmans, 1996).

Martínez, F.G. *et al., Manuscripts from Qumran Cave 11 (11Q2–18, 11Q20–30)*, DJD XXIII; Oxford: Clarendon Press, 1997).

Maspero, G. (ed.), *Mémoires publiés par les membres de la Mission archéologique française au Caire*, tome 1, 4 vols. pp. 787 + plates (Paris: Ernest Leroux, 1884–1889).

McCarter, P.K. *II Samuel*, Anchor Bible 9 (New York: Doubleday, 1984).

McKay, K.L. 'The Use of the Ancient Greek Perfect down to the End of the Second Century', *Bulletin of the Institute of Classical Studies* 12 (1965) 1–21.

——. 'On the Perfect and Other Aspects in New Testament Greek', *NovT* 23 (1981) 289–329.

McNamee, K. *Abbreviations in Greek Literary Papyri and Ostraca* (BaspSup 3; Chico, CA: Scholars Pres, 1981).

McNeile, A.H. 'Τότε in St Mattew', *JTS* 12 (1911) 127–128.

Mercati, G. *L'eta di Simmaco l'interprete e S. Epifanio ossia se Simmaco tradusse in Greco la Bibba sotto M. Aurelio il filosofo* (Modena, 1892 = *ST* (1937), 20–92).

Metzger, B.M. 'Names for the Nameless in the New Testament', in P. Granfield and J.A. Jungmann (eds.), *Kyriakon: Festschrift for J. Quasten* (2 vols.; Munster: Aschendorff, 1970) vol. 1, 79–95.

——. *A Textual Commentary on the Greek New Testament* (2nd ed.; Stuttgart: Deutsche Bibelgesellschaft, 1994).

Moule, C.F.D. *An Idiom-Book of New Testament Greek* (2nd ed.; Cambridge: CUP, 1959).

Moulton, W.F. and Geden, A.S. Marshall (ed.), *Concordance to the Greek New Testament*, Sixth edition, fully revised, I.H. (London: T&T Clark – A Continuum Imprint, 2002).

Muddiman, J. *The Epistle to the Ephesians*, BNTC (London: Continuum, 2001).

Musurillo, H. *Acts of the Christian Martyrs* (Oxford: OUP, 1972).

Neusner, J. and Green, W. (eds.), *Dictionary of Judaism in the Biblical Period* (Peabody, Mass.: Hendrickson, 1996).

Niederwimmer, K. *The Didache*, Hermeneia (Minneapolis: Fortress, 1998).

Nolland, J. *Luke 1–9:20, 9:21–18:34, 18:35–24:53*, 3 vols., WBC 35A, 35B, 35C (Dallas: Word, 1989. 1993, 1993).

——. *The Gospel of Matthew*, NICGT (Grand Rapids, MI: Eerdmans, 2005).

Oegema, G.S. *The Anointed and his People: Messianic Expectations from the Maccabees to Bar Kochba*, JSPS 27 (Sheffield: Sheffield Academic Press, 1998).

Paget, J.C. *The Epistle of Barnabas: Outlook and Background*, WUNT 64 (Tübingen: Mohr Siebeck, 1994).

Papthomas, A. 'Das agonistische Motiv 1 Kor 9.24ff. im Spiegel zeitgenossischer dokumentarischer Quellen' *NTS* 43 (1997) 223–241.

Parsons, P. *City of the Sharp-Nosed Fish* (London: Phoenix Publishers, 2007).

Plummer, A. *A Critical and Exegetical Commentary on the Gospel According to S. Luke*, ICC (4th ed., Edinburgh: T&T Clark, 1901).

Porter, S.E. *Verbal Aspect in the Greek of the New Testament with Reference to Tense and Mood* (Studies in Biblical Greek 1; New York: Peter Land, 1989).

——. 'Keeping up with Recent Studies: 17. Greek Language and Linguistics' *Exp Times* 103 (1991–92) 202–07.

——. 'Levi (person)', *ABD* 4, 295.

——. *Idioms of the Greek New Testament* (2nd ed.; Biblical Languages: Greek 2; Sheffield: Sheffield Academic Press, 1994).

Porter, S.E. and O'Donnell, M.B. 'Conjunctions and Levels of Discourse,' New Testament Philology Section, European Association of Biblical Studies Annual Meeting, Budapest, Hungary, 6–9 August 2006.

Prostmeier, F.R. *Der Barnabasbrief*, KAV (Göttingen: Vandenhoeck & Ruprecht, 1999).

Rauschen, G. *Florilegium patristicum*, III (2nd ed.; Bonn, 1914).

Rebell, W. *Neutestamentliche Apokryphen und Apostolischen Vätern* (Munich: Kaiser, 1992) 92–99.

Resch, A. *Aussercanonischer Paralleltexte zu den* Evangelien, II, *Matthaeus und Markus*, (Leipzig, 1894).

Riches, J.K. *Conflicting Mythologies: Identity Formation in the Gospels of Matthew and Mark* (Edinburgh: T&T Clark, 2000).

Roberts, C.H. '*Nomina Sacra*: Origins and Significance', chap. 2 of his *Manuscript, Society and Belief in Early Christian Egypt* (London: OUP, 1979), 26–48.

Robinson, J.M., Hoffmann P. and Kloppenborg J.S., (eds.), *The Critical Edition of Q*, Hermeneia (Minneapolis/Leuven: Fortress/Peeters, 2000).

Rowland, C.C. *The Open Heaven: A Study of Apocalyptic in Judaism and Early Christianity* (New York: Crossroad, 1982).

——. 'A Man Clothed in Linen: Daniel 10.6ff. and Jewish Angelology' *JSNT* 24 (1985) 99–110.

Sanders, E.P. *The Tendencies of the Synoptic Tradition* (SNTSMS 9; Cambridge: CUP, 1969).

Schenke, H.M. 'Das sogenannte "Unbekannte Berliner Evangelium" (UBE)', *ZAC* 2 (1998) 199–213.

Schnackenburg, R. *The Gospel according to St. John*, 3 vols. (London: Burns & Oates, 1968, 1980, 1982)

Schwarz, D.R. 'Pontius Pilate's Appointment to Office and the Chronology of Antiquities, Books 18–20', in *Studies in the Jewish Background to Christianity* (Tubingen: J.C.B. Mohr [Paul Siebeck], 1992) 182–201.

Senior, D. 'Death of Jesus and the Resurrection of the Holy Ones', *CBQ* 38 (1977) 312–329.

Slusser, M. 'Docetism: A Historical Definition', *Second Century* 1 (1986) 163–172.

Smith, D. M. 'The Problem of John and the Synoptics in Light of the Relation between Apocryphal and Canonical Gospels', in A. Denaux (ed.), *John and the Synoptics* (BETL 101; Leuven: Peeters, 1992) 147–62.

Starcky, J. 'Un texte messianique araméen de la grotte 4 de Qumrân', in *École des langes orientales ancienned d l'Institut Catholique de Paris. Mémorial de cinquatenaire 1914–1964* (Paris: Bloud et Gay, 1964).

Stillman, M.K. 'Footprints of Oral Transmission in the Canonical Passion Narratives',
   *Ephemerides Theologicae Lovanienses* 73 (1997) 393–400.
Strange, J.F. 'Magdala', in *ABD*, vol. 4, 464.
Sullivan, K.P. *Wrestling with Angels: A Study of the Relationship between Angels and
   Humans in Ancient Jewish Literature and the New Testament*, AGJU 55 (Leiden:
   Brill, 2004).
——. 'Sexuality and Gender of Angels' in April D. DeConick (ed.), *Paradise Now:
   Essays on Early Jewish and Christian Mysticism*, SBLSS 11 (Atlanta: SBL, 2006)
   211–228.
Swete, H.B. *The Gospel according to St. Mark*, (3rd ed., London: Macmillan, 1909).
Taylor, V. *The Gospel according to St. Mark*, (2nd ed., London: Macmillan, 1966).
Thackery, H. St. J. *Josephus: The Jewish War* LCL 210 (Cambridge, Mass.: Harvard,
   1928).
Thiselton, A.C. *The First Epistle to the Corinthians*, NIGNT (Grand Rapids, Michigan/
   Carlisle: Eerdmans/Paternoster, 2000) 1204.
Tischendorf, C. *Evangelia Apocrypha* (Lipsiae: Avenarius et Mendelssohn, 1853).
Traube, L. *Nomina Sacra: Versuch einer Geschichte christlichen Kürzung* (Munich:
   Beck'sche Verlagsbuchhandlung, 1907).
Tuckett, C.M. *Q and the History of Early Christianity* (Edinburgh: T&T Clark, 1996).
——. *Christology and the New Testament: Jesus and His Earliest Followers* (Edinburgh:
   EUP, 2001).
——. ' "Nomina Sacra": Yes and No?' in J.-M. Auwers and H.J. Jonge (eds.), *The Bibli-
   cal Canons*, BETL CLXIII (Leuven: Peeters, 2003) 431–458.
——. 'Nomina Sacra in Codex E', *JTS* new series 57 (2006) 487–499.
Turner, E.G. *The Typology of the Early Codex* (Philadelphia: University of Pennsyl-
   vania Press, 1977).
——. *Greek Manuscripts of the Ancient World*, (2nd ed., rev. and enl. by P.J. Parsons;
   London: Institute for Classical Studies, 1987).
Vanderkam, J.C. *The Dead Sea Scrolls Today* (London/Grand Rapids, MI.: SPCK/
   Eerdmans, 1994).
——. *An Introduction to Early Judaism* (Grand Rapids, Michigan: Eerdmans, 2001).
Van Minnen, P. 'The Greek *Apocalypse of Peter*', in J.N. Bremmer and I. Czachesz
   (eds.), *The Apocalypse of Peter* (Studies on Early Christian Apocrypha 7; Leuven:
   Peeters, 2003) 15–39.
Wallace, D.B. *Greek Grammar: Beyond the Basics* (Grand Rapids: Zondervan, 1996).
Watson, F. 'Beyond Suspicion: On the Authorship of the Mar Saba Letter and the
   Secret Gospel of Mark', *JTS* 61 (2010) 128–170.
Weigandt, P. *Der Doketismusim Urchristentum und in der theologischen Entwicklung
   des zweiten Jahrhunderts*, 2 vols. (Diss. Heildelberg, 1961).
Zerwick, M. and Grosvenor, M. *A Grammatical Analysis of the Greek New Testament*
   (4th ed.; Rome: Pontifical Biblical Institute, 1993).
Ziegler, J. *Septuaginta Vetus Testamentum Graecum*, vol. XIII Duodecim prophetae
   (Gottingen: Vandenhoeck & Ruprecht, 1984).

# INDEX OF ANCIENT SOURCES

The index of ancient sources is divided into the following sections:
A. *Gospel of Peter*
B. Hebrew Bible
C. Jewish Apocrypha and Pseudepigrapha
D. Dead Sea Scrolls
E. New Testament
F. Other Early Christian Writings
G. Philo of Alexandria
H. Josephus
I. Rabbinic Writings
J. Greek and Roman Writers

## A. Gospel of Peter

## B. Hebrew Bible

## C. Jewish Apocrypha and Pseudepigrapha

## D. Dead Sea Scrolls

## E. New Testament

## F. Other Early Christian Writings

## G. PHILO OF ALEXANDRIA

# INDEX OF MODERN AUTHORS

# INDEX OF SUBJECTS